Flanders
Northern Belgium

the Bradt Travel Guide

Emma Thomson

II0657461

www.bradtguides.com

Bradt Travel Guides Ltd, UK
The Globe Pequot Press Inc, USA

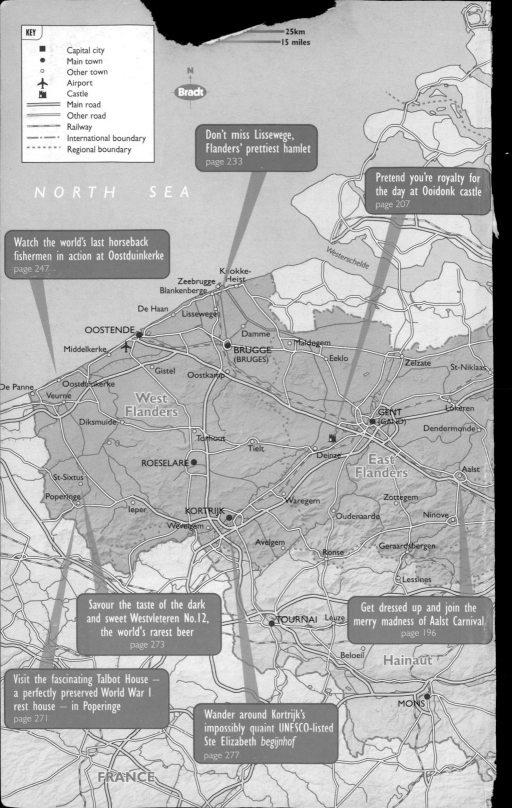

KEY

- ■ Capital city
- ● Main town
- ○ Other town
- ✈ Airport
- ♜ Castle
- Main road
- Other road
- Railway
- ·—·—· International boundary
- ·----- Regional boundary

25km
15 miles

N

Bradt

Don't miss Lissewege, Flanders' prettiest hamlet
page 233

Pretend you're royalty for the day at Ooidonk castle
page 207

NORTH SEA

Westerschelde

Watch the world's last horseback fishermen in action at Oostduinkerke
page 247

Knokke-Heist
Zeebrugge
Blankenberge

De Haan
Lissewege

OOSTENDE
Middelkerke
Damme
Maldegem
BRUGGE (BRUGES)
Eeklo
Zelzate
St-Niklaas

Gistel
Oostkamp

De Panne
Oostduinkerke
Veurne
West Flanders
GENT (GAND)
Lokeren
Dendermonde

Diksmuide
Torhout
Tielt
Deinze
East Flanders

ROESELARE
Aalst

St-Sixtus
Waregem
Zottegem

Poperinge
Ieper
KORTRIJK
Oudenaarde
Ninove

Wevelgem
Avelgem
Geraardsbergen

Ronse
Lessines

Savour the taste of the dark and sweet Westvleteren No.12, the world's rarest beer
page 273

TOURNAI Leuze

Get dressed up and join the merry madness of Aalst Carnival
page 196

Beloeil
Hainaut

Visit the fascinating Talbot House – a perfectly preserved World War I rest house – in Poperinge
page 271

MONS

Wander around Kortrijk's impossibly quaint UNESCO-listed Ste Elizabeth begijnhof
page 277

FRANCE

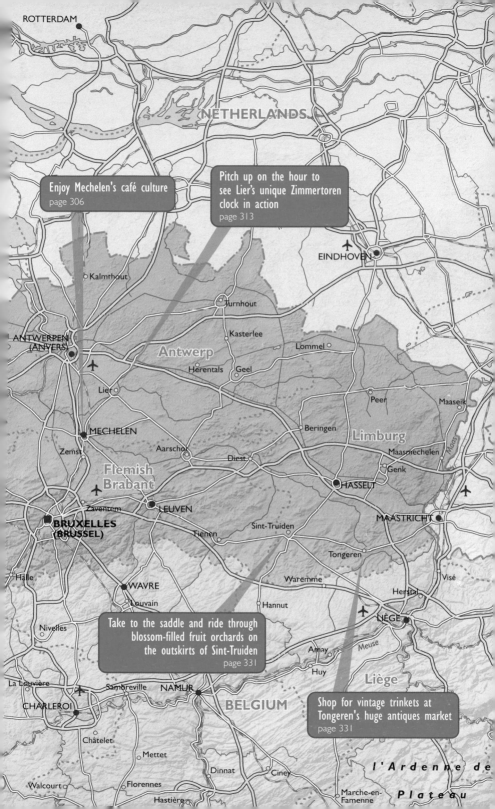

ROTTERDAM

NETHERLANDS

Enjoy Mechelen's café culture
page 306

Pitch up on the hour to see Lier's unique Zimmertoren clock in action
page 313

EINDHOVEN

Kalmthout

Turnhout

ANTWERPEN (ANVERS)

Antwerp

Kasterlee

Lommel

Herentals

Geel

Peer

Maaseik

Lier

Beringen

Limburg

MECHELEN

Aarschot

Diest

Maasmechelen

Zemst

Genk

Flemish Brabant

HASSELT

Zaventem

LEUVEN

Tienen

Sint-Truiden

MAASTRICHT

BRUXELLES (BRUSSEL)

Tongeren

Halle

Waremme

Visé

WAVRE

Louvain

Hannut

Herstal

Take to the saddle and ride through blossom-filled fruit orchards on the outskirts of Sint-Truiden
page 331

Nivelles

LIÈGE

Amay

Meuse

La Louvière

Sambreville

NAMUR

Huy

Liège

CHARLEROI

BELGIUM

Shop for vintage trinkets at Tongeren's huge antiques market
page 331

Châtelet

Mettet

Dinant

Ciney

l'Ardenne de

Walcourt

Florennes

Plateau

Hastière

Marche-en-Famenne

Flanders
Don't
miss...

**Sightseeing
from the saddle**
The whole region
is criss-crossed with
pathways — take on the
challenge of Geraards-
bergen's *Muur*
(ET) page 200

Medieval city centres
Marvel at the ancient architecture
of medieval cloth towns, including
Brugge's famous Markt
(JD/TB) page 221

UNESCO-listed *begijnhofs*
Unique to Flanders and the Netherlands, these peaceful idylls are steeped in history
(JDH/TB) page 18

Local festivals and traditions
Join the merry madness of a live concert or carnival, such as Dendermonde's decennial *Ros Beiaard*
(W) page 192

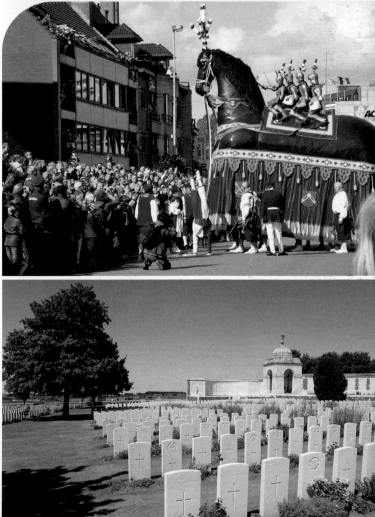

World War I sites
The atrocities of World War I were played out on Flanders' fields. Pay your respects at Tyne Cot: the world's largest Commonwealth war grave cemetery
(VF) page 268

Brussels' Grand' Place is the magnificent backdrop for the biennial Tapis de Fleurs, when more than 750,000 begonias carpet the cobblestones (HA) page 55

right   Lier's hand-built Zimmertoren features 13 clocks, which tell you everything from the tides to the phases of the moon (ET) page 313

below   Fonske, the town mascot of Leuven's university students, perfectly captures the carefree Flemish spirit (ET) page 146

bottom   Beersel is a fairytale feudal castle complete with drawbridge, moat and portcullis (AS/S) page 152

GORMAN R.A.
HODGE G.J.
HOLDER W.E.
McCLEN A.V.
MORRIS W.C.
NORRIS R.E.
PARSLEY W.
PATTERSON F
RANKINE J.G.
REGAN R.

REMEMBRANCE

left **A handful of the 54,896 soldiers' names inscribed on the Menin Gate, Ieper** (ET) page 263

below left **Fallen heroes: photos of soldiers who have passed through Talbot House, a preserved World War I B&B in Poperinge** (ET) page 271

below right **Preserved World War I trenches, Hill 62** (VS/S) page 267

AUTHOR

Emma Thomson was formerly commissioning editor at Bradt Travel Guides (but contrary to scurrilous rumours she didn't commission this one…) and now works as a freelance writer and photographer. A member of the British Guild of Travel Writers, she writes for international magazines, newspapers and publishers. She first visited Flanders ten years ago after falling for a Fleming and has been totting up her Eurostar frequent-traveller points ever since – she was even lucky enough to live in a farmhouse (complete with sheep, chickens and rabbits) near Aalst for a year.

AUTHOR STORY

Like all good stories, mine starts in a bar. Not a Flemish one, mind you, but the slightly more prosaic setting of Watford, north London. I was working as a cocktail bartender and one day in walked our new boss: a Flemish fellow called Bart – and that, as they say, was that. Within a month I was standing in Brussels' Grand' Place gawking at the gold-fringed guildhouses winking in the sun – a convert.

That was ten years ago and, in truth, I've been researching this guide ever since: jotting down a great restaurant or some nook-and-cranny bar on each successive trip. Researching this guide proper, then, has been a treat because it allowed me to delve deeper than ever before. However, it also made me nervous. From the get-go I was acutely aware of the stereotypes equated with 'boring' Belgium and her northern Flanders region. My former Bradt colleagues were quick with the quips: 'Flanders? I think I've driven through it on the way to Germany' or 'Quick, quick … name five famous Flemings!' I feared it would be an uphill struggle to convince everyone to the contrary. But I want to state it loudly here: Flanders is nothing like the clichés. She remains quirky in some quarters but achingly hip in others. In fact, her curious blend of character has won the hearts – and pens – of many a heavyweight travel writer.

So, no cajoling required: Flanders surprises at every turn. Its main cities are epicentres of culture and you could easily spend all your time visiting just these. But where possible, take the time to explore the outer towns and villages away from the regular tourist trail – they give an excellent insight into real Flemish life and its driving values. Throughout the guide I've applied Bradt's off-the-beaten-track ethos, steering clear of chain hotels and bland eateries and instead focusing on places that are classic, enchanting or quirky in character. So consider this guide a key, if you will, with which to unlock and ease open the yeasty tavern door and join the merry madness inside. My hope is that the guide will make a 'flanderophile' of you before you can finish your first beer.

PUBLISHER'S FOREWORD   *Adrian Phillips, Publishing Director*

If Belgium really were boring, it wouldn't reflect well on the Bradt office – Emma chose to resign as our commissioning editor in favour of researching this guidebook. But how could any man or woman find dull a place that produces the world's best beer and chocolate?! Emma has a genuine insider's view, having lived in a Flemish village with her sheep and chickens, and she's been able to take us to towns and villages that brim with traditional character and colour. After ditching the day job she's thrown herself into crafting a well-written, entertaining and above all joyful book built on knowledge and love; we hope it inspires you to look beyond the typical cities on the tourist trail.

First published May 2012

Bradt Travel Guides Ltd, 1st Floor, IDC House, The Vale, Chalfont St Peter SL9 9RZ, England; www.bradtguides.com
Published in the USA by The Globe Pequot Press Inc,
PO Box 480, Guilford, Connecticut 06437-0480

ISBN-13: 978 1 84162 377 1

British Library Cataloguing in Publication Data
A catalogue record for this book is available from the British Library

Photographers Hotel Amigo (HA); Krylon80/Dreamstime (K80/D); moochimages.com/Alamy (M/A); Agnese Sanvito (AS); Shutterstock (S): Europhotos (E/S); Rob Van Esch (RVE/S); Vaughan Sam (VS/S); Anthony Shaw Photography (ASP/S); Emma Thomson (ET); Toerisme Brugge (TB): Jan Darthet (JD/TB); Jan D'Hondt (JDH/TB); Visit Antwerp (VA); Visit Brussels (VB); Visit Flanders (VF): Jan Darthet (JD/VF), Choco-story Bruges (www.choco-story.be) (CSB/VF), www.milo-profi.be (MP/VF), Michel Vaerewijck (MV/VF); Wikipedia (W)
Front cover Windmill and canal, Damme (M/A), branded cover by Michel Vaerewijck (MV/VF)
Back cover Brugge's beautiful canals (K80/D), Westmalle Trappist beer brewed by monks in Westmalle, Antwerp (MP/VF)
Title page Guildhouses on the Grand' Place, Brussels (E/S); Memorial cross left at the Menin Gate, Ieper (ET); Tintin sign, Brussels (ET)
Text photos page 60 cycling sign (ET); page 268 courtesy of Volksbunde Deutsche Kriegsgräberfürsorge; page 267 (W)

Maps David McCutcheon; colour map relief base by Nick Rowland FRGS

Typeset from the author's disc by Wakewing
Production managed by Jellyfish Print Solutions; printed and bound in India

Acknowledgements

Thanks to Hilary Bradt, Donald Greig and Adrian Phillips for commissioning the guide and giving me the opportunity to work remotely for Bradt while living in Flanders for a year.

To my firm-but-very-kind project manager, Tricia Hayne; Sally Brock for typesetting; cartographer-extraordinaire, David McCutcheon; Fiona Dale for designing the colour section and cover; and Greg Dickinson and Anna Moores for endless patience concerning the colour section and cover. Thanks and appreciation also to Tim Webb for writing the section on beer; to Gordon Rattray for providing the information on disabled travel; and to Dr Felicity Nicholson for checking the health section.

An enormous *dank u wel* to Anita Rampall at Visit Flanders and the fantastic press people at the individual tourist boards, especially Nathalie De Neve and Freya Sackx (Visit Ghent), Igor Daems (Visit Antwerp), Pierre Massart (Visit Brussels), Florie Wilberts (Mechelen Tourism), Nancy Brouwers (Leuven Tourism), Petra Delvaux (Ieper Tourism), Isabelle D'Hondt (Oostende Tourism) and Anne De Meerleer (Brugge Tourism).

To the characters I met along the way, including Mark Bode and the monks of Sint-Sixtus Abbey, Elizabeth Evans, Evgenia Paparouni, Deken Roger van Bockstaele, Trees Coene and Genevra Charsley.

Thanks and love to my Flemish friends for all their support, especially Aunt Louise for sharing her wartime stories; to friends who haven't seen me for months; to my family who kept me fed and motivated; and last, but certainly not least, to Bart Wijnant – for everything.

DEDICATION

For Bart, who introduced me to his home (and *vrijdag fritjesdag*).

Contents

LIST OF MAPS

Introduction

The Flemish have a saying: 'you can't sell the skin off a bear before it's shot'. Visitors would do well to abide by this when considering the merits of visiting Flanders. For too long Belgium's northern region has been sold out as 'dull', 'small-minded', and 'characterless'. Flanders is anything but. It may lack the pomp and pride of French regions, or the self-assuredness of German states, but Flanders has a good thing going and doesn't feel the need to boast.

Invaded, occupied and ransacked, it has been the site of numerous battles between successive foreign powers over the centuries, but it is no longer just a stepping stone between France and Germany. The tables have turned. Brussels is home to NATO headquarters and the European Union and frequently hailed as Europe's business capital, while towns such as Antwerp and Zeebrugge are pulling in the heavyweights of European industry. This influx of wealth has propelled the region forward and progress is everywhere. But these achievements fail to capture what draws her fans back to her cobbled streets and cosy cafés time and time again. Flanders' appeal lies in its ability to satisfy life's fundamental desires: thirsts are quenched (or drenched?) with the choice of over 800 beers, hungry tummies are filled with home-cooked food, and bodies tired from wandering can sink into the four-postered comfort of a welcoming bed and breakfast. Take the time to experience the heavy, warm whiff of the yeast-filled air in the brasseries; to taste the custard-filled creations of the *pâtisseries*, and feast upon the works of world-renowned artists and cartoonists.

Recent reappraisals have redefined Flanders; what was once criticised as fuddy-duddy is now considered hip. Its refreshing mix of cosmopolitan towns and rural villages allows you to spend one day enjoying galleries, theatre, dinners and dancing 'til dawn amid Art Nouveau districts and medieval town squares, and the next visiting rural communities where life slips back a gear.

But why a guide to Flanders, not Belgium? Well, while the whole country is worth exploration, Flanders has its own unique character which sets it apart from the south. The region is small, but it's brimming with such a wealth of things to do that it warrants individual attention. This is, of course, thanks to the grit and good humour of its citizens who have influenced world culture in more ways than common opinion allows for. Few know that Hollywood starlet Audrey Hepburn hails from Brussels; that the Big Bang theory was actually devised by Leuven professor and priest Georges Lemaître in 1927; and that Flanders is home to Walter Arfeuille, a man who can pull eight railway coaches with his teeth. Such quirks set Flanders apart from its neighbours and place it in a league of its own. She is not a perfect place, but one you quickly learn to love because of her eccentricities, not in spite of them.

Having visited Flanders countless times now, I've learned to stop shooting bears. Every trip offers up something new. Prepare to develop a life-long devotion.

Part One

GENERAL INFORMATION

FLANDERS AT A GLANCE

Location Northern Belgium, western Europe
Size/Area 13,522km²
Climate Temperate (mild winters, cool summers)
Status Federal parliamentary democracy under a constitutional monarchy
Population 6,550,000
Life expectancy Men: 76.3; women: 82.8
Capital Brussels (1.89 million)
Other main towns Brugge, Gent, Antwerp
Economy Exports: cars, food, iron, steel, finished diamonds, textiles and plastics
GDP per capita €27,900
Languages Flanders: Dutch; Brussels: official bilingual (Dutch & French) but 80% of residents speak French.
Religion Roman Catholic 75%, other (including Protestant) 25%
Currency Euro (€)
Exchange rate £1=€1.19; US$1=€0.76 (January 2012)
National airline/airport Brussels Airlines/Brussels-Zaventem
International telephone code +32
Time GMT+1
Electrical voltage 230v AC/50Hz
Weights and measures Metric
Flag A black lion on a bright yellow background
National anthem *De Vlaamse Leeuw* ('The Flemish Lion')
Public holidays 1 January, 6 January, 14 February, Easter Monday, 1 May, 13 May, Pentecost Monday, 10 June, 11 July, 21 July, 15 August, 1 November, 2 November, 11 November, 6 December, 25 December

FEEDBACK REQUEST

Go, little book, God send thee good passage,
And specially let this be thy prayere
Unto them all that thee will read or hear,
Where thou art wrong, after their help to call,
Thee to correct in any part or all.

Preface from 1901 edition of Baedeker's *Belgium and Holland* guide

For my part, I've checked, rechecked and bitten fingernails low in the pursuit of accuracy, but inevitably things change: prices increase, restaurants are replaced and what was once hip swiftly becomes old, so if you have any comments, queries, grumbles, insights, news or other feedback, please post them on the website, email me at e info@ethomson.co.uk, or write to Emma Thomson, c/o Bradt Travel Guides, 1st Floor IDC House, The Vale, Chalfont St Peter SL9 9RZ, England.

1

Background Information

GEOGRAPHY

Flanders – or Northern Belgium – sits at the heart of western Europe, shares its northern border with the Netherlands and has a 67km coastline lapped by the North Sea.

You can drive from east to west in two hours and 30 minutes, and north to south in an hour. Flanders surrounds Brussels, which is its own independent region.

The landscape is characterised by pancake-flat coastal plains which convert to marshy areas, or polders, as you move inland. These areas sit below sea level and are drained by canals. East Flanders' southern fringes boast an area of gently rolling hills nicknamed the Flemish Ardennes, which backs onto the fertile farming grounds of Pajottenland in the Flemish Brabant region. In the northeast is the Kempen, studded with pine forests and moorland and the site of Hoge Kempen, Flanders' only national park.

Water is a huge part of Flanders' make up. The region is criss-crossed with rivers, their routes providing watery highways for early traders. The largest of these is the Scheldt, which arrives in Flanders just south of Oudenaarde, takes a detour via Gent and goes rumbling out to sea at Antwerp.

CLIMATE

Notorious for its four-seasons-in-one-day climate, Flanders lies on the same latitude as the south of England and experiences similar weather patterns – it is luck of the draw as to whether it will be a summer of heatwaves, or one of endless rain. Between spring (Apr–Jun) and autumn (Sep–Nov) you can expect temperatures to fluctuate between 14°C and 6°C and cool, sunny days to be intermingled with overcast, drizzly days. During summer temperatures hover around the 20°C mark, but in winter (Dec–Feb), when the Baltic breezes come whistling down uninterrupted from the North Pole, temperatures plummet, rarely rising above 6°C and sometimes dropping to –5°C. However, even the darkest days have their splendour. There's something incredibly romantic about dashing from café to café across soaked but sparkling cobblestone streets.

TEMPERATURE TABLE FOR BRUSSELS

	Jan	Feb	Mar	Apr	May	Jun	Jul	Aug	Sep	Oct	Nov	Dec
Max°C	4	7	10	14	18	22	23	22	21	15	9	6
Min°C	–1	0	2	5	8	11	12	12	11	7	3	0

3

As a guide, July tends to be the hottest month, January the coolest, November the wettest and February the driest. During summer, the sun rises between 05.00 and 06.00 and doesn't set until 22.00. During winter, the days shorten considerably – sunrise is between 07.00 and 08.00 and sunset between 16.00 and 17.00.

NATURAL HISTORY

Until 1989 there was no environmental planning in Flanders. Large swathes of the countryside were intensively farmed, leaving only pockets of protected areas, like Het Zwin (page 236), the Westhoek dunes (page 250) and Hoge Kempen National Park (page 338). You'll see lots of cows, horses, sheep – even the odd farmed llama – but sightings of wild mammals are rare. However, NGO Natuurpunt has strived to raise awareness and implement conservation programmes and it seems to be working. After a long absence, foxes are making a comeback across the region. Throughout West Flanders and Brussels there are populations of red squirrel, hedgehog and dwarf bat and even the occasional sighting of Siberian chipmunks. The waterways of East Flanders and Flemish Brabant are home to the odd European beaver, and Limburg has healthy populations of badger and the hazel dormouse.

Many birds use the country as a rest stop during their annual migration. One of the best places to see them is the Het Zwin wetlands and marshes on the coast north of Knokke-Heist. Seabirds include the Mediterranean, Icelandic and great black-backed gulls, curlew sandpiper, grey heron, storks and the rarely seen shoveler.

Coastal dunes support nearly 67% of the plant life found in Flanders and of this nearly a third is found in the Westhoek dunes just past De Panne. There are pockets of birch, beech and oak across the centre, but the main concentration of woodland is in the pine forests of Hoge Kempen National Park, whose mix of forest and moorland is home to deer, snakes, frogs, toads and goshawks.

HISTORY

The history of Flanders is the history of Belgium, and as far as countries go Belgium is comparatively new. Up until 1830, when it gained its independence, the country was lumped together with Luxembourg and the Netherlands. Collectively they formed the Low Countries and suffered as the pawns of successive foreign powers over the centuries. These powers played tug of war over boundaries and carved up the land to form the borders that define the countries today.

ANTIQUITY In 500BC three tribal groups covered the area: the southern-dwelling Celtic Belgae, the coastal-dwelling Germanic Frisians and the Batavians who settled in the southern Netherlands. It was these tribes that Roman General **Julius Caesar** (100–44BC) encountered during his invasion of Gaul (western Europe) in 58BC. He fought and defeated only the Celtic tribes and incorporated their land as a province of Rome under the name Gallia Belgica, including towns like Tongeren (*Aduatuca Tungrorum*). The area, which comprised much of present-day Flanders and Netherlands, was granted to the Germanic Franks – a group of Germanic tribes under forced conscription by the Romans. When the Roman Empire began to lose its grip in the north in AD500, the Franks took over, spawning the Merovingian dynasty. The long-haired kings' lazy attitude towards ruling cost them dearly and they were quickly succeeded by the Carolingians, once mayors of the Merovingian palaces, who rose to assume power. The dynasty was named after its greatest leader Carolus Magnus, better known as King **Charlemagne** or 'Charles the Great' (AD742–814), who was crowned Holy Roman Emperor in AD800. When his son, Louis the Pious, died unexpectedly, divisible inheritance laws decreed that his lands be divided between Charlemagne's three grandsons. Three years of civil war ensued until the **Treaty of Verdun** was drawn up in AD843, which carved the emperor's portion of the territory into the early divisions of France, the Low Countries and Germany, and Italy. As a result of the treaty, Flanders remained part of the Germanic Frankish lands and the remainder of the Low Countries belonged to the Roman Empire. It is at this point that the basis of Belgium's current language division was formed. Throughout the Middle Ages, the northern part of Belgium became increasingly Germanic in parlance, while the south, overseen by the Romans, was exposed to Latin dialects.

ROMANESQUE PERIOD As the threat from raiding Vikings increased, local lords and counts capitalised on the fragile authority exercised by the French kings and German emperors, and assumed control of the towns in which they lived, forming feudal states that closely resemble today's regional divisions, including the County of Flanders, the Duchy of Brabant and the Duchy of Limburg. Opportunistic characters, such as **Baldwin the Iron Arm** – who took control of Flanders by kidnapping and marrying the French king's daughter and then blackmailing him with the threat of a Norman alliance – consolidated their powers and gained autonomy often through strength of purse, not arms.

The end of the Romanesque period saw the decline of feudalism and the rise of economic prosperity, particularly in towns like Brugge, Gent and Ieper (Ypres), which not only increased their trade of Flemish cloth with merchants from Spain, Venice and Genoa, but also benefited from the newly established **Hanseatic League**. This alliance of trading guilds created a monopoly across the Baltic Sea and improved commerce with Russia, Bulgaria and England.

The influx of wealth drew a dividing line between the local counts, and the merchants and craftsmen who had gained a stronger economic foothold by uniting to form guilds. Frictions arose when the guilds, in an attempt to maintain the delivery of vital raw materials from England, began to resist centralist French policies and side with the English in conflicts between the two counties. In one particular incident, the French King, **Philip IV 'the Fair'** (1268–1314) forcibly removed the Count of Flanders, Gwijde van Dampierre, and exiled the citizens of Brugge in an attempt to suppress the uprisings. However, on the morning of 18 May 1302, the residents returned to the city and murdered as many Frenchmen as they could find in a retaliation recorded as the **Brugse Metten** (page 212). Two months later, near Kortrijk, Philip IV launched his offensive attack against an army of furious Flemings and lost in the **Battle of the Golden Spurs** – so-called for the 600 golden spurs collected from the French knights killed in battle. The defeat marked a significant development in Flemish political independence and is considered by many as the key to why Dutch is still spoken in Flanders today.

GOLDEN AGE OF THE BURGUNDIANS Amidst the sporadic struggles of the **Hundred Years' War** (1337–1453) – in which England and France respectively tried to pursue and retain the French throne – the stalemate between regional lords and French or German rulers was broken with the arrival in 1419 of **Philip the Good** (1396–1467). The first Duke of Burgundy, he inherited lands from the recently deceased Count of Flanders and in quick succession expanded these territories which spread from modern-day Netherlands through Belgium into Germany. During his reign, the work of the Flemish Primitives, like Jan van Eyck and Rogier van der Weyden, flourished and the breathtaking Grand' Place was constructed.

Philip's son, **Charles the Bold** (1433–77), was considered the last 'great duke', but his reign was cut short when he was struck in the head by a spear at the Battle of Nancy on 5 January 1477. At the age of 20 his daughter and heir, **Mary of Burgundy** (1457–82), was thrust into the political limelight and forced by the French king to sign 'the Great Privilege' charter. This restored civic rights to Flanders, Brabant etc, effectively undoing her grandfather's attempts to create a centralised state.

THE HAPSBURGS As the only heiress of the rich Burgundian Empire, Mary was not short of marriage proposals, but after much deliberation she chose the Habsburg **Maximilian of Austria** (1459–1519). For a time tensions with the French eased, but these were quickly revived when, after five short years of marriage, Mary fell from her horse and died, leaving Maximilian in charge. After countless struggles, the Duke finally squashed French rule of Burgundy and added the lands to the growing Habsburg Empire. Maximilian's first son **Philip the Handsome** (1478–1506) died of typhoid fever before he could inherit the throne which passed to Philip's second child, **Charles V** (1500–58). Born in Gent, Charles was a linguist, lover of ladies and nephew of Catherine of Aragon, Henry VIII's first wife. As a ruler, he united the 17 provinces governed by the Habsburg and Burgundian families and the Spanish Castilian and Aragonese crowns. He was only six when his father died, so for a period of nine years his empire was controlled by his aunt, **Margaret of Austria** (1480–1530). In 1519 Charles took over; aged 20 he was the most powerful ruler in Europe and his empire was enormous. He ruled Spain and her New World territories, Germany, Austria, Sardinia, Sicily, Belgium and the Netherlands, and spent much of his life sailing to or travelling between the territories, defending them against the expansionist French.

Residents were outraged at the high taxes used to fund the wars fought by their absent king, and the burghers had rebelled. They were quickly suppressed, but realising the revolts would continue, Charles tactfully granted autonomy to the 17 provinces of the Netherlands.

In 1553, an exhausted Charles returned to the Netherlands. Two years later he relinquished his titles and divided the realms by leaving the Spanish throne and rule of the Netherlands to his son Philip II (1527–98) and the crown of the Holy Roman Empire to his younger brother **Ferdinand I** (1503–64).

JACOB VAN ARTEVELDE (1290–1345)

Known affectionately as the 'Brewer of Gent', Artevelde hailed from a wealthy weaving family and rose to fame during the Hundred Years' War. When feuds between England and France began to affect the wool trade, Artevelde appealed to English King Edward III to maintain regular shipments of raw materials, on the basis that the allied cloth towns of Brugge, Ieper and Gent were neutral. His act of defiance angered the Count of Flanders and the French King Phillip IV, but unexpectedly their efforts to restrain him failed and the Count was forced to sign a treaty recognising the partnership. As a result, the textile towns flourished. However, his friendship with Edward III provoked jealousy among his peers, and when rumours surfaced that he planned to replace the existing Count of Flanders with Edward III's son, riots broke out in protest. During the uprising, Artevelde fell into the crowd and was murdered by an angry mob. A statue of him stands on Gent's Vrijdagmarkt.

THE REVOLT OF THE NETHERLANDS Born in northern Spain, Philip II had spent barely four years in the Low Countries and lacked the emotional attachment his father had formed to the territories. When his father died, Philip left his second wife – the Catholic Mary Tudor, Henry VIII's eldest daughter and Queen of England – and returned to Spain, deciding to rule the Low Countries from a distance. Disgusted by the rise of Protestantism in the territories, Philip employed the Spanish Inquisition to crush heretics and quickly passed his responsibilities on to his sister **Margaret of Parma**, Charles V's illegitimate daughter. For eight years, she ruled from Brussels with the assistance of Cardinal Granvelle struggling to calm the storm of religious discontent.

Meanwhile, **William of Orange-Nassau** – loyal subject of Charles V – found himself siding with the opposition. Despite being a Catholic, he believed in religious tolerance and was outraged at Philip's persecution of Protestants. In response, he joined other Protestant-sympathetic nobles and formed the **Confederacy of Noblemen**. Together, in April 1565, they submitted a petition which called upon the Margaret to moderate the King's anti-Protestant policies. Their appeal was dismissed, and they resorted to violence. Churches throughout the Low Countries were vandalised, their reliquaries, shrines and stained-glass windows smashed in riots labelled the **Iconoclastic Fury**.

In an attempt to squash the religious uprising, Philip dispatched his general, the **Duke of Alba**, along with 10,000 soldiers. Assisted by the Inquisition, General Alba established the **Council of Troubles** (commonly known as the 'Council of Blood' for the thousands it tried and sentenced to death) to try those who had taken part in the Fury. Among those summoned before the council were William and his cohorts, the Counts of Hoorn and Egmont. The counts were tried, condemned and executed on Brussels' Grand' Place, but William failed to appear, so Philip declared him an outlaw, seized all his property and put a price of 25,000 crowns on his head.

With nothing to lose, William embarked upon a series of attacks along the River Meuse. Having gained a foothold in the Low Countries, he finally entered Brussels, victorious, in 1576. The **Pacification of Gent**, an agreement assuring religious freedom for all, was signed, but Catholics in the south were less than keen to unite with William and the squabbles continued. Philip II capitalised on the fragmentation and sent Margaret's son, **Alexander Farnese** to provoke the discord between the Protestants and Catholics. Renowned for his cunning and powers or persuasion, Farnese convinced the southern territories to sign the **Treaty of Arras** on 6 January 1579, which promised to remove garrisons of foreign troops from the towns, in return for sworn allegiance to Philip II and the Catholic faith. Barely three weeks later, in an effort to counter balance this treaty, seven of the northern provinces met to sign the **Union of Utrecht**. The alliance formed the United Provinces, which refused to acknowledge Spanish rule; instead they appointed William as their first *stadhouder*, or governor. These divided territories became known as the Spanish Netherlands and the United Provinces. William enjoyed a short term in office, before he was assassinated in July 1584.

SPANISH RULE (1579–1713)

When Philip II died in 1598, **Philip III** (1578–1621) inherited his father's Spanish throne while his favourite daughter **Infanta Isabella** (1566–1633) and her husband **Albert Archduke of Austria** assumed control of the Spanish Netherlands. Under her rule, the area enjoyed a much-needed period of peace and prosperity. The arrival of silk-weaving, lace-making and diamond-processing revived the land's economic wealth and the arts received royal patronage.

Conscious of her father's anti-Protestant policies, Isabella attempted to wage war against the Protestant north, but with little success, so in 1609, she agreed to a ceasefire in the **Twelve Years' Truce**. The agreement temporarily granted the United Provinces their independence and over 100,000 Protestants and anti-Spanish thinkers fled north.

When **Philip IV** (1605–65) became king at the age of 16 he revived the wars against the Protestants. He suffered a series of defeats that lost him lands in the southern part of the Netherlands and compelled him to sign the **Peace of Westphalia** (also known as the Treaty of Münster) in 1648. The treaty ended the **Thirty Years' War** and formally acknowledged the independence of the United Provinces.

However, French King **Louis XIV** (1638-1715), was still intent upon adding the Spanish Netherlands to his territories and embarked upon a number of sieges, the worst of which, in August 1695, left Brussels' city centre, including the Grand' Place, in ruins. Events continued to go well for Louis when **Charles II** (1661–1700) – the last of the Spanish Habsburgs – died, leaving no heir. The crown passed to **Philip, Duke of Anjou** (1683–1746) – who also happened to be Louis XIV's grandson. The United Provinces, England, Sweden and Austria among other states knew it was only a matter of time before Louis pressured his grandson into handing the Spanish Netherlands over to France. Fearful of French domination, the countries formed an alliance and drove French troops out of the Netherlands in the **War of Spanish Succession** (1701–13). Utterly defeated, France signed the **Treaty of Utrecht** in 1713, which allowed the Duke of Anjou to keep his Spanish crown, but entrusted the rule of the Spanish Netherlands and the Holy Roman Empire to **Charles VI** (1685–1740), who belonged to the Austrian Habsburgs.

AUSTRIAN RULE (1713–94) Unfortunately, Charles VI produced no male heir either. Well aware of the inherent problems the accession of his eldest daughter **Maria Theresa** (1717–80) would cause, he announced in 1713 a pragmatic sanction that encouraged the major powers to agree to her ruling. Upon his death, however, the sanction was ignored and several contestants came forward disputing Maria's right to the throne. The disputes escalated into the **War of the Austrian Succession**, which involved most of Europe and the Spanish colonies. The distraction left the country open to invasion and France naturally obliged, managing to occupy much of the Netherlands by 1744. However, after eight years of conflict, Britain (Austria's ally) finally convinced France to sign the **Treaty of Aix-la-Chapelle**, which restored the Austrian Netherlands to Maria Theresa.

During the war, Maria had made her only sister, Maria Anna, and brother-in-law, Charles Alexander of Lorraine (1712–80), governors of the Austrian Netherlands, which went on to enjoy a period of economic prosperity. When Charles and Maria Theresa both died in 1780, her son, **Joseph II** (1741–90) assumed full control of the Empire. Unlike his Roman Catholic mother, Joseph had been heavily influenced by the Age of Enlightenment sweeping through Europe and he quickly embarked upon a prolific programme of reforms. He overhauled the education and public health systems, issued the **Patent of Toleration** in 1781 that granted Protestants freedom of worship, and moved the government from Brussels to Vienna, declaring German the official language. Although many of his reforms were of benefit to the neglected poor, his radical moves created uneasiness throughout the social scale and two groups of opposition arose: the Catholic conservatives led by **Henri van der Noot**, who opposed Enlightenment and longed to return to an absolute government and second group, led by **Jean Vonck**, who opposed the idea of a single monarch and wished to expel the Habsburgs in favour of a liberal state. Joseph attempted to quell the unrest but, unexpectedly the parties united to defeat the Austrian army near Antwerp in a retaliation known as the **Brabant Revolution**. Riding high on their success, the parties were quick to form their own Congress, with van der Noot at its head, and to declare the formation of the independent United States of Belgium. When Joseph died in 1790, his brother **Leopold II** (1747–92) wasted no time in dispatching troops to disband the Revolution and crush the fledgling attempts at Belgian nationhood; within a year the country had been pulled back into the empire.

FRENCH RULE (1794–1830) Leopold's reign was cut short when France declared war against Austria and Prussia. Despite Leopold's best efforts, Austria was absorbed into French territories in 1794. The Habsburg dynasty had fallen and for a time it seemed Belgium was without a ruler. Bu by 1795, Belgium and the Netherlands had been overpowered by the French and renamed the Batavian Republic. When Napoleon Bonaparte assumed power in 1799, he brought many improvements to the area; he rebuilt damaged docks and forced the Netherlands to relinquish control of the Scheldt, thereby opening up trade again. Furthermore, France's dependency on Belgian imports boosted the economy, breathing new life into the textile industries.

Despite the financial benefits, the populace were indignant with the French occupation and when conscription was introduced in 1797, to support Napoleon's campaigns abroad, numerous (unsuccessful) revolts were launched. Soon enough, the **Holy Alliance**, a peace-keeping coalition, was formed between Russia, Austria, Prussia and eventually England. Together, in June 1815, they met and defeated Napoleon on the battlefield at **Waterloo**. The Batavian Republic was dissolved and Belgians celebrated their apparent freedom.

THE UNITED KINGDOM OF THE NETHERLANDS (1815–31) Their celebrations were short lived. No sooner had they removed one ruler than they were saddled with another. After Napoleon's defeat at Waterloo, the **Congress of Vienna** (1814–15) met to redraw the political boundaries of the continent. It was decided that the old United Provinces should be joined with the Spanish/Austrian Netherlands to create the United Kingdom of the Netherlands and ruled by **Frederick William of Orange (William I)** (1771–1843). Patience and tolerance among the Belgians was wearing thin and William lacked tact. His decision to make Dutch the official language, secularise Church-controlled schools and refuse fair representation in parliament to the dominant south left the populace furious.

INDEPENDENCE (1830–1900) Frustrations came to a head on the evening of 25 August 1830, during the performance of French composer Daniel Auber's new opera *La Muette de Portici*. The story is one of revolution against the Spanish in 1647 and it was not long before the Belgians saw the similarity of their situation. Imbued with nationalist vigour, citizens rushed from the Théâtre de la Monnaie into the streets of Brussels and raised the flag of Brabant over the Hôtel de Ville in the Grand' Place. Uprisings like this spread in waves throughout the country and William quickly sent in the army to quash the rebels. He was successful in Hasselt and Leuven, but when Dutch troops arrived in Brussels on 23 September, four days of street fighting ensued. After bloody brawls the Dutch were finally surrounded by the nationalists and forced to make a quick retreat. The provisional government wasted no time in declaring independence on 4 October 1830. With William poised for war, the provisional government appealed to other European powers to recognise the independent Kingdom of Belgium. Great Britain and France acquiesced and at the **London Conference** in 1831, the country's independence was recognised for the first time, on the proviso that Belgium remain a neutral state and not enter into any alliances with surrounding powers.

The government then had to find a suitable king to rule their constitutional monarchy. They offered the throne to the German Prince **Leopold of Saxe-Coburg** (1790–1865), uncle and advisor to Britain's Queen Victoria. He was sworn in as King Leopold I of the Belgians on 21 July 1831. Two weeks later, a disgruntled William invaded, but Leopold managed to keep his troops at bay. These skirmishes lasted for eight years until William finally gave up in 1839 and signed a treaty acknowledging Belgium's independence.

Leopold I immediately set about regenerating the economic strength of his new country. The Société Générale bank (now Fortis) was revived and financed work on roads, canals and Europe's first public railway line between Brussels and Mechelen. These improved transport links created enormous industrial growth.

When large-nosed **Leopold II** (1835–1909) succeeded his father in 1865, he continued his programme of national development. Antwerp became an international port and the railroad companies were contracted to build lines throughout Europe and in China and South America. The proceeds financed the filling-in of the River Senne to clean up the surrounding slums and the construction of the formidable Palais de Justice, the Musées Royaux des Beaux-Arts and – for the 50th anniversary of Belgium's independence – the imposing Parc du Cinquantenaire.

However, Leopold was still not satisfied. He wanted Belgium to stand tall and equal among the other European nations, but he was hindered by a government that controlled the purse strings of the treasury. Frustrated with their lack vision, Leopold began to look elsewhere for alternative means of finance. The focus of colonialism was on Africa and Leopold joined in the race for the unconquered jungles of the Dark Continent.

THE HEART OF DARKNESS

They grabbed what they could get for the sake of what was to be got. It was just robbery with violence, aggravated murder on a great scale, and men going blind at it – as is very proper for those who tackle a darkness. The conquest of the earth, which mostly means taking it away from those who have a different complexion or slightly flatter noses than ourselves, is not a pretty thing when you look into it too much.

Heart of Darkness, Joseph Conrad

Leopold was cunning, secretive and hell-bent on his pursuit of an African colony and laid careful and meticulous plans towards its attainment. On 12 September 1876, he hosted a conference in Brussels to persuade prominent European explorers and geographers to back the foundation of the **Association Internationale Africaine** (AIA). Its aim? To suppress the slave trade, civilise the natives and create bases from which to chart and explore the continent. Leopold assured the assembly that 'Belgium may be a small country, but she is happy and contented with her lot; I have no other ambition than to serve her well.' Neal Ascherson, author of *The King Incorporated*, writes that the aims he outlined at the conference were merely 'a smokescreen to confuse stronger nations while he laid the foundations of a colony'. Leopold was elected as the first AIA chairman and once the meeting was adjourned, he wasted no time in sourcing an explorer who could found potential 'bases' for the Belgian committee of the AIA to work from.

The Welsh-born journalist and explorer **Henry Morton Stanley** (1841–1904) was by this time at the height of his fame; he had just returned from an expedition to the continent to locate the missing Scottish missionary Dr Livingstone. Known among the Congolese as *Bula Matari*, 'Breaker of Rocks', Stanley favoured firearms when it came to making 'agreements' with local tribes.

Leopold was impressed and invited Stanley to Brussels. Stanley initially declined but returned six months later and agreed to Leopold's plan.

After a while the AIA was forgotten; the other nations had now also realised that the economic benefits outweighed the philanthropic opportunities and the association soon fractured and dissipated. Leopold created the **Association Internationale du Congo** (AIC). Stanley, along with the rest of the world, remained unaware of the change. The similarity in name to the AIA was no coincidence; Leopold deliberately blurred the lines between the two organisations until it was assumed that the AIC was a remodelled version of the AIA. Leopold was now in personal control of the AIC, and financed the entire venture from his own pocket.

By 1884, Stanley had acquired an enormous chunk of central Africa through bribery and brute force and Leopold renamed it the **Congo Free State**. However, Leopold still faced challenges from France and Portugal and must have been relieved when later that year the **Berlin Conference** was held and Belgium's authority of the region was formally recognised.

By 1890 news of the atrocities taking place in the colonies had reached the ears of the European press and continued pressure from outraged Liberalist and Socialist groups forced Leopold to hand them over to the Belgian government in 1908. Life for the Congolese improved almost immediately and the Congo became one of the richest countries in Africa. However, apartheid still existed and rumblings of independence grew to a roar once World War II had ended. Belgian offered it on the condition of a three-to-four year transition period, ostensibly to prevent Congolese administration collapsing in chaos, but more realistically to prolong the immense revenue Belgium received from the mining of diamonds and gold in the colonies. But after riots broke out in protest, the Belgium government quickly gave in and granted the Republic of Congo independence on 30 June 1960.

WORLD WAR I (1914–18) On 4 August 1914, at nine o'clock in the morning, German troops breached Belgian neutrality and marched across the countries' shared eastern border, embarking upon the first phase of the **Schlieffen Plan**. The sweeping attack from the northeast relied on speed and was designed to surprise and capture French forces guarding the French–German border. Without an army, France would be forced to surrender.

The might of the German army eventually overwhelmed Belgium's attempts at resistance and by the end of 1914 the majority of the country was under German occupation. However, **King Albert I** (1875–1934) did succeed in defending the northwestern corner of the country that lay behind the River Yser and from Veurne he and the army attempted to defend their homeland.

The unexpected verve of Belgium's resistance delayed German troops for over a month and with it they lost the element of surprise. French troops re-engaged and four years of trench warfare ensued. The town of Ieper (Ypres) was obliterated during the **Ypres Salient** in which Belgian, British, French and Canadian troops found themselves surrounded on three sides by German soldiers acting on their own offensive plan, with both sides suffering huge loses for the sake of gaining a few hundred metres of land that was quickly lost at the next offensive.

Meanwhile the rest of Belgium struggled under German occupation. Forced to relinquish their crops, stores of wood and often their homes, they endeavoured to make life for the Germans as difficult as possible (see box, page 12). Germany finally capitulated and agreed to a ceasefire on 11 November 1918.

BETWEEN THE WARS In reward for their efforts in the fight against Germany, King Albert granted suffrage to the working-class population – although women were still denied – and established new social laws that would provide workers with financial security during periods of unemployment and old age, and reduced the working day from 12 hours, seven days a week to eight hours, six days a week.

By 1929 Belgium, along with the rest of Europe and North America, was experiencing the full effects of the **Great Depression**. The period was also characterised by a dip in democracy. Groups of disgruntled Flemish felt that, despite bearing the brunt of the fighting during World War I, government policy still favoured Wallonia. They were tired of French dominance and called for a unilingual Flanders and bilingual Brussels, which the government grudgingly granted in 1930.

Four years later, Albert I – the nation's beloved 'Soldier King' – fell to his death rock climbing in Namur. The country was devastated, but briefly found solace in the

LIFE DURING GERMAN OCCUPATION

Louise Wijnant has lived in Liedekerke all her life. Situated just south of Aalst, the small village invited more interest from the Germans that usual during World War II because of its radio station hidden in the nearby forest. The shack was the only facility in the area capable of receiving long-distance radio messages from the UK and US, and the Germans were keen to intercept any communication. One lunchtime, as we sat around her dining-room table eating pancakes, she told me, in her booming voice, what life had been like as a child during the war.

I was seven years old when the war started. I had one set of clothes and used to run around barefoot. We couldn't afford electricity, so used petrol lamps instead. At first we weren't really affected, but then food supplies began to run low and the rations tickets they issued were never enough to feed everyone. Instead of registering our goats and sheep, we began to hide them in the woods – that was our 'black market' for meat.

When I was nine, mum used to let me sneak up to the railway tracks at midnight with my brother, to collect coal that had fallen off the back of the wagons. One night, when we were just 100m from home, we heard voices. We threw ourselves to the ground, listening. After several minutes of hearing nothing, we decided to get up. But, as my brother wandered off into the darkness, two German police emerged from the shadows and caught me with my sack of coal. I thought they would confiscate it as usual, but instead they asked me where I lived. I silently pointed to my house a hundred yards away, fearing worse punishment, but to my surprise they let me go! I think they must have taken pity on me for dragging it all that way.

When the bombs started to fall, we were lucky to have connections with the white brigade, who warned us when the attacks might begin, so we could board up our windows. My mother owes her life to them. She was caught smuggling bread and threatened with deportation to the German work camps, so they hid the whole family. Luckily, Belgium was liberated 14 days later.

The world seemed to turn inside out after the war. There was so much of everything; everyone screamed with excitement the first time someone got a radio. We have come such a long way. I remember walking with my father, fantasising about the idea of space travel and yet, miraculously, he managed to see the first shuttle launch before he died.

beautiful face of **Princess Astrid of Sweden** (1905–35), who rose to become queen when Albert's son **Leopold III** (1901–83) inherited the throne. Her disregard of stuffy royal protocol and down-to-earth demeanour made her the most beloved queen in Belgian history and her sudden death in a car crash left the nation numb. Leopold had lost control of their car as they drove towards their villa in Switzerland, causing it to plunge into a nearby ravine.

Leopold had little time to grieve: **Adolf Hitler's** (1889–1945) rise to power in Germany was giving all cause for concern and in 1936 in an attempt to prevent Belgium being embroiled in another war, Leopold reasserted the country's neutrality.

WORLD WAR II (1939–45) Germany once again ignored Belgium's neutral status and after invading Poland, Norway and Demark, Hitler turned his attentions to Belgium, France and the Netherlands. He invaded on 10 May 1940 with a series of air attacks that left the country reeling. Within days, Leopold had surrendered without resistance and effectively made himself a prisoner of war by deciding to stay at the Royal Place in Brussels, where he was held under house arrest until he was deported to Germany in 1944. The bewildered Belgian government, meanwhile, fled to Paris and later to London to support the Allied war effort.

In 1944, three months after the D-Day landings at Normandy, Belgium was liberated. Germany made one final counter-attack in the **Battle of the Bulges** in the Ardennes, before capitulating on 8 May 1945. The same month, Leopold was liberated by the American army.

However, Leopold was among the thousands believed to have collaborated with the enemy. A confessed anti-Semite, he was under suspicion of treason after attending meetings with Hitler at Berchtesgaden. He was forbidden from returning to Belgium and spent the next five years in exile in Switzerland, while his brother **Prince Charles** took up regency. Leopold was eventually cleared of the accusations and returned to power briefly in July 1950, but abdicated a year later following protests, leaving his 21-year-old son **Baudouin** (1930–93) in charge.

MODERN BELGIUM The death of his mother when he was only five and a childhood spent in exile seemed to make Baudouin wise beyond his years. The young king succeeded where his father had not in renewing public support for the monarchy and maintaining a united nation that had been showing signs of fragmentation.

After the war, under the **Marshall Plan**, the US offered aid to the European countries hit hardest by the fighting. Belgium benefited to the tune of US$777 million and the money went into the construction of skyscrapers, self-service supermarkets, and highways so well lit that their network could be seen from space. Things improved further when Brussels was chosen as the headquarters of the **North Atlantic Treaty Organisation** (NATO) in 1949 and, two years later, as the provisional seat of the **European Coal and Steel Community**, the precursor of the European Union (EU). This blossoming of Belgium was displayed for all the world to see at **Expo '58**, for which the famous Atomium (page 130) was constructed.

In 1960 Baudouin was forced to relinquish control of the Congo, and later of Rwanda and Burundi.

His biggest challenge, though, lay closer to home. The ever-widening gap between Walloon and Flemish thought had created a chasm between government parties and revived problems of a linguistic divide. On top of this, Flanders' economy was flourishing on the back of its new light industries, while the unwanted heavy industries prevalent in the south caused the region to sink further into depression.

These events combined to bring tensions to a head and after several strikes, the country was divided into a federal state in 1993 in a series of constitutional revisions that were finalised in 2001. Today, everything from movies to government speeches must be presented in two languages, yet despite the apparent compromise, politicians continue to push for entirely separate communities. For now, though, Belgium remains the cohesive 'heart of Europe'.

GOVERNMENT AND POLITICS

Despite being one of the smallest countries in the EU, Belgium is armed to the teeth when it comes to constitutional matters. To ensure fairness and maintain neutrality between the three administrative regions (Flanders, Wallonia and Brussels), ten provinces and over 500 local authorities, powers of decision making have been divided and subdivided until the federal government was left with responsibility for major issues like defence, foreign affairs, justice, national budget, taxes and social security. All laws relating to the environment, transport, agriculture, energy etc, rest with the individual regional governments, whilst policies for education and culture are controlled by local communities. There is an overlap of administration in Brussels. The regional and local government are entirely autonomous and conduct their own elections, and their ministers have equal status with the federal party members. If you're confused, don't worry: most of the politicians are, too, and are equipped with a personal advisor to cut it all back to basics for them. The system borders on the ludicrous and is highly ineffectual.

EUROPEAN UNION

The roots of today's inter-governmental union of nation states, known as the EU, were probably inspired by Winston Churchill in 1946. World War II had ended a year beforehand and the fear of a reoccurrence was fresh in the minds of all politicians. Churchill suggested that a 'United States of Europe' would consolidate the continent's future and safeguard against future wars. Four years later, French foreign minister Robert Schuman and international economist Jean Monnet presented a proposal outlining the joint management of France's and west Germany's coal and steel industries. The proposal was solidified in 1951 by the Treaty of Paris and was extended to include Italy, Belgium, Luxembourg and the Netherlands. The European Coal and Steel Community (ECSC) heralded the birth of the EU, which gained its current name in 1993.

Today, Brussels is home to the headquarters of four of the EU's five main institutions: the European Commission, the Council of Ministers, the European Parliament and the European Council. The European Court of Justice head offices are based in Luxembourg.

These institutions have, in a short space of time, established border-free travel under the Schengen Agreement, implemented a single European currency, the euro, in 2002 thus furthering political unity and stabilising trade, and prevented war for over six decades. However, sceptics accuse the EU of being a bundle of red tape, riddled with allegations of unaccountability and corruption. The feelings of ill-will have also spread into the rest of Brussels' society, which criticises the international community for being insular and holds it responsible for rising house prices and the demolition of elegant residential neighbourhoods in favour of modern EU buildings.

Put simply, Belgium is governed as a federal parliamentary democracy under a constitutional monarch. Like Australia and Canada, the country's policies and reforms are decided by a coalition democratic government, while the king, Albert II, has theoretical authority to form and dissolve governments. This role, however, is ceremonial and symbolic; he cannot exercise personal power without the consent and cooperation of the ministers. Federal elections are held every four years; regional and community elections every five years and local elections every six years. It is compulsory for all Belgian citizens over the age of 18 to vote.

In April 2010 a caretaker government was placed in charge after Walloon and Flemish parties were unable to resolve long-running linguistic disputes. However, the risk posed by the Eurozone debt crisis galvanised the politicians and on 6 December 2011 French-speaking bow-tie-wearing Socialist Elio Di Rupo was elected as prime minister, ending a record-breaking 541 days of political deadlock. It's the longest period of a time a country has been without a government – an accolade previously held by Cambodia.

ECONOMY

Flanders was one the first European areas to undergo an industrial revolution and the development of ports and railways created an exceptionally efficient transport network. The manufacturing of textiles brought great wealth until the 1840s, when Flanders entered a depression. After World War II, regeneration money granted by the US in the Marshall Plan (page 13) was poured into development of the north and, after transferring to 'light' industries, production in Flanders caught up with, and quickly overtook, Wallonia's coal industry. The level of heavy industry once required in the south never returned and today Wallonia still suffers from 8% unemployment, double that of Flanders. To make matters worse, Flanders is forced to pour over €10 billion a year into the Wallonian economy to keep it afloat.

The ports of Zeebrugge and Antwerp – which are two of Europe's largest – handle the import of diamonds, petroleum, chemicals, clothing, machinery and food and the export of finished diamonds, cars, steel, plastics, petroleum and food. The majority of trade is with fellow EU members. In 2006, a survey conducted by the UN ranked Belgium as the 13th 'most liveable country' in the world.

PEOPLE

The Flemish are traditionally earthy in humour and character. Country lovers at heart who love to moan and make merry in equal measures, they pour heart and soul into their home cooking and prioritise the family above all else. Many remain in the town in which they were raised, so as to be close to their relatives and roles are often traditional. But don't be fooled: if the Belgian man is the head of the family, the woman is surely the neck that can turn the head any way she chooses. Her home is her domain and its appearance is important. Cleanliness is still considered next to godliness: dust-attracting carpets are despised, an untidy hedge unapproved of and it's not a rarity to see a pinafored grandma sweeping the street outside her house or soaping down the pavement until it sparkles. Indeed, a strong element of materialism informs the dreams and aspirations of the average Belgian family. Often quoted as being born *met een baksteen in de maag* ('with a brick in their stomachs'), they seek the suburban dream of a self-built house, children and a car. It seems such choices have filtered down from the generations that suffered the upheaval of the World Wars. But more recently couples have begun to break the mould, forming unmarried unions, pursuing careers and waiting until later to have children. Furthermore, women are not expected to change their maiden names if they do get married and there are egalitarian laws permitting men to take paternity leave to help their partners after the birth of a baby.

Of course, the linguistic frictions between the northern Flemish and southern-dwelling Walloons figure in daily life, but to nowhere near the extent suggested by the press. The clashes of the 1950s and 1960s have cooled and for the most part people's grumbles are ingrained dogma inherited from past generations. It's an old argument that seems relatively stale on the pallets of the younger generation and although they still identify themselves as either Flemish or Walloon ahead of any Belgian nationality, it seems the venom-infected taunts once slung between opposing language groups have lost their sting. Habit and pride ensure that the Flemish still accuse the Walloons of laziness, and perhaps the Walloons will always regard the Flemish as arrogant, but there is little bite in the bark. The rib-poking is also extended to their Dutch neighbours, and just as keenly returned. 'Why does a Belgian carry a knife in the car? So he can cut corners', is a typical dig from the Dutch who cast the Flemish as stupid and stingy. The Flemish take it on the chin and give as good as they get.

So if, like the Dutch, you have labelled the Flemish as dull you're missing the point. They *elect* to stay well-connected to the family locale, because what is more rewarding than being able to call round at your sister's or brother's, go for a bike ride among fields dotted with cud-chewing cows and finish the day off with a cool beer on a sunny terrace? While the lives of other nationalities are a frenetic imbalance of work and leisure, the Belgians usually manage to get the equilibrium right. They are an unpretentious, good-natured, hard-working bunch, who rejoice in a home life that revolves around kids, canines and cooking. All in all, a beguiling breed who quickly bring you round to the pleasures of living life at a more relaxed pace.

LANGUAGE

Flemish, or *Vlaams*, is a Dutch dialect based on the Frankish introduced by the conquering Franks following the decline of the Roman Empire. Its roots are predominately Germanic, but over time different regions developed varied dialects. Today, these exist as four main groups: West Flemish, East Flemish, Brabantian and Limburgish. Brussels also has its own dialect, but it is dying out and nowadays only heard in the Marolles district.

Residents of East and West Flanders tend to pronounce 'h' and 'g' sounds much more softly than their Brabantian neighbours, whilst Limburgians (eg: Hasselt) have a sing-song element to their dialect. All are increasingly adding English loanwords to their street Flemish. Another tendency is to add '-je' (sing), '-jes' (plural) and '-ken' at the end of a noun to imply a familiarity or fondness. For example, friends refer to me as 'Emmaken', instead of 'Emma'. The Flemish also often string several words together to create one long word, so you might need *uithoudingsdvermogen* (stamina) to wrap your tongue around all those vowels.

The Flemish delight in the fact that these dialects afford them some fun with their Dutch neighbours. In schools, Flemish children are taught Dutch and as a result speak perfect *Nederlands*, but the Dutch are left in the dark when in comes to understanding Flemish dialects. Add to this the variation of words and accents between towns, even villages, and things get really interesting. Even within a distance of 2km, the names of items (particularly culinary ones) change. For example, the *millefeuille* pastry found in bakeries is referred to as *booksken* in Denderhoutem, a *glascaken* in Denderleeuw and a *veleken* in Liedekerke.

Having said all that, the younger generations speak some, if not excellent, English (garnered mostly from the American films shown on television) and jump between the two languages with enviable ease.

Another brainteaser is the change in spelling of place names on road signs between the two regions. For a list of the most common name changes, see page 40.

THE LINGUISTIC DIVIDE

If I were king, I would send all the Flemings to Wallonia and all the Walloons to Flanders for six months. Like military service. They would live with a family and that would solve all our ethnic and linguistic problems very fast. Because everybody's tooth aches in the same way, everybody loves their mother, everybody loves or hates spinach. And those are the things that really count.

Jacques Brel

If only the politicians saw things as simply as Jacques Brel. Undeniable, discussed to death and at times looming on a fast-approaching horizon, the linguistic divide between the Dutch-speaking Flemish and the French-speaking Walloons has almost come to define Belgium, as much as it threatens to tear it apart.

The roots of the division can be traced back to the the Middle Ages when the Treaty of Verdun carved Charlemagne's lands between his three grandsons (page 5). Flanders became part of the Germanic Frankish lands, while the remainder of the Low Countries belonged to the Roman Empire and was exposed to Latin dialects. During the Burgundian Empire, French became the official language of the court, and Flemish remained the tongue of the working class. Despite the formation of the Belgian state in 1831, it was not until 1967 that the Flemish fight to equalise the status between the two languages was granted.

A few years ago a manifesto entitled *In de Warande* highlighted the ever-widening gap between Walloon and Flemish communities since the country's independence and questioned the logic of keeping the opposing regions together. It supported calls for the two communities to be split into two independent nations, leaving Brussels to be ruled jointly by the new countries and the European Union, but a separation is not broadly called for among the wider public. While no-one knows what the future holds, one hopes that the cohesive neutrality of the Royal Family, a newly formed government and the general sway of public opinion will progressively reduce the tensions and make it irrelevant to ask: what's the point of Belgium?

RELIGION

Catholicism became the religion of the masses during the Spanish occupation (1579–1713) and to this day 75% of Flanders' population is Roman Catholic. Protestantism and other religions make up the remaining 25%. Suffice to say that whilst church attendance has dropped since the 1970s and 1980s, it is still very much a part of daily life, and most towns hold an annual religious procession.

Antwerp is probably the country's most religiously diverse city. It is home to a healthy percentage of Moroccan immigrants and the country's largest concentration of Jews – based predominantly around the diamond district near the railway station – who arrived in Belgium during the 12th and 13th centuries after being expelled from France and England when persecution hit its peak during the Crusades. Numbers of Hindus and Buddhists are also on the rise in the larger cities and towns.

These walled islands of religious seclusion cropped up throughout the Low Countries during the 13th century. Comprised of a cluster of terraced homes arranged around a central garden and chapel, these *begijnhofs* were founded by pious sisterhoods of Catholic women who wished to serve God without having to observe the strict rules of Cistercian monastic life. According to historians, the networks of support arose following an increase in the number of women left as widows after the Crusades or disease took their husbands.

Making vows of chastity and obedience – but not of poverty – to the Groot Juffrouw or Mother Superior, the béguines tended the gardens, washed wool for weavers, worked in the on-site brewery and infirmary and prayed three times daily, but they were free to break their vows and leave at any time. The popularity of these self-sufficient communities allowed the sisterhood to pick and choose between applicants. Thus admission to the order was often offered to those who could afford to make donations to the financially independent community and thus the compound was home to a fair proportion of wealthy widows. These well-off residents occupied the larger rooms within the complex and spent their time caring for the elderly and sick, and weaving lace.

All of Flanders' *begijnhofs* are UNESCO listed. The prettiest can be found in Leuven, Lier, Turnhout, Tongeren, Diest, Kortrijk and Dendermonde.

CULTURE

Flanders' contribution to the arts is far-reaching and rather fantastic. From architectural firsts and world-renowned artists to colourful comic strips and international *chanson* crooners, the region is brimming with talent old and new.

LITERATURE Even after independence in 1830, works by Flemish writers were still categorised and referred to as Dutch literature. However, the denial of Flemish as an official language after independence provoked protests among Flemish writers and spawned a number of literary societies, kick-starting a transition that would eventually see Flemish literature being credited in its own right. One of the first works to contest the inequality was **Hendrik Conscience's** (1812–83) *In 't Wonderjaer 1566*, published in 1837. Disgusted that he'd written the novel in Flemish instead of French, his father threw him out of the family home and a penniless Conscience was forced to wander the streets of Antwerp. He had the last laugh though; eminent painter Wappers presented him to the royal court and it was under the patronage of Leopold I that Conscience was commissioned to write his second work, *Fantasy*. In 1845 he was made a knight of the Order of Leopold and Flemish literature became officially vogue.

Since then both Flanders has produced a handful of celebrated writers, a few of whom have achieved success abroad. Worth mentioning is **Camille Lemonnier** (1844–1913) a writer and poet from Ixelles in Brussels. His novels include the love story *Un Mâle* published in 1881 and the darker *Le Mons*, released a year later, which traces the regret of two peasants after they commit murder.

Waving the flag for women is **Marguerite Crayencour** (1903–87). Better known by her pseudonym, Marguerite Yourcenar, she remains Belgium's most prominent female writer. Born in Brussels, she received a first-class education at her father's estate in northern France. Her seminal work *Mémorires d'Hadrien* was published in

1951 and later translated by her lover, Grace Frick, into English. In 1980 she became the first woman to be elected to the distinguished Académie Française.

Also of note is the exceptional writer, poet, playwright and painter **Hugo Claus** (1929–2008). Hailing from Brugge, he wrote his seminal work *Het Verdriet van België* (*The Sorrow of Belgium*) in 1983. It tells the story of a Flemish child caught up in the German occupation of Belgium during World War II. Writing under a series of pseudonyms, Claus was nominated several times for the Nobel Prize for Literature.

POETRY Flanders is not traditionally associated with great poets but two names dominate 19th-century poetry: **Maurice Maeterlinck** (1862–1949) and Emile Verhaeren. Maeterlinck became an overnight success with his first play *La Princesse Maleine* in 1889. Born in Gent, he concentrated on exploring the themes of death and the meaning of life in the majority of his works, receiving the Nobel Prize for Literature in 1911. **Emile Verhaeren** (1855–1916) trained as a lawyer, but tried only two cases before turning to literature. Inspired by the works of Flemish painters like Jacob Jordaens and David Teniers, he published his first set of poems *Les Flamandes* in 1883. They are still admired for their raw and provocative depiction of Flemish life.

Later, many came to regard singer-songwriter **Jacques Brel** (1929–78) as a poet in his own right (page 354). Although born in Brussels, he spent most of his life in Paris. His later songs, employing numerous metaphors and linguistic styles, explored complex themes of love, death and life's hardships.

21st-century poets include **Miriam van Hee** (1952–) whose sixth collection, *Achter de Bergen* (*Behind the Mountains*), won the Flemish Culture Prize for Poetry in 1998; **Stefan Hertmans** (1951–), professor of art criticism at the Academy of Fine Arts in Gent, whose poetry focuses on the grotesque; and **Roland Jooris** (1936–) who, like van Hee, explores points of contact between poetry and day-to-day reality; he won the Flemish Culture Prize for his collection *Gekras* ('Scribblings') in 2005.

PAINTING
The Flemish Primitives
Confined to the pages of illuminated manuscripts for over 700 years, Flemish art leapt from the shadows at the beginning of the 15th century. This early Netherlandish painting flourished for over two centuries and was pioneered by a group of painters known as the Flemish Primitives – so-called for their experimentation with oil paint instead of the traditional tempera – whose work represented the transition from Middle Ages Gothic art to Renaissance. They pioneered the two-or-three painted wooden panels known as diptychs and triptychs. Artists began signing their works for the first time and became celebrities in their own right. One of the first – and best – was court painter and advisor to Philip the Good, **Jan van Eyck** (1390–1441). By mixing the oils with turpentine, he was able to layer the paint thinner than ever before; the effects were luminous and allowed him to produce works of unparalleled detail and realism. A resident of Brugge for most of his life, van Eyck produced a number of paintings that offered insight into courtly life, including the intriguing *Arnolfini Portrait* (now housed in the London National Gallery). His seminal work was the *Adoration of the Mystic Lamb,* a large polyptych painted with his brother Hubert that took over seven years to finish (page 175).

Van Eyck was eventually eclipsed by his pupil, **Rogier van der Weyden** (1400–64), who became Brussels' *stadsschilder* (official town painter) in 1436. His most famous works were the *Justice of Trajan* and *Justice of Herkenbald* retables that once hung in the Golden Chamber of Brussels' town hall, but were destroyed during the French bombardment of 1695. Among his followers, who admired his subtle and emotionally expressive style, was Weyden's pupil, **Hans Memling**

(1430–94), a German-born artist who carried on the tradition of his teacher's
painting with little innovation. Today, the Memling Museum in Brugge houses
super samples of his work, including his masterpiece the *Shrine of St Ursula*.
Another of Weyden's understudies, **Dieric Bouts** (1410–75), rose to become city
painter of Leuven in 1468. He was one of the first artists to experiment with the
single vanishing point. This method of creating depth and perspective can be
seen in his celebrated panel the *Last Supper*, which appears in the *Altarpiece of
the Holy Sacrament*.

Gerard David (1460–1523) became Brugge's leading painter following Memling's
death; his paintings cross the final bridge between Gothic and Renaissance art.
Those that remain in Flanders are the *Judgement of Cambyses*, the *Baptism of Christ*
and the *Transfiguration*, found in the Onze-Lieve-Vrouwekerk in Brugge.

Renaissance By the early 16th century the trickle of Renaissance influences had
built to a tidal wave that swept through the Flemish art world. The period also
witnessed the decline of cloth towns, like Brugge and Gent, as important centres of
art, whose epicentre moved to the booming port-town of Antwerp

Among the first to explore this hybrid of styles was **Quentin Matsys** (1464–1530).
The former ironsmith drew from the works of Dieric Bouts and van der Weyden,
and his paintings show the same attention to detail, crisp outline and transparent,
luminous layering of paint seen in the work of his predecessors. However, his work
contains the hazy landscapes reminiscent of Leonardo da Vinci, and is infused
with a strong personal religious fervour. Emotions are wrought upon the faces of
his subjects, occasionally tipping into the grotesque, as seen in the comical and
perturbing *Ugly Duchess* (now in the National Gallery in London).

Matsys' collaborator and close friend **Joachim Patinir** (1480–1524) was
renowned for his fantastical landscapes. Indeed, he showed little interest in the
figures in his paintings and often asked other artists to complete them.

Jan Gossaert (1478–1532) was one of the first artists to visit Italy in person.
He brought back techniques like *sfumato* – a hazing or blurring of layers between
paint to create a 'smoky' effect – and started using softer grey tones, instead of the
bright colours favoured by the Flemish Primitives; he was also the first to introduce
mythological nude figures into his paintings.

The work of **Pieter Brueghel the Elder** (1525–69) dominates the latter half of the
16th century. He was a fan of Hieronymous Bosch and several of his paintings are
informed by Bosch's fascination with the grotesque, most notably *The Triumph of
Death*. An accomplished landscape artist, he is praised for immortalising folk culture
in his paintings of village life. His early death prevented him from teaching his sons
Pieter Brueghel the Younger (1564–1638) and **Jan 'Velvet' Brueghel** (1568–1625);
their grandmother is believed to have taught the boys. Known to art historians as
'Pieter the Photocopier', Brueghel's eldest son is criticised for poorly copying his

father's style without innovation or individual input. Jan, on the other hand, developed his own style; preferring to focus on traditional religious iconography, landscapes and later the method of still life typical of Baroque art.

Baroque The Baroque period of Flemish art is often referred to as the Age of Rubens. Raised in Antwerp, **Pieter Paul Rubens** (1577–1640) kept Flemish art at the forefront of the cultural scene until the mid-17th century. Having visited Italy, and studied the techniques of masters such as Caravaggio, he returned to Antwerp and was appointed court painter to the Spanish rulers Infanta Isabella and Archduke Albert. Shortly after, he painted the exquisite triptych, *The Raising of the Cross,* and a year later *The Descent from the Cross*; both now hang in the Onze-Lieve-Vrouwekathedraal in Antwerp.

Whilst Renaissance work focused on encapsulating the moment immediately preceding an event, Baroque art centred on the moment of drama itself. Rich colours, the effect of *chiaroscuro* – the bold contrast between light and dark tones – and figures with muscular detail (often amply fleshed female nudes); all combined to give the works a dynamic energy. This new exuberance created ripples of excitement among artists and Rubens developed a loyal following. Those of note include **Anthony van Dyck** (1599–1641), who rose to become Rubens' best pupil. He later spent six years in Italy, before travelling to England where he was employed as court painter to King Charles I. Famed for his portraits of the royal family, van Dyck lived like a prince in London until his death; his remains are interred in St Paul's Cathedral.

When van Dyck left for Italy, he was replaced as Rubens' 'best' by head of the Antwerp artists' guild, **Jacob Jordaens** (1593–1678). Rubens employed him several times to convert his sketches into life-sized drawings and his exemplary skill earned him several commissions in his own right.

Alongside Baroque, genre painting, which captured the less poetic realities of everyday life, was beginning to emerge. At its helm was **Adriaen Brouwer** (1605–38). Brouwer by name, brewer by nature, he was a notorious drunk, but his familiarity with the taverns gave him intimate knowledge of his subject matter. His lively brushwork and muted earthy tones brought pub brawls scenes to life and immortalised the ruddy-cheeked peasants that featured in them.

Franz Snyders (1579–1657) studied under Pieter Brueghel the Younger and after experimenting with still life moved on to painting animals, often in pursuit of a hunt. His awareness of composition and uncanny ability to capture the texture of an animal's fur was greatly admired and Snyders frequently contributed to the works of Rubens and Jordaens.

Neoclassicism and Impressionism Following Rubens' death the crown of artistic significance shifted from Flanders to France. By the 18th century, Neoclassicism was in full swing, led by Parisian **Jacques-Louis David** (1748–1825). His most famous work *The Death of Marat* is housed in the Museé Royaux des Beaux Arts in Brussels and shows the murder of his good friend Jean-Paul Marat.

When Belgium achieved independence in 1830, there was an upwelling of nationalist pride and artists sought new ways of defining their art. **Antoine Wiertz** (1806–65) combined the romanticism found in the works of Michelangelo and home-grown Rubens with the neoclassical themes typical of his generation. His most distinctive work is the *Deux Jeunes Filles (La Belle Rosine),* where a luminous nude comes face to face with a menacing skeleton – symbolising the confrontation between beauty and death.

In contrast, painter and sculptor **Constantin Meunier** (1831–1905) made the average working Belgian, and later the industrial revolution, the subject of his paintings. Nature is idealised in scenes like *Trappists Ploughing* and the effects of industrialisation are captured in *In the Factory*. His contemporary, **Henri de Braekeleer** (1840–88), followed a similar course, depicting scenes of everyday life from *A Shoemaker* and *A Gardener* to his famous *The Brewer's House at Antwerp (A man sitting)*.

Impressed by the works of Monet and Renoir, **Théo van Rysselberghe** (1862–1926) dabbled in Impressionism, but abandoned it upon seeing Pointillism works of art in Paris. He brought the technique back to Belgium, much to the annoyance of his Les XX (see box, page 24) fellow **James Ensor** (1860–1949), who would remain an Impressionist painter for much of his life, albeit often tipping into the Surrealist world of the macabre, as in his masterpiece *Christ's Entry into Brussels*.

Symbolism, Fauvism, Expressionism and Surrealism During the late 19th century, Symbolism emerged alongside Impressionism, largely as an antithesis to the materialistic attitude of an industrial nation. Prominent Belgian artists in the field include **Fernand Khnopff** (1858–1921) a member of Les XX, who admired the

COMIC-STRIPS

Praised as the ninth art, the comic-strip – *stripverhalen* in Flemish, or *bandes-dessines* in French – has a cult following in Flanders. Prior to World War II, comic strips appeared as daily sketches at the back of newspapers, but shortage of paper forced publishers to relegate them to a weekly colour spread. For the first time cartoonists could develop storyboards of substance and plot. The format was much preferred by readers and the weekly colour spread stuck.

The first comic strips to gain international acclaim were the *Adventures of Tintin*, penned by Hergé (see Georges Remi, page 356). Numerous others followed in Hergé's footsteps, with many making their debut in the cornerstone comic magazine *Le Spirou* that was launched in 1938. Among the most successful series were:

BLAKE AND MORTIMER Written and drawn by Edgar P Jacobs (1904–87), the series first appeared at the front of the *Tintin* comic magazine. Apparently, the characters were modelled on two of Jacob's friends, and resident baddie, Colonel Olrik, is a self-portrait of Jacobs himself.

BLONDIN ET CIRAGE Created in 1939 for the Catholic paper *Le Croisé*, the series transferred to *Le Spirou* during the war and was considered forward thinking at the time because its two protagonists were a white child and a black child. Their creator was the prolific painter Joseph Gillain (1914–80), who went by the pen name Jijé.

BOULE ET BILL This quaint strip has appeared as a weekly gag on the back page of *Le Spirou* since 1959 and features seven-year-old Boule and his brown-and-white cocker spaniel Bill. It was created by Schaerbeek-born Jean Roba (1930–2006), who passed the series to his assistant Laurent Verron in 2003.

DE KAT Now 23 years old, Philippe Geluck's anthropomorphic, bulbous-nosed cat still appears every week in the 'Victor' supplement of *Le Soir* newspaper.

avant-garde work of the pre-Raphaelites and brought similar dreamlike qualities to his paintings; the occultist **Jean Delville** (1867–1953), chiefly remembered for his other-worldly chalk *Portrait of Mrs Stuart Merrill;* and the self-taught **Léon Spilliaert** (1881–1946) whose sickly and reclusive existence is echoed in the lone silhouettes that people his abstract watercolour landscapes.

The 20th century witnessed the arrival – albeit short-lived – of Fauvism. Led by Henri Matisse, this loosely defined genre was essentially an off-shoot of Impressionism, but was similar in style and motivation to Expressionism. Its followers, *Les Fauves* or 'Wild Beasts', distorted reality to reflect emotion, employing bold, arbitrary use of colour, unfussy lines and an exaggerated perspective. Sculptor **Rik Wouters** (1882–1916) was Belgium's most notable advocate.

Expressionism continued to strengthen in Belgium, led by **Constant Permeke** (1886–1952). Although wounded in World War I and banned from painting 'degenerate art' during Word War II by the Germans, Permeke was heavily productive during the intervening years. His success was such that the old 1,000 Belgian franc note bore his picture.

By the 1920s Surrealism had overtaken Expressionism in a big way, forcing onlookers to think in new ways by painting unexpected juxtapositions. Perhaps the

DE SMURFS Originally cropping up in a storyboard for Pierre Culliford's (Peyo) *Johan and Pirlouit* series, these sky-blue humanoids were such a success that they appeared in their own independent series, spawning collector-item miniatures, games and toys and a hugely popular TV show.

LUCKY LUKE Cowboy and keeper of the peace Lucky Luke, with his faithful steed Jolly Jumper and dim-witted dog Rantanplan, encountered real-life Western Greats like Calamity Jane and Billy the Kid. Drawn for over 50 years by Maurice De Bevère (1923–2001) – pen name Morris – it was taken over by French artist Achdé in 2003. Several of the early storyboards were penned by René Goscinny of *Astérix* fame.

QUICK ET FLUPKE Another creation of Hergé, it followed the escapades of two Bruxellois street urchins. It featured in *Le Petit Vingtième* from 1930, but Hergé abandoned it in 1940 to concentrate on the hugely successful *Adventures of Tintin*.

THE ADVENTURES OF NERO The bald, medallion-sporting, flawed, yet loveable protagonist Nero and the Porsche-driving detective van Zwam cropped up in Flemish newspapers between 1947 and 2002. Creator Marc Sleen (1922–) is a huge fan of Africa and a wildlife enthusiast; both passions crop up in his storyboards.

SUSKE AND WISKE Known as *Spike and Suzy* in English and *Willy and Wanda* in the US, the orphan and heroine team were created by Antwerp-born Willy Vandersteen (1913–90). A team of artists still produces the strips of adventures for the daily *De Standaard* newspaper.

Today, Brussels is a mecca for fans and collectors. They can browse the dense collection of comic book shops found in Rue du Midi, Boulevard Anspach and Boulevard Lemonnier; wander the halls of the Le Centre Belge de la Bande Dessinée (page 111); and follow the city's designated comic-strip walking trail.

Formed in 1883, Les XX were a group of avant-garde artists who set up an annual exhibition showcasing the work of 20 selected international artists, in the hope of inspiring and promoting new artistic developments throughout Europe. Its 11 founding members included the likes of James Ensor, Théo van Rysselberge and Symbolist Fernand Khnopff. They soon invited a further nine members and became known collectively as the *vingtistes*. Among others, their shows introduced the works of Claude Monet, Camille Pissarro, Paul Gauguin and Vincent van Gogh to the public.

However, their success was short-lived. Original founder James Ensor left the group after heavy arguments with XX fellow van Rysselberge over the scandalous nature of his *Christ's Entry into Brussels,* and after mounting disparagements from art critics Les XX disbanded in 1892.

most famous example is **René Magritte's** *Ceci n'est pas une pipe (This is not a pipe)* – with these words emblazoned beneath the image of a pipe. Another Surrealist was **Paul Delvaux** (1897–1994), whose dreamlike paintings consistently featured either railway stations or demure nudes (and sometimes both).

Modern art After World War II, Belgian art tipped into the abstract. These post-war avant-garde artists soon joined together to form **La Jeune Peinture Belge**, a group largely inspired by the work of Victor Sevranckx (1897–1965). Upon its demise, a larger-scale movement was founded encompassing artists from three European cities (Copenhagen, Brussels and Amsterdam). Nicknamed CoBrA, the movement advocated lively brushwork, vibrant colours, and warped perspectives of the human form. Belgium's most famous exponent was Brussels-born **Pierre Alechinsky** (1927–), who often worked in ink.

Working independently was **Marcel Broodthaers** (1924–76), a jack-of-all-trades who dabbled in film, poetry and collage art. He is remembered for the several large-scale installations he built inside his Brussels home.

Retired sculptor **Henri van Herwegen** (1940–), better known as Panamarenko, is based in Antwerp. The majority of his creations were modelled around the Greek mythological figure Icarus. He now promotes his PanamaJumbo coffee brand.

The latest Belgian artist to achieve international recognition was Brussels-born **Carsten Höller** (1961–), who was the talk of the town in London during 2006. His *Test Site,* set up in the grand hallway of Tate Modern in London, featured 25m-long metal and fibreglass slides that visitors could try out – at up to 50km/h!

MUSIC The Flemish love to party. Whilst older generations will be busting their groove to golden-oldie ditties in strictly over-50 dance halls, students will be head-banging to the latest techno or trip-hop tune at a club just down the road. This madness for music is reflected in the country's social events calendar, which is packed with outdoor music festivals and concert performances (see pages 52–7). Flanders' musical history features a surprising line-up of talent. Here are some of the highlights:

Jazz Brussels-born **Jean-Baptiste 'Toots' Thielemans** (1922–) achieved fame for his accomplished harmonica playing and virtuoso whistling. His career rocketed in 1949 after he joined a jam session in Paris attended by trumpeter Miles Davis, saxophonist Charlie Parker and drummer Max Roach. He moved to the US and became a member of Parker's 'All-Stars' band and recorded with the likes of Ella Fitzgerald, Billy Joel, Paul Simon and Quincy Jones. The region's love of swinging notes still runs strong and numerous jazz festivals are hosted every year, among them the world-renowned Gent Jazz Festival and the Brussels Jazz Marathon (page 53).

Folk music Before leaving for America, 'Toots' Thielemans was part of **Bobbejaan Schoepen's** (1925–) backing band. Schoepen was a jack-of-all-trades and a superb whistler, who ditched his all-singing-all-dancing vaudeville act in favour of American country music. During the 1950s, his supporting acts included Jacques Brel.

Other folk-revivalists include Wannes van de Velde, Herman Dewit, Walter de Buck and Hubert Boone, who attempted to modernise the sound by combining it with continental influences from Spain and Greece.

Chanson In 1956, Flemish singer-songwriter **Jacques Brel** (page 354) arrived on the Parisian music scene and saved Belgium's place in music history from falling into obscurity. His breakout hit *Quand on n'a que l'amour* was troubadour in style and tone, but he quickly moved on to explore more complex themes and compositions and the entire French-speaking population was entranced.

Also popular among the older generations are Helmut Lotti and Will Tura.

Popular music Flanders is extremely proud of pop group **Clouseau**. Headed by brothers Koen and Kris Wauters, Clouseau shot to fame following the 1989 Eurovision Song Contest, where they gained second place with their song *Anne*. Their English-language albums failed to make an impact on the international market and nowadays the band concentrates on playing live concerts for their adoring fans.

The other big-name duo is **Soulwax**, also known as 2ManyDJs, headed by the Dewaele brothers.

CINEMA Brussels boasts two Hollywood stars: action hero Jean Claude van Damme (page 356) and Oscar-winning actress Audrey Hepburn (page 355). However, Flanders has had much more success behind the camera. It started with the 1934 film *De Witte*, a screenplay adapted from the semi-autobiographical work of Flemish writer Ernest Claes, and expanded in the 1960s thanks to government subsidy. Often exploring gritty social problems and tainted with black humour, successes have included Poelvoorde's *Man Bites Dog* (1992), Deruddere's *Everybody Famous* (2000), which was nominated in the best Foreign Film category at the Academy Awards, the Dardenne brothers' *Rosetta* (1999), which won Palme d'Or at the Cannes Film Festival and *Rundskop* (2011), a dark police thriller nominated for the best Foreign Language Film at the 2012 Oscars.

Flanders hosts a handful of film festivals during the year (see pages 52–7).

ARCHITECTURE Flanders' rich architectural heritage ranges from the 13th-century Romanesque and Gothic to 18th-century Baroque and 19th-century Art Nouveau. At times haphazard, but always charming, the mixture of medieval houses next to modern steel and glass is a common occurrence. From Gent's Patershol quarter, lined with brick-red medieval terraces, to Brussels' ultra-modern and starlight-studded Atomium, the region's bold approach to architecture continues to evolve.

Flanders' oldest and most celebrated architectural feats are the towering belfries and secluded *begijnhofs* (see box, page 18). They cropped up during the 13th and 15th centuries when the trading of cloth created an economic boom that also financed Brussels' Grand' Place and many of the region's Gothic cathedrals and

The materials used to construct a building are a dead give away as to its age. In city centres like Gent and Brugge, a variety of architectural styles sit side by side, but how can you tell which is which? The materials and style of façade provide vital clues as to a building's age and the breakdown below should help you to classify the houses as your wander around town centres.

- **Grey limestone** is the oldest variety of building material and denotes buildings dating from the 14th century.
- **Sandstone** was a favourite throughout the 15th and 16th centuries because its crumbly surface could easily be carved into reliefs that decorated the façades of guildhouses and wealthier homeowners.
- **Red bricks and stepped gable** were made compulsory in some towns after recurring fires and popular because they were cheap; the formula is typically 17th century.
- **Bricks and painted plaster** came into style in the 18th century, a favourite of families who wished to hide their cheap brick-built houses with a prettily decorated, but inexpensive façade.

town halls; the most impressive examples of these can be seen in Antwerp's Onze-Lieve-Vrouwekathedraal and Leuven's Stadhuis.

The counter-Reformation of the 16th–17th centuries ushered in the Italian Baroque style. Characterised by twisted columns, arching domes and elaborate ornamentation, it was quickly adopted and given a Flemish twist by artists and architects and imaginatively renamed Flemish Baroque. The guildhouses of the Grand' Place were rebuilt in this design following Louis XIV's attack in 1695.

Following independence in 1830, Leopold I was keen to revive Brussels' urban cityscape and set it on par with Paris, so ordered the construction of numerous buildings. Among those commissioned were the magnificent Galeries Royales St-Hubert, famed for their arched glass-paned roof, and the formidable Palais de Justice.

Towards the end of the 19th century, Art Nouveau was in full swing. Influencing everything from buildings to bedroom furniture, the movement was characterised by the use of wrought iron, glass, marble and wood decorated with leaves and flowers in flowing, sinuous lines. Architects of note include **Paul Saintenoy** (1862–1952) – who is responsible for the elegant Art Nouveau Old England Department Store in Brussels, which now houses the Musical Instrument Museum, **Gustave Serrurier-Bovy** (1858–1910), **Henry van de Velde** (1863–1957), **Paul Hankar** (1859–1901), and the legendary **Victor Horta** (1861–1947). His most famous constructions include Hôtel Tassel, Hôtel Solvay, the Greenhouses at Laeken (which he designed with Hankar) and Maison Waucquez, which now houses the Belgian Comic Museum.

Modern architectural design was perhaps heralded by Antwerp's Boerentoren (Farmers' Tower), built in 1928 and considered Europe's first skyscraper. This was soon followed by the space-age Atomium (page 130), built for the 1958 World Fair.

The experimental design of many of the EU buildings and the conversion of Flagey – a former radio and television studio in Ixelles – into a theatre and café has inspired modern architects, and new ideas are showcased in the Museum of Modern Architecture (*18 Rue de l'Ermitage; ⊕ on appointment*) in Brussels.

2

Practical Information

WHEN TO VISIT

Flanders is best visited during spring and summer, or just before Christmas. From March to May the countryside is alive with newborn lambs and calves, and orchards are filled with blossom; July and August are marked by endless festivals and parades; and come December romantic Christmas markets line cobblestone squares. There are a few provisos: don't visit Gent in the first half of August when the locals are recovering from their Gentse Feesten hangovers and everything is closed; avoid the coast during winter when it becomes a series of ghost towns whipped by gale-force winds and rain; and be aware that from mid-November to March many of the smaller towns close their sites of interest, so plan your trip accordingly.

HIGHLIGHTS

ANDERLECHT, BRUSSELS Explore Brussels' outer communes. Up-and-coming Anderlecht is home to the capital's last working brewery, a superb off-the-beaten-track museum and boutique B&Bs. See page 122.

OOSTDUINKERKE'S HORSEBACK SHRIMP FISHERMEN Watch the world's last horseback fishermen trawling the North Sea shallows for grey shrimp – and try a few too. See page 247.

ST ELIZABETH BEGIJNHOF Wander around Kortrijk's 17th-century impossibly quaint nook-and-cranny UNESCO-listed St Elizabeth *begijnhof*. See page 277.

TRY THE WORLD'S RAREST BEER Savour the taste of the dark and sweet Westvleteren No 12, brewed by the monks of Sint-Sixtus Abbey and only available at their abbey café. See page 273.

MECHELEN Enjoy the café culture, carillon concerts and top-notch B&Bs of this buzzing, but often overlooked town. See page 306.

TALBOT HOUSE, POPERINGE Reflect on the past at this perfectly preserved World War I resthouse that's as touching as the war cemeteries. Learn about Tubby, the jolly proprietor, and the men who stayed here. See page 271.

CYCLING AROUND SINT-TRUIDEN Take to the saddle in springtime and ride through blossom-filled fruit orchards, or later, stocking up on fresh strawberries, apples and pears as you go. See page 331.

LISSEWEGE Don't miss Flanders' prettiest hamlet, made up of whitewashed cottages, concealing good restaurants and homely B&Bs. See page 233.

OOIDONK CASTLE Pretend you're royalty for the day at this fairytale castle, complete with moat and drawbridge, set in acres of forest. See page 207.

TONGEREN Shop for vintage trinkets at the antiques market in Flanders' oldest town – and visit the award-winning Roman museum. See page 331.

AALST CARNIVAL Get dressed up and join the merry madness of Aalst's three-day tourist-free carnival which features a parade, a bonfire and lots of cross-dressing and drinking. See page 196.

LIER Pitch up on the hour to see Lier's unique Zimmertoren clock in action. See page 313.

MAASEIK Discover this forgotten town snuggled against the Netherlands border. It hides a very rare hand-painted 8th-century gospel and offers lovely cross-border cycling opportunities. See page 335.

SUGGESTED ITINERARIES

It doesn't take very long to go anywhere in Flanders. All the major cities are roughly a 40-minute train ride from each other and, as a result, it's possible to fit quite a lot into a short trip. Bearing this in mind, my suggested itineraries are based around a series of themes which are designed to introduce you to the real Flanders – not just the cities – and allow you to mix and match as you see fit, or pursue a particular area of interest. Don't try to cram too much in; allow enough time to enjoy a beer while sunning yourself on a terrace, or linger over a really good meal.

BEER Devoted beer enthusiasts can visit the following breweries: Brussels' De Cantillon, De Halve Maan in Brugge, De Dolle Brouwers in Diksmuide, Gruut in Gent, Het Anker in Mechelen, Boon in Halle, Hoegaarden, Tongeren's new Au Phare microbrewery, the Hopmuseum in Poperinge, and the De Vrede café in Westvleteren.

CYCLING Flanders' most famous cycle race, the Ronde van Vlaanderen, is associated with the towns of Geraardsbergen, Sint-Niklaas, and Oudenaarde. The latter has a dedicated museum, as does Roeselare. Great cycle routes include: the Brugge to Damme canal, the entire length of the North Sea coastline and the orchard-filled Haspengouw region near Sint-Truiden.

WORLD WAR I World War I sites and cemeteries are clustered in the west and centre around the town of Ieper (Ypres), nearby Poperinge and, further north, the towns of Diksmuide and Veurne.

MEDIEVAL CENTRES A fan of medieval architecture? Be sure to visit Brussels' Grand' Place, and the city centres of Brugge, Gent, Leuven, Lier, Tongeren and Veurne.

OFF THE BEATEN TRACK To experience a real slice of Flemish life and escape the well-trod tourist trails you should add Aalst, Ronse, Maaseik, Lisswege, Laarne, Herentals and Geel to your itinerary.

TOURIST INFORMATION

The tourism infrastructure in Flanders is superb and the range of publications produced to help guide visitors around the region is vast. Even the smallest of villages has an information kiosk where you can find everything from where to stay and eat to local events going on in the area. Staff are usually very friendly, knowledgeable and enthusiastic. Tourist offices will be clearly signposted in all cities: just look for *dienst voor toerisme*.

BRUSSELS

ℹ **Visit Flanders** 61 Rue du Marché aux Herbes; ⊕ Apr–Sep 09.00–18.00 Mon–Sat, 10.00–17.00 Sun; Jul–Aug 09.00–19.00 daily; Oct–Mar 09.00–17.00 Mon–Sat, 10.00–16.00 Sun; NB closed 13.00–14.00 Sat & Sun. Pick up Art Nouveau or comic-strip trail map for free at any of these offices. ℹ **Visit Brussels** 2–4 Rue Royale; ☎ 02 513 89 40; ⊕ 10.00–18.00 daily; www.visitbrussels.be.

Formerly Brussels International, the main office is also a booking point for tours, shows etc. There are smaller kiosks inside the Hôtel de Ville on the Grand' Place (⊕ 10.00–18.00 daily), the main concourse of the Bruxelles-Midi/Brussels-Zuid railway station (⊕ 10.00–18.00 daily) & the arrivals hall at Zaventem airport (⊕ 08.00–21.00).

ABROAD There are just a few overseas tourist offices for Flanders, most of them in Europe.

ℹ **France** 21 Blvd des Capucines, Paris; ☎ +33 1 47 42 41 18; www.belgique-tourisme.be
ℹ **Germany** 46 Cäcilienstrasse, 50667 Köln; ☎ +49 221 270 97 52; www.flandern.com
ℹ **Netherlands** 86 Koninginnegracht, 2514 AJ Den Haag; ☎ +31 70 416 81 10; www.toerisme-vlaanderen.nl

ℹ **UK** 1a Cavendish Sq, London W1G 0LD; ☎ 020 7307 7738; www.visitflanders.co.uk
ℹ **US** 220 East 42nd St, Room 3402, New York, NY 10017; ☎ +1 212 758 8130; www.visitbelgium.com

TOUR OPERATORS

Flanders is a popular weekend-break destination and you should easily find deals to the major cities and towns – like Antwerp, Brugge, Brussels and Gent – online. For a tour with a certain slant see the specialist tour operators listed below.

UK

Cresta Holidays ☎ 0844 879 8036; www.crestaholidays.co.uk. Offer city breaks to Brugge & Brussels & are good for special offers.
Gold Crest ☎ 01943 433 457; www.gold-crest.com. Coach holidays to Gent, Brussels, Antwerp, Brugge & Oostende, as well as special battlefields tours & Christmas market trips.
Martin Randall Travel ☎ 020 8742 3355; www.martinrandall.com. Runs art & war-themed cultural tours led by a field expert; accommodation is mainly in 4-star hotels.
Osprey Holidays ☎ 0131 243 8098; www.osprey-holidays.co.uk. Independent family-run tour operator that offers value-for-money packages, including

everything from hand-picked accommodation to concert tickets for Brugge & Brussels.
Leisure Direction ☎ 0844 576 5504; www.leisuredirection.co.uk. Low-cost operator that can arrange everything from w/end package deals to cheap ferry fares.
Railbookers ☎ 020 3327 0800; www.railbookers.com. Arrange travel & accommodation to all of Flanders' main cities.
Shortbreaks ☎ 0844 482 2937; www.shortbreaks.com. Offer city breaks to Antwerp, Brussels, Brugge, Leuven, Mechelen & Gent with emphasis on posh hotel stays.
Thomas Cook ☎ 0844 879 8412; www.thomascook.com. Well-established agency that

organises city breaks to Antwerp, Brugge, Brussels & Gent, as well as car hire, travel insurance & foreign currency.

Travelsphere ☏ 0844 567 9961; www. travelsphere.co.uk. Its coach trips visit Brussels, Brugge & Antwerp.

US

American Express ☏ +1 800 297 2977; www. americanexpress.com/travel/. Global banking giant offers hotel & flight packages, as well as car hire; if you have an account with them you may be able to pay for the whole trip using accumulated membership points.

Austin-Lehman ☏ +1 800 575 1540; www. austinlehman.com. Runs 7-day cycling tours from Brussels to Gent.

Europe Express ☏ +1 800 927 3876; www. europeexpress.com. Organises day tours of Antwerp, Brussels, Gent & Brugge.

Eurovacations ☏ +1 877 471 3876; www. eurovacations.com. Internet company offering themed visits from diamonds in Antwerp to cooking classes in Brugge.

SPECIALIST TOUR OPERATORS
US

Beer Trips ☏ +1 406 531 9109; www.beertrips. com. This American operator offers devotees of Belgian brews the chance to visit the Flemish breweries.

In Trend ☏ +1 845 510 9630; www.intrend. com. Chocolate-themed tour visiting Brussels, Brugge & Antwerp for seriously sweet-toothed travellers.

Belgium

All About Belgium ☏ +32 53 80 98 18; www. aab-allaboutbelgium.be. This small operator arranges special-interest tours, accommodation, tickets for exhibitions, guides etc.

Holiday Pride ☏ +32 2 502 73 77; www. holidaypride.be. Tour operator specialising in trips in Flanders for gay travellers.

Itinéraires ☏ +32 2 541 03 77; www.itineraires. be. Visits to the main cities with a specialist slant: diamonds in Antwerp, Art Nouveau in Brussels.

RED TAPE

SHORT STAYS Citizens from the UK, Ireland, EU countries, Canada, Australia, New Zealand and the US do not require a visa to enter Belgium and are permitted to stay for 90 days, as long as you have three months left on your passport. If your country does not appear in this list, then you must apply for a visa. Along with your completed application form you will need to submit: your passport (preferably valid for at least six months), two recent passport photos, return travel tickets, proof of adequate travel insurance and possibly proof of sufficient financial subsistence for the duration of your trip (eg: a bank statement). Currently a short-stay visa costs €61. Applications can take up to three or four weeks to be processed, so be sure to apply well in advance.

STAYING LONGER EU nationals who plan to stay for over 90 days need to apply for a residence permit from the local town hall, within eight days of arrival. You will need to submit a valid passport, three passport-sized photos, and proof of financial independence (eg: bank statement), and pay a small commune tax charge. You may also be asked to provide your birth certificate and allow them to take your fingerprints. After that, the local police will visit you to ensure you live at the address noted, then a residence permit, valid for five months, will be granted. This will be renewed every month until proof of employment is provided; you will then be issued with a five-year permanent identity card. Non-EU nationals face a longer process. You must apply for a temporary residence permit (*Autorisation de Séjour Provisoire/Voorlopige Verblijfsvergunning*) from the consulate or embassy posted in your country of origin, before you leave.

EMBASSIES AND CONSULATES

ABROAD

Australia 19 Arkana St, Yarralumla, Canberra, ACT; ☏ +61 2 6273 2501; ⏲ 07.00–12.30 & 13.00–16.00 Mon–Thu, 09.00–12.30 & 13.00–15.00 Fri

Canada 360 Albert St, 8th Flr, Suite 820, Ottawa, K1R 7X7; ☏ +1 613 236 7267; ⏲ 09.00–13.00 & 14.00–15.00 Mon–Thu, 09.00–14.00 Fri

France 9 Rue de Tilsitt, 75840 Paris Cedex 17; ☏ +33 1 44 09 39 39; ⏲ 09.00–12.30 Mon–Fri

Germany 52–3 Jägerstrasse, 10117 Berlin; ☏ +49 3020 6420; ⏲ 08.30–13.00 & 14.30–17.00 Mon–Fri

Ireland 2 Shrewsbury Rd, Ballsbridge, Dublin; ☏ +353 1 205 7100; ⏲ 09.00–13.00 & 14.00–15.00 Mon–Fri

Luxembourg 4 Rue des Girondins, Luxembourg City; ☏ +352 44 27 461; ⏲ 09.00–14.00 Mon–Fri

Netherlands 97 Alexanderveld, 2585 DB Den Haag; ☏ +31 70 312 34 56; ⏲ 09.00–12.00 & 13.30–16.00 Mon–Thu, 09.00–12.00 Fri

New Zealand 15 Brandon St, Level 6, Wellington; ☏ +64 49 749 080

UK 17 Grosvenor Cres, London SW1X 7EE; ☏ 020 7470 3700; ⏲ 08.30–16.00 Mon–Fri

US 3330 Garfield St, NW, Washington DC 2000; ☏ +1 202 333 6900; ⏲ 09.30–12.00 & 14.00–15.30 Mon–Fri

BRUSSELS

Australia 6–8 Rue Guimard; ☏ 02 286 05 00

Canada 2 Av de Tervueren; ☏ 02 741 06 11

France 65 Rue Ducale; ☏ 02 548 87 00

Germany 8–14 Rue Jacques de Lalaing; ☏ 02 787 18 00

Ireland 180 Chaussée d'Etterbeek; ☏ 02 282 34 00

Luxembourg 75 Av de Cortenbergh; ☏ 02 737 57 00

Netherlands Av Herrmann Debroux 48; ☏ 02 512 10 40

New Zealand 7th Flr, 9–31 Av des Nerviens; ☏ 02 512 10 40

UK 10 Av d'Auderghem; ☏ 02 287 62 11

US 27 Blvd du Régent; ☏ 02 811 40 00

GETTING THERE AND AWAY

Flanders is incredibly accessible. Bang in the middle of Europe and cuddling the North Sea coastline, it can be reached by air, sea or land. It also helps that Brussels is now the second largest international business city in the world and, as a result, transport links have increased to meet the demands of countless international commuters. Companies are in a constant battle to provide competitive fares and travellers can benefit from these price wars.

BY AIR

From the UK and Ireland In the UK, you can fly direct from London, Manchester, Birmingham and Edinburgh, and, in Ireland, direct from Cork and Dublin. Flights from the UK take about an hour; those from Ireland an hour and a half.

Brussels has two major airports: the central Brussels-National (*www.brusselsairport.be*) — also known as Zaventem — and the outer lying Brussels-Charleroi (*www.charleroi-airport.com*). Brussels-National is located 13km northeast of Brussels in the small town of Zaventem. It serves most major airlines, including the national carrier Brussels Airlines. Charleroi is 60km south of the city, about an hour's drive away, and serves budget airlines. For transfers to other destinations, see pages 68–9.

✈ **Air France** ☏ 0870 142 4343; www.airfrance.co.uk. Flies from Birmingham, Edinburgh & Newcastle via Paris to Brussels.

✈ **Aer Lingus** ☏ 0870 876 5000; www.flyaerlingus.com. Flies direct from Cork & Dublin to Brussels.

✈ **British Airways** ✆ 0870 850 9850; www.
ba.com. The airline giant operates 8 flights a day,
7 days a week between Heathrow & Brussels.
✈ **Brussels Airlines** ✆ 0905 60 95 609;
www.brusselsairlines.com. Flies from Heathrow
to Brussels-Zaventem. Look out for their b.light &
b.flex ticket options. The first is the cheapest, the
second saves you paying a surcharge if you miss
your flight & need to get the next one.

✈ **City Jet** ✆ 0871 66 33 777; www.cityjet.com.
Offers direct flights from Manchester to Antwerp.
✈ **Ryanair** ✆ 0871 246 0000; www.ryanair.com
Specialises in budget flights & offers direct flights
to Brussels-Charleroi from Edinburgh, Manchester
& Dublin.

From the US and Canada

Direct flights from the US to Brussels are surprisingly limited and expensive, whilst those from Canada to Belgium's capital are virtually non-existent. The cheaper option, used by the majority of carriers, is to fly to London and pick up a connecting flight from there. These will invariably land at Brussels-Zaventem. On average, flights from the east coast to Europe take eight hours; those from the west coast take ten to eleven hours.

✈ **Air Canada** ✆ 888 247 2262; www.aircanada.
com. From Calgary, Halifax, Montreal, Ottawa,
Toronto & Vancouver to Brussels via London.
✈ **American Airlines** ✆ 800 433 7300; www.
aa.com. Chicago & New York (JFK) to Brussels.
✈ **Continental Airlines** ✆ 800 523 3273;
www.continental.com. Newark to Brussels.

✈ **Delta Airlines** ✆ 800 241 4141; www.delta.
com. New York (JFK) & Atlanta to Brussels.
✈ **United Airlines** ✆ 800 300 1547; www.
united.com. Washington to Brussels.
✈ **US Airways** ✆ 800 428 4322; www.
usairways.com. Philadelphia to Brussels.

From the rest of the world

Unfortunately, there are no direct flights to Belgium from Australia or New Zealand. The easiest and cheapest option is to fly into another European capital and catch a connecting flight from there. Those travelling from Australia will benefit from cheaper tickets by flying via southeast Asia, while flying over North America is the best option for those travelling from New Zealand. Flights from Australia and New Zealand to the UK take approximately 20 hours.

✈ **Air New Zealand** Australia: ✆ 13 24 76, New
Zealand: ✆ 0800 737 000; www.airnewzealand.
com. Flights to London from Brisbane, Melbourne
& Sydney via Hong Kong, & from Auckland via Los
Angeles.
✈ **British Airways** Australia: ✆ 1 300 767 177,
New Zealand: ✆ 09 966 9777; www.ba.com.
Flights to London from Melbourne via Hong
Kong & Singapore; from Sydney via Bangkok
& Singapore; from Perth via Singapore, & from
Auckland via Los Angeles.
✈ **KLM** Australia: ✆ 1 300 392 192, New Zealand:
✆ 09 309 1782; www.klm.com. Flies from Sydney
to Amsterdam & London via Singapore.

✈ **Qantas** Australia: ✆ 13 13 13, New Zealand:
✆ 09 357 8900; www.qantas.com.au. Flights from
Melbourne & Sydney to London & from Adelaide,
Auckland, Brisbane, Christchurch, Darwin, Perth &
Wellington to London via Asia.
✈ **Singapore Airlines** Australia: ✆ 13 10 11,
New Zealand: ✆ 09 379 3209; www.singaporeair.
com. Flights from Auckland, Brisbane, Christchurch,
Melbourne, Perth, Sydney & Adelaide to Singapore.
From here they operate daily flights to Amsterdam
where you can catch a train to Brussels.
✈ **United Airlines** Australia: ✆ 13 17 77; www.
united.com. From Auckland to London.

BY FERRY

Travel by boat has been heavily eclipsed by the faster Eurostar and Eurotunnel services, but if you're not in a rush you can benefit from huge savings offered by the cross-Channel ferries – families especially. **P&O Ferries** ✆ *08716*

64 21 21; www.poferries.com) run services from Dover to Calais, while **DFDS Seaways** (✆ *0871 574 7235; www.norfolkline.com*) sail from Dover to Dunkerque. **Transeuropa Ferries** (*www.transeuropaferries.com*) sail between Ramsgate and Oostende. P&O Ferries also run an overnight service between Hull and Zeebrugge.

BY EUROTUNNEL (*www.eurotunnel.com*) This high-speed car train runs from Folkestone to Calais 24 hours a day, with up to four departures an hour during the day and every hour between midnight and 06.00. The journey takes 35 minutes, then from Calais it's a two-hour drive along the E40 to Brussels. Standard fares for motorists and motorcyclists start from around £150 return. Travellers on a weekend break should ask about the Short Stay Saver fares. Taking an overnight train will cut the price of your ticket in half.

BY TRAIN
From the UK
Eurostar (*www.eurostar.com*) Eurostar run up to nine services a day from Kings Cross St Pancras International to Bruxelles-Midi/Brussels-Zuid; journey time one hour and 50 minutes. Tickets range from around £400 for a fully flexible business-class weekend return to £80 for a non-flexible weekend return. They frequently run weekend-break promotions combining rail travel and hotel accommodation, so check their website. Remember that your Eurostar ticket also includes an onward journey to any Belgian station, so if you are travelling on to Gent or Antwerp there's no need to purchase another ticket when you arrive in Brussels. Also, travellers with Inter-Rail and Eurail passes qualify for discounts when booking tickets on Eurostar.

Deutsche Bahn (*www.bahn.de*) Eurostar is set to lose its monopoly of the Channel Tunnel in December 2012: German rail company Deutsche Bahn are in the testing stages of high-speed routes from London to Frankfurt and Amsterdam, stopping in Brussels on the way. The journey time from London to Brussels is estimated at three hours, with three daily departures (morning, noon and afternoon) scheduled. Visit their website for up-to-date details.

From France, Germany, Luxembourg and the Netherlands Thalys (*www. thalys.com*) runs services from Paris, Cologne and Amsterdam to Bruxelles Midi/ Brussels Zuid. Over 28 trains a day depart from Paris Nord or Charles De Gaulle Airport; the journey takes 85 minutes. From Paris, trains also run to the following railway stations: Antwerp-Berchem, Brugge, Gent-Sint-Pieters and Oostende. Journeys from Cologne and Amsterdam take two hours 30 minutes.

All tickets must be bought before boarding, but booking in advance allows you to benefit from the discounted 'No-Flex' and 'Smoove' fares. Special discounts also apply to students, seniors and children. Bicycles are allowed, but they must be collapsible.

Trains from Luxembourg to Brussels depart every hour. The journey takes three hours and tickets don't need to be bought in advance.

BY BUS If you're prepared to put in the bum-numbing hours, **Eurolines** (*www. eurolines.co.uk*), a division of National Express, operate four daily departures from London's Victoria coach station to Brussels and Brugge. The journey takes approximately eight or nine hours, but coaches are fairly comfortable with reclining chairs, videos and onboard toilet. All buses use the Dover–Calais ferry route to cross the Channel. Fares are around £70 return, plus a £4 booking fee.

HEALTH *with Dr Felicity Nicholson*

There are no official vaccination requirements for entry into Flanders and no serious health issues to worry about. However, it is best to be up to date with the vaccinations recommended for Britain such as diphtheria, tetanus and polio – now given as the all-in-one vaccine Revaxis – that last for ten years. Other vaccinations would include hepatitis B for healthcare workers, plus influenza and pneumococcal vaccines for the elderly and those at special risk. If you are walking in long grass check yourself for ticks afterwards; they may carry Lyme disease which manifests as a rash accompanied by a fever, headache, neck stiffness, painful muscles and joints, swollen lymph glands, and fatigue.

Residents of EU countries, including the UK and Ireland, should obtain a **European Health Insurance Card** (EHIC) (✆ *0845 606 2030; www.ehic.org.uk*) before travelling as it allows you to receive medical treatment at a reduced cost and sometimes for free. Order it online or call the number above. The EHIC doesn't cover all eventualities, so you should still buy travel insurance that includes medical costs.

TRAVEL CLINICS A full list of current travel clinic websites worldwide is available from the International Society of Travel Medicine on www.istm.org. For other journey preparation information, consult www.tripprep.com. Information about various medications may be found on www.emedicine.com.

PHARMACIES Pharmacies are easily identified by the illuminated green cross posted outside and are generally open 09.00–18.00 Monday–Friday, 09.00–12.00 Saturday, although in the larger towns and cities some will stay open 24 hours. Consult the language section on pages 350–1 for all basic medical-related vocabulary.

HOSPITALS In case of a medical emergency dial ✆ 112. You can find out where the nearest on-call doctor (or dentist) is by calling ✆ 100. The majority of hospitals in Flanders have first-rate facilities and most staff will speak English. Like Flemish nationals you will have to pay for treatments upfront and reclaim a proportion of the costs later providing you have an EHIC card (see above).

SMOKING Smoking in cafés/restaurants serving food was banned in Flanders in January 2010. At the time of writing, you're still allowed to smoke in pubs, but this is likely to change in the near future.

SAFETY

Flanders is a safe region to visit. Like most places there are instances of bag snatching, pick-pocketing and very rarely mugging and you should be vigilant if travelling or walking late at night in the vicinity of Brussels-Zuid/Bruxelles-Midi and Brussel-Noord/Bruxelles-Nord railway stations, and in the EU quarter. There have been instances of carjacking around Brussels-Zuid/Bruxelles-Midi too, so keep your doors locked when driving around this area.

As long as you take sensible precautions to conceal the location of your wallet, aren't flashing huge sums of cash and don't leave valuables exposed in the back seat of your car, you shouldn't encounter any problems. It is probably a good idea to make photocopies of your important documents, and to store them separately from the originals.

DRUGS The most frequently occurring drug in Flanders is cannabis. Currently, it is legal for over-18s to possess less than three grams of the plant for personal consumption, as long as they are not behaving anti-socially. However, those found to be under age or in possession of more than the specified amount will face fines and possibly prison sentences. Class A drugs are present, especially in towns like Antwerp or Brussels where there is an active party scene, but the penalties for possession and consumption of these are severe.

TERRORISM There have been no attacks to date, but Brussels' profile as 'capital' of Europe and headquarters to numerous international institutions like NATO and the EU could make it a potential target. However, the threat is minimal and there is no reason to let it affect any travel plans. Check the FCO website www.fco.gov.uk/travel for the latest updates.

FOCUS ON SPECIFIC GROUPS

WOMEN TRAVELLERS I've visited Flanders countless times over the last decade and, to date, have experienced no hassles as a young female travelling independently. Women are viewed as complete equals and the quiet nature of Flemish men means you will rarely encounter the 'Romeo' or 'Casanova' types that may harass you elsewhere in continental Europe.

SENIOR TRAVELLERS Senior citizens are held in high respect in Flemish society and you can expect to be treated with courtesy. The great news is that over 60s will qualify for discounted ticket rates for many museums, theatres etc and benefit from reduced rails fares.

GAY AND LESBIAN TRAVELLERS The gay and lesbian social scene in Flanders is alive and well, albeit the flag flies at a slightly lower mast than in the Netherlands. Tolerance varies from total acceptance among younger age groups to mild indifference among the older generation and again attitudes may vary from those found in cities to those out in the country. Gay and lesbian couples have been entitled to full civil marriage rights since 2003 – the second country in the world to do so – and have had the right to adopt children since 2006. These changes are complemented by a healthy selection of gay-orientated bars, clubs and hotels in the main cities (see boxes, pages 89 and 291). For more information check out the websites listed below:

EGG www.eggbrussels.be. English-speaking gay group based in Brussels who organise parties & produce an online guide to gay Brussels & Belgium.

Rainbow House www.rainbowhouse.be. Information centre & meeting point for gays & lesbians in Brussels.
EBAB www.ebab.com. Accommodation-booking service for gays & lesbians.

TRAVELLING WITH KIDS Children are adored in Flanders and are well catered for by the majority of hotels and guesthouses, who usually have a 'family' room and, if not, are happy to supply a cot or fold-away bed. Well-behaved tots are welcomed into most restaurants and cafés and chefs are usually happy to prepare smaller

Gordon Rattray (www.able-travel.com)

Flanders is, in general, not as accessible as one might expect for a region in modern Europe. The situation is improving, and modern buildings and transport services are usually excellent, but wheelchair users would be well advised to do some research in advance to make their visit as problem-free as possible.

TRANSPORT

By air Zaventem and Charleroi airports are fully accessible and have toilet facilities for disabled people. For entering and exiting the aircraft, assistance services with equipment are also present, although those at Zaventem are more efficient and professional.

By rail Not all stations are wheelchair accessible and trains don't always have disabled toilets. Assistance can be arranged at stations, but to be guaranteed of receiving it you need to book at least 24 hours in advance. To do this phone ☏ 02 52 82 828 and follow the English-language options until you're put through to disability assistance. Be sure to turn up early and make yourself known to staff to give them time to organise your entry.

In order for your personal assistant to travel free, you need to be in possession of a 'Begeleider kaart'. Unfortunately this card is only available to residents of Flanders. However, in my experience, some conductors will turn a blind eye to this rule if you explain you are a tourist.

By bus

A large proportion of buses are accessible but it is wise to book at least 24 hours in advance. The De Lijn website (*www.delijn.be*) has English-language features, while the following numbers for 'Belbus' services will provide more information:

Antwerp ☏ 03 218 14 94	**Limburg** ☏ 011 85 03 00
East Flanders ☏ 092 10 94 94	**West Flanders** ☏ 059 56 52 56
Flemish Brabant ☏ 016 31 37 00	

It is sometimes possible to book an accessible bus if you know exactly when you want to travel. For this you need to book at least 24 hours in advance.

Brussels Few buses or trams are accessible, and only a handful of Metro stations are possible for people with mobility problems, although these do provide an assistance service. More information can be obtained by calling ☏ 0900 10 310, but the telephone number costs €1/minute.

Car and taxi The European 'Blue Badge' scheme applies in Flanders, allowing holders to park in designated spaces. In some areas, you may also use standard parking spaces without fee or time limit. More information can be found by

versions of the main meals if a children's menu is unavailable. There are numerous attractions catering to kiddies, and all museums, public transport systems etc offer special discount rates (usually half price) for children.

contacting the nearest town hall (*gemeentehuis*). If unsure, then it is worth paying, as authorities do not hesitate to remove offending cars.

Taxi companies
Taxi Verts 02 3494949; www.taxisverts.be
Taxi Peters 089 351495; www.taxipeters.be
Taxi Hendriks www.hendriks.be; Antwerp: 03 2864440; Brussels: 02 7529800; Gent: 09 2168020; Limburg: 011 809898

ACCOMMODATION Most quality hotels will have some degree of accessibility. The more restricted your budget is, the smaller your choice will be. To find suitable accommodation, the following contacts may be useful:

www.toevla.be Accessible accommodation in Flanders. At the time of writing, some features of this site didn't work in English.
www.access-able.com A database with accessible accommodation worldwide, including a few entries from Belgium.
www.eurocampings.co.uk This site can be searched by filtering for disabled-friendly establishments.
www.accessinfo.be There is a downloadable list on this site.

PUBLIC BUILDINGS AND ATTRACTIONS By western European standards, access to public buildings like libraries, banks and post offices is often poor. Many buildings are old, making adaptations difficult and costly, and legislation is not strictly adhered to. Attractions like museums and zoos are generally better, with reduced tariffs for disabled people, and an assistant may often enter free of charge. Restaurants and shops often have no step-free access and rarely have an accessible toilet.

HEALTH Although Flemish healthcare is of a high standard, it is essential to understand and to be able to explain your own medical requirements. If flying, take all necessary medication and equipment with you and pack this in your hand luggage in case your main luggage gets lost.

SECURITY As a disabled person, you are more vulnerable than most tourists. Stay aware of where your belongings are, especially during car transfers and similar activities as the confusion creates easy pickings for an opportunist thief.

FURTHER INFORMATION
Access Info 070 23 30 50; www.accessinfo.be. A branch of the Flemish Tourist Board.
VFG www.vfg.be. Flemish organisation providing support and advice for disabled people.
www.brusselvoorallen.be Searchable database with information about disability access in Brussels.
www.toegankelijkreizen.be A searchable database with information about accommodation and transportation for disabled travellers.

TRAVELLING WITH PETS Taking your dog or cat on holiday shouldn't pose too many problems. You will need to carry a veterinarian certificate, less than a year old, indicating the health status of the pet and proof of a rabies vaccination. Whether flying or travelling by ferry you will need to check airline or ship regulations. The website www.pettravel.com has good advice on what else to take into consideration.

WHAT TO TAKE

With such fickle weather, it's best to dress in layers that you can peel off and on as necessary. Outside the office, the dress code in Flanders is casual and relaxed. Even when it comes to dressing up for a night out the dress code leans more towards smart jeans or trousers and top, rather than high heels, diamonds and lip gloss. This acts as a general rule and is of course subject to change among the hipper eateries and bars in the main cities.

During the winter, a hat, scarf, gloves and windproof/waterproof jacket (with a hood, so you can ditch the unwieldy umbrella) are essential to ward off the biting northern winds. As to footwear, sturdy walking shoes or boots are more appropriate and practical among the cobblestone streets of the main towns and open fields found elsewhere. During the summer, you can switch the waterproof jacket for a light jumper and T-shirt. Practical items that you should consider taking are a conversion plug (sockets are the European two-pin style) and sunscreen (if you will be travelling during the summer).

MONEY

Belgium converted from the Belgian franc (BF) to the euro (€) in January 2002. Notes vary in colour, decrease in size corresponding to value, and come in denominations of €500, €200, €100, €50, €20, €10 and €5. Coins in circulation include the €2 and €1 with mock silver centre and outer gold band; the gold-coloured 50, 20, 10 cents, and copper-coloured 5, 2 and 1 cents.

ATMs are commonplace in all cities and towns and most accept major credit cards (Visa, MasterCard, American Express, Diners Club, as well as Cirrus and Maestro), although I have had trouble making withdrawals from ING banks. Be warned that the majority of banks at home will charge a commission fee for withdrawals made abroad. Standard banking hours are 09.00–12.00 and 14.00–16.00 Monday–Friday, 09.00–12.00 Saturday, but ATMS are usually open 24 hours. Avoid taking travellers' cheques; they're no longer widely accepted.

TIPPING Tipping is becoming more of a habit in larger cities and towns. A 16% service charge is automatically added to any restaurant bill – only leave something extra if you were really impressed. Taxi fares also immediately incorporate a gratuity. It is customary to tip cinema usherettes (except multiplexes) and your tour guide on buses and boats – €1 should cover it. It's fairly common to offer the porter or chambermaid a small note as well. By far the biggest tipping expense will be the 30 cents you are charged for using public toilets – look for the dish on the table as you enter.

BUDGETING

When it comes to expenses, Flanders is on par with most western European areas. Costs are inevitably higher in the main cities and accommodation rates are inflated during the summer high season. Some hotels charge a single supplement. The trick is to visit the main cities at weekends when businessmen decamp and rates drop significantly, especially in Brussels, and make use of the discounts hotels offer for stays of three or more days.

Entry to selected Brussels museums is free on the first Wednesday of the month. You can also save money with the multi-pass museum cards in Brussels, Gent, Brugge and Oostende (see *Mad for Museums?* boxes in this guide). Try dining in fancier restaurants at lunchtime when they offer a discounted two- or three-course *dagmenu*, or opt for the *dagschotel* (dish of the day) in run-of-the-mill restaurants.

The prices quoted below are based on a daily spend per person, on the assumption that two people will be sharing a room.

SCRIMP AND SAVE Those on a tight budget can scrape by on €35 (£30/US€45) by staying in hostels, camping where possible, visiting the free sites of interest, having a large *dagschotel* at lunchtime, snacking on *frites* in the evening and enjoying the occasional beer in a time-forgotten *estaminet*.

MAKING DO For €90 (£75/US€120) you can sleep in a two-star hotel and have change to enjoy a light lunch, paid entry to a museum and finish the day off with a modest two-course dinner in a back-street brasserie.

ABLE TO CHOOSE Those who can afford to loosen the belt a little will, for €160 (£130/US€210), be able to sleep in style at a boutique B&B, visit several museums, dine at a descent restaurant and still have change for at least a few sweet-tooth snacks throughout the day.

AFFLUENT Spending €250 (£210/US€330) a day will buy a high-star hotel room, treats such as a horse-drawn carriage tour of the town, and a lunch and dinner you can linger over, and leave a nice kitty at the end of the evening to spend on some deceptively strong Belgian beers.

MONEY NO OBJECT If you can afford to spend more than €250 a day, you'll have unlimited access to the very best hotel suites, can browse and buy designer labels in Brussels' Dansaert fashion district, enjoy first-rate cuisine at the wallet-draining and esteemed Comme Chez Soi and take in an opera performance at the legendary Théâtre de la Monnaie.

GETTING AROUND

The public transport system in Flanders is exemplary. Trains and buses service every nook and cranny of the country and, what's more, they nearly always arrive on time.

BY AIR There is no domestic air transportation between Flemish cities.

BY CAR Belgian drivers get a lot of bad press. However, tales of drivers flashing their lights to move you out of the way and acceleration speeds that would leave Michael Schumacher breathless, shouldn't put you off. The Belgian highways are some of the

ARE YOU LEGAL?

When driving in Europe, you're legally required to carry headlamp adapters, a warning triangle, GB plate, reflective vest, first-aid kit and fire extinguisher. If you are stopped and found to be missing any of the above you may be issued an on-the-spot fine, which must be paid immediately in cash to the police officer.

PRIORITÉ À DROITE

The 'priority to the right' principle exists inside most European towns. It states that, in the absence of road markings, drivers must give way to cars coming from the right, even on roundabouts. Occasionally there will be signposts bearing a yellow diamond inside a white diamond and this will be crossed through when the section ends.

best in Europe, are toll-free and, until energy-saving measures were put into place, so well lit at night that you could apparently see the network from space. Naturally, you will encounter some common irks, which include getting stuck in traffic jams during the summer exodus for the coast and driving in cities riddled with one-way systems. Then of course there are the road signs that switch from one language to another (see table below). However, with a little preparation and bravado, travelling by car will give you the freedom to drive off track and discover sights, or that special restaurant, that would otherwise pass you by as you stare out of the window of the train.

Place names Most place names have French and Flemish variations. The list below highlights the main alternatives:

City	Flemish	French
Antwerp	Antwerpen	Anvers
Bruges	Brugge	Bruges
Brussels	Brussel	Bruxelles
Ghent	Gent	Gand
Leuven	Leuven	Louvain
Mechelen	Mechelen	Malines
Ostend	Oostende	Ostende
Ypres	Ieper	Ypres
Aalst	Aalst	Alost
Tongeren	Tongeren	Tongres

Road rules You must drive on the right hand side of the road, give way to the left at roundabouts, and observe the *priorité à droite* (see box above). Speed limits range from 120km/h (75mph) on motorways to 50km/h (31mph) in towns, but be aware that 90km/h (56mph) is often allowed on open roads between villages and that near schools the speed limit drops to 30km/h (20mph). Take extra care when entering highways; cycle paths run alongside the motorway and cross at the pedestrian-stripped paths on slip roads. NB: If you see what looks like rows of abandoned cars lining the highway, you are witnessing car-pooling, a car-sharing scheme for work colleagues has cut road congestion considerably.

Fuel stations Be aware that in smaller Flemish towns, fuel stations like DAT and Gabriel accept only Bankcontact (a specialised chip-and-pin system), not international cards like Visa or MasterCard, so stick to well-known brands like Texaco and Esso. Small-town outlets open only during normal working hours of 09.00–17.00.

Car hire Rental costs start at around €380 per week, but special offers may apply to mid-week rentals. It also almost always works out cheaper to make the booking in your country of residence. Drivers will need to be over 21 and have been driving for at least a year and it is vital you carry a Vehicle on Hire Certificate (VE103).

BY TRAIN Trains are operated by the national railway company SNCB-NMBS (✆ *02 528 28 28; www.b-rail.be*) with services starting at 05.00 and ending at 23.00. Tickets may be bought online, or at the station before departure. As a last resort you can also buy them on board from the ticket inspectors kitted out in smart uniform and Postman-Pat cap. Fares start from €7.50 for a standard second-class return ticket, and travel at weekends is half price. First-class fares tend to be double the price of a standard. Students receive discounts, as do seniors (aged 65+), who pay only €4 for a return ticket anywhere in Belgium as long as they travel after 09.00. Children under 12 also travel free after 09.00. Seats cannot be reserved. Most stations have coin-operated luggage lockers. Bicycles are allowed on trains providing you buy a a one-trip card (€5) or a one-day card (€8).

Rail passes The cost of buying single train tickets mounts up, so if you are going to be taking several journeys you are better off buying a rail pass.

Go Pass 10 For under 26s this €50 pass (valid for a year) allows you to take ten single second-class trips between any two Belgian stations. It's not registered in your name, so can be used to cover trips for two people.

Rail Pass Equivalent to the Go Pass, but for adults, this pass allows ten single journeys between any two Belgian stations. Second-class passes cost €74; first-class €113.

Key Card Offers ten short single trips for the bargain price of €20 (second class) and €30 (first class) provided you travel within a designated area. Ask an operator for more details.

B-Excursion Combines rail travel with entrance to a nationwide attraction of your choice and any connecting buses or trams. Prices vary depending on the routes and attractions you want to visit.

DECIPHERING TRAIN TIMETABLES

Strange codes appear in the left-hand margin of all train timetables and if you happen to miss the small print denoting their meaning at the bottom of the poster, you could be in for a long journey.

L – stands for 'locale' or 'stoptrein' and indicates trains that will stop at every single village on the way to your destination, via Timbuktu. Suffice to say, they are painfully slow and should be avoided unless your destination is out of the way and does not appear on the faster train schedules.

IR – The InterRegio or 'sneltrein' is the faster standard service that stops at all the main cities and larger towns in between.

IC – The InterCity is the fastest of all three and acts as an express service, stopping at all the main cities.

BY METRO, TRAM AND BUS All three are operated by De Lijn (*www.delijn.be*) in Flanders and STIB (*www.stib.be*) in Brussels. Tram systems operate in Brussels, Gent and Antwerp. Trams have right of way over any other vehicle and work much like a bus service, ie: a hop-on, hop-off affair where tickets can be bought from the driver. Most fares cost €2 and allow you to get on and off as many times as you like within a one-hour period. Tickets should be validated by punching them in the yellow machines situated at the front and centre of the carriage. Alternatively, day passes (*dagpas*) cost €3, or books of ten journeys (*rittenkaart*) can be bought from De Lijn kiosks, newsagents and selected shops. Trams stop on request only when the blue button is pressed.

The bus services works in harmony with the rail network, offering access to towns and villages otherwise inaccessible by train. All timetables are available online and tickets can be bought on board from the driver, but they will not accept notes larger than €20.

BY TAXI Stands can be found outside most railway stations, airports and hotel entrances; drivers rarely do random street pick ups. Fares are based on a meter; they begin with a fixed charge of €2.40 at the start of the journey (this increases at night) and are then calculated at around €1.35/km. Tips are included, but a little extra is always appreciated.

ACCOMMODATION

Flanders is bursting at the seams with exciting accommodation options. You can sleep in a monastery one night and be lording it up in a 17th-century mansion the next. The gamut of beds on offer – from bunk to boudoir – ensures there are styles to suit all budgets and tastes.

The Benelux hotel classification was introduced in 1989 as a guide to quality and follows a blue-star rating of one to five. However, these awards are often a poor reflection of an establishment's true character because classification is not compulsory and officials from the Ministry of Tourism only follow strict criteria relating to facilities (lifts, fire exits etc). These tick lists fail to allow for individual variation in set up and in my experience the average Flemish obsession with all things 'home' tends to guarantee a good stay in even the most inauspicious of places.

Bearing in mind that where you stay can 'make or break' a trip, I have not included chain hotels in this guide, as they don't offer anything particularly memorable.

ACCOMMODATION PRICE CODES

Accommodation listings are laid out in decreasing price order, in five categories, as shown in the following key (also on the inside of the front cover), which also gives an indication of prices. Prices are based on the cost of a double room per night at high-season rates and include taxes and breakfast unless otherwise stated.

Luxury	€€€€€	€250+
Upmarket	€€€€	€176–250
Mid-range	€€€	€101–175
Budget	€€	€51–100
Shoestring	€	<€50

Rather, I've included options that reflect the character of the country and offer something special or unique. These include privately owned hotels, for those who prefer anonymity; guesthouses and B&Bs, with just a few rooms where you are likely to become friendly with your hosts; and of course budget options. However, if you are travelling for business and need a quick accommodation solution, be assured that all major cities and towns have chains such as Ibis, Sofitel, Holiday Inn and Novotel, which can be quickly contacted via their individual websites.

Best Western www.bestwestern.be   **Novotel** www.novotel.com
Holiday Inn www.holidayinn.com   **Sofitel** www.sofitel.com
Ibis www.ibishotel.com

During the summer (May–September) and at Christmas, establishments get booked up very quickly, so booking a few weeks in advance is advisable. If you are travelling on a tighter budget it pays to stay in the larger towns and cities over the weekend, when rates drop in response to the mass exodus of businessmen heading home. If you do arrive without a booking, head to the nearest tourist information office; the staff will ring round to see which establishments have vacancies. You may have to pay a small deposit but this fee will be deducted from your room rate on arrival at the hotel.

HOTELS The medieval layout of many of Flanders' oldest towns and cities has thankfully prevented a huge number of multinational mega-chains squeezing in and as a result, smaller establishments, oozing character, have managed to stay. Rooms are almost always equipped with TV, Wi-Fi, telephone, and en-suite bathroom, and a buffet breakfast, usually continental, is normally included in the price. Rates range from €70 for a standard double in a low-end hotel, to €250 plus for a double in the top-end establishments. City tax may be charged separately and it's worth enquiring about special weekend rates.

APARTHOTELS These are a combination of a hotel and a rental apartment: you have all the space of a furnished rental apartment, but all the perks of a hotel such as cleaning and breakfast brought to you.

BED AND BREAKFAST (*Chambre d'hôtes/Gastenkamer*) Flanders excels at the B&B and I am a huge advocate. These furnished rooms form part of the proprietor's home; your personal space is still your own, with the added benefits of personalised service and hosts with unparalleled insider information. What was once the territory of rural villages has now taken off in major cities and towns. The days of ageing floral bedspreads have been replaced with boutique-style bedrooms and top-quality fixtures. Often excellent value for money, prices range from €70 for a double with shared bathroom, to roughly €200 for an en-suite double in a luxury establishment. As with hotels, special rates are usually offered to those staying two or more nights. Conversely, some guesthouses charge a €10 supplement for stays of just one night, and others will accept only a minimum two-night stay.

YOUTH HOSTELS (*Auberges de jeunesse/Jeugdherbergen*) The extensive network of youth hostels throughout Flanders ensures that only in the smallest and most off-the-beaten-track towns will you be without a budget bed. Most are affiliated with Hostelling International (*www.vjh.be*). Dorm beds start at around €20; breakfast is usually included, but sheet hire may cost extra. Those without a Hostelling International card will have to pay €3 extra on top of the standard bed price, for up to six nights. After this time you will be issued with an International Guest Card, valid for one year. The social scene at these youth hostels picks in the summer, with barbecues, free town tours and bike rides often being organised.

CAMPING Campsites are graded on a 1–5-star basis: five being the best. Slightly gloomy places off season, they come alive during summer with numerous activities on offer and entertainment programmes for kids. Prices are usually calculated on individual payments for a site, cost per adult, cost per child, any pets and a car. You will also pay extra for electricity and in some instances hot showers.

I wouldn't advise camping rough. Flanders may be flat, but the majority is assigned to farming and you may anger local landowners.

EATING AND DRINKING

> Great restaurants are, of course, nothing but mouth-brothels. There is no point in going to them if one intends to keep one's belt buckled.
>
> Frédéric Raphael

A nation of gluttons or gastronomy experts? Foodies long ago decided that Flemish fare belongs firmly in the latter camp. Working from a base of burgher recipes, their rich food is often praised as the best in Europe and converts have often tried to keep the magnificence of their cuisine hush-hush, so they could guzzle its delights at leisure within time-worn, wooden-panelled eateries. Nowadays, the secret is out and visitors are often led around the country by their noses and appetites, sampling fresh fish and seafood found on the North Sea coast and beer-soaked stews. When all this can be washed down with award-winning beers or a cheeky shot of *jenever*, the appeal of Flemish dining is irresistible – gastronomes prepare to let a notch out of your belt.

FOOD When it comes to cooking, there are two types of Flanders. At-home meals are very much of the meat, potato and veg variety: filling fodder that would have kept farms hands happy until dinner time in the old days. Alongside this frill-free food, however, is the entirely different dining experience offered by haute-cuisine restaurants. There you will find delicately tiered 'tastebud teasers' informed by French and – more recently – oriental twists; but as always there is a strong emphasis on fresh, seasonal ingredients.

National favourites are undoubtedly *steak-frites* – the meat is of high quality and usually from a local butcher – and *mosselen-frieten/moules-frites*; mussels are in

---

RESTAURANT PRICE CODES

Restaurant listings are laid out in decreasing price order, in five categories, as in the following key (also on the inside front cover), which gives an indication of prices. Prices are based on the cost of a main meal (including tax) per person.

Expensive	€€€€€	€30+
Above average	€€€€	€21–30
Mid-range	€€€	€16–20
Cheap & cheerful	€€	€9–15
Rock bottom	€	<€8

FRITES

Flanders is famed for producing some of the finest cuisine in Europe, but any visit to the region will reveal that the chip is adored above all else. Even the smallest of villages houses at least two *frietkots* to cope with the locals' demand for the lovingly double-deep-fried *frites* served with mayonnaise and other sauces poured over the top.

The secret to achieving the crunchy golden exterior and light and fluffy centre is freshness. Potatoes are sliced and cooked within two hours, fried in beef fat and allowed to cool before being fried a second time. It's a serious business and it's amusing to see the chef of a newly opened *frietkot* fry feverishly for several days in a row in order to please dubious locals and assure them he's up to the task of producing crispy chips.

Sadly, traditional *frietkot* caravans are disappearing – stamped out by planning laws and hygiene standards – and only a handful remain. Permanent shop outlets are now the norm. Establishments usually stay open until 23.00 or midnight and there's nothing better than leaving a bar and picking up some piping-hot chips to tuck into on the way back to the hotel.

The most common toppings and accompaniments are listed below. A word of advice: if you don't fancy having soggy chips then you will have to ask for your sauces to be served '*apart*'.

Stoofvlees – beef chunks in brown beer sauce
Spaghettisaus – fairly self-explanatory
Vol-au-vent saus – ham, chicken and mushroom in a creamy white sauce
Goulash – strings of pork marinated with red and green peppers and onion in tomato sauce
Balletjes met tomaatensaus – small meatballs in tomato sauce flavoured with herbs
Bicky burger – hamburger served with a special pickle sauce and deep-fried chip bits
Brochette – pork steak kebab with onion
Kaaskroket – deep-fried cheese-and-potato rolls
Garnaalkroket – deep-fried prawn-and-potato rolls
Curryworst – curry sausage served with mustard and ketchup

season between September and March, or – if you take the advice of the locals – any month whose spelling contains the letter 'r'. In addition, most towns have their own specialities and I've included these under individual listings.

In winter, the Flemish like to tuck into *witloof en oven* (chicory wrapped in ham and covered in a creamy cheese sauce); *waterzooi* (a broth containing fish/chicken and vegetables); *stoemp met prei* (mashed potato mixed with leeks); *stoofvlees* (beef stew made with brown beer); *konijn en pruinen* (rabbit cooked with prunes and beer); and *paling in 't groen* (young eel cooked in a green sauce of spinach, sorrel, mint, thyme, tarragon, bay leaf and white wine).

In summer, menus feature the likes of *tomaat met grijze garnaalkes/tomate aux crevettes* (tomatoes stuffed with North Sea shrimp mixed with mayonnaise and ketchup) and *asperges op vlaamse wijze/asperges à la flamande* (white asparagus served in melted butter and with a crumbled boiled egg), which come into season at the end of May. If you are feeling really adventurous – vegetarians avert your eyes – you might like to try meaty specialties like *bloedworst* – literally 'blood sausage' – made from ground-pork leftovers, fat, breadcrumbs and pig's blood; *kop* (a chunky paté made from ground beef and tongue and set in gelatine); *paardefilet* (horse steak); and, finally, *filet américan*, which sounds deceptively like a steak, but is actually a raw patty of beef mincemeat mixed with raw egg, onion, capers and a splash of Worcestershire sauce.

Snacks: sweet and savoury Wander down almost any street and your nose will crinkle as some warm, delicious smell wafts by.

CHOCOLATE

Chocolate arrived in Europe in the 16th century when Christopher Columbus returned from his voyages to the New World and presented a handful of the beans to Emperor Ferdinand and Infanta Isabella. Barely a year later, the first official shipment arrived in the docks of Seville and by the 17th-century chocolate had become the most sought after luxury/medicinal item among European nobility.

Towards the end of the 18th and early 19th centuries, both Swiss and English chocolate makers were looking for new ways to enjoy chocolate and began re-introducing extracted cocoa butter to solidify the liquid and add alkali to neutralise the acidic flavour. These solid blocks first went on sale in 1847 and could be found in pharmacies, whose patrons recommended chocolate as a cure for stomach ache.

For years, chocolate production followed the same recipe until, in 1912 in Brussels, Jean Neuhaus created something entirely new that revolutionised the world of chocolate and made Belgium synonymous with chocolate excellence. Using the basic 'couverture' chocolate produced by chocolate makers, he crafted an individual chocolate designed to be eaten for pleasure. He filled these individual cups with flavoured creams, fruit, liquors, or crushed nut paste and named them *pralines*, after the sugared nuts favoured by the Marquis de Praslin. Originally served in paper cones, Neuhaus' wife developed the ballotin cardboard box that all confectioners use today. His original shop is still in situ in the Galeries Royales St Hubert in Brussels (see page 92) and every year at Easter and Christmas they produce elegant chocolate-inspired window displays.

Predictably, over the years the outlets of traditional chocolate makers were swallowed up by multinational conglomerates and today names like Corné de la Toison d'Or, Godiva, Leonidas and Neuhaus are all familiar Belgian brands sold worldwide. However, in recent years there has been a resurgence of new craftsmen – chocolatiers – practicing the cult of real chocolate, which is free from the vegetable fats and contains at least 52%, and often 70%, pure cocoa solids. Of particular note are Pierre Marcolini (current world champion), Jean Galler and Frédéric Blondeel. Free from artificial colours and preservatives, Belgian chocolates are superior because of their freshness – kept in the fridge, they last just seven days. Eaten at breakfast, handed out at coffee mornings, snacked on during the day and nibbled on after dinner, it's not surprising to learn that the average Belgian consumes around 13.2lbs of chocolate a year.

Savoury quick bites include the inimitable *frites* (see box, page 45), hotdogs, the Turkish *pitta*, filled baguettes (*belegd broodje*), the well-known *croque-monsieur*, and the steaming *escargot* (snail) soup ladled out at Christmas markets.

Bakers and *pâtisseries* offer several sweeter treats, from delicate cream cakes and fruit tarts to custard-filled pastries. Belgian waffles are the most famous and they come in two varieties: the Brussels and the Liège. The latter (and tastier) is a dense, doughy mixture coated in sugar and served piping hot. The Brussels variety, on the other hand, may contain fewer calories but is similar in weight and taste to polystyrene, perhaps the reason why they cover it in icing sugar, chocolate sauce, ice cream or fruit.

Also look out for the marzipan-flavoured *mattentaart* (see box, page 200), cinnamon-flavoured *speculaas* biscuits and Dikmuide's custard-filled *ijzerbollen*. Alternatively, go all out on a classic ice-cream sundae, like the *Dame Blanche* – a Belgian favourite – which is vanilla ice cream covered in molten hot chocolate, or the stomach-warming rice pudding (*rijstpap/riz au lait*).

Vegetarians and vegans Meat is the main focus of most Flemish dishes, and while exclusively vegetarian restaurants are still scarce in the smaller towns and villages, there has been a burgeoning of veggie establishments cropping up in the main cities, especially in Gent, which has the most vegetarian restaurants in Europe and hosts veggie day every Thursday. Elsewhere outlets range from health-food cafés serving quick bites to proper restaurants serving three-course menus – where these are available, I've included them in the where to eat listings. Then, of course, standard restaurants almost certainly offer one or two vegetarian options. Specialist restaurants should cover the needs of vegans, but once outside the cities it will become increasingly difficult to find restaurants that can meet your requirements. A trip to the supermarket, to stock up on essentials, might be the best solution.

DRINK Beer is to Belgium, what wine is to France – a daily essential. The two have a long and distinguished relationship and it's invariably the first word people associate with the country. With over 800 varieties, the production and consumption of beer are a source of national pride and their breadth and quality have had beer

Tim Webb (author of *Good Beer Guide Belgium*; www.booksaboutbeer.com)

Any beer drinker who comes to Flanders to drink lager such as the local Jupiler has missed the point. It is like wanting to sample the food and sticking with chips, or trying to see the region without leaving the motorways. International-brand lagers are like white sliced bread – simple, predictable, dull and everywhere. Flemish ones are no better than the rest.

The beers that make Belgian brewing world famous come mainly in bottles, usually with a yeast sediment (so pour with care) and sometimes in a size (75cl) designed for sharing, like wine. Some come bearing a logo that reads 'Authentic Trappist Product', a sign that it is made within the confines of a Trappist abbey at the behest of the Order. The monastic connection goes back to the days when abbeys were centres of scientific study, which included working out how a benign Almighty had enabled man to make alcohol out of anything that grows from the ground.

Whoever makes the beers, they come in just about every strength, shade and style imaginable. Each has its own glass, too, though this is mainly for marketing purposes.

Relatively well-known brands like Hoegaarden wheat beer, Belle Vue cherry beer, Leffe Blond and others have popularised Belgian brewing, but are not its finest achievements. What follows is a quick run through of Flanders' better brews.

WEST FLANDERS The van Eecke and St Bernard breweries of Watou, in the hop-growing area west of Poperinge, brew great beers in numerous styles under the Watou, Kapittel and St Bernardus brands. Nearby, the café opposite the abbey gates at Westvleteren (page 273) serves its remarkable Trappist ales.

Best local style Oak-aged ales like Rodenbach Grand Cru, Vichtenaar, Duchesse de Bougogne or Bavik Aged Pale come mainly from around Kortrijk.

Brewery to visit Oerbier brewed by Dolle Brouwers near Diksmuide (page 257).

LIMBURG The transformation of Limburg from the Flemish coalfield to a holiday area of forests and lakes brought with it a quiet revolution in beer making, topped off by the arrival of the new Trappist brewery at Achel, on the Dutch border.

Best local style Limburg brewers make light blond ales with a distinctive hoppy character. Try Martens Sezoens, Bink Blond, Ops-Ale, Ter Dolen Blond or the draught blond ale at the Achel cloister to get the drift.

Brewery to visit The loveliest brewery buildings in Flanders belong to Kerkom Brouwerij, near Sint-Truiden, (*469 Naamsesteenweg, Kerkom;* ⊕ *Apr–Sep 12.00–*

aficionados fizzing with delight for years. Like a fine wine – and treated with the same respect – the majority of these beers should be sipped slowly and savoured, which is no bad thing when alcohol percentages reach 12%.

Also high in the alcoholic stakes is *jenever*, a juniper-flavoured spirit unique to Flanders and the Netherlands and fondly called *witteke*. Traditionally developed from the distillation and fermentation of malt, this liver-warming shot drink

19.00 Wed–Fri, 10.00–19.00 Sat–Sun, Oct–Apr 12.00–19.00 Thu–Sun). In summer they use the old farm buildings and in winter open their traditional 19th-century café. Try the two Bink tripels.

ANTWERP The crucible of the Belgian beer revolution is going through hard times. A *bolleke* of De Koninck may still be the toast of the city but is rarely seen beyond it. Big blond Duvel, from Breendonk near Puurs, is the beer that struts its stubby-bottled stuff round the globe.

Best local style The modern incarnations of the *dubbel* and *tripel* styles of ale have their origins in beers made at the abbey of Westmalle, northwest of Antwerp, whilst the last of the great Mechelen brown ales is Gouden Carolus Classic.

Brewery to visit Het Anker, in Mechelen, is the only brewery to offer a guesthouse and it has has a massive bistro (pages 306 and 309).

BRUSSELS AND BRABANT The only Belgian beers with a European Union TSG (Traditional Speciality Guaranteed) certification are three types of lambic beers called *oude g(u)euze, oude kriek* and *faro.* The *oude* distinguishes them from (often tacky) modern derivatives.

Best local style The building blocks of lambic beers are musty, fungal, lactic, citrus fluids called lambics, made much like regular beers except that they are fermented by naturally occurring air-borne yeast, over years, in oak casks. Expert blenders then mix these and bottle them, sparking new life to create clear, ultra-dry *oude geuze.* Alternatively they may fill a cask with bucket-loads of hard, dry cherries to steep in lambic for many months before bottling as *oude kriek.*

To appreciate authentic lambic beers, suspend disbelief and anything your taste buds ever taught you. Think traditional cider perhaps, or local wines from mountain villages. The very best are from Cantillon, Drie Fonteinen, Hanssens and De Cam.

Brewery to visit The Cantillon brewery in Brussels (page 124) shows how lambic is made and sells samples. There are public brewing days in March and November.

EAST FLANDERS Most of the East Flanders' 17 breweries produce good beers but, sadly, few let in visitors. And while brand names like Witkap, Pater Lieven, Valeir and Malheur usually indicate high quality, there is no longer a specific East Flanders' style of beer.

However, if there is such a thing as the nicest pub in Belgium, the Gulzigen Bok (*48 Gentweg;* ⊕ *11.00–late Thu–Sun*) in Vurste, just south of Gent, might just be it.

Practical Information EATING AND DRINKING

2

comes in two varieties: *oude* (old) and *jonge* (young). In fact, the differentiation has nothing to do with age, but rather varying distillation recipes; younger *jenevers* are made from grain and are served chilled, tasting similar to vodka; old *jenevers* have a higher concentration of malt, are aromatic like whisky and are served at room temperature. Alcohol percentages range from a hefty 20% to a toe-curling 40%. Hasselt is particularly renowned for its production and has a dedicated museum

BASIC BEER GLOSSARY

Abbey beer A beer that imitates the monastic brewing styles of the Trappist breweries (below). Some imitations are better than the originals.

ABV Alcohol by volume. Regular beers made in the English-speaking world are generally low alcohol at 4% abv; standard international beers are 5%; speciality beers range from 4% to 12% depending on the style.

Ale Beer that is fermented at room temperature and, ideally, continues to do so (Flemish: *op gist*; French: *sur lie*) in the cask or bottle, as in British 'real ale'.

Dubbel (French: *double*) Medium-sweet brown ale of 6–7.5% abv.

G(u)euze Old pale ale. But see *oude g(u)euze* (below).

Kriek Cherry alcopop with a bearish slant. But see also *oude kriek* (below).

Lager Beer that is fermented below room temperature and, ideally, continues to mature in chilled vats for many weeks. Most do not.

Lambic Beer that is fermented very slowly by air-borne yeast, traditionally in oak casks, for anything from one to three years.

Oud bruin Oak-aged brown ale, usually of low–medium strength (5–7%), with a matured and sour character.

Oude g(u)euze A mix of old and young lambics plus a drop of sugar, refermented in champagne bottles for a year or more. Unique, brilliant and memorable.

Oude kriek Lambic steeped with a boatload of cherries for several months, then bottled.

Trappist Beer brewed at one of seven monasteries of the Trappist Order that are licensed to make beer. Six are in Belgium: Achel, Chimay, Orval, Rochefort, Westmalle and Westvleteren.

Tripel (French: *triple*) Strong, sweetish blond beer style of 7.5–9.5% abv.

White beer (Flemish: *witbier*; French: *bière blanche*) Brewed with plenty of wheat in the mash, making it naturally cloudy with a fresh-bread sweetness. Lowish alcohol (4–5.5%) and often spiced with coriander and dried peel.

(page 328). There are several specialist *jenever* bars scattered throughout the region and these have been mentioned in the bars listings.

Surprisingly, Flanders also has a modest sprinkle of vineyards, including Genoels-Elderen (page 334) on the outskirts of Tongeren, and Domaine Schorpion (*37 Kersendaelstraat, 3724 Vliermaal;* m *0477 58 12 08*), situated just outside Hasselt and renowned for its sparkling and table white wines.

Non-alcoholic drinks Belgians aren't keen on the hard water that flows through their taps, so most buy bottled water. In addition to this, all manner of fizzy drinks – Coca Cola, Orangina, Sprite and so forth – are on offer. Kids' drinks include Fristi – a strawberry-flavoured yogurt drink – and Cécémel, a syrupy chocolate shake. Coffee is more popular than tea and frequently taken with an afternoon *pâtisserie*. Most establishments offer the Lipton brand of tea, whose selection is heavy in fruit flavours.

RESTAURANTS, BRASSERIES AND CAFÉS The Flemish obsession with good cooking ensures standards are kept high, and even budget restaurants are unlikely to serve inedible food. Most offer a daily special (*dagschotel/plat du jour*) or day menu (*dagmenu*) that are excellent value for money. Also look to see if the restaurant bears a *Bib Gourmand* sign (usually posted beside the entrance); this Michelin qualification is a sign of good food sold at reasonable prices.

The popularity of eating out means venues do get very busy at weekends, so it's advisable to make a reservation for the more exclusive joints.

Children are warmly welcomed in most establishments, although not all offer high chairs or a separate children's menu. In fact, it's more common for chefs to prepare smaller servings of dishes chosen from the main menu.

Fast-food restaurants – Quick, Pizza Hut and McDonalds etc – are widespread, as are privately owned Chinese, Indian, Thai, Turkish, Italian, Greek and Japanese restaurants. However, there certainly doesn't seem to be the preoccupation with the takeaway food prevalent in the UK and US. The Flemish have full faith in their own home cooking and to that end I have tended only to include establishments that focus on or specialise in Belgian cuisine in the restaurant listings. Furthermore, most guidebooks play it safe and list only restaurants or cafés located near the city centre. I, on the other hand, believe readers are looking for eateries that are crowded with locals instead of tourists, so you can get to know the real Flanders. With this in mind, I've taken a risk and in each of the major cities suggested some sites that will require a 'bit of a walk', but are well worth the effort. Don't be alarmed though; I've included central options too for those evenings when you're just too tired after a great day's sightseeing. Be aware that expensive restaurants close in the afternoon, usually between 14.30 and 18.30/19.00, when they reopen for dinner, and close early by European standards – at around 21.00 or 22.00. Many also close

FLEMISH CAFÉS

In winter, Flemish cafés are snug warm dens in which to shelter from biting rainstorms; come summer, the doors are thrown open and tables and chairs assembled on the pavements so locals and tourists alike can enjoy the inimitable tradition known as *een terrasje doen* – 'doing a terrace'. If you're sitting inside, waiters usually expect you to set up a tab, whereas drinkers on the terrace tend to pay on a drink-by-drink basis. Closing time is determined by the last drinker, so there's plenty of time to sip slowly on a heavy-duty beer.

The Flemish refers to pubs as 'cafés', but there are in fact four subtly different types: the brown café (an old-fashioned pub decked out in wooden panelling), the *eetcafé* (the Flemish term for a café serving a small selection of meals), the grand café (a brasserie popular with elderly clients) and the *herberge* (an old Flemish term for a large tavern).

briefly to take their holidays in the first two weeks of January and perhaps the odd week in July or August.

PUBLIC HOLIDAYS

1 January	New Year's Day	Nieuwjaar
6 January	Epiphany	Driekoningen
14 February	Valentine's Day	Valentijnsdag
March/April	Easter	Pasen
	Easter Monday	Paasmaandag
1 May	Labour Day	Dag van de Arbeid
May	Mothers' Day	Moedersdag
	Ascension	Onze Lieve Heer Hemelvaar
	Pentecost	Pinksteren
	Pentecost Monday	Pinkstermaandag
June	Fathers' Day	Vadersdag
11 July	Flanders Day	Feest van de Vlaamse Gemeenschap
21 July	National Day	Nationale feestdag
15 August	Assumption	OLV-Hemelvaart
1 November	All Saints' Day	Allerheiligen
2 November	All Souls' Day	Allerzielen
11 November	Armistice Day	Wapenstilstand
6 December	St Nicholas	Sinterklaas
25 December	Christmas Day	Kerstmis

FESTIVALS

Flanders' events calendar is jam-packed, reaching its zenith during the summer months when open-air music festivals dominate the social scene. In addition to all this, most towns hold an annual carnival, which generally entails locals donning fancy-dress clothes and getting severely sloshed over the weekend. The main religious festivals are Ommegang in Brussels, Heilig-Bloedprocessie in Brugge, and Boetprocessie in Veurne. The list below highlights the main annual events, but new exhibitions and events are being added all the time, so check with the local tourist office. Events are listed alphabetically.

JANUARY
Bommelsfeesten (www.bommelsfeesten.be) Ronse is proud to host the first carnival of the year on the second weekend of January.

FEBRUARY
Aalst Carnaval Celebrates Aalst's town mascot *Voil Jeannetten* – a drunk transvestite – and features the *prince carnaval* who is allowed to 'rule' town for three days. See box, page 197.

MARCH
Bal Rat Mort (*www.ratmort.be*) The appealing-sounding Dead Rat Ball is an extravagant fancy-dress ball held on the first weekend of the month in Oostende's casino. It was conceived over one hundred years ago by artist James Ensor (page 354).

Krakelingenfeest Held in Geraardsbergen on the first Sunday of Lent, this festival sees the town dignitaries drink red wine out of a silver chalice containing tiny living fishes and throwing pretzels at the crowd. See box, page 199.

APRIL

Beaufort (*www.beaufort04.be*) An outdoor art exhibition spread along the beaches of the Flemish coast. It begins in April and lasts until October. It features large modern-art pieces from emerging artists around the world.

Choco-laté Festival (*www.choco-late.be*) Brugge's week-long celebration of chocolate, featuring demonstrations, games and the inevitable taste-tests.

Ronde van Vlaanderen (*www.rondevanvlaanderen.be*) The famous Tour of Flanders cycle race is held on the first weekend of April, departing from St Niklaas and finishing in Oudenaarde.

The Royal Greenhouses of Laeken (*www.monarchie.be*) Brussels' 19th-century greenhouses have been opened to the public for one month each year for over a century. The elegant glass structures contain specimens from King Leopold II's original collection and a large variety of rare and valuable plants.

Zythos Beer Festival (*www.zbf.be*) Held in Leuven on the last weekend of April, this knees-up attracts over 40 breweries offering over 150 varieties of beer – samples start from €1!

MAY

Belgian Lesbian and Gay Pride (*www.blgp.be*) A procession through Brussels' city centre on the second weekend in May. Participants number in their thousands and there are lots of spin-off parties and festivals.

Brussels Jazz Marathon (*www.brusselsjazzmarathon.be*) Held on the third weekend of the month, it features more than 100 concerts performed by over 450 international jazz artists at venues throughout the capital, including the Grand' Place.

Festival van Vlaanderen (*www.festival.be*) The Flanders Festival runs from May to November and features numerous world-class classical and international music events held in eclectic locations in towns throughout the region.

Hanswijkprocessie (*www.hanswijkprocessie.org*) The ancient procession of our Lady of Hanswijck, commemorating the legend which claims that the town's 1272 scourge of plague vanished when a statue of the Virgin Mary was carried through town. Held in Mechelen on the Sunday before Ascension Day.

Heilig-Bloedprocessie (*www.holyblood.com*) The Holy Blood Procession takes place in Brugge on Ascension Day and celebrates the Basilica's possession of a relic containing drops of Christ's blood. The parade starts at 't Zand at 15.00 and weaves through town via Steenstraat, Simon Stevinplein, Mariastraat, Dijver, Wollestraat, the Markt, Geldmuntstraat and Noordzandstraat.

Kattenstoet (*www.kattenstoet.be*) This 'cat parade' is held every three years on the second Sunday of May in Ieper. The next is in 2012. See box, page 262.

JUNE

Brussels European Film Festival (*www.fffb.be*) Runs from late June to beginning of July.

Brussels Ommegang (*www.ommegang.be*) Between late June and mid-July, this popular procession – held on the Grand' Place – marks the arrival of a Virgin Mary statue brought by boat from Antwerp during the 14th century. It was first performed for Charles V in 1549. Features floats, stilt walkers and giant puppets like St Gudule and St Michel.

Bivouac at Waterloo Annual re-enactment, held during mid-June, of the Battle of Plancenoit involving costumed extras from around Europe and military demonstrations.

International Cartoon Festival (*www.cartoonfestival.be*) Held in Knokke-Heist from late June to late July.

Werchter (*www.rockwerchter.be*) Held on the last weekend of June on the outskirts of Leuven, this is the social calendar's most famous open-air music event.

JULY

10 Days Off (*www.10daysoff.be*) Starting on the second Friday of July this indoor electronic music festival tends to be one hell of a party and features house, hip-hop, drum and bass, electro and lots more besides.

Antwerp City Beaches (*www.zva.be*) Throughout July and August Antwerp's Strantwerpen and Zomerbar metamorphose into trendy city beaches ideal for summer cocktails.

Boetprocessie (*www.boetprocessie.be*) Unique Penitents' Procession held on the last Sunday of July in Veurne. See box, page 252.

Brugge Zand Fests Huge flea market hosted once a month on Brugge's Koning Albertpark and 't Zand in July, August and September.

Bruxelles les Bains (*www.blb-bb.be*) Between July and August 4,500 tonnes of North Sea sand are deposited on Brussels' Quai des Péniches, transforming it into a 1km-long city beach lined with cocktail cabanas, sunbathers and impromptu volleyball games.

Cactus Festival (*www.cactusfestival.be*) Established music festival held on the second weekend of July in Brugge's Minnewaterpark, showcasing reggae, rap, rock and R'n'B bands.

Gentse Feesten (*www.gentsefeesten.be*) A must-see extravaganza of free open-air bands, street entertainers, food stands and endless parties that take over Gent city centre for the last two weeks of July. The motto is: 'Everything can be done, nothing has to be done.'

International Puppet Buskers Festival (*www.eftcgent.be*) This child-friendly festival in Gent runs performances throughout the second week in July, with free shows on Emile Braunplein, Kalandeberg and Veldstraat at 18.00 every evening.

Klinkers (*www.klinkers-brugge.be*) Held from late July to mid-August in Brugge, this music and film festival is jam-packed with well-known acts and emerging bands too, with large-scale concerts in the Markt and Burg.

Procession of the Guild of the Noose Wearers This historic ceremony takes place on the third Friday of July at approximately 20.30 and commemorates the residents' refusal to pay increased taxes levied by Charles V to fund his wars during the 16th century. As punishment the citizens of Gent had to parade through town barefoot with a noose around their neck earning the nickname *Stroppendragers*, or 'noose bearers'.

Suikkerock See page 160.

AUGUST

Antwerp Taste Festival (*www.tasteofantwerp.be*) Food fair with stalls dishing out regional delicacies; held mid-August.

Dranouter (*www.festivaldranouter.be*) A very popular folk music festival held the first weekend of the month in a field a few kilometres south of Ieper. Bring a tent.

Maanrock (*www.maanrock.be*) Flanders' largest free rock festival, held in Mechelen at the end of August on the Grote Markt and IJzerenleen.

Marktrock (*www.marktrock.com*) A mish-mash of music concerts held in Leuven's picturesque town square in mid-August.

Meyboom (*www.meyboom.be*) Follows an old folklore tradition of planting the maypole at the intersection of Brussels' Rue du Marais and Rue des Sables. Festivities include a brass band and plenty of puppets. Held on 9 August.

Pageant of the Golden Tree This enormous parade to commemorate the marriage of Charles the Bold and Margaret of York in 1468 takes place in Brugge every five years on the last weekend of August. The next is in 2012.

Patershol Feesten (*www.patershol.org*) Every year on the second weekend of August, the *Deken* (Dean) of Gent's Patershol district hosts a festival for the residents with superb toe-tapping, thigh-slapping live music.

Paulusfeesten (*www.paulusfeesten.be*) This established seven-day event, held in Oostende, features the full gamut of music, numerous film showings and theatre performances.

Pukkelpop (*www.pukkelpop.be*) Held on the third weekend of August, Hasselt's music festival showcases a broad spectrum of acts, ranging from R'n'B to indie.

Rimpelrock (*www.rimpelrock.be*) The superbly named 'wrinkle rock' music festival caters for 'oldies'. Held in Hasselt on the second Sunday of August, this concert attracts Flemish favourites Will Tura and Helmut Lotti.

Tapis de fleurs (*www.flowercarpet.be*) Every even year the cobblestones of Brussels' entire Grand' Place are covered with an elaborate pattern of thousands of begonias. A must-see.

Zand Sculptuurs (*www.zandsculptuur.be*) Towering sand sculptures are a popular attraction on the Flemish coast between mid-August and mid-September. The best can be seen at Blankenberge.

SEPTEMBER

Belgian Beer Weekend (*www.weekenddelabiere.be*) Dozens of breweries descend on Brussels' Grand' Place on the first weekend of the month. Taste tests, beer-cart processions and a brewer's parade ensue.

Floralies Procession (*www.floralien.be*) Gent's 200-year-old flower show is hosted every five years in late September. The next is in 2015.

Hoppefeesten (*www.hoppefeesten.be*) Three-day beer festival held on third weekend of September in Poperinge every three years. The next is in 2014.

Open Monumentendag (*www.openmonumentendag.nl*) Over the last two weekends of September thousands of protected monuments and historical buildings are opened to the public free of charge.

OCTOBER

Europalia (*www.europalia.be*) An annual art festival celebrating different cultures which runs between October and February. Most exhibitions are held at Brussels' BOZAR auditorium. Events range from dance recitals and music performances to art exhibitions and scientific presentations.

Flanders International Film Festival (*www.filmfestival.be*) Venues in Gent showcase hundreds of features and short films from around the world. It has become one the largest events of its kind in Europe, attracting the likes of Brad Pitt and Morgan Freeman. It takes place during the last three weeks of October.

Hasseltse Jeneverfeesten (*www.jeneverfeesten.be*) Hasselt – home of *jenever* – hosts this festival on the third weekend of October. Cafés throw open their doors, free samples abound, lives music fills the air, history walks are hosted and the winner of the waiters' race earns his own weight in the super-strong liquor.

Ostend Halloween Festival (*www.halloween-oostende.be*) A ten-day celebration of all things ghostly from mid-October to mid-November. Streets are decorated, restaurants and cafés put on special menus and a grand Halloween Gala rounds things up.

NOVEMBER

Brugge's Ice Sculpture Festival (*www.ijssculptuur.com*) 300,000 kilograms of ice are deposited on Brugges' Stationsplein and transformed into towering icy masterpieces. The exhibition runs from late November to mid-January.

I Love Techno (*www.ilovetechno.be*) Techno rave hosted on the third weekend of the month in Gent's Flanders Expo Centre, attracting over 32,000 fans every year.

Six Days of Gent (*www.sport.be/z6sdaagse*) Huge indoor cycling event, held in Gent's Het Kuipke stadium on the third weekend of the month.

Being a child in Flanders is a good gig. Every year on 6 December Sinterklaas, the patron saint of children, pays a visit accompanied by a huge sack of presents and his faithful, un-PC helper Zwarte Piet.

Originally a Turkish bishop, St Nicholas was renowned for saving children from a life of prostitution and resurrecting them from the dead. He wore a red bishop's robe, sported a long white beard, carried a big book containing every child's name and rode a white horse called Amerigo across the rooftops – sound familiar? He may have traded old Amerigo for Rudolph, but Sinterklaas is unmistakably the current mythical figure known as Santa Claus in the UK and the US. The mix up came about when English settlers arrived in New Amsterdam (modern-day New York) and mistook the Dutch pronunciation of 'Sinterklaas' for 'Santa Claus'.

According to legend, St Nicholas did not have numerous elves to help him; he had only one assistant, *Zwarte Piet* – the devil. During the 19th-century, when the slave trade was at its peak, this element of the tale morphed into 'black Pete', an African servant. This idea was eventually replaced with the less emotive idea that Pete's face was blackened from soot after climbing down chimneys to deliver presents.

Today, Flemish kids still leave a shoe under the chimney or outside the front door in the hope that Sinterklaas will visit. If they have been good they will awake to find the shoe filled with chocolate, often shaped in the first letter of the child's name, or marzipan fruit, but if they have been bad the shoe will be filled with salt.

DECEMBER

Sinterklaas On the evening of 6 December Sinterklaas and his helper Zwarte Piet come to visit children, leaving sweets and small gifts. Special celebrations are held in the town of Sint-Niklaas. See box above and page 192.

Christmas markets These unmissable markets crop up in the town squares of most towns after Sinterklaas has visited and run throughout December. Sample mulled wine, steaming *escargots* and warm waffles from the wooden huts, go ice skating on open-air rinks and pick up handmade crafts.

SHOPPING

Chocolate, beer and lace are the standard souvenirs, but Flanders offers a lot more. Why not pick up a discount diamond, a one-off fashion item or vintage Flemish pottery from one of the local markets?

As a rule of thumb, most shops are open 10.00–18.00 or 19.00 Monday–Saturday and closed on Sunday. Souvenir shops in the larger cities and towns are often open seven days a week and bakeries and *pâtisseries* are generally open on Sunday mornings.

ART AND ANTIQUES As showcased by several of the upmarket B&Bs listed in this guide, there are numerous *objets d'art* and antiques floating around the markets of Flanders. Heirlooms and valuable items were confiscated by the Germans during both World Wars and those with a keen eye can pick up everything from

Art Nouveau lamps to Pointillist paintings – I know of a family aunt who even had wooden masks and spears brought over during the Belgian occupation of the Congo. Bargains are rare, but on the whole prices are fair. The best cities for antiques are Brussels and Tongeren.

In Brussels the place for quality antiques is the Grand Sablon. The streets leading off from here are home to numerous stores – of note is the Sablon Antiques Centre (*39 Rue du Grand Sablon*) that houses collections from over 20 dealers – and hosts Europe's best antique market, the Marché des Antiquités et du Livres (page 92). Slightly cheaper items can be found along Rue Blaes and at the Marché aux Puces (page 92). It also might be worth having a roam around the *brocantes* (bric-à-brac markets) held in various communes on the first Sunday of the month. Tongeren's Sunday antiques market has over 300 stands (page 331).

BEER Flanders' has well over 800 varieties of beer which range from the internationally recognised Leffé to the revered Westvleteran Trappist beer. Of course, the best place to buy them is from the breweries themselves and lots are open to the public, including Cantillon in Brussels (page 124) and De Halve Maan in Brugge (page 228). Alternatively, you can buy them from specialist shops (page 92) and, nowadays, quite a few of the tourist offices stock locally produced beers as well.

BISCUITS The Flemish like to dunk biscuits in their coffee then spread them in a sandwich. By far the most popular biscuit is *speculaas* – a cinnamon-flavoured cookie that frequently appears in dessert recipes and melts on the tongue. Other regional varieties include Diest's *halve maantjes* (page 155), Mechelen's *maneblussertjes* (page 306), Geel's *Geels hartjes* (page 318) and Maaseik's *knapkoeks* (page 335).

CHOCOLATE Chocolate is the number one gift brought back from Flanders. Names like Godiva, Guylian, Neuhaus and Leonidas have become familiar brand names in the international market and all are good. However, for the real McCoy you need to seek out a master *chocolatier* like those listed on pages 92 and 221.

Many establishments sell pre-packed boxes, but it's much more fun to handpick your own chocolates. Specialist terms to look out for are *crème fraîche* (praline filling made from fresh whipped cream); *ganache* (chocolate, fresh cream and a stronger percentage of cocoa butter flavoured with cinnamon, coffee or liqueur); *gianduja* (milk chocolate and smooth hazelnut paste); and *praline* (chocolate mixed with finely chopped nuts or toffee).

Brussels and Brugge both have chocolate museums (pages 97 and 229) and I've included some excellent chocolate cafés in the town listings.

COMICS Brussels is a mecca for fanboys. The highlight is a visit to the Belgian Comic Strip Centre (page 111), a museum with a well-stocked gift shop. There are several comic book stores (page 92) and the Foire aux Vieux Livres et aux Vieux Papiers market (*Air Museum, Parc Cinquantenaire; ⊕ first Sat of month 08.00– 16.00*) is a good location to pick up second-hand comics.

DIAMONDS Antwerp processes more that 70% of the world's diamonds, so if you're looking for that special sparkler you could do a lot worse than coming to shop for it in this metropolitan city – the condensed-carbon carats are approximately 20– 25% cheaper than in the UK. Furthermore, you can pick up added bonuses where, if you spend more than €950 on a ring in stores like Diamondland (page 293), they will pick up the tab for an overnight stay in one of Antwerp's participating hotels. Antwerp has four official diamond exchanges, located on Hoveniersstraat, Schupstraat, Rijfstraat, and Pelikaanstraat. Dotted among them are the spin-off shops run by the city's Jewish population. All reputable jewellers should display the ADJA (Antwerp Diamond Jewellery Association) label in their window. If in doubt visit the association (*22 Hoveniersstraat 22;* ✆ *03 222 05 45; www.adja.be*). They recommend finding out about the four C's: carat, colour, clarity and cut, to ensure purchase of a quality diamond. All diamonds should have an AGS/GIA/ EGL/ IGI certificate and have earned a Kimberley Process Certificate to rule out the possibility of it being a blood diamond (ie: mined in a war zone and sold clandestinely).

FASHION Antwerp has the upper hand – or should that be cuff? – when it comes to fashion. The city owes its clothes crown to a group of avant-garde designers known as the 'Antwerp Six'. Established in the 1980s by a group of graduates from Antwerp's Royal Academy of Fine Arts, its members include Walter van Beirendonck, Dirk van Saene, Dirk Bikkembergs, Marina Yee, Ann Demeulemeester and Dries van Noten. The collections of its most successful members, Ann Demeulemeester (page 292) and Dries van Noten, regularly appear on the runways of Paris Fashion Week.

Brussels is eager to follow in Antwerp's footsteps and its fashion district centres around Rue Antoine Dansaert and the wide tree-lined Avenue Louise are famous for international brands like Louis Vuitton and Chanel. Both cities also offer a good supply of vintage clothes stores (pages 92 and 293). As in the UK, sales (*soldes/ solden*) take place in January and July and some stores offer up to a 70% discount.

JENEVER An ancestor of gin, *jenever* stored in a traditional stoneware bottle makes an excellent gift. The main brands – Filliers, St-Pol and Smeets – are sold in most supermarkets, but for superior quality it's best to buy from specialist shops. The National Jenevermuseum in Hasselt (page 328) is just the place.

LACE This medieval craft was applied almost exclusively to the robes of the clergy until the 16th century. Considered a luxury item, its popularity soared throughout the Low Countries and soon men and women who could afford it had added lace (*dentelle* in French, *kant* in Flemish) to the cuffs, hems and collars of their dresses and shirts. Its delicate white frills were sewn on to handkerchiefs, bed linen, tablecloths, hats, shawls and hair clips and at the peak of its production over 50,000 lacemakers were employed in Flanders, many of them béguines. Despite cheap imports from the Far East dominating the market, the number of outlets specialising in local cotton bobbin lace is gradually rising. Naturally, these examples are more expensive and price is determined according to the size and complexity of the design. See pages 92 and 221 for a list of shops.

MARKETS Every town holds at least one weekly market; details of these are included under each individual entry. You can find anything from old books and second-hand bikes to fresh fish or antiques among the stalls. You'll have to be up early though: most start at 06.00 or 07.00. However, if you stay until the very end some hawkers will start slashing their prices as they pack up.

SPORT

The two national obsessions are cycling and football. Come the weekend, local pitches are filled with footie teams battling it out and the bridlepaths are dotted with cyclists whizzing by in multi-coloured Lycra racing suits. During summer, the coastline also offers excellent opportunities for watersports.

BILLIARDS Bumper billiard, or *toppenbiljart*, is a unique version of the game, played with five red balls and five white balls. It's found only in Flanders and some parts of Holland and France, but even there they're still a rare sight. The In de Toewip pub in Leuven has one (page 143).

CYCLING 'Cycling is Flanders and Flanders is cycling'. It's part of the national psyche and reached fever level when Eddy Merckx (page 355) exploded onto the scene in 1966 and starting setting world records right, left and centre. His success has spawned hordes of devoted fans and prompted young and old to pick up their bikes and make use of Flanders' flat terrain.

Exploring the region by bike is an excellent way of discovering off-the-beaten-track villages – and it's easy thanks to the national network, known as **Fietskknooppuntnetwork**, which uses a green three-tier signage system (see photo). The majority of cycle paths are well maintained and safe, but watch out for the lanes that cross roundabouts and motorway exits and entrances. Cyclists have right of way in

Standard cycle route sign: the top number indicates which junction you're at, and the bottom two give you the direction for the next closest junction.

most circumstances, but remember to give way from the right and use hand signals when turning. Lock your bike when leaving it unattended, too. Tourist offices can furnish you with maps of local cycle routes, and I've suggested the best of these for most towns.

Most railway stations have a Fietspunt bike-hire shop which charge around €10 a day, and if they don't I've suggested alternative rental shops for each town. Bikes can be taken on trains if you purchase a one-trip card (€5) or a one-day card (€8).

The region hosts a number of cycling races, the most famous being the Ronde van Vlaanderen or Tour of Flanders (page 53) (*www.rondevanvlaanderen*), held at the start of April and famous for the Muur, a killer cobblestone hill in the town of Geraardsbergen which sorts the wheat from the chaff.

Other highlights of the cycling season include the one-day Omloop Het Nieuwsblad (*www.omloophetnieuwsblad.be*), which is held at the end of February and departs from outside Gent's Museum of Contemporary Art (SMAK) and concludes at Lokeren, and the indoor Six Days of Gent, held in November. The events are amazingly social, with whole villages turning out to cheer and whoop shouts of support as the fluorescent millipede of cyclists swooshes past.

FOOTBALL Football is Flanders' second favourite sport. Even the smallest of towns have their own teams and every Saturday the local playing fields are filled with players thrashing it out for a place in the provincial leagues. The league table operates

KIMMEKE

World tennis champion Kim Clijsters grew up in Bilzen, near Hasselt. Affectionately nicknamed 'Kimmeke' by the Flemish, she is known as 'Kim Kong' on the circuit and is notorious for her killing groundstrokes. She rose to fame in 1999 at Wimbledon where she made it all the way through to the fourth round, only to be beaten by childhood idol, Steffi Graf. From there she went on to win the WTA Tour Championships in 2003 after beating Lindsey Davenport (6-1, 3-6, 6-1). The win stole the crown from Serena Williams and secured her the number one spot in woman's tennis and earned her a place in the record books as the first woman to win a championship without having previously won a Grand Slam tournament. Other achievements include her victory in the 2005 US Open for which she received prize money totalling US$2.2 million – the largest pay check in woman's sports history. Then, after a month off the circuit recovering from surgery to her wrist, she returned to the WTA tour and made the biggest ranking leap in women's tennis history by starting as an unseeded entry and winning 14 straight matches to get to the top, beating five of the world's top six players along the way. She was briefly engaged to Australian tennis star Lleyton Hewitt, but today is married to basketball player Brian Lynch. She retired from tennis in 2007 to start a family.

on a similar system to that followed in the UK, with four provincial categories that teams must progress through before they qualify for the premiership. The two leading Flemish teams are Anderlecht and Club Brugge – though bear in mind that these 'big teams' are on the same annual budget as those of England's smallest clubs. Local matches between towns tend to take place every two weeks at the teams' local training grounds; tickets start from around €5/adult. The King Baudouin stadium in Brussels is reserved for matches between the premiership big boys; tickets for those start from around €40/adult.

HIKING Hiking (*wandelen*) is incredibly popular in Flanders and all the tourist offices have well-signposted local routes you can follow.

MEDIA AND COMMUNICATIONS

NEWSPAPERS AND MAGAZINES Flanders' three major newspapers are the left-wing *De Morgen*, right-wing *De Standaard* and tabloid *Het Laatse Nieuws*.

In Brussels, there are a handful of weekly English-language papers that tend to focus on EU news, including *New Europe* and *European Voice*, which is produced by London's *The Economist*. In the larger cities it's fairly easy to get your hands on major English-language broadsheets, such as *The Times* and the American *Wall Street Journal*. English-language glossy magazines are also available in specialist bookstores like FNAC. The capital also publishes a free *Metro* newspaper found on stands situated throughout all métro stations. They're in Dutch (blue version) and French (green version) only, but there's a daily weather report and sudoku quiz at the back of the paper.

There are several events' magazines. Those sold in newsagents include the weekly English-language *The Bulletin* and *Agenda* (the former also summarises the week's news, and provides art and film reviews, TV listings and job and apartment ads at the back); and *Newcomer*, a bi-annual magazine aimed predominately at expats, which covers everything from banking to baby care.

Each city also publishes a free magazine called *Zone 02* (Brussels), *Zone 03* (Antwerp) and *Zone 09* (Gent), respectively. Distributed every second Wednesday, they offer reviews on everything from films to books and provide details of upcoming exhibitions, theatre performances and concerts; there is also a short jobs section at the back.

CINEMA The majority of mainstream films are shown in English (check that the listing features the VO – *version originale* – code alongside it) with Dutch and French subtitles. Dubbed films will bear the code VF – *version française,* and if subtitles have been added look for the ST code. Ticket prices range from €2 to €9. The website www.cinebel.be provides cinema and film listings for the entire country (French and Dutch only).

TELEVISION Flanders' national television network is VRT. However, 90% of the region subscribes to Telenet, the main cable TV provider, and this means you'll be able to watch English-language channels like BBC 1, BBC 2, National Geographic Channel and Discovery Channel. VT4 and 2BE frequently show English-language films around 21.00.

RADIO You can easily tune into British radio stations; the World Service is on 648kHz medium wave, and BBC Radio 4 on 198kHz long wave. To sample what the locals listen to try the popular Studio Brussels (Stu Bru) on 102.1FM or Q-Music on 103.3FM.

TELEPHONES Belgium's international dialling code is ✆00 32. Phone booths accept both coins and pre-paid calling cards, which can be bought from post offices, newsagents, railway stations and supermarkets. Emergency telephone numbers are noted on the inside front cover of this book.

To call Flanders from abroad input the international dialling code 0032, followed by the city code and the number you require, remembering to omit the initial zero preceding the city code. Those calling from the US should dial ✆011 +0032 + city code + required number.

To call abroad from Flanders, enter the international dialling code of the required country, followed by the domestic number – again you will have to omit the initial zero. Should you encounter any problems you can call directory enquiries on ✆1405, but it charges over a euro a minute.

Mobile phones Flanders has good network coverage, but roaming fees are expensive. If you'll be staying for a while I recommend buying a local SIM card. The market is dominated by three companies: **Proximus** (*www.proximus.be*), **Mobistar** (*www.mobistar.be*) and **Base** (*www.base.be*). All have high-street outlets.

POST Belgium's national postal service is called bpost. Post offices are generally open 09.00–12.00 and 14.00–17.00 Monday to Friday, and 09.00–12.00 Saturday. You can choose from the fast *Prior* service, or slower *Non-prior*. From *Prior* experience I've found that letters and parcels sent within Europe take from three to seven days to arrive, whilst those sent to the US and Canada take around ten days. A stamp for a *Prior* letter to the US costs €1.29 and to the UK €1.09. Stamps and packaging materials can be bought at post offices, and it is also possible to buy books of stamps in supermarkets, hotels, campsites, service stations, newsstands and souvenir shops. Postboxes are red and marked *Poste*.

INTERNET Internet cafés are becoming hard to find because most hotels, hostels and cafés offer free Wi-Fi. I've listed options in towns, wherever they were possible. You can expect to pay around €1.50 for half an hour and €3 for the full hour. As a last resort most town libraries have computers you can use free of charge, but you'll need to sign up for a free library card.

BUSINESS

The majority of Flemish are skilled linguists, often speaking Dutch, French and English fluently. As a result, the bulk of business in Brussels is conducted in English. Meetings are formal and punctuality is key, as is smart attire. It is considered rude to interrupt someone when they are speaking and Belgians will always let someone finish before giving their reply. The exchange of business cards is popular and it pays to have your details translated into French or Dutch depending on the region you are working in. The sensitivity to the language divide will be appreciated.

BUYING PROPERTY

Houses for sale are marked '*te koop*'. To purchase property in Flanders, all you need is a Belgian bank account, a residence identity card and usually a copy of your work contract. However, buying property in Flanders is a commitment because if you sell it within five years of purchase you incur a heavy capital-gains tax. Legal costs are around 15–20% of the purchase price of the house, and be aware that new or highly renovated properties carry an extra 21% VAT charge. The best property websites to search are www.vlan.be and www.immoweb.be.

CULTURAL ETIQUETTE

The Flemish are exceptionally laidback and you would have to commit a serious *faux pas* in order to create offence. However, being aware of local values and customs concerning behaviour, dress and body language will enrich your experience of the region and save you from a potentially embarrassing situation. By following the few social customs listed below, you will be able to create quick rapport with the locals and quicken your understanding of the Flemish psyche.

THREE KISSES A handshake is satisfactory at formal meetings, but the Flemish do one better than the French when it comes to greeting friends or loved ones; they bestow three kisses on alternate cheeks. Younger generations and city dwellers tend to prefer the more fashionable 'kiss the air', 'darling' variety; whilst the elderly generation and country residents plump for sturdy smackers that are planted firmly on the recipient's cheek. Emotion is kept to a minimum betwixt men, who more often than not opt for the fail-proof handshake.

GIFT-GIVING The Flemish love giving gifts. When a baby is born, for example, the parents traditionally prepare cards and a small sack of *doopsuiker* (sugared chocolates) to give to visiting friends and family. Should you be invited to someone's house, it is customary to bring a small token of thanks; safe bets are flowers or pralines. Wine or beer is usually exchanged only between close friends.

TABLE MANNERS If you are invited for dinner, punctual arrival is expected. A toast is often made at the beginning of the meal, which more often than not takes the form of '*op gesondheid*' followed by a clinking of glasses. It is also polite to wish everyone '*eet smakelijk*' before they start eating – it's the equivalent of *bon appétit*. Most Flemish people are overwhelmingly hospitable and will dole out large portions until you reach the last notch on your belt. Try to eat all the food on your plate; leftovers are considered a sign of bad cooking on the part of the hostess. To signal you've finished eating, place your knife and fork together and lay them to the right at the three o'clock position on your plate.

TRAVELLING POSITIVELY

If you enjoy your travels around Flanders and would like to give something back, I suggest making a donation to the **Commonwealth War Graves Commission** (*www.cwgc.org*) who do an excellent and important job maintaining the World War I cemeteries.

Part Two

THE GUIDE

Bradt Travel Guides

www.bradtguides.com

Africa

Access Africa: Safaris for People with Limited Mobility	£16.99
Africa Overland	£16.99
Algeria	£15.99
Angola	£17.99
Botswana	£16.99
Burkina Faso	£17.99
Cameroon	£15.99
Cape Verde	£15.99
Congo	£16.99
Eritrea	£15.99
Ethiopia	£17.99
Ethiopia Highlights	£15.99
Ghana	£15.99
Kenya Highlights	£15.99
Madagascar	£16.99
Madagascar Highlights	£15.99
Malawi	£15.99
Mali	£14.99
Mauritius, Rodrigues & Réunion	£15.99
Mozambique	£15.99
Namibia	£15.99
Niger	£14.99
Nigeria	£17.99
North Africa: Roman Coast	£15.99
Rwanda	£15.99
São Tomé & Príncipe	£14.99
Seychelles	£16.99
Sierra Leone	£16.99
Somaliland	£15.99
South Africa Highlights	£15.99
Sudan	£15.99
Tanzania, Northern	£14.99
Tanzania	£17.99
Uganda	£16.99
Zambia	£18.99
Zanzibar	£14.99
Zimbabwe	£15.99

The Americas and the Caribbean

Alaska	£15.99
Amazon Highlights	£15.99
Argentina	£16.99
Bahia	£14.99
Cayman Islands	£14.99
Chile Highlights	£15.99
Colombia	£17.99
Dominica	£15.99
Grenada, Carriacou & Petite Martinique	£15.99
Guyana	£15.99
Nova Scotia	£14.99
Panama	£14.99
Paraguay	£15.99
Turks & Caicos Islands	£14.99
Uruguay	£15.99
USA by Rail	£15.99
Venezuela	£16.99
Yukon	£14.99

British Isles

Britain from the Rails	£14.99
Bus-Pass Britain	£15.99
Eccentric Britain	£15.99
Eccentric Cambridge	£9.99
Eccentric London	£14.99
Eccentric Oxford	£9.99
Sacred Britain	£16.99
Slow: Cornwall	£14.99
Slow: Cotswolds	£14.99
Slow: Devon & Exmoor	£14.99
Slow: Dorset	£14.99
Slow: Norfolk & Suffolk	£14.99
Slow: Northumberland	£14.99
Slow: North Yorkshire	£14.99
Slow: Sussex & South Downs National Park	£14.99

Europe

Abruzzo	£14.99
Albania	£16.99
Armenia	£16.99
Azores	£14.99
Baltic Cities	£14.99
Belarus	£15.99
Bosnia & Herzegovina	£14.99
Bratislava	£9.99
Budapest	£9.99
Croatia	£13.99
Cross-Channel France: Nord-Pas de Calais	£13.99
Cyprus see North Cyprus	
Dresden	£7.99
Estonia	£14.99
Faroe Islands	£15.99
Flanders	£15.99
Georgia	£15.99
Greece: The Peloponnese	£14.99
Helsinki	£7.99
Hungary	£15.99
Iceland	£15.99
Kosovo	£15.99
Lapland	£15.99
Lille	£9.99
Lithuania	£14.99
Luxembourg	£14.99
Macedonia	£16.99
Malta & Gozo	£12.99
Montenegro	£14.99
North Cyprus	£13.99
Serbia	£15.99
Slovakia	£14.99
Slovenia	£13.99
Spitsbergen	£16.99
Switzerland Without a Car	£14.99
Transylvania	£14.99
Ukraine	£15.99

Middle East, Asia and Australasia

Bangladesh	£17.99
Borneo	£17.99
Eastern Turkey	£16.99
Iran	£15.99
Iraq: Then & Now	£15.99
Israel	£15.99
Jordan	£16.99
Kazakhstan	£16.99
Kyrgyzstan	£16.99
Lake Baikal	£15.99
Lebanon	£15.99
Maldives	£15.99
Mongolia	£16.99
North Korea	£14.99
Oman	£15.99
Palestine	£15.99
Shangri-La: A Travel Guide to the Himalayan Dream	£14.99
Sri Lanka	£15.99
Syria	£15.99
Taiwan	£16.99
Tibet	£17.99
Yemen	£14.99

Wildlife

Antarctica: A Guide to the Wildlife	£15.99
Arctic: A Guide to Coastal Wildlife	£16.99
Australian Wildlife	£14.99
Central & Eastern European Wildlife	£15.99
Chinese Wildlife	£16.99
East African Wildlife	£19.99
Galápagos Wildlife	£16.99
Madagascar Wildlife	£16.99
New Zealand Wildlife	£14.99
North Atlantic Wildlife	£16.99
Pantanal Wildlife	£16.99
Peruvian Wildlife	£15.99
Southern African Wildlife	£19.99
Sri Lankan Wildlife	£15.99

Pictorials and other guides

100 Alien Invaders	£16.99
100 Animals to See Before They Die	£16.99
100 Bizarre Animals	£16.99
Eccentric Australia	£12.99
Northern Lights	£6.99
Swimming with Dolphins, Tracking Gorillas	£15.99
Through the Northwest Passage	£17.99
Tips on Tipping	£6.99
Total Solar Eclipse 2012 & 2013	£6.99
Wildlife and Conservation Volunteering: The Complete Guide	£13.99
Your Child Abroad	£10.95

Travel literature

Fakirs, Feluccas and Femmes Fatales	£9.99
The Marsh Lions	£9.99
Two Year Mountain	£9.99
Up the Creek	£9.99

3

Brussels

A capital, an independent region, an island in a language-divide dispute, the centre of Europe and seat of the European Union – Brussels wears many hats. Which side you see depends on the purpose of your visit, but most first impressions agree that the city is something of an enigma. Seated at the centre of a cultural crossroads of Latinate and Germanic traditions and home to a million people – over half of whom are of foreign descent – Brussels has a mish-mash of eurocrat and Mediterranean blood that lends her a myriad of personalities. The city isn't uniform like trendy Paris or brassy Berlin; she is composed of a hotchpotch of traditional dated buildings and ultra-modern constructions. But conventional beauty is banal and Brussels' winning card – that trumps other capital cities – is her sense of intimacy. Often described by city residents – known as *Zinnekes* – as a big village, Brussels is compact, easy to get around and not overwhelming like most European capitals.

Brussels may be an introverted city: one shy to share her secrets with those who live there, let alone with strangers on a weekend break, but therein lies the appeal. All romantics know the exhilaration is in the chase and what better thrill than to pace her streets in search of what makes Brussels tick? Look among the flea markets and the award-winning steamy kitchens of sweaty and passionate chefs, hang out in the Art Nouveau cafés and amble through the residential outer-lying communes. I guarantee that underneath the calm and composed surface you'll find the murmured heartbeat of a city with a Bohemian and eclectic spirit.

HISTORY

The capital began life on an island. St Géry, the Bishop of Cambrai, built a small chapel on a marshy mound in the River Senne and around it gathered a small settlement. Its name doesn't enter the history books until the 10th century when the Duke of Lotharingia (an area encompassing modern-day Belgium, parts of Germany and northern France) erected a fortress in a growing community called *Broeksele* – 'dwelling on the marsh'.

By the 12th century, and under the rule of the feudal Dukes of Brabant, the town was beginning to flourish. It had become a popular stop over for merchants using the Brugge–Gent–Cologne trade route and soon the marshes were drained to allow the town to expand. Independence was granted in 1229 and soon after the first city walls were erected along present-day Place Royale, Place St Gudule, Place St Cathérine and Manneken-Pis. These were replaced over a century later, in 1357–79, by medieval ramparts that encompassed a larger area and stayed in place until the 19th century. Today, they sit under the petit-ring motorway that encircles Brussels.

Brussels' status advanced rapidly in the 15th century. Child emperor Charles V had inherited the lands and when he wasn't waging war abroad, he ruled from

Brussels, lending the city financial and political pulling power. This honeymoon period ended when Charles abdicated in 1556 at the (now destroyed) Coudenberg Palace and his son Phillip II took the throne. A Catholic zealot, Phillip moved his court to Madrid and sent Spanish nobles to impose anti-Protestant edicts. Riots labelled the Iconoclastic Fury followed but were brutally crushed. Rebellion and a successful revolt led by William I Prince of Orange ensued and a Protestant government was kept in place until the end of the French Revolution, when Phillip took the city back and consolidated its status as capital of the Spanish Netherlands. Squabbles with neighbouring France had been going on for centuries, but the biggest retaliation was taken by French army commander François de Neufville, Duke of Villeroi, who, under the orders of Louis XVI, aimed his canons at Brussels and bombarded the city for 36 hours in 1695. Over 4,000 buildings were destroyed including the majority of medieval guildhouses on the Grand' Place – these were rebuilt five years later and are the examples on show today.

Control passed to the Austrian Hapsburgs and later the French, whose rule was ended when Napoleon was defeated at the Battle of Waterloo and forced to relinquish control of the area, which was incorporated into the new Kingdom of the Netherlands and ruled by William I. Uneasiness over his rule erupted in revolt in 1830 (page 9) and soon enough an independent Belgian state was formed and Brussels chosen as its capital. With a renewed sense of nationalist pride, Leopold I set about dismantling the city walls and constructing new, grand, buildings. The trend was taken up with enthusiasm by Leopold II who poured profits from his colonies in the Congo into smartening up the city, laying down wide boulevards, clearing poverty-stricken areas and covering over the remainder of the disease-invested Senne River.

The capital was occupied by German troops during World Wars I and II, but has continued to modernise exponentially ever since, attracting the headquarters of both the EU and NATO in 1958 and 1967 respectively. Its status as a region was finalised on 18 June 1989.

GETTING THERE AND AWAY

BY AIR Brussels has two major airports: the central Brussels-National (*www. brusselsairport.be*) – also known as Zaventem – and the outer lying Brussels-Charleroi (*www.charleroi-airport.com*). Brussels-National is located 13km northeast of Brussels in the small town of Zaventem. It serves most major airlines, including the national carrier Brussels Airlines. Charleroi is 60km south of the city, about an hour's drive away, and serves budget airlines.

Getting to/from Brussels-National (Zaventem)
By train The railway station is located in the basement (level -1). The express shuttle service departs every 20 minutes and takes approximately 30 minutes to reach the city centre with stops at Brussel-Noord, Brussel-Centraal and Brussels-Zuid/Bruxelles-Midi. Trains run from 06.00–midnight; a one-way second-class ticket costs €2.60, first class €4.10.

By bus The bus station is located on the ground floor (level 0). There are two operators:
De Lijn (*www.delijn.be*) operates an express service which drops at Brussel-Noord/Bruxelles-Nord (bus #471), NATO (bus #471) and the Roodebeek métro station (bus #659). All depart from platform A and a one-way ticket costs €3.

MIVB/STIB (*www.stib.be*) operates a 30-minute express service from the airport to the EU quarter. From Monday to Friday before 20.00 you need bus #12, and on the weekend or after 20.00 you need bus #21; all buses depart from platform C. A one-way fare (*un aller simple*) bought on the platform prior to travel costs €3, or €5 on the bus.

By taxi Taxis are available outside the arrivals hall 24 hours a day. A one-way fare to the city centre usually costs €45 and the journey will take around 40 minutes depending on traffic – the ring-road can get very busy during rush hour. Only taxis with a blue-and-yellow emblem are licensed.

Getting to/from Brussels-Charleroi

By bus A shuttle bus (*www.voyages-lelan.be*) departs every 30 minutes for Bruxelles-Midi/Brussels-Zuid railway station. Buses run from 08.15 to 23.45 from the airport and are arranged to coincide with the Ryanair flight timetable. A one-way ticket costs €13, a return €22, and both can be bought on the bus. The journey takes an hour. To get back to the airport, the bus stop is located on the corner of Rue de France and Rue de l'Instruction on the west side of Bruxelles-Midi/Brussels-Zuid station. Buses in this direction run from 04.00 to 20.00 every day.

By train You'll need to catch a bus (Bus A) from the airport to Charleroi railway station (⊕ *20min*), from where there are direct trains to Brussels city centre. Ask for a *billet bulk* at the airport (€10), which covers the cost of the bus and the train to the city centre.

By taxi A taxi rank is located outside the main terminal building. All companies charge a (hefty) fixed flat rate of €85 from the airport to Brussels city centre.

BY TRAIN International trains like Eurostar, Thalys, and TGV arrive and depart from Bruxelles-Midi/Brussel-Zuid, whilst most domestic trains leave from Bruxelles-Central/Brussel-Centraal. For details of getting to Brussels by train, see page 33.

Trains to other Flemish cities depart as follows from Bruxelles-Midi/Brussel-Zuid: Antwerp (*5/18/28/32/56min past the hour Mon–Fri,* ⊕ *40min; 18/33/59min past the hour Sat–Sun,* ⊕ *50min*); Brugge (*5/26min past the hour daily;* ⊕ *1hr*); Gent (*5/14/26min past the hour Mon–Fri, 5/26min past the hour Sat–Sun;* ⊕ *30min*); Oostende (*5min past the hour Mon–Fri,* ⊕ *1hr 13min; via Brugge 5/26min past the hour Sat–Sun;* ⊕ *1hr 40min*).

BY CAR Travellers arriving from the UK and landing at Calais or Dunkerque just need to follow the E40; it'll take you all the way to Brussels (*196/156km;* ⊕ *2hr/1hr 40min*). Visitors coming from Germany should also follow the E40. Visitors arriving from France should follow either the E19 or the E42.

BY BUS See page 33.

ORIENTATION

Central Brussels is encircled by the pentagon-shaped 'petit-ring' motorway that mirrors where the 14th-century city walls once stood. Within this sits the city centre that is divided in two, broadly along the weaving stretch of road that runs in front of Gare Centrale and variously named Boulevard de l'Empereur, L'Impératrice and

Berlaymont. To the left of this sits the Lower Town that spreads out from the Grand' Place to the north, south and west portions of the petit-ring. Originally a working-class area populated by Flemish speakers, the Lower Town remains the commercial heart of the city and the main swathe of restaurants, hotels and cafés are located here. To the right, and where the ground raises its head and begins to slope upwards, is the Upper Town. The area takes in sights like the Palais de Justice and Musées Royaux des Beaux Arts and was home to the rich French-speaking upper classes.

The rest of the region's 19 communes sit outside the petit-ring and stretch to the start of the second outer ring road – the R0. Immediately attached are Art Nouveau hotspots Ixelles and St Gilles; Etterbeek which is home to the EU quarter; up-and-coming Anderlecht, and Schaerbeek and St Josse-ten-Noode, which are home to concentrations of Turkish and Polish immigrants. Further out lie the affluent suburbs of Uccle in the south, the green spaces of Woluwe-St-Pierre in the east, and in the northwest the smaller communes of Koekelberg, Ganshoren and Jette.

The airport (page 68) sits on the outskirts, northeast of the town centre and the city's three main railway stations: Bruxelles-Midi, Brussels-Centraal and Brussels-Nord run through the centre of town, practically along the invisible divide between the Upper and Lower towns.

GETTING AROUND

Brussels is best explored on foot and it's easily done: all the main sights are within a 1km radius of the central Grand' Place. However, walking on uneven cobblestones all day can become tiring, so if you find yourself at the opposite end of town from your hotel at the end of the day, then make use of Brussels' excellent public transport system which combines a métro system, buses and trams. The system is efficient, but can be confusing for first-time visitors; hints and tips are listed under the relevant sections. Run by STIB/MIVB (*www.stib.be*), the network is open everyday from 05.00 to midnight.

TICKETS Tickets are valid on all three services (métro, bus and tram). They can be purchased at the métro station ticket offices, GO self-service machines, on board buses and trams, tourist information offices and most newsagents, and are available in the following formats:

One journey (allows unlimited number of changes for one hour)	€1.80
A return (within 24 hours)	€3.30
Five journeys	€7.30
10 journeys	€12.50
One-day pass (unlimited travel)	€4.50
Three-day pass (unlimited travel)	€9.80

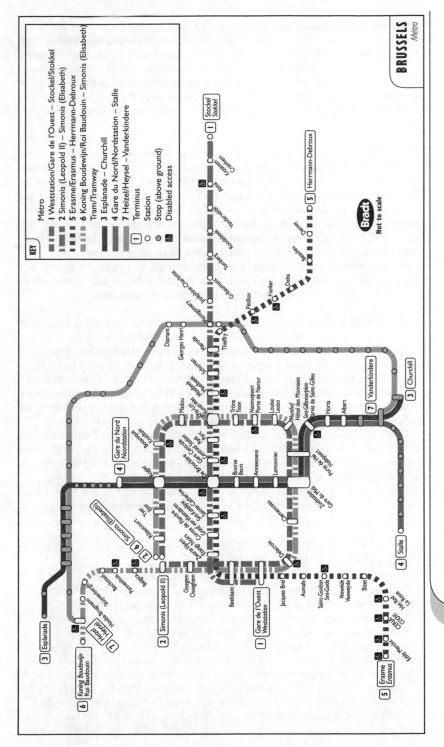

KEY

Métro
1 Weststation/Gare de l'Ouest – Stockel/Stokkel
2 Simonis (Leopold II) – Simonis (Elisabeth)
5 Erasme/Erasmus – Herrmann-Debroux
6 Koning Boudewijn/Roi Baudouin – Simonis (Elisabeth)

Tram/Tramway
3 Esplanade – Churchill
4 Gare du Nord/Nordstation – Stalle
7 Heizel/Heysel – Vanderkindere

[ ] Terminus
○ Station
● Stop (above ground)
♿ Disabled access

Bradt
Not to scale

It's cheaper to buy tickets before travel, rather than buying them from the driver. Alternatively, you can purchase the Brussels Card (*www.brusselscard.be*; see box, page 94), a museum-pass that also includes a transport ticket valid for 24, 48 or 72 hours.

Once purchased, tickets should be entered into the orange ticket-processing machines located at the start of escalators on the underground and near the doors on buses and trams. This only needs to be done once at the start of a journey or when changing mode of transport, so it's clear you've switched, say, from métro to bus.

BY MÉTRO There are six underground lines: lines #2 (orange) and #6 (blue) serve the same purpose as London Underground's Circle Line, stopping at major junctions around the city-centre ring road; lines #1 (pink) and #5 (yellow) are akin to the Central Line, running east to west through the EU district and the centre of town; and lines #3 and #4 act like the Northern Line and are serviced by trams instead of trains, running north to south through the city centre. All stations can be accessed from street level; just look out for the distinctive white 'M' on a blue background. Handy route planners suspended from the platform roof illuminate red to show the current position of the next available train and how long you have to wait until it arrives. Note that passengers are responsible for opening the doors at a station stop – pull the door lever on the old carriages, or press the green button on the new ones.

BY TRAM AND BUS There are more than 2,200 stops; pick up a full network map from the tourist office or any transport office. The rules for using the tram and bus service are very similar. First of all, stop signs are clearly labelled: at the top it indicates whether the route is serviced by tram ('T' in a circle) or by bus ('B' in a circle). Underneath this is the name of the stop followed by a list of the various lines that stop here and their final destinations. There will be a separate sign underneath indicating whether these routes are serviced by the Noctis night bus service, which runs from midnight until 03.00 every Friday and Saturday.

Trams and buses stop only on request, so raise your hand to indicate to the driver you'd like to board; similarly, when you want to get off, signal to the driver by pressing the blue button. You can buy a one-journey ticket on board, but drivers are reluctant to change anything larger than €5.

When boarding buses you enter through the front doors and exit via the back doors; with trams you can enter/exit via any door. Trams have priority over all traffic, including pedestrians.

UNDERGROUND ART GALLERY

Brussels' dingy métro system is livened up by wonderful works of art. Launched 30 years ago by CAID (Commission Artistique des Infrastructures de Déplacement) to instill an appreciation of art in the public, its instalments range from sculptures to photographs. Some of the most intriguing examples include Surrealist Paul Delvaux's 13m-long mural *Nos Vieux Tram Bruxellois* at Bourse station; fragments of demolished Art Nouveau buildings, among them the twirly and ornate barriers from architect Victor Horta's Maison du Peuple, at Horta station; and Hergé's mural (completed shortly before his death) at Stockel which features over 150 characters from his *Tintin* comic books. For a full list pick up the *Art dans le Métro* pamphlet from the tourist office. Buskers playing accordions or juggling liven up your journey too.

BY BICYCLE Brussels' bike-rental scheme, **Villo!** (✆ *078 05 11 10; www.villo.be*) has 180 bike terminals dotted around town (locations are marked on the maps), and open 24 hours a day. Just slot in your bank card and away you go! As a visitor you can purchase a one-day or a seven-day card: the first half an hour is free and thereafter you pay anything from €0.50 to €2 per hour depending on how long you keep the bike.

Alternatively, **Provélo** (*15 Rue des Londres, 1050 Ixelles;* ✆ *02 502 73 55; www.provelo.be;* ⊕ *Apr–Oct 10.00–13.30 & 14.00–17.00 daily, Nov–Mar 10.00– 13.30 & 14.00–17.00 Mon–Fri;* M̲ *Trône/Porte de Namur*) is a government-run outfit that offers bike rental (*adults €15/day, children €12/day*) and organises guided cycling tours of the city (*€17/half-day*). Most are in French or Dutch, but English tours can be arranged for groups and all tours depart from the address listed above.

BY TAXI A fixed charge of €2.40 applies at the start of all journeys (this increases to €4.40 at night) and the journey is then calculated at €1.35/km in the city centre or €2.70/km in the outer communes. You'll be given a printed receipt at the end of your journey. Tips are included, but a little extra is always appreciated. If you're hailing a taxi on the street, use only taxis bearing the official yellow-and-blue Brussels taxi sign. The following are trusted companies: **Taxis Bleus** (✆ *02 268 00 00*), **Taxis Orange** (✆ *02 349 43 43*), **Taxis Verts** (✆ *02 349 49 49*) and **Taxis for disabled travellers** (✆ *02 349 45 45/ 02 527 16 72*).

TOURIST INFORMATION

Brussels – as an independent region – has its own dedicated and dynamic tourist board known as **Visit Brussels** (✆ *02 513 89 40;* e *info@visitbrussels.be; www. visitbrussels.be*). They have two offices and kiosks at Bruxelles-Midi/Brussels-Zuid railway station and Zaventem airport.

ℹ **Brussels Info Place (BIP)** [82–3 G2] 2 Rue Royale; ⊕ 10.00–18.00 daily. The largest office, which also makes bookings for shows, concerts & hotel rooms.

ℹ **Visit Brussels** [95 D2] Hôtel de Ville (Town Hall), Grand' Place; ⊕ 10.00–18.00 daily. Doles out maps & can make hotel bookings.

ℹ **Kiosks** Bruxelles-Midi/Brussels-Zuid (opposite entrance to Eurostar), ⊕ 10.00–18.00 daily; Zaventem Airport (arrivals hall), ⊕ 08.00–21.00 daily; Place du Grand Sablon (outside Brussel-Centraal railway station), ⊕ summer 10.00–17.30 daily.

ℹ **Visit Flanders** [95 E2] 61 Rue du Marché aux Herbes; ⊕ Apr–Sep 09.00–18.00 Mon–Sat, 10.00–17.00 Sun, Jul–Aug 09.00–19.00 daily, Oct–Mar 09.00–17.00 Mon–Sat, 10.00–16.00 Sun, closed 13.00–14.00 Sat & Sun. Smart, large office suppling information on the Flanders region & Brussels. Free Wi-Fi.

ℹ **Use-It** [78–9 B4] 9B Quai à la Houille; ✆ 02 218 39 06; www.use-it.be; ⊕ 10.00–13.00 & 14.00–18.00 Mon–Sat. Superb information centre for young travellers. Their specially tailored city maps are updated yearly with off-the-beaten-track suggestions. The young, fun team also offers free internet & coffee.

🏠 WHERE TO STAY

Beds in Brussels are plentiful, but don't restrict your search to the options on offer around the Grand' Place. The majority of sights in the city centre are all within easy walking distance, so why not try a hotel outside the petit-ring motorway and stay in a less-clichéd locale?

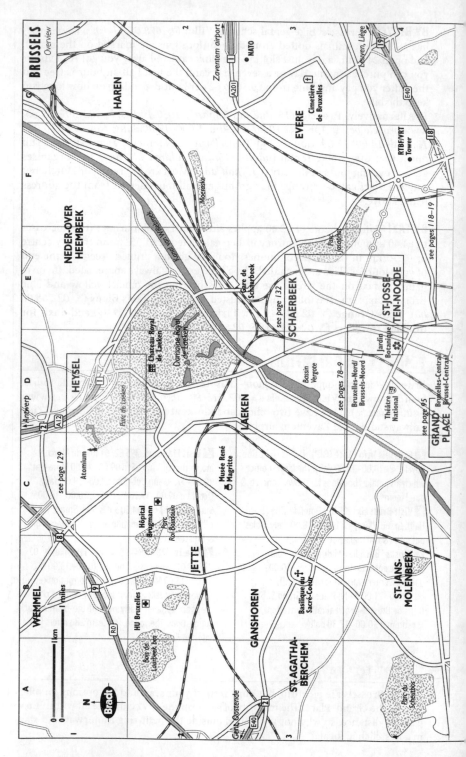

WEMMEL

NEDER-OVER-HEEMBEEK

HAREN

EVERE

Zaventem airport

• NATO

Leuven, Liège

Cimetière de Bruxelles

RTBF/VRT
• Tower

see pages 118–19

Moeraske

Parc Josaphat

SCHAERBEEK

see page 132

Gare de Schaerbeek

ST-JOSSE-TEN-NOODE

Jardin Botanique

Chateau Royal de Laeken

Domaine Royal de Laeken

Bassin Vergote

see pages 78–9

Bruxelles-Nord/Brussel-Noord

Théâtre National

HEYSEL

Atomium

see page 129

Parc de Laeken

LAEKEN

GRAND PLACE Bruxelles-Central/Brussel-Centraal

see page 95

Musée René Magritte

Hôpital Brugmann

Parc Roi Baudouin

HU Bruxelles

JETTE

GANSHOREN

Basilique du Sacré-Cœur

ST-JANS-MOLENBEEK

Bois de Laarbeek bos

ST-AGATHA-BERCHEM

Parc du Scheutbos

Gent, Oostende

Antwerp

0   1km
0   1 miles

N

Bradt

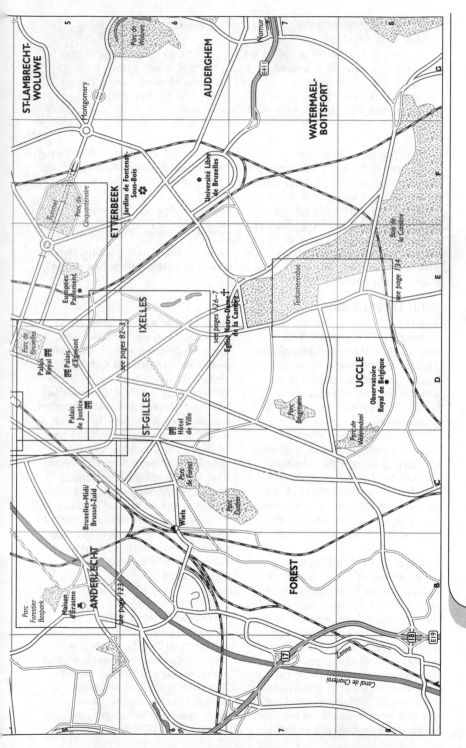

ST-LAMBRECHT-WOLUWE

Montgomery

Parc de Woluwe

AUDERGHEM

Namur

E411

WATERMAEL-BOITSFORT

Tunnel

Parc du Cinquantenaire

ETTERBEEK

Jardins de Fontenay-Sous-Bois

Université Libre de Bruxelles

Bois de la Cambre

Européen Parlement

IXELLES

see pages 126–7

Eglise Notre-Dame de la Cambre

Terkamerenbos

see page 134

Parc de Bruxelles

Palais Royal

Palais d'Egmont

see pages 82–3

UCCLE

Observatoire Royal de Belgique

Palais de Justice

ST-GILLES

Hôtel de Ville

Parc Brugmann

Parc de Wolvendael

Parc de Forest

Parc Duden

Bruxelles-Midi/ Brussel-Zuid

Wiels

FOREST

Parc Forestier Bospark

Maison d'Erasme

ANDERLECHT

see page 123

Canal de Charleroi

Zenne

E19

Brussels is busy all year round so it's advisable to book ahead, especially during the summer high-season. Be sure to check the hotel's website beforehand as many offer two-night stay or weekend discounts. Alternatively, Visit Brussels (page 73) can book a room for you free of charge.

Those on a tighter budget are well catered for: Brussels has several youth hostels dotted around town and there's a good selection of B&Bs. I've included my favourites, but www.bnb-brussels.be has the full list.

If you have an early flight to catch, there are six hotels including Sofitel, Holiday Inn and Novotel in the Zaventem area and all can be booked online (see page 43), or through the tourist board.

INSIDE THE PETIT-RING
Luxury

🏠 **Amigo** [95 D3] (173 rooms) 1–3 Rue de l'Amigo; ✆ 02 547 47 47; www.hotelamigo.com; Ⓜ Bourse. Equidistant between the Grand'Place & the wee (pardon the pun) Mannken Pis, you couldn't stay any closer to the action. Built on the site of the old prison where Karl Marx & his wife, Baroness Jenny von Westphalen, were held before their expulsion. Part of the Rocco Forte chain, but you'd never guess it thanks to the plush, individually styled rooms which are decorated with smart Flemish fabrics & prints by Magritte or Marcel Broodthaers & contain all the mod-cons. Sketches of Hergé's *Tintin* liven up the bathrooms. There's a fitness centre & attached restaurant, Bocconi, which serves high-priced Italian fare. B/fast €33. €€€€€

🏠 **Métropole** [78–9 D5] (298 rooms) 31 Place de Brouckère; ✆ 02 217 23 00; www.metropolehotel.com; Ⓜ De Brouckère. This 5-star landmark 116-year-old hotel was originally a bank – the reception & concierge desk retain the original sorting boxes – but was later bought by Villemans & Kapels brewery to be used as a café where they could sell their beer. Following complaints of too many drunken locals, it was changed to a hotel. And what a hotel! Its lavish interior has welcomed the likes of Albert Einstein & Marie Curie. Reception rooms like the magnificent Art Deco lobby & grand palm-adorned piano bar pack an impressive punch, but the modern, Art Deco or Louis XIV-style bedrooms are decidedly (& disappointingly) more demure. Nevertheless, the service & facilities are first class. €€€€€

🏠 **Le Plaza** [78–9 E4] (190 rooms) 118–126 Blvd Adolphe Max; ✆ 02 278 01 00; www.leplaza-brussels.be; Ⓜ Rogier. Brussels' oldest independent hotel still brims with character & class. Winston Churchill stayed here during World War II & during the 1960s & 1970s it became the go-to hotel for celebrities – welcoming the likes of Brigitte Bardot & Gary Cooper. A plush collection of antiques, paintings, silk rugs, sweeping staircases & marble floors are on show. The traditional rooms are good, but the deluxe rooms are a big step up in terms of design & ambiènce. The prestige rooms are larger still & have a small sitting area. Gym & Parisian-style Brasserie Estérel also on site. B/fast €27. €€€€–€€€€€

Mid-range

🏠 **Chambre d'Hôte Vaudeville** [95 F2] (4 rooms) 11 Galerie de la Reine, Galeries Royales St-Hubert; ✆ 02 512 84 56; m 0484 59 46 69; www.theatreduvaudeville.be. Lovingly renovated by stage manager of the Théâtre du Vaudeville, Thierry Denis, there are 2 smaller (cheaper) rooms with en-suite rain showers: Madame Loulou – named after Rene Magritte's dog – & the minimalist Black & White; & 2 larger rooms, the theatre-themed Diva & the travel-themed Explorateur with free-standing bathtubs in the en suite. Windows are double glazed, but there can be some noise from the galleries below. Thierry hand-prepares the delicious b/fast baskets which are left outside your room at 08.00. Free beer & water is stored in communal fridge in hallway. If no-one answers the doorbell, ask for Thierry inside the theatre. €€€

🏠 **Concept Hotel** [95 D2] (3 rooms) 39 Grand' Place; m 0474 03 24 70; www.concepthotel.be. Stunning aparthotel offering 2 en-suite dbls with views of the Grand' Place & in the rafters a family duplex with a dbl & sgl bed & private bathroom across the landing. All equipped with TV, iPod dock, bathrobe & free Wi-Fi. B/fast included. €€€

🏠 **Espérance** [78–9 E4] (12 rooms) 1–3 Rue du Finistère; ☎ 02 219 10 28; www. hotel-esperance.be; M̄ De Brouckère. Wonderful 1930s' Art Deco hotel which was saved from ruin & declared a listed building in 2008. Its tavern/b/fast room has hardly changed, while the rooms upstairs have been given a modern makeover. Rooms fall into 2 categories: 'design' or the more spacious 'superior'. All boast separate his 'n' hers shower heads in the walk-in wet room & come equipped with free Wi-Fi, safety deposit box, flatscreen TV & minibar – but no wardrobe unfortunately. Room 7 has a Jacuzzi & Room 3 is an original Art Deco room with a free-standing bathtub & gold taps. Guests have a keycard, which allows them to come & go as they please via a private entrance. B/fast €10. €€€

🏠 **Hotel Café Pacific** [78–9 B6] (12 rooms) 57 Rue Antoine Dansaert; ☎ 02 213 00 80; www. hotelcafepacific.com; M̄ Bourse. A super find on a busy street, this townhouse offers unique & sophisticated rooms that contain a blend of all-white décor & minimalist furniture, with quirky touches like writing above the bed, or a mezzanine level. TV, Wi-Fi etc, come as standard. B/fast is taken on the ground floor in the radically different Art Nouveau restaurant. €€€

🏠 **Hotel Bloom!** [78–9 H3/132 A5] (305 rooms) 250 Rue Royale; ☎ 02 220 66 11; www.hotelbloom. com; M̄ Botanique. Hip Swedish-owned hotel in the north of town, where even the staff are known by their nicknames – I was served by Edelweiss & The Voice! The very spacious rooms are decked out with IKEA-style white furniture, grass-green carpet,

& floor-to-ceiling windows so the light floods in to light up the *pièce de résistance*: a fresco unique to each room hand-painted by a European art student. Downstairs is the Smoods bar/restaurant where resident DJ Cosy Mozzy plays every Fri & Sat 22.00–02.00, & with Nintendo Wii & computers; rooftop fitness centre. Voted one of the world's trendiest hotels on Trip Advisor. The excellent b/fast costs €19 online; €25 otherwise. €€–€€€

🏠 **Hotel St-Géry** [95 B1] (24 rooms) 29–32 Pl St-Géry; m 0494 28 55 96; www. hotelstgery.com; M̄ Bourse. Boutique hotel above the classy Belmont brasserie scheduled, at the time of writing, to open January 2012. Each room is decorated by a different artist, but it's the hotel's location that's the real draw – right in the centre of St-Géry district, home of the best bars. €€–€€€

Budget

🏠 **Hotel Welcome** [78–9 C5] (17 rooms) 23 Quai au Bois à Brûler; ☎ 02 219 95 46; www. hotelwelcome.com; M̄ St-Cathérine. I loved Hotel Welcome for its sense of fun. Rooms are named (not numbered) after countries where the owners – Sophie & Michel Smeesters – have travelled & are decorated with items they brought back. Don't let the wood-panelled lobby fool you: corridors of quirkiness await… My favourites were the gargantuan 'Egyptian' suite, complete with gold mummy, a 2-person Jacuzzi & views over the Quai; the standard azure 'Zanzibar' room with ornate doors from Stonetown; & the bright-pink deluxe 'Bali' room with 1-person Jacuzzi. Free Wi-Fi. €€

🏠 **Theater** [78–9 D3] (9 rooms) 23 Rue de Gaver; ☎ 02 350 90 00; www. theaterhotelbrussels.com; M̄ Yser. Boutique townhouse with bright-white & chocolate-brown en-suite rooms. Rooms starting with '23' are located at the front of the building & are larger (& noisier) than those located in the new section – whose rooms start with the number '26' – at the back of the hotel. Triple rooms & suites are also available for families. Some travellers may find its location in the red-light district off-putting. B/fast €8 extra. €€

Shoestring

🏠 **2GO4 Grand' Place Hostel** [95 E2] (10 rooms) 6–8 Rue de Haringstraat; ☎ 02 219 30 19; www.2go4.be; M̄ Gare Centrale. Renovation incomplete at time of research, but right next to the

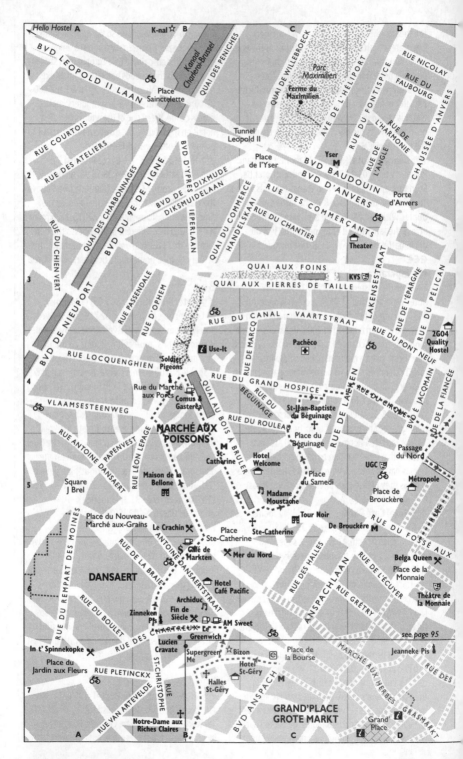

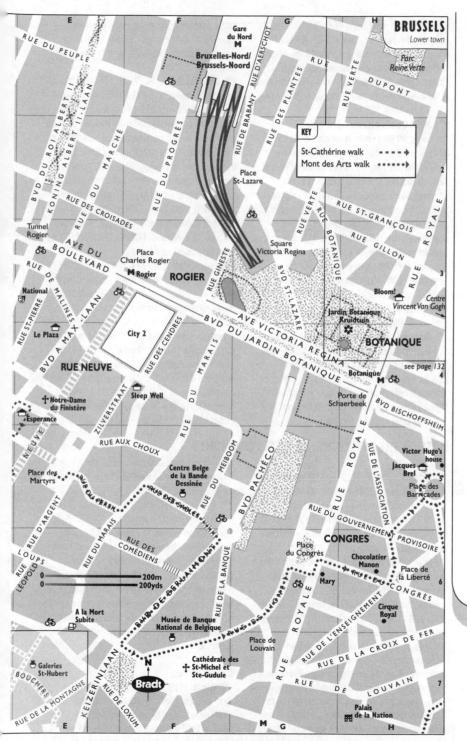

Grand' Place this promises to be the best-located budget option in the city. Mix of 6-, 8- & 10-bed dorms are finished to a high standard & en-suite bathrooms are positively luxurious. Internet & kitchen. Currently, check-in is inconveniently located at the 2Go4 Hostel (below). Bed only, no b/fast. Dbl €59–70, trpl €90–105.

🏠 **2GO4 Quality Hostel** [78–9 D3] (26 rooms) 99 Blvd Emile Jacqmain; ✆ 02 219 30 19; www.2go4.be; M̲ Rogier/De Brouckère. Excellent hostel owned by three brothers: Vincent, Xavier & Pascal. Large groups (of over 6) not admitted, so it's not rowdy. Rooms are a mix of 4-, 6-, 8- & 10-bed dorms, & dbl, triple or quadruple private rooms with en-suite shower & toilet. Rooms are spotless & modern, if a little sparse, & beds are comfortable. TV snug, internet & kitchen (no oven) are bright & trendy, but none are accessible 13.00–16.00 when reception is closed. Some rooms have baths. Free Wi-Fi, computers & towel rental. No b/fast but free hot drinks available until 10.30. Dorms €23, dbl €69.

🏠 **Bruegel** [82–3 D3] (30 rooms) 2 Rue du St-Esprit; ✆ 02 511 04 36; www.vjh.be; M̲ Gare-Centrale. The city's most central hostel, but it's popular with school groups, there's no laundry, no kitchen, & only an austere TV room & library. On the plus side, the basement pub has a happy hour & Playstation 3 & there's free Wi-Fi.

B/fast & bedding inc. Annoyingly, you have to leave the hostel between 10.00 & 14.00 for cleaning. Dorms €19.50–22, sgl € 31.30–35.50, dbl €23.50–26.50pp.

🏠 **Jacques Brel** [78–9 H5] (174 beds) 30 Rue de la Sablonnière; ✆ 02 218 01 87; www.laj.be; M̲ Botanique. Range of 2-, 3-, 4- & 6-bed dorms. Rooms are spacious & modern – if a little devoid of character – & all have a spotless en-suite shower; toilets are down the hall. The lively Babel Bar in the basement serves Belgian beers & snacks, & there's a communal kitchen. Facilities include free internet, laundry, paid luggage storage, games rooms with table tennis, a TV room & no curfew. The staff make a real effort to organise summer BBQs or city bike tours. Dorms €19.40, dbl €52. €3 extra for non-HI members.

🏠 **Sleep Well** [78–9 F4] (240 beds) 23 Rue du Damier; ✆ 02 218 50 50; www.sleepwell.be; M̲ Rogier. Has 2 dorm-room categories: Sleep Well Hostel rooms have communal showers & toilets; Hostel Luxe rooms are en suite. You're thrown out of both for cleaning 11.00– 15.00. The rooms in the adjoining 'hotel' section has Sleep Well Star rooms – Travelodge-style accommodation with en suite, TV & no lock-out in the afternoon. There's a graffiti-covered basement bar, Wi-Fi, internet, laundry, no curfew. Bedding & b/fast inc. Hostel dorms €19.50–21.50; hotel sgl €46, dbl €66.

OUTSIDE THE PETIT RING: BRUSSELS COMMUNES
Luxury

🏠 **Odette en Ville** [126–7 E5] (8 rooms) 25 Rue de Châtelain, 1050 Ixelles; ✆ 02 640 26 26; www.chez-odette.com; M̲ Louise, & tram 94. Odette 'en Ville' is the city version of a boutique hotel found in Williers, France. Odette – you can see her picture hanging behind reception – ran the local village bistro for decades, & bequeathed the restaurant to current owner Didier Thiery when she died childless in 1999. Didier has transformed it into an exclusive hideout featured in *Mr & Mrs Smith's Hotel Collection* & his Brussels' establishment is just as charming. No expense has been spared: white rabbit-skin throws adorn the bed, there's under-floor heating in the bathrooms & all the latest mod-cons. Room 2 was my favourite: the bathtub sits under the window. Everything is for sale – the bathrobes cost a cool €265. Downstairs there's a library, a candlelit bar & intimate restaurant, where the superb b/fast (€25

extra) is also served. If you're feeling lazy, room service – served on a solid silver tray, no less – is available 24hrs. €€€€€

🏠 **Be Manos** [123 G2] (60 rooms) 23–7 Sq de l'Aviation, 1070 Anderlecht; ✆ 02 520 65 65; www.bemanos.com; M̲ Lemonnier. This ultra-modern 5-star boutique hotel with monochrome black-&-white rooms offers a porter, room service, king-size bed (with leather headboard) & expensive smellies in the bathroom. Sample an in-house spa treatment or massage after a healthy b/fast in the apple-green Be Lella b/fast room. Equally chic lounge, bar & restaurant also on site. €€€€€

Expensive

🏠 **Aloft** [118–19 C5] (147 rooms) Pl Jean Rey, 1040 Etterbeek; ✆ 02 800 08 88; www. aloftbrussels.com; M̲ Schuman/Maelbeek. In the heart of the EU district, the rooms of this vibrant hotel have multi-coloured stripy blinds & pillows, & large windows. The beds – you can choose a king-size dbl, or 2 queen-size twin beds – look out the window & are very comfy. It's chockfull of extras, including an alarm clock, tea-&-coffee facilities, free Wi-Fi & a huge flatscreen TV, which link up to a 'plug & play' dock so you can connect your iPhone, iPod, or laptop. Also on site is the re:mix lounge with pool table, the re:fuel food station (which sells b/fast snacks), the wxyz bar & 24hr re:charge fitness centre. Their state-of-the-art 'touch & go' service allows you to check in & out independently. €€€€

Mid-range

⌂ **Aviation 19** [123 G2] (1 room) 19 Sq de l'Aviation, 1070 Anderlecht; m 0494 82 35 20; www.aviation19.be; M̄ Lemonnier. Live like a local while staying in this penthouse apt, which comes equipped with its own stunning rooftop terrace, kitchen, living room & free Wi-Fi. 2-night minimum stay. €€€

⌂ **Pantone** [126–7 C2] (61 rooms) 1 Pl Loix, 1060 St-Gilles; ☏ 02 541 48 98; www. pantonehotel.com; M̄ Hôtel des Monnaies. Stay in a world first! Pantone's standardised colour-matching system is used by designers & printers the world over, but this is the first time the concept has ever been applied to a hotel. All the rooms are a blank canvas of white walls & linen, with long-haired black carpet, in order to draw attention to the panel photograph mounted above each bed which features an obscure Brussels' site magnified many times to emphasise the pure Pantone colours – arty, eh? Each floor has its own colour & when you check in they can ask you what colour/mood you're in & assign you to a floor accordingly. Rooms ending in 6 (ie: 106, 206, 306, 406, 506 & 606) all have panoramic views & a terrace. Rooms 801 & 802 on the top floor don't follow the Pantone theme, but the side walls slide open & you have rooftop views of the Lower Town. Free Wi-Fi. B/fast €15. €€€

⌂ **Vintage Hotel** [126–7 C2] (29 rooms) 45 Rue Dejoncker, 1060 St-Gilles; ☏ 02 533 99 80; www.vintagehotel.be; M̄ Louise/ Hôtel des Monnaies. Childhood sweethearts Isabelle & Fabien have transformed this old people's home into a 1960s' boutique hotel. It's the attention to detail that – to quote the esteemed Austin Powers – is rather 'groovy, baby', with psychedelic

wallpaper, plastic orange phones, bubble lamps & a mini Rubik's cube on your room key. Room 1, on the ground floor, is the largest & features wooden floors. Rooms 19, 35, 36, & 41 have baths. There's a family room in the eaves. The trendy b/fast room doubles up as a wine bar offering boutique wines. Free Wi-Fi. €€–€€€

Budget

⌂ **Les Bluets** [126–7 B2] (9 rooms) 124 Rue Berckmans, 1060 St-Gilles; ☏ 02 534 39 83; www.bluets.be. Elegant, flower-adorned 19th-century townhouse B&B run by Miriam & her husband Eduardo. The spacious en-suite rooms are filled to the brim with Miriam's collection of antiques. Several rooms feature kitchenettes. No smoking allowed. Old computer for checking email. Stairlift. 3 parking places available €10/24hrs. €€

Shoestring

Å **Camping Bruxelles-Europe à Ciel Ouvert** [118–19 A7] (80 sites) 205 Chaussée de Wavre, 1050 Ixelles; ☏ 02 640 79 67; ⊕ Jul–Aug only; M̄ Trône/Maelbeek. A small, leafy campsite, just south of the EU district, belonging to the St-Sacrement church which stands in front of it. Thankfully the church bells don't chime during the night, but they do kick off at 07.00 so take earplugs (a train track runs along the back of the property too). The Albanian family living on the premises convert their living room into the campsite reception. Showers, toilets & sinks inside house are kept clean. Campervans can park in the car park outside. €6 pp/night.

⌂ **Centre Vincent van Gogh** [132 B5] (200 beds) 8 Rue Traversière, 1210 Sint-Joost-ten-Node; ☏ 02 217 01 58; www.chab.be; M̄ Botanique. Brussels' cheapest hostel underwent a major renovation in 2011 & downstairs has smart black bar, conservatory with pool table, & homely wooden kitchen. New bunk beds & mattresses due. Rooms located across the street are a bit soulless. Arranges trips to Brugge, Gent & Antwerp. Laundry, internet, Wi-Fi (€2/1hr; €5/5hr), no curfew. 18–35-year-olds only. Dorms €19, sgl €34, dbl €54.

⌂ **Hello Hostel** [78–9 A1] (17 rooms) 1 Rue de l'Armistice, 1081 Koekelberg; ☏ 0471 93 59 27; www.hello-hostel.eu; M̄ Simonis. Snug, homely option in the northwest of town offering 2-, 3-,

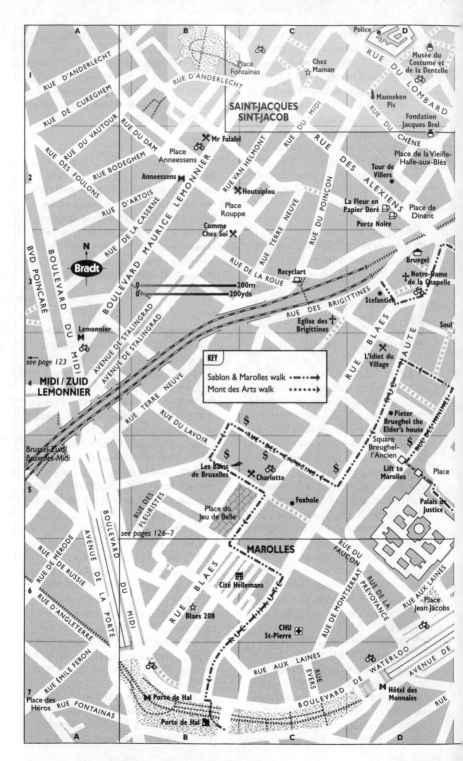

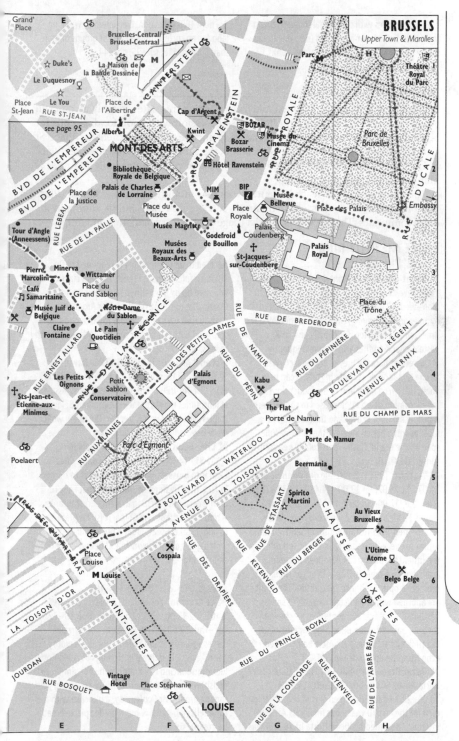

4- & 6-bed dorms with communal showers. B/fast room doubles as a common room (new one being built when I visited) & there are games, books, & a huge DVD collection. Free internet, Wi-Fi, no laundry, no curfew. Doesn't accept groups of more than 6. Dorm €18, sgl €25, dbl €44.

✗ WHERE TO EAT

Brussels' residents are nicknamed *kikefritters*, which translates roughly as 'chicken eaters': an odd moniker for a capital whose obsession with good food extends far beyond pale poultry. Each district has a distinctive style and clientele: Place St Cathérine is synonymous with fresh seafood; the Sablon district is upmarket; Place St Géry has a number of Vietnamese and Japanese restaurants, while Marolles is filling up with trendy, arty cafés.

The allure of easy-to-reach restaurants located in and around the Grand' Place is strong, but do steer clear of the infamous Rue des Bouchers and try dining in the outer communes. The hip Ixelles district (page 86) has a particularly good range.

INSIDE THE PETIT-RING
Grand' Place locale

✗ **Kwint** [82–3 F2] 1 Mont des Arts; ☎ 02 505 95 95; www.kwintbrussels.com; ⏱ 12.00–22.30 Mon–Wed, 12.00–23.30 Thu–Sat. Is dominated by an enormous bronze sculpture designed by Arne Quinze. Menu focuses heavily on fish & pasta. Caviar & truffles also feature frequently in the recipes because they're owned by Caviar Kaspia & Maison de la Truffe in Paris. It can be quiet; this isn't a reflection of the food: prior to the renovation, the homeless used to shelter here & people are used to avoiding the area. Ask for a table near the bar for views of the Hôtel de Ville spire on the Grand' Place – particularly beautiful at sunset. €€€€€

✗ **Vincent** [95 F1] 8–10 Rue des Dominicains; ☎ 02 511 26 07; ⏱ 12.00–14.45 & 18.30–23.30 Mon–Sat, 12.00–15.00 & 18.30–22.30 Sun; closed 1–11 Jan & first 2 weeks of Aug. Lively sea-themed 1905 restaurant that friends of mine return to every time they're in town. You *must* try either the rump steak flambéed in cream & alcohol on a table in front of you, or their mussels – both are house specialities. The walls are adorned with bold listed mosaics of sailors battling the oceanic elements & cows chewing the cud, baguettes are piled high for cutting, & the clink of pots & pans & orders being called echo from the open kitchen. €€€€

✗ **Bozar Brasserie** [82–3 G1] 3 Rue Baron Horta; ☎ 02 503 00 00; ⏱ 12.00–14.30 & 18.00–22.30 daily. Has been closed & gathering dust for the last 10 years, but finally its Art Deco interior – designed by Victor Horta in 1928 – was restored to its former glory & reopened in Dec 2010. Simple, elegant French/Belgian classics whipped up by Michelin-starred chef David Martin. The entrecôte cooked over Argentine coals looked very good, as did the rice pudding sprinkled with cinnamon sugar. Good-value lunch menus. €€€

✗ **Cap d'Argent** [82–3 F2] 10 Rue Ravenstein; ☎ 02 513 09 19; ⏱ 12.00–15.00 & 18.00–23.00 Mon–Sat. No-frills bistro popular with businessmen at lunchtimes thanks to their scrumptious Belgian staples like *vol-au-vent* & *filet pur*. The career waiters really know what they're doing. €€€

✗ **Chez Leon** [95 F1] 18 Rue des Bouchers; ☎ 02 511 14 15; ⏱ 12.00–23.00 daily. Chez Léon is to mussels, what McDonalds is to burgers. In fact, they've been so successful that they're on the cusp of launching a chain of restaurants – renamed Fritkot – in China. It isn't a place to linger: take a seat, order a pot of mussels with a glass of their own-brand beer & carry on sightseeing. €€

Place St-Cathérine locale

✗ **Le Crachin** [78–9 B5] 12 Rue de Flandre; ☎ 02 502 13 00; ⏱ 12.00–14.30 & 18.30–22.30 Tue–Thu, 12.00–22.30 Fri–Sun. 'The Drizzle' serves square-cut buckwheat sweet & savoury pancakes washed down with mugs of cider. Good luck pronouncing the Breton (which is similar to Welsh) names of the pancakes! Try wrapping your tongue around *Ar Poulgwenn*, a pancake with caramelised banana & homemade spiced-bread ice cream. €€

✖ **Fin de Siècle** [78–9 B6] 9 Rue des Chartreux; ☎ 02 512 51 23; ⏲ 12.00–14.00 &19.00–23.00 daily. Dishes up reliably good tummy-warming Belgian fare in traditional surroundings. Very popular with locals, so prepare to have little elbow room. €€

🍽 **AM Sweet** [78–9 B6] 4 Rue des Chartreux; ☎ 02 513 51 31; ⏲ 12.00–18.30 Tue, 09.30–18.30 Wed–Sat. Snug 2-floor café ideal for b/fast or a tea break. All the cakes are handmade by owner Anne-Marie. €

🍽 **Café de Markten** [78–9 B6] 5 Pl du Vieux Marché aux Grains; ☎ 02 513 98 55; ⏲ 08.30–00.00 Mon–Sat, 10.00–18.00 Sun. Lively café offering no-nonsense, good-quality salads, sandwiches & soups at very reasonable prices. Popular just for drinks as well. Sun loungers on street in summer. €

✖ **Mer du Nord** [78–9 B6] 45 Rue St-Cathérine; ☎ 02 511 66 71; ⏲ 11.00–17.00 Tue–Thu, 11.00–18.00 Fri–Sat, 11.00–20.00 Sun. Informal open-air seafood stand where – rain or shine – you can tuck into a chilled glass of vino & fresh seafood snacks like steaming *escargot* (snail) soup or oysters. A great place to mingle with the locals. Cash only. €

Place du Grand Sablon locale
✖ **Les Petits Oignons** [82–3 E4] 25 Rue de la Régence; ☎ 02 511 76 15; ⏲ 12.00–14.30 & 19.00–23.00 Mon–Thu & Sun, 12.00–14.30 & 19.00–00.00 Fri–Sat. Elegant brasserie serving fine French food which received glowing reviews when it opened. Has an extensive & well-considered wine list. €€€€

🍽 **Le Pain Quotidien** [82–3 E4] 11 Rue des Sablons; ☎ 02 513 51 54; ⏲ 07.30–19.00 Mon–Fri, 08.00–19.00 Sat–Sun. One of Belgium's huge success stories & my favourite place for Sunday brunch, established in 1990 by renowned Bruxellois chef, Alain Coumont; the bread baked here follows a recipe he developed when he couldn't source *pain* for his diners. 10 years later & the chain has 62 stores in 10 different countries. Famous for their *table communale* – to encourage you to natter with your neighbours, their *tartines* (open sandwiches) served on wooden boards & their out-of-this-world *bombe au chocolat* dessert. €–€€

🍽 **Claire Fontaine** [82–3 E4] 3 Rue Ernest Allard; ☎ 02 512 24 10; ⏲ 11.00–19.00 Tue–Sat. A treasure trove for foodies. The counter of this delicatessen groans with quiches, flans, salads,

freshly prepared sandwiches & cakes, all hand-cooked/prepared by Claire, the owner. She's incredibly warm & greets regular clients with '*cou cou ma belle*'. Take-away only. €

Marolles locale
✖ **L'Idiot du Village** [82–3 D4] 19 Rue Notre-Seigneur; ☎ 02 502 55 82; ⏲ 12.00–14.00 & 19.15–23.00 Mon–Fri. Established over 15 years ago by host Olivier le Bret & chef Alain Gascoin, this secluded & shabby-chic restaurant is very romantic. Old wooden desks serve as tables & there's lots of exposed brick walls, twinkly lights & funky chandeliers. Menus are inventive: imagine warm foie gras in vanilla-&-milk veal sauce & iced meringue with caramel & salt. Bookings are essential. €€€€

✖ **Soul** [82–3 E3] 10 Rue de la Samaritaine; ☎ 02 513 52 13; ⏲ 12.00–14.30 & 19.00–22.00 Wed–Fri, 19.00–22.00 Sat–Sun. The perfect antidote to all the meat-heavy menus in traditional Belgian restaurants & a lifesaver for vegans/veggies. Run by Finnish sisters Linda & Nina Rosas, this intimate 8-table restaurant serves delicious organic additive- & preservative-free vegetarian meals. Reservations recommended. €€€

✖ **Charlotte** [82–3 C5] 9 Jeu de Balle; ⏲ 07.00–19.00 Mon, Tue, Thu–Sun. Locals queue up here on market days for excellent hotdogs, burgers & sandwiches. No seating. €

🍽 **Recyclart** [82–3 C3] Gare Bruxelles-Chapelle, 21 Rue des Ursulines; ☎ 02 502 57 34; kitchen ⏲ 12.00–15.00 Tue–Fri, bar ⏲ 11.00–17.00 Tue–Fri. This rough-around-the-edges café is good for a drink or cheap lunch. Most important of all, you'll be supporting a brilliant training scheme whereby refugees, who've been unable to find work, are enrolled in a 2-year cookery course under the guidance of head chef Bruno. Together they prepare a variety of dishes, including a veggie option, which change every week. They make a real effort to use seasonal, organic ingredients. The café itself is nothing special; it's the great mish-mash of cultures & staff that make this place. Newspapers & free Wi-Fi. €

Elsewhere inside the petit-ring
✖ **Comme Chez Soi** [82–3 B3] 23 Place Rouppe; ☎ 02 512 29 21; ⏲ 12.00–13.30 & 19.00–21.30 Tue, Thu–Sat, 19.00–21.30 Wed; usually closed

during the summer holidays (mid-Jul–mid-Aug). Marie-Thérèse Wynants, the *maitre'd*, warmly welcomes guests to this 2-star Michelin restaurant run by her husband & son-in-law. 'Food' is too crass a description for their creations. Here are a few examples from the menu at the time of writing: duck liver with gin & rice pop pearls in a reduced fig vinegar, & potato mousseline with crab, shrimps, & Royal Belgian caviar in a chive & white-oyster butter sauce. Drool! The prices are exorbitant, but it'll be a meal you'll never forget. Reservations essential. €€€€€

✕ **In t'Spinnekopke** [78–9 A7] 1 Pl du Jardin aux Fleurs; ☎ 02 511 86 95; ⏰ 12.00–15.00 & 18.00–23.00 Mon–Fri, 18.00–23.00 Sat. The quaint & crooked 'spiderweb' house dates from 1762 & originally served as a post office, before being converted to a restaurant over 70 years ago. Nowadays, it's run by husband-&-wife team Elise & Jean Rodriguez & has developed a loyal following among locals. Serves all the Belgian classics such as *tomate aux crevettes d'Ostende*, *lapin à la gueuze* & *waterzooi*, but excels at mussels recipes. There's a large selection of French wines – particularly Bordeaux – to choose from. €€€–€€€€

OUTSIDE THE PETIT-RING
Anderlecht
✕ **Le Chapeau Blanc** [123 A4] 200 Rue Wayez; ☎ 02 520 02 02; ⏰ 12.00–01.00 daily. Favoured by an older clientele, this traditional *belle époque* brasserie serves excellent mussels (in season); the favourite on the otherwise meat-heavy menu is *choucroute alsacienne*. €€€

EU district
✕ **Maison Antoine** [118–19 C7] Pl Jourdan; ☎ 02 230 54 56; ⏰ 11.30–01.00 Sun–Thu, 11.30–02.00 Fri–Sat. One of the last traditional *fritkots* in the city. Locals form long queues at lunchtime to scoff their fresh chips. Warm your hands on a cornet with mayonnaise & take them to Parc Leopold for an impromptu alfresco lunch. €

Ixelles
✕ **Chez Marie** [126–7 G5] 40 Rue Alphonse De Witte; ☎ 02 644 30 31; ⏰ 12.00–14.30 & 19.30–22.30 Tue–Fri, 19.30–22.30 Sat. Just round the corner from the Flagey ponds, this snug 40-seater restaurant is run by young French chef, Lilian Devaux. She is perhaps the first chef to win a

✕ **Kabu** [82–3 G4] 48 Rue du Pépin; ☎ 02 514 28 00; ⏰ 12.00–14.00 & 19.00–22.30 Tue–Sat. Hip Japanese option with lots of clean lines, black wooden furniture & Astroturf carpet. I loved the kooky menus which are shaped like Pantone swatch strips. Be sure to try the mouth-watering scallops with white asparagus & white-truffle caviar. €–€€€

✕ **Houtsiplou** [82–3 B2] 9 Pl Rouppe; ☎ 2 511 3816; ⏰ 12.00–14.30 & 18.00–22.30 daily. Family friendly bistro with an informal home-from-home atmosphere thanks to the kitsch flower-power wallpaper (upstairs), cartoon murals (downstairs), ageing piano, books & other knick-knacks scattered along the windowsills. Serves a mixture of open sandwiches (*tartines*), salads, burgers & pastas & there's a separate children's menu. €€

✕ **Mr Falafel** [82–3 B2] 53 Blvd Maurice Lemonnier; ⏰ 12.00–00.00 daily. Tiny shop serving the best falafel in town. It's made by an Egyptian chap called Shawkat from Amsterdam & it's a bargain meal. Comes with as much free salad as you like. €

Michelin star for a burger. Food & service are reliably good. Québécoise sommelier, Daniel Marcil, looks after the 400-bottle wine list. Cheaper menus at lunchtime. Reservations essential. €€€€€

✕ **Cospaia** [82–3 F6] 1 Capitaine Crespel; ☎ 02 513 03 03; ⏰ 12.00–14.30 & 18.00–late Mon–Fri, 18.00–late Sat; kitchen closes 22.30 Mon–Thu, 23.00 Fri–Sat. Sleek & sexy option ideal for a big night out. Pre-dinner drinks are taken in the smooth bar, which is especially busy 23.00–03.00 on Sat nights. In summer, the doors to the enormous terrace (overlooking Blvd de Waterloo) are thrown open making it an ideal place for sundowners. During the day, ask to be seated in the larger, bright-white dining room, which has evocative portraits of turbaned Arabs hanging from the walls. In the evening, the 10-table all-black dining room – which features wire tree sculptures – is considerably cosier & more romantic when the lights are dimmed. My rack of lamb with a mustard crust was cooked to perfection. €€€€–€€€€€

✕ **Au Vieux Bruxelles** [82–3 H5/126–7 E1] 35 Rue St-Boniface; ☎ 02 503 31 11; ⏰ 18.30–23.30 Tue–Thu, 18.30–00.00 Fri–Sat, 12.00–15.00 &

18.30–23.30 Sun. Open since 1882 this utterly charming brasserie claims to serve the best chips in town with its array of typical Belgian dishes & Bruxellois specialities. Recommended. €€€–€€€€

✗ **Belgo Belge** [82–3 H6] 20 Rue de la Paix; ☎ 02 511 11 21; ⏰ 12.00–00.00 Mon–Fri & Sun, closed Tue afternoon. Urbane brasserie with tables spilling onto the pavement in summer. Serves all the Belgian classics at locals' prices. €€

✗ **Balmoral** [126–7 C7] 21 Pl Georges Brugmann; ☎ 02 347 08 82; ⏰ 09.00–19.00 Tue–Thu & Sat–Sun, 09.00–22.00 Fri. Fab 1960s' American-style diner serving burgers, salads, milkshakes & desserts. €€

St-Gilles

✗ **Sale Pepe Marino** [126–7 B2] 98 Rue Berckmans, 1060 St-Gilles; ☎ 02 538 90 63; ⏰ 10.00–15.00 & 19.00–00.00 (kitchen closes 23.00) Mon–Fri, 17.00–00.00 Sat. Off the beaten track & recommended by locals, it's a snug 12-table affair serving simple but exquisite Italian fare. Price–quality, it's a real find. The *saltimbocca* – pork fillet topped with Parma ham & sage leaves & drizzled with a Marsala-wine reduction – is to die for. The walls are covered with drawings sketched

by 80-year-old local, Jean Pierre Hack, who comes in every day for a few glasses of red. €€

Schaerbeek

✗ **Le Zinneke** [132 D4] 26 Pl de la Patrie, 1030 Schaerbeek; ☎ 02 245 03 22; www.lezinneke. be; ⏰ 12.00–14.00 & 18.00–22.00 Tue–Fri, 18.00–22.00 Sat, 12.00–14.00 Sun. Serves most of the Belgian staple dishes, but specialises in huge, plump 'golden' mussels that can be cooked 69 different ways! The surroundings are a typical Belgian mix of mirrored wainscot & shelves covered in bric-a-brac, but more importantly there's a good wine list to compliment the crustaceans. Locals flock here in the evening, so book in advance. €€–€€€

Uccle

✗ **Chalet Robinson** [134 B2] 1 Sentier de l'Embarcadère; ☎ 02 372 92 92; ⏰ 12.00–14.30 & 19.00–23.00 Mon–Sat, 12.00–22.00 Sun. Escape to an island in the middle of the city! Robinson is marooned in the middle of a lake & can be accessed only via water taxi. The wooden cabin conceals an ultra-modern black-&-white interior & the menu is just as sleek, with a good choice of smartly prepared meat & fish dishes. €€€€

ENTERTAINMENT AND NIGHTLIFE

Brussels' nightlife is a dynamic mix of laidback drinking sessions in time-worn bars until the wee hours, first-class live concerts and dance clubs. This city's club culture was, up until a few years ago, rather pathetic, but nowadays there are a number of edgy/raw venues, as well as some slightly classier cocktail-and-lace joints, that provide some variety to evenings spent chatting over a potent Belgian beer.

Live popular music has always been a particular strong point for Brussels and there are half-a-dozen well-established venues scattered throughout the city that bring in big-name acts on a regular basis and provide a forum for all styles of music, from jazz, reggae and hip-hop to electronic and trance. Classical music and theatre are also hosted in the city's classier venues. Tickets for most events can be bought online, at **FNAC** newsagents stores (*City 2, Rue Neuve;* ☎ 02 275 11 11; www.fnac.be; ⏰ 10.00–19.00 Mon–Thu & Sat, 10.00–20.00 Fri), or through the tourist information centre on Place Royale, which operates as an **Arsène 50** (www.arsene50.be; ⏰ 12.30–17.30 Tue–Sat) outlet that sells half-price tickets for shows up until 16.30 on the day of the performance. For the latest concert and cinema listings pick up a copy of *Agenda* magazine, free in bars and tourist information offices.

BARS Bars are an integral part of the 'Brussels experience' and virtually every street is home to at least one port in the storm; many of them have been in business for centuries. Opening hours are rarely set; most stay open until 02.00–03.00, or until the last person leaves.

Inside the petit-ring
Grand' Place locale

▣ **À la Bécasse** [95 D1] 11 Rue de Tabora; 🕾 02 511 00 06; ⊕ 10.00–late daily. Tucked away off Rue du Midi, this authentic *estaminet* is full of character. The old floor tiling, upright wooden chairs & heavy wooden panelling on the walls combine to plunge you 60 years into the past. They specialise in lambic, gueuze & kriek beers produced by the Timmermans brewery. The typically Bruxelloise *lambic doux* is still served in authentic ceramic jugs.

▣ **A la Mort Subite** [78–9 E6] 7 Rue Montagnes aux Herbes Potagères; 🕾 02 513 13 18; ⊕ 11.00–01.00 Mon–Sat, 13.00–01.00 Sun. In 1910 Theophile Vossen owned a bar called La Cour Royale. Workers from the nearby National Bank of Belgium used to visit in their lunch hour for a few cheeky kriek beers & a game of cards. Before heading back they'd play a final game nicknamed 'Mort Subite' ('Sudden Death'). When Vossens moved here in 1928 he renamed the bar after the card game & the rest is history. Still in the family, the bar retains its pre-World War I décor of high ceilings, mirror-laden walls & spindly rows of wooden tables & chairs. A classic.

▣ **Au Bon Vieux Temps** [95 D1] 4 Impasse St-Nicolas; 🕾 02 217 26 26; ⊕ 11.00–00.30 Mon–Fri, 11.00–02.00 Sat & Sun. Hidden away down a small side street off Rue du Marché aux Herbes, this charming tavern has been serving a loyal following since 1695. Take a seat at the bar by the stained-glass window of St Michel & St Gudule at the back, if you can, order a glass of Mort Subite kriek (served from the barrel here) & settle in for some first-class people watching.

▣ **La Brouette** [95 D2] 2–3 Grand' Place; 🕾 02 511 54 94; ⊕ everyday until late. I prefer 'the wheelbarrow' brasserie to any others on the Grand' Place because of its understated elegance. Overshadowed by the brassy Roy d'Espagne next door, it's enjoyably quieter, still popular with city residents & boasts equally great views of the square from the 2nd floor.

▣ **L'Imaige Nostre-Dame** [95 D1] 3 Impasse des Cadeaux; 🕾 02 219 42 49; ⊕ 12.00–00.30 Mon, Tue, Thu & Fri, 12.00–19.30 Wed, 14.30–01.00 Sat, 16.00–00.00 Sun. This property was originally two houses dating from 1664 – you can still see the divide between the first red-&-white checked floor & the lower made of old flagstones – which were joined, in 1885, to form the present café. The locals quite often play cards; you can find a pack hooked to the central column. Order your beer at the bar & the host will bring it to your table.

Place St-Cathérine, St-Géry and the Bourse locale

♀ **Bonnefooi** [95 C2] 8 Rue des Pierres; ⊕ 17.00–07.00 Mon–Wed & Sun, 17.00–08.00 Thu–Sat. Live music every night at this hip bar. Great atmosphere in summer when the crowds spill out onto the street. Jupiler €1 everyday until 22.00.

▣ **Falstaff** [95 C1] 19–25 Rue Henri Maus; 🕾 02 510 05 50; ⊕ 11.00–01.00 daily. One of the city's watering-hole highlights sits only 100m from the Grand' Place. Bought by a Miss Broeckaert in 1903, who joined the 2 houses together & invited Emile Houbbion (a pupil of Victor Horta) to design the interior. The superb organic architecture is predominately Art Nouveau & lets the light flood in. A classic.

▣ **La Fleur en Papier Doré** [82–3 D2] 55 Rue des Alexiens; 🕾 02 511 16 59; ⊕ 11.00–00.00 Tue–Sat, 11.00–19.00 Sun. Once the haunt of Magritte (page 355) & his Surrealist posse, this quirky bar has become a pilgrimage site of sorts for tourists – few actually stay to drink. Be polite: stay, & enter an unchanged world – the walls are still littered with original newspaper cuttings, photos & paintings.

▣ **Porte Noire** [82–3 D2] 67 Rue des Alexiens; 🕾 02 511 78 87; ⊕ 16.00–02.00 Mon–Fri, 18.00–04.00 Sat. A few doors up from the Papier Doré (above), but much less touristy, this underground pub is housed in the kitchen of the former Alexiens monastery. Very atmospheric & hosts live bands every Thu at 21.30.

▣ **Le Cirio** [95 C1] 18–20 Rue de la Bourse; 🕾 02 512 13 95; ⊕ 10.00–00.00 daily. Named after the original owner – an Italian grocer who used the space for his delicatessen shop – Le Cirio has been open for business since 1886. It's famous for its house speciality *half en half* – a mix of still & sparkling white wine – & the fabulous time-warp décor popular with elderly manicured ladies & moustachioed gentlemen. Be sure to spend a penny in the turn-of-the-century toilets.

▣ **Le Greenwich** [78–9 B6] 7 Rue des Chartreux; 🕾 02 511 41 67; ⊕ 11.00–01.00 Mon–Thu & Sun, 11.00–02.00 Fri–Sat. Recently renovated & well known, but one of my favourites, this period classic was another of Magritte's beloved cafés – & who can blame him? The calm quiet allows you to hear the sucking of cigarettes coming from regular customers while they pour over their chess games, or the dependable tick of the ornate clock behind the bar. It all provides perfect fodder for artistic types, who can sit & observe while relaxing with a cheap beer & a book.

Outside the petit-ring

♀ **Café Belga** [126–7 G4] Pl Eugène Flagey, Ixelles; ☏ 02 640 35 08; ⊕ 08.00–02.00 Mon–Thu & Sun, 08.00–03.00 Fri–Sat, kitchen ⊕ 09.00–16.00. Occupies the corner of Place Flagey's iconic Art Deco former broadcasting tower. Popular with a young & trendy crowd & perennially busy. €€

⊟ **Chez Moeder Lambic** [126–7 A6] 68 Rue de la Savoie, St Gilles; ☏ 02 539 1419; ⊕ 16.00–03.00 daily. A firm favourite with beerians, this tiny unpretentious corner 'brown' café is where the locals come for a good vintage

bottled beer, chunks of hearty cheese & a game or two of cards or catch-up chat. The staff are very friendly & more than happy to talk you through the 1,000-strong beer list.

♀ **L'Ultime Atome** [82–3 H6] 14 Rue St Boniface, Ixelles; ☏ 02 511 13 67; ⊕ 09.00–00.00 Mon–Thu, 09.00–00.30 Fri–Sat. Trendy brasserie constantly filled with the musical chatter of young international accents. Sexy waiters & waitresses serve food everyday until late, but it's especially popular for coffee & papers on Sunday mornings.

NIGHTCLUBS

☆ **Blaes 208** [82–3 B6] 208 Rue Blaes; ☏ 02 511 97 89; www.blaes208.be. Previously known as Fuse, it was voted the best techno club in Europe & is a *must* for clubbers. Once a month

♀ **The Flat** [82–3 G4] 12 Rue de la Reinette; ☏ 0472 18 98 73; www.theflat.be; ⊕ 18.00–03.00 Tue–Sat. An über-cool lounge bar housed in a 2-storey townhouse. Sip your champagne by the bathtub, or take your caiphriña to bed; even the most intimate rooms form part of the bar here. Doesn't get going until after midnight.

sit hosts the popular *La Démence* – a gay techno party.

☆ **K-nal** [78–9 B1] 1 Av du Port; ☏ 02 374 87 38; ⊕ 23.00–06.00 Fri–Sat. Huge warehouse

---

GAY AND LESBIAN NIGHTLIFE

Several of the city's nightclubs host gay evenings (usually Sundays), but the majority of gay bars are congregated on and around Rue des Grandes Carmes, just off the Grand' Place. The biggest crowd-puller is the monthly house and trance party *La Démence* (*www.lademence.com*) held at Blaes 208 (see above). Nightlife tailored to lesbians is more limited; start with Bitchy Butch (*www.bitchybutch.be*) and L-party (*www.lparty.be*) parties held at Biberium restaurant (*55 Cantersteen*). Brussels also hosts the annual Gay and Lesbian Film Festival in late January, which showcases a collection of documentaries and short films at the Orangerie cinema inside Le Botanique (page 136).

☆ **Chez Maman** [95 B4] 7 Rue des Grandes Carmes; ☏ 02 502 86 96; ⊕ 00.00–05.00 Thu–Sat. Feathers-&-glitter gay bar, whose resident transvestite showgirls put on regular table-top cabarets at the weekends. It gets colourful, crammed & humid. They throw a big lesbian/gay 'Cuir as Folk' party on first Thu of the month.

♀ **Homo Erectus** [95 D2] 57 Rue des Pierres; ☏ 02 514 74 93; ⊕ 16.00–05.00 daily. Oh, what subtle word play! This friendly central bar has a different vibe every night of the week. Stays open late.

♀ **La Belgica** [95 C3] 32 Marché au Charbon; ⊕ 22.00–03.00 Thu–Sat, 20.00–03.00 Sun. Small, scruffy brown café-style bar with a 1920s bar & DJ-hosted parties. Visitors have included the likes of Björk & John Galliano & it gets so busy at w/ends that punters spill out on to the street.

in the north of town & overlooking the canal, that hosts fashionable parties; entry €5 before midnight, €10 after.

☆ **Le You** [95 E4] 18 Rue Duquesnoy; ☎ 02 639 14 00; ⏰ 23.00–05.00 Thu, 23.30–06.00 Fri–Sat, 20.00–03.00 Sun; admission €10. Domain of Brussels' DJ legends Olivier Gosseries & Yves-E-Zone, this 2-tier club plays a mixture of R'n'B, house & funk. Thu is student night & Sun dedicated to the Gay Tea Dance.

LIVE MUSIC

♫ **Archiduc** [78–9 B6] 6 Rue Antoine Dansaert; ☎ 02 512 06 52; www.archiduc.net; ⏰ 16.00–05.00 daily. This Art Deco darling has been in situ since 1937. The piano in the centre belonged to Stan Brenders, the bar's first owner & songwriter for Nat King Cole. Current owner Jean-Louis has been in charge for over 25 years & organises a great programme of live jazz on Mon (May–Sep; 22.00; free) & at weekends (17.00; €8–15). Order the 'Cointreau Teese', created by by the American burlesque dancer Dita Von Teese.

♫ **Bizon** [95 B1] 7 Rue du Pont de la Carpe; ☎ 02 502 46 99; ⏰ 18.00–late daily. Cosy blues & rock bar with a 'living room' atmosphere, where you can sip on Bizon Blood vodka & listen to live performers every night of the week, or pitch up on Mon for their famous jamming sessions.

♫ **Café Samaritaine** [82–3 E3] 16 Rue de la Samaritaine; ☎ 02 511 33 95; ⏰ from 19.30

CONCERT HALLS

🎦 **Ancienne Belgique (AB)** [95 B2] 110 Blvd Anspach; ☎ 02 548 24 24; www.abconcerts.be; ⏰ closed Jul–Aug. One of Belgium's best concert venues, with events taking place most nights. Everything from pop & rock to indie. Tickets can be bought from the website or at the AB shop (23 Rue des Pierres; ☎ 02 548 24 24; ⏰ 11.00–18.00 Mon–Fri).

🎦 **BOZAR (Palais des Beaux-Arts)** [82–3 G2] Palais des Beaux-Arts, Rue Raventstein 23; ☎ 02 507 82 00; www.bozar.be; ⏰ 09.00–18.00 Mon–Sat. The heart of arts & entertainment culture in Brussels, this Art Nouveau auditorium was completed by Victor Horta in 1928 & sits mostly

☆ **Spirito Martini** [82–3 G5] 18 Rue Stassart; ☎ 02 502 30 00; ⏰ 22.30–06.00 Fri & Sat. Housed inside an old Anglican church, this swish club also has a posh restaurant on site.

☆ **The Wood** [134 B1] 3–5 Av de Flore, Bois de la Cambre; ☎ 02 741 63 20; ⏰ 23.00–06.00 Wed–Sat. The trendiest watering hole in the city at the moment. A very fashionable crowd & parties on Wed.

Tue–Sat; admission €12 adult, €8 student. Originally abandoned, this soot-blackened 17th-century cellar was bought up by proprietor Huguette van Dyck in 1984. Described as a dinner-theatre, she offers light-bites with regular music & cabaret shows. All very atmospheric.

♫ **Madame Moustache** [78–9 C5] 5–7 Quai au Bois à Brûler; ⏰ 17.00–04.00 Tue-Sun. Cabaret-style bar with wooden dance floor & 1950s' diner area. All manner of live music & dancing. Some nights attract a €5 entrance fee.

♫ **Sounds** [126–7 F1] 28 Rue de la Tulipe, 1050 Ixelles; ☎ 02 512 92 50; ⏰ 20.00–04.00 Mon–Sat. This long thin jazz bar has been in situ since 1986 & books some of the genre's best talents to perform almost every night of the week. It's run by a husband-&-wife team: Sergio makes the cocktails, whilst Rosy passes around Italian food around 20.00. Concerts kick off around 22.00.

underground because its height was not allowed to disrupt the king's view of the Lower Town. It hosts a varied programme of exhibitions, classical concerts & theatre productions. Tickets can be bought from the shop (⏰ 11.00–19.00 Mon–Sat) or by telephone. There are magazines with full monthly listings in the entrance.

🎦 **Théâtre de la Monnaie** [78–9 D6] Pl de la Monnaie; ☎ 070 23 39 39; www.lamonnaie.be. Site of the famous Belgian break for independence in August 1830 (page 9), this opera house has a stunning auditorium & a good programme that includes dance recitals. Tickets (€10–100) are snapped up quickly so it's best to book in advance.

THEATRE Brussels has two main theatres: the **National** [78–9 E3] (*111–15 Blvd Emile Jacqmain;* ☎ *02 203 53 03; www.theatrenational.be*) and the **KVS** [78–9 D3] (*146 Rue de Laeken; tel; 02 210 11 12; www.kvs.be*) that produce classical high-brow performances. Also of interest is the **Théâtre Royal de Toone** [95 E1] (*6 Impasse Schuddeveld; www.toone.be;* ☺ *12.00–00.00 Tue–Sun, closed Jan*) which puts on puppet shows in the Bruxellois dialect.

CINEMA

🎬 **Kinépolis** [129 B2] Brupark, 20 Blvd du Centenaire; ☏ 02 474 26 00; www.kinepolis. com. Located in the Heysel park, this neon-bright megaplex has 27 screens, plus a 3D IMAX screen, & is the largest cinema in the country. Films are predominately US blockbusters.

🎬 **Musée du Cinéma** [82–3 G2] 9 Rue Baron Horta; ☏ 02 507 83 85; www.cinematique.be. Situated at the bottom of the stairs on Rue Baron

Horta this museum traces the medium's early beginnings & includes 2 cosy theatres: one shows classic 'arty' films in their original language around 18.00, the other plays silent films accompanied by live piano music at 19.00 & 21.00.

🎬 **UGC De Brouckère** [78–9 D5] Pl de Brouckère; ☏ 0900 10 400. 12-screen multiplex screening a handful of American films.

SHOPPING

Brussels matches London and Paris for big-ticket fashion labels – here you can have your Gucci and wear it to breakfast too. However, the real charm of shopping here comes from riffling through the antiques shops of the Marolles district, finding a rare book in the marketplace, and letting handmade chocolates melt in your mouth.

As you'd expect, the **Grand' Place** and its surrounding streets are dominated with overpriced souvenir shops (miniature Manneken Pis, anyone?), but among them are some quality lace and chocolate shops. The covered **Galeries Royales St-Hubert** situated nearby house the boutiques of a handful of revered designers like Oliver Strelli – who designs clothes for the royal family – as well as handbag designer Delvaux's flagship store. Entrances are located on Rue du Marché aux Herbes and Rue de l'Ecuyer. Similar in style and elegance are the **Galerie Bortier** (entered via Rue de la Madeleine and Rue St Jean), filled with second-hand bookshops, and the **Passage du Nord** built in 1882 (accessed via Rue Neuve and Boulevard Adolphe Max) and lined with boutique shops ranging from cigar tobacconists to cutlery designers.

South of the Grand' Place, **Rue du Midi** – aka collectors' alley – is the go-to area for artists, philatelists and numismatists. The **Sablon** and **Marolles** districts specialise in antiques: the pricier ones are found in the immaculate boutiques of Sablon; Marolles' grittier, junk-shop style outlets are concentrated along Rue Blaes and Rue Haute. South of the Palais de Justice, just across the petit-ring motorway, you'll find the **Galerie Louise** and **Galerie de la Toison d'Or** (*Avenue de la Toison d'Or*) – lively covered arcades filled with Congolese jewellers, craft shops, hairdressers and clothes. Moving south, the wide tree-lined **Avenue Louise** – and its offshoot **Rue du Bailli** – are famous for international brands like Louis Vuitton, Chanel, Christian Dior and Hermès.

North of the Grand' Place, **Rue Antoine Dansaert** is the epicentre of Brussels' avant-garde fashion labels, where stores like Stijl (*74 Rue Antoine Dansaert*) display collections designed by the Antwerp Six. In contrast, **Rue Neuve** is the main shopping street for high-street clothing brands like H&M, Massimo Dutti, Benetton etc, and it's also the site of **City 2** (*123 Rue Neuve*) shopping centre.

ANTIQUES

Stefantiek [82–3 D3] 63 Rue Blaes & 6 Rue de la Chapelle; ☏ 02 540 81 42; www.stefantiek.com;

☺ 10.00–18.00 daily. I love these stores – they're a treasure trove of collectables. It's a complete mess, so you'll have to have a good rummage.

BEER

Beermania [82–3 G5] 174–6 Chaussée de Wavre; ✆ 02 512 17 88; www.beermania.be; ⏰ 11.00–21.00 Mon–Sat. In the Ixelles district; stocks roughly 400 varieties.

Biertempel [95 E2] 56B Rue du Marché aux Herbes; ✆ 02 502 19 06; www.biertempel.be; ⏰ 09.30–18.30 daily. Offers a good selection of gift sets.

Délices & Caprices [95 G2] 68 Rue des Bouchers; ✆ 02 512 14 51; www.the-belgian-beer-tasting-shop.be; ⏰ 14.00–20.00 Thu–Mon. Run by the personable & knowledgeable Pierre Zuber, this is a great place to stock up on some speciality beers. He occasionally runs beer-tasting sessions – email him for details; prices vary depending on the number of beers you want to try & their rarity.

CHOCOLATE

Chocolatier Manon [78–9 H6] 24 Rue du Congrès; ✆ 02 425 26 32; ⏰ 10.30–18.00 Tue–Fri, 10.00–18.00 Sat. Their award-winning chocolates are among the last still to be moulded & dipped by hand.

Mary [78–9 G6] 73 Rue Royale; ✆ 02 217 45 00; www.marychoc.com; ⏰ 10.00–18.00 Mon–Sat. A favourite of the Belgian royals, this exclusive brand was founded in 1919 by Madame Marie Delluc.

Neuhaus [95 F1] 25–7 Galerie de la Reine; ✆ 02 512 63 59; ⏰ 10.00–20.00 Mon–Sat, 10.00–19.00 Sun. See box, page 46.

Pierre Marcolini [82–3 E3] 1 Rue des Minimes; ✆ 02 514 12 06; 75 Av Louise; ✆ 02 538 42 24; www.marcolini.be; ⏰ 10.00–19.00 Mon–Fri, 10.00–20.00 Sat. The world's premier chocolatier – what more needs to be said?

Wittamer [82–3 E3] 12 Pl du Grand Sablon; ✆ 02 512 37 42; www.wittamer.com; ⏰ 09.00–18.00 Mon, 07.00–19.00 Tue–Sat, 07.00–18.30 Sun. Has been in business since 1910 & famous for their *pâtisseries* & chocolates. Good place for a cup of tea.

COMICS

Boutique Tintin [95 E2] 13 Rue de la Colline; ⏰ 14.00–18.00 Mon, 10.00–18.00 Tue–Sat, 11.00–17.00 Sun.

Espace BD [126–7 F2] 2 Pl Fernand Cocq, 1050 Ixelles; ✆ 02 512 68 69; ⏰ 10.30–18.30 Tue–Sat.

Forbidden Zone [126–7 A5] 25 Rue de Tamines; ✆ 02 534 63 67; www.forbiddenzone.net; ⏰ 12.30–19.00 Tue–Sat.

La Maison de la Bande Dessinée [95 G4] 1 Blvd de l'Impératrice; ✆ 02 502 94 68; ⏰ 10.00–18.00 Tue–Sun.

FASHION

Foxhole [82–3 C5] 6 Rue des Renards; ⏰ 09.30–18.00 Thu–Sun. Excellent vintage clothing store.

Lucien Cravate [78–9 B6] 24 Rue des Chartreux; ⏰ 12.00–18.30 Wed–Sat. Blink & you'll miss this slip of a shop which has a small selection of vintage clothes alongside reasonably priced plates, cups, jewellery etc.

Supergreen Me [78–9 B7] 10 Rue van Artevelde; ⏰ 11.00–18.30 Mon–Sat. Shop with a clear conscious here where everything – from clothing to cosmetics – is eco-friendly.

LACE

La Manufacture Belge de la Dentelle [95 F2] 6–8 Galerie de la Reine; ✆ 02 511 44 77; ⏰ 09.30–18.00 Mon–Sat, 10.00–16.00 Sun.

MARKETS Brussels was built upon the marketplace and the tradition is still thriving with literally dozens of markets – selling everything from bouquets of flowers to bikes – taking place every day of the week. Below are the highlights; pop into the tourist office for a full list. For antiques, you can't beat the **Marché des Antiquités et du Livre** (*Place du Grand Sablon; www.sablonantiquesmarket.com;* ⏰ *09.00–17.00 Sat, 09.00–14.00 Sun*) or the bric-a-brac **Marché aux Puces** (*Place du Jeu de Balle; www.marcheauxpuces.org;* ⏰ *07.00–14.00 daily, best at weekends*), where you can find everything from crockery to cupboards.

For food, the biggest is certainly **Marché du Midi** (*Blvd de l'Europe;* ⏰ *05.00–13.00 Sun*) with more than 450 stalls selling sizzling chicken, tropical fruit, and even bargain clothes – you name it! Runner-up is Anderlecht's weekend market on **Rue Ropsy Chaudron** (⏰ *07.00–13.00 Fri–Sun*). Just as big as the Marché du Midi, but with fewer pickpockets, this weekend market is held in the old abattoir warehouse and sells all manner of meat, fruit and veg. Alternatively, **Place St-Cathérine** hosts a seafood market (⏰ *07.00–17.00 Thu–Sat*) and also an organic-only market (⏰ *07.30–15.00 Wed*). **Place du Châtelain**, in the Ixelles district, holds an evening food market (⏰ *14.00–19.00pm Wed*) and there's a super fruit and veg market near **Porte de Hal** (⏰ *06.00–12.30 Tue–Sun*).

Last but not least, are the **Christmas markets** (*www.plaisirsdhiver.be*), held from around the last weekend of November until 1 January. Start on the Grand' Place, whose cobbles are usually decorated with an enormous Christmas tree and other festive decorations, and head toward La Bourse, where there are usually a handful of stalls. From there, make your way to the main market on Quai aux Briques. Here there's usually an open-air ice rink, a Ferris wheel and the famous wooden huts ladling out tummy-warming *tartiflette* and plastic cups of spicy glüwein.

OTHER PRACTICALITIES

$ Banks KBC, 9 Rue du Vieux-Marché-aux-Grains, ⏰ 09.00–12.30 & 13.30–16.30 Mon–Fri. 11 Rue d'Arenberg, ⏰ 09.00–12.30 & 13.30–16.30 Mon–Fri.

▣ Internet Aroma Coffee Lounge [95 D2], 37 Grand' Place, ⏰ 08.30–21.00 Mon–Sat, 08.30–22.00 Sun; free Wi-Fi. McDonalds [95 C1] 3 Place de la Bourse, ⏰ 24hrs; free Wi-Fi.

Luggage storage Self-service lockers at all three main railway stations; €3/3.50/4 for small/medium/large for 24hr. Need exact change. For Bruxelles-Midi/Brussels-Zuid follow signs for platforms 3–6.

✉ Post offices Bruxelles-Central, ⏰ 08.30–17.00 Mon, Wed–Fri, 09.30–18.00 Tue. 2 Galerie Ravenstein, ⏰ 07.00–20.00 Mon–Fri, 10.00–18.00 Sat. 159 Rue Arteveld, ⏰ 07.00–18.30 Mon–Fri, 08.30–13.30 Sat. 128–130 Rue Haute, ⏰ 07.30–18.00 Mon–Fri, 10.00–16.00 Sat.

✚ Pharmacies Agora, 109 Rue du Marché aux Herbes. Multipharma, 37 Rue du Marché aux Poulets.

WHAT TO SEE AND DO

The list of things to see and do is Brussels is long, and at times overwhelming, and for most visitors – who only have a day or two reserved for exploring the capital – there is a tendency to wander aimlessly without managing either to find the popular sites they were looking for or to visit lesser-known gems that perhaps reveal a truer piece of the city's identity. With this in mind, sights are instead listed not by the traditional quarters found within the Lower and Upper towns, but modelled on a series of manageable walks that will allow you to visit both the well-known museums, buildings etc, as well as the quirkier and often-left-out corners of the city. Naturally, walks only give a rough grouping of the venues and can be adjusted as you see fit, depending on your interests. Of course, a stop at a museum will limit the time available to visit other sights on that itinerary.

The surrounding communes, which lie outside the central petit-ring motorway, are often ignored – but I've provided a short history for each and listed the main sites. They're well worth a look if you have a little extra time.

LOWER TOWN
Grand' Place and the Bourse walk
Start: Grand' Place
Nearest métro: M̲ Gare-Centrale/Bourse
Walking time: 2½ hrs (although a proper tour of the Grand' Place alone can often take up to an hour in itself and can easily form the basis of a morning's exploration). See map, page 95.

This classic walk, which leads you around the heart of the old Lower Town, starts in the city's perennially impressive centrepiece – the Grand' Place. Declared '*le plus beau théâtre du monde*' ('the most beautiful theatre in the world') by French poet and playwright Jean Cocteau, the charm of the UNESCO-listed square isn't diminished by the busloads of tourists who make it their first port of call. In summer, the cobbles are covered with tables and chairs full of people sipping beer and taking in the gold-leaf inlays of the guildhouses glowing in the afternoon sun, and in winter, short days bring on early moons that cast the stepped-gabled roofs and spires in silhouette against an eerie night sky.

The square was a natural meeting point and started life during the 12th century as a marketplace – note the number of streets named after food: Rue du Beurre (butter), Rue Chair et Pain (meat and bread). As the economic wealth of the city grew, trade flourished and guilds set up home on the square. City administration and politics arrived later when the Gothic Hôtel de Ville was built in the 15th century. From then on, the square was witness and location to numerous pivotal moments in the city's history. It was here that Charles V abdicated in favour of his son in 1555, here that the Duke of Alva had patriots Count Egmont and Hoorn publicly executed (page 7), and here that the town celebrated its pageants, tournaments and processions. However, much of that history was erased on the night of 13 August 1695. King Louis VIV of France was smarting from a Grand Alliance (a coalition – pitted against France – between England, Spain, the United Provinces and the Roman Empire) attack on French-occupied Namur, so in retaliation he ordered the Duke of Villeroy and 70,000 French soldiers to attack Brussels. The Duke fired cannons and mortars at the city in an unrelenting bombardment that lasted 36 hours. The damage sustained was immense. Amazingly, the Hôtel de Ville façade survived the bombing, but only fragments of a select few guildhouses remained and the Maison du Roi was a burnt-out shell. Everything you see today was rebuilt, crafted from the ruins.

The walk begins looking at the guildhouses, which form the skeleton of the square. They replaced the covered markets that stood in place until the 14th century and were built as headquarters for tradesmen's unions, solidifying the Grand' Place's status as the commercial heart of the city. After the French bombardment, the city governor and councillors asked the guilds to submit plans for their rebuild, so the new-look square was a coherent blend of Italian and Flemish Baroque styles. The buildings were also required to be built with stone, not timber, to prevent another catastrophic outbreak of fire. The restoration took five years to complete. Touch-ups have of course taken place over the years, the most productive of which was instigated by mayor Charles Buls who directed funds towards the square between 1882 and 1923. A statue of him and his dog grace the Place Agora, a short stroll east of the square.

MAD FOR MUSEUMS?

If you're planning to visit several of the city's museums, it's worth buying the **Brussels Card** (*www.brusselscard.be*). Available for 24, 48, or 72 hours (€24/34/40), the pass grants you free access to most of Brussels' museums and includes a public-transport ticket and a full-colour city guide. The pass also entitles you to a 25% discount at participating hotels, restaurants, bars and shops. You can order it online, collect it from the tourist offices on the Grand' Place or Place Royale, or buy it from STIB transport offices.

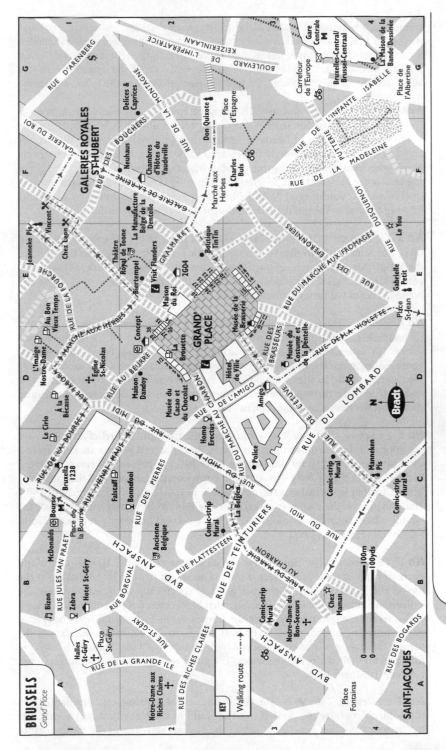

BRUSSELS
Grand' Place

KEY
--- Walking route

N

Bradt

0 ——— 100m
0 ——— 100yds

SAINT-JACQUES

Place Fontainas

RUE DES BOGARDS

BVD ANSPACH

Comic-strip Mural

Notre-Dame du Bon-Secours

Chez Maman

RUE DU MARCHE AU CHARBON

RUE DES TEINTURIERS

RUE DU MIDI

Comic-strip Mural

La Bégica

Comic-strip Mural

Police

Hanneken Pis

Comic-strip Mural

RUE DE L'ETUVE

RUE DU LOMBARD

RUE DE LA VIOLETTE

Place St-Jean

Gabrielle Petit

Le You

RUE DU MARCHE AUX FROMAGES

RUE DES EPERONNIERS

RUE DUSQUENOY

RUE DES BRASSEURS

Musée du Costume et de la Dentelle

Musée de la Brasserie

Hôtel de Ville

GRAND' PLACE

La Brouette

Maison Dandoy

Musée du Cacao et du Chocolat

Homo Erectus

Amigo

RUE DE L'AMIGO

RUE CHARBON

RUE AU BEURRE

Eglise St-Nicolas

L'Imaige Nostre-Dame

À la Bécasse

Le Cirio

Bruxella 1238

Bourse

McDonalds

Place de la Bourse

RUE DE LA BOURSE

RUE HENRI MAUS

RUE DU MIDI

Falstaff

Bonnefooi

Ancienne Belgique

RUE DES PIERRES

BVD ANSPACH

RUE BORGVAL

RUE ST-GÉRY

Place St-Géry

Halles St-Géry

Hotel St-Géry

Zebra

Bizon

RUE JULES VAN PRAET

RUE DE LA GRANDE ILE

RUE DES RICHES CLAIRES

Notre-Dame aux Riches Claires

Au Bon Vieux Temps

Concept

Maison du Roi

2GO4

Visit Flanders

Biertempel

Théâtre Royal de Toone

Jeanneke Pis

Chez Leon

Vincent

RUE DE LA FOURCHE

MARCHE AUX HERBES

GRASMARKT

RUE DES BOUCHERS

Neuhaus

Chambres d'Hôtes du Vaudeville

La Manufacture Belge de la Dentelle

GALERIE DE LA REINE

GALERIES ROYALES ST-HUBERT

GALERIE DU ROI

RUE D'ARENBERG

Delices & Caprices

RUE MONTAGNE

Don Quixote

Boutique Tintin

Marché aux Herbes

Charles Buls

Place d'Espagne

BOULEVARD DE L'IMPERATRICE / KEIZERINLAAN

Carrefour de l'Europe

Gare Centrale M
Bruxelles-Central/ Brussel-Centraal

La Maison de la Bande Dessinée

Place de l'Albertine

RUE DE L'INFANTE ISABELLE

RUE DE LA PUTTERIE

RUE DE LA MADELEINE

95

Each façade bears an ornate blend of statues and reliefs, individual markings that had a practical, as well as a decorative, use: house numbers were not applied until the French Revolution in the late 18th century, so the reliefs were clear visual markers of the trade on offer. Starting on the west side of the square, where Rue au Beurre enters the compound, the guildhouses belonged to the following trades:

Nos 1 & 2 Le Roi d'Espagne – The King of Spain – was named in honour of Charles II, whose bust dominates the upper façade, to show allegiance and celebrate his victory at the Battle of Zenda in Turkey. The building belonged to the wealthy Guild of the Bakers who bought two plots to show their importance. Statues of six Greek gods involved with the production of wheat sit atop the flat roof; from left to right these are Hercules (god of strength), Ceres (god of wheat and summer), Eoie (god of wind), Vulcan (god of fire), Neptune (god of water), Wisdom, and Fame blowing her horn. The guild's patron saint, St Aubert, sits above the door.

No 3 La Brouette – The Wheelbarrow – dates from 1644 and you can just about make out faint gold wheelbarrows above the doorway. It belonged to the Guild of the Tallow Merchants, who extracted goose fat needed by the tanners. The guild's patron saint, St Gilles, was added when the building was restored in 1912. Today, it's home to one of the better cafés on the square (page 88).

No 4 Le Sac – The Sack – was the Guild of the Joiners and Coopers, essentially cabinetmakers, and the tools of their trade can be seen in reliefs on the second storey. It's interesting to note that although the first two floors survived the bombardment, the use of a third type of ancient Greek column was used to create consistency in the façade of the building. At the bottom sit examples of the plain and vertical Doric order; above this are the scrolled tops of the Ionian column, and above this the new ornate Corinthian order.

No 5 La Louve – The She Wolf – takes its name from the bas-relief that sits above the door and depicts the founders of Rome, Romulus and Remus, suckling from a she wolf after being left for dead on the Tiber River as babies. The house belonged to the Guild of the Archers – look for the arrows on the balcony and the shield and helmet further up – and was the only façade to evade the bombardment of 1695. The phoenix on the roof was added after the rebuild to signify the rebirth of the Grand' Place. Four statues can be seen on the second floor; they represent Truth, Falsehood, Peace and War.

No 6 Le Cornet – The Horn – was the nickname of Charles II, whose bust and Spanish coats of arms are protected by two lions and flanked by two sailors at the top of the Sailors' Guild. The upper gable is specifically designed to mimic the galleon of a ship, and nautical paraphernalia, like anchors, rope, and the sun, moon and stars for navigatation, decorate the frames of the lower windows. The golden gusts spreading out from the king's bust represent the four trade winds. On the second floor are a pair of horses; if you look closely you'll see that their hooves are fins, and on their backs are fish scales. The guild was erected in 1697 and restored between 1802 and 1902.

No 7 Le Renard/ Den Vos – The Fox – dates from 1699 and takes its name from the golden fox above the door. It was the Guild of the Haberdashers, as indicated by the four bas-relief panels that depict the various activities of the trade. Further up are five statues; the middle figure wearing a blindfold and holding the scales and sword symbolises fair trade and either side of her stand the four *known* continents. From right to left they are Africa, Europe, Asia and America; Australia remained undiscovered until the first settlements took root in 1782. The statue at the top is St Nicolas – patron saint of merchants.

From here you might like to quickly pop down Rue de la Tête d'Or to visit the long-lived **Musée du Cacao et du Chocolat** [95 D2] (*9–11 Rue de la Tête d'Or;* ✆ *02 514 20 48; www.mucc.be;* ☉ *10.00–16.30 Tue–Sun; adult/concession/under 12 €5.50/4.50/free*). A sedate, privately owned, chocolate museum, it offers free tasting sessions and daily demonstrations.

Turning back to the Grand' Place you come to the towering **Hôtel de Ville** [95 D2/3] (*1 Grand' Place;* ✆ *02 279 43 65; guided tours Apr–Sep 15.15 Tue & Wed, 12.15 Sun; Oct–Mar 15.15 Tue; admission €3*). The original *stadhuis* or town hall consisted of just the left wing and the square-topped belfry built in Gothic style between 1402 and 1421 under the direction of architect Jacob van Thienen. Available funds led to the construction of the right wing and the ornate spire (which replaced the original belfry) in 1444–49, with the work being directed by popular architect Jan van Ruysbroeck. However, Charles the Bold's refusal to narrow the adjacent Rue de la Tête d'Or prevented the building reaching its proper length, and as a result the 96m tower does not appear to be placed centrally. Popular myth claims that the imbalance drove van Ruysbroeck to jump from the tower to his death. A copper statue of St Michael – the patron saint of Brussels – was placed at the pinnacle of the tower in 1455. Unfortunately, funds dried up before the 300-or-so niches created for statues of the dukes and duchesses of Brabant could be filled, and they remained empty until French writer Victor Hugo rallied funds for their instalment in 1852. The ones in place today are replacements; the originals are stowed in the Maison du Roi opposite.

After the French bombardment in 1695, all that was left of the Hôtel de Ville was the façade. The inside was gutted by fire and priceless archives and paintings, including the magnificent *Justice of Trajan* and *Justice of Herkenbald* retables by Flemish Primitive painter Rogier van der Weyden, which hung in the Golden Chamber, were lost. It was during this final rebuild that two rear wings were built to form a complete quadrangle. If you wander into the central inner courtyard you will see a brass star set into the ground. Known as '**point zero**', this is supposedly the marker from which all distances in Belgium are measured. Also here are two fountains built to represent the main rivers that cross the country: the Meuse and the Scheldt. Today, the interior has regained its splendour and you can explore a series of lavishly decorated reception rooms, council offices and the superb Council Chamber (or marriage hall), decked out with heavy oak-inlaid flooring, city-spun tapestries and majestic paintings. A tourist information centre sits beneath the arcade.

Resuming with the guildhouses, to the left of the Hôtel de Ville, is:

No 8 L'Etoile – The Star. Originally home to the city magistrate, it was knocked down in 1850 and rebuilt in 1897, this time with a passageway connecting it to the Hôtel de Ville. Rumour has it that judges would stand at the windows of this gallery to watch public executions on the square. Set on the left-hand wall under the arch is a reclining bronze statue commemorating Everard 't Serclaes, who reclaimed the city for the Duke of Brabant after the Count of Flanders, Louis de Male, tried to seize it. Under the cover of night, on 24 October 1356, 't Serclaes scaled the façade of the Star and replaced the Flanders' flag Male had set with that of the Duke, and went on to chase remaining invaders out of the city. He was hailed a hero and made an alderman of the city five times before he was assassinated by one of the Count's stooges. Parts of the escapade are highlighted in reliefs above his effigy, which is kept shiny thanks to a long-standing tradition stating that good luck follows those who rub his statue.

No 9 Le Cygne – The Swan – once belonged to the Guild of the Butchers, and today houses La Maison du Cygne restaurant. However, during its golden days in the 19th century it was a café, famous for attracting political revolutionaries, including Karl Marx and Friedrich Engels who between 1845 and 1848 penned the *Communist Manifesto* (published in February 1848) here, as well as the first chapters of *Das Kapital* – the urtext for Communism – before Marx was expelled for failing to pay his rent.

No 10 L'Arbre d'Or – The Golden Tree – is presided over by Charles of Lorraine (one of the governors during Austrian rule) on his steed and is labelled in bold gold letters as the Maison des Brasseurs. The house belonged to the Guild of Brewers prior to their abolition during the French Revolution. Today, it's the headquarters of the nationwide Union of Belgian Brewers – one of the oldest unions in the world – and houses the **Musée de la Brasserie** [95 D3] (*10 Grand' Place;* ✆ *02 511 49 87;* ◷ *10.00–17.00 Mon–Sun; adult/BrusselsCard €6/free*), a rather uninspiring museum with a lacklustre display explaining the various stages of the brewing process. A free beer is included, but doesn't justify the entrance fee.

No 11 La Rose – The Rose – is named after its original owners the van der Rosen family. Today, it houses an upmarket restaurant appropriately named La Rose Blanche.

No 12 Le Mont Tabor – Mount Tabor – dates from 1699 and underwent restoration in 1885.

On the east side of the square:

Nos 13–19 Maison des Ducs de Brabant – House of the Dukes of Brabant – dominates the east side of the square and appears to occupy a single house. In fact, it is seven separate guild buildings that share the same façade, designed by Willem de Bruyn in 1698. From right to left these are Le Renommé; L'Hermitage, which belonged to the Guild of Wine Merchants and Greengrocers; La Fortune – another of the Tanner's guilds; Le Moulin à Vent, 'The Windmill', which belonged to the Guild of the Millers; Le Pot d'Etain, 'The Pewter Pot', which housed the Guild of the Carpenters; La Colline, 'The Hill', that was home to the Guild of Masons, Sculptors and Stonecutters; and La Bourse, 'The Purse' – a private residence. Each of the pillars bears the bust of a Duke of Brabant at its base.

On the north side of the square:

No 20 Le Cerf – The Stag – was tacked on to the north end of the square in 1707 and for much of its life served as a private residence. Nowadays, it houses Le Cerf bar.

Nos 21 & 22 Named Joseph and Anna after the inscriptions found above the lower windows, it originally started life as two separate houses, but these were joined under one façade during the rebuild. Notice the iron pulley that hails from the days when large items, like furniture, were hauled up the outside of the building and taken in through the window, rather than being lugged up the stairs.

No 23 L'Ange – The Angel – was owned by a porcelain merchant.

Nos 24 & 25 La Chaloupe d'Or – the Golden Rowboat – dates from 1697 and belonged to the well-off Guild of Tailors. A bust of their patron saint, St Barbara, sits above the doorway and at the top stands St Boniface, with a plaque showing tailor's shears at his side.

Nos 26 & 27 Le Pigeon – The Pigeon – belonged to the Guild of Painters and was home to exiled French Romantic writer Victor Hugo for a few months in 1852 (look for the plaque mounted on the façade), until criticism of his writings forced his move to Guernsey.

Nos 29–33 Known as the Maison du Roi in French, the Broodhuis in Flemish, the King's House takes its name from the covered bread hall that was first erected here in the 13th century. The name was changed to Maison du Duc when the Duke of Brabant tore the bread hall down, rebuilt and moved his administration into the building in the early 15th century, and again in 1536 to Maison du Roi when the Hapsburgs assumed rule. After the bombardment it was rebuilt in 16th-century style from drawings, and today it houses the municipal museum, the **Musée de la Ville de Bruxelles** [95 E2] (*29–33 Grand' Place;* \ *02 279 43 50;* ⊕ *10.00–17.00 Tue–Sun, 10.00–20.00 Thu; adult/concession/kids/BrusselsCard €4/3/2/free*). A broad array of objects are on show, including altarpieces, tapestries, sculptures and porcelain, but the most interesting features are the paintings and drawings depicting the original town, and the rooms on the top floor containing a small selection of the 700 or so costumes donated by various dignitaries to Manneken-Pis (see box, page 101). The first was gifted after the French bombardment in 1698 by Maximilian II, ruler of Bavaria and governor of the Spanish Netherlands.

The remaining buildings – **No 28**: Le Marchand d'Or (The Gold Merchant), **No 34**: Le Heaume (The Helmet), **No 35**: Le Paon (The Peacock), **Nos 36 & 37**: Le Chêne et Le Samaritin (The Oak and the Samaritan), **No 38**: St Barbe (St Barbara) and **No 39**: L'Ane (The Donkey) – bear less decoration and were private homes. The majority of these (with the exception of Le Marchand d'Or) were rebuilt along with the others between 1695 and 1697 and restored in the late-18th early–19th centuries.

Leave the Grand' Place via Rue Charles Buls and walk until you reach Hôtel Amigo (page 76), the site of the old city prison and whose name arose as the result of a mistaken translation. Known as *vrunte*, meaning 'enclosure' in Flemish, the Spanish took it to mean 'friend' and consequently applied the Spanish equivalent *amigo*, which is certainly a more welcoming term for guests staying at the hotel today. Just opposite is Rose's Lace Boutique – look for the granite plaque that was installed in 1991 to commemorate the Ville de Courtrai mansion that once stood here and where French poet Paul Verlaine famously shot his lover Arthur Rimbaud with his revolver on 10 July 1873. Next – in order to avoid the tatty souvenir shops along Rue de l'Etuve – turn into Rue de la Violette directly opposite the hotel and visit the **Musée du Costume et de la Dentelle** [95 D3] (*12 Rue de la Violette;* \ *02 213 44 50;* ⊕ *10.00–12.30 & 13.30–17.00 Mon, Tue, Thu & Fri, 14.00–17.00 Sat–Sun; adult/concession/BrusselsCard €3/2.50/free*), which has good displays of

Brussels lace, and of costumes and embroidery collected between the 18th and 19th centuries. Continue until you reach Place St-Jean. In the centre you will see a statue of **Gabrielle Petit,** a young Walloon nurse who acted as a spy for allies during World War I. She was eventually caught by the German secret police, held at the Prison de St-Gilles and executed at the *Tir National* shooting range in Schaerbeek on 1 April 1916.

From here, head south on to Place de la Vieille Halle aux Blés to visit the **Fondation Jacques Brel** (*11 Pl de la Vieille Halle aux Blés;* ✎ *02 511 10 20; www.jacquesbrel. be;* ⊕ *12.00–18.00 Tue–Sun, Jul–Aug 10.00–18.00 daily; €5*), a multimedia library/ museum dedicated to the enigmatic *chanson* crooner (page 354). They also run a great audio-guide walking tour (€8) that last two hours and 40 minutes; you're welcome to stop off for coffee/dinner en route and return the guide later in the day. A plaque commemorating Brel's birthplace can be found outside 138 Rue du Diamant.

Turning into Rue du Chêne, walk towards the mural painted on the exposed wall of a house jutting out from the row; it depicts **a scene from the Olivier Rameau comic strip.** At the end of the street you will come to the crossroads that are home to the beloved **Manneken Pis** [95 C4] – literally 'little man peeing' in the Bruxellois dialect. The pissing boy is high on a visitor's 'must-see' list, and it's amusing to listen-out for the various translations of 'but he's so small' coming from the international clutch of tourists that file in and out of the small square.

Before continuing the walk, take a quick detour to the right down Rue de l'Etuve to see a well-known **mural** from *The Calculus Affair* in which Tintin, his dog Snowy and Captain Haddock flee from danger down a fire escape. It's hidden behind a wall on the left-hand side of the street.

Heading back to Manneken Pis, turn right down Rue des Grands-Carmes until you come out on to Rue du Marché au Charbon. Once here, first turn to the left to visit **Notre Dame du Bon-Secours** [95 B3] (*91 Rue du Marché au Charbon;* ✎ *02 514 31 13;* ⊕ *09.30–17.00 daily*). The first example of a chapel here dates from the 12th century. Known as St-Jacques, it was built flush against the old city walls and served as a resthouse for pilgrims on their way to visit the apostle's tomb in Compostela, Spain. When the popularity of this pilgrimage route died down, the chapel fell into disrepair but continued to run services. It acquired its current name in the 17th century when a church tutor, Jacques Meeus, introduced the cult of the Virgin Mary. The church became popular once again and the destruction of the city walls allowed an expansion in 1669, and the addition of the façade in 1694. Barely a year later, the whole lot was destroyed by the 1695 French bombardment and a new church (the soot-blackened version that stands today) was built in Flemish Baroque style in 1694. The emblems of the Compostela pilgrim (shell, water bottle, hat and staff) can still be seen beneath the statue of the Virgin above the door. Inside is a 14th-century oak statue of the Virgin above the main altar and nearby, four 18th-century confessionals.

Exiting the church, turn left and follow the street north. Spare a quick glance down Rue du Bons Cours to see a scene from the *Ric Hocet* (*9 Rue du Bon Secours*) a **comic strip** published in *Tintin* magazine in the 1950s, and then move on down Rue du Marché au Charbon to see two more comic-strip murals; the first is hidden behind a wall on the right-hand side of the road (*60 Rue du Marché au Charbon*) and features a scene from *Victor Sackville* by Francis Carin; the second depicts cartoonist Frank Pé's greatest creation, *Broussaille*.

Follow the curve of the road round on to Rue du Midi and then take the second street on the left, Rue Henri Maus. Here on the left is the famous Art Nouveau

MANNEKEN PIS

The first version of the Manneken Pis is believed to have been made of stone in the 1450s, but the identity of the little boy has become the stuff of legend. One story tells the tale of a hero boy who put out a firebomb by peeing on it, another relates the discovery of a lost nobleman's son eventually found peeing at this spot. We do know, however, that Jérôme Duquesnoy the Elder was commissioned in 1619 by city officials to make a bronze statue that would decorate the watering well and encapsulate the *joie-de-vivre* of Bruxellois residents. Whether it was a replica of an older version remains unconfirmed.

Since then the boy has been stolen on a number of occasions, but two attempts stick in history. He was first taken in 1745 by French soldiers who stashed him in a whorehouse, but were forced to return him when King Louis XV ordered a full-scale search for the statue and then knighted the statue to prevent him being stolen again. The second incident occurred in 1817 when an ex-convict stole the statue for its bronze. The thief was apprehended, but not before poor Manneken had been smashed to smithereens. The thief was publicly branded on the Grand' Place and given a life sentence in a forced labour camp, and a cast for the new Manneken Pis (the one that stands today) was forged from the broken pieces.

For centuries, it has been customary for visiting dignitaries to donate a costume to the wee urchin's enormous wardrobe and on special dates the small statue gets a change of attire followed by a formal ceremony. Costumes of note include the Elvis Presley outfit fitted on 8 January, Christopher Columbus fitted on 12 October and, between 21–25 December, Père Nöel. A larger display of his costumes and a full list of the costume changes are posted in the Musée de la Ville de Bruxelles (page 99).

Falstaff café (page 88); a good point to stop and refuel with a drink or bite to eat. Afterwards, continue to the end of the street until you reach Boulevard Anspach, at which point you can either dip underground into the Bourse métro station and visit the **Scientastic** museum (*Level one of métro Bourse;* \ *02 732 13 36; www.scientastic. be;* ⊕ *10.00–17.30 Mon, Tue, Thu, Fri, 14.00–17.30 Wed, Sat & Sun; adult/kids/ BrusselsCard €7.90/5.30/free*) which features a range of optical illusion experiments for kids; or turn right until you are standing in front of **La Bourse** (the old stock exchange). An impressive neo-Classical building constructed in 1873, it is guarded by two lion monuments, decorated with numerous sculptures of nudes and cherubs and – atop the six grand Corinthian columns – a mantle features various allegorical figures pertaining to Africa, nautical navigation and industry – all associated with the boom in economic wealth in Belgium during the 19th century.

Turn down Rue de la Bourse and look for the excavations located below street level and housed beneath a series of low glass arches. Uncovered in 1988, these are the remains of a Franciscan monastery, dating from 1238: hence the name **Bruxella 1238** [95 C1] (*Rue de la Bourse;* \ *02 279 43 55; guided tours in English run on the first Wed of the month, start at 10.15 from outside the Maison du Roi on the Grand' Place where tickets are also bought; €4*). Like many of the other religious buildings in Brussels, the monastery was partially destroyed during the religious wars of the 16th century and rebuilt again after the French bombardment of 1695, before it was finally dissolved in 1796 under French rule when the churches were closed and their possessions sold. It was first replaced by a butter market hall and later by the

3

stock exchange building which stands in place today. Despite several references to it in historical literature, the location of the monastery remained a mystery until 1988 when a professor and a team of archaeologists from ULB and the Société Royale d'Archéologie de Bruxelles uncovered the heart of the old chapel, including the tombs of several important persons, among them the Duke of Brabant Jean I who died in 1294. Given its central location, work is slow, and as yet the site is largely ignored by residents and tourists alike.

Further along Rue de la Bourse, you'll pass **Le Cirio** (page 88) another *fin-de-siècle* café. At the end of the street, skirt round to the right into Rue au Beurre to visit the **Eglise St-Nicolas** [95 D1] (*1 Rue au Beurre;* ❧ *02 267 51 64;* ☉ *08.00–18.30 Mon–Fri, 09.00–18.00 Sat, 09.00–19.30 Sun: mass in English at 10.00*). Named after the patron saint of traders, St-Nicolas is one of the oldest churches in Brussels. Built in the 12th century – with an asymmetric layout in order to avoid a brook that once ran through the area – it has received numerous restorations, additions and touch-ups ever since. Its right flank is studded with and concealed by shop fronts, the prettiest of which is the leaning front of the watchmaker's, and the only feature of interest inside is the relic of the Martyrs of Gorkum, which contains the remains of a group of Catholic priests murdered and martyred by the Protestants in Holland in 1572. Across the way is biscuit baker **Maison Dandoy** (*31 Rue au Beurre;* ☉ *08.00– 18.00 Mon–Sat, 10.30–18.30 Sun),* famous for his cinnamon *speculaas* biscuits.

Retrace your steps back on to Rue du Midi and follow the road around the back of the church; turn right on to Rue du Marché aux Herbes and then take the first left on to **Petite rue des Bouchers**. Press on through the famous line of wall-to-wall restaurants until you come to Impasse Schuddeveld on the right. Up here you will find the age-old **Théâtre Royal de Toone** [95 E1/2] (*6 Impasse Schuddeveld, just off Petite rue des Bouchers; www.toone.be;* ☉ *12.00–00.00 Tue–Sun, closed January),* famous for its Bruxellois puppet shows (page 91). Turn back to Petite rue des Bouchers and when you reach the end of the street turn left and take the first lane on your right, Impasse de la Fidelité. This narrow street is home to **Jeanneke Pis** [95 E1], Manneken Pis' little sister. The squatting girl (now unfortunately behind bars) was erected in 1985 by Denis Adrien Debouvrie as a symbol of feminism. Back on the Rue de Bouchers get ready to turn down Rue des Dominicains, the first road on your left.

However, before doing so look for **26 Rue de Bouchers** located on the corner. On 3 June 1960 an agreement was symbolically signed here between the mayor and a committee of city businessmen to create the Commune Libre de l'Îlot Sacré – a protected islet centring around the Grand' Place. It was established in reaction to plans for the 1958 World Expo' that had included the widening of roads, like Rue de Bouchers, Petite rue des Bouchers and Rue des Dominicains. The changes would, of course, have altered the medieval street pattern of the area, introduced modern architecture and brought cars right into the old town centre. To protect and preserve the area from other such future plans a series of regulations were laid out stipulating town-planning regulations within the islets: no signboards and the complete restoration of a façade if it contained more than 1m² of traditional stonemasonry.

Wander down Rue des Domincains until you reach the entrance to the **Galeries Royale St-Hubert** [95 F1] on your right. This glorious example of neo-Classical architecture carries the prestige of being Europe's first shopping mall and was built by Jean-Pierre Cluysenaar in 1847. Its construction caused quite a controversy at the time – a resident died of shock when the bailiff informed them they would have to vacate their property and a shop owner even slit his throat in protest. Split into three sections – Galerie du Roi, Galerie de la Reine and Galerie du Prince – the hall takes its general name from the St-Hubert passage that once connected Rue du Marché aux Herbes and Rue des Bouchers. When the covered galleries first opened, the refined clientele were charged 20 cents to wander beneath the stunning vaulted-glass ceiling and across the marble floors that today are home to the boutiques of a handful of revered designers like Oliver Strelli, who designs clothes for the Royal Family; the legendary Tropismes bookshop; the Royal handbag designer Delvaux; the renovated Vaudeville theatre; as well as a selection of pricy restaurants and cafés, including the famous writers' haunt La Taverne du Passage. Perhaps most famous, though, is the Neuhaus chocolatiers, where the first praline was concocted in 1912 by Jean Neuhaus (see box, page 46).

Exiting the galleries turn left and wander through Place Agora, where a **statue of Brussels mayor Charles Buls** and his faithful mutt sits, and up the right-hand side of Hotel Ibis to Place d'Espagne, which is dominated by a platform bearing a **statue of the fanciful (and fictional) 'knight' Don Quixote and his earthy squire Sancho Panza**, presumably because several reprints of the novel were published in Brussels during the 17th century. Also here is a sullen-looking statue of music maestro Béla Bartók (1881–1945), a Hungarian composer renowned for his folk music.

From here you can either carry straight on and come out in front of Gare Centrale, or retrace your steps and and leave Place Agora via Rue de la Colline, where there is a **commemorative plaque** situated on the corner with Rue du Marché aux Herbes to mark the sewing of the first two Belgian flags by Madame Abts on 26 August 1830 (*85 Rue du Marché aux Herbes*). Walk to the end of Rue de la Colline to arrive back on the Grand' Place and the end of the walk.

St-Cathérine walk

Start: Place St-Géry
Nearest métro: M̲ Bourse
Walking time: 2hrs; see maps, pages 95 and 78–9

On exiting the Bourse métro station, look for the **Paul Delvaux painting** *Nos Vieux Trams Bruxellois* above the escalators (see box on page 72 for other examples of métro art) and then head west along Rue J van Praet to **Place St-Géry**. Brussels' history began here when the Bishop of Cambrai founded a small chapel on this very spot – then an islet surrounded by the River Senne. A number of churches have since replaced the old St-Géry chapel, which was destroyed in AD800. When the last one was demolished under French rule during the late-18th century, the open space was made into a market square and at its centre they put a fountain and obelisk salvaged from Grimbergen Abbey. When architect Vanderheggen was commissioned to build a covered market hall in 1882, he was careful to build around the obelisk, and the Flemish-Renaissance-style **Halles St-Géry** [95 A1] (*1 Pl St-Géry;* ✆ *02 775 75 75;* ⊕ *10.00–18.00 Tue–Fri, 14.00–17.00 Sat*) are still in place today. The halls were abandoned after World War II and didn't undergo restoration until the 1980s; initially they were earmarked to become chic covered markets, similar to London's Covent Garden, but when plans failed it became an information centre for the Brussels Capital Region.

The surrounding area is now one of the trendiest in Brussels and famous for its cafés and bars with sprawling terraces.

Walk to the west side of the square and pass under the arch – known as Au Lion d'Or Gate – to the left of Le Lion St-Géry restaurant. This leads to an inner courtyard that was once home to the brewery and bakery of Notre Dame aux Riches

Throughout the Lower Town strange brass abalone (clam) shells are embedded into the pavement. These were the emblem of pilgrims traveling to visit the tomb of Apostle St Jacques in Compostela, Spain. They mark a pilgrim route that has been in place since the Middle Ages and led travellers to sites on the pilgrimage trail.

Claires convent (see below). To the left, beside the vacated offices of interior textile designers Intede, and down a trio of steps, is one of the **last open stretches of the River Senne**, which was covered over in the mid-19th century to eliminate the diseases brewing in its fetid waters.

Also on Place St-Géry you'll find a **mural of comic book hero Néro** (see box, page 23) and his buddies rescuing a cat from a tree.

Turn the corner and walk down Rue de la Grande Ile until the next intersection. Here you will find **Notre Dame aux Riches Claires** [78–9 B7] (*23 Rue des Riches-Claires;* ✆ *02 511 09 37;* ⊕ *09.30–12.30 Sun*), an elegant series of rounded church towers built in Italianate-Flemish style by Luc Fayd'Herbe (1617–97) in 1665. It was used as a hospital to treat soldiers wounded during the Belgian revolution. An outbreak of fire in June 1989 destroyed large portions of the interior, including the church organ. Restoration is now complete and the church is open to visitors on Sundays.

Return to Place St-Géry and leave via the northeast exit located on the opposite side of the square. Known as Rue Pont de la Carpe, the street takes its name from a bridge that crossed the River Senne here until the mid-19th century. Take the first left on to Rue des Chartreux and keep an eye open for Magritte's favourite café **Le Greenwich** (page 88) on the right-hand side, and just after it, a **comic-strip mural of L'Ange de Sambre** by Yslaire.

As you come to the corner with Rue du Vieux Marché aux Grains, notice the statue of a dog cocking its leg against a bollard. Sculpted by popular artist Tom Frantzen, the mutt is known as **Zinneken Pis** [78–9 B6] and completes the Manneken and Jeanneken Pis 'family' of statues dotted around the city.

Turn right into Rue du Vieux Marché aux Grains and follow the road all the way round, crossing the wide Rue Antoine Dansaert (well-known for its fashion shops), and taking the first street on the left. Half way along here, on the left-hand side, is **Maison de la Bellone** [78–9 B5] (*46 Rue de Flandre;* ✆ *02 513 33 33; www.bellone.be;* ⊕ *10.00–18.00 Mon–Fri, closed Jul*). The stunning façade of this Baroque mansion is often forgotten because it's hidden down Impasse de Roulier off Rue de Flandre, and tucked away behind two sets of glass doors. It was built in 1697 by Jan Cosyn (the sculptor responsible for the bust of King Charles II of Spain that decorates the Guild of the Bakers on the Grand' Place) for arms-trader Nicolas Bally and his wife Gertrude de Smeth. Appropriately, the house is named after the Roman Goddess of War, Bellona, whose bust sits above the doorway and Jan Cosyn's signature. Behind her is a scene depicting Austria's victory agains the Turks in 1697 and above this sits John the Baptist measuring the globe using a compass; beside him is John the Evangelist reading from the Bible. Other emblems of war are carved into the lower stone reliefs, and spread between the Ionic columns are medallions bearing the faces of Rome's great emperors: Hadrian, Antoninus Pius, Trajan and Marcus Aurelius. For unknown reasons, the building raced through a list of owners before Brussels mayor Charles Buls acquired it for the city in 1913. Since then, it has served as a police station and the offices of the Ommegang Society; today it sits resplendent under is its glass-dome covering and is home to the French theatre institute, Maison du Spectacle, which hosts concerts, workshops and exhibitions.

Come back out on to Rue de Flandre, turn left, walk to the end of the road, turn right and walk towards Square des Blindés. In the centre stands a bronze **statue dedicated to the 'soldier' pigeons** used to carry messages during World War I. Just south of this, between Quai aux Briques and Quai au Bois à Brûler, is a tree-lined plaza known as **Marché aux Poissons**. Up until 1853 the Willebroeck Canal flowed through these streets and was busy with barges delivering wares from Antwerp and the North Sea. The various street names – Quaille à la Houille (coal), Quai à la Chaux (lime) and Quai à Barques (bricks) – give away the types of cargo on board and roughly where each was delivered at the docks. After frequent floodings the canal was filled in and the space used as a fish market (hence the current name). Although this closed in 1955, the area is still synonymous with excellent fish restaurants. The stretch of land, studded with two fountains (one depicting St Michael slaying the devil) also hosts Brussels' largest Christmas market.

Continue to walk south along Quai aux Briques until you reach Place St-Cathérine. At the heart of this square stands **Eglise St-Cathérine** [78–9 C5] (*Pl St-Cathérine;* ✆ *02 513 34 81;* ⊕ *08.30–17.30 daily*). Since the beginning of the 13th century there was a Romanesque chapel dedicated to St-Cathérine on this site – it abutted the original 12th-century city walls of the **Tour Noir** [78–9 C5], on Place du Samedi, which still stands. This original chapel was replaced by a Gothic church during the 14th–15th centuries, which was remodelled and enlarged in 1629. The Baroque belfry (which took 20 years to complete) was also added at this point and is the only vestige remaining from that period. The rest of the church fell victim to rot caused by a series of floods from the Willebroeck Canal in 1850 and was torn down. Architect Poelaert (of Palais de Justice fame) was brought in to build a new church that would cover the old St-Cathérine port. Poelaert modelled his design on the neo-Gothic St-Eustache church in Paris and the Duke and Duchess of Brabant laid the first stone on 26 September 1854. True to form Poelaert progressed slowly, so in 1861 Wynard Janssens joined the project and by 1867 work was complete. Inside, in the left chapel, you'll find the legendary limestone 'black Virgin Mary' carrying the holy child. Dating from the 15th century, it was thrown in the Senne in 1744 by Protestants, but was found floating further downstream on a piece of earth and returned, albeit not before the limestone had turned an unorthodox shade of black. Behind the statue is a painted wooden panel showing the Crucifixion; it's the work of Henri de Clerck (1570–1629) who worked in the court of Archduke Albert and Archduchess Isabella for over 23 years.

Leave Place St-Cathérine, via Place du Samedi, and turn left on to Rue Cypres and walk until you reach Place du Béguinage, site of the **St-Jean-Baptiste du Béguinage** [78–9 C4] (*Pl du Béguinage;* ✆ *02 217 87 42;* ⊕ *10.00–17.00 Tue–Sat, 10.00–20.00 Sat*). Praised as one of the prettiest churches in Belgium, this Flemish Baroque church is the last remaining building of a *béguinage* that stood on this site from 1250. Far from being poor, the self-sufficient béguines possessed large amounts of land in the surrounding area and produced enough income to build a Gothic church on the site in the 14th century. Both were razed by Calvinists towards the end of the 16th century and by the time funds were available to rebuild the church, the community of béguines had started to shrink – changing times and high entry fees excluded all but the richest of women. Still, the church – built by Luc Fayd'herbe (the man responsible for Notre Dame aux Riches Claires) – was completed in 1676 and outlasted the *béguinage,* which was dissolved in 1833. The interior was damaged by an outbreak of fire in 2000, but restorations are now complete. Of note is the enormous Baroque pulpit featuring St Dominic condemning heresy and crushing the odd heretic under foot to drive the message home.

Take the north exit from the Place du Béguinage along Rue de l'Infirmerie on to Rue du Grand Hospice where, directly in front of you, stands the bulky **Hospice Pacheco,** an early 19th-century building that became a hospice in 1835 and continues to care for the elderly and infirm to this day.

Keeping the hospice on your left, walk to the end of Rue du Grand Hospice, across Rue du Laeken, and down Rue du Cirque, across busy Boulevard Emile Jacqmain and on to the equally wide Boulevard Adolphe Max. From here, head left and turn right into Rue de la Finistère and around to the entrance of **Notre Dame du Finistère** [78–9 E4] (*45 Rue Neuve;* \ *02 217 52 52;* ⊕ *08.00–18.00 Mon–Sat, 08.30–12.30 Sun*). The medieval chapel that sat here originally was placed outside the 12th-century city walls – hence the name *finis terrae,* 'end of the world'. The names of the surrounding streets, like Rue au Choux (cabbages) and Rue de la Blanchisserie (bleaching), recall the activities that took place in the fields around the chapel, namely the planting of vegetables and bleaching of sheets. In 1617, this land was bought by Hieronimus de Meester, who extended the street plan and named the central road Nouvelle Rue Notre Dame, which over the years was shortened to Rue Neuve. Soon enough the small church could not cope with the rapidly expanding community and work on the Baroque version, which stands in place today, began in 1708. However, funds for construction petered out half way through, so tombola tickets were sold to raise the necessary finances. Unfortunately, a corrupt committee member legged it with the proceeds and as a result work wasn't completed until 1730. The octangular belfry was added later in 1828, and in 1862 another chapel was built specially to accommodate the church's prize possession – a statue of Notre Dame de Bon Succès, which was originally brought over from Aberdeen in Scotland in 1625 and placed here in 1814.

On leaving the church, turn right back on to Rue de la Finistère and take the first street on the left, Rue du Colombière. This leads you briefly on to Rue St-Michel and then Boulevard Adolphe Max, which you should leave as soon as possible by turning into the ornate, but faded, **Passage du Nord** – a covered walkway filled with old tobacconist stores that leads into pedestrianised shopping street **Rue Neuve**. Once here, turn right and follow the street to its end and cross Rue de Fosse aux Loups. The walk ends in front of the **Théâtre de la Monnaie** [78–9 D6] (*Pl de la Monnaie;* \ *070 23 39 39; www.lamonnaie.be;* ⊕ *for guided visits 12.00 Sat*). Site of the famous Belgian revolt in August 1830 (page 9) and Brussels' best opera performances (page 90), this grand building stands on the site of the 15th-century Hôtel des Monnaies that served as the royal mint for the Dukes of Brabant. In 1817 it was replaced by an opera house that was destroyed by the revolt fires; the version that stands today was reconstructed by Joseph Poelaert in 1855 – although the Ionic columns and mantle were saved from the original theatre.

THE UPPER TOWN
The Sablon and Marolles walk
Start: Place de la Chapelle
Nearest métro: M̲ Lemonnier/Anneessens
Walking time: 3hrs; see map, pages 82–3

This longer walk leads you through the well-to-do Sablon area and the working-class neighbourhood of Marolles – site of the old Bruxellois dialect Marollien –

that are both located south of Brussels city centre. The walk begins outside **Notre Dame de la Chapelle** [82–3 D3] (*Pl de la Chapelle;* ⊕ *Nov–Feb 09.00–18.00 daily, Mar–Oct 09.00–19.00 daily*). A must-see, this church – shining white after extensive renovation work in the 1990s – has one of the most impressive interiors in Brussels. A chapel was first founded here in 1134, making it the oldest in the city. However, its checquered history has made the church something of a mutt and it contains a mix of styles: the Romanesque chancel and transept date from the 12th century, the Gothic nave is from the 15th century and the Baroque belltower dates from 1699. Inside the décor is predominately Flamboyant Gothic and features of note include the row of apostle statues (carved by the likes of Jan Cosyns and Luc Fayd'herbe) mounted on the aisle columns, and the incredibly detailed Baroque oak pulpit, which depicts Elijah in the wilderness. More importantly, the church is also the burial place of Pieter Brueghel the Elder and his wife, Maria Coecke – who were married here in 1563, and Frans Anneessens (1660–1719), a trades leader who was beheaded on the Grand' Place for campaigning for civil rights in the communes during Austrian rule. There's a plaque in his memory in the chapel of the Holy Sacrement. The old graveyard sits under the neighbouring Place de la Chapelle, and on the northwestern side of the square you can make out the Italian-Flemish red-brick façade of the 17th-century **Eglise des Brigittines**. It ceased to be a convent in 1784 and appears to have received little love or attention ever since; today it's used occasionally for cultural performances.

Now head north along Rue Haute on to Boulevard de l'Empereur. Here on the right-hand side of the road is **Tour Anneessens** [82–3 E3]. Also known as Tour d'Angle, the round brick tower and abutting wall are one of the last remaining portions of the 13th-century city walls. Frans Anneessens (see above) was imprisoned in this tower prior to his execution in 1719.

Turn back towards Place de la Chapelle, but take the first left into the cobbled (and pedestrianised) **Rue de Rollebeek** that is lined with pavement cafés and independent antique stores selling trinkets and furniture. Once you reach the end of the road, you can take a quick detour by turning right into Rue de Minimes and visiting the **Musée Juif de Belgique** [82–3 E3] (*21 Rue des Minimes;* ☎ *02 512 19 63; www.new.mjb-jmb.org;* ⊕ *10.00–17.00 Tue–Sun; adult/concession/under 12/ BrusselsCard €5/3/free/free*). Belgium's Jewish Museum contains a huge collection of religious paraphernalia, including genealogy charts, Hebrew bibles and books, and roughly 20,000 photographs. All this is showcased in a mixture of permanent and temporary exhibitions organised by the museum.

Retrace your steps and enter the triangular **Place du Grand Sablon** that is skirted by art and antiques stores on all sides. Chocolatier **Wittamer** (page 92) sits just on the left as you enter the square. Named after the sandy road that led up to the city gates during the 13th century, the area's status was consolidated during the 14th century when the Sablon chapel was constructed. By the 15th century, the city walls had been expanded to encompass the now new-and-improved Gothic Sablon church, and the district was becoming popular with well-to-do citizens because of its proximity to the Duke's Palais d'Egmont. Today, the fashionable plaza hosts an antiques market (page 92). In the centre is the **Fountain of Minerva**. Dedicated to the Roman goddess of war, it was a gift from English earl (and exile) Thomas Bruce: a supporter of James II who lived on the square for many years and was buried in the Eglise des Brigittines.

Walk along the right-hand pavement of the Grand Sablon towards the scaffold-covered **Notre Dame du Sablon** [82–3 F4] (*3b Rue de la Régence;* ☎ *02 511 57 41;* ⊕ *08.00–18.00 Mon–Fri, 09.30–18.00 Sat, 10.00–18.00 Sun*) spread out before you.

Its founding can be credited to one Beatrijs Soetkins who stole a statue of the Virgin Mary from a church in Antwerp and brought it to Brussels, after (she claims) a vision of the immaculate Mother had instructed her to do so. (This journey is re-enacted in the famous Ommegang procession held every summer, see page 56). The guild of the Archers pooled funds to build a chapel that could house the statue in 1304, and soon enough the site had become a major stop on the pilgrimage route to Compostela in Spain. It proved too small to accommodate the steady trickle of pilgrims, so the Archers once again reached into their pockets and spent the late-15th and early-16th centuries converting the chapel into a splendid Gothic church. In fact, Charles the Bold married Margaret of York here in 1473, while work was still in progress. The enormous interior is warmed by the series of stained-glass windows that cast technicolour light into the shadows when the sun shines. The prettiest are the row of seven windows above the altar which recount the life of the Virgin Mary, and the rose window mounted on the left as you enter via the south entrance. As was standard, a number of rich families were interred beneath the church until 1784 and numerous tombstones are embedded into the flagstones. Of particular interest, though, is the privately funded funeral chapel and crypt (located in the north transept) of the Taxis family, who controlled most of the postal service between 1516 and 1815.

Sat opposite is an excellent bakery, Le Pain Quotidien (page 85). Across the road from Eglise Notre Dame du Sablon is **Place du Petit Sablon.** This landscaped patch of grass was originally part of the main square, but was severed from it by the construction of Rue de la Régence in the late-19th century. Forty-eight statues representing the medieval guilds line its boundaries and at the centre stands a fountain topped with statues of the counts Egmont and Hoorn: members of the Confederacy of Noblemen who were famously executed on the Grand' Place in 1568 by King Philip II of Spain for taking part in the Iconoclastic Fury (page 7). The statue was once to be found in front of the Maison du Roi on the Grand' Place, marking the spot where the counts were beheaded, but it was moved here in 1890.

At the back of the park, on the other side of Rue Petits Carmes, is **Palais d'Egmont** [82–3 F4]. Closed to the public, it was originally built as a home for Count Egmont's mother, and today serves as the offices of the Ministry of Foreign Affairs.

Walk back down the other side of Place du Petit Sablon and turn left on to Rue de la Régence. Immediately on the left is the **Conservatoire Royal de Musique** [82–3 E4] (*30 Rue de la Régence;* ✆ *02 511 04 27; www.conservatoire.be*). Built between 1872 and 1876, it marks the spot where the Taxis family (see above) mansion once stood. It was replaced by the current neo-Renaissance building in the late-19th century by architect Jean-Pierre Cluysenaar, the man responsible for the Galeries Royale St-Hubert and whose bust stands in the garden, hidden behind railings. It hosts regular concerts and recitals – see the website for up-to-date listings – and groups of music students can often be seen milling around outside with their instrument cases.

Continue straight on, but take a shortcut via Rue Joseph Dupont on to Rue aux Laines and walk straight across the road into **Parc d'Egmont**. In front of you stands L'Orangerie tea room (✆ *02 513 99 48;* ⊕ *10.30–17.00*), and, to the right, a replica statue of Peter Pan gifted in 1924 by the children of London; the original still sits in Kensington Gardens. On the left you can peek over the railings to get a better look at the Palais d'Egmont.

Leave the park via the east entrance on to Boulevard de Waterloo, turn right and walk past designer shops, such as Versace, Gucci and Prada, until you reach Place Louise. Maintain your course on the right-hand side of the roundabout, head to the far side and turn into Rue des Quatre Bras, the second road on the right. This opens out on to Place Poelaert, at the centre of which stands an enormous monument dedicated to the Belgian soldiers who fought and died in World Wars I and II. Looming on the left is the mammoth **Palais de Justice** [82–3 D5/6] (*Place Poelaert;* ☏ *02 508 65 78;* ⊕ *09.00–15.00 Mon–Fri*), appropriately built on top of Galenberg or 'gallows hill' (a popular place for executions up until the 16th century) and placed here deliberately to cast a shadow over the Marolles district and remind the poor residents of what would befall them should they turn to a life of crime. Built between 1866 and 1880, it was – in its heyday – the largest building in the world. Its design was originally opened up as an international architecture contest in 1860, but a bout of poor entries led to Joseph Poelaert being asked to take on the project. It was perhaps a decision he lived to regret: the ambitious project ran massively over budget, and forced entire neighbourhoods from their homes, which were flattened to create the necessary space – a move that earned Poelaert the nickname of *skieven architek,* 'filthy architect' (still a form of slander today) – and to top things off he died insane four years before its completion. Legend has it he died at the hands of a Marollen witch who found one of his photos and began sticking pins in its head every night.

Ascend the steps towards the entrance; on the left and right are giant plaques honouring Kings Leopold I and II and Poelaert, and in front are forbidding brass doors. Renovations, which started in 2003, mean that large parts of the building are covered by scaffolding, but the inside retains its splendour and shows no traces of the fire started by German soldiers at the end of World War II. Sounds are lost in the vast central atrium and the 25 (predominantly empty) courtrooms. The building still serves as Belgium's Supreme Court of Law, and is open during working hours to lawyers meeting their clients. However, as long as you're quiet you're welcome to wander around and admire the mixture of ancient Egyptian, Babylonian and Greek-Roman architectural styles, including the Corinthian, Ionic and Doric columns that are as thick as tree trunks.

On exiting, turn to the left and take in the superb view of Brussels' skyline – you can make out the green dome of the Koekelberg Basilica in the centre, the Eglise de Chapelle behind that and – on the far right – the Atomium and, slightly closer, the Eglise Sts-Jean-et-Etienne-aux-Minimes. Viewing telescopes (costing €1) bring the view even closer.

Off to your left you'll see the free **glass lift** (⊕ *07.00–00.00 daily*) that takes you down to the Marolles district 20m below. It lands in Rue de L'Epée and from here exit via the northeast corner onto Rue des Minimes. On the left-hand side, where the path of the street shifts, turn around to see a **comic mural** (*91 Rue des Minimes*) entitled 'passe-moi l'ciel' that hides behind the house here. Further up on the right is the soot-stained **Eglise Sts-Jean-et-Etienne-aux-Minimes** [82–3 E4] (*62 Rue des Minimes;* ☏ *02 511 93 84;* ⊕ *10.00–13.00 Mon–Sat*), which was built between 1700 and 1715, at a time when architectural styles were changing from Flemish Baroque to neo-Classical. Founded in 1616 by the Minimes order of Italian monks, it was closed under French occuption and reopened in 1819. Today, it hosts classical music concerts alongside the regular church services.

Turn right as you exit the church and take the next left into Rue du Temple. Descend down the steps and then cut back left down Rue Haute towards the Palais de Justice. Just before you reach Square Pieter Brueghel again you'll pass **132 Rue Haute,** the gabled house where Renaissance artist Pieter Brueghel the Elder lived and worked between 1563 and 1569 – look for the plaque on the wall. His great-grandson, painter David Teniers, is also believed to have lived here.

Keep walking south and turn right into Rue des Capucins. On the corner stands a mural featuring Hergé's cartoon characters Quick and Flupke (*195 Rue Haute*). In the second section of Rue des Capucins that lies beyond Rue Blaes, you will

3

find two more **cartoon murals** either side of the same building. The first (*15 Rue des Capucins*) is a scene from Blondin and Cirage created by Jijé that depicts a monkey stealing fruit, and the second (*13 Rue des Capucins*) features the rotund and bearded missionary Odilon Verjus and sidekick Laurent (comic creation of Laurent Verron and Yann) offering a helping hand to an exotic beauty and her pet cheetah as seen in *Folies Zeppelin*.

Walk to the end of the street, turn left, and immediately left again on to Rue de Chevreuil. You're met with another **comic-strip scene** – this one is a sketch from *Boule et Bill* (*195 Rue du Chevreuil*) – and past this house, on the left, is **Les Bains de Bruxelles** [82–3 B5] (*28 Rue du Chevreuil;* ✆ *02 511 24 68;* ◷ *07.30–19.30 Mon–Fri; non-Bruxellois adult/concession €4/€2.30*), the last functioning public bathing house in the capital. A century ago, many households lacked private bathing facilities, and families, especially from working-class backgrounds, were reliant on these public pools to get clean. The baths are still open today and the third-floor swimming pool has large glass windows at one end offering unusual rooftop views of Rue des Capucins. It's hardly smart, but certainly off the beaten track.

Immediately to the right of Rue du Chevreuil is the open **Place du Jeu de Balle** [82–3 B/C5], site of the famous daily flea market Marché aux Puces (◷ *07.00–14.00*).

Leave via the southeastern corner, near the Skieven Architek brasserie, and walk along Rue de la Rasière, which crosses half-a-dozen streets lined with uniform rows of brick and balcony tenements. Named **Cité Hellemans** [82–3 B6] (*174–94 Rue Blaes & 174–98 Rue Pieremans*) after their architect, the social housing was built in 1913 and considered revolutionary at the time because each had ventilation and contained a flushing toilet, instead of the communal courtyard bowl that was standard in poor neighbourhoods.

Rue de la Rasière leads you back on to Rue Haute. From here turn right and walk south towards the ivy-covered **Porte de Hal** [82–3 B7] (✆ *02 534 15 18; www. kmkg-mrah.be;* ◷ *09.30–17.00 Tue–Fri, 10.00–17.00 Sat–Sun; adult/13–17/under 13/BrusselsCard €5/€4/free/free, first Wed of month free from 13.00*), which dates from 1381 and is the last rampart of Brussels' seven medieval city gates. Stronghold of the fearsome Duke of Alva during Philip II's tyrannical reign, it was saved from demolition during Leopold II's expansion plans in the mid-19th century and opened to the public as a museum of weapons in 1847, making it one of the first museums in Europe. Between 1868 and 1871 the gate was restored and the conical towerhead added. Its collections of armour were transferred to the Musée de l'Armée in Parc du Cinquantenaire and today it houses a museum showing what Brussels was like during the Middle Ages.

To return to the city centre take the prémétro from stop Porte de Hal, found just off to the right.

Place Royale, Mont des Arts and Parc des Bruxelles walk

Start: Place des Martyrs
Nearest métro: Ⓜ De Brouckère/Rogier
Walking time: 4hrs; see maps, pages 78–9 and 82–3

This walk follows on well from the St Cathérine locale route (page 103). From its conclusion in front of the Théâtre de la Monnaie, it's a short walk to the cobbled **Places des Martyrs** where this walk, which leads you through the Upper Town, begins. The neo-Classical square was created in 1775 and at its centre is a monument erected in memory of the Belgians who died in the fight for independence in 1830; their crypt still lies below.

Exit the square via Rue du Persil, turn left into Rue du Marais, and take the first right into Rue des Sables. Halfway along this street is the **Centre Belge de la Bande Dessinée** [78–9 F5] (*20 Rue des Sables;* \ *02 219 19 80; www.cbbd.be;* ⊕ *10.00–18.00 Tue–Sun; adult/concession/under 12/Brussels Card €8/6/3/free*). The Belgian Centre for Comic-Strip Art is housed in the former Waucquez warehouse – a fabric and textiles shop designed by Victor Horta in 1906. The great vaulted-glass ceiling was designed to let the daylight pour in, so that the ladies could see the true colours of the cottons and silks they were purchasing. Described by French writer Émile Zola as ' a palace of dreams', it's a heady tangle of twisted iron railings, tiered balconies and scrolled columns. The permanent exhibitions cover the various stages of production and the second floor is dedicated exclusively to Belgian comic artists, including greats like Hergé and Marc Sleen. Young children will probably not be enthralled by the bland rows of glass boxes, but there are several cartoon characters dotted around the museum that make good photo opportunities.

On leaving the museum, cut straight across Rue St-Laurent and walk up the stairs to busy Boulevard Pachéco. At the top of the flight of stairs is a giant **statue of Gaston Lagaffe** – the main character from a comic strip created by André Franquin, which follows the day-to-day life of this lazy, accident-prone office junior who works at the Journal de Spirou (the company that publishes the strip) and has a hyperactive pet cat.

Turn right and head south along Boulevard de Berlaymont, keeping the Banque Nationale de Belgique on your left. Take the first street on your left, which should lead you on to Place St-Gudule, and in front, perched on a slightly raised hill, is the commanding **Cathédrale des St-Michel et St-Gudule** [78–9 F7] (*Parvis St Gudule;* \ *02 217 83 45; www.cathedralestmichel.be;* ⊕ *07.00–18.00 Mon–Fri, 08.30–15.30 Sat, 14.00–18.00 Sun; free*). An oratory dedicated to St Michael the Archangel – patron saint of travellers and of Brussels – was first built here during the 9th century. This was replaced by a Romanesque version in the 11th century and during the same period it gained its current name when the relics of St Gudule – the daughter of a 7th-century count who tended the sick and poor and was famous for her dedication to prayer despite the devil playing tricks on her – were transferred here from the St-Géry chapel. Building of the current Gothic-style cathedral commenced in 1226 but took over 300 years to complete. As a result, the structure is a mixture of architectural styles: the nave forms the oldest part; the square towers were completed in the 15th century, and the side Chapelle du St-Sacrament and Notre Dame de la Delivérance were finished by the mid-17th century. Restoration work throughout the 1980s and 1990s uncovered preserved remnants of the old Romanesque church (⊕ *08.00–18.00 daily; €1*) and crypt; the site is located to the left of the entrance and via a series of mirrors visitors can glimpse the old 'Westbau' (a section of the church reserved as a place of refuge for residents), the original round towers and the church entrance.

Inside, the first feature to steal your attention is the magnificent 18th-century pulpit, carved from a single chunk of oak. The Tree of Knowledge growing from the base is flanked by Adam and Eve being chased from paradise and, further up, skeletons representing death and sin. The Virgin Mary stands atop the pulpit along with the infant Jesus and together they plunge a cross into the head of the serpent. The 12 stars circling her head represent the 12 tribes of Israel.

Also of note are the statues of the 12 apostles that line the nave, sculpted by Jérôme Dusquesnoy the Younger (his dad made the present-day copy of Manneken Pis) and Luc Fayd'herbe, and some splendid Renaissance stained-glass windows, the most famous of which stands in the north transept and features Charles V and

Isabelle of Portugal, kneeling in front of the holy sacrament. Left of the choir is the Blessed Sacrament of the Miracle chapel, which contains the church's 16th-century treasury (⊕ *10.00–12.30 & 14.00–17.00 Mon–Fri, 10.00–12.30 & 14.00–15.00 Sat, 14.00–17.00 Sun; €1)*. The cathedral was promoted to its current status in 1962 and is the venue for royal weddings.

Once back outside, turn right and head up Rue du Bois Sauvage. You will quickly come to the **Musée de la Banque Nationale de Belgique** [78–9 F7](*10 Rue du Bois Sauvage;* \ *02 221 22 06; www.nbbmuseum.be;* ⊕ *10.00–18.00 Tue–Sun; adult/ concession/under 12/BrusselsCard €5/4/free/free, free Sat & Sun & first Wed of month from 13.00)* situated on the right. The focus of this quiet museum is, of course, money. Learn about the stockmarkets, the secret features embedded in banknotes and the reason behind the conversion to the euro.

Afterwards, continue straight on along Rue de Ligne and walk north until you reach Place du Congrès. Standing tall on the left is the **Colonne du Congrès**. Another of Joseph Poelaert's creations, this 25m-high column was erected in 1850 to commemorate the National Congress of 1831 that laid out the Belgian Constitution. A bronze statue of Leopold I sits at the top and the figures seated at the four corners represent the freedoms of association, education, the press and public worship. An eternal flame also rests at the base of the plinth; it pays homage to the Belgian soldiers who died in World Wars I and II.

Leave the square via Rue du Congrès and when you reach Place de la Liberté, take the first street on the left and walk north along Rue de l'Association. Take your first right and follow Rue de Révolution to Place des Barricades. On the eastern edge, at Place des Barricades 4, is the former family home of French writer **Victor Hugo**, who lived here from 1866 until 1871. A plaque outside bears his signature and engraved in gold are the words: *Je me sens le frère de tous les hommes et l'hôte de tous les peuples* ('I feel myself the brother of all men and the guest of all peoples').

After this, there's a brisk stroll south along Rue du Nord, across Place Surlet and down Rue Ducale, until you come to the corner of Parc de Bruxelles. Quickly pay attention to Rue Ducale 51 (just across the road) where there is a plaque commemorating the stay of English Romantic poet **Lord George Byron** (1788–1824), who resided at the house in spring 1816 in order to escape an acrimonious separation from his wife, Anne Isabella Milbanke. He is believed to have penned the third canto of his masterpiece *Childe Harold's Pilgrimage* here.

Now turn into Rue de la Loi, passing the U-shaped **Palais de la Nation** (*1–2 Pl de la Nation*), which hosts the plenary sessions of the Belgian Senate and Chamber of Representatives.

Cross the street at the pedestrian crossing and enter the **Parc de Bruxelles** [82–3 H1/2] via the entrance opposite. Once the hunting ground of the dukes, this central 13-hectare park was laid out in 1774. Dotted with 19th-century statues, its glory days as a fighting ground for the Belgians and Dutch in the struggle for independence in 1830 are long gone and the green space seems rather bland. However, some say the uniform design is no accident. The shapes formed by the layout of the paths and positioning of the ponds easily create symbols like the compass and square that form the insignia of the Freemasons – a secret brotherhood that has been in existence since the 1600s. Charles of Lorraine, who commissioned the design, was a member, and further clues like the the small water pool (located in the bottom right-hand corner of the park) with the word 'Vitriol' – an acronym for the Latin saying: *Visita Interiora Terrae Rectificando Invenies Occultum Lapidem* which speaks of self-knowledge – carved upside down into the stone, serve to fuel the rumour mill further.

Leave the park via the southeast corner. In front of you stands the oblong and symmetrical **Palais des Académies** (*1 Rue Ducale;* \ *02 550 23 23; www.kvab. be*) that was built between 1823 and 1826 for the Prince of Orange, who stayed in residence here until 1830. It now houses the Académie Royale Flamande de Belgique des Sciences et des Arts and is closed to the public.

Now walk along the wide Place des Palais where, stretching out at the southern tip of Parc de Bruxelles, is the **Palais Royal** [82–3 G3] (*Pl des Palais;* \ *02 551 20 20;* ⊕ *Jul–mid-Sep 10.30–16.30 Tue–Sun*). Not as impressive as you might hope, the official palace is the not the seat of residence for the Belgian royal family – since the death of Queen Astrid in 1935 they have lived at the Domaine Royale in Laeken (page 128) – but used instead for state meetings. It is also where the king grants his audiences. It started life as a series of mansions constructed in 1781, and was unified by the current façade in 1904. Inside is a maze of grand rooms and royal portraits, but of more interest are the three works of modern art installed in 2002. In the mirror room is a stunning ceiling, known as *Heaven of Delight*, studded with the wings of 1.4 million emerald Thai jewel beetles; on the ground floor are seven minimalist paintings by Marthe Wéry (1930–2005); and in the rooms flanking the grand staircase are a series of portrait photographs of King Albert II and Queen Paola and the Laeken palace grounds. Perhaps most intriguing is the fourth work of art housed in the Empire Room. Entitled *Les Fleurs de Palais Royal*, it features 11 shallow, golden bowls filled with earth from each of the 11 Belgian provinces. From the earth grows glass flowers, and engraved on each are small stories (in numerous languages) relating the history of the various regions.

In the far right wing of the palace is the **Musée BELvue** [82–3 G2] (*7 Pl des Palais;* \ *02 545 08 00; www.belvue.be;* ⊕ *10.00–17.00 Tue–Fri,10.00–18.00 Sat–Sun; adult/concession/under 18s/BrusselsCard €5/3/free/free, combined ticket with Palais Coudenberg €8*), which occupies the former residence of Leopold II and Queen Astrid, and the interior retains its formal splendour. The museum relates the history of Belgium and its monarchs via a super collection of photographs, historical documents, film clips, press cuttings and uniforms donated by the royal family. The information on the country's kings is somewhat biased; for instance, there is no mention of the thousands of Congolese who died in Africa under the reign of Leopold II.

From inside the museum you can also gain access to **Palais Coudenberg** [82–3 G2] (*7 Pl de Palais;* \ *070 22 04 92; www.coudenberg.com;* ⊕ *10.00–17.00 Tue–Fri,10.00–18.00 Sat–Sun; adult/concession/under 18s/BrusselsCard €5/3/free/free, audio guide €2.50, combined ticket with Musée BELvue €8*), an archaeological site exploring the remains of the enormous medieval Coudenberg Palace that stood on Place Royale from the 11th to the late-18th centuries. It was first built as a fort that abutted the old city walls, but when these were torn down and replaced further away, the residence was transformed into a palace and the landscaped gardens and orchards expanded in all directions. It was the seat of residence of Europe's ruling powers for over six centuries and called home by the dukes of Brabant and Burgundy, Emperor Charles V, and the Archduke Albert and Archduchess Isabella. Sadly, the majority of the palace was destroyed in 1731 by a fire that started in the apartments of a governess.

What remains is a basic, albeit atmospheric and eerie, layout of under-lit brick walkways and vaulted ceilings. The programme sold at reception or the guided tours do help to bring everything to life. The biggest rooms are the kitchens and larders that sat beneath the lavish Aula Magna banquet hall built by Philip the Good in the 14th century, which hosted meetings held by the knights of the Order of the Golden Fleece and was where Emperor Charles V abdicated in 1555.

Continuing with the walk, leave Place de Palais and turn right into Rue Royale. You'll quickly come to one of the entrances for the **Palais des Beaux-Arts** [82–3 G2] (*23 Rue Ravenstein;* ✎ *02 507 82 00; www.bozar.be;* ⊕ *10.00–18.00 Tue, Wed, Fri–Sun, 10.00–21.00 Thu, see also page 90*). Better known as **BOZAR,** this fine arts centre contains a theatre and concert hall and hosts a wide range of temporary exhibitions. After several funding delays, work on the building started in 1922. However, Victor Horta (page 355), its designer, is said to have been thoroughly miffed with city officials, who insisted that shops should line the street front on Rue Ravenstein and that parts of the 'palace' should be sunk underground so the height of the building would not obstruct the King's view of the Lower Town from the Palais Royal. In his memoirs, Horta writes 'Palace? That is not how I think of it: just an arts centre'.

Now turn left down Rue Baron Horta; at the bottom of the steps on the left-hand side is the newly renovated **Musée du Cinéma** (page 91).

Further down on your left is a plaque (mounted on 23 Rue Ravenstein) that marks the spot where the **Heger** *pensionnat,* or girls boarding school, once stood. Novelists Emily and Charlotte Brontë taught English and music here in 1842 in return for French and German tuition and free board. Charlotte returned a year later and fell in love with the head of the school. The protagonist in her first novel *The Professor,* William Crimsworth, is believed to be modelled on him and her experiences in Brussels.

Cross Rue Ravenstein and walk into the covered **Galerie Ravenstein** that heads back down the hill to emerge at the back of Gare Centrale. Now turn left and within 100m you'll reach Place de l'Albertine. In the centre stands a demure Queen Elizabeth holding flowers and opposite her, marking the beginning of the Mont des Arts, is **a statue of Albert I** dressed in military regalia on horseback.

To your left is an archway that features a large **carillon clock** decorated with 12 Belgian historical figures; these move on the hour when the clock chimes and plays alternate Walloon and Flemish songs.

To your right is the massive **Bibliothèque Royale de Belgique** [82–3 E2] (*4 Blvd de l'Empereur;* ✎ *02 519 53 11; www.kbr.be;* ⊕ *09.00–19.00 (17.00 Jul & Aug) Mon–Fri, 09.00–17.00 Sat; closed during holidays*). On the third floor is the **Musée du Livre/Archives et Musée de la Littérature** (*4 Blvd de l'Empereur;* ✎ *02 519 55 82; www.aml.cfwb.be;* ⊕ *09.00–17.00 Mon–Fri; closed during holidays*), a small room which holds some of the original illuminated manuscripts owned by the Burgundians, as well as an early printed text from Japan (dating from AD770) and the earliest book printed in Europe, which is around 500 years old. The corridor leading to the museum is lined with reconstructed rooms like Emile Verhaeren's study, Henry van de Velde's library and so forth – all contain original letters, drawings, photographs and books belonging to artists. On the fifth floor is a café (⊕ *09.00–16.15 Mon–Fri*) with rooftop views of the city.

Returning to the Albert I statue, you'll be looking across landscaped gardens and the **Mont des Arts**, the collective name given to the dozen or so museums and cultural sites that cover this hill. Highlights include the Musées Royaux des Beaux-Arts, Musée Magritte, the ruins of the medieval Palais Coudenberg and the Musée BELvue. At the weekend you can buy a special one-day pass (*adult/ concession/under 13 €11/5.50/free*) that permits entry to all of the buildings in this cultural quarter.

Walk through the gardens and up the steps and turn into Rue du Musée – found immediately on the right – which opens on to Place du Musée. Right beside you, shining white and concave, is the **Palais de Charles de Lorraine** (*1 Pl du Musée;*

✎ *02 519 57 86;* ⏰ *13.00–17.00 Wed–Sat; adult/concession/under 13s €3/2/free).* Built on top of the old Palais de Nassau, it served as the grand home of Charles of Lorraine, the Governor of the Austrian Netherlands, from 1744 to 1780. A patron of the sciences and a passionate amateur art collector, Lorraine left behind a broad array of items, from scientific instruments and sculptures to hunting guns, musical instruments, porcelain, tapestries, maps and the like. All now fill the beautifully restored five salons, which are all that remain of the original palace and are certainly worth a look.

Next door to the palace is the lavish **Chapelle Protestante** (*2 Pl du Musée;* ✎ *02 513 23 25;* ⏰ *10.30–11.30 Sun*), Lorraine's private chapel that he had built in 1760. After his death it wasn't greatly used, so when Napoleon assumed power he handed it over to the city's Protestant community, hence its current name. King Leopold I attended Sunday services here, as did the Brontë sisters when they lived in Brussels in 1842.

Head up the hill towards **Place Royale**, which forms the heart of the Royal Quarter and the peak of the Upper Town. You'll notice trams rattling around a **statue of crusade leader Godefroid de Bouillon** mounted on a noble steed and raising a flag on high. Erected in 1848, it marks the spot where he urged the Flemish to join his mission in capturing Jerusalem. The rest of the square has remained virtually unchanged since the late-18th century when Charles of Lorraine employed Gilles Barnabé Guimard, a popular French architect of the day, to design a plaza that would sit on top of the ruins left by the fallen Coudenberg Palace (page 113).

Immediately on your right is the **Musées Royaux des Beaux-Arts** [82–3 F3] (*3 Rue de la Régence;* ✎ *02 508 32 11; www.fine-arts-museum.be;* ⏰ *10.00–17.00 Tue–Sun, last entry 16.00; adult/concession/under 13/BrusselsCard €8/5/free/free, free entry on first Wed of month, combi ticket with Musée Magritte €13, audio guide €4*), made up of the co-joined **Musée d'Art Ancien** and **Musée d'Art Moderne**. Their combined artworks span seven centuries and form one of Europe's most complete collections. The former is world famous for its comprehensive collection of Flemish Primitive (page 19) paintings. The main masterpieces to look for include Rogier van der Weyden's *Portrait of Anthony of Burgundy*, which depicts the illegitimate child of Philip the Good, who wears the chain of the Order of the Golden Fleece about his neck and holds an arrow to denote his membership of the Archers' Guild; *The Ordeal by Fire* from the *Justice of Emperor Otto III* panels painted by Dieric Bouts, which captures the tale of an empress who accused a man of adultery when he refused her advances, but was proven innocent after death when his widow undergoes an ordeal by fire by holding a red-hot iron bar in her hand; Hans Memling's *The Martyrdom of St Sebastian*, who was shot to death by royal archers for converting to Christianity; an assortment of paintings by Hieronymous Bosch including *Calvary with Donor* that depicts the crucifixion of Jesus; Gerard David's *Virgin and Child*, which unusually shows Virgin Mary without her halo and an ordinary (rather than divine) baby Jesus tucking into his milk soup; and *The Census at Bethlehem* painted by perhaps the best Primitive of them all, Pieter Brueghel the Elder. Renowned for his everyday life scenes and earthy tones, he relocates Mary and Joseph from Judea to a wintry Brabant village.

Moving on to the 17th and 18th centuries, you'll see Peter Paul Rubens' *The Ascent to Calvary* and Jacob Jordaen's *Allegory of Fertility,* which features the Goddess of Abundance, Pomona, draped in a red cloak.

For works produced after the 18th century, cross over to the **Musée d'Art Moderne.** At the time of research it was closed for renovations, but it's due to reopen at the end of 2012. Artworks of note include Jacques-Louis David's *Death of Marat,* Fernand Khnopff's *Caresses* featuring an androgynous figure touching heads with

3

a cheetah bearing a woman's face, and James Ensor's chilling *Shocked Masks* that shows a wife catching her husband drinking. There are also works by Surrealists Paul Delvaux and Réne Magritte, sculptor Constantin Meunier, and Impressionists Théo van Rysselberghe and Henry van de Velde.

Next door is the superb **Musée Magritte** [82–3 F3] (*1 Pl Royale;* \ *02 508 31 11; www.musee-magritte-museum.be;* ⊕ *10.00–17.00 Tue, Thu–Sun, 10.00–20.00 Wed; adult/student/under 18s/BrusselsCard €8/2/free/free, combiticket with Musées Royaux des Beaux-Arts €13*), which pays homage to the prolific Belgian Surrealist, René Magritte. It draws together works belonging to the Musées Royaux des Beaux-Arts and items donated by his wife Georgette to create the world's most comprehensive collection of his oil paintings, drawings, sculptures, films and photographs, including *Olympia*, a nude portrait modelled on Georgette that was stolen in 2009 during the museum's first week of opening. It was returned in 2012 after the €75,000 ransom was paid. Don't miss it! See also page 128. Because it's fairly new, the museum is incredibly popular. To save yourself shuffling around the exhibits with the rest of the crowds, try and visit first thing in the morning or late in the afternoon.

Exit the square via Rue Montagne de la Cour and find the unmissable and much-photographed Old England Art Nouveau building which houses the **Musée des Instruments de Musique (MIM)** [82–3 F2](*2 Rue Montagne de la Cour;* \ *02 545 01 30; www.mim.fgov.be;* ⊕ *09.30–17.00 Tue–Fri, 10.00–17.00 Sat–Sun; adult/concession/under 13s/BrusselsCard €5/4/free/free*). The building, which dates from 1899, was originally built as a department store for a British clothing company. The music museum contains a world-class collection of over 7,000 musical instruments – a fraction of which are spread over the four floors. There's a constant buzz of to-ing and fro-ing musicians heading to lessons and workshops. Kids can experiment with instruments in the Jardin d'Orphée, while adults can listen to excerpts ranging from ancient Greek melodies to Flemish folk. Regular performances (*usually 20.00 Thu*) are held on the top-floor auditorium, where you'll also find a café with excellent views over the city.

Follow the curve of Rue Ravenstein round, past the Mont des Arts gardens, and look for the stepped gable of **Hôtel Ravenstein** (*3 Rue Ravenstein*) set slightly back from the road. Henry VIII's fourth wife, Anne of Cleves, was born in this aristocratic 15th-century Gothic mansion that is the last of its kind in the city.

This concludes the walk, and from here you can either head back to Bruxelles-Central or pick up a quarter of the way through the Sablons and Marolles district walk listed on page 106.

EU Quarter and Parc du Cinquantenaire walk

Start: Square Marie-Louise
Nearest métro: M̄ Maelbeek
Walking time: 2hrs; see map, pages 118–19

Situated outside the petit-ring, the EU Quarter and Parc du Cinquantenaire form an extended pocket of Brussels city centre that was tacked on during the reign of Leopold II. He acquired the former exercise grounds of the Civic Guards and transformed them into a grand park joined to the old city centre by the arrow-straight Rue de la Loi.

Start the walk by exiting Maelbeek métro station, turning left and heading north down Avenue Livingstone. You will soon reach **Square Marie-Louise**, dominated by its large pond – one of the last remaining pools formed by the

Maelbeek River that once ran through the city. The area around the pond is littered with examples of Art Nouveau architecture, so keeping the body of water on your right, turn into Rue Ortelius, the first street on the left, and then take the next available right turn on to Rue Philippe le Bon. Here, at No 70, is the understated **Maison de Victor Taelemans**, named after the architect who built this as his own home in 1901. Just around the corner, at Square Gutenberg No 5 and No 8, are two houses built in 1898 and designed by Brussels-born architect Armand van Waesberghe (1879–1949).

Walk around the northern edge of the Square Marie-Louise pond. On the right-hand side of the grassy knoll is the **Maison van Eetvelde** (*2–4 Av Palmerston*), built by Victor Horta in 1895 for Baron Edmond van Eetvelde, colonial minister and an advisor of Leopold II. On the other side of the grass is another of Victor Horta's projects, the **Hôtel Deprez-van de Velde** (*3 Av Palmerston*) that was built just a year later in 1896. Both are closed to individual visitors, but can be visited as part of a guided tour run by Arau (✆ *02 219 33 45; www.arau.org*).

Skirt around the northern edge of **Square Ambiorix** and you'll pass the ornate façade of the **Maison St-Cyr** (*11 Sq Ambiorix*). Barely four metres wide, it is one of the prettiest (and most distinctive) examples of Art Nouveau in the city. It was built in 1903 by Gustave Straven – a pupil who had collaborated with Victor Horta on the Hôtel Deprez-van de Velde – for the painter Léonard St-Cyr. The residence is still privately owned and closed to the public.

Instead of ascending the small flight of steps up to Square Marguérite, follow the road round and take the third street on your left, Rue Archimède. Stroll to the end until you come out at the busy Rond-point Schuman. Across the road is the Council of European Communities and immediately to your right is the notorious **Berlaymont** building, designed by Lucien de Vestel. Home to the European Commission and the offices of some 3,000 cabinet members, the high-rise, cross-shaped building is the most important in the EU Quarter. It was originally unveiled in 1969, but had to be closed in 1991 to remove the asbestos wrapped around its steel structure. It was a huge job that ran massively over schedule and budget and sent waves of grumbles rippling across all levels of EU administration and city inhabitants. It was finally given the all-clear in 2006.

Head east towards the main entrance of the **Parc du Cinquantenaire** [118–19 E5] (☉ *Oct–April 08.00–18.00, May–Sep 08.00–21.00*). These spacious grounds were laid out as part of exhibition plans drawn up by Leopold II to mark the first 50 years of Belgian independence. It's fairly quiet for most of the year, popular mainly with joggers, but come summer (late-July–late-August) residents arrive in their cars to watch the latest Hollywood blockbusters that are shown on an open-air movie screen on Friday and Saturday evenings.

Several statues and monuments are dotted around the gardens, including Constantin Meunier's *The Reaper* and a statue known as the green dog – rubbing its legs is supposed to bring luck. The most notable monument in the park is the **Horta Pavilion** which houses the **Pavillon des Passions Humaines** (☉ *14.30–15.30 Tue–Fri; €2*), a bas-relief sculpture carved from great slabs of Carrara marble by Antwerp-born Jef Lambeaux (1852–1908). A young Victor Horta was employed to build a pavilion – one of his first projects – that would protect the sculpture, but he was never able to finish. Upon its unveiling in 1898 the public were horrified by the mass of naked and intertwined bodies (partaking in various sexual acts) that Lambeaux had sculpted. There was a rushed inauguration ceremony and three days later the doors to the pavilion were permanently locked. Poor Lambeaux was dubbed 'Michaelangelo of the gutter' and suffered a dramatic slump in commissions. Rules

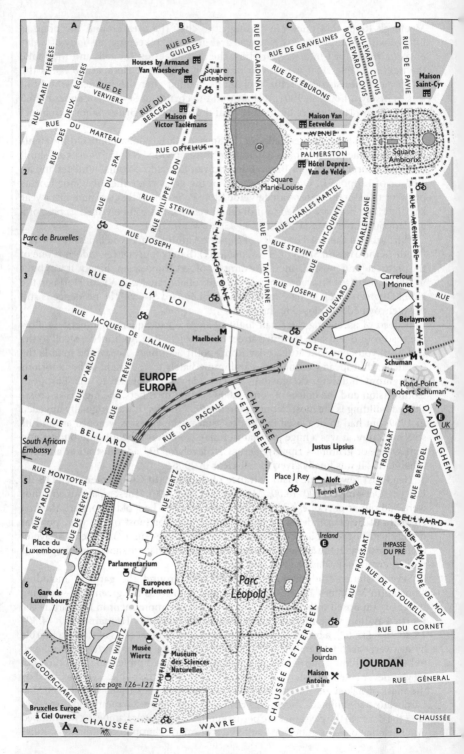

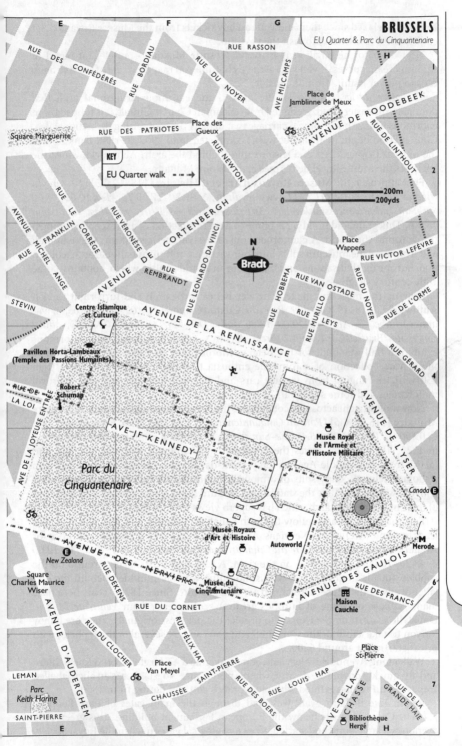

BRUSSELS
EU Quarter & Parc du Cinquantenaire

RUE RASSON

RUE DES CONFÉDÉRÉS
RUE BORDIAU
RUE DU NOYER
AVE MILCAMPS
Place de
Jamblinne de Meux
AVENUE DE ROODEBEEK
RUE DE LINTHOUT

Square Marguerite
RUE DES PATRIOTES
Place des Gueux
RUE NEWTON

KEY
EU Quarter walk

AVENUE FRANKLIN
RUE MICHEL ANGE
RUE LE CORRÈGE
RUE VÉRONÈSE
AVENUE DE CORTENBERGH
RUE LEONARDO DA VINCI
RUE REMBRANDT
AVENUE DE RENAISSANCE
RUE HOBBEMA
RUE VAN OSTADE
RUE DU NOYER
Place Wappers
RUE VICTOR LEFÈVRE
RUE DE L'ORME
RUE MURILLO
RUE LEYS
RUE GÉRARD

0 ———— 200m
0 ———— 200yds

N
Bradt

STEVIN
Centre Islamique et Culturel

Pavillon Horta-Lambeaux
(Temple des Passions Humaines)

RUE DE LA LOI
Robert Schuman
AVE-JF-KENNEDY
AVE DE LA JOYEUSE ENTRÉE

Parc du Cinquantenaire

Musée Royal de l'Armée et d'Histoire Militaire

AVENUE DE L'YSER

Canada E

M Merode

Musée Royaux d'Art et Histoire
Autoworld

New Zealand
AVENUE DES NERVIENS
Square Charles Maurice Wiser
RUE DEKENS
Musée du Cinquantenaire
AVENUE DES GAULOIS
RUE DES FRANCS
Maison Cauchie

AVENUE D'AUDERGHEM
RUE DU CORNET
RUE DU CLOCHER
RUE FÉLIX HAP
SAINT-PIERRE
Place Van Meyel
CHAUSSÉE
RUE DES BOERS
RUE LOUIS HAP
Place St-Pierre
RUE DE LA GRANDE HAIE

LEMAN
Parc Keith Haring
SAINT-PIERRE
AVE-DE-LA-CHASSE
Bibliothèque Hergé

E F G H

have been relaxed since then and you can buy tickets from the Musées Royaux d'Art et d'Histoire (see below) to visit the pavilion.

Next door to the pavilion is Brussels' **Grande Mosque** – an elegant blend of smooth cream curves. If you visit at the right time you may hear one of the five daily calls to prayer issuing from the inside.

The *pièce de la resistance* of the park is the enormous **triumphal arch** that dominates its eastern end. Designed by Frenchman Charles Girault, it is topped by an enormous bronze horse-drawn carriage that depicts Brabant raising the national flag. Construction began in 1880, but wasn't completed until 1905. Its right flank houses the Musées Royaux d'Art et d'Histoire and (behind the arch) Autoworld, whilst the left hosts the Musée Royal de l'Armée et d'Histoire Militaire.

First approach the **Musées Royaux d'Art et d'Histoire** [118–19 G5] (*10 Parc du Cinquantenaire;* \ *02 741 72 11; www.mrah.be;* ⊕ *09.30–17.00 Tue–Fri, 10.00–17.00 Sat–Sun; adult/concession/under 13s/BrusselsCard €5/4//free/free, last admission 16.00*). This grand old building is home to a vast collection of art (except paintings) from around the world. A glamorous Louis XV-style carriage adorns the main hall and from here the museum splits into four sections: antiquity, national archaeology, non-European civilisations and European arts and crafts, which contains some 18th-century sleighs.

Leaving the museum, make your way beneath the arch and turn right to visit **Autoworld** [118–19 G6] (*11 Parc du Cinquantenaire;* \ *02 736 41 65; www. autoworld.be;* ⊕ *Apr–Sep 10.00–18.00 daily, Oct–Mar 10.00–17.00 daily; adult/ concession/BrusselsCard €6/4.70/free*) A boy's fantasy realised, this enormous exhibition hall was built for the Belgian Motor Show in 1902–34. It now houses the private collection of automobile enthusiast Ghislain Mahy, with more than 450 vehicles ranging from vintage cars and steam-driven contraptions, to royal motorcycles and some super cars.

Now walk straight across the cobbles into the **Musée Royal de l'Armée et d'Histoire Militaire** [118–19 G6] (*Parc du Cinquantenaire 3;* \ *02 737 78 33; www.klm-mra.be;* ⊕ *09.00–12.00 & 13.00–16.45 Tue–Sun; free*) – a sprawling exhibition hall, established in 1923. The museum traces the development of military weapons, armour, and tactics from the Middle Ages to the present day. Explore glass cabinets filled with elaborate helmets, shiny suits of armour, cannons, tanks, guns and a hangar filled with old war planes. Take the stairs up to the third floor, where you can access the top of the Cinquantenaire arch which has superb views over the park and city.

Exit the museum and follow the path situated to the right of Autoworld, which leads out onto Avenue des Nerviens. After a few paces you will pass the entrance for **Ateliers de Moulage** (*10 Parc du Cinquantenaire;* \ *02 741 72 94;* ⊕ *09.30–12.00 & 13.30–16.00 Tue–Fri; free*) on the right. A few stray busts laying around on the cobbles outside might give away this moulding workshop hidden behind the ivy-laden walls of the Musées Royaux d'Art et d'Histoire. Since 1876, artists here have made replicas off some of Europe's greatest sculptures – from *Venus de Milo* to Donatello's *Christ on the Cross* – to protect the priceless originals. They are happy for you to take a tour of the workshop and you can buy several of the replicas, with prices starting at around €200.

Walk along Avenue des Nerviens, across Avenue d'Auderghem, onto Rue Belliard and dip quickly down Rue de Mot, where (near house No 31) there's an alley labelled **Impasse du Pré** that is lined with old worker's cottages dating from 1850.

Rejoin Rue Belliard, walk west and through the main gates of **Parc Léopold** [118–19 C6], which sits below the European Parliament building. This green park overlooks a large pond and started life as a zoological garden when the Royal Society of Zoology bought the plot of land in 1851. The stone gates at the main entrance still bear the engraving 'Jardin Royale de Zoologie'. Unfortunately, the society filed for bankruptcy and it was made a public park. Follow the footpath up the hill to an exit on Rue Vautier. Turning right will bring you into Espace Léopold, the district littered with futuristic EU offices. Forming the main focus is the **European Union Parliament** headquarters, which is made up three buildings: the most distinctive of these is the oval-shaped Paul-Henri Spaak (*43 Rue Wiertz*), which stands on the right and houses the enormous 720-seat debating chamber, and is nicknamed Le Caprice des Dieux ('whim of the gods') after a similarly shaped cheese. The complex serves as a temporary seat for the parliament, which decamps to Strasbourg roughly ten times at year at a cost of around €100 million. European Union politics can be baffling, but a visit to the new **Parlamentarium** (*60 Rue Wiertz;* ☏ *02 283 22 22;* ◷ *13.00–18.00 Mon, 09.00–20.00 Tue–Wed, 09.00–18.00 Thu–Fri, 10.00–17.00 Sat–Sun; admission free*) should make things clear. It takes you on an interactive journey through European law making. Alternatively, join a free audio-guided tour (◷ *at 10.00 & 15.00 Mon–Thu, 10.00 Fri*). Register at the entrance 15 minutes prior to the start of the tour and bring some identification with you.

Return to Rue Vautier, and just after the entrance to the park, on the right-hand side of the streets is the former studio of 19th-century painter Antoine-Joseph Wiertz. It's now the **Musée Wiertz** [118–19 B7] (*62 Rue Vautier;* ☏ *02 648 17 18; www.fine-arts-museum.be;* ◷ *10.00–12.00 & 13.00–17.00 Tue–Fri; free*). Wiertz was known for two things: his ego and his obsession with Rubens. He was so keen to be remembered that he conceived this museum well before his death. He fought hard for the government to fund the construction of his new studio and, in return, promised to bequeath all his works and the studio back to the state. A large display of his sculptures can be seen here, as well as his most famous canvases: the *Deux Jeunes Filles* (Two Young Girls), *Les Grecs et les Troyens se disputant le corps de Patrocle* (The Greeks and the Trojans fighting over the body of Patrocles) and his gargantuan *La Chute des Anges Rebelles* (Fall of the Rebel Angels). The latter is a good example of Wiertz's ambition to replicate the physicality and romanticism of his heroes Rubens and Michelangelo, but which often tipped into the macabre or erotic.

Across the road is the 160-year old **Musée des Sciences Naturelles** [118–19 B7] (*Rue Vautier 29;* ☏ *02 627 42 38; www.naturalsciences.be;* ◷ *09.30–17.00 Tue–Fri, 10.00–18.00 Sat–Sun; adult/concession/under 5s/BrusselsCard €7/6/free/free*) This child-orientated natural history museum is famous for its collection of iguanodon skeletons discovered by coal miners at Bernissart (just west of Mons) in 1878. Other highlights include the Whale Hall, Shell Gallery, North Sea Discovery room and an insect gallery. There are several interactive sections including a paleoLAB (◷ *13.30, 14.30 & 15.30 Tue–Sun; €2.50*), where kids can uncover fossils using tools.

BRUSSELS' COMMUNES

The historic heart of the city centre occupies just one of the region's 19 municipalities or 'communes'. The remainder – including the EU quarter – are located outside the petit-ring and form residential districts which each have their own distinct character. Their tempo and vibe is determined by the broad array of ethnic groups that have settled in certain quarters of the city, and lend the capital its multicultural kudos. Each is governed by a mayor and left to organise its own local elections, social welfare system, road and buildings maintenance, and local law and order etc. Communes of most interest are covered (alphabetically) below.

ANDERLECHT *Nearest métro:* Ⓜ St Guidon

Situated to the west of Bruxelles-Midi/Brussels-Zuid, Brussels' third-largest commune is most famous for its successful football team – RSC Anderlecht – who train at Le Stade Constant Vandenstock.

Just a small village – famed for its cattle – in the 10th century, Anderlecht was incorporated into Brussels territory in 1393 after Louis of Male, Count of Flanders, lost the Battle of Scheut to Joanna Duchess of Brabant. During the Middle Ages Anderlecht was a well-known area: the cult of St Guidon had attracted pilgrims en route to Santiago de Compostela in Spain and a clutch of famous residents – like Desiderius Erasmus and the Duke of Aumale – had secured the area's reputation. Events lapsed until the19th century, when the town's population suddenly exploded as city folk looked for new areas to live away from the pollution of the city centre.

Until recently Anderlecht was largely missed off the tourist-trail tick list, but visitors are slowly starting to discover the attractions of this underrated district.

Musée des Égouts [123 G1] (*Pavillon de l'Octroi, Porte d'Anderlecht;* ✆ *02 279 60 62;* ⊕ *10.00–17.00 Tue–Fri; €3; tram: 51 & 82*) The underrated Brussels Sewer Museum introduces a little-seen side of the city with a great tour that takes you into the bowels of its Victorian sewerage system, which was implemented at the same time as the fetid River Senne was being covered and filled in around 1867. There's also a quirky display of objects that cropped up in the pipes, from wedding rings to revolvers. The entrance is hidden in one of the old port gates.

Maison d'Erasme [123 A/B3] (*31 Rue du Chapitre;* ✆ *02 521 13 83;* ⊕ *10.00–18.00 Tue–Sun; €1.25, inc entry to the béguinage (see below). Guided tours in English must be booked in advance through the curator, Kathleen Leys, by calling the number above or* e *kleys@anderlecht.irisnet.be;* ⊕ *10.00–12.00 & 14.00–17.00 Tue–Fri*) A gem of a museum dedicated to the life and works of Dutch humanist and theologian, Desiderius Erasmus of Rotterdam. An exceptional scholar, the Renaissance writer is best known for his translation of the New Testament from Greek into Latin. In 1521 he lived for five months in one of the St-Guidon collegial houses belonging to friend Pieter Wychman, before moving permanently to Basel in Switzerland. Today, the house contains a museum – highlights include a first edition of his seminal work *In Praise of Folly* (1509) and Flemish Primitive artworks – plus a world-class library of Erasmus literature and a small garden filled with 16th-century medicinal plants believed to have been used by Erasmus himself.

Béguinage d'Anderlecht [123 A3] (*8 Rue du Chapelain;* ✆ *02 521 13 83;* ⊕ *10.00–12.00 & 14.00–17.00 Tue–Sun; €1.25, inc entry to Maison d'Erasme*) The only surviving *begijnhof* in Brussels, it was built in 1252 from donations bestowed by a canon visiting L'Église St-Guidon as part of a pilgrimage en route to Santiago de Compostela in Spain. It has served as a folklore museum since the end of World War II and contains a restored kitchen, parlour, private bedchamber and exhibits featuring testimonies of rural life, and Roman and Frankish artefacts.

Collégiale St-Pierre et St-Guidon [123 A3] (*Place de la Vaillance;* ✆ *02 523 02 20;* ⊕ *09.00–12.00 & 14.00–17.30 Mon–Fri*) Quoted as the prettiest medieval church in Brussels, it was founded in the 11th century but rebuilt on the old Romanesque crypt in Gothic style when Anderlecht was brought under the charter of Brussels in 1393. Interred in the ancient crypt – thought to be one of the oldest

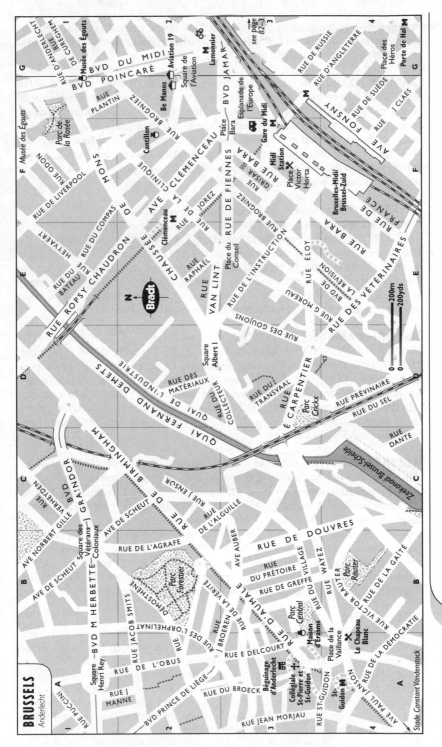

BRUSSELS
Anderlecht

see page 82–3

3

123

in Belgium – are the remains of St Guy, an 11th-century priest expelled from the Church after he squandered funds on a failed business plan and who spent the next seven years as a wandering pilgrim.

Cantillon [123 F2] (*56 Rue Gheude;* \ *02 521 49 28;* ⏰ *08.30–17.00 Mon–Fri, 10.00–17.00 Sat, €6 inc a free beer*) Seventy years ago, Brussels contained over 50 breweries. Today, Cantillon is the sole survivor. Established in 1900, the family brewery bottles it's own particular blend of three-year matured lambic, gueuze, faro and kriek beers and acts as a living museum to keep the city's history of brewing alive. You can wander around on your own, admiring century-old barrels, copper boiling vats and the cooling room, or book ahead for a guided tour – ask the son of the owner, Alastair Bouch, for more details.

ETTERBEEK *Nearest métros:* M̄ Mérode, Thieffrey and Pétillon
Etterbeek started life as a rural hamlet and took its name from the Maelbeek River – a tributary of the Senne – that meandered through it during the Middle Ages. By the 19th century Leopold II had set his sights on the area as the perfect space in which to expand and add elegance to his 'drab' newly independent capital. The result was the grand Parc du Cinquantenaire and rows of elegant mansions built as second homes by rich city traders. The commercial heart of the commune is known as 'La Chasse' and sits between arterial roads Chaussée de Wavre and Chaussée d'Auderghem.

Bibliothèque Hergé [118–19 H7] (*211 Av de la Chasse;* \ *02 735 05 86;* ⏰ *15.00– 18.00 Tue, 14.00–19.00 Wed, 10.00–18.00 Thu, 15.00–19.00 Fri, 09.00–13.00; tram: 81 & 21, Pl St-Pierre*) Hergé's greatest creations, Tintin and his dog Snowy, peek their heads out of a second-floor window on the right-hand side of this new library, whose 50,000-piece collection is open to the public – but shouldn't be confused with the Musée Hergé (page 135). You're welcome to flick through the novels, plays, essays etc in peaceful surroundings. The library often works with Fondation Hergé to produce exhibitions.

Maison Cauchie [118–19 H6] (*5 Rue des Francs;* \ *02 733 86 84;* ⏰ *first weekend of month 11.00–13.00 & 14.00–17.30; €5, cash only*) A highlight on the Art Nouveau trail, this private house dates from 1905 and was designed by architect, painter and decorator Paul Cauchie (1875–1952). The residence is most famous for its distinctive *sgraffiti* (a technique of layering, tinting and texturing plaster) façade, which bears female figures that represent the many faculties of the arts, including painting, music, sculpture and architecture. The entire building underwent careful restoration during the 1980s. Inside, the ground floor is still decorated with the original furniture, whilst the basement has been revived as an art studio and gallery displaying photographs and paintings belonging to the architect.

IXELLES/ELSENE *Nearest métro:* M̄ Louise
Ixelles is Brussels' best-known commune, famous for its Art Nouveau and Art Deco architecture, buzzing café-culture and African Matongé quarter – the most defined and celebrated of all the immigrant neighbourhoods in the region. Clustered around Porte de Namur, it sprang up during the 1950s when Belgium still owned the Congo, and grew considerably after the African state won independence in 1960 and President Mobutu's kleptocratic politics plunged the country into recession. Large numbers emigrated to Belgium, followed by citizens from other French-speaking countries like Rwanda, Burundi and Mali.

Musée d'Ixelles [126–7 G3] (*71 Rue Jean van Volsem;* ✆ *02 515 64 21; www.musee-ixelles.be;* ◷ *13.00–18.30 Tue–Fri, 10.00–17.00 Sat–Sun; free; prémétro: 81 & 82, Place Flagey*) Housed in the commune's former slaughterhouse, this small fine art museum houses a staggering 13,000 pieces of (predominately) Belgian and French art from the 19th and 20th centuries. Examples of Théo van Rysselberghe's neo-Impressionist paintings, Rik Wouters Fauvist sculptures, and Paul Delvaux and René Magritte's Surrealist paintings can all be found here, as well as Cubist pieces by Pablo Picasso.

Flagey Centre [126–7 G4] (*18 Pl Flagey*) Nicknamed *le paquebot*, or 'steamship' by locals, the mast of the Art Deco former radio broadcasting tower is highly distinctive. It was saved from demolition, and its conversion to a cultural centre has been a great success story for the commune. Café Belga (page 89) at its base is hugely popular with residents on Sunday mornings and weekday lunchtimes.

Hôtel Tassel [126–7 D4] (*9 Rue Paul-Emile Janson*) The UNESCO-listed Hôtel Tassel was built by Victor Horta for his friend Emile Tassel. Fresh from completing the Maison Autrique in Schaerbeek (page 131), and armed with a larger budget, Horta could finally implement the full extravagance of his designs to maximise light and space. When the house was completed in 1894, its exquisite attention to detail caused a sensation in the architectural community and changed the face of 19th–20th-century architecture overnight, cementing Horta's celebrity status. The house is still privately owned and therefore closed to the public, but the building's most revolutionary features – the central position of the front door, the large windows to let light in, the columns, and the rounded curves of the ironwork balconies – can still be seen from the street.

Hôtel Solvay [126–7 E/F4] (*224 Av Louise*) The construction of this house was the result of a commission hot off the back of the success of Hôtel Tassel. Built for Armand Solvay, son of the engineer and chemist Ernest Solvay, it was completed in 1898 and perhaps best known for its low balcony that allowed the family to sit and people-watch those walking along trendy Avenue Louise. The doorbell, house number, and rivets – all bear the Art Nouveau mark and in 2000 the house was added to the UNESCO World Heritage list.

Musée Constantin Meunier [126–7 F7] (*59 Rue de l'Abbaye;* ✆ *02 648 44 49; www.fine-arts-museum.be;* ◷ *10.00–12.00 & 13.00–17.00 Tue–Fri; free*) A celebrated painter and sculptor, Meunier (1831–1905) commissioned the construction of this house at the height of his fame with the sole intention it should serve as his last residence and studio. The small museum was acquired by the state in 1936 and opened to visitors in 1939. It showcases over 150 paintings and drawings executed during the latter half of Meunier's life, when he began to focus on the burgeoning industralisation in Belgium and, in particular, the mines in Wallonia. This later period of work inspired some of his greatest sculptures that are still dotted throughout Brussels today, including *Cheval à l'Abreuvoir* (*The Horse at the Pond*) on Square Ambiorix and the unfinished *Monument au Travail* (*Monument to Labour*) in Laeken. Meunier was interred at Cimetière d'Ixelles (see below).

Cimetière d'Ixelles [126–7 H7] (*Chaussée de Boondael*) One of the most important cemeteries in Belgium, the Ixelles graveyard was set up for victims of a cholera outbreak at the outset of the 19th century. It's the final resting place for a stellar line up of history's greats, including Art Nouveau master Victor Horta,

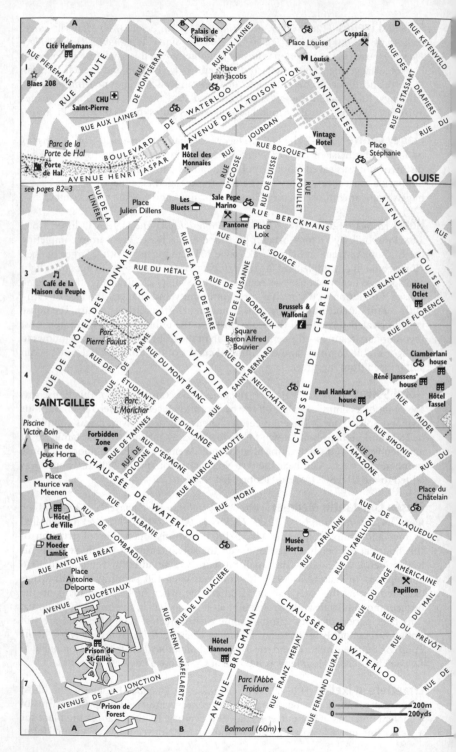

Balmoral (60m)

0   200m
0   200yds

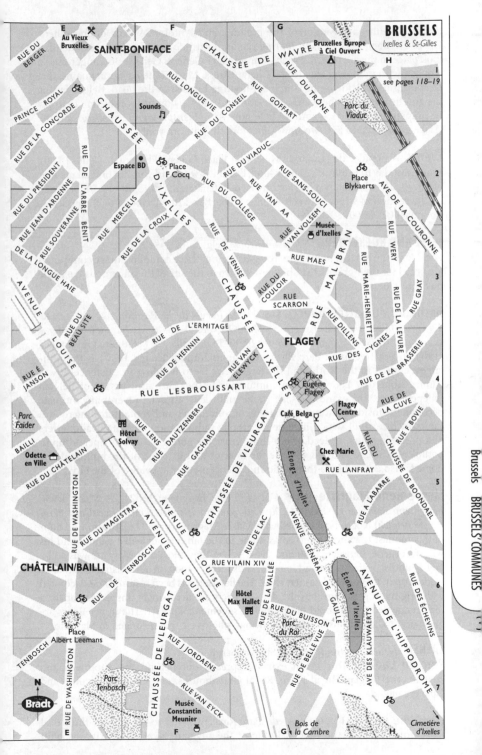

Frédéric Neuhaus (inventor of the praline), and Antoine Wiertz among others. On 10 October 1891 *Le Petit Journal* ran an illustration portraying a scandal that took place in the graveyard: French war minister General George Boulanger was so stricken with grief over the death of his mistress, Marguérite de Bonnemains, that he committed suicide on her tomb by shooting himself in the head. Before raising the gun he engraved the words *à bientôt* (and soon…) on her tombstone to imply his impending suicide – and the love note *Ai-je bien pu vivre 2 mois ½ sans toi!* (Have I managed to live two-and-a-half months without you!).

Events A popular daily market is held on Place Eugène Flagey (⏰ 07.00–13.00). From Monday to Friday it's mainly food, but at the weekend you can find all manner of things. There's usually a market on Place du Châtelain (⏰ 13.00– 19.30 Wed) and on the section of street between Avenue Gilbert and Rue Delbove on Chaussée de Boondael (⏰ 13.00–19.30 Thu).

JETTE AND KOEKELBERG *Nearest métro:* M̄ Belgica
Located in the northern tip of the Brussels region, these complimentary communes are noted for their green areas, but best known as the site of the enormous Basilique du Sacré-Coeur.

Basilique du Sacré-Coeur [74–5 B3] (*1 Parvis de la Basilique;* ☎ *02 425 88 22; www.basilicakoekelberg.be;* ⏰ *Mar–Oct 08.00–18.00 daily, viewing dome* ⏰ *summer 09.00–17.00 daily & winter 10.00–16.00 daily; €4;* M̄ *Simonis*) Ensconced at the end of tree-lined Parc Elizabeth, the mammoth Sacred Heart is the fifth-largest church in the world and the largest Art Deco building in existence. It was commissioned by Leopold II to commemorate the 75th anniversary of Belgian independence. The grandiose scale of the multi-level church prevents any intimate décor on the inside. However, the basement conceals a number of interesting rooms, the most bizarre of which include a Catholic radio station and the headquarters of a potholing club. Indeed, every three years the entire basilica is opened up to potholers who are allowed to scale the interior and exterior of the building! The dome is also accessible to the public and offers far-reaching views of the city.

Musée René Magritte [74–5 C2] (*135 Rue Esseghem;* ☎ *02 428 26 26; www. magrittemuseum.be;* ⏰ *10.00–18.00 Wed–Sun; adult/concession/BrusselsCard €7/5/ free;* M̄ *Belgica*) Not to be confused with Musée Magritte (page 116), the ground floor of this modest townhouse served as home to the famous Surrealist painter and his wife, Georgette, between 1930 and 1954. When they moved in Magritte was still a largely undiscovered artist and to make ends meet he took on advertising jobs that he worked on in the restored garden 'shed'. The flat itself has been restored and decorated with original furnishings, but the demure décor is surprisingly unspectacular for a man renowned for his bold philosophical statements and art. The upper floors are given over to collections of letters, drawings, photos etc that belonged to Magritte.

LAEKEN *Nearest métro:* M̄ Heysel/Stuyvenbergh
Parc du Laeken This green expanse spreads out behind the Atomium and contains the Belgian Royal Place, Royal Greenhouses, and Chinese Pavilion and Japanese pagoda.

Domaine Royal [129 G4] (*Av du Parc Royal*) Closed to the public, the Royal Palace of Laeken is the official home of the Belgian royal family. It was built

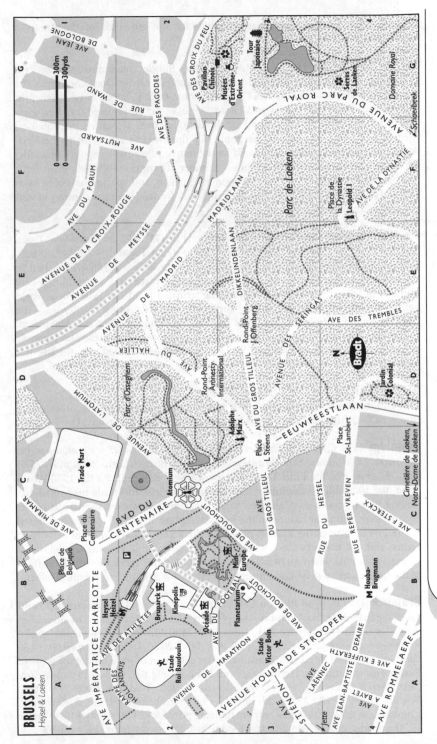

BRUSSELS
Heysel & Laeken

129

in Louis XVI-style as a summer residence for the governor of the Austrian Netherlands in 1784.

Serres de Laeken [129 G4] (*Av du Parc Royale; www.monarchie.be; €3;* M̲ *Bockstael, then bus 53*) Situated inside the gardens of the Domaine Royal, the Royal Greenhouses were built in 1873 by Alphonse Balat (Victor Horta's teacher) at the behest of Leopold II. This neo-Classical series of structures used the latest glass and metal construction technology for the time. For over a century, the botanical gardens have been opened to the public for three weeks every spring between April and May (exact dates are issued by the tourist office from January onwards) when the collections – which include a number of rare plant species, giant ferns and banana trees, an important collection of camellias, and specimens dating from Leopold's reign – come into bloom. Belgians flock from all over the country to visit the site, so be prepared to queue.

Pavillon Chinois and Tour Japonaise [129 G3] (*44 Av Jules van Praet;* ❧ *02 268 16 08; www.kmkg-mrah.be;* ☉ *09.30–17.00 Tue–Fri, 10.00–17.00 Sat–Sun; adult/concession/under 13s/BrusselsCard €4/3/free/free;* M̲ *Heysel*) Located in the northern corner of Parc du Laeken, these out-of-place oriental buildings were also commissioned by Leopold II when he returned from the 1900 Paris World Fair and wanted to erect something similar to impress visiting dignitaries – the Chinese pavilion originally served as the royal guesthouse. Each has a museum: the pavilion contains 17th- and 18th-century collections of Chinese and Japanese porcelain, whilst the new Musée d'Art Japonais has been erected near the five-tier Japanese pagoda.

HEYSEL PLATEAU *Nearest métro:* M̲ Heysel
This entertainment plateau sits north of town and is home to the Atomium, a Bruparck funpark and the countyr's largest cinema **Kinépolis** (page 91).

Atomium [129 C2] (*Blvd du Centenaire;* ❧ *02 475 47 72; www.atomium.be;* ☉ *10.00–18.00 daily; adult/concession/under 6/BrusselsCard €9/8/free/–25%*) Brussels' answer to the Eiffel Tower is a set of silver balls! Built for the 1958 World Expo, the 102m-high sculpture – that replicates an iron molecule magnified 165 million times – was never intended to be permanent. However, the structure has become such a familiar fixture on the Brussels skyline that €27.5 million was raised to fund its renovation in 2006. It now includes a new 'Kids World', an exhibition centre, and – at the very top – a restaurant and panoramic viewing station. It's at its most appealing when night falls and small white lights spread across the surface of the spheres are switched on, illuminating the sci-fi structure to beautiful effect.

Bruparck [129 B2] (*20 Blvd du Centenaire;* ❧ *02 474 83 83; www.bruparck.com*) Sat in the shadow of the Atomium, this pleasure park contains a clutch of attractions aimed at young children and teenagers. **Mini-Europe** (*www.minieurope.be;* ☉ *Mar–Jun & Sep 09.30–18.00 daily, Jul–Aug 09.30–20.00 daily, Oct–Jan 10.00–18.00 daily; adult/under 12 €13.40/10*) features a fun collection of scale models of some of Europe's most distinctive landmarks, from London's Big Ben to Rome's Colosseum. Next door is **Océade** (*www.oceade.be;* ☉ *10.00–18.00 Wed–Fri, 10.00–21.00 Sat–Sun; adult/child €16.80/13.70, kids under 1.15m go free*) a pirate-themed water park. Combination tickets that allow entry to both are priced at €24.90 adults, €18.80 under 12. The nearby '**village**' contains fast-food restaurants, sweetshops, cafés and bars.

SCHAERBEEK *Nearest métro:* $\overline{M}$ Botanique

Nicknamed the Cité des Anes – literally 'commune of the donkeys' – and bearing cherries on the commune coat of arms, it's clear that Brussels' largest municipality hails from country stock. As in St-Josse, the area's fertile slopes were used to grow the *cérises du nord* (sour cherries) used in the production of kriek beer, and donkeys would haul their fruity load to the market.

At the end of the Revolution, Schaerbeek was granted its independence from Brussels and development soon followed. By the end of the 19th and early 20th centuries it was one of the most desirable districts for property and Art Nouveau masters rushed to make their mark on the area. Interestingly, Jacques Brel (page 354) and René Magritte (page 355), were both born in this neighbourhood.

An influx of Turkish immigrants during the latter half of the 20th century marked a turning point in the commune's reputation and, until ten years ago, it was still considered down-trodden and scruffy. Recently, however, the municipality has undergone a period of rediscovery: its Art Nouveau hotspots are being salvaged and restored; the contrast of North African neighbourhoods in the north and tidy townhouses in the south has been embraced; and a fresh influx of young couples and families – attracted by low property prices and the area's shabby-chic atmosphere – have breathed new life into the commune.

Maison Communale [132 C1] (*Pl Colignon*) Schaerbeek's majestic town hall is considered one of the region's finest. Built in Flemish Renaissance style in 1887, it took 180 workers to build the hall and its 65m-high belfry, which was gutted by fire in 1911; the façade was the only feature to remain intact. The town hall is also home to the Maison des Arts, which organises a number of exhibitions, but it's worth popping in to see a sample of the 1,400 works of art the hall contains. Look out for the signed photograph of American President Eisenhower, who was made an honorary citizen for his services as Supreme Commander of the Allied forces during World War II.

Halles de Schaerbeek [132 B3] (*22b Rue Royale St-Marie;* \ *02 218 21 17; www. halles.be*) Dating from 1865, this glass-and-steel structure once housed the commune's local food market. It was gutted by fire in 1898 and quickly rebuilt, but the effects of World War I slowed trade and competition from new 'luxury' stores led traders to abandon the hall entirely. Over the years it operated as a warehouse, workshop and car park until, in 1975, it was purchased by the Brussels French Cultural Committee. Today it's a hip venue for concerts, theatre and dance productions and exhibitions. Call or check the website for upcoming events.

Maison Autrique [132 C2] (*266 Chaussée de Haecht;* \ *02 215 66 00; www. autrique.be;* ⊕ *12.00–18.00 Wed–Sun; adult/concession €6/3; prémétro 90 (stop Rogier), 92, 93 (stop St Servais)*) This dapper townhouse dates from 1893 and was Victor Horta's very first independent project. He had just completed his internship with Alphonse Balat (creator of the Royal Greenhouses of Laeken) when Eugène Autrique – a friend and mechanical engineer at Solvay – commissioned him to build their family home. Despite the limitations of Autrique's small budget, you can see Horta's flirtation with aspects of the Art Nouveau style that was still in its infancy at the time. Today, the house contains a small bookshop and hosts art exhibitions. Not suitable for disabled travellers.

Distillerie Fovel [132 C3] (*69 Rue Thiefry;* \ *02 215 58 15;* ⊕ *shop: 09.00–16.00 Mon–Fri; prémétro 90, stop Coteaux*) Makers of gin since 1863, the Fovel distillery

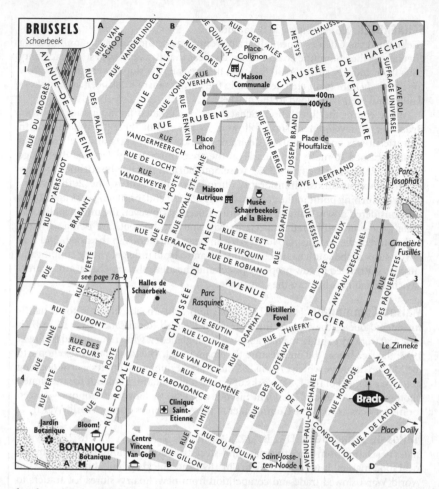

has been in the family, which hails from the original gin town of Hasselt, for over five generations and is unique to the Brussels region – a real gem. The current owner, Thierry Fovel, is happy to lead groups around the collection of pictures, huge 19th-century oak casks and the distilling machinery for free. Of course, he'll also offer you a wee dram of the gin itself, like the cherry-flavoured Griotte de Schaerbeek.

Musée Schaerbeekois de la Bière [132 C2] (*33–35 Av Louise Bertrand;* ☎ *02 241 56 27; http://users.skynet.be/museedelabiere;* ⊕ *14.00–18.00 Wed & Sat; adult/ under 14 €3/free*)

Forget the shiny commercialised beer museum on the Grand' Place and head here instead. Established by 11 locals in 1994, the ramshackle Schaerbeek beer museum was a labour of love: they convinced commune officials to sign over the underused DT building (belonging to the school on Rue de la Ruche) to serve as their premises; they cajoled and convinced breweries to donate old machinery; and then individually trawled flea markets looking for paraphernalia that would augment the collection of 300 Belgian beer bottles donated by one of its founders. Nowadays, the collection exceeds 1,000 bottles and glasses and copious beer advertisement posters and placards. The admission price includes a free beer in the café afterwards – a natural choice is the local La Schaerbeekois.

Events Weekly markets are held on Place de Helmet (☼ *08.00–13.00 Mon*), and organic foods markets on Place Dailly (☼ *08.00–13.00 Tue*), and Rue Royale St-Marie (☼ *08.00–13.00 Fri*) and Places des Chasseurs Ardennais (☼ *14.00–18.00 Fri*).

ST-GILLES Nearest métro: M̲ Porte de Hal

For centuries St-Gilles was known only as Obbrussel, literally 'beyond Brussels' – a quiet hamlet renowned for its farming of Brussels sprouts. It was naturally absorbed into Brussels city centre when the town began to expand in the Middle Ages. After independence in 1830 the area flourished, attracting Art Nouveau patrons like Victor Horta and Paul Hankar, and hit an all time high when it was chosen for the site of the new Bruxelles-Midi/Brussels-Zuid railway station in 1850. Whole sets of streets were remodelled and built, including Avenue Louise. Unfortunately, the success didn't last. By the 1950s large chunks of Brussels' prettiest commune had fallen under the construction hammer to make way for modern buildings. The south, along the border with Uccle and Ixelles, remained elegant, but the north fell into various states of disrepair and experienced an increase in crime. However, all this is set to change. The arrival of the Eurostar and TGV encouraged the municipal government to pour more money into the commune's regeneration and visitors are returning. Like Etterbeek, St-Gilles is a multicultural commune home to Moroccans, Portuguese, Greeks, Spaniards and Italians.

Hôtel de Ville [126–7 A5] (*39 Pl van Meenen;* ✆ *02 536 02 11; admission free*) St-Gilles' grandiose town hall, styled like a French Renaissance chateau, was built between 1900 and 1904 by Albert Dumont (1853–1920) – the architect also responsible for the Prison de St-Gilles. Over 107 painters were invited to decorate the interior and it's worth popping in for the resulting collections of frescoes. The one on the ceiling of the registry office was painted by Fernand Khnopff.

Hôtel Hannon [126–7 B7] (*1 Av de la Jonction;* ✆ *02 538 42 20; www.contretype. org;* ☼ *11.00–18.00 Wed–Fri, 13.00–18.00 Sat–Sun; admission €2.50*) The best Art Nouveau residence in Brussels, this corner property belonged to Edouard Hannon (1853–1931). He invited friend and architect Jules Brunfaut (1852–1942) to design the entire building – inside and out – in Art Nouveau style, just as the fashion was entering its final period of popularity. The hotel's most famous feature is the staggering fresco in the entrance hall painted by Paul-Albert Baudouin. Since its restoration in 1988, the house has been used by Espace Contretype to present contemporary photographic exhibitions.

Musée Horta [126–7 C6] (*25 Rue Américaine;* ✆ *02 543 04 90; www.hortamuseum. be;* ☼ *14.00–17.30 Tue–Sun; adult/concession €7/3.50*) Former home and studio of the celebrated Art Nouveau architect Victor Horta (page 355), this museum mustn't be missed. The building's relatively plain façade conceals four floors of spectacular features, from wrought ironwork and ornate furniture to stained glass and the arresting central spiral stairway that leads all the way up to the skylight and lets light flood in. Horta's attention to detail was unrelenting; door hinges, windows, and light fixtures – all bear his mark. Horta lived here from 1898 to 1919 before he moved to his Solvay mansion on Avenue Louise (page 125).

Wiels [74–5 C6] (*354 Av van Volxemlaan;* ✆ *02 347 30 33; www.wiels.org;* ☼ *11.00–18.00 Wed–Sun; adult/concession/under 12/BrusselsCard €7/5/free/free*) This concrete monolith was originally a brewery that fell derelict in the 1980s.

It's now Brussels' newest modern-art museum and similar in set-up and style to London's Tate Modern; expect wacky large-scale installations.

ST-JOSSE-TEN-NOODE *Nearest métro:* M̲ Botanique
Brussels' smallest commune was once covered in vineyards. When Napoleon came to power he ordered them to be destroyed and soon enough the city had expanded to cover the fertile soil. It's a little rough around the edges, but has long been popular with artistic types – Karl Marx and Friedrich Engels lived here – and the cultural centre in the botanical gardens and a handful of art galleries are testament to this.

Ferme du Parc Maximilien [78–9 C1] (*21 Quai du Batelage;* ☏ *02 201 56 09; www.lafermeduparcmaximilien.be;* ⊕ *10.00–17.00 Tue–Fri, 12.00–16.00 Sat;* M̲ *Yser*) City farmyard where kids can stroke sheep, donkeys and goats nibbling grass with a backdrop of city buildings surrounding them. You can pitch in at the vegetable garden, stroll in the orchard and help feed the ducks.

Le Botanique [132 A5/78–9 H4] (*236 Rue Royale;* ☏ *02 218 37 32; www.botanique.be;* ⊕ *10.00–18.00 daily;* M̲ *Botanique*) The neo-Classical botanical gardens were built between 1815 and 1830 and, after careful renovation, reopened in 1979 as a cultural centre. Les Serres corridor to the right still houses a few tropical plants and also on site are a museum, La Rotonde theatre hall, L'Orangerie concert space, Le Witloof Bar in the basement and the Italian Café Bota.

Musée Charlier *16 Av des Arts;* ☏ *02 218 53 82; www.charliermuseum.be;* ⊕ *12.00–17.00 Mon–Thu, 10.00–13.00 Fri; adult/student/under 18 €5/4/free;* M̲ *Arts-Loi or Madou*) Classy art gallery, which displays Belgian art dating from the end of the 19th century to the beginning of the 20th century, including works by James Ensor, Léon Frédéric, and Rik Wouters. If you can, try and coincide your visit with one of the midweek lunchtime (12.20) music recitals held in the rich turquoise concert hall.

Events St-Josse is probably most famous for its annual St-Jazz-ten-Noode (*www.saintjazz.be*) – a jazz festival held on Place St-Josse in early September. A weekly market is held on Place St-Josse and Rue des Deux Eglises (⊕ *09.00–14.00 Thu*).

UCCLE/UKKEL
Nearest métro: M̲ Churchill
As well as being Brussels' second-largest commune, Uccle is also the wealthiest – property prices are at their highest here – and its former residents

invested in Art Deco and Cubist homes. To get there take STIB/MIVB bus #38 from Bruxelles-Central and De Lijn # 134 from Bruxelles-Midi/Brussels-Zuid: both service the area.

Musée van Buuren [134 A1] (*41 Av Léo Errera;* ✆ *02 343 48 51; www. museumvanbuuren.com;* ⊕ *14.00–17.30 Mon, Wed–Sun; adult/student/under 12 €10/5/free*) One of the gems on the best off-the-beaten-track museum list. This carefully restored 1920s' Art Deco house belonged to Alice and David van Buuren, a couple of avid art collectors who spent a lifetime acquiring and filling their home with period furniture, carpets, sculptures, woodwork and paintings dating from the 15th to the 19th centuries. These included an original *Potato Peeler* sketch by van Gogh, works by Wouters and Permeke and a copy of Brueghel's *Landscape with the Fall of Icarus*. Don't miss the landscaped Art Deco gardens.

Bois de la Cambre [134 B1] The Cambre Woods were originally part of the Fôret de Soignes south of the city centre, but were annexed to the city in 1842 and a tram line set up linking it to the city centre, so residents could escape to a 'green' space at the weekends. It's a lovely spot and comes alive with runners, cyclists and groups of friends picnicking in summer. The Brussels Pony Club (*Allée des Amazones;* ⊕ *Apr–Oct 14.00–18.00 Wed, Sat, Sun*) offers pony rides, and there are a handful of restaurants scattered throughout the woods, including The Wood (page 90) and Le Chalet Robinson (page 87).

AROUND BRUSSELS

TERVUREN
Musée Royale de l'Afrique Centrale (Africa Museum) (*13 Leuvensesteenweg;* ✆ *02 769 52 11; www.africamuseum.be;* ⊕ *10.00–17.00 Tue–Fri, 10.00–18.00 Sat– Sun; adult/student/under 12/BrusselsCard €4/1.50/free/free, free first Wed of month from 13.00*) King Leopold II set up this museum on his leafy royal estate essentially to boast about the colony he'd established in the Congo – filling it with plundered treasures. Despite its dark beginnings, there's no denying the museum's beauty. Maps, photographs, stuffed animals and African artworks abound – yet incredibly just 1% of its collection is on show. The rest is rotated in a series of temporary exhibitions (which require another ticket). It's due to undergo a major renovation July 2012–2015 and, happily, the curators are working closely with the Congolese to show both sides of the story during colonial occupation.

Getting there From Bruxelles-Central take the métro to Montgomery station. Then take tram 44 until its last stop, Tervuren – the museum is 300m away. The tram journey takes 20 minutes with four trams every hour Monday–Friday and three trams every hour Saturday–Sunday.

LOUVAIN-LA-NEUVE
Musée Hergé (*26 Rue du Labrador;* ✆ *010 488 421; www.museeherge.com;* ⊕ *10.30–17.30 Tue–Fri, 10.00–18.00 Sat–Sun; adult/student/7–14/ €9.50/7/5*) A 35-minute train ride south of the city centre, in the university town of Louvain-la-Neuve, is the remarkable Hergé Museum. Open since May 2009, the building's dynamic architecture uses the same clean lines that Hergé used to make Tintin so universally recognisable. An iPod audio tour leads you through the fascinating multimedia collection of family albums, early doodles on postcards, original

sketches, and interviews – much of which comes from personal collections belonging to Hergé's second wife, Fanny Rodwell.

Getting there From Bruxelles-Midi/Brussels-Zuid take the Namur–Luxembourg train and alight in Ottignies, and from there take the train to Louvain-la-Neuve.

WATERLOO This small town 18km south of Brussels is the site of the legendary Battle of Waterloo fought between the French (led by Napoleon Bonaparte) and the English (led by the Duke of Wellington) on 18 June 1815. Napoléon's defeat ended 22 years of war and brought peace to Europe.

Getting there

By bus A bus journey takes longer than the train, but has the bonus of dropping you right outside the tourist information centre in Waterloo. Take TEC bus #W (direction Braine-l'Alleud) or #365 (direction Charleroi) from outside the Ibis hotel on Avenue Fonsny and alight at Waterloo centre; journey time 50 minutes. Ask for a day-card (€6.50) which you can use to get to Waterloo, the battlefields and back to Brussels.

By train Trains from Brussel-Zuid/Bruxelles-Midi to Waterloo depart every 40 minutes and take 20 minutes. Alternatively, direct trains to Braine-l'Alleud (€7.40 return) depart every half and hour and the journey takes 14 minutes. From Braine-l'Alleud, you'll need to take bus #W to get to the battlefield located five minutes away. From Waterloo station it's a 20-minute walk into town: turn right as you exit the station and take your first left on to Rue de la Station. Coming back it's quicker to take the train from Braine-l'Alleud.

Tourist information

ℹ Tourist information 218 Chaussée de Bruxelles; ☎ 02 352 09 10; www.waterloo-tourisme.com; ⊕ Jun–Sep 09.30–18.00 daily, Oct–May 10.00–17.00 daily.

What to see and do

Musée Wellington (147 Chaussée de Bruxelles; ☎ 02 357 28 60; www.museewellington.be; ⊕ Oct–Mar 10.00–17.00 daily, Apr–Sep 09.30–18.00 daily; adult/student/kids 6–12 €5/4/2, Pass 1815 inc entry to battlefield, Lion Mound etc adult/student/kids 6–12 €12/10/6) Seated to the left of Waterloo's tourist information centre, this 18th-century coaching inn was used as the headquarters of the British military during the campaign – and the Duke of Wellington is believe to have stayed here on the eve of the Battle of Waterloo. Its 14 rooms – which, unfortunately, are not accessible to disabled travellers – are well worth a visit while you wait for your bus to the Butte de Lion.

Waterloo Battlefield (315 Route du Lion, 1410; ☎ 02 385 19 12; www.waterloo1815.be; ⊕ Apr–Sep 09.30–18.30 daily, Oct–Mar 10.00–17.00 daily; adult/concession/kids 7–17 €12/9/7.5, inc battlefield tour, access to Lion Mound, Wax Museum & Panorama) Situated 3km south of Waterloo, the battlefields bear none of their original scars, so I highly recommend joining a **Battlefield Tour** (⊕ Apr–Sep 10.45, 11.45, 13.30, 14.30, 15.30, 16.30 & 17.30 daily, Oct–Mar 10.45, 11.45, 13.30, 14.30 & 15.30 Sat–Sun; €5.50) to help bring everything to life. Alternatively, you could try and coincide your visit with the annual re-enactment held in June (www.culturespaces-minisite.com/waterloo1815; €5.50–12). A larger one is held every five years; the next is scheduled for June 2015.

Rising 40m above the fields is the **Butte de Lion** (Lion Mound), a huge cone of earth built to mark the spot where Prince William of Orange was crowned the first king of the Netherlands. From the top there are panoramic views of the battlefield. Collected around the visitors' centre is the **Panorama**, which contains a majestic 110m-long painting by Louis Dumoulin to commemorate the first centenary of the battle in 1912, and the **Wax Museum** (with audio guide) showing various recreated battle scenes.

Getting there From town, the bus station to the battlefield is located on the left-hand side of the tourist information office, opposite the Musée Wellington. Take bus #W and alight at stop Lion, Route de Nivelles; the entrance to the Butte de Lion is 500m down the road on the left-hand side. Journey time ten minutes.

GAASBEEK

Kasteel van Gaasbeek (*40 Kasteelstraat;* \ *02 531 01 30; www.kasteelvangaasbeek. be;* ⊕ *1 Apr–11 Nov 10.00–18.00 Tue–Sun, last ticket 17.00; admission: adult/ under 26/under 7 €7/1/free, inc audio guide*) Ensconced in 17th-century parkland (⊕ *Apr–Sep 08.00–20.00 daily, Oct–Mar 08.00–17.00 daily*), just 14km southwest of Brussels, Gaasbeek Castle is a real beauty. The first version was built in the 13th-century to protect the Duke of Brabant against invasions from Hainaut and Flanders, but most of it was destroyed in 1388 – only a few of the dark-grey stone walls survive. The reconstruction of the castle you see today took over 200 years. During that time, its most famous resident was the Count of Egmond who bought the castle in 1565 and enjoyed living here for three years before he was famously executed on Brussels' Grand' Place for taking part in the Iconoclastic Fury (page 7). The last private owner, Marquise Arconati Visconti, thoroughly restored the castle in the 19th century and changed the interior considerably to suit her tastes. You can visit her bedroom chambers and other richly decorated rooms. The collection also includes a number of artworks, including *View of Gaasbeek Castle* (1805), which shows you what the castle and surrounding area looked like at the beginning of the 19th century; and *The Tower of Babel* (1595) painted by Maarten van Valckenborch, who clearly drew heavily on Pieter Brueghel the Elder's 1563 *Tower of Babel*. Graaf van Egmond brasserie (\ *02 532 29 06;* €€) is also on site.

Getting there Bus #142 (direction Gaasbeek-Leerbeek) departs from outside Brussels' Erasmus métro station and stops at the castle. By car from Brussels, Gent or Antwerp take exit 15a off the R0 ring road (direction Vlezenbeek) (*14km;* ⊕ *20min*).

138

4

Flemish Brabant

Flemish Brabant envelops Brussels and is Flanders' smallest region. The university town of Leuven is its crown jewel and shouldn't be missed. To the east lies Hageland – a patchy area of woodland couched between the provincial towns of Tienen, Diest and Aarschot – and to the west Pajottenland, an area of rural farmland that produces excellent lambic beers, asparagus and endives. Both provide lovely opportunities for cycling through proper Flemish countryside. All the tourist information offices sell Fietsknooppuntennetwerk (try saying that after a few gueuzes!) *Hageland* and *Pajottenland* cycling maps (€6), which allow you to plan routes as long, or as short, as you like. Straddle the saddle and explore a region studded with castles, old watermills and two of Flanders' best-preserved *begijnhofs*.

LEUVEN

Compact and picturesque Leuven is the capital of the Flemish Brabant region and a bustling student city. Don't be fooled by its size: the town's stupendous architecture is testament to its illustrious history. From the 11th to 13th centuries it was the stronghold of the Dukes of Brabant and the town flourished thanks to its elevated status and thriving cloth trade. However, when the Duchy moved to Brussels and the trade of cloth fell into crisis, Leuven had to look for a new role. When John IV, Duke of Brabant, appealed to Pope Martin V to build a university in 1425, it changed the city's history forever – attracting great minds from across Europe. The Catholic University of Leuven thrives to this day and shapes the character of this city which also boasts a world-famous Stadhuis, Belgium's largest *begijnhof* and the Stella Artois brewery.

GETTING THERE AND AWAY

By car From Brussels, follow the E40 and take either exit 22 or 23 (*30km; ⊕ 30min*). If you're coming from the east, eg: Hasselt, follow the E314 west and take exit 18 (*60km; ⊕ 45min*).

By train Brussels-Zuid/Bruxelles-Midi (*every 10min Mon–Fri, 10/36/58min past the hour Sat–Sun; ⊕ 30min*); Antwerp (*42/51min past the hour Mon–Fri,*

> ### COW SHOOTERS
>
> Residents of Leuven are known as *De Koeienschieters* (The Cow Shooters) after an incident that occurred one night in 1691. Leuven locals thought they were under attack from the French and opened fire on their enemy. However, when day broke they realised the 'siege' had been nothing more than a herd of cows.

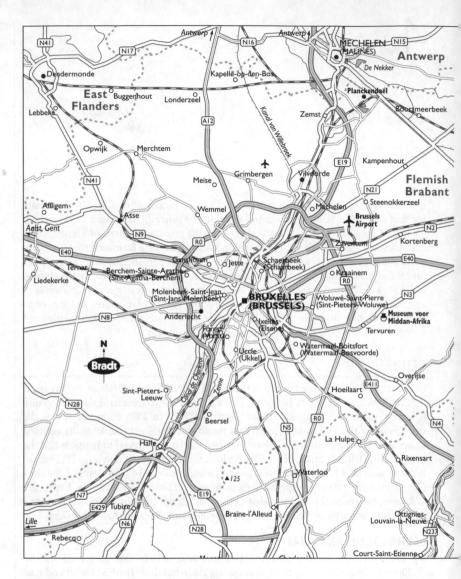

⏱ *40min/1hr; 47min past the hour Sat–Sun,* ⏱ *1hr 8min*); Brugge (*35/58min past the hour daily;* ⏱ *1hr 30min*); Gent (*3/24min past the hour daily;* ⏱ *1hr*). There's also a direct train from Brussels Zaventem Airport (*17/39min past the hour Mon–Fri, 40min past the hour Sat–Sun;* ⏱ *15min*).

It's a ten-minute walk from the to the town centre. The bus station is just to the right of the station and there's a taxi rank immediately outside the exit.

GETTING AROUND
On foot Leuven's city centre is compact and easy to navigate on foot.

By bike See page 143. Cycling maps of the Hageland can be bought at the tourist office, €6.

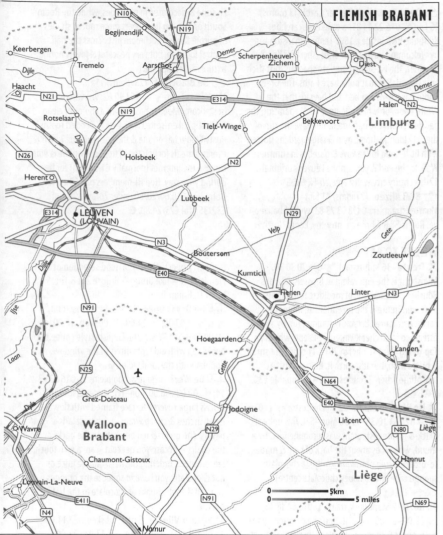

TOURIST INFORMATION

ℹ️ **Tourist office** 1 Naamsestraat; 📞 016 20 30 20; e tourism@leuven.be; www.visitleuven. be; 🕐 10.00–17.00 daily, closed 1 Nov–28 Feb. Tucked underneath the right flank of the Stadhuis, this fairly small office can book accommodation & organise private guided tours (€50/2hrs), & sells combi tickets for the Stadhuis & Sint-Pieterskerk treasury.

WHERE TO STAY

🏠 **Begijnhof Hotel** (69 rooms) 15 Groot Begijnhof; 📞 016 29 10 10; www.bchotel.be. Leuven's *begijnhof* is the largest in Belgium & as far as I know is the only one to house a luxury 4-star hotel – so grab the chance! Rooms are contemporary & fitted with all mod cons; suites have a Jacuzzi & minibar. The bar/bistro is very stylish indeed with deep-seat leather chairs & exposed wooden beams & there's a small sauna & fitness room too. **€€€–€€€€**

⌂ **Oude Brouwerij Keyser Carel** (3 rooms) 15 Lei; ☎ 016 22 14 81; www.keysercarel.be. Boutique B&B inside a 16th-century mansion run by welcoming hosts Kris & Chris (short for Kris & Kristine). The en-suite rooms are spacious, but their only downfall is that none have baths. The Green Room has a 4-poster bed, but beware that the White Room only has a floating wall separating the bedroom from the bathroom. You have the run of the arty lounge, home gym & large gardens dotted with little snug hideaways & gazebos in summer. Walk to the end & you can see Leuven's original 12th-century city walls! Free Wi-Fi. €€€

⌂ **B&B Alizée** (2 rooms) 41 Sint-Maartenstraat; m 0498 03 73 83; www.bbalizee.be. Rustic B&B whose country chic Room North is en suite & decorated in pink hues, while the Room South on the top floor bears more muted shades of purple & has a bathroom just across the hall. Central location, but very peaceful & lovely antique fixtures & fittings. €€

⌂ **De Blauwput** (28 rooms) 11a Martelarenlaan; ☎ 016 63 90 62; www.leuven-hostel.com. Modern hostel with a choice of clean & functional en-suite twin, 4- or 6-bedded rooms. Rusty Elbow bar on site & they can prepare lunch & evening meals for you too. A tip: book online & you can use the internet (normally €1/30min) for free during your stay. Non HI-members pay €3 extra. Dorm bed €18.60/20/80 under 26/over 26, sgl €32/35, dbl €23/24.80. €

✗ WHERE TO EAT

✗ **Trente** 36 Muntstraat; ☎ 016 20 30 30. Munstraat is the equivalent of Brussels' Rue des Boucher – a street full of mediocre restaurants. However, Trente is the exception: an intimate earthen-coloured 8-table restaurant run by esteemed local chef Kwinten De Paepe, who won Top Young Flemish Chef in 2011. Portions are small & prices high, but it's worth it. Perhaps visit at lunchtime when 2 courses costs a reasonable €30. €€€€€

✗ **De Blauwe Maan** 22 Mechelsestraat; ☎ 016 29 97 47; ⏲ 10.30–22.30 Mon–Sat. This upbeat black-&-white restaurant was recommended by a friend, who raves about the back of hare & made-to-order *smeuïg chocoladegebakje* (a chocolate sponge cake with a gooey chocolate centre). €€€–€€€€

✗ **Rossi** 2 Standonckstraat; ☎ 016 62 48 48; ⏲ 19.00–22.00 Tue–Sat. Don't be deterred by the basic décor & chequered tablecloths; instead trust the sumptuous smells of garlic & red wine that emanate from the open kitchen. This is real Italian food; not a pizza in sight. €€€

✗ **De Wiering** 2 Wieringstraat; ☎ 016 29 15 45; ⏲ 12.00–23.00 daily. Yesteryear-style bistro with accordions & old cameras dangling from the walls. Famous for its *grootmoedershoekje* (grandmother's kitchen) recipes like *stoofpotje framboise* (rabbit stew cooked in Lindemans raspberry beer). Also has a good selection of Flemish beers like Brugge's Brugse Zot & the hefty Delirium Tremens. €€

⌒ **De Dry Coppen** 11 Schrijnmakersstraat; ☎ 016 23 03 05; ⏲ 14.00–19.00 Mon, 10.00–19.00 Tue–Sat. Wonderful English-style coffee bar/bookshop with old typewriters in the window. Very popular with the local ladies. €

⌒ **De Werf** 5 Hogeschoolplein; ☎ 016 23 73 14; ⏲ 09.00–00.00 Mon–Fri. Students love this place's large covered terrace framed with flower-laden arches & cheap wraps, quiches, salads & pastas. The green & red blankets on the backs of the chairs – in case you get cold – are a nice touch. I recommend ordering the fresh orange juice or hot chocolate; you have to squeeze the oranges yourself & melt chunks of chocolate in the hot milk. €

✗ **Frituur Vlinder** Sint-Jacobskerk; ⏲ 11.00–14.00 & 17.00–23.00 Mon–Fri, 17.00–23.00 Sat–Sun. If you fancy something starchy & salty this traditional chip caravan serves the best chips in town. €

✗ **Kiekekot** 46 Mechelsestraat; ☎ 016 22 06 17; ⏲ 12.00–22.00 daily. Staf has run this rough-around-the-edges joint for 11 years & students love his slow-roast chicken served with apple sauce & bread. There are 4 tables inside, but most people have it as a takeaway. €

ENTERTAINMENT AND NIGHTLIFE Leuven's nightlife is incredibly lively during the week thanks to the resident student population, but much quieter at weekends when they decamp home.

The action centres around tree-lined Oude Markt just off the Grote Markt. Billed by the tourist board as 'Europe's longest bar,' its entire circumference is dominated by bars save for the occasional pharmacy thrown in – presumably to hand out doses of paracetamol for alcohol-clogged heads. There's a great vibe in summer when terraces of tables and chairs cover the square and the students arrive to sunbathe and sip after classes. The bars lining Oude Markt are all very hip, so I've provided a few traditional antidotes below.

♀ **Café Amedee** 4 Muntstraat; ⊕ 20.00–late Mon–Fri, 15.00–late Sat. This dusty café is a golden oldie which serves good Trappist beers & an interesting beer of the month. Look for the red shop front.

♀ **Café Metafoor** 34 Parijsstraat; ⊕ 11.00–02.00 Mon–Fri, 10.00–02.00 Sat, 12.00–02.00 Sun. Grab a seat in the saggy leather couch underneath the old map on the wall, order a beer & play a boardgame. Free Wi-Fi.

♀ **In den Boule** 2 Augustijnenstraat; ⊕ 11.00–06.00 Mon–Fri, 20.00–01.00 Sun. Bric-a-brac student bar with an open fire. Owner Jacqui has been in charge of this place for a staggering 42 years, so don't be put off if he's a little grumpy, the poor chap only gets a few hours sleep during the day. Gets very busy on Mon, Tue & Thu, but tends to fall quiet at the w/ends when all the students go home.

♀ **In de Toewip** 182 Diestsestraat; ⊕ 10.30–late Mon–Wed, Fri & Sat, 12.30–01.00 Sun. You can't miss the blue-&-yellow tiled façade of this pub run by twin sisters Mirella & Miranda & their father. Has a *toppenbiljart* – a pool game played with 5 red & 5 white balls – unique to Flanders & the Netherlands & rarely seen nowadays.

♀ **Nationale** 20 Tiensevest; ↘ 016 29 25 37; ⊕ 06.00– 00.00 Mon–Fri, 07.00–01.00 Sat–Sun. A real working man's bar opposite the railway station that's been around since World War II. Cash only.

OTHER PRACTICALITIES

$ Bank KBC, top of stairs to left of railway station, ⊕ 24hrs; Dexia, 16 Grote Markt, ↘ 016 27 03 80; ⊕ 06.00–00.00 daily.

♻ Bike rental Fietspunt, 1 Prof R van Overstraetenplein (railway station); ↘ 016 21 26 01; ⊕ 07.00–19.00 Mon–Fri; 1 Apr–15 Oct also open 08.30–17.00 Sat, 08.30–14.00 Sun; €9/day

◉ Internet Pay-as-you-go Telenet Wi-Fi cloud across town, otherwise try: Express Telecom; 198 Diestsestraat; ↘ 016 58 31 50; ⊕ 10.30–20.00 Mon–Sat; €1.50/hr

Markets Flower market Brusselsstraat & Oude Markt, ⊕ 13.00–18.00 Thu & artisanal food market ⊕ 09.00–18.00 Sat. General market, Ladeuzeplein & Herbert Hooverplein ⊕ 07.00–12.00 Fri.

✚ Pharmacy 14 Oude Markt, ⊕ 08.30–18.30 Mon–Fri, 08.30–12.30 Sat; 5 Mechelsestraat, ⊕ 09.00–13.00 & 14.00–18.00 Mon–Fri, 09.00–12.30 Sat

✉ Post office 12 Jan Stasstraat; ⊕ 09.00–18.00 Mon–Wed & Fri, 09.00–19.00 Thu, 09.00–15.00 Sat

WHAT TO SEE AND DO

Stadhuis (*9 Grote Markt;* ↘ *016 20 30 20;* ⊕ *guided tours 15.00 daily, predominantly in French & Dutch, but tourist office has an English-language information sheet; admission €2*) Leuven's 15th-century town hall is jaw dropping – and Flanders' best: a three-storey Gothic masterpiece with four turrets, two towers and every nook and cranny filled with statues. It's believed that the city's first town hall originally stood on Oude Markt in the 11th century. Construction of this third version began in 1439 when Sint-Pieterskerk was also being converted from a small Romanesque church to the current Gothic structure. Three different architects worked on it – the last, Matthew de Layens, decided to scrap plans for a belfry to be built on the corner of Naamesestraat, giving the town hall its unique appearance.

The building's pomp and majesty come from its 236 statue-filled niches. In fact, these were added only in 1850 and are a visual Who's Who of Leuven's history. The first rows depict eminent Leuven scholars and artists; the second shows patron saints,

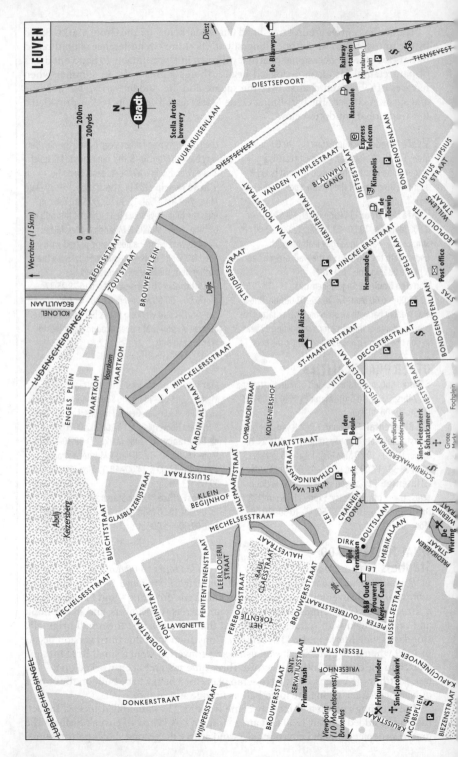

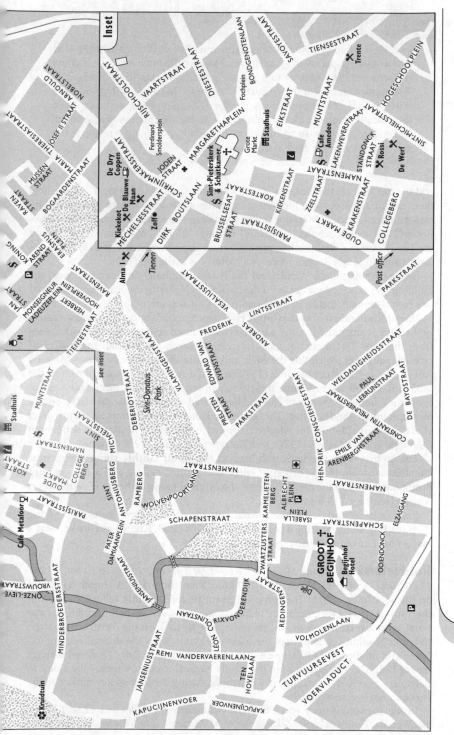

Inset

Trente ✕
TIENSESTRAAT
SAVOYESTRAAT
BONDGENOTENLAAN
Fochplein
MUNTSTRAAT
EIKSTRAAT
Café
Amedee
LAKENWEVERSTRAAT
STANDONCK
STRAAT
Rossi ✕
De Werf ✕
COLLEGEBERG
OUDE MARKT
NAMENSTRAAT
ZEELSTRAAT
KIEKENSTRAAT
PARIJSSTRAAT
KORTESTRAAT
BRUSSELSESAT
STRAAT
Sint-Pieterskerk
& Schatkamer
Grote
Markt
Stadhuis
MARGARETHAPLEIN
Ferdinand
Smoldersplein
RIJSCHOOLSTRAAT
VAARTSTRAAT
DIESTESTRAAT
SCHRIJNMAKERSSTRAAT
IJODEN
STRAAT
BOUTSLAAN
DIRK
De Dry
Coppen
De Blauwe
Maan ✕
Zoff ●
Kiekekot
MECHELSESTRAAT
SINT-MICHIELSSTRAAT
HOGESCHOOLPLEIN

Alma I ✕
Tienen ✕
ARNOULD
NOBELSTRAAT
MARIA THERESIASTRAAT
JOZEF II STRAAT
MUSSEN
STRAAT
RAVEN
STRAAT
KONING
ALBERT
BOGAARDENSTRAAT
ERASMUS
PLEIN
ARENDT
STRAAT
JAN
STRAAT
MONSEIGNEUR
LADEUZEPLEIN
HERBERT
HOOVERPLEIN
RAVENSTRAAT
TIENSESTRAAT

Stadhuis
MUNTSTRAAT
SINT
MICHIELSSTRAAT
see inset
KORTE
STRAAT
NAMENSTRAAT
OUDE
MARKT
COLLEGE
BERG
PARIJSSTRAAT

Café Metafoor
ONZE-LIEVE-
VROUWSTRAAT
MINDERBROEDERSSTRAAT
JANSENIUSSTRAAT
Kruidtuin

VESALIUSSTRAAT
LINTSSTRAAT
FREDERIK
ANDREAS
EDWARD VAN
EVENSTRAAT
PRELATEN
STRAAT
PARKSTRAAT
VLAMINGENSTRAAT
DEBERIOTSTRAAT
Sint-Donatus
Park
RAMBERG
WOLVENPOORTGANG
SCHAPENSTRAAT
PATER
DAMIAANPLEIN
SINT
ANTONIUSBERG
ZWARTZUSTERS
STRAAT
KARMELIETEN
BERG
ALBRECHT
PLEIN
ISABELLA
PLEIN
HENDRIK
CONSCIENCESTRAAT
WELDADIGHEIDSSTRAAT
PAUL
LEBRUNSTRAAT
CONSTANTIN MEUNIERSTRAAT
DE BAYOSTRAAT
EMILE VAN
ARENBERGHSTRAAT
ELZASGANG
NAMENSTRAAT
SCHAPENSTRAAT
OOIENDONCK
Post office
PARKSTRAAT
PARKSTRAAT

GROOT
BEGIJNHOF
Begijnhof
Hotel
Dijle
REDINGENSTRAAT
VONDERENDIJK
LEON COLINSTAAN
REMI VANDERVAERENLAANZ
TEN
HOVELAAN
KAPUCIJNENVOER
KAPUCIJNENVOER
VOLMOLENLAAN
TURVUURSEVEST
VOERVIADUCT

and the top features the Dukes of Brabant and the Counts of Flanders – notice how their clothing differs from the others. At the bottom look for the globe-wielding cartographer Gerardus Mercator (niche 8), painters Quentin Matsys (16) and Dirk Bouts (21), Catholic scholar Desiderius Erasmus (26), Dirk Martens, who developed the Low Countries' first printing press (27) and Pope Martinus V who founded the university (40). Holy Roman Emperor Charles V is at the top (133).

Inside, the flag-lined **Wandelzaal** (hall) was originally an open walkway; the building was accessed via doors on the back wall. Nevertheless, the original carved oak beams remain, featuring scenes from the Old Testament.

Upstairs is dominated by the **Gothic Hall** which underwent extensive renovations in the 19th century and features a similar oak-beamed ceiling, this time with scenes from the New Testament. Of most interest, however, are the four massive 19th-century paintings which line the walls and feature important city events. *Antonia van Roesmale elucidates the Bible* (1542) tells of a women who wanted to read the Bible but, unable to read Latin, unwittingly opted for a Dutch Protestant version. Emperor Charles V found out and had her buried alive in the Grote Markt. Such a pleasant, understanding chap! The others are *Pieter Coutereel tears up the privileges of the patricians* (1360), *The murdered body of burgomaster Wouter van der Leyden is brought back to Leuven* (1379), and *The official opening of the university* (1426).

The archways on the back wall lead to the **small Gothic room** where your attention is stolen by the original Gothic star-vaulted ceiling and a copy of Dirk Bout's *Judgement of the Emperor Otto* – the original hangs in Brussels' Musée d'Art Ancien (see page 115 for the story).

Back outside, and across the square, you see an irreverent statue of a young chap reading while pouring a pint of beer over his head. Known as **Fonske**, he is a mascot for Leuven university students.

Sint-Pieterskerk (*Grote Markt;* ☉ *10.00–17.0 Tue–Fri, 10.00–16.30 Sat, 14.00–17.00 Sun, 15 Mar–15 Oct 10.00–17.00 Mon; admission free*) A church has stood on this site since AD986. The current Brabantine high-Gothic version dates from the 15th century. Work began in 1425 and was overseen by architect Sulpius van Vorst, who was clearly an over achiever because he took on the construction of the elaborate Stadhuis, situated opposite, a few years later. Sadly the stress all became too much and he died in 1448 before either was completed. St Peter's suffered damage during both the World Wars, but thankfully its Gothic choir screen – the oldest in Belgium – survived. Its statues were destroyed during the French Revolution, so the current ones are new models.

Inside the ambulatory you'll find the **Schatkamer** (*adult/child €2.50/1.25 inc audio guide, combi ticket for Schatkamer & M-Museum adult/under 26/3–18/under*

13 *€9/5/3/free*) which houses a number of treasures. Carved into the walls of the radiating side chapels are 16th-century funerary reliefs financed by rich families who wished to be remembered in the prayers of churchgoers.

In the central chapel, behind the altar, is a painting depicting the tale of Proud Margaret (see box opposite), a revered local saint whose bones reside in a golden chest in the church.

Further round are two masterpieces by Dieric Bouts: the 15th-century triptych *The Last Supper* and the *Martrydom of St Erasmus*, which depicts the patron saint of mariners calmly being disembowelled.

In the last side chapel is the double tomb of Mathilde of Boulogne, wife of Henry I Duke of Brabant, and her eldest daughter Marie. Henry's tomb – the earliest surviving tomb of its kind in Belgium – is found in the centre of the choirstalls. He died on 5 September 1235 aged 70, but the carver was clearly seeking favour because the face on the tomb features a much younger, smiling Henry. Among his legacies was the land given to the Groot Begijnhof.

Before leaving, be sure to visit the crypt from the old Romanesque church.

Groot Begijnhof *(Schapenstraat; free)* A ten-minute walk south of the Grote Markt will lead you to Leuven's UNESCO-listed *begijnhof* – the largest in Belgium. This quiet world of cobblestones, red-brick houses and trickling streams was founded in 1205. It grew to accommodate 360 béguines (see box, page 18) before it was abolished by the French in 1795. The béguines were allowed to stay, with the last one only moving out in 1988. The 'mini village' was restored between 1963 and 1990 and today the picturesque houses belong to the university, which rents them out to lecturers and a few lucky students. The old infirmary, House of Chièves, is used as a conference centre so you might be able to have a peek in between proceedings.

Klein Begijnhof *(Halfmaartstraat; free)* On the opposite side of town, Leuven's small *begijnhof* is considerably less impressive, consisting of just one street and a few alleyways. Its 100 béguines worked at Sint-Geertruikerk (St Gertrude's Abbey), famous for its stone tower built without any securing pins. Again, it was closed by the French and gradually fell into disrepair before being restored and sold as private homes.

M-Museum *(28 Leopold Vanderkelenstraat; ✆ 016 27 29 29; www.mleuven.be; ⊕ 11.00–18.00 Mon, Tue, Fri–Sun, 11.00–22.00 Thu; admission: adult/under 26/3–18 €9/5/3 inc audio guide, last tickets 17.00)* The city is very proud of its newest museum which showcases a mixture of Gothic and 19th-century paintings and sculptures. Look out for the museum's crown jewels on the first floor: Rogier van der Weyden's *Edelheere Triptych* and *The Seven Sacraments* altarpiece on loan from Antwerp's KMSK until 2017.

Dijleterrassen The city has begun to install platforms along the river to create picnic spots for locals and to draw attention to Leuven's handful of canals. You'll find one in front of Oude Brouwerij Keyser Carel B&B; see map on pages 144–5 for location.

Stella Artois Brewery *(Vuurkruisenlaan; ⊕ 1 May–30 Oct 15.30 Sun; admission €7)* In 2011 the brewery opened its doors to individual visitors and although it's billed as a temporary arrangement there are lots of rumours that it will remain open in 2012 and possibly beyond that. The hour-and-a-half tour leads you through the

fermentation process and the bottling room, and concludes with a few cold ones in the Den Thuis bar. Book through the tourist office.

Day trip

Hoegaarden Brewery *(24a Stoopkensstraat, Hoegaarden;* \ *016 76 74 33; www. twitgebrouw.be;* ⊕ *10.00–20.00 Tue–Sun; admission: adult/under 12 €6/free, inc free gift)* The actual brewery isn't open to the public, but you can visit their 't Wit Gebrouw visitors' centre housed in the old brewery building. It explains the brewing process and includes an all-important tasting session of the famous white beer.

Getting there Catch the train from Leuven to Tienen, then takes bus #360 or #361 from Tienen to Jodoigne and get off at 'Au Canal'. If you're travelling by car, follow the E40 and take exit 25 towards Hoegaarden. Keep going until you reach a roundabout with a copper kettle, take the first exit and after 2km turn right into Tiensestraat. The centre is down the second street on your left.

GRIMBERGEN

Only 12km north of Brussels, Grimbergen is actually part of Flemish Brabant and retains a small-town demeanour. Before beer enthusiasts start frothing at the mouth in anticipation, I should state that the famous Grimbergen Abbey beer is no longer brewed in town. It was bought by Carlsberg/Heineken in 2008 and is now brewed in Alken, south of Hasselt. The brewing giants pay the monks of the Norbertine abbey to use their name – a real travesty.

Nevertheless, this small town has a rich history dating from the 12th century when German Christian, Norbert of Xanten, and his group of monks founded the Grimbergen Abbey in 1128 – making it one of the oldest in Belgium. At that time, the town was ruled by the rich and powerful Grimbergen family whose ruined castle can still be seen in Prinsenbos, the town park. However, disagreements with the Duke of Brabant led to the family losing their land which later fell under the rule of the House of Orange-Nassau.

Part of the Groene Gordel – or Green Belt – surrounding Brussels, it has some lovely walks along the Maalbeek River and you should certainly try and visit the old watermills, Liermolen and Tommenmolen, dotted along its banks.

Every year, on 13 May (or the first following Sunday), the town celebrates **St-Servaasommegang** – a pageant retelling the legend of the town's patron saint, St-Servaas from Bulgaria.

GETTING THERE AND AWAY

By car From Brussels follow the A12 north and take exit 3 (direction Meise) and follow N211 to Grimbergen *(15km;* ⊕ *20min)*.

By boat Arrive in style and take the Bateau Bus *(www.bateaubus.be;* ⊕ *May–Sep; admission: adult/3–11/under 2 €4/2/free)*, which sails along the Senne Canal. It picks passengers up in Brussels from the section of Avenue du Port opposite Rue Ulens, a short walk from Yzer métro station (see map on pages 78–9 B1) and drops you at Pont Brûlé on the outskirts of Grimbergen. From there it's a 2.5km walk into town or you can catch TEC bus #232 from Heienbeekstraat *(36min past the hour, every hour;* ⊕ *8min)* and alight at Hoge Steenweg, just outside the abbey.

There are sailings on Tuesday, departing Brussels between 11.30 and 12.30 and arriving in Grimbergen at 13.15, and departing Grimbergen at 13.30 and arriving in Brussels at 15.00. On Thursday there are departures from Brussels at 10.00 and 15.30 arriving, respectively, at 11.30 and 17.00, and departing Grimbergen at 13.30 and arriving back in Brussels 15.00.

By bus Three buses run regular services from Brussels Bockstael B (outside Bockstael métro station) to Grimbergen town centre: #231 (*direction: Beigem; 12min past the hour, every hour; ⊕ 26min*), #230 (*direction: Humbeek; 27/57min past the hour, every hour; ⊕ 21min*) and #232 (*direction: Grimbergen Vaart; 42min past the hour, every hour; ⊕ 25min*).

TOURIST INFORMATION

❓ Tourist information 22 Prinsenstraat; ☏ 02 270 99 30; e toerisme@brabantsekouters. be; www.brabantsekouters.be; ⊕ 08.00–11.30 & 13.00–16.00 Mon–Thu, 08.00–11.30 & 13.00–14.30 Fri, 16 Jun–12 Sep 09.00–13.00 Sat. Small, ill-equipped office & the staff don't speak much English. It's worth hiring a guide (€50/2hr) so you can visit the Beer Museum housed in the old abbey & the Liermolen & Tommenmolen. Alternatively, 2 walking routes are marked on the free town brochure: the *Prinsenwandeling* takes you past the Prinsenkasteel & the *Maalbeekwandeling* shows you how to get to Liermolen & Tommenmolen. Unfortunately, there's nowhere to rent bikes in town.

✖ WHERE TO EAT

✖ Fenikshof 20 Abdijstraat; ☏ 02 306 39 56; ⊕ 12.00–22.00 daily. Named after the phoenix that graces the labels of Grimbergen beer, this trendy orange-&-black brasserie sits round the corner from the Mira observatory. Locals recommend the *stoofvlees*. €€€

WHAT TO SEE AND DO

St-Servaasbasiliek (*1 Kerkplein;* ☏ *02 270 96 92; www.kerkgrimbergen.be;* ⊕ *09.00–17.00 daily; admission free*) Considered one of the most beautiful examples of Baroque architecture in Belgium and the Netherlands, this 17th-century church is all that remains of the Grimbergen Abbey that was dissolved during the French Revolution. Immediately your eye is drawn to the soaring ceilings and baby-blue dome high above, and then to the main altar – a mass of black and Carrara marble whose centrepiece painting the *Assumption of Mary* is flanked by statues of the apostles Peter and Paul. Also of note are the ornate choirstalls and above them four paintings depicting episodes in the life of St Norbert, the founder of Grimbergen Abbey, and the Resurrection Memorial where death (skeleton) and time (old bearded man) hold a scroll listing the many basilica's many abbots. The church boasts a 48-bell carillon, and hosts regular concerts. In good weather, locals gather on the grass or grab a seat at the picnic table posted outside.

Mira (*22 Abdijstraat;* ☏ *02 269 12 80; www.mira.be;* ⊕ *14.00–18.00 Wed & Sun; admission: adult/under 10 €3/free*) Set up by one of the abbots, this quaint observatory has several multimedia rooms and a collection of historical astronomical instruments.

Prinsenkasteel (*Princenbos*) An impressive moat-surrounded castle with its own drawbridge, Prinsenkasteel was built in the 17th century by Philip of Glymes, Prince of Grimbergen, whose tomb can be found in St-Servaasbasiliek. The castle was occupied by the Germans during World War II until an outbreak of fire left it ruined; it is now in the ownership of the city. Plans to restore it have been in place for years, but must be progressing slowly – the only sign of life on the moat are dozens of rowdy geese and ducks.

MOT (Museum for Old Techniques) (*20 Guldendal;* \ *02 270 81 11; www.mot. be;* ⊕ *09.00–17.00 Mon–Fri, Apr–Sep 14.00–18.00 Sat–Sun; admission: adult/6–12 €3/1*) Despite having the dullest museum name ever conceived, this trio of museums – comprised of the 17th-century watermills, Liermolen and Tommenmolen, and Guldendal, the former stables of Prinsenkasteel – is actually quite interesting and is housed in wonderful buildings. The **Guldendal**, which serves as the museum headquarters, has a collection of washing machines spanning 150 years, but it's the watermills that are particularly lovely. The former grain mills **Liermolen and Tommenmolen** (*8 Vorststraat & 18 Tommenmolenstraat;* ⊕ *Apr–Sep 14.00– 18.00 Sat & Sun*) sit in the north of town and, during the summer, put on milling demonstrations and open their cafés so you can enjoy a glass of Grimbergen beer.

On your way back to town, swing by **Charleroyhoeve** on Lierbaan: a 17th-century collection of farm buildings which now house the town library and an ironing shop!

HALLE

Right up against the Flanders/Wallonia border, Halle lies 15km southwest of Brussels and is the main town of Pajottenland – an area of gently rolling farmland famous for its lambic beers. The town was a major pilgrimage site from the 13th to the 15th centuries thanks to the miraculous statue of the Virgin Mary, and the church that grew up around it is still a big crowd puller. In summer, beer lovers should take the opportunity to visit the Boon Brewery which produces excellent gueuzes – and, not far away, is the picture-perfect Beersel Castle.

GETTING THERE AND AWAY
By car From Brussels follow the E19 south, take exit 21, and merge onto the E429/ N203a (direction Lille), then take exit for N6/Halle Centrum (*22km;* ⊕ *25min*).

By train Brussel-Zuid/Bruxelles Midi (*4/11/28/30/41/44min past the hour Mon– Fri, 21/26/54min past the hour Sat–Sun;* ⊕ *10min*).

TOURIST INFORMATION
🛈 **Tourist information** 1 Grote Markt; \ 02 356 42 59; e toerisme@halle.be; www.toerisme-halle.be; ⊕ 09.00–12.00 & 13.00–16.00 Mon–Fri, Apr–Oct 09.00–12.00 & 13.00–16.00 daily. Housed in the 17th-century Stadhuis, this bright office has lots of information, but unfortunately most of it is in Dutch & the ladies manning the desk don't speak much English. Pick up some treats from their regional products stand.
⑤⑤ **Bike rental** Fietspunt, 2 Vandenpeereboomstraat, Halle railway station; \ 02 360 25 55; ⊕ 06.00–20.00 Mon–Fri; €9.50/ day

🏠 **WHERE TO STAY AND EAT** In summer, the thing to eat is *plattekaas* (dark bread spread with cottage cheese and sprinkled with chopped spring onions) with a glass of locally produced Boon Gueuze (see opposite). Both the eateries below should serve it. Those with a sweet tooth should search the shops for *Halse krotten* (caramel sweets).

🛏 **Les Eleveurs** (15 rooms) 1a Suikerkaai; \ 02 361 13 40; www.les-eleveurs.be. Middle-of-the-road hotel with Holiday Inn-style rooms, smart on-site restaurant & leafy terrace. €€€

✕ **Alsput** 108 Hollestraat; \ 02 356 76 47; ⊕ 07.00–18.00 daily. Simple restaurant belonging to the Alsput hotel specialising in premier steaks & mussels. Their 3-course *dagmenu* for €11 is great value. €€€

✗ t'Groot Café 7 Grote Markt; ✆ 02 356 52 57; ⊕ 10.00–23.00 daily. A firm favourite with the locals, this brasserie/tea rooms serves Flemish classics like *witloof*. The *dagschotel* is good value at €9.80. €€€

WHAT TO SEE AND DO

Sint-Maartensbasiliek (*Grote Markt;* ✆ *02 356 42 59;* ⊕ *08.00–18.30 daily; admission free*) Don't be put off by its gleaming white exterior; the interior of this High Gothic church is very old with smatterings of ancient red paint peeling off the walls and soot-stained pillars. The current church dates from 1409, but it's been a major site of pilgrimage since 1267 when Aleydis, a daughter of the Lord of Halle, gifted a statue of the Virgin Mary. Visits from princes and popes raised enough money to build this huge shrine which is studded with interesting features.

Naturally, the main point of focus is the statue of Mary, kept on a plinth above the high altar. Legend has it she acquired her dark appearance during the siege of 1489 when she was placed on the city walls and, miraculously, caught cannonballs in her tiny lap – the gunpowder turning her black. These cannonballs are stored behind bars in a niche on the left as you enter the basilica.

Next your eye is drawn to the ornate pulpit, the base of which features Faith (woman holding the cross) and two angels destroying sin, represented by rats and other vermin. The chapel off to the right is the Old Chapel of Adam and Eve; its altar laden with flowers and candles. Following the door to the left of the altar will take you round the back of the main altar, past all the side chapels, to the sacristy at the far end which marks the entrance to the crypt, whose treasures can be viewed on selected days.

Just before going down the short flight of stairs, look to your left to see the tiny tomb of Joachim, the son of French King Louis XI, tucked into the wall.

Off to the right is the Trazegnies Chapel whose huge alabaster altarpiece, depicting the seven sacrements, was commissioned by Lord Trazegnies in 1467.

Finally, before leaving the church, have a peek at the 15th-century font in the baptistry in the chapel to the left of the exit. Made from beaten brass, its lid features figures of the 12 apostles, the patron saints St Maarten, St Hubert and St George on horseback and, at the very top, Christ being baptised in the River Jordan.

Every Whit Sunday (last Sunday in May) at 15.00, the town hosts Mariaprocessie (*www.mariaprocessie.be*) when the statue of Mary is paraded through town.

Zuidwest Brabants Museum (*7 Cardijnstraat;* ✆ *02 365 94 15; www. streekmuseum-halle.be;* ⊕ *Apr–Jun & Sep–Oct 14.00–17.00 Sun, Jul–Aug 14.00–17.00 Sat, 10.00–12.00 & 14.00–17.00 Sun; admission: adult/under 12 €2/free*) A 17th-century Jesuit school houses this Museum of Southwest Brabant which displays a hotchpotch collection of artefacts from medieval pottery to modern brewing equipment.

Boon Brouwerij (*65 Fonteinstraat;* ✆ *02 356 66 44; www.boon.be;* ⊕ *Jul–Aug 15.00 Wed; admission €4/5.50, inc one/three beers*) Located in the village of Lembeek, 2.5km southwest of Halle, the Boon Brewery produces a variety of gueuze beers, most notably the Oude Gueuze Boon and cherry-flavoured kriek Boon. During the summer, you can visit the brewery and they'll give you a one-hour guided tour and let you try the beers. Book through the tourist office. To get there, take De Lijn bus #156 (*25min past the hour, every hour*) from the railway station and get off at Lembeek kerk.

Day trips

Hallerbos (*Nijvelsesteenweg*) Five kilometres southeast of Halle, this nature-rich woodland – home to pheasant, rabbit and deer – is famous for its springtime carpets of bluebells.

Getting there You can rent bicycles from Halle railway station or take the bus. During the week catch TEC bus #114 from outside Halle railway station (*departures every few min; ☉ 9min*) and get off at Halle Vlasmarkt. On the weekend, take De Lijn bus #156 (*every 2hrs*) from the railway station and get off at Lembeek Congo; from there it's a 17-minute walk to the forest entrance.

Alternatively, if you've got a car take the N28 south from Halle and after passing Hall Horses Farm on your right, take the next left and follow Vlasmarktdreef across the motorway until your reach the woods.

Kasteel van Beersel (*Lotsestraat, 1650 Beersel;* ☎ *02 359 16 36;* ☉ *1 Mar 15 Nov 10.00–12.00 & 14.00–18.00 Tue–Sun, 16 Nov–28 Feb 10.00–12.00 & 14.00–18.00 Sat–Sun, closed Jan; admission: adult/under 12 €2.50/1.25*) Straight from the pages of a fairytale, Beersel's feudal castle – complete with moat, drawbridge, parapets and portcullis – is remarkably well preserved and one of Flanders' prettiest castles. It sits 4.5km north of Halle and was built in 1300 by Jean II, Duke of Brabant, as an early defence line for Brussels. Kids will love exploring the spiral staircases, dingy dungeons and armoury. Be sure to point out its machicolations too – the openings through which stones and boiling oil were poured onto the heads of invaders. French poet and novelist, Victor Hugo, was suitably impressed with the place to compose a few lines in its honour:

> He lies there in the valley, the mansion alone.
> The least noise was silent in its dreary poles.
> And every hour of the day sees a stone fall from its dark niche.
> The raven lodged in its ancient rooms.
> The owl reiterated his complaint there every night
> And the blade of grass between the cold tiles of its vast corridors.

Lunch can be had at Rick's Café just around the corner from the entrance.

AARSCHOT

Aarschot is largely left off visitors' itineraries, which is a shame because it's a great town to wander around, especially on Thursdays when the centre is lined with market stalls. It grew up around the chocolate-coloured Demer River, which races underneath the wonderfully preserved 16th-century Hertogenmolen, a former

---

KASSELSTAMPERS

Residents of Aarschot are known as *Kasselstampers* ('cobblestone stampers') because in the past the town was repeatedly raided by thieves. The residents decided to hire guards, but were dismayed to find that the men constantly retreated to the pub during cold weather. To solve the problem, they forced the guards to wear clogs, so they could hear them patrolling the streets and be sure they were doing their job.

grain mill that straddles the river. If you can, arrange to visit on 13 August when the town celebrates **Sint-Rochusverlichting** (⊕ *21.00–00.00*) and the centre is lit with thousands of tea lights.

A word of warning: when you pick up a map from the tourist information office you'll notice that the published street names don't match those pinned to the buildings; the latter are in the local dialect and trying to marry up the two will put your map reading skills to the test! Here's a couple to give you a head start: Eeuwigheidsstraat is Kardinaal Merciersstraat, and Cabaretstraat is Martelarenstraat.

GETTING THERE AND AWAY
By car From Leuven follow the N19 north (*18km; ⊕ 23min*); from Hasselt follow the N2 west, at exit 25 merge onto the E315 (direction Leuven) and take exit 22 for the N223 to Aarschot (*42km; ⊕ 42min*).

By train Brussels-Zuid/Bruxelles-Midi (*36min past the hour Mon–Fri, ⊕ 48min; via Leuven 10min past the hour, every hour & 58min past the hour, every 2 hours Sat–Sun, ⊕ 1hr 9min/49min*); Leuven (*5/13/34min past the hour Mon–Fri, 5min past the hour, every hour & 36min past the hour, every 2 hours Sat–Sun; ⊕ 14min*), Lier (*11/47min past the hour Mon–Fri, 5/58min past the hour Sat–Sun; ⊕ 30min*); Hasselt (*8/22/39min past the hour Mon–Fri, 10min past the hour, every hour & 38min past the hour, every 2 hours Sat–Sun; ⊕ 30min*).

TOURIST INFORMATION
📆 **Tourist information** 103 Elisabethlaan; ☎ 016 56 97 05; e toerisme@aarschot.be; www.toerismeaarschot.be; ⊕ 09.00–12.00 & 13.30–16.30 Tue–Fri, 13.30–16.30 Sat–Sun. Very friendly office a 10-min walk from centre that houses the modern Stedelijkmuseum, the public toilets & has free Wi-Fi. It also has a traditional-style bar that,

as of October 2012, will be reviving the local beer Aarschotse Bruine, which stopped being brewed when the Tielemans brewery, on the banks of the Demer River, closed in 1960.
🚲 **Bike rental** Velo, 18a Statieplein; ☎ 016 48 23 79; www.velo.be; ⊕ 07.00–19.00 Mon–Fri, 08.30–17.00 Sat; €10/day

WHERE TO STAY AND EAT
🏠 **'s Hertogenmolens** (25 rooms) 1a Demerstraat; ☎ 016 67 98 03; www.lodge-hotels.be. Located in the beautifully restored 16th-century former watermill, the en-suite rooms are a lovely hybrid of modern & old, with ageing white-brick walls & exposed wooden beams. The upmarket brasserie downstairs is calm & cosy & has views over the river. **€€€**

✕ **Kop of Munt** 7 Capucienenstraat; ☎ 016 43 94 39; ⊕ 12.00–14.00 & 18.00–22.00 Tue–Fri, 18.00–22.00 Sat–Sun. 'Heads or Tails' may be the name of this chic restaurant, but which ever way the coin lands you're guaranteed to have a good night munching on the likes of wild sea bass & Argentine steak. View of the city park from their terrace. **€€€€**

WHAT TO SEE AND DO
Onze-Lieve-Vrouwekerk (*Kardinaal Mercierstraat; ⊕ 09.00–12.00; admission free*) Built from the area's distinctive brown bricks, Aarschot's 15th-century church is very large considering the small size of the town, whose population was greatly diminished during an outbreak of the plague. Prior to this, the town flourished on the back of the Flanders–Rhineland trade route, which ran along the Demer River, and under the patronage of William de Croÿ, Lord of Aarschot, who became Charles V's tutor. Indeed, the emperor attended de Croÿ's funeral held at the church in 1521 before the body was moved to Leuven. The dim interior is lit only by the

flicker of candles and the glint of coloured light from the stained-glass windows. Amazingly, it survived the Iconoclasm, but lost most of its treasures during Spanish raids, except a lavish wrought-iron chandelier designed by Quentin Metys.

Begijnhof *(Begijnhof;* ⊕ *daily)* The town's original 13th-century *begijnhof* was looted and burned during the 15th and 16th centuries by Austrians and later the Spanish. The béguines fled to Leuven, but returned in 1609 and built the uniform brick buildings you see now. Unlike Flanders' other *begijnhofs*, it lacks charm because it's open to the road, but notice the statue of a saint above each doorway.

Stedelijkmuseum *(103 Elisabethlaan, inside tourist information office;* ⊕ *09.00–12.00 & 13.30–16.30 Tue–Fri, 13.30–16.30 Sat–Sun; admission €1.20, audio guide Dutch only)* The tourist office have obviously put a lot of effort into their town history museum, which starts with a caveman wearing trendy fur anklets and continues all the way up to the present day. Highlights include a room dedicated to Arthur Meulemans, an Aarschot-born composer who famously wrote the music for Brugge's Heilig-Bloedprocessie; an old Singer shoe-making machine which brought much-needed work to the town during the 1900s because it allowed people to work at home making clogs; and the sounds of the market singer, who sang the local news to passers-by until the 1960s/70s.

Day trips

Horst Kasteel *(28 Horststraat, 3220 Holsbeek;* ✆ *016 62 33 45;* ⊕ *Apr–Oct 14.00–17.00 Mon & Wed, 14.00–18.00 Sun, Jul–Aug 14.00–17.00 Mon, Wed–Fri, Nov–Mar 14.00–17.00 Mon, Wed & Sun; admission: adult/under 12 €4/1 inc audio guide)* Sitting calm and tranquil, 10km south of Aarschot, this beautiful 15th-century moated castle has barely changed since the last owner, Maria-Anna van den Tympel, moved out in the 17th century. The new audio guide gives you the full history of the castle and highlights the fabulous ceiling of the great hall decorated with scenes from Ovid's *Metamorphoses*. Take lunch at on-site restaurant Het Wagenhuis (✆ *016 62 35 84;* ⊕ *11.30–23.30 Mon & Wed–Sun;* €€€€) and walk it off in the surrounding gardens.

Getting there The castle is not accessible by public transport. By car, follow the N223 south, turn right into Luttelkolen, then first right onto Horststraat *(10km;* ⊕ *18min)*.

DIEST

For nearly 300 years, between 1499 and 1795, the attractive town of Diest was home to the Princes of Orange-Nassau – who still rule the Netherlands today. It subsequently became known as the 'Orange City' and benefited from its location on the River Demer and the Cologne–Brugge trading route that operated along it. By the 16th century the linen trade had declined and the city's status nosedived as it was caught up in rebellions against the Spanish. Only under Austrian rule did stability and commerce return. Most of the action centres around the contorted Grote Markt, but be sure to visit the town's *begijnhof* – one of Flanders' prettiest.

GETTING THERE AND AWAY

By car From Hasselt follow the N2 west *(24km;* ⊕ *30min)*; from Leuven follow the N2 east *(30km;* ⊕ *35min)*; from Aarschot follow the N10 west *(17km;* ⊕ *20min)*; and from Tienen follow the N29 north *(24km;* ⊕ *30min)*.

By train Hasselt (8/22/39min past the hour Mon–Fri, 10min past the hour, every hour & 38min past the hour, every 2 hours Sat–Sun; ⊕ 15min); Leuven (13/34min past the hour Mon–Fri, 5min past the hour, every hour & 36min past the hour, every 2 hours Sat–Sun; ⊕ 25min); Brussels-Zuid/Bruxelles-Midi (36min past the hour Mon–Fri, ⊕ 1hr; 58min past the hour, every 2 hours Sat–Sun, ⊕ 1hr 7min).

TOURIST INFORMATION

⁊ Tourist information 16a Koning Albertstraat; ☏ 013 35 32 74; e toerisme@diest. be; www.diest.be; ⊕ Apr–Sep 10.00–12.00 & 13.00–17.00 daily, Oct–Mar 10.00–12.00 & 13.00–17.00 Mon–Sat. A surprisingly large & modern office with very helpful staff.

♿ Bike rental Fietspunt, railway station; ☏ 013 66 51 47; ⊕ 08.30–17.00 Mon–Fri; €10/day

🏠 **WHERE TO STAY, EAT AND DRINK** Diest has several local specialities to look out for. Perhaps the most famous are the moon-shaped biscuits known as *halve maantjes*, and *patatjestaart*, a custard cake with crumble topping. In springtime (April/May), keep an eye out for *Diestse cruydtcoeck* on restaurant menus; it's a local herb pancake containing the flowering plant tansy. Out of season, you can usually pick some up at Thomfro (*72–4 Hasseltsestraat;* ⊕ *07.00–18.30 Tue–Sun*) delicatessen. Local beers worth trying are Gildenbier and Loterbol (page 158).

🏠 **The Lodge** (20 rooms) 23 Refugiestraat; ☏ 013 35 09 35; www.lodge-hotels.be. Known locally as Het Spijker, this 16th-century building belonged to the Abbey of Tongerlo refuge & was used as a grain store. Today it's an elegant 3-star with high-ceiling rooms & on-site restaurant. €€€

🏠 **B&B@Home** (2 rooms) 3 Heilige Geeststraat; ☏ 013 31 22 82; m 0477 91 55 49; www.bbbegijnhof.be. Homely apartment right in the centre of the *begijnhof*, with private garden, kitchen, living room, bathroom & 2 rooms (1 dbl bed & 1 twin). The exposed beams, brick walls & farmhouse kitchen table give it lots of character. Have a peek through the window of your neighbour at No 7 Heilige Geestraat – the lady restores ancient books. €€

✕ **Gasthof 1618** 18 Kerkstraat; ☏ 013 67 77 80; ⊕ 11.30–22.00 Tue–Sun. Inside the *begijnhof*, this ancient room is incredibly atmospheric thanks to all the medieval candle chandeliers & a central fireplace. There's a lot of crowd pleasers on the menu – shockingly, even fajitas – but I'd opt for the *Diesterse stoverij* or *konijn op Diestse wijze* – stew or rabbit cooked the local way. €€€–€€€€

✕ **Nicky's Catwalk** 26 Grote Markt; ☏ 013 31 36 40; ⊕ 09.00–01.00 daily. Its fish dishes, steaks & salads are recommended by the locals, but the real treat here is *rundswangetjes* (beef cheeks). Plump for a seat on the terrace overlooking the square, or a table right at the back of the restaurant. €€€

☕ **Stuckens** 5 Zoutstraat; ☏ 013 32 52 20; ⊕ 09.00–18.00 Tue, Thu–Sat, 08.00–18.00 Wed. Upmarket café with fun butterfly stencils on the walls & you can see the bakers at work thanks to a glass screen. It's also the best place in town to try/buy *halve maantje* biscuits. They come in 3 versions: original, apple or half-dipped chocolate. €

☕ **De Kozak** 26 Koning Albertstraat; ⊕ 07.00–19.00 Mon–Wed & Fri–Sun. A tiny & scruffy bakery that prepares *patatjestaart* a few paces from the tourist office.

♀ **De Molensteen** 33 Schaffensestraat; ☏ 013 33 36 11; ⊕ 09.30–late Mon, Wed–Sun. Diest's oldest brown café has Gildenbier on tap & it's served in chunky ceramic mugs.

WHAT TO SEE AND DO

Stadhuis (*Grote Markt*) Diest's brick-and-sandstone town hall dates from 1731. However, a much early version had stood on the site since 1337 and its medieval cellars now house **De Hofstadt** (*1 Grote Markt;* ☏ *013 35 32 09;* ⊕ *1 May–30 Sep 10.00–12.00 & 13.00–17.00 daily, 1 Oct–30 Apr 10.00–12.00 & 13.00–17.00 Tue–Sun, closed last 2 weeks of Dec & 1st week Jan; admission: adult/under 12*

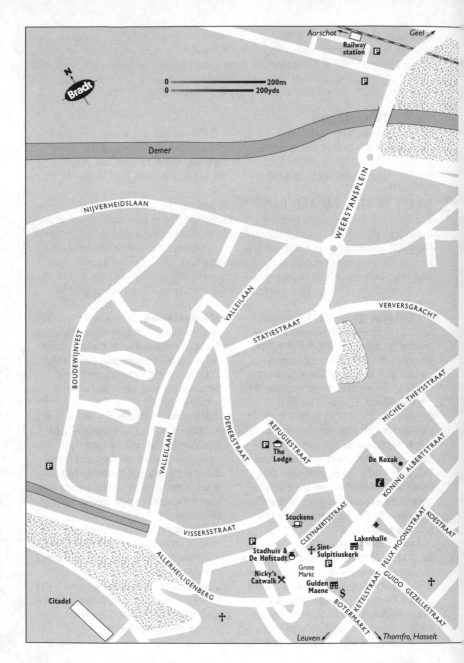

€4/free, inc entrance to *Museum voor Religieuze Kunst in Sint-Sulpitiuskerk*), a museum devoted to the town's history. There's no audio guide, but ask for the laminated explanation sheets in English and start in the Gothic room, round the corner from the entrance. Here look for the 14th-century Virgin and Child statue – a copy of the original now stands in New York's Metropolitan Museum of Art – and the five bells from Sint-Sulpitiuskerk carillon. The room on the left,

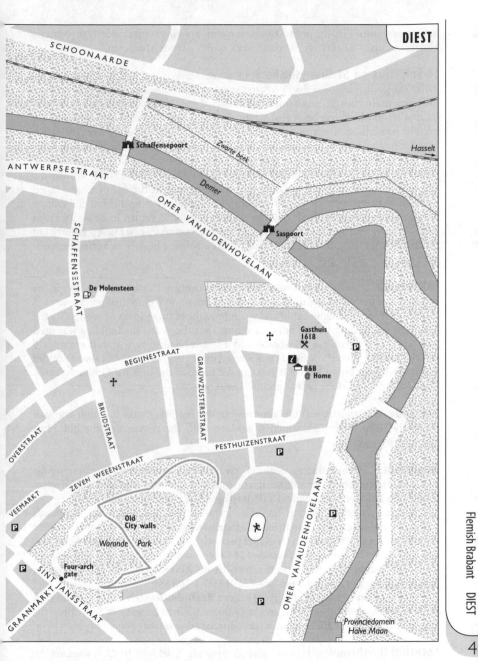

SCHOONAARDE

Schaffensepoort

Zwarte beek

Hasselt

ANTWERPSESTRAAT

Demer

OMER VANAUDENHOVELAAN

Saspoort

SCHAFFENSESTRAAT

De Molensteen

Gasthuis
1618

BEGIJNESTRAAT

GRAUWZUSTERSSTRAAT

B&B
@ Home

BRUIDSTRAAT

OVERSTRAAT

PESTHUIZENSTRAAT

ZEVEN WEEENSTRAAT

VEEMARKT

Old
City walls

OMER VANAUDENHOVELAAN

Warande   Park

Four-arch
gate

SINT JANSSTRAAT

GRAANMARKT

Provinciedomein
Halve Maan

the Orange Nassau room, has portraits of René of Chalon, the founder of the House of Orange-Nassau, and his wife, Anna of Lorraine, and next to these a painting of Philip William – whose tomb is found in Sint-Sulpitiuskerk – lying in state in Brussels. Hanging on the back wall of the Linden room you'll find Theodoor van Loon's *Adoration of the Magi* (1645) and *The presentation of Christ in the temple and Simeon's Prophesy* (1635). The lovely *Esschius* triptych is in the

Beguines' room. Finally, in the Treasure room, are two remarkable 17th-century Horti conclusi – effectively 3D patchwork quilts – from Mechelen.

St-Sulpitius en St-Dionysiuskerk (*1 Grote Markt;* ⊕ *15 May–15 Sep 14.00–17.00 Tue–Sun; admission free*) Walk to the other side of the square to get a full view of Diest's main church, nicknamed the 'Mustard Pot'. It's unique thanks to its two-tone mish-mash of red brick and white sandstone and because the construction became something of a farce, taking 18 architects 200 years to complete. The lavish interior has a number of treasures, most of which are held in the **Museum voor Religieuze Kunst** (⊕ *as above; admission: €2, or combi ticket with De Hofstadt €4*). However, the main attraction here is the tomb of Filips Willem (Philip William), a Prince of Orange and Lord of Diest. He was kidnapped at the age of 13 and taken to Spain to be brought up as a strict Catholic, in retaliation for his father, William the Silent, ignoring the Spanish Duke of Alba's order to return to Brussels. Filips Willem didn't return until he was 42, but from then on he visited Diest regularly. On his death, after lying in state in Brussels, his embalmed body was buried between the choirstalls on 1 April 1618.

Lakenhalle (*Koning Albertstraat*) Diest's 14th-century Cloth Hall was built at the height of the town's economic success when its linen was found throughout western Europe and the trading of cattle and grain brought in huge sums of money. By the 17th century, trading had all but ceased and, over the years, the building was used as a school, an abattoir, a fire station and a festival hall; it now stands empty and can't be visited. The yellow façade was altered in the 19th century, but if you wander down the streets either side of it you can see more of the original Gothic features. The 15th-century 'Holle Griet' cannon stands outside.

Warande (*Sint-Jansstraat*) On your way to the *begijnhof*, take a detour through the fairly steep town park which is studded with the remains of the old 19th-century city walls.

Begijnhof (*Begijnenstraat; admission free*) Diest's 18th-century *begijnhof* (page 18) is wonderful to wander around, its chocolate-box cottages studded with original fixtures and hidden among them a B&B (page 155), a restaurant and a pub.

Entering via the elaborate Baroque archway you encounter the *begijnhof*'s crumbling red-sandstone church, **Sint-Catharinakerk**, which is closed for renovation until 2014. Around the back is **De Kapel** pub (which may be closing down) and, just down the lane, the atmospheric **Gasthof 1618** restaurant (page 155). During summer it's worth visiting the information centre **In de Zevende Hemel** (*21 Kerkstraat;* ⊕ *Apr–Sep 14.00–17.00 Sat–Sun, Oct–Mar 14.00–17.00 Sun*).

Every year, on 13 May, the *begijnhof* hosts a **Begijnhoffeesten** with food and craft stalls to celebrate Mothers' Day, and at 19.00 on the first Sunday of September the streets and doorways are lined with tea lights, bathing the *begijnhof* in golden light.

Loterbol Huisbrouwerij (*58 Michel Theysstraat;* ✎ *013 77 10 07; www.loterbol. be;* ⊕ *16.00–00.00 first Sat of month; admission free*) Die-hard beer lovers will be pleased to hear that Belgium's smallest brewery – it produces only around 650 crates a year – opens the doors of its on-site café the first Saturday of every month. You can try the Loterbol vat, a bitter banana-scented beer (6%), and the fruitier Blond and Bruin (8%), and they usually open up the brewing rooms as well.

TIENEN

This often-overlooked town has the biggest Grote Markt in Belgium after Sint-Niklaas, thanks largely to its status as a major market town during the Middle Ages when an important trade route ran from Flanders to the Rhineland. Most of the action now centres around this square, which still hosts a weekly market on Tuesdays and Fridays (⏱ *07.00–13.00*) – and which is dominated by the former town prison on the north side and the flag-adorned Stadhuis (town hall) on the southern side. The rose compass which is embedded into the pavement outside the Stadhuis marks the spot where the town gallows stood and where, macabrely, Belgium's last beheading took place in 1845. Now known as 'Sugar Town' thanks to the large sugarbeet-processing factory to the south, its main attractions are the Suikermuseum and the Suikkerock festival it hosts every July.

GETTING THERE AND AWAY

By car From Leuven follow the N3 southeast (*19km;* ⏱ *25min*); from Hasselt, take the N80 to Sint-Truiden and then follow the N3 west to Tienen (*38km;* ⏱ *45min*); from Diest follow the N29 south (*24km;* ⏱ *30min*). You can park on the Grote Markt.

By train Leuven (*38/42/59min past the hour Mon–Fri, 5min past the hour, every hour & 38min past the hour, every 2 hours Sat–Sun;* ⏱ *11min*); Brussels-Zuid/Bruxelles-Midi (*7/31min past the hour Mon–Fri, 36min past the hour Sat–Sun;* ⏱ *40min*); Hasselt (*35min past the hour Mon–Fri, 1min past the hour Sat–Sun;* ⏱ *35min*). To get to the Grote Markt from the station, take Ijzerenwegstraat to your left and at the end turn right into Avendorenstraat; follow it all the way, crossing Goosensvest, past the park on your left, and you'll arrive at the southwestern edge of the main square.

TOURIST INFORMATION

ℹ Tourist information 4 Grote Markt; ☏016 80 57 38; e toerisme.tienen@skynet.be; www.tienen.be; ⏱ 10.00–17.00 Tue–Sun) Has a concealed entrance: through the archway of the Suikermuseum, turn left & walk through the *streekproducten* shop to the tourist information display stands at the front of the building. You can also enter via the Suikermuseum café at 4 Grote Markt. Has a few pamphlets in English.
🚲 Bike rental €3.75/half day from tourist office; deposit of €12.50 required.

WHAT TO SEE AND DO

Suikermusem (*6 Grote Markt;* ☏ *016 80 56 66; www.erfgoedsitetienen.be;* ⏱ *10.00–17.00 Tue–Sun, last ticket 16.00; admission: adult/under 26 €5/4, combi ticket with Toreke €6/5, inc audio guide*) Tienen's main attraction is this very – apologies for the pun – sweet museum which explains the four stages of harvesting sugar in inventive ways. On the lively 90-minute audio tour, narrated by Professor Zucchero, you'll visit the quirky maternity ward for young sugarbeets and a room of giant cakes.

Het Toreke (*6 Grote Markt;* ⏱ *10.00–17.00 Tue–Sun, last ticket 16.00; admission: adult/under 12 €4/2, combi ticket with Suikermuseum €6/5*) Remarkably the building which houses the Suikermuseum and the tourist information centre served as the town prison for over 500 years until 1975. It now contains an exhibition on Roman death rituals.

Onze-Lieve-Vrouwe-ten-Poelkerk (*Grote Markt;* ⏱ *09.00–19.00 Mon & Thu, 09.00–18.00 Tue, Wed & Fri, 15.00–18.00 Sat, 09.00–12.30 Sun*) Standing proud on the eastern side of the Grote Markt and gleaming white, Our Lady of the Lake Church is deceptively small on the inside. High Gothic on the outside and Baroque on the inside, it's named after a lake that once stood on the site and was drained to make way for the Grote Markt.

Suikerrock (*www.suikerrock.be*) During the last weekend of July, Tienen hosts this hugely popular rock/pop festival with stages set up on Grote Markt and Veemarkt. Tickets can be bought online and range from €25 to €45, depending on which day you attend.

5

East Flanders

East Flanders – or *Oost Vlaanderen* – is my favourite region. Spend a couple of days in the vibrant regional capital of Gent strolling the pretty cobbled streets and dining in some of Flanders' best restaurants, then head out into the countryside and have a go at the legendary Ronde van Vlaanderen cycling route – which runs from Sint-Niklaas to Oudenaarde – stopping off to try Geraardsbergen's delicious *mattentaart*. In Sint-Niklaas learn about the legend of Reynard the Fox, and take the kids to see Santa's workshop; explore Ronse's rarely visited 13th-century St Hermes crypt, and dance like a fool at the tourist-free Aalst Carnival (see box, page 196).

GENT (GHENT)

Victor Hugo described Gent as 'a kind of Venice of the North'. He wasn't exaggerating. Brugge may have more waterways, but its beauty has been somewhat tarnished by the tourist trade. Gent, on the other hand, receives fewer visitors but has equally pretty medieval architecture and real Flemish residents, who are immensely proud of their buzzing university town. Trams rattle through the cobbled streets of the compact city centre that is strong on boutique B&Bs and excellent restaurants, and home to fine and contemporary art museums, three *begijnhofs* and its lauded treasure: the *Adoration of the Mystic Lamb* triptych in Sint-Baafskathedraal.

HISTORY The city's name is believed to be a derivative of the Celtic word 'ganda' meaning 'confluence', which perfectly describes Gent's location at the crux of the Scheldt and Leie rivers. First records of the city spring up in AD630 when French missionary St-Amand founded the St-Pieter and St-Baafs abbeys. A settlement grew around them and despite a couple of Viking raids the city flourished from the 11th century onwards. Originally, Gent's wool industry was served by the sheep reared on the fertile flats surrounding the rivers, but this was soon eclipsed by trade with England and the import of grain from northern France. The speed of trade improved further when Margaret of Constantinople, Countess of Flanders, gave permission for the Lieve canal to be dug in 1251, linking Gent with Damme and thus the Zwin estuary that led out to the North Sea. As a result, from 1000 to 1550, Gent was the largest and most powerful city in western Europe (excluding Paris).

Gent's economic decline began at the outset of the Hundred Years' War between France and England. France's fleet of ships controlled much of the seas and as a result the trade of wool between England and Flanders was interrupted. It was restored for a time when Jacob van Artevelde (page 6) convinced France and England to recognise the neutrality of the Flemish cloth towns, but the resident's distrust of the counts was kept up for centuries and when the Philip II, Duke of Burgundy, attempted to levy

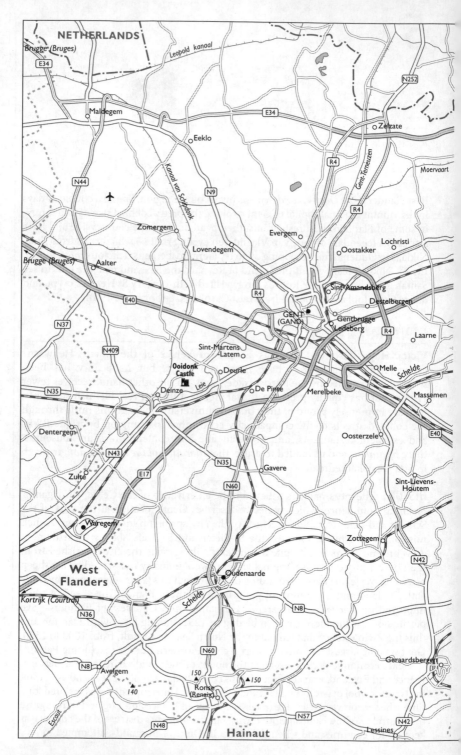

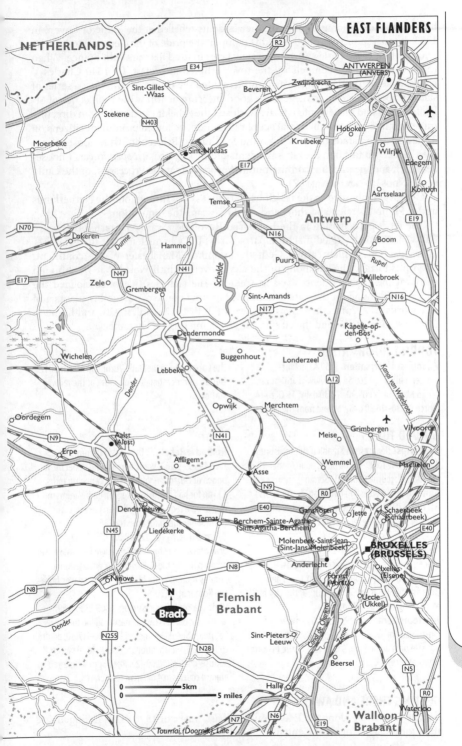

NETHERLANDS

Sint-Gilles
-Waas

Beveren

Zwijndrecht

ANTWERPEN
(ANVERS)

Stekene

N403

Hoboken

Moerbeke

Kruibeke

Wilrijk

Edegem

Sint-Niklaas

E17

Aartselaar

Kontich

N70

Temse

Antwerp

E19

Lokeren

Durme

Hamme

Schelde

N16

Boom

Rupel

Zele

N47

N41

Puurs

Willebroek

Grembergen

N16

Sint-Amands

E17

N17

Dendermonde

Kapelle-op-
den-Bos

Wichelen

Buggenhout

Londerzeel

Dender

Lebbeke

A12

Kanaal van Willebroek

Oordegem

Opwijk

Merchtem

N9

Aalst
(Alost)

N41

Meise

Grimbergen

Vilvoorde

Erpe

Affligem

Asse

Wemmel

Machelen

N9

Denderleeuw

R0

E40

Ganshoren

Jette

Schaerbeek
(Schaarbeek)

E40

Ternat

Berchem-Sainte-Agathe
(Sint-Agatha-Berchem)

N45

Liedekerke

Molenbeek-Saint-Jean
(Sint-Jans-Molenbeek)

**BRUXELLES
(BRUSSELS)**

N8

Ninove

N8

Anderlecht

Ixelles
(Elsene)

Forest
(Vorst)

Dender

N

Bradt

**Flemish
Brabant**

Uccle
(Ukkel)

Canal de Charleroi

Zenne

N255

Sint-Pieters-
Leeuw

N28

0   5km

0   5 miles

Halle

Beersel

N5

R0

Waterloo

Tournai (Doornik), Lille

N7

N6

E19

**Walloon
Brabant**

higher taxes on the import of grain the residents rebelled at the Battle of Gavere in 1453. It wasn't a success, but that didn't dampen the pride of the Gent residents, who rejected Emperor Charles V's vote for new taxes to fund his wars with France. When the taxes were made compulsory the town erupted in protest. By 1540 Charles V had had enough and as punishment implemented the *Concessio Carolina*; a series of statutes abolishing city privileges. For good measure he threw the monks out of St-Baafs Abbey and made it into a fortress, closed the Scheldt canal and began directing trade north to Antwerp; in a final act of retribution, he forced prominent citizens on 3 May 1540 to parade barefoot from the Stadhuis to Princenhof with nooses about their necks. To this day, the city's residents are nicknamed *Stroppendragers* ('noose-bearers'), and the march is commemorated every year at the Procession of the Guild of the Noose Wearers (page 57).

Gent was embroiled in the religious wars that swept throughout the Netherlands under Philip II's reign and thousands fled to escape the inquisition.

The city's participation in the Industrial Revolution was kick-started by Lieven Bauwens, who smuggled machine parts across the Channel and set up a number of textile mills, which earned Gent the moniker 'Manchester of the continent'. The mills formed the backbone of the city's revenue until World War II, although many of the city's residents lived in squalor. The factories that once clogged the city are still found on the outskirts today, but now house car-assembly plants and steelworks. The Universiteit Gent that was built in 1817 is still in situ and home to 50,000 students who lend the city its convivial, intellectual character.

TOURIST INFORMATION

Tourist information [169 A2] 5 Sint-Veerleplein; 09 266 56 60; www.visitgent.be; 15 Mar–14 Oct 09.30–18.30 daily, 15 Oct–14 March 09.30–16.30 daily. Moved from the crypt of the Lakenhalle to the Oude Vismijn in March 2012. During summer there's also a kiosk at the railway station.

GUIDED TOURS

Boat trips Depart from Kraanlei/Vleeshuisbrug 1 Apr–30 Oct 10.00–18.00 daily; adult/under 12 €6.50/3.50; journey time 40–50min.

Gandante 16 Woestijnegoedlaan; 09 375 31 61; m 0479 51 52 42; www.gandante.be. Offer tours of the Belfort every Sat at 15.30 for €3, not including entry.

Gentse Gidsen 5 Sint-Veerleplein (tourist office); 09 233 07 72; www.gentsegidsen.be. Run guided walking tours May–Sep 14.30 daily, Oct–Apr 14.30 Sat for €8pp & tours of the city hall at 14.30 Mon–Thu for €5pp.

Jog-Tours Gent m 0499 53 23 65; www.jog-tours.com. Combine your city tour with some exercise on a guided jog. A 6km tour of the historic city centre costs €12pp.

Nomad & Rebel 73 Octaaf van Dammestraat; m 0495 99 93 63; www.nomad-and-rebel.be. A bunch of Canadians who run city canoeing tours. €11pp for half day, €16pp for full day. Minimum of 2 people required. They'll even pack you a champagne lunch for an extra €35.

Town criers 09 220 48 02/ 09 222 67 43; www.towncriers.be. A free tour available May–Sep accompanying the *Belleman* or town crier on a Sunday morning tour of the markets. Leaves from the Kouter at 10.30.

Vizit 4a Corduwaniersstraat; 09 233 76 89; www.vizit.be. Run two culinary walking tours every Saturday: 'Sneukelen met Stijl' (15.30–17.30; adult/child €12/5) which introduces Gent's local sweets & 'Amuse-gueule' (18.00–22.00; €55pp) where you enjoy 4 courses in 4 different restaurants.

GETTING THERE AND AWAY

By car Travelling along the E40 from the coast, take exit 13 towards Drongen and then follow signs for Gent Centrum.

By train Brussels-Zuid/Bruxelles-Midi (*5/14/26min past the hour Mon–Fri; 5/26min past the hour Sat–Sun;* ⊕ *30min*); Antwerp (*on the hour & 18/52min past the hour Mon–Fri, 34/52min past the hour Sat–Sun;* ⊕ *55min*); Brugge (*18/25/37/58min past the hour Mon–Fri; 5/35/37/58min past the hour Sat–Sun;* ⊕ *25min*).

GETTING AROUND

By tram Gent city centre is about a 20-minute walk from the Gent-Sint-Pieters railway station (☏ *02 528 28 28; www.nmbs.be*), so it's worth catching tramline #1 (direction Everhem) and alighting at Korenmarkt. At the time of writing, there was a huge amount of construction work going on around the station. It's scheduled to finish around 2016 and, until then, trams for the city centre depart from the terminal on Koningin Maria Hendrikaplein opposite – and a little to the left – of the entrance. To get back to the station take tram #1 direction Flanders Expo.

By bus If you're coming from Gent-Dampoort station, De Lijn buses #3,17,18,38 and 39 will take you to the city centre.

By bike See page 174 for bike rental. The tourist office has four themed cycling route maps. The most interesting are the 'Religieus erfgoed' or Religious Heritage trail (14.7km) and the 'Onstann can een stad aan het water' (10.8km) which follows the waterways.

By boat Numerous companies offer tours of the waterways (see opposite).

⌂ **WHERE TO STAY** Gent excels in the bed and breakfast. Choose from plush mansions, an artist's studio, and even an eco-friendly barge. The choice is wide-ranging and in comparison to Brussels and Brugge, prices at even the most upmarket establishments are incredibly reasonable. I've listed my favourites below, but a full list can be found at www.bedandbreakfast-gent.be. Otherwise there are about 20 hotels in the city centre, and budget accommodation is catered for well too: there's a campsite and a clutch of really good youth hostels. The tourist office (opposite) is happy to make bookings free of charge. A deposit is required, but this will be deducted from your hotel bill.

Luxury

⌂ **Hotel Verhaegen** [166–7 C4] (4 rooms) 110 Oude Houtlei; ☏ 09 265 07 65; www. hotelverhaegen.be. This palatial 18th-century private mansion has the 'wow' factor in bucketfuls. Renovated by interior designers Marc Vergauwe & Jan Rosseel, the building is alive with detail & lush furnishings. Ceilings are adorned with original frescoes, the walls decorated with turquoise panelling & Rococo paintings, & the windows framed by huge heavy drapes. Each room is individually named & styled: the Balcony room with its enormous bath; the blue Italian room; the Paola that has a magnificent *lit à la Polinèse* (4-poster-bed with drapes) & my personal favourite, the Chambre des Amoureux, which has views of the garden &

mirrors round the bath. These classic surroundings are blended seamlessly with state-of-the-art flatscreen TVs & motion-activated lights. What's more, most items are for sale. Marc & Jan are happy to arrange a tour guide for you. B/fast €15pp; dinner is available on request. €€€€– €€€€€

Mid-range

⌂ **De Waterzooi** [166–7 B2] (2 rooms) 2 Sint-Veerleplein; ☏ 09 330 77 21; www.dewaterzooi.be. Right opposite Het Gravensteen castle & housed in an 18th-century townhouse, the luxurious, country-chic Felix & mezzanine-level Phara suites feel very decadent with private sitting rooms, rain showers & exposed wooden beams. Minimum 2-night stay at w/ends. Excellent price/quality. €€€

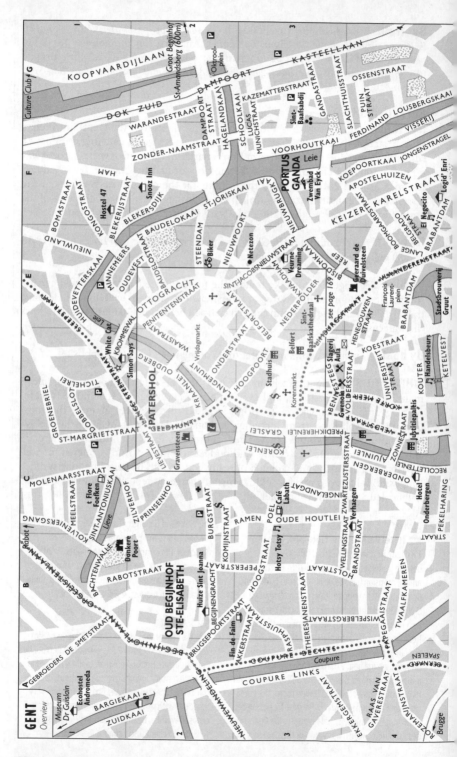

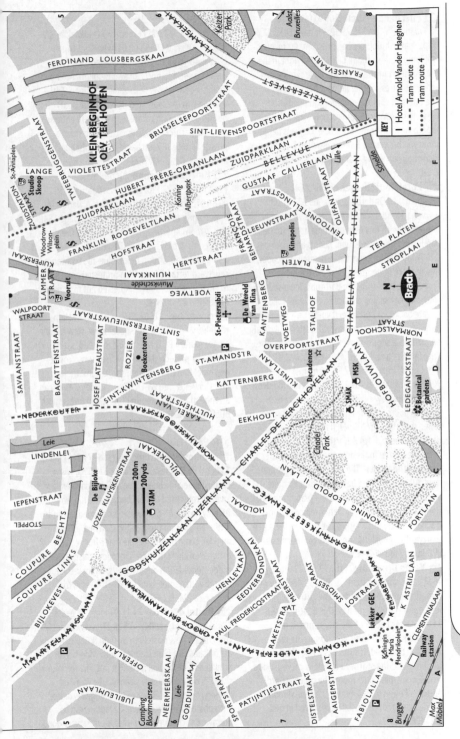

5

167

🏠 **Puerto Patershol** [169 B1] (1 room) 55 Kraanlei; ☎ 09 225 75 32; m 0476 645 557; http://patersholbb.ceciliajaime.com. Art lovers will jump at this unique B&B located right in the historic heart of the city & run by Argentinean artist/sculptress Cecilia Jaime & her husband. She offers the Suite Patagonia equipped with en-suite bathroom, living room & a kitchen with superb views over the River Leie. Cecilia is happy to show you her studio & offers drawing & painting workshops on Wed & Sat afternoons. Cash only. €€€

🏠 **Hotel Onderbergen** [166–7 C4] (12 rooms) 69 Onderbergen; ☎ 09 223 62 00; www.hotelonderbergen.be. Friends were really impressed with this new boutique hotel situated barely 50m from the action. Rooms are spacious & decorated with funky hand-painted wallpaper; the beds are huge, there's free Wi-Fi & some rooms have free-standing bathtubs. You also have your own key so you can access the hotel via a private backdoor entrance. If you're on a romantic getaway, pay €50 extra & they'll scatter rose petals on the bed & supply flowers, chocs & champagne. Price/quality a real gem. €€–€€€

🏠 **Logid' Enri** [166–7 F4] (5 rooms) 201 Brabantdam; ☎ 09 328 80 93; www.logidenri. be. Stunning new B&B whose rooms have real wooden floors & come equipped with Nespresso coffee machines, free Wi-Fi, flatscreen TV & iPod dock. The South, Fifth & North rooms have twin beds; the former looks onto the street, the latter two onto the garden. The Fourth has a mezzanine level. All except Noord have high-spec en-suite bathrooms. The Suite bathroom – featuring a free-standing bathtub with modern fireplace alongside it & floor-to-ceiling window overlooking the green courtyard – is nothing short of breathtaking. Free DVD library too. €€–€€€

🏠 **Verne Dreaming** [166–7 E3] (2 rooms) 46 St-Jacobsnieuwstraat; ☎ 09 233 48 55; www. vernedreaming.be. Lavish in the extreme, yet such good value for money, this boutique B&B on the eastern edge of the city centre is run by photographers Annie & Herman. The pink Shanghai opium-den suite has a huge bed, a laughing Buddha statue, a fabulous carved-wood arch & open-plan bathroom; the green Oxford suite is all open plan & features a free-standing purple claw-foot bath. B/fast is served in bed. €€–€€€

Budget

🏠 **B³** [166–7 A2] (1 room) 43 Zuidkaai; ☎ 09 324 49 50; m 0477 54 00 03; www.bnbtriple. be. For 40 years this barge delivered barrels of Antwerp sand to ports all over Belgium. After a loving 1-year conversion, owners Sabina & Carl (who live in the loading quarters of the boat) offer guests the Captain's Suite with a private entrance, en-suite bathroom, kitchenette, living room & private terrace. €5 surcharge for 1-night bookings at w/ends. Cash only. €€

🏠 **Huize Sint Joanna** [166–7 B2] (1 apartment) 27 Proveniersstersstraat; ☎ 055 49 66 07; www.huizesintjoanna.be. A wonderful opportunity to stay in Gent's *begijnhof* (page 184). This 3-room apartment features original fireplaces, oak beams & old clay floor tiles, can sleep 3 & has a small kitchen, sitting room, blue-tile bathroom & courtyard terrace. Since it's a protected area, home to elderly people, you're requested not to make any noise after 23.00. €€

🏠 **Snooz Inn** [166–7 F2] (1 room) 89 Ham; m 0496 24 14 26; www.snoozinn.be. New highly contemporary B&B with a king-size bed, satin sheets, TV projected onto wall, Nespresso coffee-machine, foldaway kitchenette, chromotherapy rain shower & free Wi-Fi. Bikes €10/day & they can arrange massages. Regular b/fast €10; b/fast with bubbly €20. €€

Shoestring

🏠 **Ecohostel Andromeda** [166–7 A1] (4 rooms, 16 beds) 35 Bargiekaai; m 0486 67 80 33; www. ecohostel.be. All aboard! Liselot & her partner have lovingly converted this old barge into a hip, eco-friendly hostel. All dirty water is siphoned upwards & filtered through the roof-top reed bed, all waste recycled & the mattresses are made from eco-latex & cotton. Fun chalk messages in toilets, trust-operated fridge stocked with organic beers, & hippy-style lounge with games, books & Wi-Fi. Bikes €7/day. Dorm €22–24, dbl €65. €

🏠 **Hostel 47** [166–7 F1] (9 rooms, 38 beds) 47 Blekerijstraat; m 0478 71 28 27; www.hostel47. com. Trendy new hostel run by Youri & Georg. Dorms are finished to a high standard with wide-berth bunkbeds & individual reading lights. The communal showers & sinks are very swanky. Free Wi-Fi, no laundry, no curfew. B/fast room/lounge decorated with photos from their travels. 2 laptops can be borrowed to check email. Includes b/fast (very good

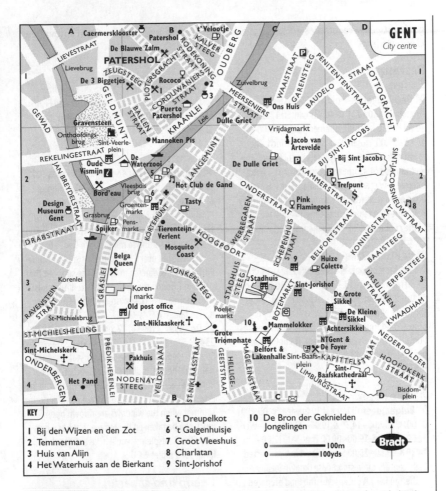

GENT
City centre

KEY

1 Bij den Wijzen en den Zot	**5** 't Dreupelkot	**10** De Bron der Geknielden
2 Temmerman	**6** 't Galgenhuisje	Jongelingen
3 Huis van Alijn	**7** Groot Vleeshuis	
4 Het Waterhuis aan de Bierkant	**8** Charlatan	
	9 Sint-Jorishof	

0 — 100m
0 — 100yds

Bradt

N

coffee) & sheets, but not city tax (€2.50pp). Cash only. Dorm €24, sgl €45, dbl €66. **€**

⚠ Camping Blaarmeersen [166–7 A6] (206 places) 12 Zuiderlaan; ☎ 09 266 81 60; www.gent. be/blaarmeersen. Part of an outdoor activity park,

Gent's 5-star campsite is a 10-min bus ride (#38) from the Korenmarkt. Facilities include a library, café, takeaway kitchen, shop & laundry room. Jul–Aug €5.50 per adult, plus €5 per tent; Sep–Jun €4.50 per adult, plus €4 per tent. **€**

✗ WHERE TO EAT The city has a particularly good range of restaurants, but Patershol ('Hole of the Monk') is without a doubt the word on the street when it comes to dining out in Gent. During the 17th and 18th centuries the area belonged to poor textile manufacturers, but was revived in the 1960s by a group of artists. Its winding medieval streets and brick-red façades now conceal top-class restaurants.

The city is famous for its tummy-warming *Gentse waterzooi* (made with chicken instead of eel) and *Gentse stoverij* (a beef, liver and kidney stew). Vegetarians will be happy as carrots in Gent, which has the largest number of veggie restaurants in Europe. Moreover, every Thursday is vegetarian day and restaurants make a special effort to offer at least one or two veggie options.

For a complete change, head to Klein Turkije, Gent's Turkish quarter, on Sleepstraat and try the oven-cooked Turkish pizza pockets filled with meat, goats' cheese, vegetables and egg. And remember to look out for Gent's new beer, Gentse Strop.

Restaurants

Expensive

✘ **De 3 Biggetjes** [169 B1] 7 Zeugsteeg, Patershol; ☎ 09 224 46 48; ⊕ winter: 12.00–14.00 & 19.00–21.00, summer: 12.00–15.00 & 19.00–23.00, closed Wed, Sun & Sat lunch. The '3 Little Pigs' is revered by locals. Lychi Cuong, the Vietnamese chef, originally came over as a boat-refugee & was adopted by Belgians. He has since gone on to receive a *Bib Gourmand* for his culinary flair. I prefer a table near the front with views of the cobbled street. Lunch menus good value. €€€€€

✘ **De Blauwe Zalm** [169 B1] 2 Vrouwebroersstraat; ☎ 09 224 08 52; ⊕ 19.00–21.30 Mon, 12.00–13.30 & 19.00–21.30 Tue–Fri, 19.00–21.30 Sat. Faultless seafood restaurant in the heart of the Patershol district. The décor is crisp & modern – look for the fish-shaped ceiling lights – & the service is excellent. It's not cheap, but it's lauded as the best fish restaurant in town. €€€€€

Above average

✘ **Belga Queen** [169 A3] 10 Graslei; ☎ 09 280 01 00; ⊕ 12.00–14.30 & 19.00–23.00 Mon–Wed, 12.00–14.30 & 19.00–00.00 Thu–Sat, 12.00–14.30 & 18.30–23.00 Sun. Housed in a converted 13th-century grain storehouse (known locally as the 'Spijker') & oozes style. The food prepared in the open kitchen is delicious & pretentious in equal measures & the Belgian-Congo-styled bar hosts DJ sessions Thu–Sat in the Cigar Lounge Bar. Beware: the ladies' toilet has transparent doors! €€€€–€€€€€

✘ **Bij den Wijzen en den Zot** [169 B1] 42 Hertogstraat, Patershol; ☎ 09 223 42 30; ⊕ 12.00–14.00 & 18.30–22.00 Tue–Sat. The 'Wiseman & the Fool' was the first restaurant on the scene in the Patershol area. Set up over 25 years ago by a circle of artist friends, this unpretentious nook-&-cranny spot holds the prestigious title of 'beste Gentse viswaterzooi' – an obvious dish to start with when choosing from the French/Flemish menu. €€€€

✘ **Bord'eau** [169 A2] Sint-Veerleplein, Oude Vismijn; ☎ 09 223 20 00; ⊕ 12.00–14.30 & 18.30–22.00 Mon–Thu, 12.00–14.30 & 18.30–22.30 Fri–Sat, 12.00–15.00 Sun. Urbane restaurant/bar inside the newly renovated Fish Market (page 180) with stunning views of the Grasbrug & Korenlei €€€€

Mid-range

✘ **Pakhuis** [169 B4] 4 Schuurkenstraat; ☎ 09 223 55 55; ⊕ 12.00 – 14.30 & 18.00– midnight Mon–Sat, closed Sun. Transformed by renowned Portuguese chef & designer, Antoine Pinto, this former iron warehouse (tucked down a side-alley) is a stunning setting to mingle with Gent's hip residents. Split over 2 levels, the restaurant echoes with chatter & diners can bask in the sunlight that pours in through the vaulted glass ceiling, whilst they sample first-class oysters & posh Flemish/Italian fare. €€€–€€€€

✘ **De Foyer** [169 C4] 17 Sint-Baafsplein; ☎ 09 234 13 54; ⊕ 12.00–14.00 & 18.30–22.00 Wed–Sun. An elegant brasserie on the first floor of the National Theatre. It dishes up seafood, *waterzooi* & light bites & is at its liveliest on Sun when brunch is served 09.00–11.00. It's also very popular during summer when the windows are thrown open & lunch can be taken on the terrace that has views over Sint-Baafsplein – you'll have to fight the locals for a table! €€€

Cheap and cheerful

✘ **Gwenola** [166–7 D3] 66 Voldersstraat; ☎ 09 233 17 39; ⊕ 11.00–19.00 Mon–Sat. This old-fashioned café with sturdy brown tables & porcelain plates on the walls has been serving its famous Breton crêpes for over 50 years – testament to their quality. €€

✘ **Mosquito Coast** [169 B3] 28 Hoogpoort; ☎ 09 224 37 20; ⊕ 11.00–late Mon–Sat, 15.00–late Sun. I always takes friends to this laidback travellers' café for a glass of Gent-made aperitif Roomer (see box opposite). Has bookshelves of guides, two terraces & a menu of filling wraps & salads. €€

✘ **Slagerij Aula** [166–7 D3] 24 Voldersstraat; ☎ 09 225 05 14; ⊕ 11.30–14.40 Mon–Sat. Locals head to this respected butchers at lunchtime for their hot, good-value meals served at the bar. €€

Shoestring

✕ **De Blauwe Kiosk** [166–7 D4] Kouter;
☎ 0496 51 95 60; ⏰ 11.00–14.00 Sat,
10.00–16.00 Sun. Locals flock to this classy,
open-air stand on w/ends for an indulgent snack
of fresh oysters & champagne. Half a dozen of
the aphrodisiac inducers & a glass of bubbly costs
€13.60. €

✕ **Lekker GEC** [166–7 B8] 5–6 Koningen Maria
Hendrikplein; ☎ 09 242 87 50; ⏰ 12.00–22.00

Cafés

🍺 **Simon Says** [166–7 D1] 8 Sluizeken; ☎ 09
233 03 43; www.simon-says.be; ⏰ 09.00–18.00
Tue–Fri, 10.00–18.00 Sat–Sun. Charming
coffee house run by Cardiff-born Simon Turner
& his boyfriend Christopher. Mosaic-tile tables,
Panamarenko (page 24) drawings on the walls &
coffee served in elegant Turkish silver pots. Grab a
newspaper & relax. 2 very stylish en-suite rooms
on second floor also available (€€). €€

🍺 **Café Labath** [166–7 C3] 1 Oude Houtlei;
☎ 09 225 28 25; ⏰ 08.00–19.00 Mon–Fri, 09.00–
19.00 Sat. Coffee house serving healthy soups &
sandwiches. Try the Malteser hot chocolate. €

🍺 **Fin de Faim** [166–7 B3] 73 Hoogstraat;
☎ 09 225 10 25; ⏰ 08.00–16.00 Mon– Fri.
Homely ye olde 4-table café serving soups, salads,
pasta dishes, paninis (€6 eat-in, €4 takeaway) &
cakes – all homemade by Diana, the owner. €

Tue–Sat, 12.00–15.00 Sun. A self-service
restaurant dishing up delicious, 100% organic,
vegetarian meals prepared by chefs in training.
Essentially, they are locals who have had real
trouble finding employment, so the restaurant
trains them up for a year & a half so they can find
jobs elsewhere. The cost is measured by the weight
of your plate, so you don't pay for what you don't
eat. Try the house aperitif *vierbloesemsiroop* –
white wine with elderflower cordial. €

🍺 **Huize Collete** [166–7 C3] 6 Belfortstraat;
📱 0478 90 64 73; ⏰ 09.00–19.00 Tue–Fri,
10.00–19.00 Sat–Sun. Co-owned by the lovely
Aline & Ottelien, it's named after Aline's mother
who kindly stumped up the cash to allow them
to open this café/bookstore inspired by their
travels through England. The house specialities
are sumptuous homemade cakes & hot chocolate
made by melting lumps of top-quality chocolate
into steaming milk – no cheap powders here!
Upstairs there's a second-hand bookstore with
sofas & tables which are popular with studying
students. €

🍺 **Tasty** [166–7 B2] 1 Hoogpoort; ☎ 09
225 74 07; ⏰ Apr–Sep 11.00–20.00 Mon–Sat,
Oct–Mar 11.00–19.00 Mon–Sat. Fun vegetarian
café serving a range of veggie burgers, smoothies,
soups & wheatgrass shots. €

ENTERTAINMENT AND NIGHTLIFE The university city has buzzing nightlife. The
historical centre is strong on traditional bars, while the south of the city is home to
theatre, concert halls and Blandijnberg, the lively student area. Above all, the city
excels in live music and hosts several important festivals during the summer (pages
52–7). Tickets for most concerts and shows can be bought at FNAC newsagent (*88
Veldstraat;* ☎ *09 223 40 80*).

Pubs

🍺 **De Dulle Griet** [169 C2] 50 Vrijdagmarkt;
☎ 09 224 24 55; ⏰ 16.60–01.00 Mon, 12.00–
01.00 Tue–Sat, 12.00–19.30 Sun. Named after

the enormous 15th-century red cannon nearby,
this bric-a-brac pub serves over 250 types of beer
but the real draw is the 'shoe challenge.' There are
2 stories behind this tradition. The first claims the

ROOMER

If you're looking to try a local tipple, I highly recommend Gent-made Roomer:
an elderflower-flavoured aperitif with real flowers in it. Brothers Maarten
and Jeroen have revived their grandmother's recipe and its been a roaring
success. You can visit their factory (groups only unfortunately) at Krevelstraat
3, or buy a bottle at the Groot Vleeshuis (page 174).

landlord got rather peeved with everyone stealing the specially designed Kwak beer glasses, so required a deposit of 1 shoe that was hoisted up to the ceiling in a basket & let down only when the glass was returned. The second story claims it's a bit of fun that challenges contestants to finish the litre of beer the Kwak beerstands holds. The rules are simple: if you finish the beer, you get your shoe back, if not, well…you don't.

🍺 **Het Waterhuis aan de Bierkant** [169 B2] 9 Groentenmarkt; ☎ 09 225 06 80; ⏱ 11.00–late daily. Situated right beside the River Leie, this pub is especially popular as a terrace-hopping spot in summer. It stocks over 160 types of beer, so you could settle in until morning. It specialises in gueuze & kriek, but ask for the beer of the month on special offer.

🍺 **'t Dreupelkot** [169 B2] 12 Groentenmarkt; ☎ 09 224 21 20; ⏱ 16.00– late daily. Run by the inimitable Pol Rysenaer for 25 years, this small café is the ideal place to sample *jenever* (page 48). Furnishings are sparse (you seat yourself round upturned barrels) & you may have to wake Pol up if he's sleeping in his armchair, but there are more than 225 flavours of schnapps on offer here, from garlic to grapefruit.

🍺 **t' Velootje** [169 B1] 2 Kalversteeg, Patershol; ☎ 09 223 29 34; ⏱ 18.00–03.00 Tue–Sat. Don't miss this wacky bar crammed with old bicycles, antiques & knick-knacks – you can barely get in the door. Owner Lieven De Vos works at the local Volvo car factory during the day, & has run this beloved place at night for 25 years – he even has fan mail from Russia & Arabia! Find a space on the wooden benches & Lieven will bring you 1 of the 2 beers on tap: usually Westmalle Dubbel & Delirium Tremens.

🍺 **Spijker** [169 A2] 3–5 Pensmarkt; ☎ 09 329 44 40; ⏱ 09.00–04.00 daily. Cosy candlelit bar housed in a 13th-century former leprosy shelter. Terrace out the back with lovely views of the canal. Free Wi-Fi. Try the honey beer.

Bars

♀ **Pink Flamingo's** [169 C2] 55 Onderstraat; ☎ 09 233 47 18; ⏱ 12.00–00.00 Mon–Wed, 12.00–03.00 Thu–Fri, 14.00–03.00 Sat, 14.00–00.00 Sun. A Gent institution, this fun-loving bar celebrates all things kitsch with a Barbie-doll chandelier & music ranging from swing to soul & a bit of boogie.

♀ **Rococo** [169 B1] 57 Corduwaniersstraat; ☎ 09 224 30 35; ⏱ 22.00–late Tue–Sun. Cosy time-worn room with candelabras on ancient wooden tables, an old piano in the corner & dried sausages hanging from a rack at the small bar presided over by the owner, Betty.

♀ **Trefpunt** [169 D2] 18 Bij Sint-Jacobs; ☎ 09 225 36 76; ⏱ 17.00–late daily. The famous Gent Festival (page 54) started here in 1968 when Walter de Buck took to the stage of this bar with a couple of friends & their guitars. A lively local haunt that hosts free Monday concerts 21.00.

Nightclubs

☆ **Culture Club** [166–7 G1] 174 Afrikalaan; ☎ 09 233 09 46; ⏱ 22.00–late Fri & Sat. This is *the* place to party in Gent. It's filled with fashionistas & the odd celebrity, moving between the chill-out & R'n'B rooms & the main hall blasting out techno-tunes mixed by live DJs. Admission Sat €8; €10 after midnight.

☆ **White Cat** [166–7 D1] 40 Drongenhof; ☎ 0496 18 91 89; www.white-cat.be; ⏱ 20.00–04.00 Wed–Thu, 20.00–05.00 Fri–Sat, closed Wed May–Jul. Underground funk/jazz bar in the Patershol district with a fish-tank bar.

Live music

🎵 **Charlatan** [169 D2] 6 Vlasmarkt; ☎ 09 224 24 57; www.charlatan.be; ⏱ 19.00–late Tue–Sun. Gent's biggest live-music bar with free shows at 22.00 on Thu, Sun & occasionally Sat too.

🎵 **El Negocito** [166–7 F4] 121 Brabantdam; ☎ 09 329 87 01; ⏱ 18.00–late daily. A stone's throw from the red-light district, don't judge this Bohemian bar by its scruffy appearance. Run by Chilean refugee Juan Carlos, it's great fun with free Latin/jazz concerts on Mon, Tue & Wed & a good selection of rums & cocktails. Juan whips up some delicious tapas too.

🎵 **Hot Club de Gand** [169 B2] Schuddenvisstraatje, 15b Groentenmarkt; m 0486 53 94 55; ⏱ 17.00–late Tue–Sun. Tucked down a side-alley (look for the sign next to the optician's) on the right-hand side, this cosy nook hosts weekly acoustic concerts & jam sessions featuring everything from jazz bands to gipsy quartets. Inspired by a similar club in Paris, the guitarist Django Reinhardt opened the club in May 2005. The candles, exposed brick-work & toe-tapping tunes combine to create a memorable evening.

♪ **Hotsy Totsy** [166–7 C3] 1 Hoogstraat; ✆ 09 224 20 12; ⊕ 18.00–late Mon–Fri, 20.00–late Sat–Sun. On the corner of the street, inside a stepped-gabled house, this legendary bar is usually humming with locals, who sit surrounded by black-&-white pictures of past acts with a beer in hand listening to the brilliant line up of singers, jazz musicians, comedians & poets.

Concert halls

🖰 **De Bijloke** [166–7 C5] 2 Jozef Kluyskensstraat; ✆ 09 269 92 92; www.debijloke.be; ⊕ ticket office: 10.00–12.00 & 13.00–17.00 Tue–Fri, 13.00–17.00 Sat. Housed in the Gothic former infirmary of Bijlokeabdij this renovated concert hall puts on respected classical & contemporary music concerts. Events usually start at 20.00 & take place every night except Sun & Mon.

🖰 **Vooruit** [166–7 E5] 23 Sint-Pietersnieuwstraat; ✆ 09 267 28 28; www.vooruit.be. This Art Nouveau building was built by the socialist party 1910–14 & finally opened after World War I in 1918. It flourished as an arts centre for the working classes who couldn't afford opera, but during World War II the Germans set up offices in the Majolica room & kept livestock in the concert hall. It was left a shambles, & furthermore had lost its relevance among the new 'Americanised' generation. Unused, it fell into disrepair & was earmarked for demolition until two students from Gent university wrote a thesis on the building & evoked overwhelming public response to save & restore it. It now hosts all manner of performances from music to theatre & dance.

Theatre

🖰 **NT Gent** [169 C4] 17 Sint-Baafsplein; ✆ 09 225 01 01; www.ntgent.be. Home to Nederlands Toneel Gent (NTG), the Gent & East Flanders repertory company that runs regular productions of classical & contemporary theatre in Flemish. They use 2 other venues as well: NT Gent Arca (3 Sint-Widostraat) & Minnemeers (Minnemeers 8). The De Foyer brasserie is also on site (page 170).

Cinema

🖰 **Kinépolis Gent** [166–7 E7] 12 Ter Platen; ✆ 09 265 06 00; www.kinepolis.com. Gent's most modern cinema shows the latest blockbusters.

🖰 **Studio Skoop** [166–7 F5] 63 Sint-Annaplein; ✆ 09 225 08 45; www.studioskoop.be. Opened in the 1970s & has 5 screens showing a mixture of mainstream movies & foreign-language films.

SHOPPING Gent is not associated with a particular shopping highlight; it doesn't share Antwerp's monopoly on diamonds, or produce the lace long associated with Brugge. However, much of the town centre is pedestrianised (save for the trams) and, as a result, shopping among the hotchpotch mix of boutiques, run-of-the-mill fashion branches and traditional stores is a relaxing and enjoyable affair. These shopping areas are situated south of the Korenmarkt and Emile Braunplein and concentrated around Veldstraat, Langemunt, Mageleinstraat, Volderstraat, Kalandenberg square and – feeding off of this – Koestraat. The new Gent Zuid shopping centre (*4 Wilsonplein; www.gentzuid.be*) in the southeast of town has a

---

MAD FOR MUSEUMS?

The Gent Museum Pass costs €20, is valid for three days and grants entry to all the city's museums and monuments, including the Belfort, Het Gravensteen, SMAK and St Baafskathedraal and *The Mystic Lamb*. Free travel on the trams is also included. Passes can be bought from tourist information centre, the museums themselves, or De Lijn offices. Be aware that entry to selected museums is free on Sundays, last admission is usually one hour before closing time, and many museums are closed on a Monday.

Travellers under the age of 26 pay only €1 for entry to the following museums: SMAK, Design Museum, MIAT, MSK and Museum Dr Guislain. Visit www.1euromuseum.be for full details.

good collection of shops, cafés, and music stores. Some of my favourite stores are listed below:

Groot Vleeshuis [169 B2] 7 Groentenmarkt; ⟋ 09 223 23 24; ⏲ 10.00–18.00 Tue–Sun. The old meat market dates from 1419 & has a stunning oak ceiling. It sells regional food products & East Flanders specialities, including Roomer (see box, page 171). There's a café too.

Temmerman [169 B1] 79 Kraanlei; ⟋ 09 224 00 41; ⏲ 11.00–18.00 Tue–Sun. 80 year-old family-run confectioner selling old-fashioned sweets housed in big glass jars, including the plum-coloured *cuberdon's* or *neuzekens*: a local cone-shaped purple sweetie with a gooey centre.

Tierenteijn-Verlent [169 B2] 3 Groentenmarkt; ⟋ 09 225 83 36; ⏲ 10.00–18.00 Mon, 09.00–18.00 Tue–Thu, 08.30–18.00 Fri, 09.00–12.30 & 13.00–18.00 Sat. This delicatessen has been in situ since 1790 & is famous for its homemade mustard. It's pumped up from the cellars into a big wooden barrel & ladled into a jar of your choice. Be sure to buy a wooden spoon with it, otherwise the ingredients will 'split' when stirred – it's that fresh! The secret behind its bite is closely guarded, but I'm told it's definitely not horseradish!

Markets

Bird market Vrijdagmarkt; ⏲ 07.00–13.00 Sun
Book market Ajuinlei; ⏲ 09.00–13.00 Sun
Christmas market Sint-Baafsplein; ⏲ Dec 13.00–21.00 daily
Craft & art market Groentenmarkt; ⏲ Apr–Sep 10.00–18.00 Sat–Sun
Flea market Bij Sint-Jacobs/Beverhoutplein; ⏲ 08.00–13.00 Fri–Sun

Flower market Kouter; ⏲ 07.00–13.00 daily
Food markets General: Sint-Michielsplein; ⏲ 07.30–13.00 Sun; organic: Groentenmarkt, ⏲ 07.30–13.00 Fri
Poultry market Oude Beestenmarkt; ⏲ 07.00–13.00 Sun

OTHER PRACTICALITIES

$ Banks KBC: 10 Vlasmarkt, ⏲ 24hrs; 57 Burgstraat, ⏲ 09.00–12.30 & 14.00–16.30 Mon–Fri; 175 Kouter, ⏲ 09.00–16.30 Mon–Fri, 09.00–12.00 Sat.
Bike rental [166–7 E2] Biker, 16 Steendam, ⟋ 09 224 29 03, ⏲ 09.00–12.30 & 13.30–18.00 Mon–Sat, €9/day; [169 C3] Max Mobiel, 27 Voskenslaan (behind Gent-Sint-Pieters station), ⟋ 09 242 80 46, ⏲ 07.00–18.45 Mon–Fri, €7.50/day, €30 deposit
Internet [169 C3] Coffee Lounge, 6 Botermarkt, ⏲ 10.00–19.00 Mon, Wed–Sun, €2.50/hr

Luggage storage Gent-Sint-Pieters railway station, opposite the Travel Centre Office; ⏲ 06.15–21.30 daily; €3/3.50/4 for a small/medium/large locker.
✚ Pharmacies 19 Groentenmarkt, ⏲ 13.30–18.30 Mon, 08.30–18.30 Tue, Thu–Sat, 08.30–13.30 Wed; 42 Sint-Niklaasstraat, ⏲ 08.00–18.30 Mon–Fri, 08.30–18.00 Sat; 34 Burgstraat, ⏲ 09.30–12.30 & 13.30–18.30 Mon–Fri, 09.30–12.30 Sat.
✉ Post office [166–7 D3] 55 Lange Kruisstraat; ⏲ 09.00–18.00 Mon–Fri, 09.00–15.00 Sat.

WHAT TO SEE AND DO
Sint-Baafskathedraal (St Bavo's Cathedral) [169 D4] (*Sint-Baafsplein*; ⟋ 09 269 20 45; www.sintbaafskathedraal-gent.be; ⏲ Apr–Oct 08.30–18.00 Mon–Sat, 13.00–18.00 Sun, Nov–Mar 08.30–17.00 Mon–Sat, 13.00–17.00 Sun; admission free)

The oldest of Gent's 59 churches, St-Baafskathedral started life as a wooden chapel and originally went by the name of St Janskerk (St John's). As the wealth of the city grew, so did the church, and despite his feuds with the city residents, Emperor Charles V retained a soft spot for the church he was baptised in and donated money to its upkeep and expansion. Indeed, the majority of the current exterior dates from the 16th century. However, by 1540 his patience with the unruly residents had ended. He was short of buildings that could accommodate his Spanish soldiers posted to keep the citizens in check, so turfed out the monks living in St Bavo's Abbey in the east of town. They moved into St John's and the church adopted its current name. It was elevated to cathedral status in 1559 by Pope Paul IV.

The cathedral is home to a treasure trove of artworks. A good place to start is the crypt. It's the largest of its kind in Belgium and belonged to the original Romanesque St John's Church. Until 1784, it was the burial ground of numerous bishops and rich families whose gravestones and plaques line the floor and walls. Relics that survived the religious wars and are housed here include the 'Willibrordus' Bible dating from 1528, the *Mystery of the Cross* triptych, and the silver reliquary of St Macarius that was a gift from the town of Mons who believed the relic saved them from a plague epidemic.

Hanging opposite the crypt exit is Rubens' enormous *St-Baaf Enters the Convent at Ghent* (1624). St Baaf was a 6th-century Frankish noble who abandoned his drinking and extra-marital affairs and converted to Catholicism when his wife died. He accompanied St-Amand on his missionary work for a number of years before retiring to the woods outside Gent. The moment of his conversion is captured in Rubens' painting, which depicts a red-cloaked St Baaf kneeling before St Amand, while his daughter and her maids look on. It's said St Baaf's face is actually that of Rubens.

Also of note are the coats of arms of the Order of the Golden Fleece mounted along the right aisle (just before the choir); a cenotaph of bishop Antonius Triest carved by Jerome Duquesnoy; a triptych entitled *Viglius Aytta* (1751) by Frans Pourbus the Elder; the monumental oak-and-marble Rococo pulpit and the 17th-century Baroque organ.

In a closed-off side chapel, behind bullet-proof glass, is the church's – and city's – greatest treasure: the altarpiece entitled *The Adoration of the Mystic Lamb* (⊕ *Apr– Oct 09.30–17.00 Mon–Sat, 13.00–17.00 Sun; Nov– Mar 10.30–16.00 Mon–Sat, 13.00–16.00 Sun; admission: adult/under 12/under 7/MuseumPass €4/1.50/free/ free includes audio guide*). An inscription on the oak-panel polyptych claims it was completed on 6 May 1432 and credits it as the collaborative eight-year work of Jan van Eyck (page 356) and his brother, Hubrecht. Art historians are unable to distinguish who painted which bits, but its now thought Hubrecht did most of the work and Jan added a few finishing touches and his name because he was the better known of the two at the time. Regardless of ownership, it is considered to be the single most remarkable work of Flemish Primitive art. The pin-point accuracy and level of detail was far beyond what other painters were achieving at the time, and even more extraordinary is the luminosity of the paint that still glistens after more than 500 years. The secret was a new technique: they waited until the oil-paint mixture had begun to dry before applying it in thin layers.

The lamb, in the centre, was a common symbol for Christ. The words of its most well-known reference are found in the Gospel of St John (1:29) 'Behold the

WHAT'S WITH ALL THE MESS?

The stretch of open square between Sint-Niklaaskerk and the Belfort – Poeljemarkt – was, at the time of writing, a real mess. Construction of a contemporary city hall is underway and due for completion at the end of 2012. However, Gent projects notoriously run over schedule – the restoration of the Oud Vismijn took three years longer than expected – so you may have to tiptoe around the madness for a while yet.

Lamb of God, which taketh away the sin of the world!' and are inscribed around the rim of the altar where the lamb stands. Above shines the light of the Holy Ghost and the city of Jerusalem; in front stands the Fountain of Life. Figures from the Old and New Testaments congregate in worship, including the brothers Cain and Abel off to the left. Sitting above, in the upper central panel, is God (again there's some debate about this), flanked by the Virgin Mary on the left and John the Baptist on the right. Either side of them are groups of angels making music in celebration. Amazingly, experts claim you can tell which notes the angels are singing by the varying shapes of their mouths. On the outer edges stand Adam and Eve. Keeping the enormous painting in one piece throughout history has proved a challenge: it survived the riots of the 16th-century Iconoclastic Fury, but in 1794 the central panels were stolen by French soldiers and taken to Paris. These were returned in 1815, but a year later the side panels were stolen and sold to a buyer in Prussia. In was 1920 before all the pieces were reunited, and then during World War II it was stolen by the Nazis and hidden in an Austrian salt mine, where it was found by American allied soldiers in 1946. Unfortunately, one of the panels – *De Rechtvaardige Pechters* (the Fair Judges) – is a copy; the original was stolen in 1934 and is still missing.

BELFORT [169 C4] (*Sint-Baafsplein;* ✆ *09 233 39 54; www.belfortgent.be;* ⏲ *10.00–18.00 daily; admission: adult/under 19/MuseumPass €5/free/free; 45-min guided tours at 15.30 daily, €3*) The town watchtower and a symbol of civic autonomy, Gent's belfry was first erected in 1314 and topped with a wooden spire; after several replacements the current stone version was installed in 1913. The tower held the city's first carillon bell, known as Klokke Roeland (see opposite), which would sound to keep time, announce the arrival of special visitors, or signal the start of public executions. Today the carillon – one of the best in Belgium – is home to some 53 bells that are located on the fifth floor and can be visited using the glass lift.

From the sixth floor there are stunning views over the square and rooftops of Gent. Merchants would send boys up the tower to look for incoming trade ships and until 1869 four guards – known as *kannenschijters* ('can shitters') – would be posted at the top of the tower overnight to keep watch for fires or surprise attacks. The climb to the top took so long that they were unable to descend if they needed the toilet, so instead they were given a pot in which to perform their nightly 'functions' – hence the nickname. The guards have since been replaced by stone tower guardians posted at each of the four corners.

High above is the copper dragon weathervane. The current version dates from the 1980s, but the first was installed in 1377 and is believed to have been a gift from raiding Vikings who detached the mast from their ship and presented it to the city residents in admiration of their bravery.

Lakenhalle [169 C4] (*18 Emile Braunplein*) Adjoining the belfry is the cloth hall. Weaves approved by the textile guild were sold here, but unfortunately its construction was rather ill-timed: work on the building came to an abrupt halt in 1441 when the textile trade dried up during the Hundred Years' War. The basement was used as the city prison until 1902. Look for the relief on the upper façade which marked the entrance to the jail. Known as **Mammelokker**, it shows old Cimon (a Greek revolutionary), who was imprisoned by the Greek king and sentenced to death by starvation. However, months later he was still alive and well. Bemused, the guards decided to spy on his daughter, Pero, who visited him every day. To their amazement, they saw her breastfeeding her father. The king was so impressed by the ingenious plan that he freed Cimon.

Emile Braunplein [169 B/C3/4] Named after Baron Emile Braun (1849–1927) – a Belgian politician, textile-factory owner and Gent burgomaster who help organised the city's World Fair in 1913 – the area has two important features. The first is the statue **Bron der Geknielden Jongelingen (Fountainhead of Kneeling Youths)** carved by Gent-born sculptor Georges Minne (1866–1941). Rubbing the boys' feet is supposed to grant good luck and eternal youth. Also on the square is **Grote Triomfante** – a bell forged in 1660 from the remains of Klokke Roeland, a mighty bell that had hung in the belfry since 1314.

Sint-Niklaaskerk [169 B3] (*Korenmarkt;* ⏱ *14.00–17.00 Mon, 10.00–17.00 Tue–Sun; admission free*) St Nicholas' Church is one of the oldest buildings in town. The Romanesque version that was first erected in the 11th century was demolished in 1200 to make room for the church that stands today. The congregation was made up almost entirely of the merchants and guildsmen who worked nearby, and appropriately the church was consecrated in the name of St Nicholas – better known as Santa Claus – patron saint of merchants, sailors and children. The church tower was used as a lookout post until the Belfort was built in 1314.

Korenmarkt and the old post office [169 B3] Stretching out in front of St-Niklaaskerk is the cobblestone Korenmarkt. Grain and corn unloaded at the nearby Graslei canal was sold here and horses would bring mail to and from the old post office, which sits opposite St-Niklaaskerk. Completed in 1909, it's a mixture of Gothic Revival and neo-Renaissance and heavily decorated with busts of European heads of state who visited during the 1913 World Exhibition (Florence Nightingale sits oddly among them). It's now a shopping arcade.

Sint-Michielsbrug [169 A3] Leaving the Korenmarkt along Pakhuisstraat will lead to the Leie canal and Gent's famous St Michael's bridge, which offers great views of the guildhouses that line Graslei and, looking back, the city's three famous towers belonging to St Niklaaskerk, the Belfort, and St Baafskathedraal.

Graslei and Korenlei [169 A3] This stretch of canal was the city's first commercial port. Known as Tusschen Brughen (Between the Bridges), it became active in the 11th century and even busier during the 13th century when it was linked via canals

LET THERE BE LIGHT

Gent is pretty by day, but come darkness its iconic buildings and waterways are lit up to create dramatic and romantic night-time scenes. In fact, in October 2004 Gent won the International City-People-Light Award hosted by Philips Lighting Company. The award is given to the city that can enhance its cultural and architectural heritage and night-time identity, whilst at the same time respecting the environment. Travellers and residents can now trundle around the city centre in safe well-lit areas; it's a far cry from 18th-century Gent when residents were ordered to carry a flame torch with them if venturing out after the 22.00 curfew, or risk be arrested and interrogated for suspicious behaviour. Ask the tourist office for a Light Plan Gent walking-tour map.

to the North Sea. It closed in 1575 as a result of the religious wars. The gabled guildhouses that line its banks have been well maintained and on the Graslei side, from near right to far left, served as the following:

Gildehuis van de Vrije Schippers (Guildhouse of the Free Boatmen) (*14 Graslei*) The Free Boatmen had complete control of Gent's waterways from the mid-14th to mid-17th centuries. This meant all members of the Unfree Guild of Boatmen (see below) had to hand over their goods to the brother guild on the outskirts of the city, and the Free Boatmen towed it into the centre. The guild decorated it with Gent's coats of arms and a carving of a caravel – the sailing ship Christopher Columbus was aboard when he discovered America.

Coorenmeterhuis (House of the Corn Measures) (*12–13 Graslei*) This fruit-and-cartouche-laden building is where officials would keep track of the amount of grain delivered at the port and later sold at the city markets. By way of a standard measuring system they filled huge bronze tubs to the brim.

Tolhuisje (Toll house) (*11 Graslei*) This slip of a building squeezed between its bigger neighbours housed the offices of the customs officers who collected taxes on the products passing through the port.

Spijker (Staple House) (*10 Graslei*) The squat Romanesque-style Spijker is the oldest building on the street. Dating from AD1200 it was built with grey Tournai limestone at a slight slant – notice that the upper floors overhang the bottom of the building – which made it easier to haul sacks of grain, unloaded at the port, up the outside of the building into the warehouse. A fire in 1896 gutted the interior, but happily the façade and side walls remained intact. It's now home to the classy Belga Queen restaurant (page 170), whose entrance, down a short flight of steps, marks the original street level.

Den Enghel (The Angel) (*8 Graslei*) This six-turreted house had its façade replaced by the Guild of the Masons in 1912, but an angel with a banner was added to show the old name. It features four statues of the guild's patron saints, the Roman martyrs Severinus, Victorinus, Carpophorus and Severianus.

Along Korenlei, on the opposite side of the river, is another row of historic houses. Those of most interest are noted below:

De Lintworm (The Tapeworm) (*24 Korenlei*) Flush against St-Michielsbrug, this Renaissance-style house is named after the long wagons used by the Guild of Beer Exporters that once occupied the premises.

De Zwaene (The Swan) (*9 Korenlei*) At the other end of the street, the Swan was the site of an old brewery. The building underwent extensive renovations in the 1940s, but parts of it still date from the 16th century.

Gildehuis van de Onvrije Schippers (Guildhouse of the Unfree Boatmen) (*7 Korenlei*) Sat diagonally opposite the Guild of Free Boatmen, this flamboyant Regency-style gabled house was built in 1739 and is littered with sea-faring symbols such as dolphins, anchors and, at the very top, a caravel ship weathervane: an obvious boast of grandeur intended to impress the Free Boatmen.

Sint-Michelskerk [169 A4] (*St-Michelsplein;* ⊕ *Apr–Sep 14.00–17.00 Mon–Sat; admission free*) Across St-Michielsbrug on the left-hand side stands St Michael's Church. Its construction was financed by the Guild of Brewers and work on the current version started in 1440 and dragged on for over 200 years, largely due to looting and fire attacks during the Iconoclastic Fury. Designs for a 134m spire – one that would out-do the Notre Dame Cathedral in Antwerp (123m) – were put in place, but lack of funds left the church with its low flat-topped roof. A stroke of luck it turns out: recent research revealed that a higher tower would have toppled the whole building. Its principal treasures are the *Crucifixion* (1630) in the north transept by Antoon van Dyck; Gent-born Gaspar de Crayer's *Assumption of St-Cathérine*; and a copy of Michelangelo's *Madonna and Child* from Onze-Lieve-Vrouwekerk in Brugge.

Het Pand [169 A4] Adjoining St-Michelskerk this 13th-century soot-blackened stretch of building was home to the Predikheren, or Gent Dominican Friars. The grounds contained guesthouses and dormitories, as well as an infirmary where the friars cared for the sick, and a library containing a brilliant collection of medieval works. Sadly, the majority of these were thrown into the river by iconoclasts during the Fury; indeed, a local, Marius van Vaernewyck, wrote in his diary that so many volumes were discarded into the Leie that they rose above the water line to form a bridge enabling citizens to cross the river without getting wet. The establishment of a Calvinist university ousted the friars from their home for a few years, and after a brief return they were expelled for good 1823. It was bought and restored by Gent University in 1963 and now serves as a conference and exhibition hall. Tours are available on request.

Interestingly, Hugo Claus (page 354), the famous Flemish writer, lived across the river in the white house on Predikherenlei from 1955 to 1965. A native of Brugge, he never warmed to the Gent residents and numerous derogatory references to them crop up in his works.

Design Museum Gent [169 A2] (*5 Jan Breydelstraat;* ☏ *09 267 99 99; www.designmuseumgent.be;* ⊕ *10.00–18.00 Tue–Sun; admission: adult/under19/MuseumPass €5/free/free*) Contains a vast range of furnishings and is composed of two parts: the 18th-century Hotel de Connick (named after a rich linen merchant) and a new extension. The first section is filled with period furniture, including King Louis XVIII's writing desk used during his 100-day stay in Gent, and Art Nouveau furniture designed by Henry van de Velde, Paul Hankar and Victor Horta. The stark white walls of the add-on at the back houses collections from the 1970s and '80s, including glass and ceramic works.

Groentenmarkt [169 B2] Trams thread through this former vegetable market that formed the first commercial centre in the city outside the Graslei port. It actually started life as a fish market: canals once ran under the Groot Vleeshuis (Great Butchers' Hall) on the west side of the square allowing the shipments of mussels and fish to be easily unloaded. It transferred to the sale of fruit and veg in the 18th century.

The low-slung **Groot Vleeshuis** dates from the early 15th century and is the work of master-builder-of-the-times Gilles de Suttère. Here the Guild of Butchers graded the meat for sale until 1884. Today, it houses a café and shop promoting East Flanders specialities (page 174). Tacked on to the side is Gent's smallest pub **Galgenhuisje**, named after the gallows that once stood on the square.

Sint-Veerleplein [169 A2] This picturesque square is named after patron saint, St Pharaildis, commonly known as Veerle and sister to St-Gudule (page 111), who remained a virgin until her death despite receiving beatings from the husband she was forced to marry. Other tales commonly link her to the miraculous resurrection of a goose. Legend has it a local villain had stolen and eaten the bird leaving only bones. Veerle prayed to God for its revival and the next morning it was clucking around her bedroom floor!

Round about are numerous façades dating from the 17th and 18th centuries. The most impressive is the **Oude Vismijn** (Old Fish Market): a grand Baroque gateway dominated by a statue of a trident-bearing Neptune. Below him are allegorical figures of the Scheldt (represented by a man) and Leie (woman) rivers. Fish was sold here until 1966, and after a decade of dereliction it's now the home of the new tourist information centre and the swanky waterside Bord'eau restaurant (page 170).

On the west side of the square, at Veerleplein 8–9, are the remains of the **Het Wenemaerhospice**, a hospital/almshouse founded in 1323 by well-off cloth merchant Willem Wenemaer. The 15th-century façade, old entry porch and a passage are all that remain of the original building, but of most interest is the statue of St Laurence – the hospice's patron saint – who stands above the doorway.

Gravensteen (Castle of the Counts) [169 A2] (*11 Sint-Veerleplein;* \ *09 225 93 06; www.gent.be/gravensteen;* ☺ *Apr–Sep 09.00–18.00 daily, Oct–Mar 09.00–17.00 daily; admission: adult/under 19/MuseumPass €8/free/free inc movie guide*) The unlikely positioning of this moat-surrounded medieval fortress, right in the centre of town, makes it all the more impressive. Built in 1180 by Philip of Alsace to make the masses cower, it was modelled on the Krak des Chevaliers stronghold in Damascus that Philip visited during the Crusades. For 150 years it served as the dark (and damp) seat of residence of the Counts of Flanders, but towards the beginning of the 14th century Charles V's new castle in the Prinsenhof quarter became the favoured residence of the counts when they were in town – they constantly travelled around the country to keep an eye on their domain. It was still used to host the odd banquet and on one occasion, in 1445, it hosted a chapter of the Order of the Golden Fleece. After that it housed the counts' mint, but soon enough it became the city prison and court of law. Grisly punishments, from flogging to burning at the stake, were administered either in the central courtyard or on St-Veerleplein opposite. A selection of these instruments of torture are on show in the **Museum voor Gerechtsvoorwerpen** inside. The castle's feared reputation hit a peak during the Inquisition under Philip II's reign and the 17th-century witch hunts.

At the end of the 18th century the complex was sold to a private owner and converted to house two cotton mills, with workers living in the castle grounds or in shacks leant against the outer walls. These were all torn down in 1872 when the city bought the castle back and restored it. The portions of most interest today are the torture chambers, dank dungeons and upper ramparts that offer good views over the city.

Onthoofdingsbrug [169 A2] To the left of the castle is 'Decapitation bridge', named after the beheadings that took place on Sint-Veerleplein until the 16th century. Looking south (with the castle behind you) there is a row of houses on the right-hand bank. The fourth in line bears the last surviving wooden façade in the city and dates from the 16th century. It was painted yellow in honour of Isabella, Charles V's grandmother, who was associated with the colour after she refused to remove her yellowing vest until the siege of Granada was won.

Vrijdagmarkt [169 C1/2] Named after the Friday market held here since 1199, this large square has been the stage for the official receptions of rulers and dignitaries, medieval jousting tournaments, tussles between guildhouses, a public execution platform, and one memorable winter when 11-year-old Charles V – in celebration of his coronation – flooded the square with water, which froze to create an enormous skating rink for the residents.

The centre point is the straight-faced **statue of Jacob van Artevelde** (see box, page 6) addressing the crowds. The outskirts of the square are lined with 17th- and 18th-century gabled guildhouses, but disrupting the roofline in the north corner is **Ons Huis** (*9 Vrijdagmarkt*). The impressive building dates from 1900 and bears the embossed gold letters *Socialistische Werkervereenigingen* on its façade: it has served as the headquarters of the socialist labour union since 1902. It was originally designed as a department store, but was instead used by Bond Moyson health insurance company, whose banner also appears on the façade.

At the other end is the former **Lakenmeterhuis** at Vrijdagmarkt 25. It dates from 1770 and housed the Linen Measurers' headquarters.

The Gothic-style **Toreken** – former guildhouse of the Tanners – sits in the southeast corner at Vrijdagmarkt 37. It's the oldest guildhouse on the square and dates from 1422. Melusine – the mermaid statue at the top – was a symbol of courage and the tanners' mascot. Look for the large metal ring attached to the façade: poor quality cloth sent to the tanners was hung here to embarrass the weaver who had made it.

Dulle Griet [169 C1] On the corner of Grootkanonplein is 'Mad Meg' – a 5m-long, 12,500kg red cast-iron cannon that dates from the 15th century. It's the largest of its kind in Europe and was once capable of firing cannonballs weighing 250 kilos. It was made in Oudenaarde (page 203) and dragged all the way to Gent, but unfortunately the barrel split on the firing of the first shot. Oudenaarde refused to give a refund, relations between the two towns soured, and it's sat there, useless, ever since.

Bij Sint Jacobs [169 D2] (*Bij Sint-Jacobs;* ❧ 09 223 25 26; ⊕ Apr–Oct 09.30–12.30 Fri–Sat) St James' Church is the only one still to bear its Romanesque outer structure. Inside the artworks of note are a black-and-white marble Renaissance tabernacle depicting scenes from the Bible and several paintings by popular Flemish artists Gaspar de Crayer and Jan van Cleef.

Hoogpoort and Nederpolder [169 B–D3] Hoogpoort, together with its add-on Nederpolder, form the oldest street in town. The show stealer is the city's **Stadhuis** (*1 Botermarkt*). Construction of the ornate Gothic façade began in the late 15th century, but ground to a halt barely a quarter of the way through the build. Emperor Charles V's quibbles with the city residents had begun and as punishment he retracted all the building funds – notice the still-unfilled statue niches. The 19 that are filled were installed only in the 19th and early 20th centuries, and those of Charles V and his aunt Margaret of Austria on the corner date from the year 2000. By the time sufficient funds had been saved to continue with the project, late-Gothic style was no longer in vogue and the remainder, facing Botermarkt, was completed in Renaissance style. The building still contains the offices of Gent's burgomaster and alderman, but visitors are only allowed to explore the main rooms with a guide, including the *Pacificatiezaal*, or Court of Justice, with its distinctive blue-and-white tile maze floor. It's said that crawling around it on your hands and knees would suffice as punishment instead of a pilgrimage to Jerusalem.

Across the street, on the corner, is the sandstone-built **Sint-Jorishof**, former guildhouse of the Crossbow Archers (who were responsible for defending the city) and site of the oldest hotel in western Europe. The Flemish-Gothic building was inaugurated in 1477 by Mary of Burgundy, who laid the first stone and slept in one of the rooms still on offer at the fancy Cour St-Georges hotel. A statue of dragon-slaying St George – the guild's patron saint – graces the top of the façade.

De Grote Sikkel and De Kleine Sikkel [169 D3] (*64 Hoogpoort & 2 Neder-polder*)
Split either side of Biezekapelstraat, these Gothic stepped-gabled mansions date from 1481. The façade of the Grote Sikkel bears an upside-down horn beside the entrance; it's a torch snuffer, where visitors carrying flares to guide the way at night could stub out the flames before entering the compound. Just around the corner, down Biezekapelstraat, is **Achtersikkel** – a jigsaw of building materials that date from medieval times to the 20th century. The handsome red-brick tower hugging the arcade is the oldest portion and dates from the 14th century.

Geeraard de Duivelsteen (Castle of Gerald the Devil) [166–7 E4] (*1 Geraard de Duivelstraat*)
This 13th-century Romanesque castle was named after its first owner – a knight called Geerard Vilain. His surname lent itself nicely to rumours of his devilish behaviour: stories claim he beat his wife and plotted to murder his own son, so he could steal the young man's pretty fiancée. The family property was sold in 1328 and has since served variously as a monastery, a school, a boy's orphanage, a madhouse, and a prison. It was sold back to the state at the end of the 19th century and now holds the public record office.

Hotel Arnold van der Haeghen [166–7 C4] (*82 Veldstraat;* \ *09 269 84 60;* ⊕ *10.00–12.00 & 14.00–16.00 Mon–Fri; admission free*)
This white mansion originally belonged to Joost Clemmen, a cotton-mill owner whose house guests included the Duke of Wellington, who stayed here during discussions with Louis XVIII in 1815. Inside you'll find a reconstruction of Nobel Prize winner Maurice Maeterlinck's writing studio and the opulent Chinese Room, whose walls are wrapped in fragile 18th-century silk wallpaper.

Justitiepaleis (Palace of Justice) [166–7 C4] (*23 Koophandelsplein*)
Further south, on the right-hand side of the street, are the Law Courts, which took ten years to build between 1836 and 1846. The façade was the only section to survive a catastrophic fire in 1926. The triangular pediment on the south side of the building features the allegorical figure of Justice surrounded by lawyers, suspects and the guilty.

Stadsbrouwerij Gruut (Gruut Brewery) [166–7 E5] (*10 Grote Huidevettershoek;* \ *09 269 02 69; www.gruut.be;* ⊕ *11.00–17.00 Mon–Tue, 11.00–01.00 Wed–Sat, 15.00–19.00 Sun; admission: adult €8 inc 3 tasters*)
Tours of Gent's local brewery are normally reserved for groups, but if you call the tourist information office they may be able to match you with an existing group booking. Of course, you can alway visit the on-site café (⊕ *11.00–late daily*) and try the Gruut Amber (6.6%), the sweet and herby Blond (5.5%), the very light Wit (5%), the light but mighty Inferno (9%) or the nutty Bruin (8%) – all of them unique because a mixture of herbs (*grut*) is used instead of hops.

Patershol
This tiny district – comprised of just 13 streets – sits north of the historic city centre across the River Leie. It roots date back to medieval times

and the maze of narrow streets have been well preserved thanks to an ongoing refurbishment project that has transformed the once working-class district into a hip neighbourhood containing many valuable buildings and a superb restaurant scene. The transformation is only recent, mind you; the area bordered by Lange Steenstraat, Geldmunt, Kraanlei and Oudburg was originally the residential area of guild members. They were ousted during the 17th century by magistrates who wanted to be based near Gravensteen, but when the castle of the Counts was sold at the end of the end of the 18th century the magistrates left and their grand homes were divided into rows of smaller houses that could accommodate the workers toiling in the cotton mills that had been set up inside the castle. However, at the end of the 19th century industry relocated to the outskirts of the city and Gravensteen was forced to close. The residents left and the district descended into a period of poverty, well-known for its brothels and dingy drinking dens. Change came only in the 1980s and now the picturesque district is home to a handful of sights:

Manneken Pis (*17 Kraanlei*) Above the doorway of this house, Gent boasts its own statue of the miniature pissing boy famously attributed to Brussels. It's thought the small figure was a reference to the Tanners' Guild that often bought samples of strong urine to soften the leather hides.

Huis van Alijn [169 B1] (*65 Kraanlei;* \ *09 269 23 50; www.huisvanalijn.be;* ⊕ *11.00–17.00 Tue–Sat, 10.00–17.00 Sun; admission: adult/19–26/under18/ MuseumPass €5/1/free/free*) This U-shaped bundle of almshouses is the former 14th-century Alijn's Children Hospice. Their construction is attached to a Shakespearian-style story of scandal. Two boys – one from the Rijms family, the other from the Alijn family – had fallen in love with the same girl. Driven mad by jealousy the young Rijm murdered Hendrik and Seger Alijn while they were at mass in St-Janskerk (the present-day St-Baafskathedraal). The Rijm family were banished, but a few years later given the option of a pardon by the count on the condition they build a series of almhouses on land donated by the Alijn's. Despite its name, the hospice cared for elderly women who were chosen by a committee for pious or good behaviour. Bought by the city council in the 1950s, the museum has lovely little exhibitions that recreate scenes from 19th-century daily life. Every Saturday there are afternoon puppet shows (⊕ *Oct–May 14.30–16.00; admission €3.50*) and across the courtyard is a quaint 19th-century tavern that serves *Plumetje*, a Gent *jenever* served half & half (half cherry and half straight schnapps).

Zeven Werken van Barmhartigheid and De Fluitspeler [169 B1] (*79 & 81 Kraanlei*) Stop to admire the façades of these two terraced houses. The first belongs to Gent's famous Temmerman sweet shop (page 174). The house is known as the Seven Works of Mercy and gets its name from the illustrations on the façade: burying the dead, ministering to prisoners, visiting the sick, feeding the hungry, giving drink to the thirsty, and clothing the naked; the seventh work, sheltering a stranger, was performed inside, as the building was originally an inn.

On the corner is the mid-17th-century 'Flute Player' house. Also known as Het Vliegend Hert (The Flying Deer), its bright-red terracotta reliefs depict female figures displaying the five senses: sight, smell, hearing, taste and touch. The reindeer in the middle of the top row symbolises new life. The three figures on the mantle are Faith, Hope and Charity.

Patershol [169 B1] The whole district is named after this unremarkable blue door that sits at the corner of Rodekoningstraat and Trommelstraat. Flemish for 'monk's arsehole' because of it's small size, the low door was the entrance to a series of steps leading down to the waterside from which locals could draw their water.

Caermersklooster (Carmelite Friary) [169 B1] (*6 Vrouwebroersstraat;* ⟍ *09 269 29 10;* ◷ *during exhibitions 10.00–17.00 Tue–Sun; admission free*) The former Friary of the Carmelites – an order of Roman Catholic monks – was established in 1329. Today its vacuous white interior and vaulted wooden ceiling form the spellbinding backdrop of a contemporary art museum. The 17th-century infirmary has an impressive ridged roof dotted with wooden carvings of animals and men.

Prinsenhof

Prinsenhof (*Prinsenhof; admission free*) Once a lavish 300-room castle, Prinsenhof was the birthplace of Emperor Charles V (page 6), who took his first breaths within its walls on the night of 24 February 1500. In the 12th-century castle it was known as Hof ter Walle and owned by the Deputy Count of Flanders. It acquired its current name in the mid-14th century when it fell into the hands of Louise de Male, Count of Flanders. He was tired of the chilly and dark Castle of the Counts across town, so poured funds into the redecoration of Prinsenhof that now reached all the way to Burgstraat. In its prime, the residence hosted guests like Mary of Burgundy and the English King William III. However, by the mid-17th century its heyday was over: sections were sold off and, like Gravensteen, it was filled with factories during the 18th century. Several outbreaks of industrial fire destroyed most of the castle and today only fragments remain. The most distinctive of these is the Donkere Poort (Dark Gate) [166–7 B1] that sits at the north end of Prinsenhofplein. It served as the north entrance gate to the castle and now bears a plaque showing a picture of the once-complete castle. The bottom rampart is original, but the upper levels made from brick were added in the 19th century. On the other side of the gate, is a statue of a *stroppengrager* (page 55).

Oud Begijnhof St-Elisabeth [166–7 B2] (*Begijnhofdries; admission free*) Gent's largest *begijnhof* was once a sprawling estate home to over 700 béguines who spun lace for sale. Like many others, it sprung up in the 13th century. Changes to the street layout in the 19th century led to several homes and gardens being bulldozed, so Duke Engelbert-Auguste Arenberg built the Groot Begijnhof St-Amandsberg (see opposite) for the béguines who moved there in 1874, leaving the St-Elisabeth cottages as housing for the elderly. The best preserved portions are clustered around Proveniersstersstraat, and worth visiting are the 17th-century Baroque church, the Groothuis (the former residence of the Mother Superior) in the corner of the adjoining cemetery, and the pretty grassy knoll behind the church, which contains the Ecce Homo chapel dating from 1793.

Rabot [166–7 C1] (*1 Opgeëistenlaan*) A short stroll north of the former site of the Prinsenhof castle, these two distinctive turreted towers and stepped gable form the last of Gent's city gates. The Lieve canal flowing through the town walls formed a weak spot for the city's defences; only by luck and a modest earth rampart did the citizens of Gent ward off a 40-day siege launched on the city by Maximilian of Austria in 1488. To celebrate, these slightly more robust ramparts were built between 1489 and 1491. They also performed as flood gates and an inspection and toll gate for trading ships up until the 16th century.

Museum Dr Guislain [166–7 A1] (*43 Jozef Guislainstraat;* \ *09 216 35 93;* ⊕ *09.00–17.00 Tue–Fri, 13.00–17.00 Sat–Sun; admission: adult/12–26/under12/ MuseumPass €6/1/free/free*) Set in the northern outskirts of town, this psychiatric hospital is the oldest in Belgium still in use today. The large new wing houses patients, but the museum is housed in the old wing and tells you a bit about the doctor himself, as well as tracing the history of psychiatry through collections of photographs and props. There is also an interesting studio displaying works of art created by psychiatric patients. It certainly appeals to those with an interest in the macabre. To get there taken tram #1 from Korenmarkt (direction Evergem) and get off at Guislainstraat.

East of the centre
Portus Ganda This port marks the confluence of the Scheldt and Leie rivers and was recently renovated to create a new marina for pleasure yachts. The restored docks are now a chic eating and shopping area, and home to the Art Deco Zwembad van Eyck (*1 Veermanplein*) – Belgium's oldest indoor swimming pool.

Sint-Baafsabdij (St Bavo's Abbey) [166–7 G3] (*Spanjaardstraat;* ⊕ *11 Apr–24 Oct 13.00–18.00 Sun, 31 Oct–7 Nov 12.00–17.00 Sun; admission free*) St-Bavo's Abbey was one of two (the other was St-Pietersabdij, page 186) founded by a missionary named Amand in AD630. Sadly Amand's teachings weren't received well by the locals: they drowned him in the nearby Scheldt River and later named the church after his successor – a wealthy nobleman and landowner called Adlowinus who had taken the name Baaf when he entered the monastery and who was elevated to the status of saint upon his death. When the Vikings arrived in AD879 they destroyed the abbey, and used the grounds as a base for raids throughout the country. When they left, the monks returned, rebuilt the abbey, and adopted the Benedictine order. On the back of the wool industry, the abbey became rich and Gent grew up around it. An important site of pilgrimage, the church received many famous visitors and hosted the birth of John of Gaunt and the marriage of the Philip the Bold, Duke of Burgundy.

The sections of the abbey still standing today are surrounded by wild flowers. Most impressive of these is the intact refectory and its 12th-century vaulted timber roof found up a flight of stairs above the north cloister. The room forms part of the **Museum voor Stenen Voorwerpen**, or Lapidary Museum (*43 Voorhoutkaai;* \ *09 225 15 85;* ⊕ *11 Apr–24 Sep 13.00–18.00 Sun, 31 Oct–7 Nov 13.00–17.00 Sun; admission free*), which displays a collection of tombstones, among them the tomb of painter Hubert van Eyck, who contributed to the world-famous *Adoration of the Mystic Lamb* altarpiece.

Groot Begijnhof St-Amandsberg [166–7 G2] (*Jan Roomsstraat;* \ *09 228 23 08;* ⊕ *06.30–23.00 daily; admission free*) Quite a trek from the city centre but well worth it, the St-Amandsberg is the newest of Gent's three *begijnhofs*. It was built during the late 19th century to replace the Oud Begijnhof St-Elisabeth (see opposite) across town. A glimpse of their old way of life can be seen in the **Museum Groot Begijnhof** (*67 Groot Begijnhof;* \ *09 228 23 08;* ⊕ *09.00–12.00 Mon, Wed & Sat*), found near the entrance on Hertog Engelbert van Arenbergstraat.

South of the centre Known as the Kunstenkwartier (Arts Quarter), the south of Gent is dotted with art museums, theatre complexes and the city's parks, which cover the 2km stretch between the Gent-Sint-Pieters railway station and the historical city centre. It's also home to the Blandijnberg district that forms the heart of the Gent University campus.

Stadmuseum Gent (STAM) [166–7 C6] (*2 Godshuizenlaan;* ☏ *09 267 14 00;* ⊕ *10.00–18.00 Tue–Sun; admission: adult/under 26/under 19/MuseumPass €6/1/ free/free*) This new city history museum is housed in the grounds of Bijlokeabdij, a former Cistercian convent. Its giant Google Earth map of the city is fun, and the 14th-century murals in the old abbey dining room are impressive too.

Boekentoren [166–7 D6] (*9 Rozier*) The University of Gent's library and its distinctive 64m-high 'book tower' were designed by Art-Nouveau master Henry van de Velde. He was a professor at the university between 1926 and 1936. Often quoted as the city's 'fourth' tower (after the three spires of St-Baafs, the Belfort and St-Niklaaskerk) the building stocks some three million books.

Onze-Lieve-Vrouw St-Pieterskerk [166–7 D6] (*2 Sint-Pietersplein;* ☏ *09 225 44 37;* ⊕ *10.00–17.00 Tue–Sat, 10.00–12.15 Sun*) A chapel dedicated to St Peter cropped up at roughly the same time as the St Peter's Abbey (see below), but the Romanesque construction was demolished completely during the Iconoclasm and the Baroque version that stands today was placed in its stead. The dome-topped church is modelled on St Peter's Church in Rome and was completed in 1722. Inside, there are a number of paintings, but of most interest are the tombs of five counts of Flanders laid to rest under the Lady Chapel, and the remains of Isabella of Austria's tomb (sister of Emperor Charles V) in the far right-hand corner.

St-Pietersabdij [166–7 E6] (*9 Sint-Pietersplein;* ☏ *09 243 97 30;* ⊕ *10.00–18.00 Tue–Sun; admission: adult/under 19/MuseumPass €5/free/free, last admission 17.00, movie guide €3*) St Peter's Abbey is the other chapel founded by missionary St-Amand in the 7th century. The abbey was partially destroyed on a number of occasions: first by Viking raids and later by the Iconoclasm. After each incident the abbey was rebuilt and as the preferred residence and burial site of the Counts of Flanders, it continued to grow into one of the richest and most important abbeys in the Low Countries. The brotherhood of Benedictine monks was finally expelled under French rule in 1796 and the abbey was sold at public auction. It was bought by the city and the grounds were used as army barracks until World War II. The old infirmary now houses the **De Wereld van Kina** natural history museum [166–7 D7] (*14 Sint-Pietersplein;* ☏ *09 244 73 73;* ⊕ *09.00–17.00 Mon–Fri, 14.00–17.30 Sun; admission: adult/concession/under12/MuseumPass €2.50/1.25/ free/free*), while the old dormitories are used as an exhibition space. Its one permanent exhibition retells the history of the abbey and its monks via an iPod tour. Interestingly, the vineyard that once covered the south-facing slopes has been revived and a modest number of bottles are produced ever year bearing the Monte Blandino label.

Klein Begijnhof Onze-Lieve-Vrouw ter Hoyen [166–7 F/G5] (*209 Lange Violettestraat;* ⊕ *until 21.00 daily*) Gent's third *begijnhof* was first established in 1235, but most of the buildings visible today date from the 17th century. The highlight of the central Baroque church is the 16th-century *Fountain of Life* polyptych painted by Lucas Horenbaut II. Located on the left-hand side of the church, the central panel features two fountains – the upper is the Fountain of Life, the lower is the Fountain of Mercy – and to either side stand figures from the Old and New Testaments. The right panel depicts the Pope worshipping the Holy Sacrament of the Eucharist, and on the left King David pays homage to the ark of Jehovah.

above Escape to the country – take to the saddle and explore poplar-lined canals (ET) page 60

below Board a boat tour of Brugge's romantic canals (RVE/S) page 213

Be led around the region by your tastebuds: visit a brewery (*left* MP/VF; page 28); try a glass of the revered Westvleteren — the world's rarest beer (*below left* ET; page 273), or local varieties such as Witkap Pater brewed by Brouwerij Slaghmuylder in Ninove (*below* ET; page 48) or the additive-free Oerbier by De Dolle Brouwers in Diksmuide (*bottom* ET; page 257)

Watch master chocolatiers at work (*right* CSB/VF; page 46); let local chocolates like Antwerpse handjes melt in your mouth (*bottom* VA; page 289); or gorge on a cornet of salty chips (*below* ET page 45)

above left Brugge's Heilig-Bloedprocessie — when a vial containing a few drops of Christ's blood is paraded through the city — has been held every May for over 700 years (TB) page 53

above right Brussels' annual Ommegang is a lively show featuring stilt-walkers, actors in medieval dress and free beer! (VB) page 54

below Join the tourist-free drunken revelry of Aalst Carnival (ET) page 196

left See the world's last horseback shrimp fisherman in action at Oostduinkerke (ET) page 247

below The coast comes alive in summer with festivals, markets, sand-sculpture competitions and open-air film screenings (JD/TB) page 234

right **Try your hand at sandsurfing in Middelkerke** (ET) page 246

below **Every few years, the Flemish coastal towns host Beaufort: a series of thought-provoking artworks scattered along the North Sea sands** (ET) page 53

above left Brussels boasts numerous Art Nouveau residences, including Hôtel Hannon and its stunning central staircase (VB) page 133

above In complete contrast are the ultra-modern silver balls of the Atomium (ET) page 130

below left Leuven's spectacular 15th-century town hall is covered with statues of famous Flemish figures (ET) page 143

below left The capital is littered with comic-book murals — including this one of Tintin and his loveable dog, Snowy (AS) page 100

Municipal Museum for Contemporary Art (S.M.A.K) [166–7 D8] (*Citadelpark;* ✆ *09 221 17 03; www.smak.be;* ⊕ *10.00–18.00 Tue–Sun; admission: adult/19–26/under18/MuseumPass €6/1/free/free*) Housed in a 90-year-old former festival hall, this minimalist-white contemporary art museum is hailed as one of the best in Europe. Its permanent collection contains works by Magritte and Broodthaers, but it's most famous for its inspiring temporary shows that feature installations, videos, sculptures and paintings by artists from around the world. On one memorable occasion it showcased, for four days, 12 statues of hat-wearing penises – until it was discovered to be a hoax.

Museum voor Schone Kunsten (M.S.K) [166–7 D8] (*Citadelpark, 1 Fernand Scribedreef;* ✆ *09 240 07 00; www.mskgent.be;* ⊕ *10.00–18.00 Tue–Sun; admission: adult/19–26/under18/MuseumPass €5/1/free/free*) The regal Museum of Fine Arts displays around 300 permanent works of art dating from the Middle Ages until the first half of the 20th century.

LAARNE

The leafy village of Laarne, some 15km east of Gent city centre, is full of hocus pocus. Along with the neighbouring village of Kalken it was the site of witch burnings in 1607. Today, a Witches Guild has been revived and in between promoting the local Toverhekske beer they have set up *heksenpad*: a 20km walk through Laarne that pinpoints the homes and meeting places of former witches.

GETTING THERE AND AWAY

By bus Bus #34 runs a direct service from Gent-Sint-Pieters to Laarne Dorp (*13min past the hour, every two hours;* ⊕ *40min*).

By car From Gent follow the signs for the E17 and follow it east for 5km, then take exit labelled Destelbergen. Merge onto the R4, then take exit 5 (direction Laarne) (*14km;* ⊕ *20min*).

TOURIST INFORMATION

🛈 **Tourist information** 2 Dorpsstraat; ✆ 09 365 46 00; e toerisme@laarne.be; www.laarne. be/toerisme; ⊕ 09.00–11.45 Mon & Thu, 09.00–11.45 & 14.00–18.45 Tue & Wed, 09.00–12.35 Fri.

Not an official tourist information office, but the staff in the town hall are happy to help & they sell the *heksenpad* walking routes (€1.80).

WHAT TO SEE AND DO

Kasteel van Laarne (*Eekhoevestraat;* ✆ *09 230 91 55;* ⊕ *14.00–17.30 Sun*) This looming medieval fortress complete with moat and turreted towers is praised as one of the best-preserved castles in Belgium. Built in the late-12th century it served as residence to Diederik of Alsace when he returned from the Crusades in 1157 with the relic of the Holy Blood (now housed in Brugge, page 223). The fort protected a garrison of the Count of Flanders from several sieges in 1362 and 1382, before falling under the private ownership of – variously – local lords, the De Vos family, the van Vilsterens (who started extensive renovations in the 17th century) and later the counts of Ribaucourt who donated it to the Koninklijke Vereniging voor Historische Woonsteden (Society for Historic Houses) in 1952. The first courtyard was the domain of the castle coachmen, garderners and chaplain – on the right, a fancy **restaurant** (✆ *09 230 71 78;* ⊕ *12.00–14.00 & 19.00–21.00 Wed–Sat, 12.00–*

14.00 Sun; €€€€€) occupies the former farm buildings. At the other end, across the bridge, is the grey-stone castle. Rooms of note include the Renaissance loggia, or entrance hall, whose large fireplace bears the crest of the van Vilsteren family and is flanked by paintings of Holy Roman Emperor Charles VI and his wife Elizabeth; and the Knight's Hall decorated with Brussels-made tapestries. Upstairs is the fort's excellent collection of 17th- and 18th-century silverware, including chocolate pots and utensils.

SINT-NIKLAAS

Equidistant between Antwerp and Gent, Sint-Niklaas belongs to Waasland – a formerly swampy region which served as the backdrop of the ancient fable of Reynard the Fox (see box below). The Flemish know it best as the start point for the Ronde van Vlaanderen (page 53), but it also boasts Belgium's largest market square which hosts a weekly market every Thursday and where, on the first weekend of September, dozens of hot-air balloons are launched during the Vredefeesten (Peace Festival) and subsequent three-day Villa Pace music festival.

REYNAERD DE VOS

The legend of Reynard the Fox comes from a Frankish fable that originated in Germany and spread all over Europe before being committed to the page in the mid-13th century by a Dutch scholar. The original author is unknown, but it's believed his name was Willem because the name appears in the first stanza. An English version was printed by William Caxton in 1481. The rhyming prose is similar in style and tone to Chaucer's Canterbury Tales – so similar that some scholars believe Chaucer stole the story during his European travels. It tells the tale of an anthropomorphic fox that is constantly tricking his fellow animals. It's a dark story which is used to highlight the lies, hypocrisy and greed of humankind. Over time, details of the legend have been changed, but the basic story is as follows:

King Noble the lion had called all the animals to an annual feast at his court in the forest, where they might air their grievances. The only one not present was Reynard the Fox and it soon became clear he had committed several crimes. Isegrim the wolf complained that the fox had blinded three of his children, and Henning the cockerel told the congregation that Reynard had killed five of his sons and daughters. Grimbart the badger stepped forward to defend his uncle, but the king was outraged and sent Brown the bear to fetch him from his castle in Malpertus. Brown never returned. Reynard had led the bear to a log filled with honey and encouraged him to stick his head through a tight hole to get it. The bear got stuck and his cries for help alerted the local peasants who set upon the bear with knives. He managed to escape, and returned to court bruised and bleeding.

Next King Noble sent Hintze the tom cat. Reynard tells the cat he'll follow, but asks if he'd like a meal of mice before starting their journey. He leads the cat to a nearby barn and lures him into the mouse trap set by the parson's son. His squeals of pain bring the men running, and after a fight the cat flees back to the forest missing an eye.

The king was now so angry that Grimbart the badger feared for his uncle's life and begged the king to allow him to go and fetch the fox. After listening to his nephew's concerns, Reynard agrees to accompany him back to court where

Finally, as you may have guessed, Sint-Niklaas has become the hometown of Sinterklaas, otherwise known as Santa Claus. In 1217 the local clergy founded Sint-Nicolaas Church and dedicated it to the Greek bishop. Around this grew the cult of Sinterklaas and, as well as boasting a huge statue of the saint which stands outside the Stadhuis, the city organises several events. The highlights are his arrival on the Grote Markt, every year on 13 November at 13.00, astride a white horse and complete with red velvet robes and a real long white beard; and a present workshop set up in the Salon voor Schone Kunsten (page 19). It's a great experience for children.

Sint-Niklaas may not be an immediately pretty town, but it has some quirky charms if you spend a few hours getting to know it.

GETTING THERE AND AWAY
By car From Antwerp follow the E17 southwest and take exit 15 to Sint-Niklaas (*25km;* ⏰ *21min*). From Brussels follow the A12 north, take exit 7, and follow the N16 for 19km to Sint-Niklaas (*47km;* ⏰ *46min*). From Gent follow the E17 northeast and take exit 15 (*37km;* ⏰ *30min*). There's a huge underground car park beneath the Grote Markt.

the king condemns him to death. Reynard concocts an escape plan. Before heading to the gallows he begs the king to listen to his story. He claims Isegrim the wolf corrupted him and took all his money, and if it wasn't for his secret store of treasure he would have starved to death. Furthermore, Isegrim and Brown the bear were plotting to kill the king. The king falls for Reynard's trap, imprisons the other animals and agrees to release the fox in return for the treasure. Reynard tells the king the location of the gold, but says he cannot accompany him and instead will make a pilgrimage to atone for his sins. He asks the king to release two of the animals – Lampe the hare and Bellyn the ram – to serve as companions. On arriving home, Reynard and his family eat poor Lampe and he parcels up her head in a patch of skin from Brown the bear (which the king had gifted to Reynard for warning him of the assassination plot). He orders Bellyn to return to court with the parcel, without looking inside, and tell the king he had helped Reynard to prepare the parcel and should be duly rewarded for his services. When the parcel was opened to reveal Lampe's head, the king fed Bellyn to Brown the bear and Isegrim the wolf, whom he released, realising he too had been tricked.

The tale ends with the king once more summoning Reynard to court and the fox outwitting the gullible king. He claims Lampe insulted his children and therefore couldn't be blamed for his murder, and he volunteers to fight Isegrim to prove his innocence. He shaves off his fur and covers himself in butter, so Isegrim is unable to get a grip of him and loses the fight. The king, assured of Reynard's innocence, pardons him and makes him his privy councillor.

Sint-Niklaas has a close association with the legend because it was found – when local scholars started to study the text in detail during the 1950s and '60s – that many of the places mentioned in the text related to real-life woods, rivers and villages located in the region. The city created a route dotted with benches bearing excerpts from the story. You can buy these walking maps and a car route from the tourist information office (€2.50), but at the moment they're only in Dutch. There are also several statues of the fox dotted around town.

By train Antwerp (*every 20min Mon–Fri, 12/34/52min past the hour Sat–Sun; ⊕ 20min*); Gent (*5/16/47min past the hour Mon–Fri, 16/33min past the hour Sat–Sun; ⊕ 30min*); Brussel-Noord/Bruxelles-Nord via Dendermonde or Antwerp-Berchem (*14/30min past the hour Mon–Fri, ⊕ 1hr; 8/40/42min past the hour Sat–Sun, ⊕ 1hr 5min*).

TOURIST INFORMATION

ℹ️ Tourist information 45 Grote Markt; 📞 03 760 92 60; e toerisme@sint-niklaas.be; www.sint-niklaas.be; ⊕ 08.00–17.00 Mon–Fri, 15 May–15 Sep also open 10.00–16.00 Sat–Sun. Can arrange tours of the Stadhuis €50/2hr, but they must be booked at least a week in advance.

🚲 Bike rental Fietspunt, 2 Leopold II-laan (railway station); m 0493 51 64 76; ⊕ 07.00–19.00 Mon–Fri; €10/day

🏠 WHERE TO STAY, EAT AND DRINK

Sint-Niklaas is heavily associated with the legend of Reynard the Fox (see box, pages 188–9), so it's only fitting their local cake is named after him. The *Reynaertgebak* has a cake base, a thick layer of marzipan coated in chopped almonds and a disc bearing a picture of the tricksy fox.

🏠 Moon Eat Sleep (5 rooms) 18b Richard van Britsomstraat; 📞 03 337 14 02; www.moon-eat-sleep.be. Fashionable & welcoming B&B with dark, dramatic suites & 3 dbls with walk-in showers, flatscreen TV & coffee-making facilities. B/fast taken in the café downstairs. €€€

🏠 Ibis (85 rooms) 2 Hemelaertstraat; 📞 03 231 31 41; www.ibishotel.com. Sint-Niklaas has a dearth of good accommodation, so I'm including this bright & modern chain. There's a bar & Wi-Fi. €€

✕ Merlot 4 Regentiestraat; 📞 03 777 06 08; ⊕ 10.00–22.00 Wed–Fri, 10.00–23.00 Sat, 12.00–22.00 Sun. Upmarket restaurant with intimate black-&-white interior, & small terrace out the back for use in summer. Menu is a mix of French/Flemish dishes & it's popular for tea & coffee too. €€€€

✕ Kasteel Walburg 35 Walburgstraat; 📞 03 766 21 15; ⊕ 11.00–late Tue–Sun. Yesteryear bar/restaurant inside Walburg Castle in Romain de Vidtspark. There are angel-themed murals, low-hanging lights & candles. During the week they offer a bargain 3-course lunch on a first-come first-served basis, with the choice of meat or fish, for €11.80. Recommended. €€

Thierens 47–9 Kokkelbeekstraat; 📞 03 776 15 80; ⊕ 06.30–12.30 & 13.30–18.30 Mon–Sat. Bakery that almost always has *Reynaertgebak* for sale; €1.75 for a small one.

WHAT TO SEE AND DO

Mercatormuseum (*49 Zamanstraat;* 📞 *03 760 37 83;* ⊕ *14.00–17.00 Tue–Sat, 11.00–17.00 Sun; admission: adult/concession/under 12 €2.50/2/free, combi ticket with STEM & Salon voor Schone Kunsten €6*) Hidden at the back of the small garden, this modest museum is dedicated to cartography, but its real draw are the ancient maps drawn by Gerardus Mercator. Head to the right of the information desk and walk straight to the back room, which contains yellowing atlases and Mercator's wonderful 16th-century maps of Europe (1554 and 1572) and the world (1569), as well as two of his globes – all of them illustrated with the weird and wonderful creatures believed to live in these strange lands.

STEM (*14 Zwijgershoek;* 📞 *03 760 37 50;* ⊕ *14.00–17.00 Tue–Sat, 11.00–17.00 Sun; admission: adult/concession/under 12 €4/3/free, combi ticket with Mercatormuseum & Salon voor Schone Kunsten €6*) Many Flemish towns have museums dedicated to their city history, but Sint-Niklaas' is different: it's a fun assembly of items ranging from an old barber's chair and mirrorstand and looms, to mosaic-tiled floors and old guns. There's even a velvet-curtained tent containing small sketches of naked women.

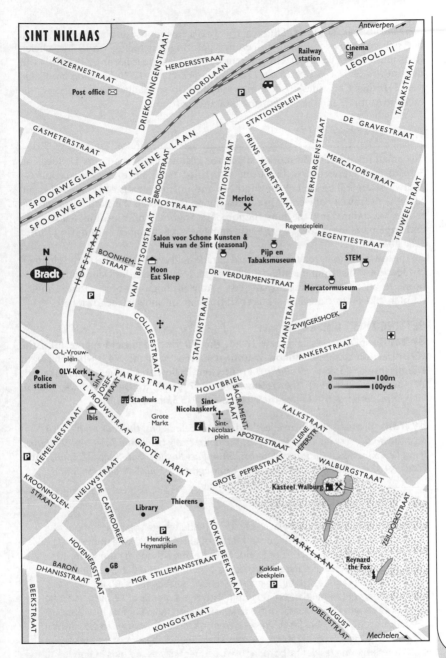

Pijp en Tabakmuseum (*29 Regentiestraat;* **m** *0473 70 77 57;* ⊕ *10.00–13.00 Sun; admission: €1.50*) Set back from the street, down an inner alley, this independent museum has a pipe collection dating from 1492 and owns the world's largest cigar.

Salon voor Schone Kunsten (*85 Stationstraat;* ✆ *03 778 17 45;* ⊕ *14.00– 17.00 Tue–Sat, 11.00–17.00 Sun; admission €1.50, combi ticket with STEM &*

Mercatormuseum €6) Most of the year this 1920s' townhouse displays the city's small but rich collection of 16th–20th-century paintings, including works by Felicien Rops and Henri Evenepoel. However, at Christmas time it becomes the **Huis van de Sint** (⊕ *12 Nov–6 Dec 16.00–17.30 Mon–Fri, 10.00–17.30 Sat–Sun; admission free*) – Father Christmas' workshop. Kids can also see Santa Claus' bedroom, his exercise room (!) and the present-manufacturing room.

DENDERMONDE

The small town of Dendermonde sits at the confluence of the rivers Dender and Scheldt and, consequently, has been a fortified town since the 12th century – archways can still be seen at the southern and northern ends of Leopold II Laan. Like the nearby city of Gent, it grew wealthy on the back of the cloth trade and the money was poured into the construction of its Stadhuis and Vleeshuis. Sadly, these and large parts of the town were badly damaged in September 1914 during World War I bombings.

The town is famous for its Ros Beiaard parade held every ten years (see box below), but few know that from the mid-19th to the mid-20th centuries Dendermonde was home to an esteemed Academy of Arts – one of Belgium's best – that schooled painters like Franz Courtens, whose paintings are on show in the town hall.

GETTING THERE AND AWAY

By car From Brussels take exit 10 on the R0 ring road, and merge onto the N9 (direction Asse) and follow it until it merges with the N47, which leads to Dendermonde (*33km;* ⊕ *40min*). From Gent, follow the E17 east and take exit 12 (direction Lokeren), then follow the N47 south to Dendermonde (*35km;* ⊕ *35min*). From Aalst, follow the N406 north (*15.5km;* ⊕ *25min*).

By train Brussels-Zuid/Bruxelles-Midi (*21/34/59min past the hour Mon–Fri, 32min past the hour, every hour & 36min past the hour, every two hours Sat–Sun;* ⊕ *40min*); Gent (*25/53min past the hour Mon–Fri, 5min past the hour Sat–Sun;* ⊕ *23min*); Sint-Niklaas (*31min past the hour Mon–Fri, 15min past the hour Sat–Sun;* ⊕ *26min*).

ROS BEIAARD

The UNESCO-listed Ros Beiaard parade is held every ten years in honour of a medieval folk song that recounts the tale of King Charlemagne punishing the four sons of Aymon, Lord of Dendermonde, for fighting by drowning their prized horse Beiaard. Its centrepiece is an enormous oak horse measuring 5.2m long and 4.8m high and weighing a staggering 800kg. *Pijnders,* members of the guild of bearers, split into three groups of 12 men and take turns carrying the colossal horse through town. On its back sit four armour-clad brothers known as *heemskinderen.* It's a huge honour to be chosen because the rules of eligibility are very strict: the brothers must be the sons of Dendermonde residents, born in town, sequentially (ie: no girls in between), and aged between seven and 21. This explains why its only held only once a decade! Following the horse, are three giants named Indiaan, Mars and Goliath. The next parade takes place in May 2020. A statue of the chosen boys on horseback stands in the middle of the roundabout between Stationsstraat and Brusselsestraat.

TOURIST INFORMATION

ℹ Tourist information Stadhuis, Grote Markt; 052 21 39 56; e toerisme@dendermonde.be; www.dendermonde.be; Apr–Sep 09.00–12.00 & 13.30–16.30 Mon–Fri, 10.00–12.00 & 13.30–18.00 Sat–Sun, Jul–Aug 09.00–18.00 Mon–Fri, 10.00–18.00 Sat–Sun, Oct–Mar 09.00–12.00 & 13.30–16.30 Mon–Fri, 10.00–12.00 & 14.00–16.30 Sun. Sells Reuzenroute cycling maps (€1.80).

Bike rental €8.60/day from tourist office.

✗ WHERE TO EAT AND DRINK

Local meaty treats to look out for are *Dendermondse paardenworstjes* (horse sausages) and *kopvlees* (pig's head paté) served with mustard, which is tastier than it sounds, and the sweeter *Ros Beiaardkoekjes*. You may be able to pick some up at the weekly market held on Kerkstraat, Oude Vest, Brusselsestraat (⊕ *08.00–12.00 Mon*). You can also find an excellent range of beers here, including the award-winning Tripel Karmeliet and touristy Kwak brewed by Brouwerij Bosteels in Buggenhout – 8km east of Dendermonde – and the locally produced Dendermonde Tripel and Vicaris Tripel.

✗ Den Ommeganck 18 Grote Markt; 052 22 66 01; ⊕ 09.00–23.00 Mon, 11.30–00.00 Tue, Thu, 11.30–01.00 Fri, 14.00–01.00 Sat, 14.00–00.00 Sun. This building served as the Academy of Fine Arts until 1861 & has been a café since 1953. Has a good selection of Trappist & Abbey beers & serves tasty sandwiches, spaghetti & croque monsieurs. €€

☿ Charles Quint 26 Grote Markt; 052 21 03 92; ⊕ 10.00–late Mon, Thu–Sun. Just before you enter, look to your left; the wall holds a painting of the city showing the extent of the damage after the town succumbed to bombing in World War I. Traditional pub with old wooden interior & good selection of local beers (see above).

☿ Honky Tonk 12a Leopold II laan; 052 52 04 66; www.jazzcentrumvlaanderen.be; ⊕ 13.30–16.30 Tue–Sat. Legendary jazz bar that's been running since 1965. Midweek it operates as a museum & there are live events most Saturday evenings around 20.00; tickets usually cost €10.

WHAT TO SEE AND DO

Stadhuis (*Grote Markt;* ⊕ *Apr–Sep 10.00–12.00 & 13.30–16.30 Tue–Fri, 10.00–12.00 & 13.30–18.00 Sat–Sun, Jul–Aug 10.00–18.00 Tue–Sun, Oct–Mar 10.00–12.00 & 13.30–16.30 Tue–Fri, 10.00–12.00 & 14.00–16.30 Sat–Sun; admission free*) Dendermonde's symmetrical town hall is very pretty in summer, with regional flags fluttering in the breeze and flower boxes perched on the windowsills. The original 14th-century stadhuis was destroyed during the bombardments of World War I – only fragments remain – and it had to be rebuilt after the war. A painting in the lobby of the Charles Quint bar (see above) shows the extent of the damage. Tours are available only for large groups, but they're happy for you to wander around on your own.

The interior boasts a number of paintings by the Dendermonde School of Art which stood at 18 Grote Markt until 1861 and is now found at Bogaerdstraat 125. In the entrance hall, look for the portrait of a chap sporting a heavy moustache and long sideburns. This is Polydore de Keyser. He was born in Dendermonde, but moved to England in his teens, established a hotel and rose to become Lord Mayor of London (1887–88).

Next enter the new part of the building, located to the left of the main staircase. In the Trouwzaal is a view of the royal park from Laeken painted by Franz Courtens, the most famous painter to graduate from Dendermonde's School of Art. Another of his paintings depicting a frozen river hangs next to the Ritsaertzaal, and two more – one of men gathering hay and the other of cows grazing – hang in the Aymanzaal council chamber.

Back in the old part of the building, the small Jumelagezaal contains a trio of treasures: a wonderfully emotive plaster sculpture of kids fighting by Jef Lambeaux, a glass case containing the four suits of armour worn by the Ros Beiaard brothers (see box, pages 188–9) and a huge painting commemorating the Ros Beiaard parade held when Polydore de Keyser visited in 1888. You can pick him out sitting in front of the town hall thanks to his red military attire. Also notice the Union Jack flags erected in his honour. One of the giants, Indiaan, appears on the left.

When the hour strikes, the belfry plays the Ros Beiaard song – try and listen out for it.

Vleeshuismuseum (*32 Grote Markt;* ⊕ *Apr–Oct 09.30–12.30 & 13.30–18.00 Tue–Sun; admission free*) Across the square, it's easy to pick out the slender turret of the former Meat Hall. The current building is a reconstruction of the 15th-century version which was badly damaged in September 1914. It now houses an archaeology and town-history museum. Worth a visit, if just to see the skeleton of a 28,000-year-old mammoth.

Onze-Lieve-Vrouwekerk (*Kerkstraat;* ⊕ *Apr–Sep 14.00–16.45 Sat–Sun, Jul–Aug 14.00–16.45 Tue–Sun; admission free*) The 13th-century Church of Our Lady proudly houses two paintings by Antony van Dyck – the *Adoration of the Shepherds* (in the north aisle) and the *Crucifixion* (in the baptistry) – and a 12th-century font crafted from blue Tournai marble. The church hosts carillon concerts every Monday and Sunday (⊕ *11.00–12.00*).

Opposite the church entrance stands a statue of Pieter Jan de Smet, a Roman Catholic priest who emigrated to America in the early 19th century. De Smet became well known in the US for successfully implementing the Treaty of Fort Laramie in 1868 between the government and American Indian clans. His statue stands outside Washington's Capitol building; not bad for a local Dendermonde boy!

Sint-Alexiusbegijnhof (*Brusselsestraat; admission free*) It's easy to walk past the *begijnhof* gateway buried between the ING bank and Passerella Fashion shop on Brusselsestraat. The cobbled path opens out to reveal a spacious triangular compound of 61 17th-century houses. No 11 retains its authentic béguine furnishings and can be visited, as can No 25 which belonged to Miss Ernestine De Bruyne – Dendermonde's last béguine who died in 1975 – and now houses the **Begijnhofmuseum** ⊕ *Apr–Oct 09.30–12.30 & 13.30–18.00 Tue–Sun; admission free*). Before you leave, pay your respects at Sint-Alexius cave at the back of the church, which is lit with prayer candles every evening.

AALST

Aalst is an up-and-coming city which, for the moment, still remains off the beaten track. This is bound to change quickly: moving to new premises has galvanised the tourist office and they're feverishly working to promote the city to visitors. The biggest draw is the city's annual carnival (see box, page 196), which is held in February and involves a great deal of beer and bad behaviour.

Locals are known as *ajuinen* (onions) due to the massive amount of onions that were once grown on the fertile banks of the River Dender. Residents flaunt their nickname with pride because they feel it perfectly sums up their spicy humour and ability not to take things too seriously. Amusingly, there's lots of rivalry between

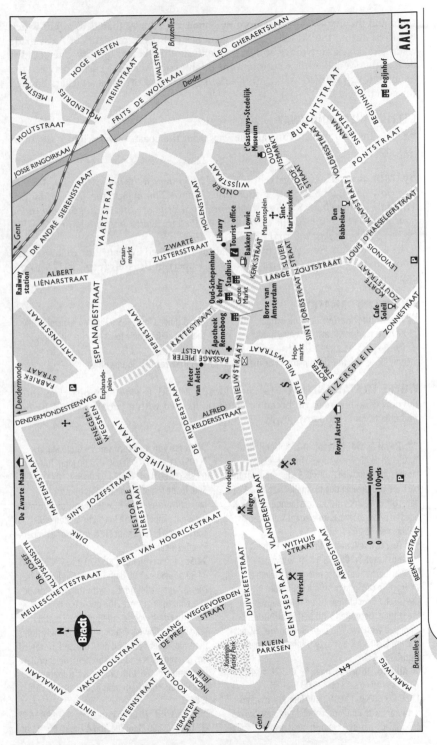

AALST

them and the *wortels* (carrots) from neighbouring Ninove thanks to a raid which occurred during the Middle Ages. Legend has it that the residents of Aalst made a surprise attack on Ninove and in the confusion the key to the city gate couldn't be found. As a makeshift solution, some bright spark wedged a carrot between the handles, which worked well … until a donkey ate it and the Aalst attackers flooded through the gates.

GETTING THERE AND AWAY

By car The E40, which runs all the way from the coast, travels right past Aalst; take exit 19.

By train Brussels-Zuid/Bruxelles-Midi (*32/55min past the hour Mon–Fri, 4/32/56 min past the hour Sat–Sun;* ⊕ *30min*); Gent (*8/20min past the hour Mon–Fri, 11/27min past the hour Sat–Sun* ⊕ *30min*); from Brugge (*direct trains 5min past the hour Mon–Fri,* ⊕ *1hr 20min & via Gent-St-Pieters, 35min past the hour Mon–Fri,* ⊕ *1hr; 35/58min past the hour Sat–Sun,* ⊕ *1hr*).

It's a short walk from Aalst railway station – designed by Jean-Pierre Cluysenaer, who also designed the Galeries Royales St-Hubert in Brussels (page 102) – to the city centre.

TOURIST INFORMATION

🖪 **Tourist information** 45 Molenstraat; ☎ 053 73 22 70; e toerisme@aalst.be; www.aalst.be; ⊕ 09.00–11.45 & 13.00–16.45 Mon–Fri. Small, friendly office with free town maps, cycle maps

(€3) & guided tours (€50/2hrs) on request. Sadly the MP3 audio-guide tours are currently only in Dutch.
🚲 **Bike rental** Tourist office.

🏠 **WHERE TO STAY AND EAT** The city's local speciality is *vlaai*, a moist cinnamon-flavoured cake spread on bread or eaten on its own with a cup of coffee. The best place to try it is Bakkerij Lowie.

🏠 **Royal Astrid** (13 rooms) 27 Keizerplein; ☎ 053 70 65 00; www.royal-astrid.be. Classy family run 3-star with 8 dbls & 5 sgls; rooms at the back are €10 cheaper due to smaller size & lack of bath. Other facilities including a lounge with TV & bar. The b/fast room has an elegant stained-glass ceiling. €€–€€€

🏠 **De Zwarte Maan** (1 room) 11 Dirk Martensstraat; ☎ 053 78 37 29; www. dezwartemaan.be. Hosts Kristien & Lieven & their white cat Spooky offer a B&B room on the second floor of their listed townhouse near the station. Decorated with period furniture, & equipped with free Wi-Fi, an electric fire, TV, tea-making facilities & a snazzy bright-pink en-suite bathroom. €€

✗ **Allegro** 16 Gentsestraat; ☎ 053 78 44 46; ⊕ 11.45–15.00 & 18.00–23.00 Tue–Fri. 11.00–23.00 Sat, 12.00–23.00 Sun. Ivy-covered restaurant with romantic, candlelit interior. Serves good salads, pastas & Flemish meat dishes. €€€€

✗ **Borse van Amsterdam** 26 Grote Markt; ☎ 053 21 15 81; ⊕ 09.30– 22.00 Mon, Tue & Fri, 09.30–13.00 Wed, 10.00– 22.00 Sat, 10.00–13.00 Sun. To the left of the belfry, this upmarket brasserie occupies the beautifully restored former meat hall. Popular with lunching 'golden oldies', you can pop in for a pancake & coffee or a proper Flemish meal. €€€€

✗ **So** 1 Keizerplein; ☎ 053 70 05 55; ⊕ 12.00– 14.30 &18.30–23.00 daily, closed Sat lunch. *Très chic* restaurant/loungebar with theatrical drapes adorning the entrance. The décor is a blend of über-cool dark woods, studded white leather seats, exotic flowers & a flourish of twinkly lights. Here you linger over wild duck dressed in stewed figs & lavender & end with homemade chocolate ice cream scented with orange & Campari. Yum! The 3-course lunch menu is good value at €19. €€€€

✗ **T'Verschil** 70 Gentsestraat; m 0474 98 16 98; ⊕ 12.00–22.00 Mon, Tue, Thu & Fri, 12.00–15.00

Wed, 18.00–23.00 Sat. Homely collection of wooden tables, candles & theatrical red drapes hanging from the ceiling. You're waited on personally by the spectacled (& bald) owner, Peter Maertens. The scampi spaghetti is very popular, but I'd opt for the *Américain* – the raw mincemeat may not be to everyone's liking, but it's seasoned to your preference at the table & slated to be the best for miles around – followed by the *sabayon* for dessert. Superb. It's very popular, so booking isn't a bad idea. €€€–€€€€

🖳 **Bakkerij Lowie** 16 Molenstraat; ✎ 053 77 43 00; ⏰ 08.00–18.30 Mon, Tue, Thu–Sat. The best place in town to try Aalst speciality *vlaai*. They also sell chocolate onions, a gimmicky homage to the city residents' nickname. €

WHERE TO DRINK

🍸 **Den Babbelaer** 3 Klapstraat; ✎ 053 77 58 96; ⏰ 11.30–late Tue–Sat. Very cosy bar owned by Els Verbraekel who serves a superb selection of local beers, including Gilladeken – the official city beer of Aalst – & Ondineke, brewed at De Glazen Toren brewery in the nearby town of Erpe-Mere. Also serves tapas & Abazjoer, a regional *jenever*.

🍸 **Café Soleil** 43 Korte Zoutstraat; ✎ 0496 28 70 57; ⏰ 12.00–late. Laidback Mediterranean-style bar on the corner of Keizerplein. Has a very busy terrace on sunny days.

WHAT TO SEE AND DO

Grote Markt Aalst's main square is dotted with several buildings of note. Standing tall and gleaming white is the Gothic **Oud-Schepenhuis** (Old Courthouse). Parts of it date back to the 13th century, making it the oldest of its kind in the Netherlands.

AALST CARNIVAL

This tourist-free folkloric feast dates back to the Middle Ages when local rulers allowed the townsfolk to enjoy three days of no-rules debauched behaviour prior to Ash Wednesday – the start of Lent. I'll warn you now: this is partying like you've never seen it before. It's a three-day bender of non-stop beer swigging and drunken dancing, with only brief pauses to catch a few winks on the bar top or in the gutter.

In 1851 they introduced the procession of flotillas which parade through town and mark the arrival of carnival. Local groups spend months preparing these floats, which take the mickey out of local figures and events that took place in the past year – events like those of 2011 when the mayor of Aalst, Ilse Utterrsprot, was caught on camera having sex on the rooftop of a castle while on holiday in Spain.

The procession starts on the Sunday/Monday before Ash Wednesday and ends with Aalst dignitaries throwing thousands of candy onions from the balcony of the Stadhuis into the crowd, including one lucky golden onion.

Tuesday is Voil Jeanetten day. Men arrive dressed in old stockings, wigs and bras and stumble around on their high-heels drunkenly embracing each other. As evening falls, everyone gathers on the Grote Markt and, with genuine tears of sadness, watches the Carnival Prince light a bonfire which signals the end of the party. A statue of Voil Jeanetten usually stands outside the post office on Hopmarkt, but at the time of writing can be seen in the entrance of t'Gasthuys-Stedelijk Museum (page 198).

Happily, the carnival joined the UNESCO list of cultural events in 2010. Dates for the next five years are as follows: 19 February 2012, 10 February 2013, 2 March 2014, 15 February 2015 and 7 February 2016.

The eight-cornered UNESCO-listed belfry forming its left flank dates from 1460. Look for the inscription *Nec Spec, Nec Metu* ('Without hope, Without fear') below the statue reliefs. It's a quote by Philip II who became Count of Aalst in 1595. The clocktower contains one of the oldest sets of still-working bells in Belgium but unfortunately they can't be visited. Locals refer to the tower as Tettentoeren (Titty Tower) because of the raised balls which form the hour markers on the modern clock face.

The **statue of Dirk Martens** in front of the Courthouse has stood here since 1856. Thanks to the colour of the oxidised bronze locals call him De Zwart Man ('the Black Man'). In 1473 Martens developed the first printing press in the Southern Netherlands and published works by Christopher Columbus as well as Thomas More's *Utopia*. To the left of the Courthouse is the 17th-century **Borse van Amsterdam**; once the meat market, it's now an upmarket restaurant (page 197). To the right is the neo-Classical **Stadhuis** (town hall), erected in 1830. If you wander through its archway to an inner courtyard, you'll see the Rococco **Landhuis** (country house), which contains the city administration offices. A statue of Ondineke – a character from Louis Paul Boon's famous novel *De Kapellekensbaan* – stands at the back of the courtyard.

t'Gasthuys-Stedelijk Museum *(13 Oude Vismarkt;* \ *053 73 23 45;* ☉ *10.00– 12.00 & 13.00–17.00 Tue–Fri, 14.00–18.00 Sat–Sun; admission free, explanations in Dutch only)* Notice the statue of Louis Paul Boon – the famous Dutch author and painter – located to the left of the entrance. Inside the town's only museum, on the first floor, is a lively exhibition about the history of Aalst Carnival (see box, page 196) with old film footage and photos, a jukebox playing carnival tunes, a recreation of a traditional *estaminet* (bar) and a line-up of the carnival 'princes'. A separate room houses paintings by Valerius De Saedeleer, a Flemish painter born in Aalst. Downstairs there's an exhibition about the history of the town. The Voil Jeanette statue which usually sits outside the post office on Nieuwstraat has been moved to the museum for safekeeping while renovation take place on the Hopmarkt. It'll move back at the end of 2013 once works have finished.

Sint-Martinuskerk *(5 Sint-Martensplein;* \ *053 21 31 95;* ☉ *09.00–12.00 & 14.00–17.00; admission free)* Aalst's neo-Gothic parish church is a real beauty. Work on the current building started in 1650 and, incredibly, still isn't finished! Inside it's bursting at the seams with no fewer than 22 chapels – each one belonging to a different guild – and over 400 works of art, including the catchily titled *Christ appoints St Rochus as Patron Saint of the Plague Victims* by Rubens.

Begijnhof *(Sterherenstraat; admission free)* Aalst's *begijnhof* still survives and it looks promising as you enter via the honeysuckle-laden archway, but apart from the pretty church (closed to the public), it's rather disappointing. The terraced houses are painted the characteristic white, but look more akin to a 1950s' housing estate, and behind them smoke belches from the sugar-factory chimneys.

Cycling Two cycle routes span out from the city centre: you can loop north via Dendermonde (45km) or head south to the town of Ninove (42km). Ask for the *Denderende Stedentocht* cycle-route map at the tourist office; it costs €3 and highlights what you'll see along the way. Bikes can be rented from the tourist office (page 196) from July to September; four hours costs €6, or €9 for the day.

GERAARDSBERGEN

The hilly town of Geraardsbergen (known as Grammont in French) sits at the southeastern edge of the Flemish Ardennes and is famous for its three Ms: the Muur, *mattentaart* (see box, page 200) and – the real – Manneken Pis. Amazingly, it's also believed to be Flanders' oldest city, with a charter dating from 1068. Later, on 29 May 1815, it enjoyed its five minutes of fame when the Duke of Wellington reviewed his troops in the fields surrounding the town prior to the pivotal Battle of Waterloo.

GETTING THERE AND AWAY

By car From Brussels follow the N8 west and take the N42 exit towards Geraardsbergen (*41km;* ⏱ *50min*). From Gent follow the N422 south, merge onto the E40 and take exit 17 (direction Wetteren); follow the N42 for 25km (*41km;* ⏱ *45min*). Free car parks are located on the edge of town, or there's paid parking in the centre; follow the P-route signs.

By train Aalst (*43min past the hour daily;* ⏱ *44min*); Gent (*11min past the hour Mon–Fri, 15min past the hour Sat–Sun;* ⏱ *50min*); Brussels-Zuid/Bruxelles-Midi (*fast train 28min past the hour Mon–Fri,* ⏱ *41min; 32min past the hour Sat–Sun,* ⏱ *55min*).

TOURIST INFORMATION

📧 Tourist information De Permanensje, Markt; 📞 054 43 72 89; e toerisme@geraardsbergen. be; www.geraardsbergen.be; ⏱ Mar–Sep 09.00– 12.00 & 13.00–17.00 Oct–Mar 09.00–12.00 & 13.30–16.00 Mon–Fri, Mar–Aug 10.00–13.00 & 13.30–17.30 Sep–Mar 10.00–13.00 & 14.00–

17.00 Sat–Sun. Staff don't speak English, but there's a useful interactive aerial map of the town & surrounding countryside with English subtitles. **🚲 Bike rental** €24 (electric) or €9 (standard)/ day from the tourist office.

🏠 WHERE TO STAY AND EAT

🏠 Grupello (10 rooms) 17 Verhaegenlaan; 📞 054 41 60 07; www.grupello-vijverhof.be. Landmark 105-year-old building that was previously a luxury clothes shop, now an intimate hotel with modern en-suite rooms run by married couple Carina & Kristoff. Free Wi-Fi & a superb b/fast – served beneath exquisite arches of

stained-glass window. Swish brasserie also on site. If you're planning to coincide your visit with the Ronde van Vlaanderen, you'll need to book up to a year in advance. €€€ **🍴 De Erfzonde** 3 Brugstraat; 📞 0478 82 33 79; ⏱ 06.30–13.00 Mon, 07.30–18.00 Wed–Sun. Snug café owned by a beard-

---

KRAKELINGEN

Every year, on the last Sunday of February, Geraardsbergen celebrates **Krakelingen** and **Tonnekensbrand** – a UNESCO-listed pagan procession that marks the end of winter. Townsfolk dress up in ye olde clothes and put together a parade recounting the town's history. It departs from outside Hunnegem church and climbs to the top of Oudenberg hill. From here town officials throw *krakelingen* (bagels) that have been blessed in Oudeberg Chapel to the crowds, city notables drink from glass bowls containing a dash of red wine and a live fish, and as evening falls, the Tonnekensbrand (bonfire) is lit. It's all meant to pay homage to life's basic elements: fire, food and wine.

enthusiast father-&-son team serving soups, croques monsieur & salads. Mary statuettes are everywhere & fun Manneken-Pis taps in the bathrooms. Also the best place to try *mattentaarten* (see box below). €

WHAT TO SEE AND DO

Markt Perched on the slopes of Oudenberg hill, Geraardsbergen's old market square is a regal space. The **Stadhuis** (town hall), which sits on its northern flank, has undergone several renovations. The current neo-Gothic façade dates from 1891. At the foot of its steps is the **Manneken Pis** fountain. Most people are familiar with Brussels' statue of the peeing boy (see box, page 101) but, in fact, Geraardsbergen's version dates from 1459 making it 160 years older. Like its Brussels' counterpart, the statue has a wardrobe to rival that of Kate Moss: more than 189 outfits gifted by various visiting dignitaries, some of which are on show at the Geraardsbergse Musea (see opposite).

To the left of the Stadhuis is a copy of the **Marbol**, a Gothic-style fountain where the townsfolk used to draw their water, and the former **Lakenhalle** (Cloth Hall) which now houses the tourist information centre.

To the east is the late-Gothic **Sint-Bartholomewskerk** (*Markt*; ⊕ *Apr–Oct 08.30–18.00 daily, Nov–Mar 08.30–16.00 daily; admission free*), which first appeared in 1476 but, again, has undergone several renovations. Inside, the Onze-Lieve-Vrouwe-Kapel holds a particularly beautiful triptych composed of rich reds, golds and greens. The chapel on the right behind the altar houses the relic of St Bartholomew in a silver chest, whose lid is adorned with his bust and flanked by angels. It was moved here in 1515 from the Carthusian Monastery in Sint-Martens-Lierde, a relocation commemorated every year on 24 August (or nearest Sunday) in the **Processie van Plaisance**, when the chest is paraded through town.

Also worth a quick gander is the cute **Brandstraat** tunnel located on the south side of the square and, a short walk along Borenhall and through the archway, the **Dierkosttoren**, the only tower remaining from the 12th-century city walls which were demolished in the 19th century.

Oudenberg and De Muur

Climbing the Oudenberg hill, which sits 110m above sea level, offers great views of the town and surrounding countryside. Leave the Markt via Hooiweg, keeping the church on your right. Soon you'll pass **Grupello Park**, which contains a statue of an elephant to commemorate those that lost their lives in the Belgian Congo (page 10) and, further up, a golden statue of an angel called **Heilig-Hartbeeld** (Holy Heart). The park is named after local sculptor Gabriel Grupello who was born on Pentitentenstraat in 1644.

MATTENTAART

Geraardsbergen is famous for its marzipan-flavoured *mattentaart*. They were first made during the Middle Ages as a way of putting soured milk to good use: the curds were mixed with eggs, sugar and almonds and covered in puff pastry. They are so beloved that they have their own dedicated song, feature in the *Guinness World Records* book and in 1985 became the first food to appear on a special-issue national stamp. Only bakers from Geraardsbergen and Lierde are allowed to sell *Geraardsberges Mattentaart* and they must use local milk. Every year, on the first Sunday of August, the town celebrates the curdled cake with festivities on the Markt.

Exiting the park, cross Pachtersstraat and make your way along the steep cobbled path known as **De Muur** (The Wall). Cycling fans will have heard of it. It forms the final leg of the **Ronde van Vlaanderen (Tour of Flanders)** cycle race and every year, on the first Sunday of April, thousands come from all around to watch cyclists pit their wits and calve muscles against the punishing slope. On the crest of the hill sits the domed **Oudenbergkapel** (Oudenberg Chapel). It was once a popular 17th-century pilgrimage site, but the current version only dates from 1905. Have a peek inside: the walls are plastered with 'thank you' plaques.

Geraardsbergse Musea *(26 Collegestraat;* \ *054 43 72 89;* ⊕ *2 Mar–30 Sep 14.00–17.00 Tue–Fri, 14.00–18.00 Sat–Sun, 1 Oct–1 Mar 14.00– 17.00 Sat–Sun; admission: adult/under 12 €1.75/0.75)* The town's only museum houses the real Manneken-Pis in a glass box – the one on the Markt is a replica in case it gets stolen – and a selection of his costumes. Other rooms are crammed with paraphernalia based on themes of tobacco, beer and lace. It's hardly show-stopping stuff, but the room devoted to matchsticks (the first on the right) is worth a look. In 1850 a matchstick factory was established on Gaverstraat in the nearby village of Overboelare, which – at the height of its power – was the largest of its kind in the world, employing over 2,000 people. It closed in 1999.

Hunnegem and Oud-Hospitaal Along Gasthuisstraat you'll find the oldest hospital in Flanders. The appropriately named **Oud-Hospitaal** (Old Hospital) was built in 1238, but most sections now date from the 16th and 17th centuries. Also on site is a Rococo chapel and next to it the original spire of the Marbol fountain – a copy of which stands on the Markt. Later on it served as an orphanage, and today houses an Academy of Arts. At the end of the street is the **Hunnegem** parish (⊕ *visits by appointment only; enquire at tourist office*). It was established in the 8th century, long before the town of Geraardsbergen grew around it. In the 17th century a group of Benedictine nuns built a convent next to the original Romanesque church.

Cycling If you want to have a go at tackling De Muur yourself, you can rent a bike from the tourist office and follow the 45km M-Route or, if you're feeling really fit, you can follow the 114km Ronde van Vlaanderen trail. Maps of both routes can be bought from the tourist office.

RONSE

Ronse – or Renaix in French – is known as a 'facility town' because it lies mere metres from the Flanders/Wallonia border. Consequently, the locals switch easily back and forth between the two languages. However, it's a rather technical term for a rather quaint town, which boasts two century-old pubs and a remarkable 1,000 year-old crypt, which has to be one of Flanders' most overlooked treasures.

During the 1920s and 1930s, Ronse was a textile town, home to over 24,000 residents and a staggering 500 factories, one of which is now a museum. The trade brought great riches to the textile barons, who built themselves Art Nouveau and Art Deco mansions. One manufacturer, Valère Carpentier, even went so far as to employ master Art Nouveau architect Victor Horta to design his summerhouse, Villa Carpentier (*9–11 Doorniksesteenweg*).

The town also kicks off the Flemish events' calendar with Bommelsfeesten on the second weekend after New Year. The dates for the next couple of years are 5–7 January 2013 and 11–13 January 2014.

GETTING THERE AND AWAY

By car From Brussels follow the N8 west; at the Brakel roundabout take the second exit and follow the N48 to Ronse (*57km; ⏲ 1hr*). From Gent follow the N60 south past Oudenaarde to Ronse (*41km; ⏲ 43min*).

By train Oudenaarde (*38min past the hour daily; ⏲ 10min*); Gent (*1min past the hour daily; ⏲ 47min*); Brussels-Zuid/Bruxelles-Midi via Oudenaarde (*41min past the hour Mon–Fri, 36min past the hour, every 2 hours Sat–Sun; ⏲ 1hr 7min*).

TOURIST INFORMATION

🖪 Touist information 2 De Biesestraat; ☎ 055 23 28 18; e toerisme@ronse.be; www.ronse.be; ⏲ Apr–Sep 09.00–12.00 & 13.00–17.00 Mon–Fri, 10.00–12.00 & 14.00–17.00 Sat–Sun, Oct–Nov 09.00–12.00 & 13.00–17.00 Mon–Fri, 14.00–17.00 Sat–Sun, Dec–Feb 09.00–12.00 & 13.00–16.00 Mon–Fri. Housed in a lovely 17th-century building inside a compound known as 'Hoge Mote', which was originally part of a line of 9 defence buildings along the Molenbeek River. I recommend booking a guided tour with the personable Chris van Thujne (€30/hr), who brings the Hermes Crypt to life.

🚲 Bike rental Tourist office. From April 2012 you'll be able to rent electric bikes with sites programmed into the GPS system €50/4hrs.

✗ WHERE TO EAT AND DRINK

The town has number of local beers: the high-malt Hoge Mote (6.1%), the light brown Bommelsbier (8.5%), the dark Ronsischen Dubbel (7.4%) and amber-coloured Ronsischen Tripel (8%). Savour them with a serving of HogeMotekaas, the local cheese. All of these can be found at Harmonie.

✗ De Acte 27 Grote Markt; ☎ 055 38 56 58; ⏲ 11.30–22.00 Mon–Wed & Fri–Sun. Smart dining room/tearoom studded with stained-glass windows & large terrace & lawn out the back. 2-course *dagmenu* with a beer or glass of wine costs €15. €€€

🍷 Harmonie 10 Grote Markt; ☎ 055 21 11 74; ⏲ 10.00–late daily. Another classic pub on the main square, it was built in 1900 & modelled on bars the rich textile barons had seen in Paris. German soldiers spent a lot of their down time here during World War II.

🍷 Local Unique 25 Grote Markt; ☎ 055 21 38 00; ⏲ 10.00–22.00 Mon–Fri, 10.00–01.00 Sat–Sun. Over 100 years old, the walls of this spacious bar are filled with old tile mosaics & it's also the meeting place for participants in a wonderful, but rarely seen, local sport: dove racing. Every w/end between Apr & Sep old men gather here with their best birds, waiting for the truck to come & take them to the racing start line. Serves Ename & Liefmaans beer.

WHAT TO SEE AND DO

St Hermeskerk (*Sint-Hermesstraat; ⏲ Apr–Sep 14.00–17.00 Tue–Sun, 1 Oct–30 Nov 14.00–17.00 Sat–Sun, 1 Dec–30 Mar closed; admission: adult/under 12 €2.50/ free, combi ticket with MUST €6*) St Hermes is a rare Catholic saint: only five churches in Europe are dedicated to him. He was a Roman who converted to Christianity, and the decision landed him a lengthy jail sentence before he was beheaded. He became a martyr and the saint of mental illnesses thanks to his association with the head – or loss of it in his case. His relics came to Ronse in the 9th century. A church and crypt was built around the chest and throughout the Middle Ages pilgrims came from far and wide to be cured of depression, schizophrenia and epilepsy. The constant influx of travellers brought the town great wealth and status. This Romanesque church collapsed in 1267 – some of the remains still lie outside to the left of the crypt entrance – but parts of the 1089 crypt survive to this today; look for the jumbled bricks on the ceiling near the entrance. The crypt – which technically isn't a crypt because it sits above street level – was repaired and a new church built on top. It was given a new wing in 1517 which was constructed in the late-Gothic style, marked by the use of red brick.

To be eligible to enter, pilgrims had to complete two tasks. The first was a physical offering: they had to walk at least 25km on foot to reach the church, which stupidly meant Ronse locals couldn't enter. To solve the problem, they started the Fiertelommegang, a 32km procession around town which is still celebrated on Trinity Sunday when St-Hermes' relic chest is paraded around town. The dates for the next few years are 3 June 2012, 26 May 2013 and 15 June 2014.

Second, the pilgrims had to make a monetary offering. They were placed on weighing scales and had to pay their own weight in goods or food. The system was actually fairly democratic since only the rich could afford to eat a lot and therefore weighed the most. The scheme was a profitable one for the church, which sold the offerings of chickens and goats back at market the next day – it's highly likely the poor chickens saw the inside of the crypt day after day on an endless cycle of buying and selling.

Pilgrims were then allowed to enter the crypt and walk around the relic chest, touching it gently to absorb its healing powers. The wooden version on display today is a copy; the original silver one was destroyed in the 16th century during the religious wars.

The sick would then enter the two side rooms, which served as separate male and female bathing rooms with wooden tubs, which were filled from the well in the centre of the crypt. The effects of the bath were twofold: it symbolically washed away their sins, and cleaning off the dirt probably made them feel better too. It's believed pilgrims could listen to mass through the small window in the wall while they were bathing.

There are a number of interesting features to look out for. The walls are studded with slivers of terracotta, which are old Roman roof tiles, and at the back of the crypt, is a support stone recovered from the church that collapsed. It stands on a pillar on the right-hand side. Look closely and you'll see it has a clear engraving of a vagina on it – a common fertility symbol.

Today, many people are dubious about the contents of relics like those of St-Hermes, but a few years ago the church consented to have the whole box placed in a hospital scanner. Amazingly, the scan revealed the relic wasn't empty and did indeed contain human bones, not those of St-Hermes, but of a man, a woman and a child. Who they are remains a mystery.

Textielmuseum (MUST) (*De Biesestraat;* ⊕ *Apr–Sep 14.00–17.00 Tue–Sun, Oct–Nov 14.00–17.00 Sat–Sun, Dec–Mar closed; admission: adult/under 12 €5/ free, combi ticket with crypt €6*) Across the courtyard from the tourist information office, this former textile mill has over 40 looms of varying ages, all of them in working order. The curator will give you a demonstration, so you can grasp the deafening level of noise the workers had to ensure when there were hundreds of the machines all working at once. Notice the original triangular Rackham roof; the windows deliberately point north to allow the maximum amount of neutral light for the workers.

OUDENAARDE

Oudenaarde sits on the River Scheldt in the heart of the Flemish Ardennes – an area of rolling green hills studded with hamlets and crops of woodland. Its riverside

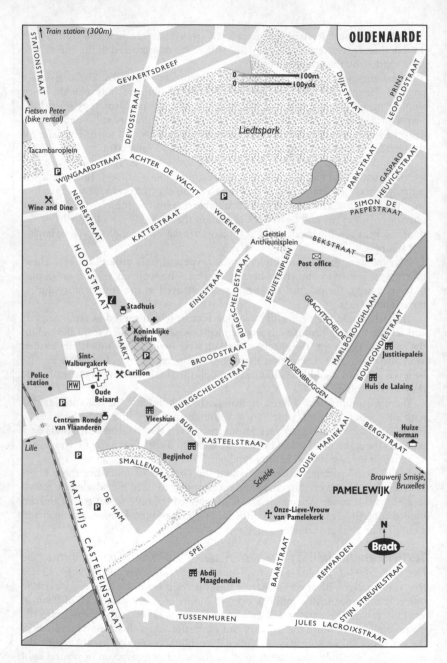

Train station (300m)

STATIONSTRAAT

GEVAERTSDREEF

DEVOSSTRAAT

Fietsen Peter
(bike rental)

Liedtspark

DIJKSTRAAT

LEOPOLDSTRAAT

PRINS

Tacambaroplein

WIJNGAARDSTRAAT

ACHTER DE WACHT

PARKSTRAAT

GASPARD
HEUVICKSTRAAT

Wine and Dine

NEDERSTRAAT

KATTESTRAAT

WOEKER

SIMON DE
PAEPESTRAAT

HOOGSTRAAT

Gentiel
Antheunisplein

BEKSTRAAT

EINESTRAAT

BURGSCHELDESTRAAT

JEZUIETENPLEIN

Post office

Stadhuis

Koninklijke
fontein

GRACHTSCHELDESTRAAT

MARLBOROUGHLAAN

BOURGONDIESTRAAT

Justitiepaleis

MARKT

Sint-
Walburgakerk

BROODSTRAAT

TUSSENBRUGGEN

Huis de Lalaing

Police
station

MW

Carillon

Oude
Beiaard

BURGSCHELDESTRAAT

BERGSTRAAT

Huize
Norman

Centrum Ronde
van Vlaanderen

Vleeshuis

BURG

KASTEELSTRAAT

LOUISE MARIEKAAI

Lille

Begijnhof

SMALLENDAM

Schelde

Brouwerij Smisje,
Bruxelles

PAMELEWIJK

DE HAM

MATTHIJS CASTELEEINSTRAAT

Onze-Lieve-Vrouw
van Pamelekerk

SPEI

N

Bradt

BAARSTRAAT

REMPARDEN

STIJN STREUVELSTRAAT

Abdij
Maagdendale

TUSSENMUREN

JULES LACROIXSTRAAT

0 — 100m
0 — 100yds

location allowed it to join the linen trade and the town flourished from the 11th century onwards. When the linen trade dipped, the residents transferred their skills to tapestry weaving and later silverwork, which lasted for over 300 years until the 18th century. The tapestries were highly admired and sold the world over and it was during this period of prosperity that Oudenaarde's flamboyant-Gothic Stadhuis – which rivals that of Leuven and Brussels – was built.

The town was equally famous for its brewing industry, which remains strong to this today (see *Where to sleep, eat and drink* below). Local breweries converge on the Markt on the last weekend of June to celebrate **Adriaen Brouwer Bierfeesten** – a beer festival named after Adriaen Brouwer, a local 17th-century artist famous for his paintings depicting peasant life.

Despite this glorious history, Oudenaarde isn't well known by travellers. However, this is set to change when the Ronde van Vlaanderen cycle race terminates here from 2012 to 2014. It's a huge coup for the city. Be sure to book your accommodation well in advance if you plan to coincide your visit with the April race.

GETTING THERE AND AWAY

By car From Brussels the fastest route is to take the E40 to Gent, take the Zwijnaarde exit and merge onto the E17 (direction Kortrijk). Soon after take exit 8 (direction De Pinte) and follow the N60 south to Oudenaarde (*73km;* ⊕ *1hr*). From Aalst take the N9 west out of town and follow signs for the E40. On the E40 take exit 18 (direction Erpe Mere) and follow the N46 to Oudenaarde (*40km;* ⊕ *43min*).

By train Brussels-Zuid/Bruxelles-Midi (*41min past the hour Mon–Fri,* ⊕ *46min; 36min past the hour Sat–Sun,* ⊕ *52min*); Gent (*fast train 1min past the hour daily;* ⊕ *28min*); Kortrijk (*5/15min past the hour Mon–Fri, 15min past the hour Sat–Sun;* ⊕ *20min*).

TOURIST INFORMATION

🛈 **Tourist information** Stadhuis, Hoogstraat; ☏ 055 31 72 51; e toerisme@oudenaarde.be; www.oudenaarde.be; ⊕ Apr–Oct 09.00–17.30 Mon–Fri, 10.00–17.30 Sat–Sun, Nov–Mar 09.30–12.00 & 13.30–16.00 Mon–Fri, 14.00–17.00 Sat. Modern, glass-fronted building which sells town-walk maps in English (€1.50) – bonus! See page 206 for information on cycling.

🚲 **Bike rental** Fietsen Peter, 119 Beverestraat; ☏ 055 31 16 53; ⊕ 08.30–12.00 & 13.30–18.30 Tue–Fri, 08.30–12.00 & 13.30–18.00 Sat

🏠 **WHERE TO STAY, EAT AND DRINK** Oudenaarde has a number of local breweries. Brouwerij Roman produces the dark chocolate-coloured Adriaen Brouwer, the Liefmans brewery is famous for its refreshing fruit beers, and micro-brewery Smisje creates the cheeky amber-coloured Smiske. The pubs and bars I've listed below sell a good selection of them, but to try Smiske you'll have to visit the brewery café (page 206). As a treat, locals love to chew on *lekkies* made by Jan van Gent (see below).

🏠 **Huize Norman** (4 rooms) 30 Bergstraat; m 0473 21 76 78; www.huizenorman.be. Norman's House is a very trendy retro-style B&B a short walk south of the central Markt. Has 3 rooms, 1 suite, a zesty lime b/fast room & bikes for hire. Good price/quality. €€

✗ **Wine and Dine** 34 Hoogstraat; ☏ 055 23 96 97; ⊕ 11.30–14.30 & 18.00–22.30 Tue–Sat. *The* place among locals for an affordable dinner out, this urban bistro has black décor broken up with flashes of red & serves a varied menu of pastas, salads, fish & meat dishes. €€€

🍴 **Jan van Gent** 98 Kerzelare; ☏ 055 30 49 00; ⊕ Oct–Feb 10.00–18.00 Mon–Thu & Sat–Sun, Mar–Sep 09.00–20.00 Mon–Thu & Sat–Sun. Rent a bike & cycle to this delightful tearoom, 2.5km southeast of town, which turned 200 years old in 2012 & is famous for its *lekkies* – pieces of nougat – which are sold in the attached traditional sweet shop. €

🍺 **Carillon** 49 Markt; ☏ 055 31 14 09; ⊕ 09.00–late Tue, Wed & Fri–Sun, 08.00–late Thu. Sits in the shadow of Sint-Walburgakerk. Does serves food, but locals come here in summer to sit on the large terrace & listen to the church's carillon concerts while sipping on a Liefmans Kriek.

WHAT TO SEE AND DO

Stadhuis (*Markt;* ⊕ *Apr–Oct 11.00–15.00 Tue–Sun; admission €6*) Standing tall and proud at the northern end of the Markt, Oudenaarde's ornate UNESCO-listed town hall cannot fail to impress. Built between 1525 and 1536 in Brabantine Gothic style, its great rooms house a number of treasures, which as of March 2012 visitors will be able to explore without booking a guide. There will also be a new museum, on the second floor, describing the town's history and displaying its collection of silver and tapestries.

Sint-Walburgakerk (*Sint-Walburgastraat;* ⊕ *Jun–Sep 14.30–17.00 Tue–Sat, 10.00–12.00 & 14.30–17.00 Thu, 14.00–17.30 Sun, Oct 14.30–17.00 Tue & Sat, 10.00–12.00 & 14.30–17.00 Thu, Nov–Feb 10.00–12.00 Thu; admission free*) Perched on the southwestern edge of the Markt, this bell-topped church is in fact two churches joined at the transept: the choir, in dark-grey limestone, dates from the 13th century and the rest from the 15th century. The church lost most of its treasures during the religious wars, but has a reasonable collection of statues and tapestries inside. Every Sunday, between 12.00 and 13.00, it hosts a carillon concert and also in July and August on Thursdays from 20.30 to 21.30.

Centrum Ronde van Vlaanderen (*43 Markt;* \ *055 33 99 33; www.crvv. be;* ⊕ *10.00–18.00 Tue–Sun, closed 2nd & 3rd week of Jan; admission: adult/ under 14 €7.50/4*) Across the road from the church, this museum is dedicated to the illustrious Tour of Flanders and a must-see for cycling enthusiasts. Lots of newspaper clippings, new footage and films. Relive the races by discussing them with the locals over a beer at the on-site Flandrien bar.

Begijnhof (*Achterburg;* ⊕ *summer 06.00–21.00, winter 06.00–19.00; admission free*) Oudenaarde's béguines originally lived behind St Walburga church and moved to this quaint enclave in 1449. A statue of St Rochus – the patron saint of plague victims – guards the entrance. The uniform rows of whitewashed buildings largely date from the 18th and 19th centuries. Wander round to the back to find the *begijnhof's* minuscule chapel.

Huis de Lalaing (*9 Bourgondiëstraat;* \ *055 31 48 63;* ⊕ *Apr–Oct 13.30–17.00 Tue–Sun; admission: adult/12–18/under 11 €3/1.50/free – ring bell to enter*) This 16th-century mansion on the banks of the Scheldt River belonged to Philip De Lalaing, the town governor, and is rumoured to be the birthplace of Emperor Charles V's illegitimate daughter Margaret of Parma. The building now houses a selection of Oudenaarde's enormous 17th-century tapestries and a restoration studio on the second floor. Before entering the house, look for the ancient ginkgo biloba tree – with its fan-shaped leaves – in the garden.

Browerij Smisje (*1 Driesleutelstraat;* m *0475 36 44 89; www.smisje.be;* ⊕ *Jun–Oct 14.00–21.00 first Sat of the month*) Those with a real interest in Belgian beers should visit Oudenaarde on the first Saturday of the month when this local micro-brewery opens its café doors and offers a tour of the brewery at 16.00.

Cycling Bang in the middle of the Flemish Ardennes and – as of 2012 – the terminal of the Ronde van Vlaanderen, Oudenaarde is one of the best towns in which to base yourself while having a go at Flanders' most famous cycle routes. Channel your inner Eddy Merckx and have a go at the *Ronde van Vlaanderen* (€3), or even his own personalised *Eddy Merckxroute* (€1.80). For something easier, ie: flatter, try the *Scheldt Vallei* route (€1.80). The tourist office also sells a regional cycling map of the Flemish Ardennes entitled *Vlaamse Ardennen* (€6), but if you'd prefer to explore the area by car they have a driving map (€2.50) too.

DEINZE

Deinze is a small, fairly bland town on the southwestern outskirts of Gent. Its advantageous position, at the confluence of the Kanaal van Schipdonk and the River Leie, led to a strong start in life during the 12th century when the village prospered from the trade of textiles. However, it all went down hill from there. During the 14th and 15th centuries, Deinze was besieged alternately by Gent and Brugge troops, in the 16th century it got caught up in the Iconoclastic Fury and suffered from a bout of plague, and throughout the 17th and 18th centuries it was virtually empty. The main reason for visiting is the picture-perfect 16th-century Kasteel van Ooidonk.

GETTING THERE AND AWAY
By car From Gent follow the N466 southwest to Deinze (*18.5km;* ⊕ *26min*). From Kortrijk follow the E17 northeast and take exit 7 (*35km;* ⊕ *27min*). From Brugge follow signs for the E40 Oostende/Kotrijk, follow the motorway southeast for 19km, then take exit 11 (direction Aalster) and follow the N409 south to Deinze (*44km;* ⊕ *45min*).

By train Gent (*9/51min past the hour daily;* ⊕ *13min*).

TOURIST INFORMATION
▪ Tourist information 4 Emiel Clausplein; ⧀ 09 380 46 01; e toerisme@deinze.be; www.deinze. be; ⊕ 16 Jun–15 Sep 09.00–12.00 & 13.00–16.00 daily, 16 Sep–15 Jun 10.00–12.00 & 14.00–16.00 Mon–Fri

♂♂ Bike rental Deinze railway station; Stationsstraat; m 0476 46 53 17

WHAT TO SEE AND DO
Onze-Lieve-Vrouwekerk (*Markt;* ⊕ *daily; admission free*) The first version of this church was founded in the 9th century by Abbot Poppo, who was born in Deinze and died in the Holy Lands. His relics were returned to the church. The current version dates mainly from the 1920s, but parts of the side chapels are 12th century and the altar and its wooden retable date from the 14th century. Look for the paintings above the main arch and admire the central columns studded with statues of the apostles.

Museum van Deinze en de Leiestreek (*3–5 Lucien Matthyslaan;* ⧀ *09 381 96 70; www.museumdeinze.be;* ⊕ *14.00–17.30 Tue–Fri, 10.00–12.00 & 14.00–17.00 Sat–Sun; admission: adult/6–16/under 6 €2.75/1.25/free*) Displays the work of Symbolists and Impressionists including Constant Permeke who were inspired by the River Leie landscape. One floor also serves as the town history museum with a wonderful vintage coffee shop and bakery.

Kasteel van Ooidonk (*9 Ooidonkdreef;* ⧀ *09 282 35 70; www.ooidonk.be;* ⊕ *castle: 1 Apr– 15 Sep 14.00–17.30 Sun, Jul–Aug 14.00–17.30 Sat–Sun, garden: 1 Apr–15 Sep 14.00–17.30 Tue–Sun; admission castle: adult/under 12 €7/2, admission* *gardens: adult/child €1/0.30*) People come from far and wide to visit Flanders' most complete, and beautiful, castle. Surrounded by a moat and rich woodland, Ooidonk Castle once belonged to Philippe II de Montmorency-Nivelle, also known as the Count Hoorn who was executed on Brussels' Grand' Place alongside Count Egmond for resisting Spanish rule (page 7). The castle suffered extensive damage during the religious wars of 1579 and was rebuilt in the Flemish-Spanish style you see today. You're free to wander the lovely gardens all week, but the interior is only open at weekends because the current owner, Earl Juan t'Kint de Roodenbeke, still lives in the castle. Its collection of period furniture, paintings, tapestries and silver is sumptuous.

Getting there
On foot The tourist office sells a 7.5km walking route, *Ooidonk wanderlroute*, that takes you past the castle (€1.25).

By bike The tourist office sells the *Leiestreekroute* (55km; €1.80) cycling map, which takes you past the castle.

By bus During the week bus #14 departs every hour from Deinze railway station and stops in Sint-Martens-Leeme (stop: Mulderstraat); from there it's a ten-minute/1km walk south to the castle. At the weekend, you'll have to call the Belbus (✆ 09 211 91 91; ⊕ 07.00–20.00 Sat, 07.00–13.30 Sun) to come and collect you. Book it two hours in advance and tickets cost the same as a regular bus journey.

By car Follow the N466 west for 10km; once you reach the village of Sint-Martens-Leeme take the second left onto Ooidonkdreek and follow signs for the castle (14km; ⊕ 25min).

West Flanders

This coastal region is home to Flanders' most evocative place names: Brugge (Bruges), Ieper (Ypres), Passchendaele and Poperinge. Many are famous for their involvement in World War I, which was played out on the polders between Nieuwpoort on the coast and Menen on the French border. Between 1914 and 1918 the fluctuating Western Front reduced many towns to rubble and left lasting scars on the landscape. It was a dark period, which has been carefully preserved by the War Graves Commission and the Flemish Government, who have allocated generous funds to the 2014 centenary.

Outside these cities, stretch flat green fields drained in the 10th century by the dykes still seen either side of the raised roads. These pathways join up to form some of the prettiest and most interesting cycling routes in the country, leading you past picture-perfect villages like Damme and Lissewege, working windmills and rural Flemish hamlets.

Explore the romantic canals and B&Bs of Brugge, whizz along the North Sea sands while trying sandsailing at De Panne, step into the shoes of World War I soldiers at Poperinge's incomparable Talbot House and taste the world's rarest beer at Sint-Sixtus Abbey.

BRUGGE (BRUGES)

The capital of West Flanders, Brugge has long been a major port of call for travellers. Indeed, until the 15th century it was a port; connected to the North Sea via the town of Damme (page 231) and the Het Zwin canal.

Shaped like a spider's web, the city is spun from numerous spindly streets and framed by canals. Its legendary status as the best-preserved medieval city in Europe attracts hordes of tourists every summer, but somehow this doesn't diminish its beauty. Your days will be easily filled admiring the ancient architecture, sleeping in historic hotels and perhaps spoiling yourself at dinner time, because the city boasts no fewer than eight Michelin-starred restaurants. Don't miss the *begijnhof* – one of Belgium's best; the revered Basiliek van het Heilig-Bloed; and the De Halve Maan city brewery.

HISTORY It's hard to overstate Brugge's importance. Mentions of *Municipium Brugense* crop up in the history books as early as the 7th century. Baldwin the Iron Arm, first Count of Flanders, built the first fort (Burg) here in the 9th century and erected city walls to guard against Viking attacks. At that time the town was closely connected to the sea by a series of short canals, and Baldwin revived trade routes with England and Scandinavia that had been established by the Romans. This natural channel silted up in the 11th century, but fortunately a storm caused the

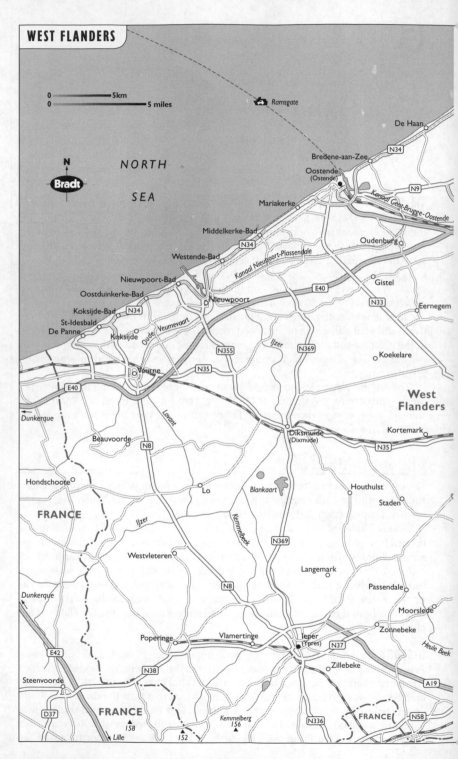

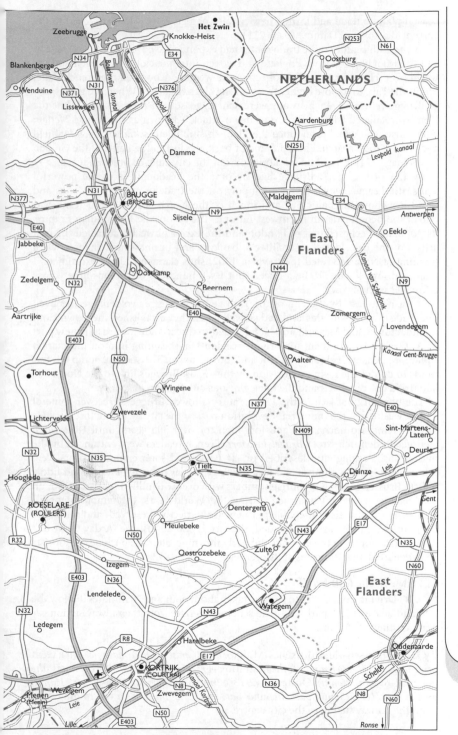

coastal plain to flood and form a new canal – named Zwin – that stretched to the current-day town of Damme (page 231).

By the 13th century these trade routes had expanded to cover the Mediterranean and the wool brought from England and woven into fine cloth was in demand the world over. However, the influx of economic wealth encouraged the French King, Philip the Fair, to impose higher taxes on the city's residents. When the guildsmen of Brugge refused, French troops were sent in to squash their rebellion, but the Flemish retaliated with a murderous dawn attack – known as the *Brugse Metten*; only those who could pronounce the Flemish shibboleth *schild en vriend* (shield and friend) were spared. Philip IV fought back and lost in the Battle of the Golden Spurs (page 274) in 1302, so for a brief period the city enjoyed independence.

By the 14th century, Brugge had become the headquarters of the powerful Hanseatic League, which had a monopoly on the trade of gold, spices, silks and furs throughout the Baltic Sea and much of the North Sea, and as a result was one of the richest cities in northwest Europe. The seat of the Burgundian Empire, its population eclipsed that of London and the excess of wealth attracted the best artists of the day, as well as architects, bankers and businessmen. Indeed, when Johanna of Navarre visited the town in 1302, she's claimed to have exclaimed, 'I imagined myself alone to be a queen, but I see hundreds of persons here whose attire vies with my own.'

It wasn't to last. By the end of the 15th century Brugge's golden age was over. The trade of wool with England had slowed when they established their own cloth manufacturers, and Maximilian I had decided to direct trade towards the new port of Antwerp as punishment for Brugge residents imprisoning him on the market square. Merchants had followed suit and moved north. The sudden slump left few funds to dredge the Zwin estuary and by the 1530s, Brugge's link to the North Sea had dried up completely and the once glorious city fell into obscurity.

The popularity of lace in the 17th century allowed Brugge to recover some of its lost wealth, but the Industrial Revolution passed the city by. Like a lost fairytale town it remained unchanged and forgotten for over 300 years, until 1892 when Georges Rodenbach wrote *Bruges-la-Mort*. French readers were entranced by the mysterious, sleeping city described on its pages and soon enough visitors were returning to catch a glimpse of a forgotten age. Today, Brugge plays second fiddle only to Brussels in terms of tourist numbers with over two million traipsing through its streets every year. Unharmed during the World Wars, the famous stepped-gabled houses, canals and cobbled streets are perfectly preserved, and whilst it's sometimes criticised as overcrowded, the city is still a must-see. A day trip won't do it justice, for it's in the evening and early morning, after the busloads of tourists have departed, that Brugge is at its prettiest.

GETTING THERE AND AWAY

By car Driving from Calais to Brugge takes about hour and 20 minutes. Follow the E40 and take exit 7. A park-and-ride scheme operates from the railway station car park, costing €2.50/24hr.

By train Brussels-Zuid/Bruxelles-Midi (*5/26min past the hour daily;* ⊕ *1hr*); Gent (*on the hour, 15/38/41min past the hour Mon–Fri, on the hour/29/38/41min past the hour Sat–Sun;* ⊕ *25min*); Oostende (*2/13/42min past the hour Mon–Fri,* ⊕ *15min; on the hour/18/47/55min past the hour Sat–Sun,* ⊕ *34min*). It's a ten-minute walk from the railway station to the city centre.

GETTING AROUND

On foot Brugge and all its winding alleyways are best explored on foot. The city centre is compact – just 2km wide and 3km long – but, nevertheless wear sturdy walking shoes that can cope with all the cobbled streets.

By bike See bike rental on page 221.

By boat Half-hour boat tours depart from various locations along the canal – see map on pages 214–15 for locations – and run between March and November (⏰ *10.00–18.00 daily; adult/4–11/under 4/BruggeCard €7.60/3.40/free/free*).

By bus The bus station is situated outside the railway station. Buses # 1, 3, 4, 6, 11, 13, 14 and 16 all stop in the central Markt square on 't Zand for the tourist information office. Tickets can be bought from the De Lijn office outside the station.

By horse-drawn carriage Brugge is famous for its romantic horse-drawn carriage tours. You can hail one down on the Markt and the driver will clop around town for half an hour, with a five-minute stop at the *begijnhof*, before returning to the main square. A carriage holds up to five people and currently costs €39 per tour, paid direct to the driver.

TOURIST INFORMATION

ℹ Main office [214–15 B6] 34 't Zand; ☎ 050 44 46 46; www.brugge.be; ⏰ 10.00–18.00 daily. Has 3 computer terminals for checking hostel/hotel bookings/availability & suggesting where to eat & drink, plus selection of Brugge guidebooks to flick through. There's a ticketing system in place if you want to talk to a tourism guide.

ℹ Railway station ☎ 050 44 46 46; ⏰ 10.00–17.00 Mon–Fri, 10.00–14.00 Sat–Sun

GUIDED TOURS

City bus tour Sightseeing Line; ☎ 050 35 50 24; www.citytour.be. The bright-yellow minibuses depart from the Markt, ⏰ Jan–Feb 10.00–16.00, Mar & Nov–Dec 10.00 17.00, Apr–Jun 10.00–19.00, Jul–Sep 10.00–20.00, Oct 10.00–18.00; adult/ 6–11 €14.50/8.50.

Koninklijke Gidsenbond 3 Kleine Hertsbergestraat; ☎ 050 33 22 33; www.brugge-guides.com. The Royal Guides Association run a series of themed private walking tours. as well as tours of Damme (page 231), which cost €60 for 2hr & €30 for each additional hour after that.

Pink Bear ☎ 050 61 66 86; www.pinkbear.freeservers.com. Run 4hr guided bike tours through the polders to the village of Damme; depart under the Belfort on the Markt at 10.25; adult/under 25/under 8/BruggeCard €22/20/free/21.

QuasiMundo ☎ 050 33 07 75; www.quasimundo.eu. Run guided bike tours of the city Mar–Nov 10.00–12.30; adult/under 26/under 8 €25/23/free. Depart from the Toyo Ito pavilion on the Burg.

Q-rius ☎ 050 44 12 81; www.q-rius.be. Run a wide range of gastronomic walking, bike & horse tram tours. To whet your appetite: a 4.5hr bike ride with 3 courses costs €65; a 4hr horse-tram ride with 3 courses costs €71.

Walking tour 34 't Zand; ⏰ Apr, Jul–Aug 14.30 daily, May, Jun, Sep & Oct 14.30 Sat–Sun, Nov–Mar 17.00 Mon, Wed & Sat–Sun; adult/under 12 €9/free. 2hr tour of all the main sights. During winter, Brugge City Card holders can join the tour for free.

WHERE TO STAY Tucked away among the winding medieval streets of Brugge are some exciting, one-off accommodation options. Large chain hotels simply cannot squeeze into the narrow corridors paved out between canals and as a result exclusive B&Bs have been able to proliferate. However, this does put strain on the proprietors

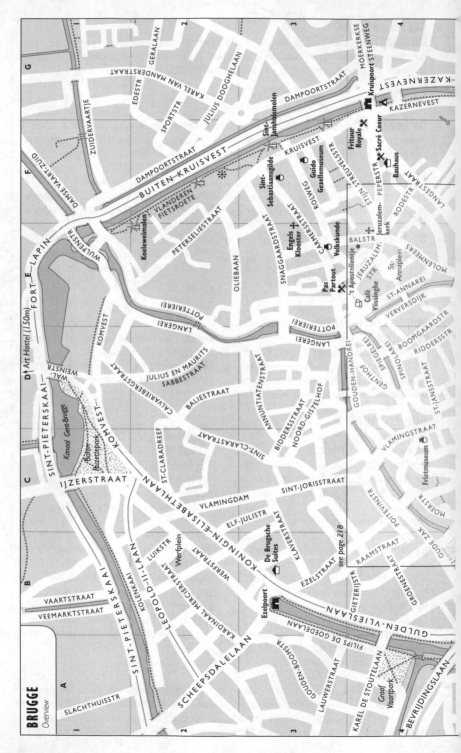

BRUGGE
Overview

SLACHTHUISSTR

VEEMARKTSTRAAT

VAARTSTRAAT

SINT-PIETERSKAAI

Art Hostel (150m)

FORT-E-LAPIN

DAMSE VAART-ZUID

ZUIDERVAARTJE

SPORTSTR

EDESTR

KAREL VAN MANDERSTRAAT

JULIUS DOOGHELAAN

GERALAAN

DAMPOORTSTRAAT

BUITEN-KRUISVEST

MOERKERKSE STEENWEG

Kruispoort

KAZERNEVEST

KAZERNEVEST

Koeleweimolen

Sint-Janshuismolen

DAMPOORTSTRAAT

VLANDEREN FIETSROETE

PETERSELIESTRAAT

KRUISVEST

Sint-Sebastiaansgilde

CARMERSSTRAAT

ROLWEG

Guido Gezellemuseum

Frituur Royale

Sacré Coeur

PEPERSTR

Bauhaus

LANGESTRAAT

RODESTR

JERUZALEM STR

JULIEN STREVELSSTR

Engels Klooster

Volkskunde

Jeruzalem-kerk

St-Annaplein

BALSTR

MOLENMEERS

WULPENSTR

OLIEBAAN

SNAGGAARDSTRAAT

Pas Partout

't Apostolientje

Café Vlissinghe

JERUZALEM STR

ST-ANNAREI

VERVERSDIJK

BOOMGAARDSTR

RIDDERSSTR

POTTERIEREI

LANGEREI

KOMVEST

LANGEREI

POTTERIEREI

GOUDEN-HANDREI

GENTHOF

SPIEGELREI

SPINOLAREI

ST-JANSSTRAAT

JULIUS EN MAURITS SABBESTRAAT

CALVARIEBERGSTRAAT

WAL-WEINSTR

KOMVEST

SINT-PIETERSKAAI

IJZERSTRAAT

KOMVEST

Kanaal Gent-Brugge

Baron Ruzettepark

ST-CLARADREEF

SINT-CLARASTRAAT

BALIESTRAAT

ANNUNTIATENSTRAAT

BIDDERSSTRAAT

NOORD-GISTELHOF

VLAMINGSTRAAT

Frietmuseum

VLAMINGDAM

SINT-JORISSTRAAT

POITEVINSTR

MOERSTR

OUDE ZAK

SCHEEPSDALELAAN

LEOPOLD-II-LAAN

KONINGIN-ELISABETHLAAN

ELF-JULISTR

KLAVERSTRAAT

EZELSTRAAT

see page 2/8

RAAMSTRAAT

GROENESTRAAT

KARDINAAL MERCIERSTRAAT

LUIKSTR

KOLENKAAI

Werfplein

WERFSTRAAT

De Brugsche Suites

Ezelpoort

GIETERIJSTR

GULDEN-VLIESLAAN

FILIPS DE GOEDELAAN

LAUWERSTRAAT

GOUDEN-BOOMSTR

KAREL DE STOUTELAAN

Graaf Visartpark

GRAAF DE STOUTELAAN

BEVRIJDINGSLAAN

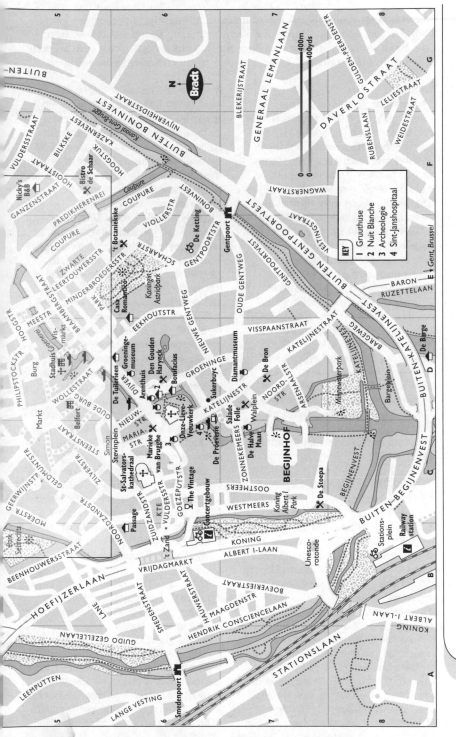

KEY
1 Gruuthuse
2 Nuit Blanche
3 Archeologie
4 Sint-Janshospitaal

0 400m
0 400yds

N

→ Gent, Brussel

when busloads of tourists arrive in summer, so it's essential to book ahead, even for budget accommodation. During the winter and early spring months, when trade dips, about 35 hotels participate in a three-for-two-night offer, which is open to guests arriving on Sunday, Monday or Tuesday, so it's worth enquiring before you book.

Luxury

🏠 **Bonifacius** [214–15 D6] (3 rooms) 4 Groeninge; ✆ 050 49 00 49; www.bonifacius.be. Right beside the canal, this exclusive & romantic guesthouse hosted Colin Farrell & Ralph Fiennes while they were filming In Bruges. The 3 suites – the junior Guinevere, standard Ambusson & the master Clair Obscure – are decorated with plush fabrics, motif wallpaper, antique furniture & (in the first & latter) 4-poster beds. Special features include the roof terrace with views of Onze-Lieve-Vrouwekerk & a Gothic-style b/fast room. The Michelin-starred De Gouden Harynck restaurant (see opposite) is close at hand. €€€€€

🏠 **De Tuilerieen** [214–15 D6] (45 rooms) 7 Dijver; ✆ 050 34 36 91; www.hoteltuilerieen. com. The De Tuilerieen is opulent in the extreme & judging from the line of photographs showing off the hotel's famous guests, it's keen to let everyone know just how grand it is. Admittedly, the rooms are wonderful & the facilities, like the pool & Turkish hammam, are top notch, but it's the bar & dining room that will really blow your socks off. Black-&-white chequered floors, chandeliers & enormous 15th-century fireplaces – you won't be able to concentrate on your croissants. B/fast €25pp. €€€€–€€€€€

Upmarket

🏠 **Casa Romantico** [214–15 D/E6] (3 rooms) 37 Eekhoutstraat; ✆ 050 67 80 93; www.casa-romantico.be. It's all in the name really. Rooms are very well presented, but what separates this from other upmarket B&Bs is its sauna, Jacuzzi & lawn-fringed heated outdoor pool. It does cost €35pp for 2hrs, but what a treat! Children not allowed. Cash only. €€€€

🏠 **De Brugsche Suites** [214–15 B3] (3 rooms) 20 Koningin Elisabethlaan; ✆ 050 68 03 10; www. brugschesuites.be. The unassuming plain-white façade of this townhouse conceals a rich explosion of colour within. Highlights of the lavish interior include motif wallpaper, restored parquet floors, ancient portraits, tapestry rugs, studded leather sofas & an array of intriguing & pricy antiques. Each period suite – the (red) Roi Albert I, the (blue)

Prince Imperial & the (green) Reine Elisabeth – has an en-suite bathroom & private lounge with an open fire. The latter 2 have rooftops views of the city, while the first overlooks the medieval Ezelpoort gate. Be warned though: you could end up spending more than you bargained for; every *objet d'art* on show is for sale. B/fast is taken in the elegant drawing room downstairs. €€€€

🏠 **Die Swaene** [218 E4] (38 rooms) 1 Steenhouwersdijk; ✆ 050 34 27 98; www. dieswaene.com. You cannot fail to fall in love with Brugge's beacon hotel. Die Swaene has won heaps of awards, but nothing prepares you for the faded opulence & lavish attention to detail it exudes from every nook & cranny. The original 18th-century building contains 30 rooms, as well as the heated indoor pool & sauna, but I'd opt for one of the 8 much-newer 'pergola' dbls. Situated across the canal, these have an oriental twist & a breathtaking blend of rich fabrics, high-tech gadgets, palatial bathrooms & views of the canal. When you emerge for nourishment, you can choose between the highly praised gastronomic restaurant or the low-key Kaffee Pergola, which has a peaceful waterside terrace. €€€€

🏠 **Nuit Blanche** [214–15 D6] (2 rooms) 2 Groeninge; 📱 0494 40 04 47; www.brugge-bb. com. A stay here plunges you back to Brugge's heyday. The owner, Flemish painter David De Graef, has kept the rooms simple so the mass of original features can claim centre stage. Picture heavy oak-beamed ceilings, enormous Gothic fireplaces & incredible views of OLV-kathedraal & the medieval courtyard garden. Recommended. €€€€

Mid-range

🏠 **Côté Canal** [218 E3] (2 rooms) 8–10 Hertsbergestraat; 📱 0475 45 77 07; www.brugge-bedandbreakfast.be. Once the priory of the Canons of St-Austin, this beautiful canal-side renovation is run by Brugge-born host Caroline van Langeraert. She's managed the adjoining Huyze Hertsberge for years, but now offers these 2 newer suites, the regal Clin d'Oeil with free-standing bathtub & the French shabby-chic Clair de Lune with views of the garden & its 100-year-old pear tree. Cash only. €€€

La Maison Zenasni [218 D2] (3 rooms) 10 Riddersstraat; m 0478 23 21 07; www. lamaison-zenasni.be. This new luxury guesthouse is named after the host, Djamil Zenasni, who restored the 1787 house with his wife. They live on one side of the house; the B&B is on the other – & it's quite special. The Blue (standard dbl) & Red (suite with its own sitting room) rooms are very Victoriana chic, while the White apartment (dbl & 2 twin beds), situated on the floor above, is a very clean space where everything is white except the wooden floorboards & exposed beams. €€€

Budget

De Barge [214–15 D8] (20 rooms) 15 Bargeweg; 050 38 51 50; www.hoteldebarge. be. Brugge is famous for its waterways, so why not moor yourself for a couple of nights on this restored canalboat in the south of town? The snug en-suite cabins are predictably decked out in nautical blues, but the orange lifejackets on your bed are fun. Also on board is the Captain's Table restaurant (19.00–22.00 daily; €€€€). €€–€€€

De Loft [218 G2] (3 rooms) 34 Timmermansstraat; 050 49 08 49; www.de-loft. be. You're guaranteed a warm welcome & pleasant rooms by owner (& architect) Thomas Coucke & his wife Bieke. I'd opt for the spacious & funky Red suite which, like the Green room, has a bath. The Chocolate room (should be called the Chocolate-Orange room thanks to the brightly coloured walls) only has a shower, but it does boast a 4-poster bed. €€

Nicky's B&B [218 G3] (3 rooms) 37 Ganzenstraat; 050 33 12 33; e nicky.s.b.b@ skynet.be. These bright funky rooms are run by Nicky, owner of the Ganzespel (page 220). Choose from the spacious pink-&-purple Amethyst, ideal for a family with a dbl & 2 twin beds, & the 2 dbls: the red-&-white Onyx & the smaller Moroccan-blue Sapphire. Minimum 2-night stay at w/ends. €€

Shoestring

Arthostel [214–15 D1] 2 Havenstraat; 050 67 82 78; www.arthostel.be. Just over the canal in the north of town, this stylish hostel opened in 2006. Run as a budget hotel, the beds are still bunks, but the décor is a boutique-hotel blend of extrovert oranges & Gothic chandeliers & – true to name – the walls of the 'arthostel' are decorated with the works of local artists. Further benefits include free internet access, luggage storage, lockers & bike hire. Ladies-only dorms are available. If you don't fancy the 15-minute walk, buses #14, 41 & 42 depart from the railway station; get off at Haven & from there it's a 150m walk. Dorm bed €14; dbl €36; b/fast €3. €

Bauhaus [214–15 F4] (22 rooms) 133 Langestraat; 050 34 10 93; www.bauhaus. be. Cheerful hostel with its own nightclub (145 Langestraat; 23.00–07.00 Fri–Sat) – reception (located at No 145) supplies free earplugs. Ask for a bunk in the new section: 'pod' beds have curtains around them for privacy & locker drawers. Perks include 10% off bill & free beer at hostel's excellent Sacré Coeur bar/restaurant. Free Wi-Fi or internet €1/15min; no curfew. Bedding & b/fast included. Dorms €14, sgl €26, dbl €40. €

Passage [214–15 B6] (10 rooms) 26–8 Dweerstraat; 050 34 02 32; www. passagebrugge.com. A long-term favourite with backpackers thanks to its lovely Art Deco Grand Café which serves b/fast & very good Belgian classics. Choose to sleep in the hostel section, which is let down only by the slightly musty showers, or the Passage Hotel next door which has chintzy dbls. Rooms 3, 12, 14 or 15 are en suite; otherwise you'll have to tiptoe down the hall. Hostel: dorm bed €16, b/fast €5. Hotel: dbl €52–67. €

✗ **WHERE TO EAT** Flanders' most touristy town has lots of restaurants and quality runs the full gamut. Try to branch out from the eateries that populate the Markt and Burg and head into the maze of surrounding streets for gastronomic, rather than quick, meals. Prices remain inflated year round.

Restaurants
Expensive
✗ **Den Gouden Harynck** [214–15 D6] 25 Groeninge; 050 33 76 37; 12.00–14.00 & 19.00–21.30 Tue–Fri, 19.00–21.30 Sat. One of Brugge's best & housed in an ancient fairytale building where the chef prepares flamboyantly

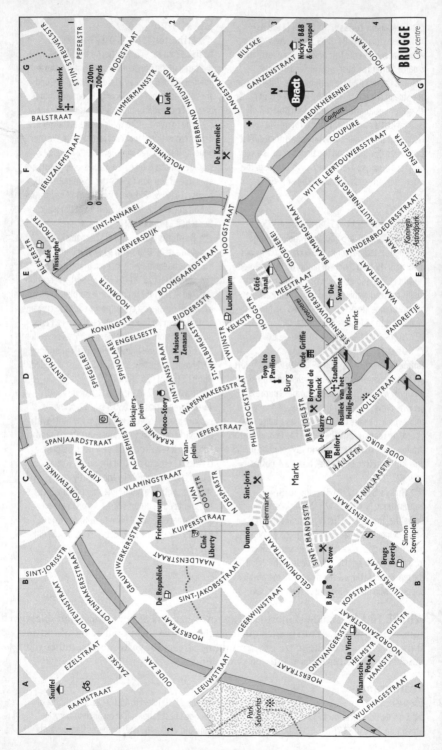

BRUGGE
City centre

Jeruzalemkerk ✝
BALSTRAAT
JERUZALEMSTRAAT
STIJN STREUVELSSTR
PEPERSTR
RODESTRAAT
TIMMERMANSSTR
De Loft
VERBRAND NIEUWLAND
BILKSKE
GANZENSTRAAT
Nicky's B&B & Ganzespel
HOOISTRAAT
Bauhaus
LANGESTRAAT
MOLENMEERS
De Karmeliet ✕
PREDIKHERENREI
Coupure
COUPURE
WITTE LEERTOUWERSSTRAAT
KRUITENBERGSTR
BRAAMBERGSTRAAT
MINDERBROEDERSSTRAAT
WAALSESTRAAT
ENGELSTR
Koningin Astridpark
PARK

SINT-ANNAREI
VERVERSDIJK
BOOMGAARDSTRAAT
HOOGSTRAAT
GROENEREI
MEESTRAAT
Die Swaene
Café Vlissinghe
BLEKERSTR
STROTSTR
HOORNSTR
KONINGSTR
ENGELSESTR
SPINOLAREI
SPIEGELREI
GENTHOF

RIDDERSSTR
Lucifernum
KELKSTR
Côté Canal
HOOGSTR
STEENHOUWERSDIJK
Groenerei
Oude Griffie
Vismarkt
PANDREITJE

La Maison Zenasni
SINT-JANSSTRAAT
ST-WALBURGASTR
TWIJNSTR
Toyo Ito Pavilion
Burg
Oude Griffie
Stadhuis
Basiliek van het Heilig-Bloed
Breydel de Coninck ✕
WOLLESTRAAT

Biskajersplein
Choco-Story
KRAANREI
WAPENMAKERSSTR
PHILIPSTOCKSTRAAT
IEPERSTRAAT
De Garre
Belfort
HALLESTR
OUDE BURG

SPANJAARDSTRAAT
ACADEMIESTRAAT
VLAMINGSTRAAT
Kraanplein
Markt
ST-NIKLAASSTR

KIPSTRAAT
KORTEWINKEL
Frietmuseum
J VAN OOSTSTR
N DESPARSTR
Sint-Joris
Eiermarkt
SINT-AMANDSSTR
STEENSTRAAT

SINT-JORISSTR
GRAUW WERKERSSTRAAT
KUIPERSSTRAAT
Ciné Liberty
Dumon
De Stove ✕
B by B
Brugs Beertje
ZILVERSTRAAT
Simon Stevinplein

POTTENMAKERSSTRAAT
POTTERIESTRAAT
NAALDENSTRAAT
De Republiek
SINT-JAKOBSSTRAAT
GEERWIJNSTRAAT
GELDMUNTSTRAAT
KOPSTRAAT
NOORDZANDSTRAAT
GISTSTR
Da Vinci
HELMSTR

EZELSTRAAT
ZAKSKE
OUDE ZAK
MOERSTRAAT
LEEUWSTRAAT
ONTVANGERSSTR
MOERSTRAAT
De Vlaamsche Pot ✕
HAANSTR
WULFHAGESTRAAT

Snuffel
RAAMSTRAAT
Park Sebrechts

200m
200yds

I 2 3 4
G F E D C B A

218

named dishes such as 'candied shoulder of Pyrenean milk lamb' to bamboozle diners. Tue–Thu they offer a 3-course dinner menu for €55. Very smart. €€€€€

✖ De Karmeliet [218 F3] 19 Langestraat; ☎ 050 33 82 59; ⏰ 12.00–13.30 & 19.00–21.30 Tue–Sat, closed mid-Jun–mid-Jul. Whisper this name into the ear of a food critic & they'll be putty in your hands. The 3 Michelin-starred De Karmeliet is synonymous with the finest, freshly prepared & inventive cuisine. You don't just 'eat' here – *nee, nee*; you 'savour flavours' prepared by revered head chef Geert van Hecke. The décor is elegant – original artworks adorn the walls – & the dress code is, predictably, a tie & your best set of manners. Reservations are essential, with mid-week bookings made 2 weeks ahead & w/end sittings often up to a month in advance, but pop in at lunchtime & you may get lucky. €€€€€

Above average

✖ Bistro de Schaar [214–15 F5] 2 Hooistraat; ☎ 050 33 59 79; ⏰ 12.00–14.30 & 18.00–22.00 Mon, Tue & Fri–Sun. Look for the charming bronze scissors sign hanging above the door & enter this cosy restaurant famous for its steaks cooked over an open fire & its artistic desserts. Lovely terrace overlooking the water too. €€€€

✖ De Stove [218 B3/4] 4 Kleine Sint-Amandsstraat; ☎ 050 33 78 35; ⏰ 19.00–21.00 Mon–Tue & Fri, 12.00–14.00 & 19.00–21.00 Sat–Sun. Often-reviewed & with good reason, this white townhouse is tucked away on an alley behind the Markt. Run by a husband-&-wife team it has an intimate modern interior & a continually changing seasonal menu. You'll be greeted by Erica Travers while Gino will feverishly prepare all the homemade bread, ice cream & sorbets. Reservations are encouraged. €€€€

✖ De Vlaamsche Pot [218 A4] 3–5 Helmstraat; ☎ 050 34 00 86; ⏰ 12.00–22.00 Mon–Wed & Fri–Sun. Tucked away just off Noordzandstraat, this cosy, gingham-laden, converted terrace house is famous for its *waterzooi*, but I'd also recommend the *stoofvlees* or *witloef en oven* washed down with the local Brugge Zot beer. Only local Flemish products are used (you can even trace your meat back to its original farm) & all meals are prepared freshly when ordered, hence the motto on the back on the waiters angel-winged T-shirts: '*volamus si convenit*' – 'we fly when you have a reservation'.

Also good for pancakes & waffles, it's worth peeking into the kitchen on your left as your enter to see the chefs at work. One of my favourites. €€€€

✖ Marieke van Brugghe [214–15 C6] 17 Mariastraat; ☎ 050 34 33 66; ⏰ 12.00–22.00 Mon–Wed & Fri–Sun. Artistic bistro with a loyal following who come for the *rundsstoverij in Kasteelbier* or *mosselen natur* while dining beneath a replica of the *Creation of Adam* panel from the Sistine Chapel. €€€€

Mid-range

✖ Sint-Joris [218 C3] 29 Markt; ☎ 050 33 30 62; ⏰ 10.00–22.00 Mon, Thu–Sun, 10.00–15.00 Tue. The good grape from the bunch of restaurants that populates the main Markt square. It's worth paying the inflated prices for standard Flemish fare because it offers the best views of the belfry, which sits directly opposite. €€€–€€€€

✖ Breydel de Coninck [218 D3] 24 Breidelstraat; ☎ 050 33 97 46; ⏰ 12.00–15.00 & 18.00–22.00, closed Wed. Run by a local family for over 50 years, this is *the* place to try mussels & chips in Brugge. €€€

Cheap and cheerful

✖ 't Botaniekske [214–15 E6] 26 Minderbroedersstraat; ☎ 050 33 27 90; ⏰ 18.00–late Wed–Sat, 12.00–14.30 & 18.00–late Sun. Housed in a building dating from 1612, it claims to be one of the oldest restaurants in Brugge. People come here to try the house speciality of pork ribs in 4 sauces, sip slowly on a glass of house red & soak up the old-world charm of the interior. The inscription above the original fireplace '*vrienden zien hier thuus*' (friends are at home here) is testament to the warm welcome you are likely to receive. Bookings are advised, especially at w/ends. €€

✖ Passage [214–15 B6] 26 Dweerstraat; ☎ 050 34 02 32; ⏰ 18.00–23.30 daily. A well-worn tourist spot, this Art Deco restaurant still deserves a mention because despite the numerous buttocks grazing the upright wooden chairs, the tasty food & cheap beer are served at unbeatable prices. Lovely at night when the tables are adorned with candles. €€

✖ Salade Folle [214–15 D7] 13–14 Walplein; ☎ 050 34 94 43; ⏰ 11.30–21.30 Mon & Thu–Sun, 11.30–15.00 Tue. A fresh, bright café with reliably good, predominately vegetarian, meals. Be sure to leave some room for their homemade apple tart & ice cream. Visit at lunchtime & takes advantage of their filling 3-course menu for €16. €€

Shoestring

✕ De Bron [214–15 D7] 82 Katelijnestraat; ✆ 050 33 45 26; ⏰ 11.45–14.00 Tue–Sat. Well-loved for its seasonal, organic, vegetarian fare – from summer salads to tummy-warming pies – all served at unbeatable prices. €

✕ De Stoepa [214–15 C7] 124 Oostmeers; ⏰ 11.45–02.00 Tue–Sun. Mediterranean-style bar/café serving tapas with wood-burning stove in winter & a quiet leafy terrace to escape the tourist hordes in summer. €

✕ Ganzespel [218 G3] 37 Ganzenstraat; ✆ 050 33 12 33; ⏰ 18.00–22.00 Fri–Sun. Charming time-worn dining room which dishes up superb dinner: soup, a main meal & a glass of beer or wine for just €9.35! €

✕ Pas Partout [214–15 E3] 1 Jeruzalemstraat; ✆ 050 33 62 43; ⏰ 11.45–14.00 Mon–Sat. Hearty dishes of *stoofvlees* & *witloof* prepared by once-unemployed individuals who are now learning a new trade. They serve the cheapest *steak frites* in town & the dish of the day is just €8. Cash only. €

Cafés

☕ De Proeverie [214–15 C6] 6 Katelijnestraat; ✆ 050 33 08 87; ⏰ 09.30–18.00 daily. You can't come here without trying the homemade *chocolademelk Proeverie*, a rich hot chocolate drink that goes nicely with the freshly baked scones on offer. Milkshakes, ice creams & other fancy desserts are also available in this Victoriana-style café.

☕ Da Vinci [218 B4] 34 Geldmuntstraat; ✆ 050 33 36 50; ⏰ 11.00–22.00 Mon–Thu, 11.00–23.00 Fri–Sat, 12.00–23.00 Sun. The city's best gelateria. Sit in, or order a cornet of Ferrero Rocher, limoncello, or pannacotta ice cream & continue your wanderings.

ENTERTAINMENT AND NIGHTLIFE
Pubs

🍺 Brugs Beertje [218 B4] 5 Kemelstraat; ✆ 050 33 96 16; ⏰ 16.00–01.00 Mon, Tue, Thu & Fri, 16.00–02.00 Sat–Sun. Very tourist orientated, but still charming & one of the few places to serve local beers Brugse Zot & Straffe Hendrik.

🍺 Café Vlissinghe [218 E1] 2 Blekerstraat; ✆ 050 34 37 37; ⏰ 11.00–00.00 Wed–Sat, 11.00–19.00 Sun. Supposedly founded in 1515, Café Vlissinghe is the oldest pub in Brugge. During the 19th & early 20th centuries it became a favourite haunt of notable writers & artists who gathered here for meetings, & today the faded yellow wallpaper, heavy wood-panelled bar, dusty paintings & creaky wooden stools hark back to the days of yore. There's a lovely stone-walled terrace out the back too.

🍺 De Garre [218 D4] 1 De Garre; ✆ 050 34 10 29; ⏰ 12.00–00.00 daily. Down a hidden alley, just off the Burg, this joint is the only place in town to serve De Garre – a whopping 11% amber beer. Be prepared to wrestle other tourists for a table.

🍺 De Republiek [218 B2] 36 St Jakobsstraat; ✆ 050 34 02 29; ⏰ 11.00–late daily. Large time-worn bar with mustard-yellow walls & a large terrace out the back. The menu is printed & presented as a newspaper! Choose either from their huge selection of rums or a cocktail.

Bars

🍷 Lucifernum [218 E3] 6 Twijnstraat; m 0476 35 06 51; ⏰ 18.00–22.00 Sun. It's hardly ever open, but do dress up & visit this bizarre bar if you can. Once famous among locals for its debauched drink-fuelled parties, this scaffold-clad mansion belongs to Willy Retzin who now serves quiet cocktails (& his Peruvian wife's paella) amongst his enormous collection of paintings, religious icons & statues.

🍷 The Vintage [214–15 C6] 13 Westmeers; ✆ 050 34 30 63; ⏰ 11.00–02.00 Mon–Fri, 11.00–17.00 Sat–Sun. Lively bar entered via stable-doors with leather sofas & vintage paraphernalia (an old Vespa hangs from the ceiling). Vincent, the owner, is clearly a man of principle: house rules state girls get a free drink if they show a nipple!

Cinema

🎬 Ciné Liberty [218 B2] 23 Kuipersstraat; ✆ 050 33 20 11; www.cinema-liberty.be. A cinema has stood on this site since 1908 – you can see the old seats & projection equipment in the hall – & proprietor, Patrick, takes pride in showing the latest blockbusters in the ornate theatre. When was the last time you went to the movies & velvet curtains were drawn at the end of the film?

SHOPPING Most visitors to Brugge shop for lace and chocolate, but a determined search often gets waylaid among the more eclectic shops mingled between the picturesque medieval buildings. The city's main run of shops spreads west from the Markt along Steenstraat, Zuidzandstraat, Simon Stevinplein, St Amandsstraat, Geldmuntstraat and Noordzandstraat. There are a number of galleries dotted along these streets, including the Ter Steeghere shopping mall that links the Burg and Wollestraat, but the biggest and prettiest is **Zilverpand** (🕐 *10.00–18.00 Mon–Sat*), an inner courtyard containing a collection of 25 shops with entrances from Zilverstraat, Zuidsandstraat and Noordzandstraat.

A concentration of lace shops can be found along Breidelstraat – the pedestrianised path running between the Markt and the Burg – but **'t Apostolientje** (*11 Balstraat;* 🕐 *09.30–17.00 Mon–Sat, 09.30–13.00 Sun*) has also been recommended. Brugge has 52 chocolate shops, so there's plenty of choice. My favourites are the family-run **Sukerbuyc** [214–15 D6] (*5 Katelijnestraat;* 🕐 *08.30–18.30 daily*), traditional **Dumon** [218 C3] (*16 Eiermarkt;* 🕐 *10.00–18.30 daily*) and (*27 Sint-Amandsstraat;* 🕐 *10.30–18.30 Mon–Sat, 14.00–18.00 Sun, closed Wed*), and über-modern **BbyB** [218 B4] (*39 Sint-Amandsstraat;* 🕐 *10.00–18.00 Mon–Sat*).

Markets

Christmas market Markt; 🕐 Dec 11.00–19.00 daily

Flea market Dijver; 🕐 Mar–Nov 10.00–18.00 Sat–Sun

Fish market Vismarkt; 🕐 07.00–13.00 Tue–Sat.

Fresh catches from the seas around Zeebrugge are brought to the famous weekly fish market

General market Markt, 🕐 08.00–13.00 Wed; 't Zand & Beursplein, 🕐 08.00–13.00 Sat

OTHER PRACTICALITIES

$ Bank [218 B4] KBC, 38 Steenstraat, 🕐 09.00–12.30 & 13.30–16.30 Mon–Wed & Fri, 09.00–12.30 & 13.30–18.00 Thu, 09.00–12.00 Sat

🚲 Bike rental B-bike, next to tourist information centre, m 0479 97 12 80; 🕐 1 Apr–15 Oct 10.00–19.00 daily; €12/day; Fietspunt, Stationsplein, 🕐 07.30–19.00 Mon–Sat, 09.00–21.40 Sat–Sun, €12/day or €9/day with BruggeCard; De Ketting [214–15 E6], 23 Gentpoortstraat, ✆ 050 34 41 96, 🕐 09.00–18.30 Mon–Sat, €6/day – the cheapest rates in town.

🖥 Internet The city has free Wi-Fi zones ('ZapFi') in the 't Zand, Markt & Burg squares. Otherwise try Bean around the World [218 D1], 5 Genthof; 🕐 10.00–19.00 Mon & Thu–Sun, 12.00–19.00 Wed; €1/15min

Luggage storage Located at main station entrance on left; €3/3.50/4 for small/medium/large self-service locker

➕ Pharmacy [218 F3] 36 Langestraat, ✆ 050 34 05 53, 🕐 09.00–12.30 & 14.00–18.30 Mon–Wed & Fri, 09.00–12.30 Thu & Sat

WHAT TO SEE AND DO

The Markt [218 C3] Come summer, the city's central cobblestone square is thronging with tourists and clattering horse-drawn carriages. The domain of the guildsmen, it was the commercial and social focal point of Brugge and today their gabled houses host the cafés and restaurants that flank two sides of the square. Following two major fires at the end of the 14th and 16th centuries, the city administration dictated that the original medieval wooden houses be replaced with brick. The houses in place today are reconstructions and date from the 18th to 20th centuries. The building with the richest history is Markt 16, which now houses the Craenenburg café. It was here that the guildsmen of Brugge imprisoned the soon-to-be emperor Maximilian I for three months, in 1488, as punishment for restricting the city's privileges. It was probably the worst mistake they ever made; Maximilian conned his way out of incarceration and for the rest of his reign made deliberate decisions to direct all trade north to the port of Antwerp.

On the eastern side of the square stands the Provinciaal Hof (Provincial Court). In the medieval era, a covered *lakenhalle* or 'water hall' stood here and before the Reie canal was covered over ships would sail right up to the building and unload their wares for sale in the Hallen market. When it was destroyed by fire in 1787 the Provincial Court was rebuilt in the current neo-Gothic style.

In the middle of the square stand the statues of butcher Jan Breydel and weaver Pieter de Coninck, the guildsmen who participated in the Brugse Metten (page 212) against the French in 1302. Breydel provided meat for the soldiers during the battle.

Belfort [218 C4] (⊕ *09.30–17.00 daily, last tickets 16.15; admission: adult/6–25/ under 6/BruggeCard €8/4/free/free*) Brugge's belfry, which stands proud over the Markt, took over three centuries to complete. The original foundations date from the 13th century and stretch up to the first four ramparts of the tower. However, a lack of funds put building on hold until the 14th century, when the rest of the tower was completed, and the final octagonal steeple was added between 1482 and 1486. For approximately three centuries a wooden spire also stood atop the steeple, but after being destroyed by fire for a second time in 1741, it was never rebuilt. Now standing at a respectable 83m (and leaning a worrying one metre to the east) the Belfort offers superb views over the city. Visitors who wish to climb the 366 steep steps to the top should enter the Hallen – whose courtyard once served as the city's market hall – and make for the steps immediately on the right. The climb leads you past the Treasury Room, whose wooden box with ten locks originally held the town documents and could only be opened when the mayor and nine appointed town officials were present with their individually assigned keys. When a new law was passed all had to agree before the boxes could be opened and the amendment made. This arrangement was common throughout Europe and is said to be the origination of the saying 'being in a key position'. Climb higher and you pass the Carillon Room which controls the tower's 47 bells played at regular **carillon concerts** (⊕ *mid-Jun–Sep 21.00–22.00 Mon, Wed &Sat, 14.15–15.00 Sun; Oct–mid-June 14.15–15.00 Wed, Sat & Sun*).

The Burg [218 D3] Set just to the southeast of the Markt square, down Breidelstraat, is the smaller Burg square. It was here that the city was born, when Baldwin the Iron Arm, the first Count of Flanders, built 'Grafenburg' – the castle from which the square takes its name – to guard against invading Normans and Vikings during the 9th century. Today, remains of the castle and the vestiges of St Donatian's Cathedral, which fell in 1799, are buried under – and integrated into – the Crowne Plaza Hotel at the north end of the square. Incidentally, visitors can see the remains of the choir gallery– among which painter Jan van Eyck (page 356) is believed to have been buried – in the hotel's cellar. The ruins were uncovered in 1988 during excavations for the proposed hotel car park.

Happily, the Stadhuis (town hall), Oude Griffe (municipal records office), Gerechtshof (law courts) and Basiliek van het Heilig-Bloed (Basilica of the Holy Blood) are all still standing:

Stadhuis [218 D4] (*12 Burg;* ⊕ *09.30–17.00 daily; admission: adult/6–25/under 6/BruggeCard €2/1/free/free, inc an audio guide & entry to Brugse Vrije, see opposite*)

Construction of Brugge's Gothic town hall began in 1376, making it one of the oldest in Belgium. The 49 statues that decorate the elaborate sandstone façade are relatively new (1989); the originals were destroyed by French revolutionaries in 1792. The majority depict the counts and countesses of Flanders, but the bottom row features prominent religious figures. Notable characters include Adam and Eve (the first statue on the left of the bottom row), Baldwin the Iron Arm (the fourth figure from the left on the bottom row), the ill-fated Maria of Burgundy with the falcon on her shoulder (the last statue on the right of the third row) and beside her, Leopold II.

The highlight of the interior is the dramatic **Gotische Zaal** (Gothic Hall), whose exquisite vaulted polychrome wooden ceiling dates from 1402. Twelve vault-keys, depicting scenes from the New Testament, appear where the ribs of the arches converge, and where the arches meet the walls you will see 16 consoles illustrating the 12 months and four seasons. The original and long-ago-faded 1410 paintings were replaced by frescoes painted by Flemish artists Albert and Julian De Vriendt between 1895 and 1905. They depict key events of the city's history: the foundation of the Order of the Golden Fleece by Philip the Good in 1430 can be seen on the left-hand side of the chimneypiece and on the right, Diederik d'Alsace brings the relic of the Holy Blood to the church of St Basil. Above these frescoes are painted figures of Flemish alumni: a mixture of counts, artists and scientists.

Oude Griffie [218 D3] (*11a Burg*) Sat to the left and in stark contrast to the Gothic town hall is the municipal records office. Built between 1535 and 1537, its vibrant Renaissance façade features ornate scrolled gables topped by the renovated bronze statues of Justice, Aaron and Moses.

Gerechtshof (*11 Burg;* ⊕ *09.30–12.30 & 13.30–17.00 daily; admission: adult/6–25/under 6/BruggeCard €2/1/free/free, inc entry to the Stadhuis*) Adjacent to the Oude Griffie is the Burg's second-largest building, the former Court of Justice. Built on the site of the 15th-century Landhuis van het Brugse Vrije (Mansion of the Liberty of Brugge – headquarters of an administrative council in charge of inhabitants who lived outside the city gates) the neo-classical law courts date from 1722. One room of the former palace – the Alderman's Room – remains and is the main draw for visitors. Known as the **Renaissancezaal 't Brugse Vrije**, it contains an enormous 16th-century Renaissance chimneypiece carved from black marble and oak. Designed by Lanceloot Blondeel (1496–1561) it commemorates Charles V's victory against the French at Pavia in 1525. Take a seat and let the free audio guide talk you through the full story.

Basiliek van het Heilig-Bloed [218 D4] (*15 Burg;* ⊕ *Apr–Sep 09.30–12.00 & 14.00–18.00 daily, Oct–Mar 10.00–12.00 & 14.00–17.00 Mon, Tue & Thu–Sun, 10.00–12.00 Wed; admission €1.50*) At the opposite end of the square, tucked discreetly into the southeast corner, sits the Basilica of the Holy Blood. Named after the holy relic it houses, this 12th-century church is composed of two parts. Under the two arches on the left-hand side of the 'Steeghere' façade sits the entrance to St Basil's Chapel. Bereft of decoration, this Romanesque chapel contains a statue of the Virgin Mary dating from 1300. Back outside and up the stairs is the chapel and museum of the Holy Blood. Here, within a silver tabernacle, you will find an intricately designed rock-crystal phial purported to contain a cloth stained with a few drops of blood and water washed from the body of Christ by Joseph of Arimathea. Legend has it that Diederik d'Alsace returned from the second Crusades in Jerusalem in possession of the relic, but further investigations have revealed that it did not arrive in Brugge until 1250 so was probably part of the loot acquired from the sacking of Constantinople in 1204. Nevertheless, the medieval relic remains heavily venerated and every year in May it is paraded through town in the Heilig-Bloed Processie (ask the tourist office for tickets).

Toyo Ito Pavilion [218 D3] On the northwest side of the square is a modern aluminium bridge over a shallow pool of water. Known as the 'pavilion', it was commissioned as part of the festivities surrounding Brugge's election as the 2002 cultural capital of Europe. It was meant to be dismantled, but has ended up staying despite locals hating it.

Along and around the Dijver
Leaving the Burg via Blinde Ezelstraat and crossing the canal leads you to the **Vismarkt**. Fish is still sold here among the Tuscan colonnades (page 221). Turning right on to **Huidenvettersplein** you enter the old tanners' square. On house No 10 you will notice six reliefs showing how to produce leather from cow's hide. It is interesting to note that the houses carry motifs of the family name above the door here; street names and numbers were not implemented until Napoleon's invasion in 1799. Continuing westwards leads you on to Rosenhoedkaai (which offers picture-perfect views of the Markt's belfry) and past Wollestraat bridge – look out for the statue of **St Johannes Nepomucenus**. Also known as St John Nepomuk, this vicar was elevated to the status of martyr after being thrown from Charles Bridge in Prague by King Wenceslas in 1393. His body floated, proving his innocence, and today he is worshipped as a protector from floods. Moving on to the Dijver, you pass the prestigious **College of Europe**, where up-and-coming politicians from over 40 countries take their masters in European studies, law, economics and political sciences. Just up the road is the Groeningemuseum.

MAD FOR MUSEUMS?

The Brugge City Card (*www.bruggecitycard.be*) grants free access to the main museums and attractions, and includes a free canalboat ride, a free guided winter walking tour and 25% discount on bicycle hire and public transport. It costs €35/40 for 48/72hr, and is cheaper for those under 26 (€32/37). Tickets can be bought from any of the museums or at the tourist information centre.

The city also runs several penny-saving double- or multiple-entry tickets, costing €8 each. For example, instead of buying individual tickets for the Groeningemuseum and Arentshuis, you can buy a one-day combi ticket and save yourself €2. Options are as follows:

Groeningemuseum covers entry to Groeningemuseum and Arentshuis;
Hospitaalmuseum covers entry to Memling Sint-Jan and OLV-ter-Potterie
Bruggemuseum covers entry to Gruuthuse, Archeologie, Stadhuis and BrugseVrije, Volkskunde, Gezelle, Molens, Gentpoort and Onze-Lieve-Vrouwekerk.

Alternatively, you can purchase a three-day card which grants entry to all of the above for €15. You can't criticise the tourist board for not allowing you lots of choice!

Groeningemuseum [214–15 D6] (*12 Dijver;* ☻ *09.30–17.00 Tue–Sun; admission: adult/6–25/under 6/Brugge Card €8/1/free/free; inc audio guide & entry to Arenthuis*) Designed by architect Joseph Viérin, the Groeningemuseum houses the world's most complete collection of Flemish Primitive and Brugge Renaissance artworks and is a must see. A refurbishment in 2003 provided more space for the modern artistic movements like Flemish Expressionism, Surrealism etc, but it is clear the spotlight still rests on the 20-or-so masterpieces found in rooms one, two and three. Their positions move, but look for the following:

Hieronymous Bosch's Dali-esque triptych of *The Last Judgement*. Heaven is depicted in the left panel, hell in the right, and in the middle, earth. This central panel is perhaps the most disturbing: filled with mayhem and lewd sexual imagery – the harp and the bagpipes were well-known references to sexual organs – Bosch makes his opinions of the stupidity of the human race clear.

The enormous and equally graphic *The Judgement of Cambyses* (1498), painted by Gerard David (page 20) tells the story of the corrupt judge Sisamnes, who was sentenced to be flayed alive by the Persian king after accepting a bribe. It is interesting to note David's experiment with perspective and the lack of knowledge of human anatomy at the time – veins and sinew do not lie directly beneath the skin.

Jan van Eyck's *Portrait of Margaretha van Eyck* (1439) – featuring van Eyck's rather plain looking 33 year-old wife – and *Madonna with Canon Joris van der Paele* (1436), which depicts the commissioner, van der Paele, dressed in white on the right. Noteworthy features include the reflective armour worn by St George (also on the right) and the texture of the blue velvet robe worn by St Donatian who stands on the left of the painting.

Also of note is Hans Memling's *Moreel Triptych* (1484), whose central panel features patron saint St Christopher carrying the Christ child aloft his shoulders. He is flanked by St Maurus (left) and St Gilles (right) and on the side panels kneel the commissioners of the painting, Moreel and his wife Barbara van Vlaenderberch, and their children.

Pieter Pourbus' interpretation of *The Last Judgement* (1551) depicts the physicality of the fight between angels and demons over human souls, strongly reflecting the wars of religion, known as the Reformation, sweeping through Europe at the time Pourbus was painting. Look for his signature, which can just be seen on the stone in the bottom right of the painting.

Also a highlight is the Surrealist room, which contains René Magritte's *L'attentat* (1932) and Paul Delvaux's *Serenity* (1970).

Arenthuis [214–15 D6] (*16 Dijver;* ☻ *09.30–17.00 Tue–Sun; admission: adult/6–25/under 6/Brugge Card €2/1/free/free*) The ground floor of this 18th-century mansion is used as an overspill gallery for the Groeningemuseum collection, as well as hosting temporary exhibitions. The first floor exhibits the etchings and paintings of Welsh – but Brugge-born – artist Frank Brangwyn (1867–1956). Inspired by the Orientalism art movement – as seen in the later works of van Gogh – Brangwyn travelled as far as South Africa in search of different palettes of colour, but is better remembered for his versatility with different media. He worked as an official UK war artist during World War I, but retained strong links with Belgium and was made an honorary citizen in 1936.

Gruuthuse [214–15 D6] (*17 Dijver;* ✎ *050 44 87 51;* ☻ *09.30–17.00 Tue–Sun; admission: adult/6–25/under 6/Brugge Card €6/1/free/free, inc an audio guide & entrance to Onze-Lieve-Vrouwekerk*) The Gothic building of the Gruuthuse

Museum (so-called for the original owner's right to tax the *gruut* – a dried flower and herb mixture added during brewing until the 14th century to improve the flavour of the beer) houses a bizarre array of antiques and art dating from the 13th to the 19th centuries. Highlights include a strong collection of tapestries hung in the Hall of Honour, a guillotine, a terracotta bust of 20-year-old Emperor Charles V, and the 15th-century oak oratory overlooking the high altar of Onze-Lieve-Vrouwekerk.

Onze-Lieve-Vrouwekerk

Onze-Lieve-Vrouwekerk [214–15 D6] (*Mariastraat;* ⊕ *09.30–17.00 Mon–Sat, 13.30–17.00 Sun; museum admission: adult/6–25/under 6/Brugge Card €4/1/free/ free*) Sitting beside the Gruuthuse Museum you cannot miss the Church of Our Lady – thanks in large part to its 122m steeple (Europe's tallest brick tower). The church is a hotchpotch blend of Gothic and Romanesque architecture, but its star attraction is Michelangelo's surprisingly small statue of the *Madonna and Child*. Carved from one solid piece of Carrara marble, it was originally commissioned by the Bishop of Sienna, but banker and friend Giovanni Mouscron fell so deeply in love with the Rococo-style sculpture that he begged Michelangelo relentlessly to sell it to him instead. The master artist finally acquiesced when a price of 4,000 florins was named and Mouscron returned to Brugge with the only piece of Michelangelo art to leave Italy during his lifetime; the bishop eventually received a similar, but inferior, version. Michelangelo's depiction of the mother and child is unique when compared to the popular renditions of a virginal maiden smiling down upon her holy infant child: Michelangelo's Mary looks vacantly towards onlookers, seemingly unaware of the child at her feet and devoid of the usual royal crown, whilst the infant Christ is empty-handed (he usually carries a cross) and seems to be on the verge of toddling away from his mother. The effect serves to humanise these holy figures.

Also worth a look are the 16th-century ceremonial tombs of Charles the Bold and his daughter Maria of Burgundy (see page 6) in the chancel, and Adrian Isenbrant's *Madonna of the Seven Sorrows*.

Archeologie

Archeologie [214–15 C6] (*36a Mariastraat;* ⊕ *09.30–12.30 & 13.30–17.00 Tue–Sun; admission: adult/6–25/under 6/BruggeCard €2/1/free/free*) A light-hearted, hands-on museum that traces the city's history through the ages, with particular emphasis on the everyday themes of work, home and death.

Sint-Janshospitaal and the Memlingmuseum

Sint-Janshospitaal and the Memlingmuseum [214–15 C6] (*38 Mariastraat;* ⊕ *09.30–11.45 & 14.00–17.00 Tue–Sun; admission: adult/6–25/ under 6/Brugge Card €8/1/free/free, inc an audio guide & entry to OLV-ter-Potterie*) Originally a haven for the sick and a resting place for pilgrims, this medieval hospital (founded in 1150) is one of the oldest in Europe. Still in use until the 19th century, the complex features the former ward, which contains a museum filled with paintings and *objets d'art* documenting the hospital's history; the old *apotheek* (also a museum); and the Cornelius chapel, better known today as the Memlingmuseum and home to six works by Flemish Primitive Hans Memling (page 20). The highlight of the collection is the *Reliquary of St Ursula*. Housed in a glass case, the miniature Gothic wooden church purportedly contains relics of the beautiful British princess, St Ursula. Legend has it she was murdered, alongside the 11,000 virgins accompanying her on a pilgrimage, by Huns near Cologne for refusing to abandon her faith. In the same room you will find the impressive *Mystic Marriage of St Catherine* triptych and in a nearby side chapel look for *Our*

Blessed Lady and Maarten van Nieuwenhoven and the Sibylla Sambetha; both are fine examples of Memling's skill as a portraitist. Also worth seeing is the peaceful herb garden outside.

Sint-Salvatorskathedraal [214–15 C6] (*Steenstraat; www.sintsalvator.be;* ⊕ *church: 14.00–17.30 Mon, 09.00–12.00 & 14.00–18.00 Tue–Fri, 09.00–12.00 & 14.00–15.30 Sat, 09.00–10.00 & 14.00–17.00 Sun; free*) When the St Donatius Church on the Burg was destroyed in the 18th century, the Holy Saviour Church – the city's oldest Gothic parish church – was upgraded to the status of cathedral to take its place. To fits its new role, it was subsequently rebuilt in Romanesque style by English architect William Chantrell. Its most important treasures, like Dirk Bout's *Martyrdom of St Hippolytus*, are housed in the *schatkamer* (treasury) (⊕ *14.00–17.00 Mon–Fri & Sun, closed mid-Jan–mid-Feb*), but several Flemish tapestries, works of art and medieval tombs can be found inside the church.

't Zand [214–15 B6] The 't Zand square is one of the town's oldest and takes its name from the sand dunes that 13th-century settlers started building on (until 700AD the sea reached as far as the city's western gates). Today, the square is host to the town's largest underground parking area, whilst above ground the open expanse is a popular place for meeting friends. At its centre sits a fountain composed of four nudes. Designed by local artists Stefaan Depuydt and Livia Canestraro, each woman represents one of the four major cities in Flanders: Kortrijk, Brugge, Antwerp and Gent. The **Concertgebouw** (Concert Hall) (*34 't Zand; www.concertgebouw.be;* ⊕ *09.00–19.00 Mon–Fri, 09.00–00.30 Sat*) in the southeast corner – famously built on a foundation of springs to avoid vibrations from the traffic affecting the music – hosts modern art exhibitions and is also the new location of the city's tourist In&Uit information centre (page 213). Regular performances and presentations are held in the venue's two concert halls; ask at the information desk for up-to-date listings and tickets.

Smedenpoort [214–15 A6] One of the four remaining city gates, the 'Blacksmith's Gate' was originally constructed in 1367. Note the raised sandbanks (now covered in grass) that were made to catch cannonballs. The bell that was tolled to announce the closure of the gate at dusk still remains. Look also for the bronze skull mounted high up on the left-hand side of the gate. In 1688 a dastardly Gent citizen opened the gates to invading soldiers under France's Louis XIV. He was promptly killed and his head mounted where this bronze copy stands to remind locals of their fate should they allow enemies through the city walls.

Monasterium de Wijngaard – Begijnhof [214–15 C7] (*24–30 Begijnhof;* ☎ *050 33 00 11;* ⊕ *06.30–18.30 daily*) Come spring, golden daffodils carpet the lightly wooded gardens of Brugge's lovely *begijnhof* (see box, page 18). Established by Margaret of Constantinople, Countess of Flanders, in 1245 the medieval compound is one of the best preserved in Belgium and like all the others was designated a UNESCO World Heritage site in 1998. Since 1927, it has been home to a handful of Benedictine nuns and all of the houses are closed to the public save No 1, the *begijnhuisje*, which serves as a **museum** (⊕ *10.00–12.00 & 14.30–17.00 Mon–Sat, 14.30–17.00 Sun; admission: adult/child/BruggeCard €2/1/free*). Visitors can explore four preserved rooms – look out for the traditional béguine cupboard or *schapraai* in the dining room; from top to bottom its three compartments housed china, a dining table and a larder – and an inner courtyard. Look also for the mid-

16th- century painting by Pieter Clasessens the Elder on the right-hand wall, as you enter, which depicts the seven wonders of Brugge. Nearby, house No 4 serves as the liturgical shop and sells a wide variety of biblical knick-knacks –including Jesus-shaped perfume bottles.

Pop into the Baroque church to see the canvas on the high altar, which features the *begijnhof's* patron saint – St Elizabeth of Hungary – kneeling before Christ in Eisenach church; it was painted by Jacob van Oost the Elder. Also of note are the gilt Romanesque statue of Notre Dame de Spermalie, which dates from 1240 and is the oldest statue of Mary in Brugge; the intricately carved pulpit designed by artist Jan van Hecke that depicts Jesus, the Virgin Mary, John the Baptist, John the Apostle, and the Holy Spirit in the form of a dove; and the memorial stones set into the floor among the choir pews – look for the 'Lourdes Stone': a blue-grey stone cut from the Massabielle cave in Lourdes in which the Virgin Mary appeared to St Bernadette Soubirous.

De Halve Maan [214–15 C7] (*24 Walplein;* ✆ *050 33 26 97;* ⏱ *Apr–Oct 11.00–16.00 Mon–Fri, 11.00–17.00 Sat, 11.00–16.00 Sun; Nov–Mar 11.00–15.00 Mon–Fri, 11.00–17.00 Sat, 11.00–16.00 Sun; 45-min tour €6.50*) Brugge was once home to a handful of working breweries, but today the soul survivor is De Halve Maan or 'half moon', which first crops up in record books in 1564! The current business was established in 1856 by Leon Maes and, incredibly, remains in the family. Maes' great, great, great, great granddaughter developed the Straffe Hendrink and her son, Xavier, the blond Brugse Zot (see box below). You can try both in the converted maltery and bottling room, which now acts as the brewery's café.

Diamantmuseum [214–15 D7] (*43 Katelijnestraat;* ✆ *050 34 20 56;* ⏱ *10.30–17.30 daily; admission: adult/child/BruggeCard €10/8/free, inc demonstration*) Covering two modest floors, Brugge's diamond museum traces the city's early entanglement with the carbon sparklers before it lost its trade to Antwerp in the 16th century. Daily demonstrations in diamond cutting and polishing take place at 12.15.

Minnewater [214–15 D8] Dubbed the 'lake of love' by writer Victor Hugo (the epithet has stuck and quite rightly so; see box opposite), this willow-lined pond is popular with hand-holding lovers and lady luck is rumoured to visit those who throw coins over their backs towards the lockhouse. Two such lockhouses once stood upon the site, which was originally the city harbour, and controlled the exit and entry of the numerous barges travelling between Brugge and Gent. The remaining one is known as Poertoren because it was used as a store for gunpowder and weapons.

CLOWNING AROUND

Take a sip of the beer produced by Brugge's De Halve Maan brewery and you'll notice the name on the label – Brugse Zot. Translating as 'Brugge Fool', it refers to the city's inhabitants. Legend has it the name was bestowed on the people of Brugge by Holy Roman Emperor Maximilian I in the 15th century. The story goes that in order to please the reigning emperor, a colourful procession of fools and merrymakers was assembled to welcome his arrival to the city. As the festivities drew to a close the residents of Brugge put forward their request for a new lunatic asylum, to which Maximilian replied: 'I have seen nothing but fools here today. Brugge is one great lunatic asylum!'

According to folklore, the Minnewater lake is named after star-crossed lovers. During the Roman rule of Gaul, Brugge was just a small village. Among the inhabitants was a girl named Minna, who had fallen in love with Morin Stromberg, a warrior from a neighbouring tribe. Her father disapproved of the match, but nonetheless promised Stromberg he could marry his daughter when he returned from fighting in the wars. No sooner had he left, than Minna's father revealed he had set in place an arranged marriage for the girl. Distraught, Minna fled to the nearby forest and managed to evade her father's searches. When Moren returned victorious from battle and learnt of his beloved's disappearance he raced to the forest to find her. However, when he eventually discovered Minna it was too late. Exhausted and malnourished, she died in his arms. The inconsolable Morin carried her body to a dried-up lake bed and then burst the banks of the nearby dyke, burying her body and naming the lake Minnewater – an immortal symbol of their everlasting love.

The view from the arched footbridge – over which Audrey Hepburn is rumoured to have stepped during filming for *The Nun's Story* – is lovely. Nearby stands a statue of Flemish writer Maurits Sabbe who penned the story *De filosofoof van 't sashuis* ('The Philosopher in the Lockhouse') in 1907.

Gentpoort [214–15 E/F7] (*Gentpoortstraat;* ☉ *09.00–12.30 & 13.30–17.00 Thu–Sun; admission: adult/6–25/under 6/Brugge Card €2/1/free/free*) In July 2011 another of Brugge's four remaining city gates was opened up. It now houses a museum about how they were built and the imports and exports that were ferried through them every day.

North and east of the city centre

Choco-Story [218 C2] (*2 Wijnzakstraat;* ☎ *050 61 22 37;* ☉ *10.00–17.00 daily; admission: adult/6–11/under 6/BruggeCard €7/4/free/free*) Housed in the 15th-century Maison de Croon (a former taverne), it covers the cocoa bean's migration from the hands of the Aztecs and Mayans (who used cocoa as currency) to the clutches of the Spanish who introduced the luxury into the royal courts of Europe. The second floor explains the extraction and production process, whilst the third details the history of chocolate in Belgium. The best bit is of course the demonstration and tasting session held on the ground floor just before the exit.

Frietmuseum [218 C2] (*33 Vlamingstraat;* ☎ *050 34 01 50;* ☉ *10.00–17.00 daily; admission: adult/6–12/under 6/BruggeCard €6/4/free/free*) Dedicated solely to the humble chip, this three-floor museum is housed in the elegant 14th-century Saaihalle. The ground floor describes the potato's peaty Peruvian roots and upstairs how they came to Belgium. Like its sister museum, Choco-Story, the best bit is the demonstration area in the cellars where you can munch on freshly cooked frites.

Jeruzalemkerk and Kantcentrum [218 G1] (*3a Peperstraat;* ☎ *050 33 00 72;* ☉ *10.00–17.00 Mon–Sat; admission: adult/6–25/under 6/BruggeCard €2.50/1.50/ free/free*) Refreshingly different in structure, this church is a copy of the Holy Sepulchre in Jerusalem and the interior is just as surprising. The altarpiece is

West Flanders   BRUGGE (BRUGES)

6

decorated with skulls and ladders and the small chapel at the back contains a replica of Christ's tomb, including a model of his corpse.

Nestled behind the church are the almshouses containing the **Kantcentrum** (Lace Centre) museum. During the 14th century this art form was in heavy demand – lace was added to the hems of skirts to prevent them from fraying – and Brugge was renowned worldwide for its production, but today a handful of women run afternoon demonstrations to keep the once-famous *bloemenwerk, rozenkant* and *toveresseteek* designs alive. They also have a shop.

Volkskunde [214–15 E3] (*43 Balstraat;* ⊕ *09.30–17.00 Tue–Sun; admission: adult/6–25/under 6/BruggeCard €2/1/free/free*) Housed in a row of eight 17th-century whitewashed almshouses, the Folklore Museum is a charming series of rooms decked out in yesteryear décor to recreate traditional scenes from the 19th and early 20th centuries. These include a classroom, a pharmacy, a hatter's workshop and best of all a confectioner's (fresh sweets are prepared here every Thursday afternoon using traditional recipes). Explanations are exclusively in Flemish, so it's worth buying the English guidebook sold at reception. Before leaving, duck into the museum pub, De Zwarte Kat, for a drink or two.

Guido Gezellemuseum [214–15 F3] (*64 Rolweg;* ⊕ *09.30–12.30 & 13.30–17.00 Tue–Sun; admission: adult/6–25/under 6/BruggeCard €2/1/free/free*) The life and works of celebrated poet-priest Guido Gezelle (1830–99) are displayed in the house in which he was born. His father, Pieter Jan Gezelle, was the gardener of the property and Guido grew up here until the age of 16 when he left to study in Roeselare. He briefly moved back to Brugge at the age of 20 to be ordained as a priest, but quickly returned south to resume his teaching position. His poetry is predictably pious, but also explores themes of nature and Flemish nationalism. He had a flair for sound and metaphor and is believed to have invented over 150,000 words to augment Flemish vocabulary.

Sint-Sebastiaansgilde [214–15 F3] (*174 Carmersstraat;* ⟍ 050 33 16 26; ⊕ *summer 10.00–12.00 Tue–Thu, 14.00–17.00 Sat; winter 14.00–17.00 Tue–Thu & Sat*) Distinguishable by its Rapunzel-like tower, the St Sebastian's Archers' Guild dates from the 15th century and contains a museum with a collection of interesting rooms. King Charles II is rumoured to have participated in archery competitions with the guild's members during his banishment from England. Ever since, all British sovereigns have been honorary members and the walls of the elongate Koningszaal are lined with paintings gifted by the British monarchy.

Engels Klooster [214–15 E3] (*85 Carmersstraat;* ⟍ 050 33 24 24; ⊕ *14.00–15.30 & 16.15–17.15 Mon, Tue, Thu–Sat; admission free*) A hidden gem, the English Convent is based on the site of a house founded by five English nuns in 1629. As their numbers grew, they were given permission by the Bishop of Brugge, Henry van Susteren, to build a new church, completed in 1739. The resident nuns will happily show you around the Baroque church, whose star-emblazoned marble floor and richly painted ceilings are worth the walk.

Sint-Janshuismolen & Koeleweimolen [214–15 F3+E2] (*Kruisvest; Sint-Janshuismolen:* ⊕ *May–Aug 09.30–12.30 & 13.30–17.00 Tue–Sun, Sep 09.30–12.30 & 13.30–17.00 Sat–Sun; Koeleweimolen:* ⊕ *Jul–Aug 09.30–12.30 & 13.30–17.00 Tue–Sun; admission: adult/6–25/under 6/BruggeCard €2/1/free/free*) On the eastern outskirts of town, four windmills perch on mounds that mark the position of the old city walls. Of these, St John House Mill and Koelewei Mill are still active and during summer the millers are happy to show you around their flour mills. The 18th-century Sint-Janhuis still stands on its original site, whilst the slightly younger Koelewei was transplanted from a nearby village to the north of town in 1996.

AROUND BRUGGE

DAMME The beautiful village of Damme presents the perfect postcard of Flemish life: a small cobbled market square surrounded by ancient buildings, an atmospheric church and traditional restaurants all surrounded by waterways – it even has its own windmill, whose red sails turn gently in the coastal breeze. As an added bonus, it's also a book town – similar to Hay-on-Wye in the UK – with nine independent bookshops to browse through and a bi-monthly book market.

The village sprang up in the 12th century when the Het Zwin creek was created and Brugge dug a canal to meet it and gain access to the North Sea. As a halfway port between the two, Damme handled the import of everything from grain and wine to herring. The village was razed in 1213, but locals – determined to start again – erected Onze-Lieve-Vrouwekerk and established St-Janshospital. The Stadhuis was built in 1468 with the last of the money just as the Het Zwin canal was silting up. Damme was largely untouched during World War I, but the fighting came very close in 1944 when the Battle of Mill was fought at Moerkerke, just 5km to the east.

Getting there and away
By boat From 1 April to 15 October the *Lamme Goedzak* (*www.bootdamme-brugge.be; adult/concession/3–11 €8.50/7.50/6.50, €1 cheaper one-way*) sails between Brugge and Damme. Sailings depart from Brugge (*31 Noorwegse Kaai*) at 10.00, 12.00, 14.00, 16.00 and 18.00, and from Damme (*12 Damse Vaart-Zuid, opposite the windmill*) at 09.15, 11.00, 13.00, 15.00 and 17.20. Sailing time is 35 minutes.

By bike If you're staying in Brugge, I highly recommend cycling to Damme. It's a simple 5km route along Noorweegse Kaai, which runs straight from the north of Brugge to Damme, so it's impossible to get lost. You cycle next to the canal and through lovely sections of poplar-lined paths, then put your bike on the boat for the return to Brugge.

By bus From April to October bus #43 departs from Brugge railway station (*33min past the hour except 10.33, 12.33 or 16.33*) and from the Markt (*39min past the hour*). The journey time is ten minutes. From Damme, buses depart for Brugge from the main square (*55min past the hour, but no buses at 10.55, 12.55 & 16.55*). From mid-October to March buses depart from Brugge station at 12.20 and 17.33 and the Markt at 12.26 and 17.39, and depart from Damme to Brugge at 07.39, 12.55 and 18.09. Otherwise, you have to call the Belbus (☏ 059 56 52 56).

By car From Brugge's R30 follow the Damse Vaart-Zuid north for 4.7km (*7km; ⏱ 12min*).

Tourist information
🔢 **Tourist information** 3 Jabob van Maerlantstraat; ☏ 050 28 86 10; e toerisme@ damme.be; www.toerismedamme.be; ⏱ 16

Apr–15 Oct 09.00–12.00 & 13.00–18.00 Mon–Fri, 10.00–12.00 & 14.00–18.00 Sat–Sun, 16 Oct–15 Apr 09.00–12.00 & 13.00–17.00 Mon–Fri, 14.00–

17.00 Sat–Sun) Inside the Huyse de Grote Sterre, a 15th-century patrician house that belonged to the Spanish governor, this modern tourist information office can organise a guide (€60/2hr) (who can arrange for you to visit the windmill out of season). It houses the Uilenspiegelmuseum on the 2nd floor.

۶۶ **Bike rental** Tourist office €10/day.

✗ Where to eat and drink
Two local products to look out for here: Damse Moeke, a cheese similar to camembert, and Uilenspiegel (8%) beer. You can find both at Tijl and Nele (below).

✗ **Damse Poort** 29 Kerkstraat; ☎ 050 35 32 75; ⏰ 10.30–22.00 Mon, Tue, Thu–Sun. 1900s' house serving Flemish classics like *paling in 't groen* & *stoofvlees*. €€€

▭ **Tante Marie** 38 Kerkstraat; ☎ 050 35 45 03; ⏰ 10.00–19.00 daily. Upmarket tearoom/brasserie that makes its own jams & pastries. For lunch their speciality is *drie hartige gerechtjes*: a trio of small savoury dishes, usually including their homemade cheese or shrimp croquettes. €€€

▭ **Tijl & Nele** 2 Jabob van Maerlantstraat; ☎ 050 35 71 92; ⏰ 09.00–18.00 Mon–Thu & Sat–Sun. Low-key sandwich & gift shop run by Debbie & Bert who also rent bikes €9.95/day.

Other practicalities
$ **Bank** There's an ATM concealed in a niche on the right-hand side of the Stadhuis; look for a small flight of stairs leading down from the street level.

Markets There a general market on the Markt (⏰ 08.00–12.00) every Thu, & every 2nd Sun there's a book market in the town hall & on the Markt.

What to see and do
Stadhuis (*Markt;* ⏰ *only during exhibitions & book fairs*) Built in 1464, the Gothic town hall is studded with six statues: Philip of Alsace; Joan and Margaret of Constantinople; Philip of Thiette; and Charles the Bold and his wife Margaret of York, who were married just around the corner at Huis St Jean d'Angély (*13 Jacob van Maerlantstraat*) in 1468. On the right flank of the building, two stones protrude from the wall: they were punishment stones which wrong-doing women – men were given an alternative punishment – had to wear around their necks while walking around the marketplace; a public form of embarrassment similar to the stocks. A **statue of Jacob van Maerlant** – a Damme local who rose to become the greatest Flemish poet of the 13th century – stands outside.

Onze-Lieve-Vrouwekerk (*Kerkstraat;* ⏰ *May–Sep 14.00–17.00 Mon–Thu, Sat & Sun; admission free*) Bulky 14th-century church, made all the more impressive by the attached ruins of its nave, transept and spire which were pulled down in 1725. You can climb the 43m tower (€1) for great views, and inside is the tombstone of Jacob van Maerland which, from 1300 to 1600, was believed to be the grave of Till Uilenspiegel (below) until it was determined he was a purely fictional character.

Uilenspiegelmuseum (*Above tourist information office;* ⏰ *as tourist office; admission €2.50*) Till Eulenspiegel is a character from an ancient Germanic fable. The first written version of the tale was penned in 1500 by Hermann Bote, a resident of Damme, who portrayed Till as a villain who stood for everything society shouldn't be. However, this story was eclipsed by the version Charles de Coster wrote in 1867, which depicts Thyl Ulenspiegel – note the change in spelling – as a loveable rogue: a trickster who fights for freedom and has adventures with his girlfriend Nele and his best friend Lamme Goedsak. The museum explores these different takes on the character and displays the range of engravings, books, sculptures and paintings modelled on Till.

St-Janshospital (*33 Kerkstraat;* ✆ *050 46 10 80;* ⊕ *Apr–Sep 14.00–18.00 Mon & Fri, 11.00–12.00 & 14.00–18.00 Tue–Thu, Sat & Sun; admission €1.50*) St John's Hospital was founded in the first half of the 13th century by Augustine friars (and nuns) who cared for the sick and provided lodging for pilgrims. It has operated as an old people home since the 19th century, but they've now converted the central, oldest, building into a museum to show what the hospital was like back then.

Schellemolen (*Damse Vaart-West;* ⊕ *Apr–Sep 09.30–12.30 & 13.00–18.00 Sat–Sun; admission free*) Whether you arrive by boat, bike or car this windmill catches your eye as soon as you enter Damme. It was built in 1867, on the base of an earlier 13th-century mill. During summer, miller Johan Denys is happy to show you around.

Terra Flamma (*17 Jacob van Maerlantstraat;* ⊕ *Jan–Mar 10.00–19.00 Sat–Sun, Apr–Dec 10.00–19.00 Mon, Tue, Thu & Sat–Sun, 13.00–19.00 Fri*) The small pottery studio is owned by Bart and Marina Missiaen, who produce the ceramic bowls, mugs and vases themselves. You can even see them at the wheel!

Cycling The area surrounding Damme is wonderful to explore by bike. There's a free map on the back of the tourist information map which takes you past the tiny, but typically Flemish villages of Hoeke and Oostkerke. You can rent bikes from the tourist information office or Tijl & Nele sandwich shop (opposite page).

LISSEWEGE Just north of Brugge, Lissewege is a tiny conglomeration of whitewashed cottages nestled around an ancient Gothic church. It's one of Flanders' prettiest villages and home to a close-knit community of 2,700 inhabitants. However, this number can seem considerably greater during summer when groups of locals and tourists stop off for lunch during cycling tours of the surrounding polders. Visit at the beginning of September when the season is dying down and you'll be able to wander its cobbled streets in peace. I guarantee you'll start enviously eyeing up the '*Te Koop*' (For sale) signs in some of the cottage windows.

Getting there and away

By car From Brugge follow the N9 northwest, merge onto the N31 and follow it for 7km to Lissewege (*12km;* ⊕ *17min*).

By train Brugge (*7min past the hour daily;* ⊕ *13min*).

Tourist information

ℹ **Tourist information** 5 Oude Pastoriestraat; ✆050 55 29 55; e vvv.lissewege@zeelandnet. nl; www.lissewege.be; ⊕ 15 Jun–15 Sep 14.00–17.30 daily. Informal information centre shared with the local police & town administration. In one of the back rooms they have 7 oil paintings depicting the village & surrounding polders.

🏠 Where to sleep, eat and drink

🏠 **Hof ter Doest** (6 rooms) 4 Ter Doeststraat; ✆050 54 40 82; www.terdoest.be. Part of the 13th-century abbey, rooms are a hybrid of old beams & modern fittings, with open-plan bathrooms. Rates include access to the beach-hut wellness centre; there's also bike rental (€10/day) & a 1st-class restaurant. €€€

🏠 **Lisdodde** (3 rooms) 1 Oude Pastoriestraat; m 0476 97 51 40; e info@lisdodde.be; www. lisdodde.be. Lore Brouns & her daughter Eva run this fresh, modern B&B behind the church. It was planned as a retirement dream for Lore & her husband, but when he was sadly killed in a construction accident in 2008, Lore decided to go ahead. She's done a great job. Rooms are painted in calming whites, baby blues & spring greens & have stunning views of the polder meadows out the back. €€€

✕ De Valckenaere 1 Lissewegsvaartje; ✆ 050 54 57 59; ☉ Jul– Aug 12.00–14.30 & 18.00–21.30 Mon–Wed & Fri–Sun, Sep–Jun 12.00–14.30 & 18.00–21.30 Mon, Tue & Fri–Sun, 18.00–21.30 Wed. The wife of 15th-century painter Hans Memling is believed to have lived in this cosy house, which now operates as a tearoom & restaurant. Best to visit at lunchtime when a 3-course menu costs €17. €€€€

♀ Den Ouden Tijn 14 Onder de Toren; ✆ 050 54 40 86; ☉ 10.00–late Mon, Tue, Thu–Sun. This pub has been running for 77 years & has had only 4 owners. Kurt & his brother Freddy have only had the place 2 years, & in their words they've 'got a while to go yet'. Black-&-white photos line the walls & upturned barrels serve as tables.

What to see and do

Onze-Lieve-Vrouwekerk (*Willem van Saeftingestraat;* ☉ *10.00–17.00 daily, Jul–Aug 09.00–20.00 daily; admission free*) The flat-topped tower of the Church of Our Lady can be seen for miles around. She stands amid a collection of large marble tombstones, in the centre of the village, and dates from the 13th century. She's unusually large for such a small village because she was one of the first stops for pilgrims on their way to Santiago de Compostela in Spain. They came to see the miraculous statue of OLV van Lisswege, and their offerings to Our Lady allowed the church to be extended several times. The current statue, carrying Jesus, is made of lime wood after the original was destroyed by Iconoclasts in 1586. Every first Sunday of May she's paraded in a Rococo chair from the church to Ter Doest barn (see below).

Also on show in the brick-heavy interior are Jan Maes' *Adoration of St James in Compostela,* painted in 1665, and 13 panels spread across both side walls depicting Christ's crucifixion. Unusually, explanations of the artworks are given in English. It's also possible to climb the **church tower** (✆ *050 55 24 55;* ☉ *15 Jun–15 Sep 14.00–17.00 daily, 16–30 Sep 14.00–16.30 Sat–Sun, 1 Oct–14 Jun on appointment; admission: adult/child €1/0.50*), which affords great views over the landscape.

Ter Doest (*4 Ter Doeststraat;* ☉ *10.00–18.00 daily; admission free*) I highly recommend the 15-minute walk along country roads to visit this enormous oak-beamed barn which, amazingly, dates from 1280. It, and a few annexes, are all that remain of a farm affiliated with Koksijde's 13th-century Ten Duinenabdij (page 248). The compound is littered with modern sculptures and one of the annexes now houses a smart restaurant and the romantic Hof Ter Doest hotel (page 233).

Getting there On exiting the church, you'll notice the road forks: follow the road on the right, then take the tarmac-covered Ter Doeststraat, the first street on the left, and follow it for a kilometre. Turn right when you reach a small side chapel; you'll see the barn 300m away.

THE FLEMISH COAST

Most guidebooks give the Flemish coastline a bad write up and perhaps with good reason. In the 1900s, it was *the* holiday destination for northern Europe's rich and famous. King Leopold I regularly holidayed here with his wife and poured money into the development of Oostende. Belle-Epoque mansions sprung up and the sweeping beaches were dotted with wooden beach huts. Today, the beach huts remain but the mansions have been replaced by ugly high-rise apartment blocks; only smaller towns like Knokke and De Haan have escaped the hands of contractors. However, the coast's heritage is only hidden, not lost. You can see the world's last group of shrimp fishermen trawling the shallows on horseback in Oostduinkerke, visit the medieval remains of Ten Duinenabdij and pay your respects at World War I sites. The area also boasts a jam-packed calendar of summer events: from mountain-bike races across the beach and giant sand sculptures to festivals and fireworks. Not to mention the avant-garde Beaufort art festival where huge thought-provoking sculptures are dotted along the coast every three years. The next takes place from 31 March to 30 September 2012 (*www.beaufort04.be*).

It's also incredibly easy to visit the various coastal municipalities thanks to the Kusttram, which runs along the entire length of the coast: at 67km it's the longest tram line in the world. However, I urge you to rent bikes and make use of the excellent promenade that also runs the length of the coast. The tourist offices sell a selection of maps, including the specially tailored *De Kust*, the *Westhoek Noord* which covers De Panne–Oostende, and *Westhoek Zuid* which covers Diksmuide to Ieper. Unfortunately, you can't rent bikes from one town and drop them off in another, so you'll need to return to your starting point.

So then, the Flemish coastline may no longer rival the French Riviera but when the sun is shining it offers something better: not glitz and bronzed beauties, but refreshingly wholesome scenes of kids building sandcastles, grandmothers reclining in deckchairs, toes in the sand, and teenagers tucking into huge ice creams. The way holidays used to be.

KNOKKE-HEIST As the hyphen suggests, Knokke and Heist are two separate towns subsumed under one umbrella. Spread between the two are the beaches and villages of Duinbergen, Albertstrand and, on the otherside of Knokke, Het Zoute. Each has its own characteristics: Heist is cosy, Duinbergen is residential, Albertstrand is sporty, Knokke is upmarket and Het Zoute is exclusive and elegant. The restaurants along this stretch serve the best seafood on the coast thanks to their proximity to Zeebrugge. There is a clutch of museums, but the main draw is Het Zwin nature reserve which sits right up against the Dutch border.

Getting there and away On the Kusttram (see box below) alight at Heldenplein for the centre of Heist, Duinbergen for Albertstrand, and Station for Knokke. By train from Brugge (*33min past the hour, every hour;* ⏱ *21min*).

Tourist information
ℹ️ **Knokke** 660 Zeedijk, ☎ 050 63 03 80, ✉ toerisme@knokke-heist.be, www.knokke-heist.   info, ⏱ 08.30–18.00 daily. Knokke has the best office of the 2: a very large, modern affair where you

KUSTTRAM

De Lijn operate a cheap-as-chips (or should that be *frites*?) tram service that visits over 70 destinations along the entire 67km stretch of North Sea coast. Trams run every 20 minutes during winter and every ten minutes in summer. A €5 day pass allows you unlimited jumps on and off within a 24hr period and this can be extended to three (€10) or seven days (€18) depending on the length of your stay; a single journey costs €2.

Tickets can be bought from tourist offices/kiosks of various towns or at De Lijn ticket booths posted at various points along the tracks. Visit www.flemishcoast.co.uk for more information.

can book hotel rooms, organise a guide (€50/2hr), check your email free of charge for 15min – get the code from reception. It sells cycling maps: *Riant Polder* (44km; €2) which includes Damme (page 231) & the hamlets of Hoeke & Oostkerke & the *Zwinroute*

(39km; €2) which takes you across the border into the Netherlands.
ᗐᗑ **Bike rental** Knokke tourist office (€11/day).
🄸 **Heist** 22 Knokkestraat; 🔧 & e as above; 🕐 09.00–12.30 & 13.30–17.30 daily

What to see and do
The old primary school houses the **For Freedom Museum** (*91–3 Ramskapellestraat*; 🔧 *050 68 71 30; www.forfreedommuseum.be;* 🕐 *1 Apr–15 Nov 10.00–17.00 Tue–Sun; admission: adult/concession/7–11/under 6 €6/4/3/free, combi ticket with Sincfala €7*), a private collection of World War II memorabilia. There's more history at **Sincfala** (*140 Pannenstraat;* 🔧 *050 63 08 72; www.sincfala. be;* 🕐 *10.00–12.00 & 14.00–17.30 daily; admission: adult/concession/6–26/under 6 €3.50/1.75/1/free*), which covers the local fishing industry and what life was like on the coast in the 19th century. However, the main attractions is **Het Zwin** (*8 Graaf Leon Lippensdreef;* 🔧 *050 62 20 00; www.zwin.be;* 🕐 *Apr–Sep 09.00–17.30 Tue–Sun, Oct–Mar 09.00–16.30 Tue–Sun; admission: adult/concession/6–11/under 6 €5.20/4.40/3.20/free, audio guide walk €2.50*), a 222ha wetland reserve attracting various species of birds on their way to winter nesting grounds. Visit in April and you have a good chance of seeing stork chicks, while in December the herons descend. The red-billed shelduck used to be a big draw but numbers have dropped, so they're letting sections of the reserve lie fallow in hope the ducks will return. Also sharing the land are mouse-eared bats, foxes, Polish horses, and highland ponies and cattle. You can see the storks being fed daily at 15.00. A snazzy new visitor centre, with an observation deck overlooking the reserve, is scheduled to open in 2014.

Heist has a general market (*Maasplein & Boereboonplein;* 🕐 *07.00–13.00 Tue*) and Knokke a food market (*Gemeenteplein;* 🕐 *07.00–13.00 Wed & Sat*). From July to August Heist hosts a popular **folkloric market** every Thursday (🕐 *14.00–18.00*) with a live band and regional food and antiques stalls spread along Knokkestraat and Graaf d'Ursellan.

ZEEBRUGGE To this day, residents of Brugge still regard the port town of Zeebrugge (literally 'sea Brugge') as an adjunct to the city. The town is dominated by a huge international port, which handles one of Europe's largest fish markets as well as the delivery of cars, agricultural products and passengers who arrive by ferry from Hull (page 33). It was the site of two major historical events. The first was the Zeebrugge Raid of 23 April 1918, when the British Navy sunk two concrete-filled cruisers at the mouth of the port to prevent German U-boats – which presented a serious threat to Allied shipping – from leaving. The second was the 1987 Zeebrugge ferry disaster when the MS *Herald of the Free Enterprise* capsized and 193 passengers drowned.

Getting there and away
On the Kusttram, alight at Zeebrugge-Kerk. At certain times of the year there are trains to and from Brugge: Brugge–Zeebrugge (*1 Jan–24 Jun & 29 Aug–31 Dec, 7min past the hour, every 2 hours on Sat & Sun, 25 Jun–28 Aug 7min past the hour daily*); Zeebrugge–Brugge (*1 Jan–24 Jun & 29 Aug–31 Dec, 33min past the hour, every 2 hours Sat–Sun, 25 Jun–28 Aug 32min past the hour daily*). The Zeebrugge-Vaart tram stop is 200m from the railway station.

Tourist information
🄸 **Tourist information** Zeedijk; 🔧 050 54 50 42; www.brugge.be/zeebrugge; 🕐 Jul–Aug

10.00–13.00 & 13.30–18.00 daily. Outside these hours visit the Brugge office, page 213.

What to see and do Zeebrugge is keen to dispel its reputation as 'just an international port', but aside from the **beach** (tram stop: Strandwijk), which has formed the other side of the harbour, there's little do.

You can join a 75-minute **boat tour** of the harbour (*Tijdokstraat;* ✆ *059 70 62 94; www.havenrondvaarten.be;* ⊕ *9 Apr–16 Oct 14.00 Sat–Sun, Jul–Aug 14.00 & 16.00 daily; admission: adult/concession/under 12 €9/8.50/6.80*), and visit **Seafront** (*7–9 Vismijnstraat;* ✆ *050 55 14 15; www.seafront.be;* ⊕ *Jul–Aug 10.00–19.00 daily, Sep–Jun 10.00–18.00 daily; admission: adult/concession/under 12 €10.50/10/8.50*), a maritime museum which includes a Russian submarine and the old fish market.

BLANKENBERGE Blankenberge is to Flanders, what Blackpool is to northwest England. During summer, the coast's second-largest town is filled with noisy bars and restaurants and its 350m-long seafront crowded with people. It's not everyone's cup of tea, but it's a good place for kids thanks to a clutch of animal-themed attractions and the huge range of sports on offer.

Getting there and away On the Kusttram alight at Blankenberge-Station or Blankenberge-Pier. By train from Brugge (*36min past the hour Mon–Fri, 10/36min past the hour Sat–Sun;* ⊕ *13min*).

Tourist information
ℹ️ **Tourist information** (Koning Leopold III-plein; ✆ 050 41 22 27; e toerisme@blankenberge. be; www.blankenberge.be; ⊕ Oct–Mar 09.00–11.45 & 13.30–17.00 daily, Apr–Jun & Sep 09.00–11.45 & 13.30–17.00 daily, Jul–Aug 09.00–19.00 daily. Can arrange a huge number of land- & water-based sports & sells walking maps of the local polders.

What to see and do It's impossible to be unimpressed by the annual **Sand Sculpture Festival** (*116 Koning Albert I-laan; www.zandsculptuur.be;* ⊕ *Jun–Sep 10.00–19.00 daily; admission: adult/concession/4–12/under 3 €11/9/7/free*), with towering dunes moulded into different themes each year.

Kids will love the penguin corner, interactive rockpools and sharks at the nearby **Sealife Centre** (*116 Koning Albert I-laan;* ✆ *050 42 43 00; www.sealife.be;* ⊕ *Jul–Aug 10.00–19.00 daily, Apr–Sep 10.00–18.00 daily, Oct–Mar 10.00–17.00 daily; admission: adult/concession/3–11 €16.50/15.50/13*), as well as the slithery creatures on show at the **Serpentarium** (*146 Zeedijk;* ✆ *050 42 31 62; www. serpentarium.be;* ⊕ *Jan–Mar & Oct 13.00–17.00 Mon–Fri, 10.00–18.00 Sat–Sun, Apr–Jun, Sep & Nov 10.00–18.00 daily, Jul–Aug 10.00–19.30 daily, Dec 13.00–17.00 Wed; admission: adult/concession/3–12/under 3 €10/8/8/free*). It's also possible to find nature on walks through the **Zeebos, Fonteintjes and Uitkerkse nature reserves** – ask the tourist information office for details.

WENDUINE AND DE HAAN Windy Wenduine and De Haan are a complete contrast to Blankenberge. They are residential areas with quieter beaches and De Haan, in particular, is lovely. It is one of the few coastal towns to have escaped high-rise development and is filled with Belle Epoque villas. There's not much to do, but if you're looking for somewhere quiet to stay on the coast, De Haan is your man.

Getting there and away On the Kusttram alight at Wenduine-Centrum for Wenduine, or De Haan-Aan Zee for De Haan centre.

Tourist information

De Haan Tram station, Koninklijkplein; ☏ 059 24 21 34; e toerisme@dehaan.be; www.dehaan.be; ⊕ Jul–Aug 09.30–18.00 daily, Apr–Jun & Sep–Oct 09.30–12.00 & 13.30–17.00 daily, Nov–Mar 09.30–12.0 & 14.00–16.30 Mon–Sat, 10.00–14.00 Sun.

Wenduine Tram station, Leopold II-laan, De Haan; ☏ 050 41 24 69; e info.wenduine@skynet.be; www.wenduine.be; ⊕ as De Haan. **Bike rental** André, 9 Leopoldlaan; ☏ 059 23 37 89; ⊕ 09.00–18.00 Tue–Sat. €13/day.

What to see and do Rent bikes, purchase the *Brugse Ommeland* cycling map from the tourist information office and visit the old polder villages of Vlissegem and Klemskerke, roughly 2km and 7km inland from De Haan. The former has an ancient barn, De Schamelweke, that you can visit and the latter a Gothic church and windmill. The nature reserves of Duinbos and Kijkuit, spread either side of De Haan, are pleasant to explore too.

On the first Saturday of August De Haan celebrates Trammelant, a Belle-Epoque Festival, and in mid-July Wenduine hosts Reuzenfeesten, a Giant's Parade.

OOSTENDE (OSTEND)

Oostende once sat at the eastern end of an island called Testerep – which included Middelkerke and Westende – but when the sea level dropped during the Middle Ages it became part of the mainland. By the 15th century, this small fishing village was doing very well for itself, but it hit the jackpot in 1717 when local merchants established the Oostendse Compagnie – a fleet that traded with India and China. Despite the riches it brought, the route was closed in 1731 as part of the Treaty of Vienna, when the Austrian Netherlands joined forces with Britain against the French and Spanish. The town's life as a seaside resort started not long after in 1784 and by 1850 it was the playground of the European aristocracy. The Dover–Calais ferry route was established and the construction of the Brussels–Oostende railway line allowed easier access to the town.

Today, the 'pearl' of the Flemish coastline has lost some of her shimmer, but is working hard to reinvent itself. Thanks to a number of first-class restaurants, snug bars and high-design hotels it's an ideal base from which to explore the other seaside towns. Its docks harbour two historical ships, Napoleon's fort, and a thriving fish market. The painter James Ensor lived here all his life and, unbelievably, soul legend Marvin Gaye called the town home for a few months as well (see box, page 246).

Getting there and away

By car From Calais (*94km;* ⊕ *1hr 4min*) or Dunkerque (*55km;* ⊕ *43min*) follow the E40, then take exit 5 and follow the N33.

By train Brussels-Zuid/Bruxelles-Midi (*5min past the hour Mon–Fri,* ⊕ *1hr 13min; via Brugge, 5/26min past the hour Sat–Sun,* ⊕ *1hr 40min*), Brugge (*4/30/44min past the hour Mon–Fri,* ⊕ *14min; 2/9/11/35min past the hour Sat–Sun,* ⊕ *35min*), Gent (*15/38min past the hour Mon–Fri,* ⊕ *40min; via Brugge, on the hour/29/38min past the hour Sat–Sun,* ⊕ *1hr 10min*).

By tram On the Kusttram, get off at Oostende-Marie-Joseplein. Oostende's De Lijn ticket office can be found at 110 Nieuwpoortsesteenweg (☏ *059 56 52 31;* ⊕ *08.45–12.00 & 13.45–16.00*). See box on page 235.

Getting around

By bike For bike rental, see opposite.

By bus The bus station is on the left-hand side as you exit the railway station. Buses #1 into town depart every 15 minutes from Perron 1; a single journey costs €2.

By ferry A free tug boat *Het Rode Vierkant op Zee (Apr–Sep 06.30–10.00 & 10.30–18.30 & 19.00–21.00 daily, last departure west–east 20.40 & east–west 20.50; Oct–Mar 07.45–13.00 & 13.30–18.17, last departure west–east 17.55 & east–west 18.05)* ferries passengers back and forth between the west coast and east coast, where sights like Fort Napoleon (page 245) are located. Departs from next to the aquarium [242 D3] every ten minutes.

Tourist information

i **Tourist office** [242 A2] 2 Monacoplein; ✆ 059 70 11 99; e info@visitoostende.be; www. visitoostende.be; ⏱ Sep–Jun 10.00–18.00 daily, Jul–Aug 09.00–19.00 daily. Large office with helpful staff, who sell City Passes (see box, page 244) & can book tickets for the Kursaal (casino) & the Kusttram (see box, page 235). Alternatively,

the 'Plus Card' offers you discounts by combining transport & passes for attractions.

&ᴥ **Bike rental** Gino Carts & Bikes, 40 Kemmelbergstraat, ✆ 059 50 06 23, www. ginocarts.be, ⏱ 08.30–20.00 daily; Nico Karts, 44 Albert 1-Promenade, ✆ 059 23 34 81, www. nicokarts.be

Guided tours

Lange Nel 67 Christinastraat; ✆ 059 80 73 81; e lange_nel@hotmail.com. Ostend Guides' Association arrange a number of guided walking tours.

City walks The tourist office offers 2 digital city walks – the Perfume of Oostende trail & the Marvin Gaye tour – which can either be downloaded on to your own iPhone, iPod or Android or played on iPods

rented from the tourist office. The first is a tour of Surrealist painter James Ensor's favourite spots in the city, as well as those of other Ostend locals Constant Permeke & Léon Spilliaert; the latter – developed with the help of Gaye's second wife Janis Hunter – details the singer's favourite haunts while in Ostend (see box, page 246), & includes rare archive footage & photos.

⌂ Where to stay

⌂ **Andromeda** [240–1 A1] (90 rooms) 60 Albert-1 Promenade; ✆ 059 80 66 11; www. andromedahotel.be. Overlooks the beach & has everything on site for a luxury stay: 4-star rooms, 2 restaurants, cocktail bar, swimming pool, sauna, gym & Thalassa spa offering all manner of massage, body wraps & facials. Splash out on a Junior Suite for sea views. B/fast €16. €€€

⌂ **Mondo** [240–1 A2] (59 rooms) 1 Leon Spilliaertstraat; ✆ 059 70 08 06; www. mondohotels.eu. Fun, vibrant 3-star Art Deco hotel. The standard Cosy rooms live up to their name, so upgrade to a Superior which are much more spacious. The 2 Suites are very beach house chic – with a curtain separating the sleeping area from the huge lounge. The neon-coloured graphic art all over the back wall of the b/fast room will wake you up in the mornings. €€–€€€

⌂ **Oesterhoeve** [240–1 G6] (3 rooms) 84 Schietbaanstraat; ✆ 059 33 08 73; www.oesterhoeve. be. On the eastern shore, this quiet beach house-chic

B&B is owned by the Oyster Farm (page 245) who can prepare a special seafood & champagne dinner for you. As an added bonus, from autumn 2012 there will be a sauna for guests too. €€

⌂ **Polaris** [242 C3] (18 rooms) 19 Groentemarkt; ✆ 059 27 90 06; www.restorpolaris.be. Design hotel with listed 1902 Art Deco façade. The rooms – all dbls – are decorated in black & white. 2 luxury rooms have Jacuzzi baths & room 206 is equipped especially for disabled travellers. Ask for a room at the back of the hotel if you can: the square hosts a market every Tue & Sat morning. The hotel is closed throughout Oct when a funfair overruns the market square. B/fast served in restaurant downstairs. Excellent price/quality. €€

⌂ **De Ploate** [242 C2] (21 rooms) 82 Langestraat; ✆ 059 80 52 97; www. jeugdherbergen.be/oostende.htm. Maritime-themed youth hostel with Mess restaurant, a library/ chartroom with maps plastered to the tabletops & a bar. It's a bit dated now, but this will change when

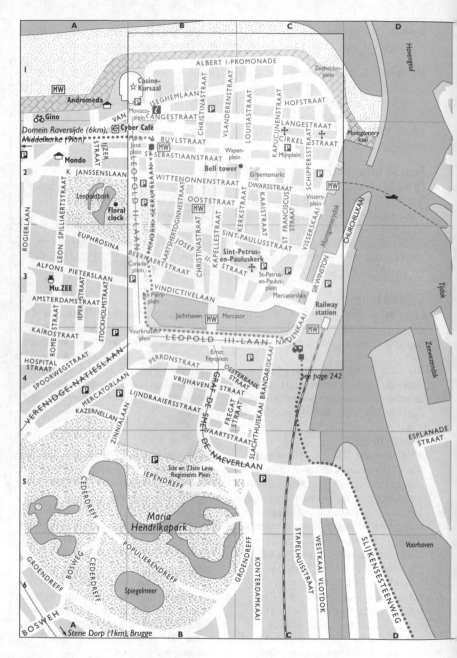

A · B · C · D

Hovengeul

ALBERT I-PROMONADE
Zeeheldenplein

MW
☆ Casino-Kursaal
▲ Andromeda
🚲 Gino
Monaco-plein
Cyber Café
VAN ISEGHEMLAANGESTRAAT
CHRISTINASTRAAT
VLANDERENSTRAAT
LOUISASTRAAT
KAPUCIJNENSTRAAT
HOFSTRAAT
LANGESTRAAT
CIRKEL STRAAT
Montgomery kaai

Domein Raversijde (6km),
Middelkerke (9km)
▲ Mondo
Marie-josé plein
ST SEBASTIAANSTRAAT
BUYLSTRAAT
Wapen-plein
Mijnplein
IJZER STRAAT
K JANSSENSLAAN
Leopoldpark
● Floral clock
WITTENONNENSTRAAT
Bell tower ●
Groentemarkt
DWARSSTRAAT
MW
OOSTSTRAAT
KERKSTRAAT
ST FRANCISCUS STRAAT
Vissers-plein
MW
✈
ROGIERLAAN
EUPHROSINA
ALFONS PIETERSLAAN
AMSTERDAMSTRAAT
IEPERSTRAAT
STOCKHOLMSTRAAT
KAÏROSTRAAT
ROMESTRAAT
HENDRIK SERRUYSLAAN
LEOPOLD II-LAAN
AARTSHERTOGINNESTRAAT
JOSEF
CHRISTINASTRAAT
KAPELLESTRAAT
BEERNAERTSTRAAT
SINT-PAULUSSTRAAT
Sint-Petrus-en-Pauluskerk ✝
St-Petrus-en-Paulus-plein
ST FRANCISCUS STRAAT
SCHIPPERSSTRAAT
VISSERSKAAI
Montgomerydok
CHURCHILLKAAI
Tijdok

🏛 Mu.ZEE
Canada-plein
Inn Piers-plein
VINDICTIVELAAN
Jachthaven
MW Mercator
Mercatorsluis
SIR WINSTON CHURCHILLKAAI
Railway station
MW
Zeewezendok

VERENIHDGE-NATIESLAAN
HOSPITAAL STRAAT
SPOORWEGSTRAAT
MERCATORLAAN
KAZERNELLAN
LIJNDRAAIERSSTRAAT
Vuurkruisen-plein
LEOPOLD III-LAAN
NAGENKAAI
MW
PERRONSTRAAT
Ernst Feysplein
VRIJHAVEN STRAAT
GRAAF DE SMET DE NAEVERLAAN
FREGAT STRAAT
Oesterbank STRAAT
SLACHTHUISKAAI
BRANDARISKAAI
See page 242
ESPLANADE STRAAT

ZINNIALAAN
IEPENDREFF
3de en 23ste Linie Regiments Plein
STAPELHUISSTRAAT
WESTKAAI VLOTDOK
Voorhaven

CEDERDREFF
BOSWEG
Maria Hendrikapark
POPULIERENDREFF
GROENDREFF
KONTERDAMKAAI
SLIJKENSESTEENWEG

GROENDREFF
Spiegelmeer
CEDERDREFF

BOSWEH
▲ Stene Dorp (1km), Brugge

---

the current hostel closes at the end of 2013 & moves to 72 Langestraat down the street. The new property will have sgl beds. Non HI-members pay €3 extra. Dorm bed under 26/over 26 €20.30/22.80. €

✗ **Where to eat** Look out for local speciality *sole à l'ostendaise* (sole in a shrimp-and-mussel cream sauce) and locally farmed mild and sweet oysters – to get them extra fresh visit the oyster farm on the eastern shore (page 245).

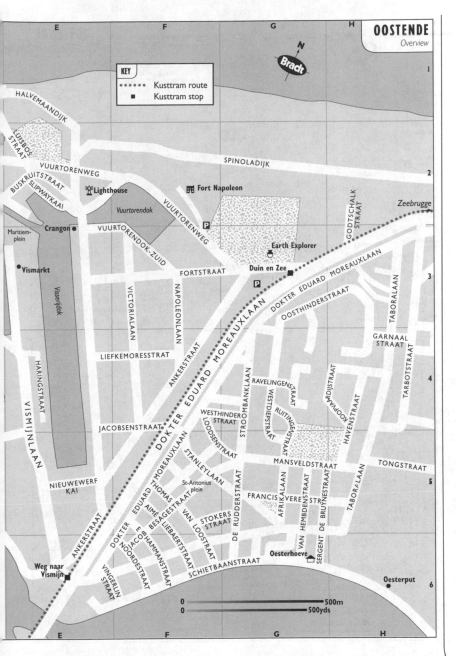

KEY
•••••• Kusttram route
■ Kusttram stop

HALVEMAANDIJK
LUTSBOS STRAAT
VUURTORENWEG
BUSKRUITSTRAAT
SLIPWAYKAAI
Maritiem-plein
Crangon ●
Vismarkt ●
VUURTORENDOK-ZUID
Visserijdok
Lighthouse
Vuurtorendok
VUURTORENWEG
FORTSTRAAT
SPINOLADIJK
Fort Napoleon
Earth Explorer
Duin en Zee
Zeebrugge
GODTSCHALK STRAAT
DOKTER EDUARD MOREAUXLAAN
OOSTHINDERSTRAAT
TABORALAAN
GARNAAL STRAAT
TARBOTSTRAAT
VICTORIALAAN
NAPOLEONLAAN
ANKERSTRAAT
LIEFKEMORESSTRAT
HARINGSTRAAT
VISMIJNLAAN
JACOBSENSTRAAT
DOKTER EDUARD MOREAUXLAAN
STROOMBANKLAAN
RAVELINGENSTRAAT
WESTHINDERO STRAAT
WESTDIEPSTRAAT
RUITINGSTRAAT
LOODSENSTRAAT
KOOPVAARDIJSTRAAT
HAVENSTRAAT
NIEUWEWERF KAI
STANLEYLAAN
St-Antonius plein
DOKTER EDUARD MOREAUXLAAN
T THOMAS
AIMÉ BESAGESTRAAT
JACOB B HAMMANSTRAAT
NOORDESTRAAT
E LIEBAERTSTRAAT
VAN LOOSTRAAT
DE RUDDERSTRAAT
STOKERS STRAAT
MANSVELDSTRAAT
FRANCIS AFRIKALAAN VERESTR
VAN HEMBDENSTRAAT
SERGENT DE BRUYNESTRAAT
TABOR LAAN
TONGSTRAAT
Weg naar Vismijn
ANKERSTRAAT
VINGERLIN STRAAT
SCHIETBAANSTRAAT
Oesterhoeve
Oesterput

0   500m
0   500yds

✗ **Ostend Queen** [242 A1] Kursaal, Monacoplein; ✆ 059 44 56 10; ⊕ 12.00–14.00 & 19.00–21.30 Mon, Thu–Sun. Billed as the best restaurant in town, it occupies the top floor of the casino & has stunning sea views. The food is first class, but it can be somewhat lacking in atmosphere. €€€€€

✗ **Mathilda** [242 A3] 1 Leopold II-laan; ✆ 059 51 06 70; ⊕ 12.00–22.45 Wed–Sun. According to French newspaper *Le Monde*, this bistro serves the best steak in the world. Quite a claim, but it's hard not to be impressed when the *rundvlees Blonde d'Aquitaine* is cooked at your table. €€€€

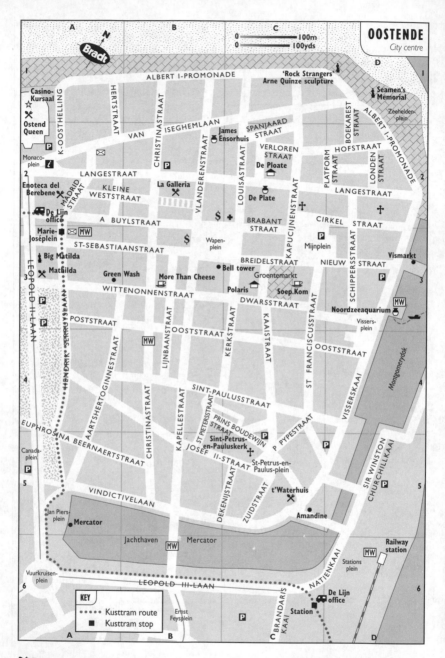

OOSTENDE
City centre

KEY
····· Kusttram route
■ Kusttram stop

✗ **Enoteca del Berebene** [242 A2]
6 Madridstraat; ☎ 059 80 19 84; ⊕ 18.00–23.00
Tue, 12.00–14.00 & 18.00–23.00 Wed–Sat. Italian
wine bar with over 150 different bottles; you get to
taste before buying. All go well with the *antipasti*
& delicious classic Italian dishes. Cash only. €€€

✗ **La Galleria** [242 B2] 32 James Ensorgaanderij;
☎ 059 70 01 50; ⊕ 11.30–21.00 Mon, Thu–Sun.
Bonhomie bistro that serves some darn good
garnaalkroketten (shrimp croquettes). Best
visited on a Mon, when it's also lobster day!
€€–€€€€

✕ t'Waterhuis [242 C5] 35 Vindictivelaan; ☎ 059 80 32 73; ⊕ 10.00–22.30 Mon–Sun. Oostende's oldest restaurant was one of few places allowed to sell water to sailors & breweries until the town was connected to the potable water of the Bocq River in 1923. Today, locals head here for the excellent pasta & good selection of beers. €€

⊒ More Than Cheese [242 B3] 89 Witte Nonnenstraat; ⊕ 09.00–12.30 & 14.00–18.30 Tue–Sat. Delicatessen with 8-table bistro upstairs serving exciting cheese & meat platters, salads & sandwiches. Recommended. €€

⊒ Soep.Kom [242 C3] 6 Groentemarkt; ☎ 0498 44 28 80; ⊕ 10.00–18.45 Tue–Sat, 12.00–18.45 Sun. 3 different kinds of soup deals include soup served with croutons, cheese, bread & a fruit salad for dessert. On offer every day, all are homemade by the owner Chantelle. €

What to see and do

Mercator [242 A5] (*Mercatordok;* ☎ *059 51 70 10; www.zeilschip-mercator.be;* ⊕ *10.00–12.30 & 14.00–17.30 daily, Jul–Aug 10.00–17.30 daily; admission: adult/6–14/under 6/CityPass €4/2/free/free*) Designed by Antarctic explorer Adrien de Gerlache and built in Scotland, the 78m *Mercator* – named after the 16th-century cartographer Gerardus Mercator – took to the seas in 1932. Designed mainly as a Belgian Navy training ship, in 1935 she sailed across the world to Easter Island to collect a Belgian research team, who brought back two colossal Moai statues as souvenirs; and in her late 60s, she won the 1960 Oslo–Oostende tall ships' race. Now retired, she sits gleaming on Oostende docks after a 2011 restoration. It's great fun exploring the commander's cabin, the wood-panelled officer's mess, the infirmary and the kitchen. Lots of old photos and film too.

Amandine [242 C5] (*35 Vindictivelaan;* ☎ *059 23 43 01; www.museum-amandine. be;* ⊕ *10.00–17.00 daily, closed Jan; admission: adult/6–14/City Pass €4/2/free*) From 1974 to 1995, this fishing trawler sailed 1,000 nautical miles between Oostende and the fishing grounds off southern Iceland to catch cod, sea bream, haddock and red mullet. The crew of nine were confined to the boat for months on end and worked in freezing conditions. However, Oostende's status as a major fishing port effectively ended overnight in 1995 when Iceland extended its protected-water boundaries forcing trawlers like the *Amandine* out of the good fishing grounds. They've done a great job of bringing 'life on board' to, well, life: the smell of fish and the cries of seagulls permeate the sorting bays in the hull, and the smell of bacon wafts from the galley kitchen. Remember to look out for the wooden grid on the dining-room table – put in place to prevent the plates sliding around during stormy weather.

Nordzeeaquarium (North Sea Aquarium) [242 D3] (*Visserskaai;* ☎ *059 50 08 76;* ⊕ *10.00–12.00 & 14.00–17.00 Mon–Fri, 10.00–12.30 & 14.00–18.00 Sat–Sun; admission: adult/under 14/CityPass €2/1/free*) Oostende's aquarium has been going

---

NEW YEAR'S DIVE

Balls of steel? Join the locals on the first Saturday of January for a bracing dip in the North Sea. Buy your €5 tickets online at www.nieuwjaarsduik.be. On the day take the tram west to Koninginnelaan and head to the Stedelijk Zwembad (Municipal Swimming Pool) to sign in and collect your wristband that will give you access to the beach. Everyone gathers on the sand at 14.30, waiting for the gun to go off at 15.00. At the sound of gunfire everyone runs shrieking and squealing into the water. You may well end up on local TV! Warm up with a hot chocolate or a tot of gin afterwards.

The City Pass grants free entry to Oostende's main attractions and includes a free 'Perfume of Oostende' digital walk, where an actor pretending to be local painter James Ensor leads you around his favourite city haunts. Tickets can be bought from the tourist office and cost €12/15/20 for adults, €4/5/6 for children and are valid for 24/48/72 hours.

for 30 years and, I'm sorry to say, is showing her age. It's a rather lacklustre display of anemones, polyps, crabs and brown fish.

Fish market [242 D3] (*Visserskaai;* ☉ *07.00–12.00 daily; admission free*) Just north of the aquarium, this small fish market is worth a peek. Locals still come here to buy bundles of fresh North Sea shrimp and fish. Have a whiff.

Arne Quinze sculpture [242 D1] (*Zeeheldenplein & Albert I Promenade*) Installed in June 2012, this series of ten red metal shapes is entitled 'Rock Strangers' and cost the city a cool €400,000. They're meant to inspire you to consider your identity ... Hmmm ...

Museum de Plaaten [242 C2] (*69 Langestraat;* ☎ *059 51 67 21; www.deplate.be;* ☉ *closed until end of 2012, but usually 10.00–12.00 & 14.00–17.00 Sat; admission: adult/14–18/under 14/City Pass €2/1/free/free*) Between 1834 and 1922 this house served as the summer residence of King Leopold I and his wife Louise-Marie, who died here from tuberculosis on 11 October 1850. Napoleon Bonaparte is also said to have stayed here on his first visit to Oostende in 1798 – presumably while surveying sites for Fort Napoleon (see opposite). Now a marine history museum displaying model boats, paintings and tools, it should reopen at the end of 2012.

Ensorhuis [242 B2] (*27 Vlaanderenstraat;* ☎ *059 50 81 18;* ☉ *10.00–12.00 & 14.00–17.00 Mon & Wed–Sun; admission: adult/13–26/under 13/City Pass €2/1/free/free*) Surrealist painter James Ensor inherited this house from his aunt and uncle, who ran a small souvenir shop, when he was 57 and lived here until his death in 1949. Prior to that he'd had to make do with a studio in the attic of his parents' house situated just up the road. He didn't achieve success as a painter until he was 35 years old, but rose to become a baron and honoured local figure. The house is filled with his vivacious paintings and personal effects, including the harmonium he used to compose music. A group guided tour costs €60. Not suitable for disabled travellers.

Mu.ZEE [240–1 A3] (*11 Romestraat;* ☎ *059 50 81 18; www.muzee.be;* ☉ *10.00–18.00 Tue–Sun; admission: adult/13–26/under 12/City Pass €5/1/free/free*) Oostende is very proud of its provincial collection of modern and fine art. Highlights include James Ensor's *De Gendarmen*, which depicts a fight between Oostende fishermen and police that occurred in August 1887; Léon Spilliaert's unnerving *Zelfportret met rood potlood* and Constant Permeke's vibrant *De Sjees*.

Domain Raversijde [240–1 A2] (*696 Nieuwpoortsesteenweg;* ☎ *059 70 22 85; www.west-vlaanderen.be/raversijde;* ☉ *24 Mar–11 Nov 14.00–17.00 Mon–Fri, 10.30–18.00 Sat–Sun; admission: adult/under 12/CityPass 3 museums €9.75/free/free; per museum €6.50/free/free, inc audio guide*) This 50ha site west of the city centre comprises three sights: the restored fishing village of Walraversijde, the Atlantikwall World War II war museum and the Prince Charles Memorial exhibition. To get there take the Kusttram west, direction De Panne, and get off at Raversijde.

Atlantikwall The Atlantic Wall was a series of coastal fortifications built by the Germans between 1942 and 1944. It stretched from the French/Spanish border to the tip of Denmark and continued along Norway's coastline to northern Finland. Oostende's 2km stretch of superbly preserved bunkers and trenches is one of the most complete in Europe. You can book 90-minute walking tours through Raversijde.

The Eastern Shore Visitors rarely venture across Oostende harbour to the eastern shore and that's a shame. It has a handful of lovely sights and provides the rare opportunity to visit an oyster farm. The best way to get there is by ferry (page 239), but if you haven't got a good pair of sea legs you can catch the Kusttram (see box, page 235) and get off at 'Duin en Zee'.

Fort Napoleon [240–1 F2] (*Vuurtorenweg;* \ *059 32 00 48; www.fortnapoleon.be;* ⊕ *Apr–Oct 10.00–18.00 Tue–Sun, Jul–Aug 10.00–18.00 daily, Nov–Mar 13.00–17.00 Wed–Fri; adult/6–12/CityPass €5/2/free, inc audio guide*) Built by Napoleon in 1798 to defend himself against a British attack – which never came – the fort was used as an artillery store by the German army during World War I and II, but was left abandoned. Following restoration in 1995, it now houses a bistro and restaurant (\ *059 33 21 60;* €€€€) with wonderful views of the harbour and Lange Nelle lighthouse. Limited access for disabled travellers.

Earth Explorer [240–1 G3] (*128b Fortstraat;* \ *059 70 00 11; www.earthexplorer.be;* ⊕ *10.00–18.00 daily; admission: adult/4–12/CityPass €15/11/free*) Next door to the fort, this brilliant interactive museum explores how earth, wind, fire and water have shaped our earth with gusto. Kids will be blown around in a simulated tornado, shaken by an earthquake and ride through a river of lava.

Oesterput (Oyster Farm) [240–1 H6] (*Schietbaanstraat;* \ *059 33 08 73; www. aquacultuur.be;* ⊕ *Feb–Nov 09.00–12.00 & 13.00–17.00 Mon, Wed–Sat, 09.00 12.00 Sun; admission €12*) Few outsiders know about this oyster farm that was revived in the 1990s. You can only visit as part of a group of 15, but if you call the tourist board they should be able to match you up with other people. A visit includes a 30-minute presentation about the pearly beauties, a tour of the farm and the all-important taste test at the end with a lovely cold glass of wine. To get there take the Kusttram direction Knokke and get off at Weg naar Vismijn.

Shrimp fishing on the Crangon [240–1 E3] (*2 Hendrik Baelskaai;* m *0476 75 63 57; www.crangon.be; departures 08.30 &13.30 daily; €30pp cash only*) Fancy catching your own shrimp? Roll up your sleeves and board the *Crangon* – a traditional shrimp trawler named after the species' family name Crangonidae. On the four-hour round trip you'll be put to work sorting, washing and cooking the grey prawns and at the end given a share of the haul as a reward.

Day trips
Stene Locals like to escape to the rural village of Stene, 1km south of Oostende, to enjoy its pleasant square lined with restaurants dishing up rich traditional dishes. A good off-the-beaten-track day trip.

Did you know that soul-singer legend Marvin Gaye penned his hit song 'Sexual Healing' while living in Oostende? It was December 1980 and Gaye's life and career had hit an all time low: his relationship with Motown Records had soured after they'd rushed out an unedited album, he'd just split from his second wife Janis Hunter after only 18 months of marriage and he was in the throes of a serious drug addition. He also owed the IRS millions in taxes. So when Oostende-born fan Freddy Cousaert invited him to come and stay at his house, Gaye accepted and turned up two weeks later on Valentine's Day 1981 with his son Bubby. Freddy and his wife organised an apartment for him and Gaye ended up staying for over a month. 'He loved the rain and the wind, the honesty of the sea' recalled Freddy. A bronze statue of Marvin playing the piano graces the entrance of the Kursaal (casino) and the tourist office run a digital walking tour covering his favourite haunts.

To get there you can either walk (10km), take bus #6 which departs from outside the railway station or Marie-Joséplein every ten minutes, or you can rent bikes (page 239) and cycle there.

Jabbeke: Permekemuseum (*341 Gistelsteenweg, 8490 Jabbeke;* \ *059 50 81 18;* ⊕ *Apr–Sep 10.00–12.30 & 13.30–18.00 Tue–Sun, Oct–Mar 10.00–12.30 & 13.30–17.30 Tue–Sun; admission: adult/13–26/under 13 €3/1/free*) Located in the village of Jabbeke between Oostende and Brugge, this house was the home and studio of artist Constant Permeke. As per his wishes, the house was opened as a museum in 1961 and you can see 121 of his dark and brooding paintings, as well as his sculptures – an art form he only started to explore in his 50s.

To get there take bus #52 from Oostende railway station and alight at Constant Permekelaan (⊕ *1hr 5min*).

MIDDELKERKE AND WESTENDE Middelkerke and Westende are quiet resorts favoured by families. The former's wide beach attracts sandsurfers, horseback riders and kite flyers.

Getting there and away On the Kusttram alight at Middelkerke-Casino for Middelkerke centre, and Westende-Bad for Westende centre.

Tourist information

ℹ Middelkerke 1 Joseph Casselaan, \ 059 30 03 68, e toerisme@middelkerke.be, www.middelkerke.be; ⊕ Jan–Jun & Sep–Dec 09.30–12.00 & 13.30–17.00 daily, Jul–Aug 09.00–18.00 daily

ℹ Westende 173 Henri Jasparlaan, \ 059 30 06 40, ⊕ as Middelkerke.

What to see and do Learn about the development of tourism on the coast at **Kusthistories** (*1 Joseph Casselaan;* \ *059 30 03 68; www.kusthistories.be;* ⊕ *Sep–Jun 09.30–12.00 & 13.30–17.00 Tue–Sun, Jul–Aug 09.00–18.00 daily; admission: adult/concession €2/1*), which shares the same building as the tourist information centre, and see inside an original 1930s' apartment at **Villa Les Zéphyrs** (*173 Henri Jasparlaan;* \ *059 30 06 40;* ⊕ *as Kusthistories*). Alternatively, take a stroll through

Warandeduinen nature reserve, south of town between Koninklijkebaan and Miamiwijk.

In mid-June, Westende hosts the **Fish Weekend** with food stalls and competitions in wood sculpting, straw plaiting and chair mending. It also coincides with the international **Kite Festival** held on the stretch of beach opposite Meeuwenlaan (nearest tram stop: Westende-Bad).

OOSTDUINKERKE Quaint and quiet Oostduinkerke is famous for its *paardenvissers* (horse fishermen), who trawl the shallows at low tide fishing for the grey North Sea shrimp used in dishes like *tomates-crevettes*.

Getting there and away The Kusttram has four stops in Oostduinkerke; get off at Bad, which drops you right in front of Astridplein – the central square in front of the beach.

Tourist information

𝑖 Tourist information 6 Astridplein; ☏ 058 51 13 89; ◌ Apr–Sep 10.00–12.00 &14.00–17.45

daily, Oct–Mar 10.00–12.00 & 14.00–16.45 Sat–Sun

What to see and do A hundred years ago *Paardenvissers* (horse fishermen) could be seen plying the shallows along the length of the Flemish coast, northern France, the Netherlands and the south of England. Today, Oostduinkerke is the only place in the world where it still takes place. From late June to mid-September, ruddy cheeked, bearded fishermen wearing yellow oilskins ride Clydesdale-like Flemish Brabander horses up to their chests into the muddy North Sea and spend two to three hours wading up and down the beach pulling nets behind them and occasionally coming ashore to empty their catch into the wicker baskets slung either side of their (wooden) saddles. Fishing spots are located on the stretch of beach in front of Astridplein, or a kilometre west toward Koksijde-Bad (where G Scottlaan meets the beach). The local tourist office publishes a leaflet detailing the latest fishing times. Bags of the freshly washed and cooked *garnaalen* can be bought on Mondays from the De Peerdvisser café next door to the **Nationaal Visserijmuseum (National Fishery Museum)** (*5 Pastoor Schmitzstraat;* ☏ *058 51 24 68; www.visserijmuseum.be;* ◌ *Apr–Oct 10.00– 18.00 Tue–Fri, 14.00–18.00 Sat–Sun, Nov–Mar 14.00–18.00 Tue–Sun; admission: adult/ concession/6–18/under 6 €5/3/1/free)* an hour or so after the fisherman have finished fishing (on Fridays they go to the restaurants). The Oud-Gemeentehuis (*Leopold II-Laan 2*) houses an exhibition detailing the history of the ancient fishing method and the annual **Garnaalfeesten (Shrimp Parade)** is held on the last weekend of June.

KOKSIJDE AND SINT-IDESBALD These two family-orientated towns have two of the best museums on the coast, bar Oostende: the Ten Duinen Abdijmuseum and the former studio of artist Paul Delvaux, famous for his paintings of nudes.

Getting there and away On the Kusttram alight a Koksijde-Bad for the centre; there's only one stop for Sint-Idesbald.

Tourist information

𝑖 Koksijde 303 Zeelaan, ☏ 058 51 29 10; e toerisme@koksijde.be, www.koksijde.be, ◌ Apr–Sep 10.00–12.00 & 14.00–17.45 daily, Oct–Mar 10.00–12.00 & 14.00–16.45 daily

𝑖 Sint-Idesbald 26a Zeedijk, ☏ 058 51 39 9, ◌ Apr–Sep 10.00–12.00 & 14.00–17.45 daily, Oct–Mar 10.00–12.00 & 14.00–16.45 Sat–Sun

What to see and do In the last few years, harbour **seals** have returned to Koksijde and when the tide is high you can often see them basking on the stone barriers which point into the sea on the stretch of beach opposite Ster der Zee tram stop. Don't get too close.

Koksijde is also home to the medieval **Ten Duinenabdij** (*6–8 Koninkllijke Prinslaan;* \ *058 53 39 50; www.tenduinen.be;* ⊕ *Apr–Oct 10.00–18.00 Tue–Fri, 14.00–18.00 Sat–Sun, Nov–Mar 14.00–18.00 Tue–Sun; admission: adult/6–18/child €5/1/free; tram stop: Koksijde-Ster der Zee*) a fascinating archaeological site and museum built around the remains of an abbey founded in 1138 by a Cistercian hermit known as Ligerius. Also part of the complex, and a two-minute walk south, is **Zuid-Abdijmolen** (*van Buggenhoutlaan;* \ *058 53 39 50;* ⊕ *Apr–Sep 10.30–12.00 & 15.00–17.00 Mon–Fri, 10.30–12.00 Sat; admission €1*), an impressive working grain mill once owned by the Abbey of the Dunes and, incredibly, one of only eight still found worldwide.

To the east of Koksijde are the **Schipgatduinen and Doornpanne nature reserves** – the latter the site of **Hoge Blekker**, Belgium's highest sand dune at 33m.

In Sint-Idesbald you can visit the studio of Surrealist painter **Paul Delvaux** (*42 Av Paul Delvauxlaan;* \ *058 52 12 29; www.delvauxmuseum.com;* ⊕ *Apr–Sep 10.30–17.30 Tue–Sun, Oct–Dec 10.30–17.30 Thu–Sun; admission: adult/concession/ under 6 €8/6/free*) and the higgledy-piggledy **T'Krekelhof** (*237 Koninklijkebaan;* \ *058 51 23 32;* ⊕ *11.00–15.00 Fri, 10.00–17.00 Sat, 10.00–12.00 Sun; admission: adult/child €3.50/2, inc drink*) – a museum-cum-café filled with artefacts from the 1900s collected by the Vandamme family.

DE PANNE Right up against the French border, De Panne has the widest beach on the coast and locals love to race sail wagons across the compact sand. It also has a pretty collection of early 20th-century holiday mansions and extensive nature-rich sand dunes.

Getting there and away On the Kusttram alight at De Panne-Kerk for the centre. By train from Veurne (*3min past the hour;* ⊕ *7min*).

Tourist information

🄸 **Tourist information** 21 Zeelaan; \ 058 42 18 18; e tourism@depanne.be; www.depanne. be; Jul–Aug 08.00–18.00 Mon–Fri, 09.00–18.00 Sat–Sun, Apr–Jun & Sep–Dec 08.00–12.00 & 13.00–17.00 Mon–Fri, 09.00–12.00 & 14.00–17.00 Sat, 10.00–12.00 Sun. Hidden inside the police headquarters, the tourist office can organise accommodation & guided tours across the Westhoek & Oosthoek nature reserves, & has free Wi-Fi & public toilets.
🚲 **Bike rental** €12/day from tourist office.

What to see and do In town have a wander around the **Dumont Wijk** – an area of streets bordered by Zeelaan, Duinkerkelaan and Witteberglaan that contain a high concentration of original 1900s' holiday homes. Then head inland to explore the **Westhoek and Oosthoek dunes**, home to an array of flora and fauna, including foxes, plovers, larks, nightingales and the short-eared owl, to name a few. You can book a guide through the tourist office or at **De Nachtegaal** (*2 Olmendreed, De Panne;* \ *058 42 21 51; www.vbncdenachtegaal.be;* ⊕ *Apr–Jun 10.00–17.00 Mon– Fri, 10.00–18.00 Sat–Sun, Jul–Sep 10.00–18.00 daily, Oct–Mar 10.00–17.00 Mon– Fri, 14.00–17.00 Sat–Sun*).

Two-and-a-half kilometres inland, in the village of Adinkerke, is **Plopsaland** (*68 De Pannelaan, 8660 Adinkerke;* \ *058 42 02 02; www.plopsa.be;* ⊕ *Apr–Jun & Sep 10.00–18.00 Mon–Fri, 10.00–19.00 Sat–Sun, Jul–Aug 10.00–21.00 daily; admission:*

adult/child 85cm–1m/child under 85cm €29.90/8.50/free, 10% cheaper if you book online), a popular kids' theme park which centres around the world of TV gnome Plop and his friends – it's hugely popular with Flemish children.

De Panne also hosts a number of festivals, including **Dranouter** (*www. dranouteraanzee.be*) at the end of April, **De Drie Dagse van De Panne**, a three-day cycling tournament held at the end of March, and **Beach Endurance**, a mountain-bike race across the sand in November.

And, being so close to the border, if you fancy a foray into France buy the Cobergher (47km; €2) cycle map from the tourist office; it starts from De Panne railway station and travels via Adinkerke and across the French border.

VEURNE

Just four miles from the French border and the North Sea coastline, Veurne – or Furnes as it's known in French – retains an ancient charm that Flanders' other coastal towns have lost. Established in the 9th century as part of a chain of fortified towns built to defend locals from pillaging Vikings, it benefited for a short while from the Hanseatic League, but when relations with London soured, the town entered a dark period and became embroiled in numerous wars. It also suffered under the thumb of the Spanish Inquisition, which held their court in the Landhuis. Peace and prosperity returned in the late 16th century when Infanta Isabella and her husband Albert Archduke of Austria assumed control of the Spanish Netherlands. Many of the town's finest buildings date from this period. Indeed, Veurne boasts one of Flanders' most authentic market squares because the town was situated 9km from the Front Line during World War I and, as a result, many of its 16th-century buildings avoided destruction. It's a lovely town to wander around and there are ample local specialities to tuck into too. The surrounding countryside, known as Westhoek, is a rich agricultural region studded with windmills, and is ideal cycling territory.

GETTING THERE AND AWAY

By car From Ieper follow the N8 northwest (*31km; ⊕ 35min*). From Oostende take the N33 south, merge onto the E40 (direction Veurne) and take exit 1a, then follow N8 into town (*33km; ⊕ 27min*). From Brugge R30 follow signs for the E40 and follow it west for 33.5km, then take exit 1a (*54km; ⊕ 42min*).

By train Brugge via Lichtervelde (*7min past the hour daily; ⊕ 54min*); Gent (*51min past the hour daily; ⊕ 1hr 10min*); Ieper–Kortrijk–Lichtervelde–Veurne (*39min past the hour daily; ⊕ 2hr 20min*); from Oostende go via Brugge and Lichtervelde.

TOURIST INFORMATION

🛈 **Tourist information** 29 Grote Markt; 📞 058 33 55 31; e infotoerisme@veurne. be; www.veurne.be; ⊕ 1 Apr–14 Jun & 16–30 Sep 09.00–12.00 & 13.30–17.00 Mon–Fri, 10.00–12.00 & 13.30–17.00 Sat–Sun. 15 Jun–15 Sep 09.00–17.00 Mon–Fri, 10.00–17.00 Sat–Sun, Oct–Mar 09.00–12.00 & 13.30–17.00 Mon–Thu, 10.00–12.00 & 14.00–16.00 Fri–Sun. Large, modern office inside the Landhuis with information covering the whole of West Flanders & an interactive museum about the area & the war; one exhibit plays a song sung in the local dialect. 🚲 **Bike rental** Wim's Bike Centre, 35 Pannestraat; 📞 058 31 22 09; ⊕ 08.00–12.00 & 13.30–18.30 Tue–Fri, 09.00–12.00 & 13.30–18.00 Sat; €9/day

🏠 **WHERE TO STAY, EAT AND DRINK** Veurne has a number of local specialities, ranging from the acquired taste of *potjesvlees* (gelatinous paté made from boiled-

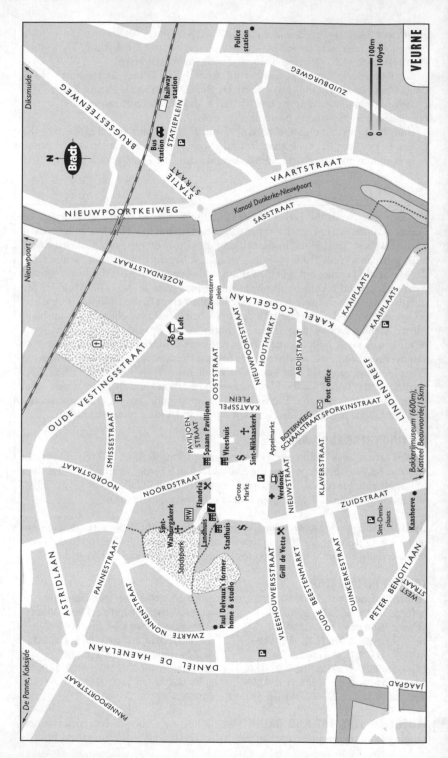

VEURNE

0 _____ 100m
0 _____ 100yds

down chicken, veal and rabbit), hearty *boudin blanc* (pork and veal sausage) and Walhoeve and Moerenaar cheeses, to the sweeter *kletskoppen* (wafer-thin almond and hazelnut snaps) and *babelutten* (hard butter-flavoured toffee). Tipples to try are the Boeteling (6.6%), and Sporkin beers and Veurnsche Witten (*jenever*). Most of these goodies can be bought from Kaashoeve delicatessen (see below).

🏠 **De Loft** (8 rooms) 36 Oude Vestingstraat; 📞 058 31 59 49; www.deloft.be. Modern rooms, above a tearoom/brasserie, decorated in mocha browns & azure blues. Dogs allowed & bike rental (€10/day). €€

✘ **Grill de Vette** 1 Zuidstraat; 📞 058 31 31 10; ⏱ 18.00–02.00 Mon, Tue, Fri & Sat, 12.00–14.30 & 18.00–02.00 Sun. My pick of the bunch, this romantic dining room is covered in candles. Try the house speciality of half chicken. Best to reserve a table at w/ends. €€€

✘ **Flandria** 30 Grote Markt; 📞 058 31 11 74; ⏱ 10.00–20.00 Mon, Tue, Fri–Sun, 10.00–18.00

Wed. Lovely terrace overlooking the square in summer. They serve snacks including *boudin blanc*, & Boeteling beer. €€

☕ **Verdonck** 11 Grote Markt; 📞 058 31 22 86; ⏱ 09.00–18.00 Mon, 09.00–21.00 Wed–Sun. Respected tearoom which makes its own ice cream & sells *kletskoppen* & *babelutten*. €

De Kaashoeve 35–7 Zuidstraat; 📞 058 31 18 47; ⏱ 14.00–18.30 Mon, 08.00–12.30 & 14.00–18.30 Tue–Sat, 08.00–12.30 Sun. Run for 20 years by husband & wife, Marc & Hilde, this fabulous delicatessen stocks heaps of regional cheeses, beers, *jenevers* & sweet treats.

WHAT TO SEE AND DO

Grote Markt The star of Veurne's main marketplace is the **Stadhuis** (*27 Grote Markt;* ⏱ *tours: 1 Apr–15 Nov 10.00, 11.00, 14.00, 15.00 & 16.00 daily: 16 Nov–30 Mar 15.00 daily; admission €3*), a pretty little thing tucked away in the western corner of the square. It consists of two parts: the Stadhuis – easily recognisable thanks to its colonnade decorated with golden angels on a blue background – and the adjacent Landhuis. Unusually, the Stadhuis, which dates from 1596 (left side) and 1612 (right side), played second fiddle to the Renaissance-style Landhuis, serving as a hotel of sorts for officials attending meetings in the Landhuis. They were merged at the end of the French Revolution and served as headquarters of the Belgian Army during World War I when they narrowly avoided destruction – a series of photos in the Mayor's Cabinet show how the bombs destroyed the row of four houses of the square and came within mere metres of the Landhuis.

A tour of the rooms reveals a number of ancient items. In the entrance hall, in the far right corner, stands an original 1759 fireplace and just above it a niche which in 1612 contained an external window. On the right of the entrance is the former drawing room where card games would be played. It's now the Trouwzaal (Wedding Room); getting married here must be quite an occasion, surrounded by the sumptuous golden leather wallpaper decorated with flowers and birds which dates from 1725. Also note the trio of chairs lined up in the left-hand corner which date from 1693. The former dining room also boasts a floral mural made from a single swathe of leather. Le Salon Bleu (the Blue Room) was once a bedroom (Austrian Emperor Joseph II slept here on 10 June 1781) and is decorated with luxurious 'camelotte' (velvet-embossed wallpaper) and *grisailles* (paintings using multiple shades of grey). Last, but not least, is the elaborate Albert Hall which King Albert I used as an office during World War I and where he met Britain's King George V. Above the fireplace hang portraits of Archduke Albert and Archduchess Isabella and below is a portrait of local hero Karel Cogge (see box, page 253).

Crossing over to the Landhuis, you'll enter the Oude Zittingzaal (Court Room) with cold stone floors and a 19th-century painting of Philip the Fair taking his oath as Prince of Veurne. Leading off from the court room is the 17th-century chapel, where the condemned could offer a last prayer before their execution. Today, it houses two paintings by Paul Delvaux – *Le Parc* (on the right) and *La Dames de Veurne* (on the left) – who lived the last 23 years of his life in Veurne at 19 Zwarte Nonnenstraat.

On the other side of the Grote Markt, flanking the entrance to Oostraat, are the **Vleeshuis** (on the right) and the red-windowed **Spaans Pavilljoen** (on the left). The latter was built as the original town hall in 1530, but takes its name from when Spanish officers used it as their quarters in the 17th century.

Sint-Walburgakerk
(*Sint-Walburgastraat, to the right of the Landhuis;* ⊕ *Apr–Sep 09.00–17.30 daily, Oct–Mar 09.00–14.00 Wed, 09.00–16.00 Sat; admission free*) Hidden behind the Landhuis, this buttressed red-brick church dates mainly from the 14th century, but had its transept added in 1907. Numerous works of art are on show, but its pride and joy are the skull of St Walburga and a relic of the True Cross brought back from Jerusalem during the Crusades.

Sint-Niklaaskerk
(*Appelmarkt;* ⊕ *mid-Jun–mid-Sep 10.00–11.45 & 14.00–17.15 daily; admission free*) Bulky 14th-century church, which was plundered by French soldiers during the Revolution. They stole the medieval carillon, leaving only the heaviest bell, 't Bomtje, which dates from 1379 and is the bell you'll hear tolling solemnly during the Boetprocessie (see box below). The new 1960s' set of bells plays concerts twice a week in summer (⊕ *Jul–Aug 10.30–11.30 Wed, 20.00–21.00 Sun*) and you can climb the tower (⊕ *15 Jun–15 Sep 10.00–11.30 & 14.00–17.00 daily*) too.

Bakkerijmuseum
(*2 Albert I-laan;* ✆ *058 31 38 97; www.bakkerijmuseum.be;* ⊕ *Sep–Jun 10.00–17.00 Mon–Thu, 14.00–17.00 Sat–Sun, Jul–Aug 10.00–17.30 Mon–Fri, 14.00–17.30 Sat–Sun; admission: adult/12–18/6–12/under 6 €5/3.50/2/ free, last tickets 16.00*) Two kilometres south of town, this independent bakery

BOETPROCESSIE

Veurne's famous Procession of the Penitents (*www.boetprocessie.be*) has been held on the last Sunday of July since 1646. Its origins are debated, but it's either based on a tale of Robert II Count of Flanders returning from Jerusalem in 1099 with a fragment from Christ's cross (which currently resides in Sint-Walburgarkerk), or a 1644 procession held by residents, re-enacting Christ carrying the cross before his crucifixion, in an effort to protect the town against an outbreak of plague. Either way, the event is unique because it's not performed for entertainment or as a tourist attraction; the participants apply to take part so they can atone for real sins.

The penitents don coarse brown robes and walk barefoot through the centre of town carrying heavy wooden crosses, marching to a slow and steady drumbeat. Meanwhile, members of the organisational group dress as characters from the New and Old Testaments.

Starting and finishing at Sint-Walburgakerk the procession passes though the Grote Markt, Noordstraat, Zwarte Nonnenstraat, Zuidstraat, Spoekijnstraat, Appelmarkt, and Oostraat. In 2012, it will be held on 31 July at 15.30. If you'd like to take part you can apply via email (e *info@boetprocessie.be*).

Intent on completing the first phase of the Schlieffen Plan – to capture Paris – the German Army advanced rapidly towards the Belgian coastline during the first few months of World War I. To halt their advance, Belgian troops established a Front Line 22 miles behind the Yzer Canal, which ran from Nieuwpoort to Arras in France. However, during the Battle of Yzer the Germans crossed the river and it was feared the Allies were on the verge of losing their hold in Belgium. (Diksmuide publishes a car route map that takes you past monuments and memorials associated with the battle, page 255).

Karel Cogge, a Veurne local who worked for the water board, suggested they open the sluice gates at Nieuwpoort and slowly flood the area to halt the Germans. The idea was approved and on 26 and 29 October 1914 the gates were raised, creating a marshland which spread as far as Diksmuide and was over a mile wide. Cogge's plan had single handedly prevented Belgium becoming fully occupied, and ended the German's 'Race to the Sea' for control of Calais and Dunkerque. In recognition of his services, Cogge was knighted in the Landhuis by King Albert I. Two paintings of him can be found in the Mayor's Cabinet of the Stadhuis and the Albert Hall of the Landhuis. His bust stands on Noordstraat.

museum is contained within 17th-century farm buildings and aims to preserve traditional baking methods. The highlights are the bakery demonstrations held in the former barn and freshly made 'daily cake' on sale in the café. To get there take bus #32, 50, 56, 68 or 69 from Veurne railway station and get off at Veurne-Kliniek. From there it's a five-minute walk to the museum: walk straight on until you reach the large roundabout, take the first exit right and the entrance to the compound is half way along the street.

Cycling Until 1627, the Moeren marshes on Veurne's eastern outskirts were unsafe and useless. That all changed when Antwerp engineer Wenceslas Coberger dug canals and drained them using a system of 22 windmills – the Charles Mill is the only original one to survive – transforming the region into a fertile plain, which is lovely to explore by bike. The tourist office sells the tailored *De Moeren* (37km; €2) map, which extends to the French border and takes in a handful of windmills; *Veurne-Ambacht* (48km; €2) is a longer route which takes you to Oostduinkerke; and the *Westhoek Nord* (€6) covers the surrounding region and takes in the village of Lo (page 254). See page 249 for bike rental.

AROUND VEURNE

BEAUVOORDE The appeal of Beauvoorde district is the tiny hamlet of Wulveringem and its **Kasteel Beauvoorde** (*10 Wulveringemstraat;* \ *058 29 92 29; www.kasteelbeauvoorde.be;* ⏱ *Apr–Oct 14.00–17.30 Thu–Sun, Jul–Aug 14.00–17.30 daily, Nov–Mar closed; admission: adult/6–12/under 6 €5/2/free, inc audio guide*), which was first built in 1408 but burned down 200 years later. The dark-grey 17th-century version seen today is built in Renaissance-style and is surrounded by trees and a moat. It was lovingly restored by the last private owner, Arthur Merghelynck, who filled it with *objets d'art* and gifted it to the state after his death.

Getting there Beauvoorde Castle is clearly marked on the *Westhoek Nord* cycling map sold by Veurne tourist office. By car, follow Ieperse Steenweg south out of town and merge onto the N8. After 3.8km turn right onto Gouden-Hoofdstraat and 2km later you'll see the castle on your right (*7.9km; ⊕ 12min*).

LO The hamlet of Lo, 12km south of Veurne, was put on the map by none other than Julius Caesar. It's claimed he passed through the area in 55BC on his way to his Roman territories in Britain and rested at a very famous tree (see below). The pretty village has a smattering of other ancient sites too.

Getting there and away Lo is best visited by cycling from Veurne – buy the *Westhoek Nord* map from the tourist office – but you can also catch bus #50 (direction Ieper) from the De Lijn bus stop on Lindendreef (*departures at 06.53, 09.47, 12.55, 16.18 & 18.15 Mon–Fri; ⊕ 28min*) and return with the same bus from Lo's Eiermarkt (*departures at 09.32, 13.02, 15.39, 18.02 & 19.37 Mon–Fri*).

Tourist information

🛈 **Tourist information** 17a Markt; ☎058 28 91 66; www.lauka.be; ⊕ 09.30–12.00 & 12.00–17.00 Mon–Thu, 09.30–12.00 & 13.00–16.00 Fri. Tucked around the corner from the Markt. They run a 6hr guided tour of the village (€12pp) where you get to try the local Destrooper biscuits, tour the village's historical sites in the morning & enjoy a nature walk in the afternoon.
🚲 **Bike rental** €8.50/day from tourist office.

What to see and do The village's highlight is **Caesarsboom (Caesar's Tree)**, a yew believed to be over 2,000 years old and a Belgian national monument. Legend has it that Roman Emperor Julius Caesar tethered his horse to the tree and caught a few winks beneath its boughs. True or not, the ancient tree survives to this day and sits beneath the slender turret of **Westpoort**, the last remaining gatepost from Lo's 14th-century city walls, and next to **Het Damberd**, site of the town's former 1499 brewery. To learn more about the village's history, I highly recommend joining the tourist office's guided tour (see above).

Bezoekercentrum Jules Destrooper (*5 Gravestraat* ☎ *058 28 09 33; www. destrooper.be; ⊕ 09.00–12.30 & 13.30–17.30 Mon–Thu, 09.00–12.30 & 13.30–16.30 Fri, 13.30–17.30 Sat; admission: adult/under 6 €4/free*) This family-run bakery has been producing its Lo-speciality butter crisp, butter crumble and almond thin biscuits for over 125 years. Learn about their history and sample some at the daily (bar Saturdays) demonstrations.

DIKSMUIDE

Wandering around Diksmuide's pleasant Grote Markt listening to the golden-oldie tunes being softly piped out across the square, it's hard to imagine the intense conflicts played out here during World War I. From the very start, the town became embroiled in the Battle of Yzer/Ijzer, which effectively dismantled Germany's Schlieffen Plan and established the boundaries of the Front Line that would barely move for the next four years.

The main sites of interest are the Ijzertoren peace monument and the preserved Dodengang trenches, but do take the time to buy a couple of *ijzerbollen* – heavenly custard-filled creations – and visit the town's tiny *begijnhof* and art-filled Sint-Niklaaskerk.

GETTING THERE AND AWAY

By car From Ieper follow the N369 south (*22.6km;* ⏲ *30min*); from Veurne follow the N36 westwards (*17.4km;* ⏲ *20min*); from Oostende take the N33 south and join the E40 (direction Veurne), take exit 4 (direction Middelkerke) and follow the N369 south (*28km;* ⏲ *32min*); from Brugge follow the N31 south and merge with the E40 (direction Oostende), take exit 4 (direction Middelkerke) and follow the N369 south (*50km;* ⏲ *47min*).

By train Brugge via Lichtervelde (*7min past the hour daily;* ⏲ *43min*); Gent (*51min past the hour daily;* ⏲ *59min*); Oostende via Brugge and Lichtervelde (*42min past the hour Mon–Fri,* ⏲ *1hr 8min; 18min past the hour Sat–Sun,* ⏲ *1hr 32min*); Veurne (*3min past the hour daily* ⏲ *11min*); Kortrijk via Lichtervelde (*on the hour Mon–Fri, 2min past the hour Sat–Sun;* ⏲ *50min*); Ieper via Kortrijk and Lichtervelde (*39min past the hour daily;* ⏲ *2hrs 11min*).

TOURIST INFORMATION

🛈 Tourist information 28 Grote Markt; 🕾 051 51 91 46; e toerisme@stad.diksmuide.be; www. diksmuide.be; ⏲ 1 Apr–15 Nov 10.00–12.00 & 14.00–17.00 daily, 16 Nov–30 Mar 10.00–12.00 & 14.00–17.00 Mon–Fri. Small, friendly office which sells the *Yzer Front* 79km car route map and booklet (in English; €3) which takes you on a tour of the sites & memorials associated with the Battle of Yzer (see box, page 253). It will be available as an iPhone download from 2013. They're also really keen to promote their cycling routes, so they've installed a free bicycle pump outside the office &

sell the *Nooit meer Oorlog* map (37.5km; €3) which takes you past Vladslo cemetery, the trenches & Ijzer tower. They can also arrange guided tours (€50/2hr): off season at short notice; during the summer try & give a week's notice.

🚲 Bike rental Catrysse, 56 Kaaskerkestraat; 🕾 051 50 46 70; ⏲ 08.00–12.00 & 13.00–18.30 Mon–Fri, 09.00–12.00 & 13.00–17.30 Sat; €8/day, tandem bike €18/day

Markets General market, Grote Markt, ⏲ 07.00–12.00 Mon; Farmers' Market, Grote Markt, ⏲ 14.00–17.00 Sat

✗ WHERE TO EAT AND DRINK

The nearby brewery De Dolle Brouwers produces a number of speciality beers (page 257), and the local sweet treat is the delicious custard-filled doughnut known as *ijzerbollen*.

✗ De Brooderie 11 Generaal Baron Jacquesstraat; 🕾 051 50 59 98; ⏲ 07.00–18.00 Mon–Fri, 08.00–14.00 Sat. A bright & trendy café serving freshly prepared sandwiches & salads. €

Bakkerij Desender 13 Kiekenstraat; 🕾 051 50 15 44; ⏲ 07.00–18.30 Mon, Tue, Thu–Sat, 06.30–12.30 Sun. Prepares plump & whisper-light *ijzerbollen*.

WHAT TO SEE AND DO

Sint-Niklaaskerk (*Sint-Niklaastraat;* ⏲ *08.00–18.00 daily; admission free*) This Gothic-style church boasts a number of artworks, the most interesting of which is the *disbank*, a rarely seen charity bench, located to the left of the entrance, from which food would be dispensed to the needy at rich people's funerals. It's engraved with seven scenes depicting the seven works of charity: give bread to the poor, give drink to the poor, clothe the poor, provide lodging, visit the sick, give prisoners freedom and bury the dead. On the right-hand side of the church, you'll find a 1950s' copy of Jan van Eyck's *Adoration of the Mystic Lamb*; the original is to be found in Gent's Sint-Baafskathedraal (page 175).

Begijnhof (*South of the Vismarkt, just across the river;* ⏲ *daily; admission free*) It is said that this tiny *begijnhof* hid the Archbishop of Canterbury, Thomas Beckett,

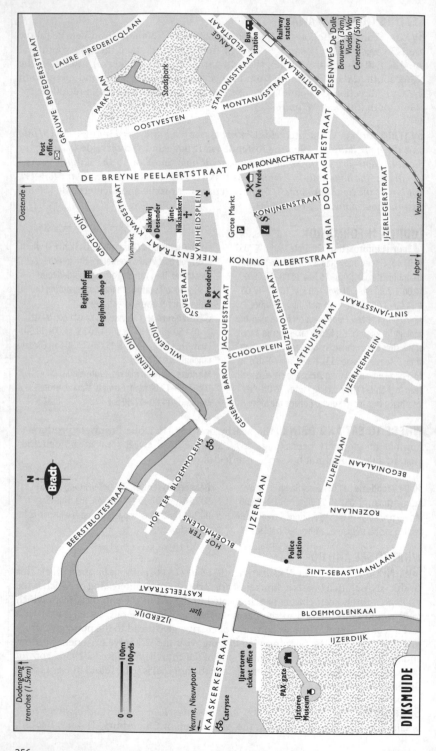

DIKSMUIDE

Dodengang
trenches (1.5km)

Oostende

Veure, Nieuwpoort

Veurne

Ieper

LAURE FREDERICQLAAN

GRAUWE BROEDERSSTRAAT

Post office

GROTE DIJK

Begijnhof
Begijnhof shop

KLEINE DIJK

PARKLAAN

Stadspark

OOSTVESTEN

KNAPDESTRAAT

Vismarkt

WILGENDIJK

STOVESTRAAT

BEERSTBLOTESTRAAT

HOF TER BLOEMMOLENS

HOF TER BLOEMMOLENS

KASTEELSTRAAT

IJZERDIJK

IJzer

KAASKERKESTRAAT

Catrysse

STATIONSSTRAAT

LANGE VELDSTRAAT

MONTANUSSTRAAT

Bus
Bus station

Railway
station

BORTIERLAAN

ESENWEG

De Dolle
Brouwers (3km),
Vladslo War
Cemetery (5km)

DE BREYNE PEELAERTSTRAAT

ADM RONARCHSTRAAT

Bakkerij
Desender

Sint-
Niklaaskerk

VRIJHEIDSPLEIN

KIEKENSTRAAT

Grote Markt

De Vrede

KONIJNENSTRAAT

MARIA DOOLAAGHESTRAAT

IJZERLEGERSTRAAT

KONING ALBERTSTRAAT

De Broderie

JACQUESSTRAAT

SCHOOLPLEIN

REUZEMOLENSTRAAT

GASTHUISSTRAAT

SINT-JANSSTRAAT

GENERAAL BARON

IJZERHEEMPLEIN

IJZERLAAN

TULPENLAAN

ROZENLAAN

BEGONIALAAN

Police
station

SINT-SEBASTIAANLAAN

BLOEMMOLENKAAI

IJZERDIJK

IJzertoren
ticket office

PAX gate

IJzertoren
Museum

N

Bradt

0   100m
0   100yds

256

when he was on the run from King Henry II in the 12th century, but that is dubious as most historical records place the first *begijnhof* as being built in the 13th century. Nevertheless, it's one of Flanders' smallest and cutest *begijnhofs*, whose collection of whitewashed cottages were restored after World War I. They now provide homes for 18 mentally handicapped adults, who spend their days making candles and delicate ornaments sold in the *begijnhof* shop (⊕ *11.00–12.00 & 14.00–17.00 Mon–Fri*).

Ijzertoren (*49 Ijzerdijk;* ✆ *051 50 02 86; www.ijzertoren.org;* ⊕ *Jan–Mar & Oct–Dec 09.00–17.00 Mon–Fri, 10.00–17.00 Sat–Sun, Apr–Sep 09.00–18.00 Mon–Fri, 10.00–18.00 Sat–Sun, closed 9–29 Jan; admission: adult/7–25/under 6 €7/1/free*) The cross-shaped Ijzertoren protrudes 84m above the horizon: a giant, and defiant, monument to peace. Erected in 1965, its base is inscribed with the words 'No More War' in four languages and its 22 levels are dedicated to the retelling of the war (and a bit on Belgian politics too). Starting at the very top of the tower, which offers sweeping 360° views of the landscape, you work your way down, experiencing dim and frightening recreated trenches (level 3), the smell of mustard and chlorine gas (level 15) and the tale of Hoge Brug.

Prior to entering the tower, you buy your tickets from the 1960s' building on the right, just after the bridge. They feed you out the back of the building and through a replica trench – complete with sandbags and smoke machines – and across a duck pond with bomb sound effects timed with splashes in water, so it feels like you're under attack. This leads you to the **PAX gate**, a monumental archway built in 1950 from the ruined remains of the first Ijzer tower. This was itself built in 1928 but was blown up on 15 March 1946 by pro-French Belgian military members who opposed the growing strength of the Flemish Independence Movement. The tower was a target because it contains the graves of eight leading Flemish freedom fighters.

Passing by the gate, you enter a compound where the first tower stood – button No 4 on the right-hand wall gives an explanation of its various elements in English. What's most important to notice is the inscription on the eight freedom-fighters' graves: AVV, VVK 'Alles voor Vlaanderen, Vlaanderen voor Kristus' (All for Flanders, Flanders for Christ). Prior to World War I, the Flemish were at a distinct social disadvantage to their French-speaking Wallonian countrymen: there were no Flemish schools, and if you couldn't speak French you couldn't qualify as an officer. The discrepancies angered Flemish soldiers, who began to question why they should fight and die for their country when the government would place a tombstone bearing a French motto on their grave. The Flemish Independence Movement came up with the above inscription.

Dodengang (*65 Ijzerdijk;* ✆ *051 50 33 44;* ⊕ *1 Apr–15 Nov 10.00–17.00 daily, 16 Nov–31 Mar 09.30–16.00 Tue–Fri; admission free*) Located 2km north of the Ijzertoren, this 400m stretch of preserved trenches has been carefully maintained, 'lest we forget'. Allied troops called it the 'trench of death' and spent four years here bravely holding the Front Line.

De Dolle Brouwers (*12b Roeselarestraat, 8600 Esen;* ✆ *051 50 27 81; www. dedollebrouwers.be;* ⊕ *09.00–19.00 Sat, 14.00–19.00 Sun*) In the village of Esen, 3km east of Diksmuide, this family-run brewery produces a number of unique beers, most notably the additive-free Oerbier (7.5%), the pure-malt Arabier (8%), Boskeun, a special Easter beer, and the extremely sweet Stille Nacht which is only brewed at Christmas time. You can visit the café at the times listed above, but if you'd like a one-hour tour in English pitch up at 14.00 on Sunday; it costs €3.50 per person and includes a bottle of Oerbier.

Getting there On Saturdays, take bus #31 from Diksmuide Markt (*departures 08.09, 13.09 & 18.09*) and get off at Esen Dorp. From there it's a 200m walk to the brewery (🕒 *12min*). On the way back, bus #31 departs from Esen (*12.47 & 17.47*). Outside these hours, and on Sundays, call the Belbus (📞 *059 56 52 56*) two hours in advance to arrange a pick up.

Vladslo War Cemetery (*3 Houtlandstraat, 8600 Vladso-Diksmuide;* 🕒 *daily; admission free*) Over 25,000 soldiers are buried at this German war cemetery, which also contains the hugely moving *Grieving Parents* sculpture created by Käthe Kollwitz, whose 18-year-old son, Peter, was killed in the war.

To get there you can cycle or call the Belbus (📞 *059 56 52 56*) two hours before you want to travel. It'll pick you up from an agreed spot and drop you on Houtlandstraat, a 300m walk from the cemetery.

IEPER (YPRES)

Ieper – or 'Wipers' as it was known by British soldiers – is a relatively small town with a very famous history. Most people associate it, of course, with World War I but its great buildings – the Lakenhalle and Sint-Maartenskathedraal – were built on the back of the town's lucrative cloth trade with England. During the medieval period, Ieper was the third-largest city in Flanders after Gent and Brugge – so important that Chaucer refers to it in *The Canterbury Tales*:

> 'A good wif was there, of biside Bathe, but she was somdel deef and that scathe. Of clooth-makyng she hadde swich an haunt, she passed hem of Ypres and of Gaunt.'
> (There was a wife of Bath, or a near city, who was somewhat deaf, it is a pity. At making clothes she had a skilful hand, she bettered those of Ypres and of Ghent.)

Close to the border, Ieper was caught up in various fights with the French, including the Battle of the Golden Spurs (page 5) in 1302, and by the 16th century the cloth trade had died. The weavers left for richer pastures and the town gradually shrunk from memory. Baedeker's 1901 edition of *Belgium & Holland* dedicates just two pages to the town, simply praising the 'many memorials of its golden period'. However, less than 13 years later, World War I was declared and it wasn't long before these 'memorials' lay in ruin – flattened by artillery.

War arrived in Ieper on 7 October 1914 when 10,000 German troops entered the town, kidnapped the burgomaster, stole 62,000 francs from the city coffers and demanded the local bakers prepare 8,000 loaves of bread to feed the soldiers. The next morning they released the burgomaster and marched west towards Vlamertinghe. Germans never entered the city again and residents felt safe enough to stay put until May 1915 when chlorine gas was deployed on the battlefields. As the war progressed, Ieper became a strategic defence point of the Ypres Salient (page 263) and was battered by artillery fire. When locals returned at the end of the war, it was barely recognisable. It's said you could sit on horseback and look over the town without a single building interrupting your view.

GETTING THERE AND AWAY

By car From Calais or Dunkerque leave the E40 at exit 14 and follow N8 south to Ieper (*53km; ⏀ 50min*). From Brussels, the quickest route is via the E40: head west towards Gent, then take E17/A14 to Kortrijk, exit at junction 2 and follow the ring road round to exit 10, then follow A19 west to Ieper (*122km; ⏀ 1hr 24min*).

By train Brussels-Zuid/Bruxelles-Midi (*41min past the hour Mon–Fri, 36min past the hour Sat–Sun; ⏀ 1hr 45min*); Brugge via Kortrijk (*32min past the hour daily; ⏀ 1hr 49 min*); Gent via Kortrijk (*9min past the hour daily; ⏀ 1hr 12min*).

TOURIST INFORMATION

i Tourist information Lakenhalle, 34 Grote Markt; ☏ 057 23 92 20; e toerisme@ieper.be; www.toerisme-ieper.be; ⏀ 09.00–18.00 Mon–Sat, 10.00–18.00 Sun. Well-equipped office that organises hotel bookings & battlefield tours, & sells self-guided tour maps for bikes & cars (see box, page 261).

🚲 Bike rental Standard bikes can be rented from Ambrosia Hotel (*54 d'Hondtstraat;* ☏*057 36 63 66*); electric bikes with GPS tours built in can be rented from Solex (see box, page 261).

GUIDED TOURS

Flanders Battlefield Tour 29 Boeschepestraat, Poperinge; ☏ 057 36 04 60; e info@ypres-fbt. com; www.ypres-fbt.com. Englishwoman Genevra Charsley & her Flemish husband study & conduct research all winter, so come summertime their tours are the city's best. Very knowledgeable, friendly & accommodating. Their standard tour includes Essex Farm, Tyne Cot, Hill 62, Vancouver Corner & the New Zealand Memorial (⏀ *Apr–Oct 10.00–12.30 daily, Nov–Mar on request; €30pp*). The larger North & South Salient tours cost €35. Their silver minibuses depart from the public bus stop on Grote Markt.
Frontline Tours 3 Willebeek, Kemmel; ☏ 057 85 99 35; e info@frontline-tours.com; www. frontline-tours.com. Has a great 2hr tour explaining the Mine Battle, €20pp.

Over the Top Tours 41 Meensestraat; ☏ 057 42 43 20; e tours@overthetoptours.be; www. overthetoptours.be. Daily morning tour of the North Salient which departs at 09.30 & returns at 13.30, & an afternoon tour of the South Salient which departs at 14.00 & returns at 17.30; both cost €35pp. Most visitors combine the 2. Meet at the address above. Credit cards accepted.
Salient Tours British Grenadier Bookshop, 5 Meensestraat; ☏ 057 21 46 57; e tours@ salienttours.be; www.salienttours.be. Their standard tour of the whole Salient departs daily at 10.00, returns at 14.00 & costs €38pp. The Short Tour departs at 14.30, returns at 17.00 & costs €30pp, & visits Hill 60, Bayernwald trenches & Bedford House cemetery.

🏠 WHERE TO STAY

🛏 Sabbajon (4 rooms) 6 Boezingepoortstraat; ☏ 057 20 30 06; www.sabbajon.be. 4-star

boutique B&B with spacious open-plan rooms: Denim Thoughts & Sweet Chocolate overlook

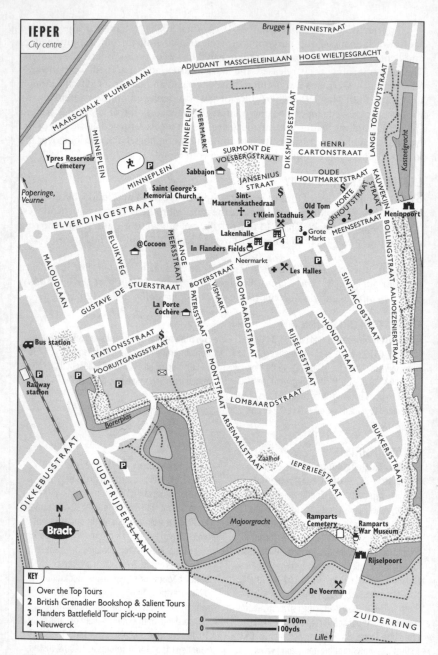

IEPER
City centre

Brugge ↑ PENNESTRAAT

ADJUDANT MASSCHELEINLAAN   HOGE WIELTJESGRACHT

MAARSCHALK PLUMERLAAN

MINNEPLEIN

Ypres Reservoir Cemetery

SURMONT DE VOLSBERGSTRAAT

HENRI CARTONSTRAAT

DIKSMUIDSESTRAAT

LANGE TORHOUTSTRAAT

Kasteelgracht

VEERMARKT

Sabbajon

JANSENIUS STRAAT

OUDE HOUTMARKTSTRAAT

KAUWEKIJNSTRAAT

MINNEPLEIN

Saint George's Memorial Church

Sint-Maartenskathedraal

Old Tom

KORTE TORHOUTSTRAAT

Meninpoort

Poperinge, Veurne

ELVERDINGESTRAAT

t'Klein Stadhuis

MEENSESTRAAT

@Cocoon

Lakenhalle

Grote Markt

BELUIKWEG

LANGE MEERSSTRAAT

In Flanders Fields

Neermarkt

BOLLINGSTRAAT

AALMOEZENIERSTRAAT

MALOUDLAAN

Les Halles

GUSTAVE DE STUERSTRAAT

BOTERSTRAAT

VISMARKT

BOOMGAARDSTRAAT

RIJSELSESTRAAT

SINT-JACOBSTRAAT

D'HONDTSTRAAT

La Porte Cochère

DE MONTSTRAAT

PATERSSTRAAT

Bus station

STATIONSSTRAAT

VOORUITGANGSSTRAAT

BUKKERSSTRAAT

Railway station

Borerplas

ARSENAALSTRAAT

LOMBAARDSTRAAT

IEPERLEESTRAAT

Zaalhof

DIKKEBUSSTRAAT

OUDSTRIJDERSLAAN

Majoorgracht

Ramparts Cemetery

Ramparts War Museum

N

Bradt

Rijselpoort

De Voerman

ZUIDERRING

Lille ↓

KEY
1 Over the Top Tours
2 British Grenadier Bookshop & Salient Tours
3 Flanders Battlefield Tour pick-up point
4 Nieuwerck

0 ——— 100m
0 ——— 100yds

the street, while Gentle Grape & Orange Delight overlook the garden. The Grape also has lovely views of Sint-Maartenskathedraal. The only downside is that dbls are comprised of 2 twins pushed together & check-in is at the late hour of 18.00. Otherwise excellent. €€€

🏠 **@Cocoon** (2 rooms) 9 Sint-Niklaasstraat; m 0495 96 26 04; www.cocoon-bedandbreakfast. be. Highly recommended 3-star B&B in the centre of town with bright, trendy rooms, flower-power bedspreads & a 2-table minimalist chic b/fast room. Cash only. €€

La Porte Cochère (3 rooms) 22 Patersstraat;
057 20 50 22; www.laportecochere.com. A 5-min
walk from the Menin Gate, this aristocratic house is
filled with original features, including a gorgeous
stained-glass skylight. Owners Steven & Katrien
are warm & welcoming & rustle up a great b/fast.
Unusually, rooms don't have a TV, but there's one
downstairs in the lounge. Cash only. €€

✗ WHERE TO EAT Ieper has a number of local specialities. The two you're most likely to
find are *tapjesvlees*, bacon-infused braised pork or veal, and the *kattenklauw*, a claw-
shaped Danish pastry filled with custard, apples and raisins and covered in icing.

✗ De Voerman 10 Rijselseweg; m 0497 50 58
49; ⏰ 18.30–22.00 Thu, 18.30–23.00 Fri–Sat,
12.00–23.00 Sun. Serves the best steak in town
– it's cooked over an open fire. Try & get a table
downstairs underneath the heavy oak-beam
ceiling; it's much cosier than the dining room up in
the eaves. Large terrace out the back & a separate
children's menu. €€€€
✗ Old Tom 8 Grote Markt; 057 20 15 41;
⏰ 12.00–15.00 & 18.00–21.30 Mon, Tue, Thu–
Sun. Started as a street stall after World War I
had left Ieper in ruins & has risen to be one of the
most respected restaurants in town. If you order in

advance they'll happily prepare *tapjesvlees* for you.
Also good for eel, oysters & lobster. €€€€
✗ t'Klein Stadhuis 32 Grote Markt; 057 21
55 42; ⏰ 11.30–14.30 & 18.00–22.30 Mon–Fri,
11.30–14.30 & 18.00–23.00 Sat–Sun. Tucked
away in the corner of the Grote Markt this 2-floor
medieval-style bar serves salads, soups & good
Flemish stews & steaks. €€€
✗ Les Halles 35 Grote Markt; 057 36 55 63;
⏰ 09.00–22.00 Mon & Wed–Sun. Locals love to
come to this laidback brasserie at lunchtime & sink
their teeth into the homemade hamburgers. €€

WHAT TO SEE AND DO
Lakenhalle (*34 Grote Markt*) Ieper's original Cloth Hall was built in 1304, a
covered hall for the sale and storage of linen. It was almost completely flattened
by artillery fire during World War I, although some of the foundations survived
and you can still make out pockmarks hollowed into the stone. Winston Churchill
wanted to preserve the entire area as a memorial, but residents protested and the
hall was carefully reconstructed in its original style and finished in 1967. Its sheer
size is testament to the former wealth of the city. When the Flanders Fields Museum

EXPLORING ON YOUR OWN

Visiting sites where family members may have died in battle is emotional and for
many a pilgrimage of sorts. If you'd prefer privacy, why not rent a bike and take off
on your own? The tourist board sells two maps. The 35km *Ypres Salient* route (€3)
uses Flanders' regional numbered cycling network. The accompanying booklet
comes in English and has useful aerial photographs, diagrams and explanations
of the various sites. Or, if you're feeling a bit more confident, there's the un-
signposted circular 45km *Vredes* route (€2), which departs from the Grote Markt
and, among others, takes in Essex Farm Cemetery, Langemark, the Vancouver
Corner, Tyne Cot and Hill 62. Explanations are in Dutch only.

If you don't fancy all that peddling or are worried about getting lost, you
can rent an electric bike from Solex (e *info@rentasolex.be; www.rentasolex.
be; €50/day*). These have GPS routes programmed into them and guide you
around the sites – it couldn't be simpler. You'll need to book ahead so they
can bring the bikes to Ieper.

Alternatively, you can take the car and follow the 82km *In Flanders Fields*
route (€3), which takes in Poperinge, Messines and Zonnebeke.

KATTENSTOET

Every three years on the second Sunday of May, Ieper hosts the Cat Parade (*www.kattenstoet.be*). Considered an ill omen during the Middle Ages, cats were burned or thrown alive from the top of the town's belfry. Thankfully, this practice was ditched in 1817 and nowadays *snoezepoezen* (cuddly kitties) are thrown to the crowds from the Belfry balcony on the Grote Markt and an enormous parade of cat-themed flotillas, and enormous cat puppets weaves through town. One takes place in 2012, the next is in 2015.

reopens in June 2012 you'll be able to access the belfry (€2) and climb its 260 steps for great views of the city. The **Nieuwerck** (town hall) sits on the building's eastern flank, facing the Grote Markt. It houses the council chamber and when it's open you can pop inside and get a glimpse of its stunning stained-glass window.

In Flanders Fields Museum (*34 Grote Markt;* ☎ *057 23 92 20; www. inflandersfields.be;* ☺ *1 Apr–15 Nov 10.00–18.00 daily, 16 Nov–31 Mar 10.00–17.00 Tue–Sun; admission: adult/7–25/under 7 €8/1/free*) At the time of writing the museum was undergoing a major renovation as part of the 2014 centenary programme and due to reopen in June 2012. Located on the second floor of the Lakenhalle, the new museum will be twice as big and feature a Knowledge Centre (which replaces the documentation centre previously located at 9 Janseniusstraat) with access to maps and books without a prior appointment. The highlight, though, will be the new 'poppy bracelet' experience: after leaving a €1 deposit you declare where you're from and your bracelet will be programmed with the personal stories of people from your town or county who participated in the war. You'll then be able to print or email the stories to your iPhone and create an itinerary to visit the areas where they fought. You can keep the bracelet as a souvenir and forego the deposit.

Sint-Maartenskathedraal (*Jules Coomansstraat;* ☺ *daily, closed 12.00–14.00; admission free*) Like the Lakenhalle, the first version of St Martin's Cathedral – which was built between 1230 and 1370 – was destroyed during the war and rebuilt with a cheekily taller tower to make it the tallest building in Belgium. Outside, just off Vandenpeerboomplein, are recovered fragments of the original church.

St-George's Memorial Church (*1 Elverdingestraat;* ☎ *057 21 56 86;* ☺ *Apr–Sep 09.30–20.00 daily, Oct–Mar 09.30–16.00 daily; admission free*) This unassuming church was built by Sir Reginald Bloomfield – the architect responsible for the Menin Gate – in 1929. It's filled with brass plaques honouring fallen soldiers and furniture donated by the victim's families. The stained-glass windows dedicated to various individuals and regiments are moving too, especially the window on the right above the baptistry which remembers Captain Boyce Combe. He was killed on 11 November 1912 at the tender age of 26 and his name appears on the Menin Gate.

Ramparts War Museum (*208 Rijselsestraat;* ☎ *057 20 02 36;* ☺ *10.30–20.00 Mon, Tue, Fri–Sun; admission €3*) Owned by the old-fashioned 't Klein Rijsel pub located next door, this small museum has a lovely private collection of war artefacts displayed in patiently recreated scenes of the trenches and bunkers. A short walk west will bring you to the Ramparts Commonwealth Cemetery.

Meninpoort (Menin Gate) (*Meensestraat*) Erected in July 1927, the Menin Gate marks the spot where soldiers would leave town on their way to the Front Line. Carved into the interior walls are the names of 54,896 British and Commonwealth soldiers killed in World War I and whose graves are unknown. Soldiers who went missing after 16 August 1917 have their names inscribed on the arches at Tyne Cot cemetery (page 268). As a mark of respect, the road is closed every evening at 20.00 and members of the local fire brigade sound their bugles in the Last Post. One member, Anton Deon, has been sounding his horn for over 57 years. This tribute to the fallen has continued uninterrupted since 2 July 1928, except under German occupation during World War II when then the ceremony was conducted in Brookwood Military Cemetery in Surrey.

THE YPRES SALIENT

A salient is a military defence line that bulges into enemy territory and is surrounded on three sides. The one which developed around the town of Ieper (Ypres) during World War I was a result of the failure of the German Schlieffen plan. Their aim was to avoid fighting a war on two fronts by invading France, then capturing its sea ports and Paris, via Belgium, before Russian troops could mobilise on the east German border. The attack relied on speed and the element of surprise. The Germans lost both when they were caught unawares by the Belgian resistance who delayed German troops for over a month until French and British soldiers arrived. Both sides dug in: the Allies (British, French, Canadian and Belgians) defending the coastline and the Germans pushing towards it. Both built trenches in the soil that stretched for 400 miles from Nieuwpoort to the French/Swiss border, a line known as the Western Front. The contours of this line were established during the First Battle of Ypres when Allied forces fought the Germans for control of Ieper and won, securing the last major town that stood between the Germans and the coast.

Over the next four years, this line would barely move. Vicious trench warfare ensued with increasingly bloody (and muddy) battles being fought in a bid to reach ridges, like Tyne Cot and Hill 60, that would provide elevated views of the battlefield and enemy lines. Evermore ruthless tactics were employed to weaken the enemy, including the use of chlorine and mustard gas, and casualties soared, culminating in the Third Battle of Ypres (see box, pages 266–7), which claimed the lives of over half-a-million soldiers. By the time the Armistice was signed on 11 November 1918, 1.5 billon shells had been fired on the Western Front and an estimated 750,000 soldiers had lost their lives in the Salient. The entire area was a wasteland of death, decay and

---

IN FLANDERS' FIELDS — Lt Colonel John McCrae, 8 December 1915

In Flanders' Fields the poppies blow,
Between the crosses, row on row,
That mark our place; and in the sky,
The larks, still bravely singing, fly
Scarce heard amid the guns below.

We are the dead. Short days ago
We lived, felt dawn, saw sunset glow.
Loved, and were loved, and now we lie
In Flanders' Fields.

Take up our quarrel with the foe:
To you from failing hands we throw
The torch; be yours to hold it high.
If ye break faith with us who die
We shall not sleep, though poppies grow
In Flanders' Fields.

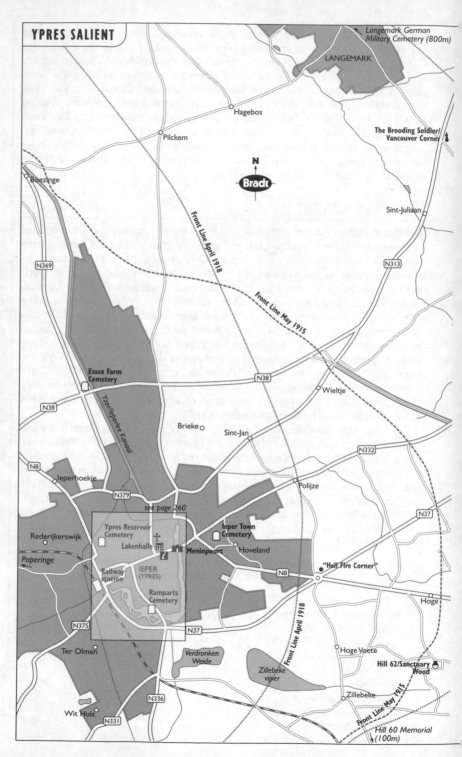

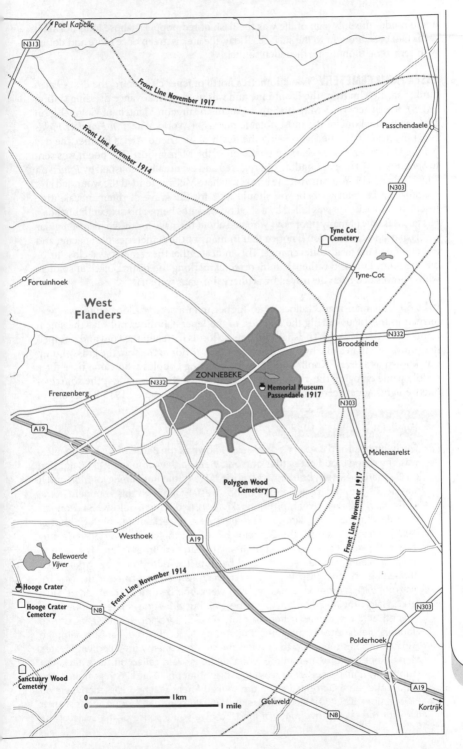

liquid mud – the only sign of life was the flash of red poppies, whose long-dormant seeds had been brought to the surface. Today, the area is green once more and dotted with cemeteries honouring the fallen soldiers.

ESSEX FARM CEMETERY Two kilometres north of Ieper city centre, the Essex Farm bunker sat 1,800m from the Front Line and was used as an advance dressing station (ADS). It was here on 3 May 1915 that Canadian surgeon Lieutenant Colonel John McCrae penned one of the most notable poems of World War I, *In Flanders Fields* (see box, page 263), after witnessing the death of his friend Alexis Helmer the day before. Helmer's name appears on panel ten of the Meninpoort. The poem was sent to *Spectator* magazine in London, but rejected and eventually published by *Punch* on 8 December 1915. You can visit the bunkers where McCrae tended the wounded and the adjacent cemetery, where you should look for the grave of rifleman Valentine Joseph Strudwick – he was killed by a shell two months before his sixteenth birthday. His tale was true of many poor boys who lied about their age for the chance of regular meals, pay and clothes. You'll notice that in many of the cemeteries the spacing and orientation of the headstones change. This indicates that the cemetery sat close to, or on, the Front Line and rather than incorrectly marking the resting place of soldiers whose graves had been destroyed by artillery fire, gaps were left.

HILL 60 This man-made hillock – no higher than a second-floor window – was formed in the 1860s during the creation of the Ieper–Comines railway. The steam trains had struggled with the slight incline, so locals flattened the land and dumped the leftover earth in a pile by the side of the tracks. Prior to the war, the grassy bump was known as Lovers' Knoll, popular with courting couples who came here for a cuddle while enjoying the views. But it was these views that made it the source of intense fighting between the Allied and German forces, and by 1915 it was one of

THIRD BATTLE OF YPRES

The infamous Third Battle of Ypres – also known as the Battle of Passchendaele – was one of the bloodiest battles of World War I. In the summer of 1917, fighting on Germany's eastern border had stopped due to the Russian Revolution and it was possible to redeploy German troops west. Faced with this imminent surge in German military strength, Britain knew it had to act quickly. Sir Douglas Haig developed a plan whose main aims were to reclaim the high ground at Passchendaele and push the Germans back from the coast in order to destroy their submarine bases, which continually threatened Britain's supply lines and the American reinforcements arriving by ship. Buoyed by success at the Battle of Messines in June, the plan was given the go ahead and to 'clear the way' for his troops Haig ordered a massive two-week bombardment. Then on, 31 July 1917, Haig sent Allied troops over the top, but a few days later the heavens opened and the worst deluge of rain to hit the region in 30 years turned Flanders' fields into a quagmire. Tanks got stuck, gun mechanisms jammed and crater holes that used to provide shelter from enemy fire filled with water. Men and horses drowned in the worst sections. Haig called off the attack, but stubbornly issued another on 16 August, another on 20 and 26 September, and yet another on 4 October. By the time Allied forces reached Passchendaele on 6 November, 325,000 Allied soldiers and 260,000 German troops had lost their lives for the sake of five miles of land. To give you a sense of the scale of the

the most feared places on the Front Line. Control of the hill passed back and forth between British and Germans is a series of suicidal attacks and counter attacks. The biggest breakthrough came on 7 June 1917, during the Battle of Messines, when British tunnellers detonated 53,000 pounds of explosives under German lines – the resulting crater can still be seen today.

To get there troops had to march past **Hell's Fire Corner**, an infamous roundabout on the Menin Road where German artillery reached within one yard of the road. Several soldiers were killed here before even making it to the Front Line.

SANCTUARY WOOD/HILL 62 *(26 Canadalaan;* \ *057 46 63 73;* ⊕ *10.00–18.00 daily; admission: adult/under14 €8/5)* This superb privately owned museum doesn't sanitise the war. The land belonged to a farmer, who left the British trench system and shell holes in place when he returned after the war. It's one of the last original trench systems to survive; most have been filled in. The museum rooms are bursting with accumulated rifles, shell casings, helmets and, best of all, stereoscopes containing original 3D war photographs – although be warned: some of them are quite graphic.

HOOGE CRATER MUSEUM *(467 Meenseweg;* \ *057 46 84 46; www.hoogecrater.com;* ⊕ *1 Feb–15 Dec 10.00–18.00 Tue–Sun; admission: adult/child €4.50/2)* Housed in a 1920s' chapel, this quaint two-room museum contains the private collection of curator Niek Bennot and his friend Phillipe Oosterlinck. They've amassed a good collection of clothing (displayed on mannequins), helmets and shells, as well as a 1916 ambulance and Fokker DR1 German warplane. The now-flooded Hooge Crater lies 100m east. It was created by the British during the Second Battle of Ypres when they smuggled 1,700kg of dynamite down specially built tunnels that ran under the German Front Line and detonated them on 19 July 1915 in an effort to break up the enemy's formation.

loss, it is estimated that for every square metre gained, 435 men died. Aerial photographs of Passchendaele after the war show a pock-marked lunar expanse of complete devastation (see right).

In an attempt to gain an advantage before American troops arrived in Europe, the German army embarked on the Lys Offensive in April 1918 and in the space of three days pushed the Allies all the way back to the outskirts of Ieper, reoccupying the land taken by the Allies during the Third Battle of Ypres. However, the effort exhausted the final reserves of the German army and it was unable to resist the Allies' Hundred Days Offensive in August 1918. A few months later, on 11 November, the Armistice was signed in a railway carriage in Compiègne Forest, just north of Paris.

Aerial photographs of Passchendaele taken before and after WWI

MEMORIAL MUSEUM PASSCHENDAELE 1917 *(5 Ieperstraat, Zonnebeke;* ✆ *051 77 04 41; www.passchendaele.be;* ⊕ *Feb–Nov 09.00–17.00 daily; admission €5)* Inside Kasteel Zonnebeke, a 1920s' mansion, this museum explains the 100-day Battle of Passchendaele (see box, pages 266–7) that claimed the lives of hundreds of thousands of soldiers in 1917. Its centrepiece is the immersive indoor trench 'experience' complete with corrugated-iron walkways, bunker rooms, dim lights and war-sounds soundtrack. An eerie and sobering reminder of how horrific life was for the soldiers.

TYNE COT Tyne Cot is the world's largest Commonwealth war grave cemetery and the final resting place of 11,954 souls. The sight of its uniform graves stretching into the distance is utterly humbling. Over 70% of them belong to unidentified British or Commonwealth soldiers and simply bear the words 'Known unto God'. The cemetery takes its name from a barn that once stood at the centre of this German strongpoint, and which British troops presumably thought resembled a Tyneside cottage. The Germans had a couple of blockhouses or 'pillboxes' here which they used as advance dressing stations. Several have been preserved, including the one beneath the mighty Cross of Sacrifice erected in 1922. Gently climb a few of its steps, and you get a glimpse of the German's advantageous viewpoint overlooking the British lines and Ieper. It was this high ground that the British fought for at the Third Battle of Ypres (see box, pages 266–7).

VANCOUVER CORNER This small garden is dominated by the statue of the **Brooding Soldier**. Carved from a single piece of solid granite, it was erected in memory of the First Canadian Division who were wiped out by a gas attack on 24 April 1915. The ferns planted round about are meant to symbolise the creeping green-tinted gas.

LANGEMARK GERMAN MILITARY CEMETERY Dotted with oak trees – the national symbol of Germany – Langemark is one of four German cemeteries left in Flanders. Originally there were 68, but many of the graves were consolidated or the bodies reinterred back home. Hitler visited the cemetery in June 1940 while Flanders was under German occupation following the Battle of France.

Inside the entrance arch, carved into oak panels, are the names of the **Student Soldiers**: university students who volunteered to join the war, but were given only six weeks' training before being sent to the Western Front – and often the worst parts.

On the other side of the gate sits a square mass grave containing the remains of 24,000 unknown soldiers and beyond this, at the back of the compound, is the statue of the **Mourning Soldiers**: four slumped figures modelled on a 1918 photograph of the Reserve Infantry Regiment 238 mourning at the graveside of their comrade (see photo). The trios of basalt crosses dotted throughout the cemetery are symbolic rather than specific.

German soldiers of the 238 Reserve Infantry Regiment mourning the death of a comrade. The second soldier from the right was killed in action two days after the photograph was taken.

BOEZINGE

Most people have heard of Passchendaele and Messines and the great battles associated with them, but few have heard of Boezinge – a small village north of Ieper on the banks of the Ieperlee canal. In April 1915, during the Second Battle of Ypres, the German army was forcing French troops back across Pilkem Ridge. The French dug in just before reaching the canal and held the Allied Line until the British 4th Division relieved them in June. They began advancing across no man's land on 6 July 1915. They sustained heavy losses, but were able to push the Allied Line forward until it was less than 100m from the Germans. General Sir Herbert Plumer claimed that 'the attack… [was] one of the great battles of the campaign'.

When the war ended, the fighting ground was left fallow and forgotten until the late 1990s when a local volunteer group of archaeologists and historians called The Diggers obtained a permit to excavate. After digging barely 1m they uncovered trenches, dugouts, thousands of artefacts and undetonated bombs (incredibly the Belgian Army still uncover 200 tonnes every year). Most poignantly, in 2002, behind the Boezinge Industrial Estate, they uncovered the remains of 120 British, German and French soldiers believed to have died in a gas attack. They lay hunched on the ground, still holding their guns and wearing their helmets. Sadly, any identifying markers such as dog tags or uniforms had long since rotted away and none could be identified. Their remains were reinterred in the surrounding cemeteries. The land will be built over soon to make way for the expansion of the estate, and if it hadn't been for The Diggers the efforts of the British 4th Division would have remained buried and forgotten.

POPERINGE

Like its neighbours, the middling-sized town of Poperinge joined the cloth trade in the 14th century and flourished until competition with Ieper forced them to bow out (see box, page 273) and resort to cultivating hops for use in the production of beer. However, it wasn't enough and the town slipped into economic depression until the 18th century when the region came under Austrian control.

Of course, Poperinge is most famously associated with World War I. Like Veurne, it was one of the few towns to remain under Allied control throughout the war and, as a result, was a haven for soldiers travelling to and from the Front Line. Troops referred to it affectionately as 'Pops'. Talbot House, in particular, became a legendary place of respite where soldiers could take much-needed rest and let off steam. The compact town, which incidentally boasts some of the best regional dishes in Flanders, makes an excellent day trip from Ieper and shouldn't be missed.

GETTING THERE AND AWAY

By car From Ieper follow the N308 west (*13.5km;* 🕘 *20min*). From Veurne follow the N8 south and when you reach the village of Oostvleteren turn right onto the N321 to Poperinge (*30km;* 🕘 *37min*).

By train Ieper (*21min past the hour Mon–Fri, 22min past the hour Sat–Sun;* 🕘 *7min*); Kortrijk (*50min past the hour Mon–Fri, 51min past the hour Sat–Sun;* 🕘 *38min*); Brugge via Kortrijk (*32min past the hour daily;* 🕘 *1hr 56min*).

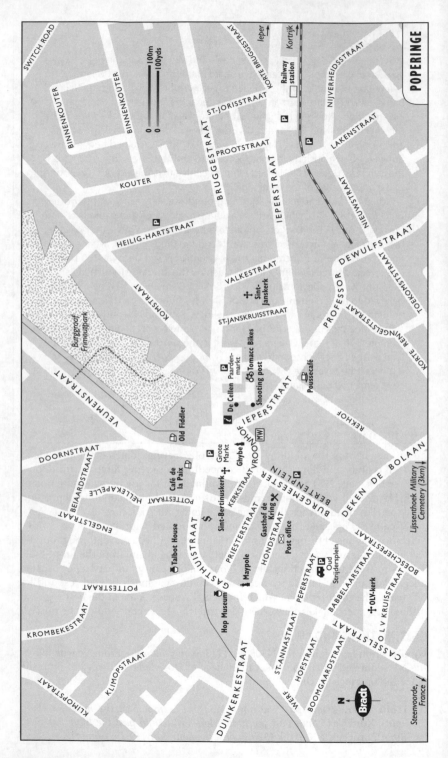

POPERINGE

TOURIST INFORMATION

ℹ Tourist information 1 Grote Markt; ☏ 057 34 66 76; e toerisme@poperinge.be; www. toerismepoperinge.be; ⊕ Apr–Sep 09.00–12.00 & 13.00–17.00 Mon–Fri, 09.00–12.00 & 13.00–16.00 Sat–Sun, Oct–Mar 09.00–12.00 & 13.00–17.00 Mon–Fri, 09.00–12.00 & 13.00–16.00 Sat. Narrow office in the basement of the Stadhuis.

⓸ Bike rental Tomacc Bikes, Paardenmarkt; ☏ 057 33 66 25; ⊕ 13.30–19.00 Mon, 08.30–12.00 & 13.30–19.00 Tue–Sat; €10/day

⌂ WHERE TO STAY, EAT AND DRINK

At the time of writing, Poperinge is the undisputed queen of regional food. In 2011 it was named Vlaanderen Lekkerland – 'most tasty town' – and won the coveted Vlaamse Streekvork (proudly displayed in the tourist information office) for the best regional dishes in Flanders.

Look out for *potjesvlees* (also known as *hennepot*), literally 'potted meat' made from boiled-down veal, chicken and rabbit; *kabeljauw aan de Schreve*, cod in a beer and cream sauce; *hopscheuten*, fresh hop shoots available between January and April; and *mazerinetaart*, a dense cinnamon-flavoured syrup-soaked cake.

⌂ **Talbot House** (10 rooms) 43 Gasthuisstraat; ☏ 057 33 32 28; www.talbothouse.be. Talbot House is steeped in history & offers a once-in-a-lifetime opportunity to stay in an authentic World War I soldiers' house. No meals are provided, but there's a fridge you can store food for b/fast in & tea- & coffee-making facilities. Just wonderful. See below for further details. €

✗ **Gasthof de Kring** 7–9 Bertenplein; ☏ 057 33 38 61; www.dekring.be; ⊕ 10.00–15.00 & 18.00–21.30 Tue–Sat, 18.00–21.30 Sun. Hotel restaurant with an unspectacular dining room & gruff owners, but it serves lots of local dishes, including *hennepot* & *mazerinetaart*. €€€

☕ **Poussecafé** 45a Ieperstraat; ☏ 057 33 32 89; ⊕ 08.00–20.00 Mon, Wed–Sun. Always busy with locals who come for the homemade *mazerinetaart* prepared in the bakery next door. Run by Kurt & his Siamese cat – which the café is named after. €

WHAT TO SEE AND DO

De Cellen (*Guido Gezellestraat;* ⊕ *09.00–17.00 daily; admission free*) Just around the corner from the Stadhuis and tucked away off the street, this courtyard is the site of a very dark chapter in British World War I history. British soldiers who refused to return to the Front Line or were caught deserting – often as a result of trauma – were held in these two cells and executed at the wooden post standing at the back of the courtyard. A priest would read them their last rites, the attending medical officer would place a white cloth over their heart and a line of six riflemen would face the accused – although only one of the guns was loaded.

Now a memorial, the cells bear five pictures of soldiers known to have been shot here. A button by the doorway triggers a chilling audio recreation of a solider being sentenced and facing the firing squad. The last execution took place on 8 May 1919.

Talbot House (*43 Gasthuisstraat, entrance via Pottestraat;* ☏ *057 33 32 28; www. talbothouse.be;* ⊕ *16 Feb–14 Nov 09.30–17.30 Tue–Sun, 15 Nov–15 Feb 13.00–17.00 Tue–Sun; admission: adult/7–18/under 7 €8/5/free, last ticket 16.30, combi ticket with Hopmuseum €10*) Talbot House is a very special living museum that was established in December 1915 by Reverend Philip Clayton – best known as 'Tubby' – and chaplain Neville Talbot as a bed and breakfast for soldiers travelling to and from the Front Line.

Tubby was born in Queensland, Australia, in 1885, but after losing their property several times to floods the family moved back to England when Tubby was two years old. He was a sharp, brilliant student, but decided to become a priest; when World War I broke out he was assigned to the 6th Division as an army chaplain and

West Flanders POPERINGE

6

posted to the Salient. He visited the trenches, or 'slums' as the called them, several times and narrowly escaped death on a number of occasions. He saw first hand the unspeakable horrors soldiers faced, so he and Talbot opened the B&B as a place of 'light, warmth and laughter', a shelter from the ugliness of war. Here soldiers could make as much noise as they liked, play card games and have an undisturbed night's sleep. Indeed, the 'real sheets' room (the General's Room) was famous as the only the room in the house with a bedsheet – a luxury which cost five francs and was the prize of many a card game. By the summer of 1917, it's estimated that 5,000 soldiers a week were passing through the house in preparation for the Third Battle of Ypres (see box, pages 266–7).

Tubby was a jovial landlord, famous for his love of humorous adages, such as 'Never judge a man by his umbrella, it might not be his', and several are pinned above the doorways. In the chapel, which sits on the fourth floor beneath the eaves, he baptised 50 soldiers, performed 800 confirmations and delivered communion to tens of thousands of soldiers.

The house is filled with original items, but the two most poignant artefacts are found in the hallway on the ground floor. The first is 'Friendship corner', a visitors' book where soldiers would leave messages for friends, or notes asking others if they knew of their whereabouts. The second is a map of the area. Poperinge and Ieper have been wiped away by the fingerprints of soldiers pointing to where they were stationed or had lost friends – you can even make out the salient, marked by a smudgy bulge.

After the war, Tubby was made an honorary citizen of Poperinge. He returned to England in March 1919, accompanied by his dog Chippy, and became the vicar of All Hallows' Church near the Tower of London.

Talbot House was, and will remain, a hugely important place of remembrance for World War I veterans, like Harry Patch – the last surviving soldier to have fought in the trenches during World War I – who visited the house before his death in 2009 and was able to sit in the same lounge chair he'd last sat in while talking to friends in 1917.

Renovations are ongoing, but take your time to wander around and soak up the atmosphere, or even spend the night (page 271).

Hopmuseum (*71 Gasthuisstraat;* ✆ *057 33 79 22; www.hopmuseum.be;* ⊕ *Mar–Nov 10.00–18.00 Tue–Fri, 14.00–18.00 Sat–Sun, closed Dec–Feb; admission: adult/6–25/under 6 €5/2.50/free, last ticket 17.00*) Poperinge sits at the centre of Hoppeland, Belgium's main hop-growing region, and until the 1960s this building was the *Stadsschaal* or municipal scales, the main headquarters for inspecting, weighing and pressing the hops. An interactive museum now explains the various stages of production.

Sint-Janskerk (*St-Janskruisstraat;* ⊕ *07.30–19.00 daily; admission free*) This Gothic church is venerated thanks to the miraculous statue of the Virgin Mary, which stands bathed in candlelight on the ornate Lady Altar on the left-hand side of the church. In 1479 a local woman, Jacquemyne Bayaerts, gave birth to a stillborn son, who had to be buried in unconsecrated ground because he wasn't baptised. Distraught, the parents prayed to the Virgin Mary and pleaded for the child to be disinterred. Three days later their wish was granted and the child was found alive. They were able to quickly baptise the infant before it died an hour later. The miracle was officially recognised by the Pope in 1481 and has been celebrated ever since at the annual Maria-Ommegang in March.

Poperinge residents are nicknamed *keikoppen*, or 'pigheads', as a mark of their stubborn refusal to stop producing linen when the city of Ieper threatened them for impinging on their trade. The statue of Ghybe riding a donkey backwards, which stands in front of Sint-Bertinuskerk, is a satirical representation of the rivalry. The jester making an – pardon the pun – ass out of the donkey represents the three clothes towns of Ieper, Gent and Brugge.

Sint-Bertinuskerk (*Vroonhof;* ☺ *09.00–18.00 daily; admission free*) This 15th-century late-Gothic church with curling blue paint on the walls has a large oak-panelled entrance which holds the organ. It contains a number of artworks, but look out for the baldachin: a white-and-gold 18th-century Rococo procession canopy in the right-hand chapel and, embedded above it, a Christmas-themed stained-glass window featuring Mary, Joseph, Jesus, the shepherds and the three wise men.

Lijssenthoek Military Cemetery (*Boescheepseweg; admission free*) One-and-a-half miles west of Poperinge, Lijssenthoek is the second-largest Commonwealth cemetery in the world, after Tyne Cot (page 268). Originally a farm, it operated as a field hospital and now contains over 10,000 tombstones. A new information centre is scheduled to open in September 2012.

Day trip

Sint-Sixtus Abbey (*www.sintsixtus.be*) Whisper 'Westvleteren' into the ear of any beer enthusiast and they'll be putty in your hands. Sat in seclusion 17km north of Poperinge, this small village is home to the revered Sint-Sixtus Abbey. Inside its walls, 29 Cistercian monks brew award-winning Trappist beers, including the elusive No 12 – repeatedly ranked as the rarest variety in the world. The recipe of this beer remains undisclosed and for a long time its production was shrouded in mystery; the unlabelled bottles are sold only from an obscure side entrance at the abbey itself.

However, visitors can find out more about the abbey in the **Claustrum** information centre (☺ *14.00–17.00 Mon–Thu, Sat & Sun)* and try the beers in the **In de Vrede** café (*12 Donkerstraat, 8640 Westvleteren;* ☏ *057 40 03 77; www.indevrede. be;* ☺ *Jul–Aug 10.00–19.00 Mon–Thu, Sat & Sun, Sep–Jun 10.00–19.00 Mon–Wed, Sat & Sun, closed 1–15 Jan, 29 Mar–6 Apr, 13–30 Sep*). Choose from the bitter blond (5.8%), the brown No 8 (8%), or the surprisingly sweet and oh-so-smooth No 12 (12%). Orders of the Abbey cheese with mustard and homemade pâté are essential nibbles to enhance the flavour of the beers. It's a great place to marvel at the old ladies who pitch up every day and knock back three or four of the No 12s. You can buy small mixed cases of the beer from the café shop, but if you join the ranks of addicts and want to get your hands on a crate then you'll have to phone the beer hotline (☏ *070 21 00 45*) well in advance; a crate of 24 bottles ranges from €30 to €39, not including the €12 deposit for the crate. The system was introduced after a queue of over 400 cars made national news in 2005. You'll be given a date and time for collection and then have to go to a side entrance located to the west of the abbey.

Getting there

By bike Poperinge tourist office sells the Hoppeland (43km; €2) cycling map which takes you past Westvleteren and Sint-Sixtus Abbey. For bike rental, see page 271.

By car From Poperinge, take the N308 west out of town and turn right onto Diepemeers/N347; after 750m turn left into Krombeekseweg and take your fourth right into Nonnenstraat; follow it round and turn left into Donkerstraat; the café is on your left (*7.7km;* ⏲ *14min*).

KORTRIJK

The course of Flemish history was changed forever in the Groeninge fields on the outskirts of Kortrijk in July 1302. A group of lightly armed Flemish foot soldiers went head to head with a calvary of professional French knights – and won. Known as the Battle of the Golden Spurs (pages 5 and 214), it was the first time in history a horseback army had been defeated by footmen and is considered by many the reason why Dutch is still spoken in Flanders today. In revenge, the city was razed by French King Charles VI in 1382 but Kortrijk bounced back by joining the clothing trade, and despite suffering severe damage during World Wars I and II it still has 200 listed monuments dotted around town.

The city is very close to the Wallonian border, and consequently is quite French with good shopping and a burgeoning café culture. The city also blends old and modern very well: from the traditional Sint-Elizabeth*begijnhof* to the seven modern bridges, which connect Buda Island to the city centre and span the newly widened River Leie.

GETTING THERE AND AWAY

By car From Gent follow the E17 southwest and take exit 2 (direction Hoog Kortrijk) and follow signs for Kortrijk Centrum (*49km;* ⏲ *36min*). From Brugge follow signs for the E40 out of town and join the E403, then follow it south for 43.8km and take exit 1; follow the R8 and take exit 12 (direction Marke) and follow Pottelberg into the centre of town (*57km;* ⏲ *45min*).

By train Gent (*9/46min past the hour daily;* ⏲ *33min*); Brugge (*7/32min past the hour daily;* ⏲ *45min*); Brussels-Zuid/Bruxelles-Midi (*41min past the hour Mon–Fri,* ⏲ *1hr 4min; 36min past the hour Sat–Sun,* ⏲*1hr 9min*); Ieper (*39min past the hour daily;* ⏲ *30min*).

TOURIST INFORMATION

🛈 Tourist information Begijnhofpark; ☏ 056 27 78 40; e toerisme@kortrijk.be; www.tourismkortrijk.be; ⏲ Apr–Sep 10.00–18.00 Mon–Fri, 10.00–17.00 Sat–Sun, Oct–Mar 10.00–17.00 daily. Brand new office & site of the 1302 history museum (page 276). They can organise a guide (€65/2hr) so you can visit the Belfort, medieval crypt & Broel Towers; book tickets for the Tasty Ticket culinary themed city walk (€7/9); & sell the local Goedendag (45km; €2) cycling map which departs from the tourist office. NB: In the

begijnhof compound you'll see a bunker with a tree growing on top; it used to be a well where the local women washed their laundry.

ﾃﾞﾞ Bike rental Tourist information centre (€12/day) – limited number. Centre Mobiel, 57 Minister Tacklaan; ☏ 056 24 99 10; ⏲ 07.00–18.50 Mon–Fri, 10.00–17.50 Sat

Markets General market, Grote Markt, Doorniksestraat & Schouwburgplein, ⏲ 08.00–12.00 Mon, 08.00–12.30 Tue; Food market, Sint-Amandsplein, ⏲ 15.00–19.00 Fri

🏠 **WHERE TO STAY, EAT AND DRINK** At the savoury end of the scale is *Kortrijkse bil* (smoked veal), but save room for the delicious *kalletaart*, apple pie flavoured with Calvados and marzipan. You'll also see *begijntjes* – nun-shaped chocolates – in the shops, but the best are sold at **Kortrijks Chocolathuis** (*35 Leiestraat;* ⏲ *09.00–*

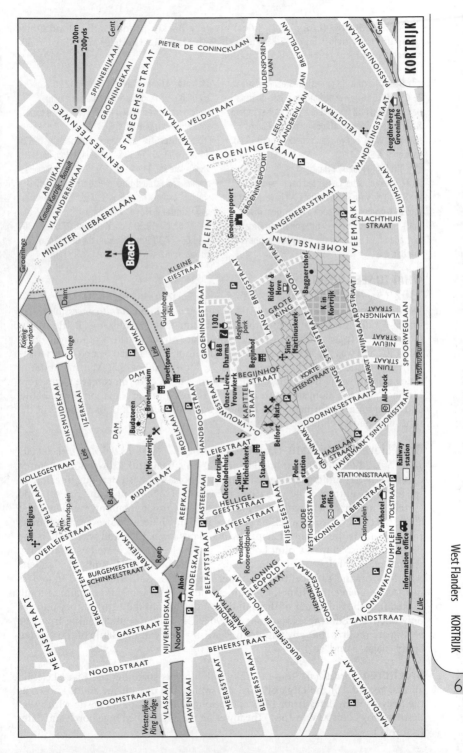

KORTRIJK

Gent

Gent

200m
200yds

SPINNERIJKAAI

GROENINGEKAAI

PIETER DE CONINCKLAAN

STASEGEMSESTRAAT

VAARTSTRAAT

VELDSTRAAT

GULDENSPOREN
LAAN

LEEUW VAN
VLANDERENLAAN

JAN BREYDELLAAN

PASSIONISTENLAAN

Gent

VELDSTRAAT

Jeugdherberg
Groeninghe

WANDELINGSTRAAT

PLUIMSTRAAT

GENTSESTEENWEG

ABDIJKAAL

VLAANDERENKAAI

Kanaal Kortrijk - Bossuit

MINISTER LIEBAERTLAAN

GROENINGELAAN

GROENINGEPOORT

Groeningepoort

LANGEMEERSSTRAAT

VEEMARKT

SLACHTHUIS
STRAAT

Groeninge

Koning
Albertpark

Dam

KLEINE
LEIESTRAAT

Guldenberg
plein

PLEIN

ROMEINSELAAN

Ridder &
Hove

Baggaertshof

K in
Kortrijk

VLAMINGEN
STRAAT

VLAMINGEN
STRAAT

College

Leie

GROENINGESTRAAT

GROENINGESTRAAT

1302

B&B
Dharma

Begijnhof
park

LANGE BRUGSTRAAT

Begijnhof

GROTE
KING

NOORD STRAAT

SPOORWEGLAAN

NIEUW
STRAAT

DIKSMUIDEKAAI

IJZERKAAI

DAMKAAI

DAM

Broeltorens

Budatoren

Broelmuseum

t'Mouterijtje

Leie

HANDBOOGSTRAAT

BROELKAAI

O.-L.-VROUWSTRAAT

Onze-Lieve-
Vrouwkerk

O.-KAPITTEL
STRAAT

BEGIJNHOF
STRAAT

Sint-
Martinuskerk

KORTE
STEENSTRAAT

LANGE STEENSTRAAT

LANGE STEENSTRAAT

WIJNGAARDSTRAAT

TUIN
STRAAT

Vlasmuseum

Leie

Buda

Buda

DAM

KAPELSSTRAAT

KOLLEGESTRAAT

KASTEELKAAI

REEPKAAI

LEIESTRAAT

Kortrijks
Chocoladehuis

Sint-
Michielskerk

Stadhuis

Belfort

Nata

DOORNIKSESTRAAT

HAZELAAR
STRAAT

GRAANMARKT

All-Stock

HAVERMARKT SINT-JORISSTRAAT

Sint-Eligius

Sint-
Amandsplein

OVERLEIESTRAAT

FABRIEKSKAAI

BUDASTRAAT

Reep

Ahoi

BELFASTSTRAAT

KASTEELSTRAAT

HELLIGE-
GEESTRAAT

President
Rooseveldtplein

RIJSELSESTRAAT

Police
station

Post
office

STATIONSSTRAAT

OUDE
VESTIGINGSSTRAAT

KONING ALBERTSTRAAT

De Lijn
information office

Railway
station

MEENSESTRAAT

REKOLLETTENSTRAAT

BURGEMEESTER
SCHINKELSTRAAT

HANDELSKAAI

NIJVERHEIDSKAAI

Noord

HENDRIK
BEHERSTRAAT

KONING
LEOPOLD I-
STRAAT

HENDRIK
CONSCIENCE
STRAAT

CONSERVATORIUMPLEIN TOLSTRAAT

Parkhotel

Casinoplein

Lille

GASSTRAAT

NOORDSTRAAT

DOORNSTRAAT

VLASKAAI

HAVENKAAI

MEERSSTRAAT

BLEKERSSTRAAT

BEHEERSTRAAT

BURGEMEESTER

MAGDALENASTRAAT

ZANDSTRAAT

Westerlijke
Ring bridge

N
Bradt

West Flanders   KORTRIJK

6

275

12.30 & 13.30–18.00 Mon–Sat). Local brewery Bockor produces the blond Omer (8%) and the Bockor lager (5.2%) as well as the Jacobins Gueuzes and Max Krieks, and there's a local *jenever* called Sint-Pol.

🏠 **B&B Dharma** (3 rooms) 18 Groeningestraat; \ 056 29 36 56; www.bedandbreakfast-dharma. be/. Beautiful B&B finished to a very high standard & decorated with one-off design pieces. Rooms have TV & Wi-Fi, but you can't check-in until 18.00. Cash only. €€€

🏠 **Ahoi** (10 rooms) 1 Handelskaai; \ 056 29 90 27; www.ahoi.be. Converted barge moored on the River Leie with simple rooms. All have en-suite capsule bathrooms, but book a large room if you can – the normals are very tight on space. Organic, fairtrade b/fast served in the funky beach-house-chic bar. €€

✗ **Nata** 4 Grote Markt; \ 056 20 12 20; ⏱ 08.00–23.00 daily. Smart brasserie with large terrace overlooking the *belfort*. Serves local speciality *Kortrijkse bil*. €€€

✗ **'t Mouterijtje** 25a Kapucijnenstraat; \ 056 20 14 14; ⏱ 11.45–14.30 & 18.00–late Mon, Tue & Fri, 18.00–late Sat, 11.45–15.15 & 17.30–late Sun. Has a wonderful vaulted-brick ceiling & menu offering scallops, prawns, frogs' legs & salads. €€€

🍴 **Ridder & Hove** 7 Voorstraat; \ 056 22 44 42; ⏱ 07.15–18.30 Mon, Wed–Sat, 07.00–12.30 & 14.00–17.30 Sun. Dishes up the best slice of *kalletaart* in town. €

WHAT TO SEE AND DO

1302 (*Begijnhofpark;* \ *056 27 78 40; www.kortrijk1302.be;* ⏱ *Apr–Sep 10.00– 18.00 Tue–Sun, Oct–Mar 10.00–17.00 Tue–Sun; admission: adult/concession/6–16/ under 6 €6/4/2.50/free*) A multimedia museum that explains the Battle of the Golden Spurs (pages 5 and 214), which took place on the outskirts of Kortrijk on 11 July 1302 and was the first time in history that foot soldiers had beaten a horseback army. The audio guide is narrated by Gilles le Muisit, Abbot of St-Martins Abbey in Tournai, who wrote the original history of the battle, and you can see pages from his book upstairs alongside spur artefacts. There's a full explanation of the battle, and background information on Gwijde van Dampiere, Count of Flanders at the time, who had 16 children.

Onze-Lieve-Vrouwekerk (*Deken Zegerplein;* ⏱ *08.00–18.00 Mon–Fri, 09.00– 18.00 Sat, 11.00–18.00 Sun; admission free*) This beautiful 13th-century Church of our Lady has undergone many repairs and boasts a lavish Baroque interior. To the left of the entrance, there's a silver memorial plaque for poet and priest Guido Gezelle; further down hangs the *Raising of the Cross* by Antoon van Dijk; and above the choir gallery is a ceiling covered in Flemish lions. However, the church's real treasure is the Counts' Chapel, which dates from 1370 and was built as the personal mausoleum of Count Lodewijk van Maele. It is decorated with stunning stained-glass windows and 18th-century murals of all the Counts of Flanders. Also look for the 14th-century alabaster statue of St Catherine stored in a glass box. As you leave the chapel, keep an eye out for the anonymous painted tomb tucked into the far corner of the building; it dates from the 15th century but was only uncovered during excavations in 1963. The golden spurs hanging from the ceiling are replicas, but pay tribute to Flemish victory in the Battle of the Golden Spurs (pages 5 and 214).

Broeltoren (*Broelkaai*) These chunky watchtowers spanning the River Leie are all that remains of the city's original city walls. The one on the right, known as the Speye Tower, dates from 1385 and belonged to the Count's castle which was destroyed by Louis XIV in 1684. The tower on the left is called Ingelborch and dates from 1413.

Broelmuseum (*6 Broelkaai;* ✆ *056 27 77 80; www.kortrijk.be/musea;* ⏱ *10.00–12.00 & 14.00–17.00 Tue–Fri, 11.00–17.00 Sat–Sun; admission: adult/ concession/13–26/under 12 €3/2/1/free, includes audio guide*) This creaky 18th-century mansion which overlooks the River Leie houses a museum that displays an interesting collection of art created by Kortrijk locals. Highlights include Roeland Savery's 16th-century *Plundering van een dorp* ('Plunder of a village'); the 19th-century *Bevroren Leie in Kortrijk*, which depicts Sint-Maartenskerk and the Broel Towers and was painted by Louis Pierre Verwee; Vincent de Vos' huge oil painting *Rest after the hunt*; Constantin Meunier's haunting and sombre *Begrafenis van een Trappist* ('Burial of a Trappist monk'); Robbe Louis' *Grazende Koeien* featuring anatomically correct cows and similar paintings of sheep by his pupil Edward Woutermaertens; and Roger Ravel's modern *Ruimte in her Atelier* ('Space in a studio'). Definitely worth a detour.

Stadhuis (*54 Grote Markt;* ⏱ *Jul–Aug 15.00–17.00 Tue, Thu & Sat; admission free*) The richly decorated 15th-century town hall is studded with sculptures of the Counts of Flanders. Inside, its Schepenzaal (Aldermen's Hall) and Raadzaal (Council Chamber) have impressive chimneys, but these can only be visited with a guide.

Belfort (*Grote Markt*) Unusually, Kortrijk's belfry stands alone in the middle of the Grote Markt; a squat red-brick affair that dates from the 13th century. It belonged to the cloth hall which was destroyed in 1944 and still houses a 48-bell carillon. At the top stand Kalle and Manten, the hourly bell ringers.

Sint-Elizabethbegijnhof (*Begijnhof;* ⏱ *summer 07.00–21.00 daily, winter 07.00–20.00 daily; admission free*) Kortrijk's *begijnhof* is one of my favourites: a totally secluded cobblestone enclave full of nooks and crannies to explore. Be sure to visit the 15th-century Kapel Sint-Matthews (*2 Begijnhof;* ⏱ *13.00–17.00 Tue–Sun*) with its rich interior and gold chandeliers. Its adjoining museum is closed for renovation until 2014, but there's a small room behind the welcome desk displaying old photos. Silver medallions and candles are on sale if you'd like to make an offering.

Sint-Maartenskerk (*Sint-Maartenskerkstraat;* ⏱ *07.30–18.00 Mon–Fri, 10.00–18.00 Sat–Sun; admission free*) A pretty 15th-century church with an intricately carved entrance and 83m-high Brabantine-Gothic tower. Near the entrance hang ten modern paintings depicting the life of St Martin, as described by his biographer Sulpicius Severus, and numerous paintings completed by students from the school of Rubens. The treasury in St-Eligius Chapel (⏱ *Apr–Aug Sun afternoons*) displays 16th-century textiles and a silver collection spanning three centuries.

Baggaertshof (*37 Sint-Jansstraat;* ⏱ *14.00–18.00 Tue–Thu & Sat–Sun; admission free*) This miniature *begijnhof* was established in 1638 and contains its original row of 17th-century cottages – one of which houses a lace workshop – and a medicinal herb garden littered with womanly sculptures in various stages of repose. A real hidden gem. Pause and take a whiff of the rosemary-scented air.

Groeningepoort and monument (*Plein*) The Groeninge Gate looks older, but was installed in 1908 to commemorate the Battle of the Golden Spurs. Follow the path through the park and you'll come to the gilded Groeninge monument of Flanders' virgin – a symbol of freedom – keeping a lion at bay.

Vlasmuseum (*4 Etienne Sabbelaan;* \ *056 21 01 38; www.vlasmuseum.be;* ⊕ *Mar–Nov 09.00–12.30 & 13.30–18.00 Tue–Fri, 14.00–18.00 Sat–Sun; admission: adult/concession/13–26/under 12 €3/2/1/free, inc audio guide*) Kortrijk is one of the few 'linen towns' that still produces textiles, and this flax museum, 2.5km south of town, was established to honour that history. Housed in an authentic 19th-century flax farm, it has life-size models performing the various cultivation and processing techniques and displays of unique lace and linen. Bus #13 from Kortrijk railway station departs every 20 minutes and stops outside the museum (⊕ *10min*).

Vannestes Molen (*Abdijmolenweg, 8510 Marke;* ⊕ *Apr–Sep 14.00–17.00 Tue, Thu & Sun; admission: adult/6–12/under 6 €2/0.50/free*) This windmill dates from 1841 and was used to grind grain and press flax seeds for linseed oil. It now contains a bakery museum. You can cycle there – see the Goedendag cycling map – or take bus #83 (*22min past the hour, every hour*) from Kortrijk railway station and get off at Marke, Vannestesmolen (€2.40 return; free if you return within 1hr).

ROESELARE

Roeselare is a commercial town where even the locals are nicknamed *Nieuwmarkters* because of their love of shopping. The city centre is pleasant enough, but the highlight is the dynamic WieMu cycling museum. Frustratingly, all the other interesting sights, such as Kasteel van Rumbeke and Brouwerij Rodenbach, can only be visited as part of a large group.

GETTING THERE AND AWAY
By car From Kortrijk follow the E403 north and take exit 7 (direction Izegem) (*24km;* ⊕ *21min*).

By train Kortrijk (*on the hour/48min past the hour Mon–Fri, 2/48min past the hour Sat–Sun;* ⊕ *18min*).

TOURIST INFORMATION
🔳 **Tourist information** 35 Oostraat; \ 015 26 96 00; e toerisme@roeselare.be; www.roeselare. be; ⊕ 09.00–12.30 & 13.30–17.00 Mon–Fri.

The old post office now houses the large, modern tourist information office; at the w/end you'll need to visit the Wielermuseum.

WHAT TO SEE AND DO
Sint-Michielskerk (*Sint-Michelsplein;* \ *051 26 96 00;* ⊕ *Jun–Sep 09.00–11.00 & 14.30–18.00 Mon–Fri, Oct–May 09.00–11.30 daily; admission free*) This 18th-century church houses a handful of art treasures, including the tomb of 17th-century Flemish painter Jan van Cleef and his wife, and the largest organ in West Flanders, which is put to use every Thursday at the weekly **carillon concert** (⊕ *20.30–21.30*).

Wielermuseum (WieMu) (*15 Polenplein;* \ *015 26 87 40; www.wiemu.be;* ⊕ *10.00–17.00 Tue–Sat; admission: adult/12–26/under 12 €5/1/free*) For cycling enthusiasts this must-see museum covers the history of the sport in Flanders, has a collection of the earliest bikes (including penny-farthings), an old-fashioned bicycle workshop where saddles and bike frames are forged and a room dedicated to cycling legend and world champion Jean-Pierre Monseré. Known as 'Jempi', the Roeselare native was killed in a collision with a car while racing in 1971.

7

Antwerp

Home to over 1.7 million people, Antwerp is Flanders' most populous region and shares its northern border with the Netherlands. Most of the action is weighted in the west, where the dynamic city of Antwerp clusters around its enormous port and, a little to the south, the underrated city of Mechelen. Move eastwards and you enter the Kempen, a relatively undeveloped region of moors and woodland, which is popular with walkers and cyclists following the *Provincie Antwerp* cycling route. Laid across this landscape are the small towns of Turnhout, Herentals and Geel. And not forgetting adorable Lier with its famous Zimmer clocktower.

ANTWERP

Belgium's second-biggest city has bite, verve and a seductive carefree vibe that gives it a lead in the 'best city' stakes. Similar in many ways to the Dutch towns just across the border, its open-minded attitude is summed up in one version of the city's coat of arms, which features a nude male and female with wooden clubs slung over their shoulders. Its residents are incredibly proud of their northern 'metropolis' and they are justified in their boasting: it was here that Sir Thomas More conceived his *Utopia*, that William Tyndale wrote the first English translation of the Old Testament, and where the world's first stock exchange was established. The world headquarters of diamond processing; the tramping ground of revered fashion designers, like the Antwerp Six; and home turf of Europe's greatest Baroque artist, Pieter Paul Rubens – Antwerp is an accomplished cultural city.

Laid out like an inverted 'C', the city cuddles its Scheldt River port with the medieval centre 'De Leien' at its heart, followed by the 19th-century neighbourhoods, which are separated from the outer 1960s' housing developments and the city's parks by the ring-road motorway. The central area is split into 12 neighbourhoods, each with a slightly different character, from the rough red-light district in Schippersquartier to the Art Nouveau and Art Deco architecture along Cogels-Osylei street in Zurenborg.

HISTORY Antwerp was settled during the 4th century by the Germanic Franks – a group of united Germanic tribes under forced conscription by the Romans. By the time the Empire's clutch in the north began to weaken around AD500, the tribes had built a fortified town. This was destroyed by the Vikings in AD836 and expansion was limited until the end of the 15th century, when the town suddenly began to blossom. The Zwin canal that fed trade to Brugge had begun to silt up and as a result sea traffic was forced north to Antwerp. This move was backed by Maximilian I, who snubbed the cloth town of Brugge and instead patronised the burgeoning port town. Within 25 years, over a hundred ships a day were passing through the port and more than 2,000 carts laden with pepper, silver and silks were

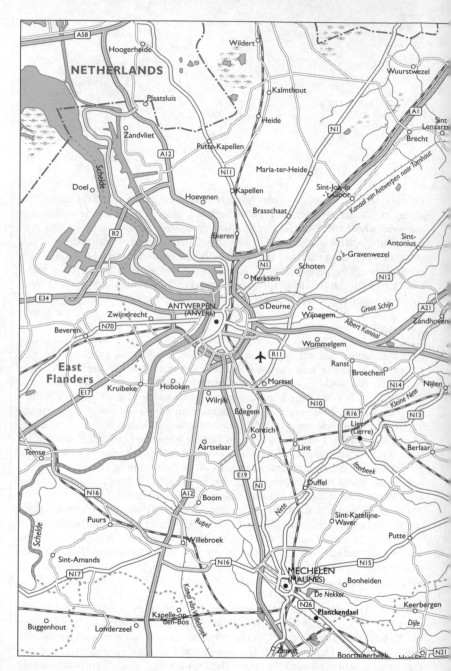

being unloaded at the docks. Foreign and domestic trading companies had moved their headquarters here and rich families set up home, building grand mansions. All flocked to the new 'centre of international economy'. The new-found wealth attracted the best artists and scientific minds of the day, including Pieter Brueghel and cartographer Gerardus Mercator.

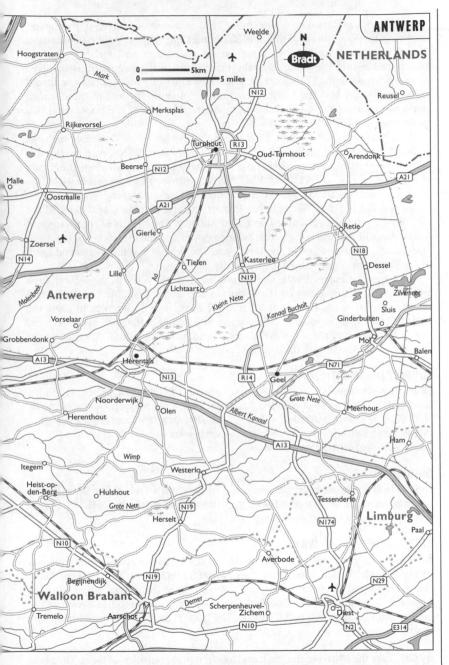

This 'golden age' came to a halt less than a century later, when Philip II came to power. He was appalled by the Reformation riots sweeping through the Netherlands at the time and when Protestants destroyed the inside of the city cathedral during an Ommegang Procession in 1566, Philip sent in his troops and the Inquisition to banish or hang participants. After nine years the unpaid

Spanish troops mutinied on 4 November 1576 and went on a three-day rampage, known as the Spanish Fury, that left 800 homes burned and over 8,000 citizens dead. They were expelled, but returned six years later and forced Antwerp's incorporation into the Spanish Netherlands. Part of the negotiations involved Antwerp becoming a Catholic city, and thousands of Protestants were forced across the border into the United Provinces (Holland). The loss of these skilled workers weakened the city's economy further and by 1800 the population had fallen from 100,000 to just 42,000.

There was a slight revival in 1609 when the Twelve Years' Truce between the United Provinces and the Spanish Netherlands was signed. However, during this period the Dutch increased their hold over the waterways and when the Treaty of Munster (part of the Peace of Westphalia agreement) was signed in 1648, the newly independent Dutch closed the Scheldt to all foreign shipping. The agreement ended the Thirty Years' War between Protestants and Catholics, but sounded the economic death toll for Spanish-controlled Antwerp. The city didn't regain some of its glory until 1797, when Napoleon came to power and the French rebuilt sections of the docks for use as a military naval base. The Scheldt was finally opened again in 1863 and Antwerp regained its prosperity.

The city was occupied by the Germans in both World Wars. In the second, their army was finally forced out by the British in September 1944, but bomber planes returned to batter the port with V1 and V2 missiles in an attempt to sever the trade links bringing supplies to Allied soldiers. Amazingly, the port remained fairly intact, but the rest of the city was devastated and had to be rebuilt. After the war, it rose to become the world's third-largest port.

TOURIST INFORMATION

i Tourist information [287 C2] 13 Grote Markt; ✆ 03 232 01 03; www.visitantwerpen. be; ⊕ 09.00–17.45 Mon–Sat, 09.00–16.45 Sun. They run historic walks in English every weekend (every day Jul–Aug), departing from outside the office at 11.00. Tickets adult/under 12 €5/2.50. The office can also arrange private guided tours at €65/2hrs, though you'll need to give a couple of weeks' notice.

GUIDED TOURS

Antwerp by Bike 40 Kronenburgstraat; www. antwerpbybike.be. Offer 3hr 18km guided bike tours that visit all the main sights. Departures Jul–Sep every Sat & Sun at 13.45 from Steenplein (near Flandria kiosk); adult/under 12 €16/13.

GETTING THERE AND AWAY

By train Brugge (*18min past the hour Mon–Fri, direct 5min past the hour Sat–Sun;* ⊕ *1hr 25min*); Brussel-Noord/Bruxelles-Nord (*5/14/37/42min past the hour Mon–Fri, 8/42min past the hour Sat–Sun;* ⊕ *40min*); Gent (*5/16/47min past the hour Mon–Fri, 16/33min past the hour Sat–Sun;* ⊕ *50min*). Antwerp has two mainline railway stations, Berchem and Centraal. The latter is the one you want for the city centre.

By car Take the E40 from the coast and follow it to the outskirts of Gent. Then take exit 9 and follow signs for the E17. Take exit 5a for Antwerp city centre.

GETTING AROUND Antwerp has an integrated bus, métro and tram system. A flat-rate one-way ticket on any part of the city's transport system costs €2; a 24hr pass (*dagpas*) €5.

By tram Trams #2 and #15 (direction Linkeroever) depart from just outside Centraal Station to the city centre (stop: Groenplaats).

🏠 **WHERE TO STAY** Antwerp has a huge choice of central hotels and a good selection of B&Bs. Those of most interest are listed below, but a full list can be found at www.bedandbreakfast-antwerp.com. However, where Antwerp really excels is in budget accommodation. It boasts a handful of excellent independent hostels, and good campsites, including the new **Zomer Camping** [284–5 E2] (*Kempenstraat;* m *0483 66 20; www.zomercampingantwerpen.be;* ⊕ *1 Jul–12 Sep*) which should open every summer if it proves a success.

Luxury

🏠 **De Witte Lelie** [287 F1] (11 rooms) 16–18 Keizerstraat; ✆ 03 226 19 66; www. dewittelelie.be. Quite rightly a member of the Small Luxury Hotels of the World, the White Lily occupies a 17th-century mansion & has a rich interior with fresh flowers everywhere. Rooms & suites feature queen- or king-size beds & Hermès bath products. Personal guide/shopper, limo service & pets welcome – darling. B/fast €25, but when you're spending this much why not upgrade to the €35 champagne b/fast! €€€€€

🏠 **Huis Ergo** [284–5 C4] (3 rooms) 16 Venusstraat; ✆ 03 292 66 00; www. huis-ergo.be. Owners Kenneth & Robert have painstakingly restored this patrician house, whose spacious, light, bright rooms combine classic & contemporary design features. Chantilly is the smallest of the 3, the Florentine has its own fireplace & the Jules suite has an elegant free-standing bathtub. There's a heated swimming pool in the basement & they can book a guided tour with the suave & moustachioed Tanguy Ottomer – one of Antwerp's best city guides. €€€€–€€€€€

Upmarket

🏠 **Home@Feek** [284–5 C4] (3 rooms) 52 Klapdorp; ✆ 03 485 82 84; http://home.feek. be. A vivacious B&B/showroom for Frederik van Heereveld's über-contemporary furniture. The Luxe & Executive suites each have a private Jacuzzi, while the smaller Standard has views over the city. The Luxe suite, in particular, takes your breath away with 3 mezzanine levels & a private terrace. Bike rental €5/day. €€€–€€€€

🏠 **Hotel Les Nuits** [284–5 C6] (24 rooms) 12 Lange Gasthuisstraat; ✆ 03 225 02 04; www. hotellesnuits.be. Brand new design hotel with faultless rooms which (quirkily) range from Solo

Slim to Just Friends. Mainly black & white with lots of high-gloss surfaces & shiny tiles. A sauna, steam room & the Flamant Dining restaurant are also on site. €€€–€€€€

Mid-range

🏠 **Atelier 20** [284–5 B4] (2 rooms) 20 Sint-Paulusstraat; m 0479 74 14 55; www.atelier20. be. Aparthotel with brilliant central location, right in the shadow of Sint-Pauluskerk. The 2 all-white shabby chic suites are very homely & equipped with Wi-Fi, huge flatscreen TV, tea & coffee facilties & share a small garden. Owners Nathalie & Paul bring you a lovely continental b/fast every morning. Word of these great suites has spread quickly, so book well in advance. Cash only. €€€

🏠 **Banks** [287 C4] (70 rooms) 55 Steenhouwersvest; ✆ 03 232 40 02; www. hotelbanks.com. Just 3min from the Grote Markt, this wonderful über-modern art hotel refreshes its collection every 2 months. Albeit well equipped, the Compact & Economy rooms are very small so upgrade If you can to the more spacious Backyard or Square View rooms. Better still are the Executives with either private sauna or rooftop terrace. Bathrooms are glass capsules embedded into the rooms. Excellent price/quality. €€€

🏠 **The Black** [284–5 B7] (5 rooms) 113 Amerikalei; ✆ 03 298 42 98; www. hoteltheblack.be. Run by interior designer Kim Soeffers, this minimalist all black-&-white hotel is a real bobby dazzler. The open-plan rooms each have a free-standing claw-foot bath in the middle of them. Oozes luxury. €€€

🏠 **Yellow Submarine** [284–5 C3] (2 rooms) 51 Falconplein; m 0475 59 59 83; www. yellowsubmarine.be. Very close to the new MAS museum, this fun B&B has 2 luxury rooms with huge baths & rain showers. Its sits above a coffee shop of the same name, but the owner Elke is

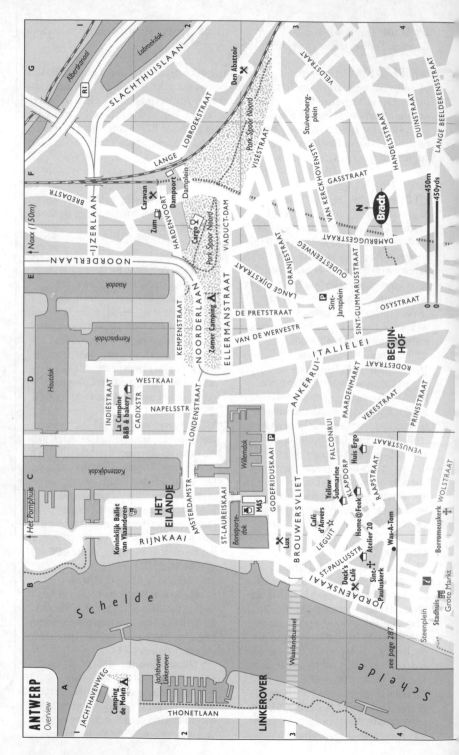

ANTWERP
Overview

Schelde

LINKEROVER

Camping de Molen ⚑

Jachthaven Linkeroever

JACHTHAVENWEG

THONETLAAN

Waaslandtunnel

see page 287

Het Pomphuis

Koninklijk Ballet van Vlaanderen ♫

HET EILANDJE

RIJNKAAI

AMSTERDAMSTR

ST-LAUREISKAAI

Bonapartedok

Willemdok 🅿

Lux ✗

Café d'Anvers ★

LEGUIT

GODEFRIDUSKAAI

Home@Feek ★

Atelier 20

Yellow Submarine

KLAPDORP

Huis Ergo

FALCONRUI

Dock's Café ✗

Sint-Pauluskerk ✝

ST-PAULUSSTR

JORDAENSKAAI

BROUWERSVLIET

Was-A-Tom ●

RAAPSTRAAT

PAARDENMARKT

ANKERRUI

ITALIËLEI

VEKESTRAAT

RODESTRAAT

PRINSSTRAAT

VENUSSTRAAT

WOLSTRAAT

Borromeuskerk ✝

Grote Markt

Stadhuis 🏛

Steenplein

i

BEGIJN-HOF

RODESTRAAT

SINT-GUMMARUSSTRAAT

OSYSTRAAT

Sint-Jansplein 🅿

VAN DE WERVESTR

DE PRETSTRAAT

Lange Dijkstraat

ELLERMANSTRAAT

LANGE DIJKSTRAAT

ORANJESTRAAT

OUDESTEENWEG

DAMBRUGGESTRAAT

OSYSTRAAT

VAN KERCKHOVENSTR

GASSTRAAT

N

Bradt

HANDELSSTRAAT

DUINSTRAAT

LANGE BEELDEKENSSTRAAT

VELDSTRAAT

Stuivenbergplein

Den Abattoir ✗

Pork Spoor Noord

VISÉSTRAAT

LOBROEKSTRAAT

SLACHTHUISLAAN

Lobroekdok

Albertkanaal

R1

Damplein

Dampoort

LANGE

HARDENVOORT

Caravan ⚑

Zum 🍴

Cargo 🍴

Pork Spoor Noord

VIADUCT-DAM

NOORDERLAAN

KEMPENSTRAAT

Zomer Camping ⚑

Noorderlaan

NOORDERLAAN

IJZERLAAN

BREDASTR

← Noxx (150m)

E

Asiadok

Kempischdok

Houtdok

D

INDIÉSTRAAT

La Campine B&B & bakery

CADIXSTR

WESTKAAI

NAPELSSTR

LONDENSTRAAT

Kattendijkdok

C

Het Pomphuis →

MAS 🏛

B

A

Schelde

0 450m
0 450yds

284

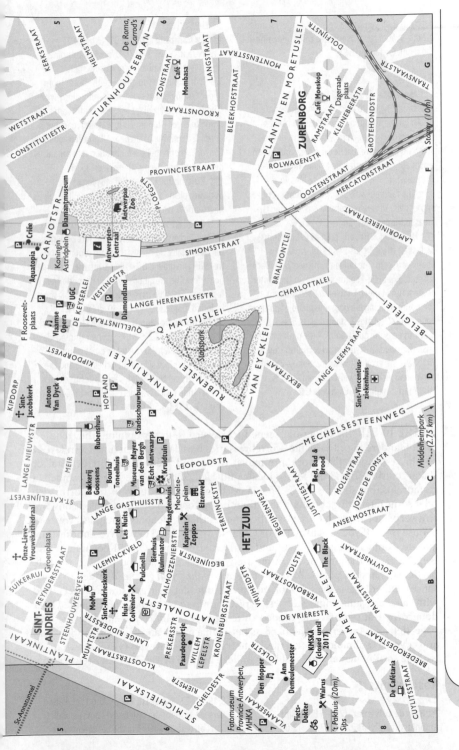

285

happy to spoil you with a delicious made-to-order brekkie in your room. Nespresso coffee machine in the room. Cash only. €€€

Budget

🏠 **Matelote** [287 B2] (11 rooms) 11a Haarstraat; ☎ 03 201 88 00; www.hotel-matelote. be. An intimate boutique hotel that combines 16th-century architecture with modern décor. Standard rooms are functional & pleasant, but the reasonably priced suites are a huge improvement. The all-white Junior suites & Suite Matelote up in the fabulous oak-beamed eaves are very impressive. All very welcoming & cosy when the fire is roaring in the lounge. €€–€€€

🏠 **Bed, Bad & Brood** [284–5 C7] (3 rooms) 43 Justitiestraat; ☎ 03 248 15 39; www. bbantwerp.com. The brilliantly named 'Bed, Bath & Bread' is a Belle-Époque mansion in the centre of town run Marleen Engelen & Koen Ribbens. The entire building is a gorgeous blend of parquet floors, stucco ceilings & stained glass. The 3 spacious en-suite guestrooms – the pink-Stucco Sissi, the Swedish-style Gustav & English-country Victoria – are excellent value for money. Victoria is joined to Vicky – a twin-bed room for kids. Minimum 2-night stay. Cash only €€.

Shoestring

🏠 **La Campine** [284–5 D1] (6 beds) 53 Cadixstraat; ☎ 03 293 59 80; www.lacampine. be. It's a steep climb up very narrow stairs to the 3rd floor, but once you get there the dorm room above Campine bakery is wonderfully hippy with 6 beds reached via giant ladders, a bathroom home to a free-standing tub, washing machine & dryer, & a communal kitchen. All proceeds go to Convoi Exceptionnel – a foundation that organises neighbourhood events. Dorm bed €15. €

🏠 **Pulcinella** [284–5 B6] (48 rooms) 1 Bogaardeplein; ☎ 03 234 03 14; www.vjh.be. Sleek new black-&-white minimalist hostel. A mix of 2-, 4- & 6-bed en-suite dorms with individual reading lights & lockers. Female-only dorms too. Designer bar downstairs, no kitchen, TV room coming soon, free Wi-Fi on ground & 1st floor & internet terminals, no curfew. Theatre groups occasionally perform in b/fast room. Disabled traveller friendly. B/fast & sheets included. Dorms €22, sgl €35.50, dbl €53. €

🏕 **Camping De Molen** [284–5 A1] (72 places) Thonetlaan; ☎ 03 219 81 79; www.camping-de-molen.be; ⊕ Apr–Sep. A leafy, quiet campsite that sits the other side of the Scheldt, facing the historic city centre. Facilities are basic but clean & the St-Anna beach is a short stroll north. €4/tent, adult/3–12 €3/1.50. €

🍴 **WHERE TO EAT** The eating-out scene in Antwerp is, in my opinion, the trendiest of all Flanders' big cities. Time-worn brasseries have largely been ditched in favour of hip restaurants that sport minimalist décor and menus that flirt oriental or Italian cuisine. The Grote Markt locale and Het Zuid have the largest number of restaurants, but streets such as Spanjaardsteeg, near the docks in the north, also offer some interesting options. The listings below focus on Belgian food options, but Antwerp's hotch-potch of nationalities means there's plenty of foreign flavours to choose from. If you're hankering for Chinese or Thai head to van Wesenbekestraat and de Coninckplein; for Italian and Turkish stroll down Oude Koornmarkt and Pelgrimstraat. The city's position on the river means it's a good place to try fish, particularly oysters and the Antwerp favourite *palingen in groene saus* (eels in green sauce). Other local edibles to look out for include *filet d'Anvers* (smoked beef cured with salt, herbs and juniper berries), typical fair food *smoutebollen* (fermented beer dough fried in pork fat and dipped in icing sugar), *Antwerpse handjes* (see box, page 289) and *Antwerps gebak* (a cross between a biscuit and cake with apricot jam and covered in almonds). Local tipples to try are Elixir d'Anvers (yellow spirit made with 32 sorts of herbs) and local beer Bolleke brewed by De Koninck Brewery.

Restaurants

Expensive

🍴 **Huis de Colvenier** [284–5 B6] 8 Sint-Antoniusstraat; ☎ 03 226 65 73; ⊕ 12.00–15.00 & 19.00–22.00 Tue–Fri, 19.00–22.00 Sat. Eating here is a treat for the tastebuds – not the wallet. Start off with an aperitif in the basement wine

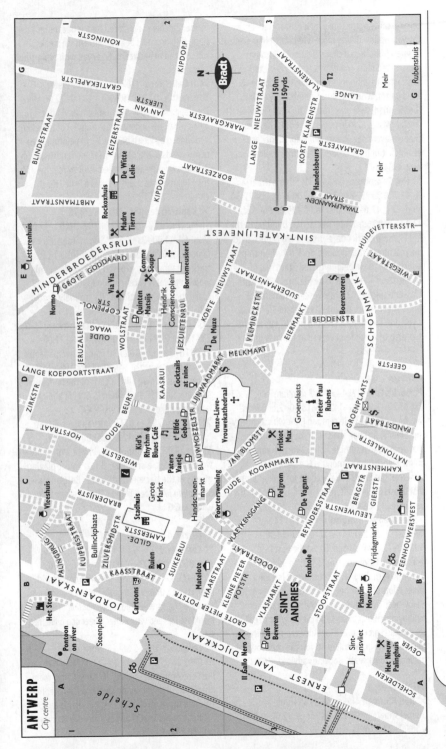

ANTWERP
City centre

Scheldē

N

Bradt

150m
150yds

cellar – some bottles are over a century old. Enter the yolk-yellow dining room where the elegance of finely upholstered chairs & smooth Baroque music serenading you from speakers is in stark contrast with enormous paintings of cabbages & a red parrot. When the sun is shining, try & sit in the Victorian-style glasshouse: the white linen & crystal glasses sparkle under the light. The menu changes every day. Reservations for dinner are essential, but try your luck at lunchtime. Dress your best. €€€€€

✗ **Het Pomphuis** [284–5 B1] Siberiastraat; ☎ 03 770 86 25; ⏰ 12.00–15.00 & 18.00–22.30 Mon–Thu, 12.0–15.00 & 18.00–23.00 Fri–Sat, 12.00–22.00 Sun. This spectacular building in the Het Eilandje district dates from 1920 & once held the machinery that drained dock #7 when ships – including those belong to Red Star Line, of *Titanic* fame – came in to be maintained. A chic brasserie since 2002, it serves an equal mix of fish & meat dishes despite its dockside location. If you don't want to spend too much, opt for the 3-course €45 set menu served at lunch & dinner. €€€€–€€€€€

Above average
✗ **Dock's Café** [284–5 B4] 7 Jordaenskaai; ☎ 03 226 63 30; ⏰ 12.00–14.30 & 18.00–23.00 Mon–Sat. An industrial-style seafood joint with a chunky (but trendy) interior filled with copper & bronze that's meant to resemble a ship. Worth trying on the French/Italian menu is the Dock's Café casserole, but locals usually come for the oyster bar that boasts 8 eight different sorts & is hailed as the best in town. €€€€

✗ **Het Nieuw Palinghuis** [287 A4] 14 Sint-Jansvliet; ☎ 03 231 74 45; ⏰ 12.00–14.30 & 18.00–22.00 Wed–Sun. Rated the best fish restaurant in Belgium by *Guide des Connoisseurs*, this no-frills traditional fish restaurant has long tables & lots of customers. Owner Erik Haentjens is elbow-deep in the running of the restaurant from scrubbing shellfish to advising clients what to eat. Try the eel in green sauce (an Antwerp speciality) & spend a penny in the toilets so you can check out the traditional toilet seats. Bookings advised. €€€€

Mid-range
✗ **Den Abattoir** [284–5 G3] 65 Lange Lobroekstraat; ☎ 03 271 08 71; ⏰ 12.00–14.30 & 18.00–22.00 Mon–Fri, 18.00–22.00 Sat. This

former butcher's was closed for a while, but is now back, dishing up its beloved ultra-fresh steaks & ribs, cooked to perfection & served with piping-hot *frites*. €€€

✗ **Il Gallo Nero** [287 A3] 36 Grote Pieter Potstraat; ☎ 03 231 19 60; ⏰ 18.00–22.00 Mon, Thu–Sun. This kooky & romantic Italian joint is run by a husband-&-wife team. A handful of tables are surrounded by kitsch photos & old paintings, & a piano stands in the corner. The food is quite simply delicious & you're well looked after by Milanese Mr Nero (who speaks only Italian & a little French). €€€

✗ **Kapitein Zeppos** [284–5 C6] 78 Vleminckveld; ☎ 03 231 17 89; ⏰ 10.00–22.00 Mon–Fri, 11.00–23.00 Sat–Sun. Named after a famous 1960s' cartoon hero, this off-the-beaten-track restaurant has exposed brick walls, chunky wooden tables & excellent food. The *dagschotel* (daily special), in particular, is extremely good value for money. Cash only. €€€

✗ **'t Pakhuis** [284–5 A7] 76 Vlaamsekaai; ☎ 03 238 12 40; ⏰ 11.00–22.00 Mon–Thu, 11.00–23.00 Fri–Sat, 12.00–21.30 Sun. Antwerp's family-run brewery serves hearty Belgian classics that you can wash down with a glass of the homemade Antwerp blond (5.1%), bruin (5.5%) or almighty Nen Bangelijke (9.5%) beers. €€€

✗ **Walrus** [284–5 A7] 2 Jan van Beersstraat; ☎ 03 238 39 93; ⏰ 12.00–22.00 Mon–Fri, 11.00–22.00 Sat–Sun. Calm *eetcafé* with simple wooden tables, a small bar & jazz music playing quietly in the background. Serves Belgian classics like *paling in t'groen* & the €10 *dagschotel* is good value. €€€

Cheap and cheerful
✗ **Caravan** [284–5 F2] 17 Damplein; ☎ 03 297 68 52; ⏰ 10.00–21.00 Mon–Wed & Sun, 10.00–23.00 Thu–Sat. Vintage-style *eetcafé* with open kitchen that puts together picnic hampers, & is famous for its weekend *koppijn ontbijt* ('hangover breakfast') served with either a beer or a painkiller! €€

✗ **Carrod's** [284–5 G6] 18 Krugerplein; ☎ 0498 06 23 21; ⏰ 18.00–23.00 Mon–Sat. I can't recommend this tiny 10-table living-room restaurant highly enough. Owner & chef Stephanie Wouters shops, cooks & serves her clients a 3-course menu that changes every day & costs a bargain €15. €€

✕ **Stanny** [284–5 F8] 1 Stanleystraat;✆ 03 289 54 67; ⊕ 11.00–03.00 Mon–Fri, 17.00–03.00 Sat, closed Jul–Aug during summer hols. Locals are always recommending this café to me. Once a run-down drinking hole, it was transformed into a homely neighbourhood haunt by a young local couple who smartened it up with a lick of paint & started serving generous portions of wholesome food. 3 specials & a couple of soups are on offer each day. €€

✕ **Via Via** [287 E1/2] 43 Wolstraat;✆ 03 226 47 49; ⊕ 11.30–22.30 Mon–Sat, 15.00–22.30 Sun. Branches of this welcoming traveller's café can be found in Arusha (Tanzania), Dakar (Senegal), Zanzibar & Buenos Aires. Tibetan flags line the bar, foreign banknotes are stuck to pillars & there's a big world map on the back wall. Serves a great selection of international dishes at traveller-friendly prices. €€

Cafés

⌓ **Bakkerij Goossens** [284–5 C5] 31 Korte Gasthuisstraat;✆ 03 226 07 91; ⊕ 07.00–19.00 Tue–Sat. In situ for over 121 years, the city's oldest bakery makes Antwerp speciality *roggeverdommeke*, a dark rye bread stuffed with raisins. Give them a quick wave of your Antwerp Museum Card & they should deduct 10% off your bill.

⌓ **De Cafétaria** [284–5 A8] 21 Montignystraat;✆ 03 294 45 70; ⊕ 09.00–18.00 daily. Shabby-chic café with paper butterflies strewn across the bar & plenty of magazines for reading. Serves healthy sandwiches, milkshakes, pastries & excellent coffee. Terrace with rainbow-coloured tables & chairs in summer.

Shoestring

✕ **Comme Soupe** [287 E2] 11 Hendrik Conscienceplein;✆ 03 234 35 33; ⊕ 11.30–17.00 Mon–Fri, 11.30–18.00 Sat. A friend in the know recommended this cute-as-a-button rustic bar, where the patron, Charlotte, cooks up 3 different soups every day & prepares sandwiches too. €

✕ **Fritkot Max** [287 C3] 12 Groenplaats; ⊕ 12.00–00.00 Mon–Thu & Sun, 12.00–03.00 Fri–Sat. Hankering for some starch & salt? This *fritkot* has being going for donkeys years & still serves the best chips in town. €

✕ **Madre Tierra** [287 E1] 47 Minderbroedersrui;✆ 03 232 42 40; ⊕ 10.00–17.00 Mon, 08.00–17.00 Tue–Thu, 08.00–16.00 Fri. Arty veggie *eetcafé* run by Sandra & Linda with slap-dash painted chairs & cupboards & a yummy selection of pastas, soups & sandwiches. €

⌓ **La Campine** [284–5 D1] 55 Cadixstraat;✆ 03 293 59 80; ⊕ 08.00–20.00 Mon–Fri, 09.00–20.00 Sat, 10.00–20.00 Sun. I was chuffed to bits when I discovered this organic bakery owned by Rosy Simoens, with blue mosaic floor tiles, loaves of bread stacked on traditional wooden dressers, handwritten labels for homemade quiches & cakes. Try their bread & butter pudding & fresh ginger tea. Also has a great hostel upstairs (page 286).

⌓ **Normo** [287 E1] 30 Minderbroedersrui; ⊕ 10.00–19.00 Mon–Sat. Quickly becoming *the* coffee shop to hang out in, Normo is rough around the edges & owned by a guy called Jens, who takes his coffee very seriously. He roasts the beans on site

ANTWERPSE HANDJES

Legend has it that Antwerp was named after a grisly battle between a giant and a Roman centurion. Back then, traffic entering the city via the Scheldt River had to pay a toll at Het Steen bastion levied by a giant named Druoon Antigoon. If a skipper refused (or was unable) to pay, the giant lopped off his right hand. One day Silvius Brabo, a centurion from the Roman army, arrived at port and, furious at the expense, challenged the giant to a duel. Brabo won and in retribution chopped off Antigoon's hand and threw it in the Scheldt to signal it was a free waterway. Over time, this 'Hand-werpen' (or 'throwing the hand') lost the accented 'h' and the city's present name was arrived at. To this today, Het Steen and the severed hand feature on a version of the city's coat of arms and local chocolate shops and bakers sell 'Antwerpse handjes' – hand-shaped biscuits and chocolates.

& has added yummy extras to the menu, including a heavenly Maltesers hot chocolate. **Zum** [284–5 F2] 1 Viaductdam; \ 03 345 03 36; ⏱ 09.00–20.00 Tue–Sun. Just across the street from Caravan (page 288), this bright, lively café is run by Femke whose friend, Ludwina, makes the delicious pink cupcakes piled up by the till.

ENTERTAINMENT AND NIGHTLIFE Antwerp probably has the best nightlife in Flanders. There's the complete spectrum of bars, from smoke-filled pubs to trendy cocktail joints. Hotspots include the Het Zuid neighbourhood and the streets clustered around OLV-Kathedraal, while Stadswaag square and Hendrik Conscienceplein are student hangouts. The tourist board's *Use-It* guide, aimed at backpackers and students, is a good source of information for popular bars and clubs.

The theatre and music scene is just as active, and don't miss taking in a film at the elegant De Roma cinema. For listings of what's on, pick up a copy of *Zone 03* magazine, published weekly and found in stands around the city centre and in the tourist office. Tickets for concerts, theatre etc can be bought from FNAC in the Groenplaats shopping centre (*tel: 0900 00 600;* ⏱ *10.00–18.15* daily) and Prospeckta, which has the same address as the tourist office. And a final word: as you can probably tell from the street names – Oudemaanstraat (Old Man street), Leguit (Leg Over), Schipperstraat (Shippers' street) – Antwerp's red-light district sits between the city centre and the docks. The area is perfectly safe to walk through.

Pubs

Bierhuis Kulminator [284–5 B6] 34 Vleminckveld; \ 03 232 45 38; ⏱ 20.00–00.00 Mon, 11.00–00.00 Tue–Fri, 17.00–00.00 Sat. Run by husband-&-wife team, Dirk van Dyck & Leen Boudewijn, this beloved traditional pub is famous for its 600+ varieties of aged beer with bottles dating back to the 1970s. There's a telephone-book-sized menu on hand to help, but it's often more fun to pick one of the dusty bottles lined up behind the bar. Look out for EKU-28 – it's reputed to be the strongest beer in the world.

Café Beveren [287 A3] 2 Vlasmarkt; \ 03 231 22 25; ⏱ 13.00–late Thu–Mon. A favourite with locals young & old, this age-old pub has a wonderful atmosphere in the evening. It starts off with some quiet drinking, but come 22.00/23.00 someone usually puts a euro in the 1937 Wurlitzer organ & the party gets going. Couples take to the dance floor & start crooning to ye olde tunes. Join in!

Paters Vaetje [287 C2] 1 Blauwmoezelstraat; \ 03 231 84 76; ⏱ 11.00–03.00 Sun–Thu, 11.00–05.00 Fri–Sat. 2-floored old-fashioned drinking den, which serves more than 100 varieties of beer, including Karmeliet Tripel – voted the world's best beer in 2008. Try to get a seat downstairs; there's a better atmosphere.

Pelgrom [287 C3] 15 Pelgrimstraat; \ 03 234 08 09; ⏱ 17.00–late daily. Very cosy 15th-century merchant cellar that's now a tavern/restaurant serving the local Antwerp tipple Elixir d'Anvers. Nibble on hearty chunks of sausage & cheese washed down with a beer.

Quinten Matsijs [287 E2] 17 Moriaanstraat; \ 03 225 01 70; 12.00–late Tue–Sat, 12.00–20.00 Sun. Established in 1545, this is Antwerp's oldest bar. The regal dark-wood interior is ideal for a relaxed quiet drink & there's a nice garden out the back.

t' Elfde Gebod [287 D2] 10 Torfbrug; \ 03 289 34 66; ⏱ 11.00–late daily. Ivy-covered on the outside & crammed with statues of the Virgin Mary on the inside, this unusual (& admittedly touristy) bar is definitely worth a visit. Sits just off the Grote Markt, in the shadow of OLV-Kathedraal.

Bars

Café Moeskop [284–5 G7] 17 Dageraadplaats; ⏱ 11.55–01.00 Mon–Fri, 14.55–02.00 Sun. Moeskop's strange opening hours are no mistake: 'vijf voor twaalf' in Flemish translates as 'the eleventh hour' – a play on words to say 'drink up – it's your last chance!' A lovely Bohemian bar with long wooden tables, tulips hanging from the ceiling & lanterns spreading coloured light. Donovan, the manager, serves only the best coffee & is rather proud of his tapas too.

Cargo [284–5 F2] Park Spoor Noord; ⏱ 10.00–00.00 daily. Laidback cocktail bar that occupies the corner of 'The Shelter' – an old railway repair shed; you can still see the rail tracks embedded in the floor. Especially popular in summer when guest mixologists arrive & the BBQ is fired up at 14.00 Thu–Sun. Overlooks a fountain & a playground for the kids. If you get peckish they serve pizzas, pastas & tapas.

🍸 **Cocktails at nine** [287 D2] 9 Lijnwaadmarkt; 📞 03 707 10 07; ⏱ 18.00–01.00 Mon–Fri, 15.00–01.00 Sat–Sun. Grown-up cocktail bar where bartender Piotr prepares the city's best cocktails. Not cheap, but worth it.

🍸 **Sips** [284–5 A7] 8 Gillisplaats; 📞 0477 63 91 52; ⏱ 17.00–late Mon–Fri, 18.00–late Sat. Classy, pretentious cocktail bar run by Manuel Wouters, a superstar bartender who used to mix drinks on the *QE2* & knows over 1,000 cocktail recipes by heart. Well, if they're good enough for the likes of Tom Cruise & Dolly Parton …

Nightclubs

☆ **Café d'Anvers** [284–5 C3] 15 Verversrui; 📞 03 226 38 70; www.café-d-anvers.com; ⏱ 23.00–06.00 Thu, 23.00–07.30 Fri–Sat. Around

since the late 1980s, Anvers is Antwerp's original nightclub & it's still considered hip. Hugely popular on Fri & Sat. Tickets can be bought online €7.

☆ **Noxx** [284–5 E1] 1 Kotterstraat; www. noxxantwerp.eu; ⏱ 22.00–06.00 Thu, 23.00–06.00 Fri, 23.00–07.00 Sat. Located in the Het Eilandje district, Noxx has 4 rooms, including the Salle Noire with a 360° LED wall. Music varies. Entry on Thu free, Fri varies, Sat €15.

Live music

🎵 **De Muze** [287 D2] 15 Melkmarkt; 📞 03 226 01 26; ⏱ 11.00–03.00 daily. Jazz bar that attracts all ages. Live performances almost every night, but arrive early if you want a good view of the stage.

🎵 **Den Hopper** [284–5 A7] 2 Leopold De Waelplaats; 📞 03 248 49 33; ⏱ 10.30–late daily. Named after the great American painter Edward Hopper, this smart jazz bar near the MSK hosts concerts every Mon at 21.00 & Sun at 16.00 & feature acts by jazz students, as well as the occasional master.

🎵 **Kid's Rhythm & Blues Café** [287 C2] 50 Grote Markt; 📞 03 289 05 79; ⏱ 12.00–06.00

GAY ANTWERP

Antwerp's lesbian and gay scene is the most active and accepted in Flanders, perhaps due to its proximity to the Dutch border. To find out what's on, it's worth visiting Het Roze Huis (*1 Draakplaats;* 📞 *03 288 00 84; www. hetrozehuis.be;* ⏱ *11.00–17.00 Mon–Fri*), an umbrella organisation for all gay and lesbian associations in Antwerp. The streets north of Centraal Station – in particular van Schoonhovenstraat – have a high concentration of gay and lesbian-friendly bars. Every year the Red & Blue dance club (*11 Lange Schipperskapelstraat*) organises Navigaytion (*www.navigaytion.be*), a gay festival held on a weekend in June on Steenplein. Various bars get involved and there's lots of party boats on the Scheldt. Tickets can be ordered online. The city also has its own rainbow radio station, O Radio, at 107.0FM.

🏠 **Villa T** (3 rooms) 17–19 Verversrui; 📞 03 231 23 00; www.villat.be. Of interest to the open-minded, this trendy gay-friendly B&B in the heart of the Shippers' Quarters sits above Europe's largest brothel. Designed & built by couple Hein Knapen & Frederik de Witte, its funky rooms feature bright wallpaper & simple beds. Not fancy, but it's a chance to stay in one of Antwerp's up-&-coming quarters. Cash only. **€€–€€€**

☆ **Hessenhuis** 53 Falconrui; 📞 03 231 13 56; ⏱ 11.00–late Mon–Fri, 13.00–late Sat–Sun. Old converted warehouse near the docks; serves as a café during the day, but is converted to a chic dance club at night.

🍸 **Body boys** 42 van Schoonhovenstraat; 📞 03 203 05 43; ⏱ 16.00–02.00 Wed–Thu, 16.00–05.00 Fri–Sat, 16.00–03.00 Sun. Hugely popular, disco-crazy bar that gets very busy, especially during their Fri & Sat late-night happy hour between 23.00 and 00.00.

Mon–Fri, 12.00–08.00 Sat–Sun. As-central-as-they-come blues bar with bags of atmosphere. Signed pictures of jazz greats with the bar's owner, Kid, line the walls & the stage is given over every Sun to promising young musicians & the odd big-name professional.

Theatre and cinema
Antwerp's thriving theatre district is concentrated in the Kruidtuin neighbourhood – otherwise known as the *Quartier Latin* (Latin Quarter). Most of the productions will be in Flemish, but some establishments produce the occasional play in English. Instead, I'd recommend catching a play in the local dialect (see Echt Antwaarps Teater). The latest listings & programmes can be found on the theatres' websites or in the local papers.

Theatre
🎭 **Het Toneelhuis** [284–5 C6] 18 Komedieplaats; ☏ 03 224 88 44; www. toneelhuis.be. Also known as Bourla, Antwerp's largest theatre is run by a co-operative of 5: a choreographer, director, playwright, performer & fixed troupe of actors whose productions are a mixture of theatre, music & dance.
🎭 **Echt Antwaarps Teater** [284–5 C6] 10 Arenbergstraat; ☏ 03 231 64 64; www. echtantwaarpsteater.be. Nightly performances (20.15) of modern plays in traditional Antwerp dialect. Cheap seats (€18) can be bought on Thu.
🎭 **Stadsschouwburg** [284–5 D6] 1 Theaterplein; tel: 0900 69 900; www. stadsschouwburgantwerpen.be. Runs well-known shows like *Fame* & *Equus*, as well as other national productions. It's also home to the *Het Paleis* childrens' theatre.

Cinema
🎭 **De Roma** [284–5 G6] 286 Turnhoutsebaan; ☏ 03 292 97 40; www.deroma.be. They don't make them like this any more. Fabulous Italian-style theatre with wooden stage, red velvet curtains & gold filigree details. Has 14.00 matinee showings of art-house movies, classics & blockbusters. Tickets can be bought up the road at 327 Turnhoutsebaan or online.
🎭 **UGC Cinema** [284–5 E5] 17 van Ertbornstraat; www.ugc.be. Modern 17-screen complex showing the latest Hollywood blockbusters.

SHOPPING
Antwerp is a superb city for fashion – it even has its own fashion label *WIT0708*. Its *haute-couture* fashion district congregates around Nationaalstraat, Kammenstraat, Lombardenvest and Steenhouwersvest, but also worth visiting are the eclectic bundle of boutiques, shoe shops and jewellers lining De Keyserlei boulevard situated opposite the side entrance to Antwerp's Centraal Station. The Hylitt Gallery, the Century Center and Quellin Shopping Center also sit on this avenue and down side streets like Quellinstraat and Frankrijklei you will find big international fashion labels and chic interior-design stores.

Less expensive European high-street fashion names can be found along the Meir and as you move further towards the centre of town you will find the Grand Bazar Shopping Center (*2 Beddenstraat; www.grandbasarshopping.be;* ⏲ *10.00–18.00 Mon–Sat*) with a choice over 50 shops, including familiar brands like Mango, Accessorize and The Body Shop.

Streets surrounding the Grote Markt, like Kloosterstraat, Wolstraat and Lange Koepoortstraat, also contain a number of bric-a-brac and antiques stores; although it's also worth visiting the shops on Mechelsesteenweg and Volkstraat, which are situated slightly further away.

Nearing the harbour, you enter first the Wilde Zee area – whose streets Huidevetterstraat and Lange Gasthuisstraat are synonymous with trendy fashion and home to the Den Oudaan and Nieuw Gaanderij galleries – and then the Quartier Latin where you can find the posh boutiques of acclaimed Belgian designers on Schutterhofstraat and Hopland.

Ann Demeulemeester [284–5 A7] Leopold de Waelplaats; ☎ 03 216 10 33; ☺ 10.30–18.30 Mon–Sat. A famous member of the Antwerp Six (page 59), this designer clothing shop is one of Ann's 4 stores worldwide. The clothes hang, like pieces of art, inside a minimalist studio.
Diamondland [284–5 E6] 33a Appelmansstraat; ☎ 03 229 29 90; ☺ 09.30–17.30 Mon–Sat. Here's a chance to sweep your lady off her feet. At this diamond showroom, you can select a rough diamond & watch the craftsman polish & set it in your own ring. Because you're buying direct from the source, prices are very reasonable. Once you've settled on a stone, it's customary among Jewish retailers to seal the deal with a handshake & the words 'Mazel und Broche' – 'luck & blessing'.
Foxhole [287 B3] 10 Reyndersstraat; m 0476 95 88 72; ☺ 12.30–18.30 Tue–Sat. Renowned vintage clothes store that they ladies will love.
T2 [287 G4] 21 Lange Klarenstraat; ☺ 11.00–18.00 Mon–Wed, 11.00–19.00 Thu–Sat. Second-hand & vintage clothes shop that locals rave about.

Markets
Antiques markets Lijnwaadmarkt, ☺ 09.00–17.00 Sat; Sint-Jansvliet, ☺ 09.00–17.00 Sun.
Art market Lambermontplaats; ☺ May–Sep last Sun of month 12.00–17.00.
Bird market Oude Vaartplaats & Theaterplein; ☺ 08.30–13.00 Sun. Flowers, pets, antiques & jewellery.
Christmas markets Grote Markt & Groenplaats; ☺ Dec 11.00–19.00 & later on w/ends.

Exotic market Oudevaartplaats & Theaterplein; ☺ 08.00–16.00 Sat. Turkish & Moroccan foods.
Friday market Vrijdagmarkt; ☺ 09.00–13.00 Fri. Second-hand furniture & antiques.
Markt van Morgen Kloosterstraat & Riemstraat; ☺ May–Sep first Sun of month 12.00–18.00. The 'market of tomorrow' showcases the work of interior & clothes designers.
Organic market Falconplein; ☺ every 1st & 3rd Sun of the month 07.30–18.00.

OTHER PRACTICALITIES
$ Bank [287 E4] KBC, 20 Eiermarkt, ☺ 09.00–12.30 & 14.00–16.30 Mon–Wed & Fri, 09.00–12.30 & 14.00–19.30 Thu
♻ Bike rental De Fiets-Dokter, 48 Verschansingstraat, ☎ 03 237 82 54, ☺ €7/day; Fietshaven, Centraal Station, ☎ 03 203 06 73, ☺ 09.00–13.00 & 15.00–18.30, €13/day
Internet Famous Cyber, 92 Nationalestraat; ☺ 10.00–20.00 Mon–Thu & Sun, 10.00–21.00 Fri; €1.50/hr

Luggage storage Self-service lockers in the railway station under the stairs, €3/24hr.
➕ Pharmacies 42 Groenplaats; ☎ 03 225 11 74, ☺ 09.00–18.30 Mon–Fri, 10.00–17.00 Sat; 33 Melkmarkt, ☎ 03 226 08 97, ☺ 08.30–18.30 Mon–Fri
✉ Post office 43 Groenplaats; ☺ 09.00–18.00 Mon–Fri, 09.00–12.00 Sat

WHAT TO SEE AND DO
Grote Markt [287 C2] The focus of Antwerp's UNESCO-listed city centre, this triangular town square is dominated by the gilded façade of the Stadhuis and the towering, turquoise mass of **Brabo Fountain**, which was sculpted by Jef Lambeaux in 1887 and depicts the legend which gave the city its name (see box, page 289). Round about sit the smart guildhouses topped with gold figurines depicting the various trades, the majority restored 19th-century constructions. The striking **Stadhuis** (town hall) (*1 Suikerrui*; ☺ *closed to public*) was built between 1561 and 1565 using pink marble. The various column styles formed a new blend of Flemish-Italian Renaissance that was copied all over Europe. Either side of the city coat of arms are the figures of Justice and Wisdom. At the top of the main staircase, the main hall was originally an open courtyard; the roof was added during repairs in the 19th century and the walls adorned with frescoes painted by Baron Hendrik Leys.

Handschoenmarkt [287 C2] Leaving the Grote Markt from the south corner leads you into the cobbled Handschoenmarkt square. Sitting in the shadow of

Onze-Lieve-Vrouwekathedraal, it was (rather predictably) used as a cemetery until the 16th century. After this, it developed into a market that became the tramping ground of fur and glove sellers – hence the street name. Just off centre is a well, topped with a statuette of town legend Brabo (see box, page 289). The saying on the ironwork, 'the smith who came to be a painter out of love', has led many to believe the it's the work of Renaissance artist Quentin Matsys, who originally started out as a smithy, but learned to paint so he might court the daughter of a painter whose father disapproved of his lowly guild trade.

Onze-Lieve-Vrouwekathedraal [287 D2/3] (*Handschoenmarkt;* ✆ *03 213 99 51; www.dekathedraal.be;* ⊕ *10.00–17.00 Mon–Fri, 10.00–15.00 Sat, 13.00–16.00 Sun; admission: adult/under 12/MuseumCard €5/free/free*) A chapel has stood on this spot since the 12th century, but work on the current version started in 1352. Original plans envisaged two towers, but the south spire was never completed. This was perhaps a blessing in disguise because the cathedral and its exceptional 123m north tower alone took 169 years to complete. Even today, it is the largest Gothic construction in the Low Countries. In 1533 the lavish interior was ruined by fire, in 1566 it was plundered during the Iconoclastic Fury, and in 1794 it was looted by French Republicans. Very little of the original Gothic interior remains, but a 20-year restoration programme presents the Baroque additions and seven-aisled interior at its best.

Luckily, the cathedral's treasures survived and by far the best works on display are Pieter Paul Rubens' (page 356) four masterpieces: the *Assumption of the Virgin* positioned over the altar, the *Resurrection of Christ* in a right-hand side chapel, the *Raising of the Cross* in the left transept, and the serene and luminous triptych *The Descent from the Cross*, which is displayed in the right transept. In the painting, Mary reaches up to touch Jesus as he is removed from the cross; to the right, dressed in red, is John the Baptist and at Jesus' feet, Mary Magdalene. The painting was commissioned by the Guild of Arquebusiers, who requested an altarpiece of their patron saint St Christopher (whose name means 'bearer of Christ'). As payment, Rubens would receive a plot of land from the Arquebusiers' estate. However, there was some dispute between him and the guild over the construction of a wall that would divide their properties, so Rubens craftily took a broad view of the 'bearer of Christ' theme. All the figures in the painting are seen to be 'carrying Christ' in some form: St John carries Christ down from the cross; Mary in the left-hand panel is pregnant; and Simeon on the right-hand side is holding the baby Jesus aloft. Naturally, the guild wasn't amused, so Rubens added St Christopher to the outside of one panel and on the other he painted a hermit and owl, well-known characters from the saint's legend – no doubt after the payments for the wall were settled of course. Booklets with full decriptions of the artworks are on sale at the entrance. Carillon concerts are held on Monday, Wednesday and Friday between 12.00 and 13.00, and in summer guided tours (⊕ *15 Jul–31 Aug 11.00, 14.15 & 15.45 Mon–Fri, 13.15 & 15.00 Sun*) are available in English.

MAD FOR MUSEUMS?

The tourist offices sell the Antwerp City Card which costs €31, is valid for 48 hours, and grants free access to all city museums and churches, as well as 25% discount on numerous other attractions and bike rental. Be aware that many museums and exhibitions issue their last tickets at 16.30 and won't allow you in if you arrive after this time.

Kitted out in green wellies and protective overalls, it's possible to take a tour of Antwerp's underground sewers or 'ruien' (*21 Suikerrui;* \ *03 232 01 03*). You can opt for a quick look (⊕ *10.00–18.30 Mon & Thu–Sun; admission €2.50*) or book a three-hour guided tour which is quite arduous and muddy (⊕ *for individuals 13.00 Mon, Thu & Fri, 11.00 & 13.00 Sat–Sun; €16pp plus €2 admin fee; bookings 3 weeks in advance essential, not suitable for under 12*). You'll see the remnants of old bridges, the foundations of century-old architecture, old street signs and even an underground cathedral where the hip aristocracy partied in privacy. You'll need to wear trousers and jumper, and bring a bag to carry your own shoes, handbag etc.

Hendrik Conscienceplein

[287 E2] Head east to Hendrik Conscienceplein, the prettiest square in the city. It's named after the Antwerp-born writer, Hendrik Conscience, who is best remembered for *De Leeuwe van Vlaanderen* (*The Lion of Flanders*) and whose statue sits in an alcove of the city's library façade. The majority of the buildings were designed and funded by the Jesuits in the 17th century.

Sint-Carolus Borromeuskerk

[287 E2] (*6 Hendrik Conscienceplein;* \ *03 231 37 51; www.topa.be;* ⊕ *10.00–12.30 & 14.00–17.00 Mon–Sat; admission free*) Standing out on the square, this ornate church was built in typical Baroque style by the Jesuits between 1614 and 1631 and hailed as 'heaven on earth'. The church once bore Rubens' stamp everywhere, from the 39 paintings covering the ceiling, to the tower and sculptural decorations on the façade, but a fire in 1718 destroyed the roof artwork. Happily, the Onze Lieve Vrouwekapel (Chapel of Our Lady) on the right-hand side still houses some good pieces of art. Also inside is an unspectacular lace museum (⊕ *10.00–12.30 & 14.00–16.00 Wed; admission: adult/under 12 €1.50/free*).

Groenplaats

Also known as Groen Kerkhof (or 'Green Cemetery'), this square is where the dead were buried until the 18th century when the Austrian rulers moved the practice outside the city walls. The bronze statue in the centre of Baroque artist extraordinaire Pieter Paul Rubens replaced a crucifix in 1843.

Poorterswoning

[287 C3] (*15 Pelgrimstraat;* \ *03 234 08 09;* ⊕ *12.00–18.00 Sat–Sun; admission: adult/under 12 €2/free*) This gem of a museum sits above Pelgrom's cellar restaurant and is often overlooked because of its limited opening hours. If you can, stop by to wander through the restored rooms of this 16th-century burgher's house. Enormous working fireplaces, the kitchen and bedroom are all filled with original knick-knacks – it's as if the family has just popped out for an hour.

Vlaeykensgang, and Grote and Kleine Pieter Potstraat

Across the way from Poorterswoning is Vlaeykensgang – a 16th-century alleyway lined with old cobblers' shops. They were scheduled to be torn down in the 1960s, but thankfully saved by a wealthy antiques dealer who paid for their restoration. Exiting on to Hoogstraat, stroll across the street (steering slightly to the left) and into Kleine Pieter Potstraat. Forming a T-junction with Grote Pieter Potstraat, these two streets are the oldest in Antwerp. They're named after wealthy banker, Pieter Pot, who lived during the 15th century and funded the construction of the Priory of St Salvador, of which only the chapel remains (on the corner of the two streets).

Steenplein From Grote Pieter Potstraat it's a short walk north along van Duckaai to Steenplein, site of Antwerp's impressive fortress castle **Het Steen**. Documents suggest it was built as an outpost of the Holy Roman Empire in 900AD, but what remains today dates from the early 13th century when it was used as a prison. It gained its current name, Heeren Steen (King's Stone) – later shortened to Het Steen – in 1520 when Emperor Charles V paid for its reconstruction. Above the entrance you can make out the enormous erect penis of Semini, the Scandinavian god of youth and fertility. It's a reference to a generation of Antwerp residents whose mothers prayed to the virile god for children after the outbreak of the plague. Nearby, is the crucifix where condemned convicts were allowed to issue their last prayers. Thankfully, the castle escaped demolition when the docks were expanded in the 19th century, but the change heralded the demise of its period as a prison and wrong-doers ceased to be impounded here in 1827.

Vleeshuis [287 C1] (*38–40 Vleeshouwersstraat;* \ *03 233 64 04; http://museum. antwerpen.be/vleeshuis;* ⊕ *10.00–17.00 Tue–Sun; admission: adult/12–26/under 12/MuseumCard €5/1/free/free*) The imposing red-and-grey brick butchers' guildhouse with its two turreted towers was built between 1501 and 1504. Throughout the 16th century it was the tallest private building in the city and conveyed the might of a guild that controlled the preparation and sale of meat in the city. The guild was abolished in 1793 under French occupation and the Vleeshuis now houses a 'sounds of the city' museum.

Centraal Station (East) The area around Centraal Station forms the city's second focal point. Until the 19th century, social and business affairs had been focused on the river, but when the Scheldt was reopened in 1863 the port had to be expanded to cope with the boom in shipping traffic. Hundreds of riverside buildings were demolished (only the Het Steen castle was saved) and the 16th-century city walls were pulled down. A new railway was built and residential neighbourhoods such as Zurenborg, Het Zuid and Stuivenberg sprang up. The dynamics of the metropolis had been changed forever. Today, the area's main attractions are the station itself, Antwerp Zoo, and above all the trade of diamonds; dozens of Jewish-owned spin-off stores line Pelikaanstraat and Vestingstraat. Other nationalities have taken root in this area too, and the surrounding streets are home to Chinese restaurants, Turkish bars and African clothing shops.

Centraal Station [284–5 E5/6] This stunning building cannot fail to impress. Arching 44m above you as you alight on the platform is the great iron-and-glass vaulted ceiling of the trainshed designed by Clement van Bogaert, while the main terminal building displays all the self confidence you'd expect from this new era in the city's history. Referred to as the railway cathedral, its grand tree-trunk pillars, turreted gables and vast dome were built in neo-Renaissance style between 1895 and 1905 by Brugge-born architect Louis Delacenserie (1838–1909).

Antwerpse Zoo [284–5 F6] (*26 Koningin Astridplein;* \ *03 202 45 40; www. zooantwerpen.be;* ⊕ *Jan–Feb & Nov–Dec 10.00–16.45 daily, Mar–Apr & Oct 10.00–17.30 daily, May–Jun & Sep 10.00–18.00 daily, Jul–Aug 10.00–19.00 daily; admission: adult/3–17/under 3/MuseumCard €21/17/free/25% off*) At the back of

Centraal Station is Antwerp Zoo, its entrance located to the right of the station's exit. Founded in 1843, it's one of the oldest in the world and, to be honest, looks its age. The animal enclosures are small, particularly the gorilla paddock. However, there have been successful attempts at breeding elephants and lions here.

Diamantmuseum [284–5 E5] (*19–23 Koningin Astridplein;* \ *03 202 48 90; www. diamantmuseum.be;* ⊕ *10.00–17.30 Mon, Tue, Thu–Sun; admission: adult/12–25/ under 12/MuseumCard €6/4/free/free, inc audio guide*) An audio tour takes you through a series of interactive displays covering the history, geology and mining of the carbon carats. The highlight is probably the historical tiaras, necklaces, brooches and a replica of the British Crown Jewels that sparkle under the watchful eye of a security guard.

Aquatopia [284–5 E5] (*7 Koningin Astridplein;* \ *03 205 07 40; www.aquatopia. be;* ⊕ *10.00–18.00 daily; admission: adult/3–12/under 3/MuseumCard €13.95/9.50/ free/25%off*) Huge amounts of cash have obviously been poured into this aquarium that sits opposite Centraal Station. With ocean sounds, interactive displays and plenty of sharks, it's worth a visit.

Criée and Chinatown A short walk north from the Diamantmuseum, at van Schoonhovenstraat 21, is the entrance to a 19th-century covered market hall. Called *criée* after the 'shouts' of the vendors coming from within, this market stills opens every day to sell fruit, veg and meat to residents. Exiting the market via the west entrance leads you directly on to van Wesenbekestraat, the heart of Antwerp's Chinatown.

St-Jacobskerk [284–5 D5] (*73–5 Lange Nieuwstraat;* \ *03 225 04 14; www.topa. be;* ⊕ *Apr–Oct 14.00–17.00 Mon–Fri; admission: adult/under 12/MuseumCard €2/ free/free*) Over 150 years in the making, this lavish Gothic church has a Baroque interior containing more than 100 types of marble. Notably, it was one of the very few churches in the city not to have been plundered by the French, so still contains many of the treasures and tombs of the Antwerp elite who poured money into the construction of family side chapels and the artworks that adorn them. Of particular interest is the burial vault belonging to the Rockox family located in the third chapel from the transept. However, the main attraction is Rubens' tomb, which lies behind the main altar in the Chapel of Our Lady, beneath the *Our Lady and the Christ Child Surrounded by Saints* painting that he produced for the purpose. Interestingly, the faces of St George, St Jerome, the Virgin Mary and Mary Magdalene are purported to be portraits of Rubens, his father, Isabella Brant (his first wife) and Hélène Fourment (his second wife).

Rubenshuis [284–5 D5] (*9–11 Wapper;* \ *03 201 15 55; www.rubenshuis.be;* ⊕ *10.00–17.00 Tue–Sun; admission: adult/12–26/under 12/MuseumCard €8/1/free/ free, inc free audio guide*) Rubens did for Antwerp what Elvis did for Memphis, so it's no surprise that the artist's former home and studio is the city's top sight. Rubens (page 356) bought the courtyard complex in 1611 and lived, taught and entertained here until his death in May 1640. On the right is his studio, and on the left his living quarters and personal art gallery. In the centre is a landscaped garden. The town failed several times in their attempts to acquire the complex after the artist's death, and when they finally did in 1937 it was little more than a ruin. Careful restoration ensued and period furniture from his era brought in to furnish the rooms. Only

— *margin text:* Antwerp ANTWERP

ten of the maestro's works are on show here, but these include a portrait of himself aged 50 – he wears a hat to conceal his baldness; an early work of *Adam and Eve in Paradise*; *The Annunciation*; his unfinished *Battle of Ivry* featuring French king-to-be Henry IV in Paris; and a portrait of young Anthony van Dyck.

Handelsbeurs [287 F3] Hidden down Twaalfmaandenstraat is Antwerp's glorious former stock exchange building. The trade centre was the first of its kind in Europe and history tells that Sir Thomas Gresham, financial advisor to King Edward VI of England, visited the exchange and promptly returned to Britain and ordered the construction of an equivalent that later became the London Stock Exchange. The building suffered several outbreaks of fire, but one in 1858 destroyed it completely. The ornate neo-Gothic galleries on display today date from 1872.

Boerentoren [287 E4] Standing 97m tall on the corner of Eiermarkt and Schoenmarkt is the 'farmers' tower' – Europe's first skyscraper, and the final building of note to be found along the Meir. The blockish Art Deco building was designed by Jan van Hoenacker for Antwerp's 1930 World Exhibition and kept its hold on the world record until the 1950s, when it was replaced by the 32-storey Torre de Madrid in Spain. It's now used as the city headquarters of banking giant KBC.

Sint-Andries, Het Zuid and Kruidtuin (South)
Spanning south from the historic city centre, these three neighbourhoods developed during the latter half of the 19th century and are home to the majority of the city's museums, theatres and art galleries.

Sint-Andries is a quiet working-class area intersected by shopping thoroughfare Nationaalstraat and antiques hot-spot, Kloosterstraat, and Het Zuid is referred to locally as 'Little Paris' because of its high concentration of Art Nouveau architecture. Kruidtuin, which is also known to as Antwerp's Latin Quarter, sits off to the west and is slightly classier; it's famous for its theatre and weekend markets on Theaterplein.

Vrijdagmarkt [287 B4] This 16th-century marketplace marks the boundary between Sint-Andries and the historic centre. The space was created for a second-hand clothes market – a statue of St Cathérine, patron saint of haberdashers and spinners, stands in the middle – but was largely destroyed during World War II. It was rebuilt and now an antiques markets is held here (⊕ *09.00–13.00 Fri*). The main building of note, however, is the Museum Plantin-Moretus in the west corner.

Museum Plantin-Moretus [287 B4] (*22–3 Vrijdaagmarkt;* \ *03 221 14 50; http:// museum.antwerpen.be/plantin_moretus;* ⊕ *10.00–17.00 Tue–Sun; admission: adult/12–26/under 12/MuseumCard €8/1/free/free*) This wonderful museum was formerly the home and offices of Christoffel Plantin (1520–89), a French bookbinder who moved to Antwerp in 1549 and six years later founded De Gulden Passer (The Golden Compasses) publishing house. A shrewd businessman, Plantin secured contracts for all Spain's liturgical publications from King Philip II and yet was the official printer of the Protestant State-General. On the side, he indulged his love of humanism and published works of scholar Justus Lipsius and anatomist Andreas Versalius. As a result, the business rose to become the largest printer-publisher in the Low Countries and the family was Antwerp's richest. When Plantin died, his son-in-law, Jan Moretus, took over the business. He in turn passed it onto his son Balthasar, who was a close friend of Rubens; the family portraits he made for his friend can still be seen in the museum. The family kept things going until 1866, then a year later the building and its contents were sold to the city. In 1877 it opened as a museum. The offices, letter room, library and shop of this Baroque house narrowly avoided German bombs during World War II and have been preserved in their original state. You can peruse ancient presses, copper plates and rare manuscripts, including a copy of the precious Gutenberg Bible.

ModeNatie [284–5 B5] This bright-white corner building started life as the chic Hotel Central in the 19th century. It attracted top-notch haberdashers and the trend continued. Today, it houses the Royal Academy of Fine Art Fashion Department and the Flanders Fashion Institute, as well as the **Modemuseum (MoMu)** (*28 Nationalestraat;* ✆ *03 470 27 70; www.momu.be;* ⊕ *10.00–18.00 Tue–Sun; admission: adult/under 26/under 12/MuseumCard €8/1/free/free*). The fashion museum covers the work of the Antwerp Six (page 59) and exhibits the work of the Academy students and avant-garde designers.

Paardepoortje [284–5 A6] In the south of the Sint-Andries neighbourhood, along Willem Lepelstraat 14, is the quiet Paardepoortje alleyway. The white painted walls and flower-lined paths are one of the last examples of 19th-century working-class housing in the city. Until 1869, the entire Sint-Andries area would have been covered with these small enclaves that shared basic facilities such as a communal toilet and central water pump. Almost all were lost during redevelopment projects.

Museum van Hedendaagse Kunst Antwerpen (MHKA) [284–5 A7] (*32 Leuvenstraat;* ✆ *03 260 99 99; www.muhka.be;* ⊕ *11.00–18.00 Tue–Wed & Fri–Sun, 11.00–21.00 Thu; admission: adult/under 26/under 13/MuseumCard €8/1/free/free*) Antwerp's Museum of Contemporary Art is housed in a vast 1920s' converted grain silo. Showcasing art produced from the 1970s onwards, its main point of focus is the Matta-Clark Foundation that's named after American architect, Gordon Matta-Clark, who started creating urban art structures from derelict buildings when the area was still run down in the early 1970s. There are great views of the city from the top-floor café (⊕ *as above*).

Fotomuseum Provincie Antwerpen [284–5 A7] (*47 Waalse Kaai;* ✆ *03 242 93 00; www.fotomuseum.be;* ⊕ *10.00–18.00 Tue–Sun; admission: adult/under16/ under 2/MuseumCard €7/1/free/free*) This well-respected photography museum has a smart, white, minimalist interior with permanent exhibitions of old and new photography equipment, plus a mixture of temporary exhibitions and workshops. Check the website for listings.

Koninklijk Museum voor Schone Kunsten (KMSKA) [284–5 A7] (*Leopold de Waelplaats;* ✆ *03 238 78 09; www.kmska.be;* ⊕ *closed until 2017*) Art lovers will have to go in search of Antwerp's exceptional fine arts collection, parts of which have been scattered to different parts of the country while the building undergoes a huge renovation. The museum is scheduled to reopen in 2017. Lier has been lent a couple of Brueghel paintings (page 315) and Mechelen is looking after Rik Wouters' artworks (page 311). Sadly the others are in storage or abroad.

Justitiepaleis At the southern tip of the neighbourhood sits Antwerp's new Law Courts. The exceptional piece of architecture was designed by Richard Rogers – the man responsible for London's Millennium Dome – and it's no mistake that the white jutting fixtures on the roof look like the wind-blown sails of a ship.

Elzenveld [284–5 C6] (*45 Lange Gasthuisstraat;* \ *03 202 77 04; www.elzenveld.be;* ☉ *daily*) With a name taken straight from *Lord of the Rings*, this former 13th-century hospital is just as secretive. Hidden behind a row of houses, it has to be accessed via a passageway built into the façade, labelled Gasthuis St-Elizabeth. Taking an immediate right brings you in front of an engraved archway with wrought-iron gates and a lantern hanging dead centre. The hospital originally started life in the shadow of Onze-Lieve-Vrouwekathedraal, but was moved to the current location in 1238 to bring infection out of the city centre. When the city expanded again, it all had to be knocked down and rebuilt. It was run much like a *begijnhof* by a religious community of men and women until 1797, when city funds were withdrawn, and under French rule it was used as a classroom for training medical and pharmacy students until 1849. Today, the series of buildings surrounding the inner courtyards has been converted into a business centre and hotel. You can wander around the chapel and quiet gardens littered with spectral statues.

Maagdenhuis [284–5 C6] (*33 Lange Gasthuisstraat;* \ *03 223 56 28;* ☉ *10.00–17.00 Mon, Wed–Fri, 13.00–17.00 Sat–Sun; admission: adult/12–26/under 12/MuseumCard €5/1/free/free*) The 'Maidens' House' was a 16th-17th-century girls' orphanage that now houses Antwerp's social services office. Often the girls did have families, but the parents were either too poor to raise them, or felt the skills (sewing, lace-making etc) they learned here would serve them better later on in life. Babies were often left in purpose-built compartments, known as 'drawers', which were dug into the façade of the orphanage. The intention for many was to reclaim the child once things had improved, so to identify them later on, a token – often a playing card – was ripped in half. One portion was given to the parents, the other to the child; if the child was then reclaimed the pieces were joined together as proof of a legitimate reunion. Examples of these are held in a cabinet to the right of the entrance. Other rooms contain a good collection of paintings, including *St Hieronymus* by van Dyck, a study of *The Descent from the Cross* by Jordaens, *Orphan Girl at Work* by Cornelius de Vos, and *Invocation of Christ in Favour of the Poor Families* by Rubens. The old chapel, opposite the entrance on the right-hand side, has a display of the girls' gruel bowls.

Museum Mayer van den Bergh [284–5 C6] (*19 Lange Gasthuisstraat;* \ *03 232 42 37; http://museum.antwerpen.be/mayervandenbergh;* ☉ *10.00–17.00 Tue–Sun; admission: adult/12–26/under 12/MuseumCard €8/1/free/free*) The tapestries, paintings, sculptures, stained glass, manuscripts, drawings and other *objets d'art* that make up this 5,000-strong private art collection are revered and range from the Middle Ages to the Renaissance period. All belonged to self-taught collector Fritz Mayer van den Bergh (1858–1901), who hailed from a family of rich merchants and died at the age of just 43. Bergh had a real eye for art and picked up some incredible bargains: he bought Pieter Brueghel the Elder's apocalyptic and Bosch-inspired *Dulle Griet* for €12 at an auction in Cologne in 1897; an early 14th-century walnut carving of Christ and St John by Heinrich of Constance; and Quentin Matsys' *Crucifixion* triptych. His mother – with whom he lived with until his death – had the Gothic Revival house built especially for the collection and opened it as a museum in 1904.

Schipperskwartier and Het Eilandje (North)

North of the old town centre, these three neighbourhoods have a distinctly maritime atmosphere. Schipperskwartier ('Sailor's Quarter') is an unofficial area straddling the boundary between the historic city centre and Stadswaag, and home to Antwerp's red-light district. Here Europe's largest legal brothel, Villa Tinto (*17–19 Verversrui*) and Belgium's biggest collection

of brothels and all-night bars are spread between St-Paulusplaats, Verversrui, Vingerlingstraat, Schippersstraat, and particularly along Oude Manstraat. Its seedy streets contain a few secrets, like art-treasure church Sint-Pauluskerk.
Close by is Stadswaag, the old merchant quarter. Home to Antwerp's only *begijnhof* and the excellent Rockoxhuis museum, it's also kept hip by students attending the city university.

Antwerp's famous docks, known as Het Eilandje ('Little Island'), sit in the far north and extend well beyond the city limits. The sections closest to town are developing quickly thanks to the city's newest museum, MAS.

Begijnhof [284–5 D4] (*39 Rodestraat;* \ *03 232 52 97;* ◒ *09.00–17.00 daily*) On the eastern edges of the neighbourhood, Antwerp's only *begijnhof* is exceptionally well preserved. Built in the 16th century against the old city walls, it has survived virtually intact and the old béguine houses now belong to elderly residents. Definitely worth a detour.

Rockoxhuis [287 F1] (*10–12 Keizerstraat;* \ *03 201 92 50; www.rockoxhuis.be;* ◒ *10.00–17.00 daily; admission: adult/under 26/under 19/MuseumCard €2.50/1.25/ free/free*) This 17th-century townhouse is the former home of Mayor Nicolaas Rockox (1560–1640). An avid patron of the arts, he was good friends with painter Pieter Paul Rubens, humanist Justus Lipsius and publishers Jan and Balthazar Moretus (page 298), and as president of the Arquebusiers' Guild he commissioned Rubens to paint *The Descent from the Cross* now hanging in the OLV-Kathedraal. Rockox bought the two houses at Keizerstraat 10 and 12 in 1603 and joined them under one façade. At his request, the entire contents of his house were given to the poor after his death, so when the building was bought by banking giant KBC in 1970 the restorers had to salvage pieccs mentioned in an inventory taken after Rockox's death in 1640. Apart from the beautifully restored rooms, the museum's main wealth is its modest collection of first-class artworks. In Room 1 is Quentin Matsys' *Holy Virgin and Child*, and tucked into a corner, Joachim Patenier's *St Christopher Bearing the Christ Child*. In Room 2 you'll find Rubens' *The Virgin in Adoration Before the Sleeping Child* to the right of the fireplace and a study by van Dyck. In the centre of Room 3 is Joachim Beuckelaer's *Woman Selling Vegetables*; Room 5 holds Frans Snyders' *Antwerp Fish Market*; whilst Room 6 has Pieter Brueghel the Younger's *Proverbs*, a chaotic country scene that depicts 108 Flemish proverbs. Many are indecipherable, but those that can be picked out are cakes on the roof (prosperity), a pig opening the tap of a barrel (gluttony), and the monk giving Jesus a false beard (blasphemy).

Letterenhuis [287 E1] (*22 Minderbroedersstraat;* \ *03 222 93 20; www.letterenhuis. be;* ◒ *10.00–17.00 Tue–Sun; admission: adult/12–26/under 12/MuseumCard €5/1/ free/free*) Part of a serious archive of Flemish literature, this museum shows off a selection of manuscripts, private correspondence and photographs belonging to Flemish authors from the 19th century onwards; these include Hugo Claus and Antwerp's godfather of literature Hendrik Conscience. The space was renovated a few years ago and is looking all the better for it. Now you can watch clips of documentaries and films, and dip into computer programs that tell you more about the authors.

Sint-Pauluskerk [284–5 B4] (*14 Veemarkt;* \ *03 232 32 67; www.topa.be;* ◒ *1 Apr – 14 Oct 14.00–17.00 daily; admission free*) Once part of a Dominican monastery, this Baroque jewel was consecrated in 1517. Over the years it suffered several fires, the last of which was in 1968. A restoration project was recently completed and several Baroque artworks are now on show, including van Dyck's *The Bearing of the Cross*, Jacob Jordaen's *Crucifixion* and Rubens' *Scourging at the Pillar*.

Museum aan de Stroom (MAS) [284–5 C3] (*1 Hanzestedenplaats;* \ *03 338 44 00; www.mas.be;* ⊕ *10.00–17.00 Tue–Fri, 10.00–18.00 Sat–Sun; admission: adult/12–26/under 12/MuseumCard €5/1/free/free*) The stunning MAS – constructed from red Indian sandstone and waves of perspex – brings together the collections of the former Ethnographic, National Shipping and Folklore museums in a dynamic new display spread over floors four to eight. Giant games of snakes and ladders will keep the kids entertained too. The ground-floor Storm Café has become very popular with locals and the top floor offers superb panoramic views of the city. Don't miss it!

Bonapartedok and Willemdok Het Eilandje's two central docks were constructed on the orders of Napoleon towards the end of the French occupation; he wanted the port to be like 'a pistol aimed at the heart of England'. The Bonaparte was completed in 1803 and named after the French general, but the Willem was only partially completed when Napoleon's occupation ended in 1814. The dock was finished and named after the country's new ruler, William I of the Netherlands, instead. Numerous bars and clubs are scattered through the streets fringing the docks.

Stuivenberg (Northeast) A short stroll from the docks and close to the railway tracks, the Stuivenberg neighbourhood, in the northeast, is distinctly working class and home to several different nationalities. The majority of its sights of interest are the old 'public service' facilities set up for poor labourers and dockworkers in the 19th century. Worth walking by are the old police office on the corner of Biekorkstraat and Sint Jobstraat, and the Art Deco fire station on the corner of Viséstraat and Halenstraat.

Zurenborg and Middelheim (Southeast & far south) Divided in two by the railway line that runs through it, Zurenborg is home to Antwerp's middle and upper classes. Here – between 1894 and 1914 – they embarked on an architectural frenzy that made Zurenborg famous throughout Europe for its condensed collection of architecture. Everything from Art Nouveau to neo-Flemish Rennaissance is on show along Cogels-Osylei and the streets that radiate out from Draakplaat/Tramplein roundabout. Those to look out for in particular are the Art Nouveau De Morgenster (*55 Cogels-Osylei*), the Baroque Witte Paleizen (*Circus Cogels-Osylei*), and the Greek neo-Classical Euterpia (*2 Generaal Capiaumontstraat*). Plans to demolish the area in the 1960s had to be abandoned following protests. With tree-lined streets and flower boxes in the windows, it's now considered the most exclusive place to live in the city and it's worth visiting its central square, Dageraadplaats, which is wonderfully free of tourists and lined with great bars and restaurants. The tourist board produce a free booklet containing two walking tours of the area.

Stuck in the outskirts, and virtually never visited by tourists, Middelheim's golden ticket is its green spaces. Its three parks – Den Brandt, Middelheim, and Vogelenzang – are the legacy left by rich nobility who once owned them as private grounds.

Linkeroever (The Left Bank) The oft-ignored west bank of the Scheldt affords great views of Antwerp's skyline. It's reached through St-Anna pedestrian tunnel that runs under the river; to find it look for the 1930s' brick building on St-Jansvliet square.

Inside, an escalator takes you down to the footpath, then it's about a 15-minute walk to the other side. On exiting, the Linkeroever park sits right in front of you; pause to take in the views. Then head north towards De Molen, an open-air swimming pool with nearby restaurants serving good mussels. At the headland is Sint-Anna beach, a stretch of white sand great for sunbathing during summer.

MECHELEN

Mechelen (Malines in French) is one of Flanders' most underrated cities. Today, it's overshadowed by its big brothers, Brussels and Antwerp, but in the late 15th century it was the most important town in the southern Netherlands. Charles the Bold, Duke of Burgundy, established his Great Council in the Schepenhuis in 1473 and Holy Roman Emperor Charles V lived here as a child in 1501 with his aunt Margaret of Austria in the Paleis van Margaretta van Oostenrijk. The city faded from centre stage when Margaret of Austria died in 1530 and her niece Mary of Hungary – who had agreed to look after the territories for her brother Charles V – moved the royal court to Brussels, her place of birth.

Home to 80,000 inhabitants (14% of whom are of Moroccan descent) and just 2.81km², the city may be small, but it's certainly not short on attractions. It boasts more UNESCO-listed sights than any other art city in Flanders – St Rumbold's Tower (page 308), the town hall's *belfort* (page 308), the large *begijnhof* (page 309) and the Ommegang Procession (page 308); it is home to the world's top carillon school, and has a wonderful historic quarter, good museums and restaurants.

GETTING THERE AND AWAY

By car Mechelen is 25 minutes (27km) from Brussels and 30 minutes (25km) from Antwerp. For both, follow the E19, and take either exit 9 (north Mechelen) or exit 10 (south Mechelen). From Leuven it's 35 minutes (25km); follow the N26. From Gent it's 50 minutes (78km); follow the E17 and then the E19. From Brugge it's one hour 20 minutes (110km); follow the A11, then the E19. There's free parking at Douaneplein car park, east of the city centre.

By train Brussels-Zuid/Bruxelles-Midi and Brussels-Centraal (*every 10min daily*; ⊕ *20min*); Antwerp (*every 10min Mon–Fri, 3/7/11/38min past the hour Sat–Sun*; ⊕ *20min*). Mechelen has two railway stations: Mechelen-Centraal and Mechelen-Nekkerspoel; both are a 10–15-minute walk from the city centre. Most trains stop at Mechelen-Centraal.

GETTING AROUND

By bus It's only a 15-minute walk from the station to the city centre, but buses #1, 2, 3, 5 and 7 depart from outside the station and all stop in town should you need them. Tickets €2 when bought on board.

By boat Take to the water and explore the city's canals on a 45-minute boat trip (*Haverwerf;* ✆ *03 213 22 54; www.v-zit.be/en/malinska-bootjevaren-op-de-binnendijle/;* ⊕ *3 Apr–31 Oct departures at 13.30, 14.30, 15.30, 16.30 & 17.30; admission: adult/4–12 €6/4*).

By foot Mechelen is compact and easy to explore on foot. Be sure to have a wander along the **Dijle Path** – a waterside walkway that runs along the south side of the river from Haverwerf to the Kruidtuin (botanical gardens).

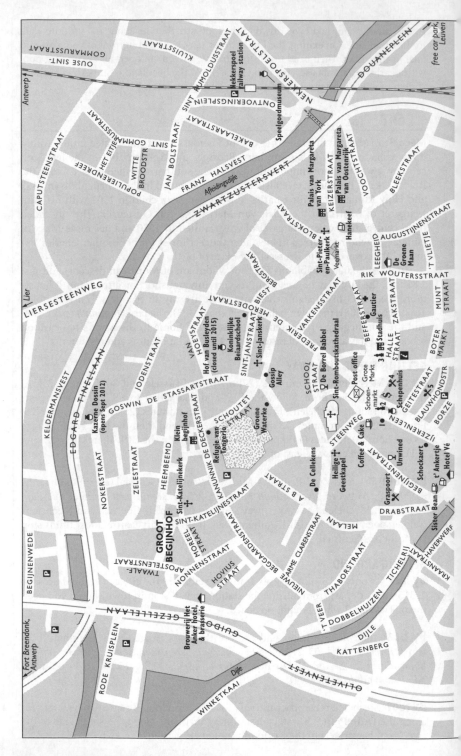

Antwerp

OUSE SINT-
GOMMARUSSTRAAT

SINT-
GOMMARUSSTRAAT

KLUISSTRAAT

SINT-RUMOLDUSSTRAAT

KAKELAARSTRAAT

NEKKERSPOELSTRAAT

DOUANEPLEIN

free car park,
Leuven

Nekkerspoel
railway station

Speelgoedmuseum

ONTVOERINGSPLEIN

NEKKERSPOELSTRAAT

Speelgoedmuseum

CAPUTSTEENSTRAAT

POPULIERENDREEF

HET EITJE

WITTE
BROODSTR

JAN BOLSTRAAT

SINT-GOMMARUSSTRAAT

FRANZ HALSVEST

Afleidingsdijle

ZWARTZUSTERSVEST

BLOKSTRAAT

Palais van Margareta
van York

KEIZERSTRAAT

Palais van Margareta
van Oostenrijk

VOOCHTSTRAAT

BLEEKSTRAAT

Hanekeef

Lier

LIERSESTEENWEG

EDGARD TINELLAAN

KELDERMANSVEST

Kazerne Dossin
(opens Sept 2012)

VAN HOEYSTRAAT

Hof van Busleyden
(closed until 2015)

Koninklijke
Beiaardschool

SINT-JANSTRAAT

Sint-Janskerk

BIEST

FREDERIK DE MERODESTRAAT

BERGSTRAAT

Sint-Pieter-
en-Paulkerk

Veemarkt

LEEGHEID

AUGUSTIJNENSTRAAT

De
Groene
Maan

'T VLIETJE

RIK WOUTERSSTRAAT

BEFFERSTRAAT

Gautier

MUNT
STRAAT

GOSWIN DE STASSARTSTRAAT

JODENSTRAAT

Gossip
Alley

SCHOUTET
STRAAT

Groene
Waterke

SCHOOL
STRAAT

De Borrel Babbel

Sint-Romboutskathedraal

Post office

Grote
Markt

Schoen-
markt

Stadhuis

HALLE
STRAAT

ZAKSTRAAT

Schepenhuis

GEITESTRAAT

BLAUWHONDSTR

BOTER
MARKT

BORZE

NOKERSTRAAT

ZELESTRAAT

HEEMBEEMD

Klein
begijnhof

SINT-KATELIJNE KANUNNIK DE DECKERSTRAAT

Refugie van
Tongerlo

Sint-Katelijnekerk

A B STRAAT

De Cellekens

STEENWEG

Heilige
Geestkapel

Coffee & Cake

Unwined

Schockaert

Graspoort

Sister Bean

't Ankertje

Hotel Vé

IJZERENLEEN

BEGIJNENSTRAAT

BEGIJNENWEDE

GROOT
BEGIJNHOF

SINT-KATELIJNESTRAAT

MOREEL
STRAAT

TWAALF-
APOSTELENSTRAAT

NONNENSTRAAT

NIEUWE BEGGAARDENSTRAAT

NIEUWE ARME CLARENSTRAAT

MELAAN

HOVIUS
STRAAT

THABORSTRAAT

DRABSTRAAT

KRAANSTRAAT

HAVERWERF

TICHELRIJ

'T VEER

'T DOBBELHUIZEN

DIJLE

Fort Breendonk,
Antwerp

RODE KRUISPLEIN

GEZELLELAAN

GUIDO

Brouwerij Het
Anker hotel,
& braserie

Dijle

WINKETKAAI

OLIVETENVEST

OUSE DIJLE

KATTENBERG

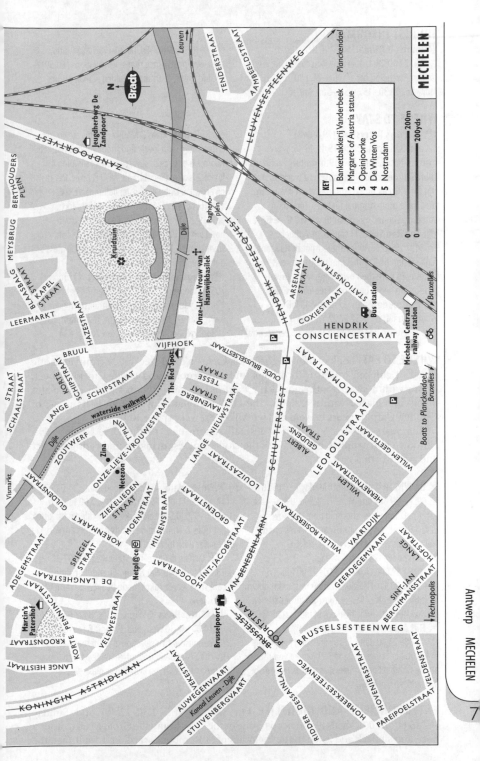

KEY
1 Banketbakkerij Vanderbeek
2 Margaret of Austria statue
3 Opsinjoorke
4 De Witten Vos
5 Nostradam

0   200m
0   200yds

Leuven ↑

Planckendael

Jeugdherberg De Zandpoort

ZANDPOORTVEST

BERTHOUDERS PLEIN

MEYSBRUG

BLAASBALG

LEERMARKT

KAPEL STRAAT

HAZESTRAAT

Kruidtuin

Dijle

Ragheno-plein

LEUVENSESTEENWEG

AAMBEELDSTRAAT

TENDERSTRAAT

Bruxelles

STATIONSSTRAAT

ARSENAAL-STRAAT

COXIESTRAAT

Bus station

HENDRIK CONSCIENCESTRAAT

Mechelen Centraal railway station

Boats to Planckendael, Bruxelles

HENDRIK SPEECVEST

Onze-Lieve-Vrouw van Hanswijkbasiliek

VIJFHOEK

The Red Spot

waterside walkway

OUDE BRUSSELSESTRAAT

TESSE STRAAT

RAVENBERG STRAAT

LANGE NIEUWSTRAAT

SCHUTTERSVEST

ALBERT GEUDENS STRAAT

COLOMASTRAAT

LEOPOLDSTRAAT

WILLEM GEETSTRAAT

WILLEM HERETHSTRAAT

WILLEM ROSIERSTRAAT

LOUIZASTRAAT

GROENSTRAAT

SINT-JACOBSTRAAT

VAN-BENEDENLAARN

HOOGSTRAAT

MILSENSTRAAT

MOENSTRAAT

ZIEKELIEDEN STRAAT

ONZE-LIEVE-VROUWESTRAAT

Zina
Netezon

ZOUTWERF

Dijle

Vismarkt

GULDENSTRAAT

KORENMARKT

SPIEGEL STRAAT

DE LANGHESTRAAT

Netpl@ce

SCHAALSTRAAT

STRAAT

LANGE KORTE

SCHIPSTRAAT

SCHIPSTRAAT

BRUUL

ADEGEMSTRAAT

VELEWESTRAAT

KRONINGSTRAAT

Martin's Patershof

KROONSTRAAT

KORTE HEISTRAAT

LANGE HEISTRAAT

KONINGIN ASTRIDLAAN

AUWEGEMVAART

Kanaal Leuven - Dijle

STUIVENBERGVAART

Brusselpoort

BRUSSELSE-POORTSTRAAT

BRUSSELSESTEENWEG

GEERDEGEMVAART

VAARTDIJK

RIDDER DESSAINLAAN

HOMBEEKSESTEENWEG

PAREIPOELSTRAAT

HOVENIERSSTRAAT

BERCHMANSSTRAAT

SINT-JAN

LANGE HOFSTRAAT

VELDENSTRAAT

Technopolis

Bradt

N

TOURIST INFORMATION

ⓘ Tourist information 2–6 Hallestraat; ☎ 070 22 00 08; e toerisme@mechelen.be; www.tourismmechelen.be; ◷ Nov–Mar 09.30–16.30 Mon–Fri, 09.30–15.30 Sat–Sun, Apr–Oct 09.30–17.30 Mon–Fri, 09.30–16.30 Sat–Sun. Well-equipped office that sells city maps (€0.50) & cycling maps, & arranges guided walking tours.

⌂ WHERE TO STAY

⌂ **Martin's Patershof** (79 rooms) 4 Karmelietenstraat; ☎ 015 46 46 46; www.martins-hotels.com. This 19th-century Franciscan church turned chic 4-star hotel is a world first. Opt for a 'Great' or 'Exceptional' room if you can: they have more original features, including stunning stained-glass windows. €€€–€€€€

⌂ **The Red Spot** (3 suites) 14 Vijfhoek; m 0497 22 46 27; www.theredspot.be. Elegant high-design B&B with 3 minimalist white-&-red suites each with their own living room, private terrace, kitchen & bedroom. Free Wi-Fi. €€€

⌂ **De Groene Maan** (2 rooms) 19 Rik Woutersstraat; m 0497 67 22 17; www.degroenemaan.be. 'The Green Moon' is a very central eco B&B run by Klaas & Marijke. Rooms are en suite & decorated with lovely finds from antique markets. Room 1 is a spacious suite capable of sleeping 4; Room 2 is a smaller dbl. Free Wi-Fi & bikes. Pay cash on arrival or by bank transfer beforehand. €€

⌂ **Hotel Vé** (36 rooms) 12–14 Vismarkt; ☎ 015 20 07 55; www.hotelve.com. A chain hotel with a difference: it was formerly a fish smokehouse. Extras inc free drink in bar & glass of bubbly with b/fast. €€

⌂ **Jeugdherberg De Zandpoort** (37 rooms) 70 Zandpoortvest; www.mechelen-hostel.com. Modern youth hostel on the southeastern edge of town. Has 2-, 3-, & 4-bed rooms, restaurant, bar & TV lounge. Dorm beds for +26s €20, sgl €34.

✕ WHERE TO EAT

Look out for *Mechelse koekoek* – a local stew made from an exotic breed of chicken mixed with onions and mushrooms and cooked in local beer. Those with a sweet tooth should try *maneblussertjes* – moon-shaped chocolates or biscuits glazed with marzipan. The city's pride and joy though is its range of Gouden Carolus beers brewed by Het Anker Brewery (page 309).

Ten years ago the Vismarkt – a small square next to the Dijle River – was rundown and avoided, but today it's the city's trendiest drinking and eating district and well worth a visit.

✕ **De Witten Vos** 30 Grote Markt; ☎ 015 20 63 69; ◷ 09.30–late Mon–Fri & Sun, 09.00–late Sat. A safe bet when choosing from the slew of restaurants on the Grote Markt. Serves good Flemish classics, salads & pastas. €€€€

✕ **Graspoort** 28 Begijnenstraat; ☎ 015 21 97 10; ◷ 12.00–14.00 & 18.00–22.00 Tue–Fri, 18.00–22.00 Sat. Health-conscious restaurant down a cobbled alleyway. Pastas, couscous dishes & open sandwiches with huge helpings of fresh salad. €€€

✕ **Het Anker** 49 Guido Gezellelaan; ◷ 11.00–23.00 daily. Rustic brasserie belonging to Het Anker Brewery (page 309) where you can try all the Gouden Carolus beers, as well as local dish *Mechelse koekoek*. €€

✕ **Nostradam** 25 Blauwhondstraat; ☎ 015 21 14 99; ◷ 11.00–15.00 & 17.00–22.00 Tue–Fri, 10.00–22.00 Sat. Laidback *eetcafé* filled with kitsch antiques & whose huge salads & pastas are very popular with locals. €€

⊒ **Coffee & Cake** 18 Steenweg; ◷ 07.30–18.00 Mon–Thu, Sat & Sun. Chandelier-laden café that serves cakes made by local Savarin *pâtisserie*. €

⊒ **Sister Bean** 26 Vismarkt; ☎ 0497 67 22 17; ◷ 10.00–18.30 Wed–Sun. Organic & Fairtrade coffeehouse with a selection of homemade cakes. Try the 'Sister Bean' iced coffee made with chocolate & *speculaas* & served in a Martini glass. €

ENTERTAINMENT AND NIGHTLIFE

On Saturday (◷*11.30–12.30*) and Sunday (◷ *15.00–16.00*), locals like to head to one of the cafés lining the Grote Markt, order a beer, and sit back and listen to the melodies of St Rombout's carillon. In summer, the

Beiaardschool (Royal Carillon School) organises live **carillon concerts** (◷ *6 Jun–12 Sep 20.30 Mon*), which are best appreciated on Cultuurplein. Otherwise, Mechelen is a city for enjoying good beers and conversation, not for late-night dancing.

⌂ **'t Ankertje** 26 Vismarkt; ☏ 015 34 60 34; www.tankertje.be; ◷ 15.30–01.00 Tue–Thu, 15.30–02.00 Fri, 11.00–02.00 Sat, 14.00–20.00 Sun. A charming brown café where it's easy to while away the houses nursing a Gouden Carolus. All the varieties are served here thanks to the bar's close relationship with the Het Anker Brewery.

♀ **De Borrel Babbel** 7 Nieuwwerk; ☏ 0477 72 48 04; ◷ 09.00–late Mon–Fri, 11.00–late Sat–Sun. Mechelen's smallest bar – there are just 3 tables inside – is hidden down an alley behind the cathedral. Lovely terrace spilling out on to private square.

⌂ **Hanekeef** 8 Keizerstraat; ☏ 015 20 78 46; ◷ 09.00–late Mon–Sat, 12.00–late Sun. Pub established in 1880 with free Wi-Fi & a small terrace overlooking St-Pieters & Pauluskerk.

♀ **Unwined** 23 Begijnenstraat; ☏ 015 41 81 85; ◷ 18.00–00.00 Thu, 12.00–00.00 Fri–Sat. Koen Vanoverbeke runs this refreshingly unpretentious *bodega*, which aims to eliminate the snobbery surrounding wine bars by using a simple selection chart based on country of origin & occasion.

SHOPPING Mechelen's shopping district centres around the pedestrianised triangle of streets: Bruul, Ijzerenleen and Onze-Lieve-Vrouwstraat. On Bruul you'll find the usual commercial high-street shops, while the other two are lined with specialist one-off stores.

Banketbakkerij Vanderbeek 36 Steenweg; ☏ 015 20 32 66; ◷ 07.00–18.30 Wed–Sat, 07.00–14.00 Sun. Family baker, established in 1786; sells *maneblusser* biscuits & *potdommeke*, a local brown bread with raisins so named after a baker mistakenly mixed the raisins with brown, instead of white, flour & exclaimed *potdommeke* ('damn it!').

Gauthier 12 Befferstraat; ☏ 015 21 95 90; ◷ 09.30–12.30 & 13.30–18.00 Tue–Sat. This family-run business is *the* place to buy chocolates: they're handmade from scratch without preservatives by the father Edouard; his daughter, Pascale, makes the ice cream sold next door at No10.

OTHER PRACTICALITIES

$ **Bank** 27 Grote Markt; ☏ 015 29 82 00; ◷ 09.00–12.30 & 12.00–16.30 Mon–Fri. Notice the plaque outside: Victor Hugo wrote a poem on carillons while staying here in 1837.

♻ **Bike rental** Fietshaven, Centraal Station, ☏ 03 203 06 73, ◷ 09.00 –13.00 & 15.00– 18.30, €13/day; Freewieler, 1 Steenplein, ☏ 03 213 22 51, ◷ 15 Mar–31 Oct 10.00–18.00 daily, €15/day

MOON EXTINGUISHERS

Residents of Mechelen are known as *maneblussers* ('moon extinguishers'). The nickname was coined one misty night on 28 January 1687 when a local stumbled out of one of the bars on the Grote Markt and, looking upwards, recoiled in horror to see St Rumbold's Tower on fire. He raised the alarm and the city's residents started ferrying buckets of water up the 500 steps to the top of the tower to douse the flames. Only when they reached the top did they discover that the 'fire' was, in fact, the orange glow of a winter moon shining through the mist. Mortified at their mistake, the locals tried to keep the incident hush-hush, but word of the blunder soon spread to Antwerp whose residents delight in calling people from Mechelen *maneblussers* to this day. In true Flemish fashion, locals have embraced the nickname and name their local biscuits and chocolates after it.

✉ Internet Netpl@ce, 28 Hoogstraat, \ 015 64
01 54; t' Netkot, 81 Leopoldstraat, \ 015 43 14 44
Markets General market, Grote Markt
🕐 08.00–13.00 Sat; Flea market, Veemarkt,
🕐 May–Oct 11.00–17.00 Sun; Guido Gezellelaan,
🕐 08.00–13.00 Mon, Wed & Fri

✚ Pharmacy 26 Befferstraat; \ 015 20 13 24;
🕐 08.45–12.30 & 13.30–18.30 Mon–Fri, 08.45–
12.30 & 13.30–17.00 Sat, closed Wed afternoon
✉ Post office 1 Grote Markt; 🕐 09.00–18.00
Mon–Fri, 09.00–12.30 Sat

WHAT TO SEE AND DO

Grote Markt Mechelen's impressive market square is dominated by **Sint-Romboutskathedraal** (*St Rumbold's Cathedral, Grote Markt;* \ *070 22 00 08;* 🕐 *Nov–Mar 09.00–16.00 Tue–Sun, Apr–Oct 09.00–17.00 Tue–Sun*), named after an Irish (or possibly Scottish, no one is sure) missionary, St Rumbold, who visited the area in the 8th century. Sadly, two locals took offence at his attempts to convert them to Christianity and murdered him, but an abbey was built in his honour. Work on the current Gothic-Brabant cathedral started in 1200 and wasn't completed in full until 1520. Inside, look for the solid-oak pulpit depicting Earthly Paradise (get up close to find the carvings of a pelican, squirrel, snakes and snails) and St Norbert being flung from his horse as he repents; Anthony van Dyck's *Christ on the Cross* in the right transept; 25 15th- and 16th-century paintings depicting the life of St Rumbold in the choir aisle; and the relics of St Rumbold kept behind the golden doors of the 17th-century high altar. However, it's the cathedral's soaring blunt-ended **tower** (🕐 *10.00–18.00 Tue–Sun, last visit 16.30; adult/under 12 €7/€3.50*) that steals the show. The 97m-high belfry was never finished due to a lack of funds. It's one of the few cathedrals in Flanders where you can glimpse the carillon as you ascend the 538 steps to the top. It's not an easy climb, so take your time. A new glass Sky Walk offers 360° views of the town and on a clear day you can see Brussels and Antwerp.

On the southern side of the square stands a **statue of Margaret of Austria**. When Belgium gained independence in 1830 the government ordered every city to raise a statue of a local hero and, interestingly, Mechelen is the only town that chose a woman. *Ons Margriet* – as she's affectionately known – used to stand in the centre of the Grote Markt, but was moved to the side in 2005 to make way for the new underground car park.

To the east is the UNESCO-listed **Stadhuis** (town hall) comprised of the former Lakenhalle (Cloth Hall) – with its unfinished belfry – and the Palace of the Great Council. The belfry is, in fact, hollow; funds for its completion dried up when trade dipped in the 14th century and the tower stood empty for 200 years before the city could afford to add a roof. A tour of the town hall, its impressive council chamber and the *Battle of Tunis* tapestry can be booked at the tourist information office adjacent. A **bronze statue of Opsinjoorke** (see box opposite) stands outside the office.

North of the Grote Markt Head west along Onder-den-Torenstraat and look for the 13th-century **Heilige Geestkapel** (Chapel of the Holy Ghost) on the corner of

---

OMMEGANG

Most people have only heard of Brussels' Ommegang – a procession of giant puppets. But Mechelen, too, has it's own UNESCO-listed version which takes place after the Hanswijk Cavalcade, a huge horse-filled extravaganza that most people only get to experience three times in their lives because it takes place every 25 years. The next is in 2013, on 25 August and 1 September.

Mechelen and Antwerp enjoy a light-hearted rivalry, but things weren't always so amicable. Tensions arose in 1301 when Antwerp lost is *staplerechten* (staple rights) to Mechelen, meaning that all fish, salt and corn brought in by boat had to be offered for sale in the city markets for three days before it could be reloaded and taken to Antwerp. However, the rivalry reached new heights on 4 July 1775 while Mechelen was celebrating its annual procession of *Sotscop* ('Dumbhead') – a doll symbolising drunken abusive husbands which was symbolically humiliated by being paraded through town and thrown up in the air on a sheet. On this occasion, the doll was thrown too high and landed in the crowd. An onlooker from Antwerp reached out to catch it, but was accused of trying to steal the doll. The crowd was furious and the poor chap had to attend a court hearing. He was eventually cleared, but ever since the doll has been known as *Opsinjoorke* – a bastardised version of the Italian *signor* used by Mechelen residents to mock Antwerpens for their snobby attitude.

Minderbroedersgang. It survived various attacks on the city and is believed to be the oldest building in town.

Follow Minderbroedersgang. Halfway along, on the right-hand side, you'll see **De Cellekens** (The Cells), a U-shaped building with a beautiful courtyard garden. It's private property now, but try and get a glimpse of the garden and its border of small 19th-century houses; each used to provide shelter (well, a bed, table and chair) for destitute single women.

Moving on, you reach a newly uncovered section of canal known as the **Melaan**. It last saw daylight in 1913 when it was covered to prevent the spread of disease.

Crossing the water, walk down Arme-Clarenstraat. The end of this streets marks the beginning of the **Groot Begijnhof** (*Nonnenstraat, Conventstraat, Hoviusstraat, Acht-Zalighedenstraat*), Mechelen's UNESCO-listed *begijnhof* (see box, page 18). Originally, it stood outside the city walls but these buildings were destroyed in 1560 during the religious wars so the béguines moved closer to the centre, buying existing property and building a few new houses as well. This led to a mix of architectural styles that make Mechelen's *begijnhof* unique in Flanders – others follow a uniform layout.

On its western flank sits the **Brouwerij Het Anker** (*Het Anker Brewery; 49 Guido Gezellelaan;* \ *015 28 71 41;* e *brasserie-hotel@hetanker.be; www.hetanker.be;* ⊕ *tours 11.00 Fri–Sun, minimum 4 people; €7.20*). Founded by Jan uit den Anker in 1369, Het Anker is one of Belgium's oldest breweries. Charles V famously enjoyed a mug of den Bruynen, which is still brewed and known as Gouden Carolus Ambrio. Today, Het Anker produces several varieties, but I recommend the Classic (8.5%) – which won gold medal at the 2010 World Beer Awards – and the Cuvée van de Keizer, a knee-buckling 11% brew released on 24 February every year to commemorate Charles V's birthday. Groups of four or more can book a tour of the brewery and a tasting session afterwards – email the address above – or you can visit the on-site brasserie.

Retrace your steps and exit the Groot Begijnhof via Moreelstraat. In front of you stands **Sint-Katelijnekerk** (Church of St Catherine) (⊕ *Apr–Oct 13.00–17.00 Tue–Sun, Nov–Mar 13.00–16.00 Tue–Sun; admission free*) built in honour of a lass called, you guessed it, Catherine who was sentenced to death by the Romans

Antwerp MECHELEN

7

for refusing to renounce Christianity. She was strapped between two wheels and 'driven' through town, but instead of tearing her in two the wheels broke. Sadly, the Romans weren't impressed so they resorted to beheading her.

Behind the church, just off Kanunnik de Dekerstraat, is the city's **Klein Begijnhof** – a U-shaped alley leading off from Klein Begijnhofstraat – but it's currently a bit shabby, so skip it. Carry on and turn right into Schoutetstraat where you'll find **Refugie van Tongerlo** (⊕ *09.00–12.00 & 13.00–15.00 Mon–Fri*). The high walls of this 15th-century former abbey conceal a green oasis: a hidden garden of box hedges and gravestones embedded in paths, where the only sound is the soothing trickle of the courtyard fountain. Enter quietly and enjoy a few moments of peace. The compound now belongs to **De Wit** (*7 Schoutetstraat;* ☏ *015 20 29 05; www. dewit.be;* ⊕ *10.30 Sat; adult/children 12–18 €6/€2*), a family-run company that cleans and restores tapestries. I realise it's a subject that initially doesn't get everyone excited, but the company is the world's best – they've even restored tapestries that hang in the Vatican. Their guided tours, hosted every Saturday, offer a real off-the-beaten-track experience; you'll get a tour of their prestigious collection of ancient and modern tapestries and see a demonstration.

Follow Schoutetstraat to its conclusion. Here you can turn left to see the **Groene Waterke** (Green Water), another area of exposed canal named after the green weed which grows there, or cross the road and dip through the small archway which conceals **Klapgat** (Gossip Alley) where the town's women used to gather for a gossip after attending mass at **Sint-Janskerk** (St John's Church) (⊕ *Apr–Oct 13.00– 17.00 Tue–Sun, Nov–Mar 13.00–16.00 Tue–Sun; admission free*). Members of the Great Council attended this parish and consequently it contains a great number of treasures, including a triptych by Pieter Paul Rubens placed above the altar. In 2008, exquisite 14th-century murals of St Christopher and St George were uncovered in the church tower and can now be visited with a guide.

Moving on you reach Frederik de Merodestraat. Walking left will quickly lead you to the **Koninklijke Beiaardschool** (Royal Carillon School) which occupies the white Rococo-style building on the corner. If you look through the window you can sometimes see students practising. However, the real trial runs take place in the tower of **Hof van Busleyden** (*65 Frederik de Merodestraat;* ⊕ *closed for renovation until 2015*), the private home of Hieronymus van Busleyden, an advisor to Charles V.

Cross the road and follow the Biest, through to the Veemarkt, site of the Jesuit **Sint-Pieter-en-Paulkerk** (Church of St Peter and St Paul) (⊕ *Apr–Oct 09.30–11.30 Mon–Sat, 13.00–17.00 Sun; Nov–Mar 09.30–11.30 Mon, 09.30–11.30 & 12.00–16.00 Tue–Sat, 13.00–16.00 Sun*), famous for its ten enormous paintings depicting the life of missionary Francis Xavier and the large number of confessionals brought in to absolve the sins of all the wrong-doers hanging out on the Veemarkt before they touched the church's relics.

Next door, on Keizerstraat, is the **Palais van Margareta van York** (Margaret of York's Palace). Margaret was the third wife of Charles the Bold, Duke of Burgundy. She moved to Mechelen after being banished from Gent for meddling in the affairs of her stepdaughter Mary of Burgundy who was left in charge when Charles died in 1477. Don't be fooled by the paltry façade you see today; the palace once occupied the huge triangle of land which sits between Keizerstraat, Blokstraat and Zwartezustersvest.

Across the road is **Paleis van Margareta van Oostenrijk** (Margaret of Austria's Palace), which was designed Keldermans – the same architect responsible for St Rumbold's Tower – and the first Renaissance-style building to be constructed in the Low Countries. Walk through the green door on the left and you enter a regal courtyard lined with box hedges and vines climbing the high walls.

Before heading south of the river, walk to the northern tip of the city where, from September 2012, you'll find **Kazerne Dossin** (*Goswin de Stassartstraat;* ✆ *015 29 06 60; www.kazernedossin.be*). From 1942 to 1944 more than 25,000 Jews and gypsies were deported from SS Sammellager Mecheln, a Nazi barracks based in Mechelen, to Auschwitz-Birkenau concentration camp. Only 5% (1,221 people) escaped the gas chambers. The city was chosen due to its proximity to both Brussels and Antwerp, which were home to large concentrations of Jewish families. The new museum is a memorial to those who lost their lives and will include the collections of the former Joods Museum van Deportatie en Verzet (Jewish Museum of Deportation and Resistance). The first, second and third floors will feature a permanent exhibition on the Holocaust and Mechelen's involvement. The fourth floor will be for changing exhibitions on the topic of human rights. Its floor-to-ceiling windows offer a view over the former barracks to encourage visitors to reflect on the atrocities that took place there.

South of the Grote Markt
Follow **Ijzerenleen**, the broad pedestrianised boulevard leading south of the Grote Markt. It was once a stream linked to the Dijle River, and site of the city's fish market. Margaret of Austria complained about the smell, but it was only filled in after her death in 1531. Today it's lined with smart boutiques with (fake) 16th-century façades. Almost immediately you'll pass the 13th-century **Schepenhuis** (Alderman's House) (*1 Steenweg;* ⊕ *10.00–17.00 Tue–Sun; admission €8*), which served as the city's first town hall and later as the parliament and law courts of the Burgundian empire. It currently houses the world's most complete collection of Rik Wouters' sculptures and Fauvist paintings with pieces on loan from Antwerp's KMSKA. Its seven *Besloten Hofjes* altarpieces have been relocated to Den Grooten Zalm (⊕ *10.00–12.00 & 13.00–17.00 Tue–Sun*) – the former Fishmongers' Guildhouse – on Zoutwerf.

Walk to the end of Ijzerenleen, turn right and enter the **Vismarkt**, a trendy café-lined square that was originally – as you can probably guess from the name – the city's fish market; indeed there are still one or two shops selling their fishy wares. Also on the square is the glass-fronted former **Lamot brewery** which was active until the 1980s but now serves as a modern conference centre.

Retrace your steps and cross the Dijle River via the 13th-century **Grootbrug**, a sandstone bridge that's the oldest of its kind in Flanders. The embankment on the left-hand side is known as **Zoutwerf** (Salt Wharf), where salt used to preserve fish and meat was traded. Look for two wooden façades: the one on the left is De Steur (the Sturgeon) where the salt was stored; the one on the right is De Waag (the Weighhouse) where the salt was weighed. Bills were settled in Innhuysken located next door to De Waag. The building was destroyed by fire in the 17th century, rebuilt by the Fishmongers' Guild and renamed Den Kleinen Zalm to match their taller Renaissance Den Grooten Zalm guildhouse which sits beside it and easily identified by the gilded salmon above the door.

Return to the bridge and head south, through the Korenmarkt, until you reach the outer ring road. In the centre stands **Brusselpoort** (*Kruispunt Hoogstraat*), the only remaining gate from the city walls that surrounded the town in the 13th century.

If you follow the main road around to the left, it's a ten-minute walk to visit **Onze-Lieve-Vrouw van Hanswijkbasilek** (Church of Our Lady of Hanswijk) (*Hanswijkstraat;* ⊕ *Apr–Oct 13.00–17.00 Tue–Sun, Nov–Mar 13.00–16.00 Tue–Sun; admission free*), an atmospheric soot-stained basilica that arose as a result of a miracle. In 988AD a barge carrying deliveries for the burgeoning town was sailing up the Dijle River when it ran around at this very spot in the hamlet of Hanswijk. The cargo was unloaded, but still the boat didn't budge. Only when a statue of the Virgin Mary, which was stored among the deliveries, was moved to dry ground did the barge lift free. Locals took it as a clear indication that Mary wanted to stay where she was, so they built a church in her honour. The episode is celebrated with the Hanswijk Procession (*www.hanswijkprocessie.org*), held every year on the Sunday before Assumption. A huge parade kicks off around 15.00 and weaves its way through town along Keizerstraat, Veemarkt, Befferstraat, Grote Markt, IJzerenleen, Guldenstraat, Onze-Lieve-Vrouwestraat, Vijfhoek and Hanswijkstraat. Tourists are welcome to join in; just notify the organisers beforehand and they'll provide you with a costume.

Day trips

Technopolis (*Technologielaan;* \ *015 34 20 00; www.technopolis.be;* ⊕ *09.30– 17.00 daily; adult/3–11 €11.50/9*) Interactive science museum that explains all those things you never learnt in school, and allows kids to race a leopard, stand inside a giant soap bubble or sleep on a bed of nails.

Getting there It's a ten-minute bus ride from the city; buses #282/682 depart every 30 minutes from the main station.

Plankendael (*582 Leuvensesteenweg, Muizen;* \ *015 41 49 41; www.planckendael. be;* ⊕ *Jan–Feb, Nov & Dec 10.00–16.45 daily, Mar–Apr & Oct 10.00–17.30 daily, May–Jun & Sep 10.00–18.00 daily, Jul–Aug 10.00–19.00 daily; adult/3–17/under 3 €21/17/free*) Normally, I don't recommend zoos, but Plankendael is a little different: it's a 40ha safari park which runs a research and conservation programme with Antwerp Zoo (page 296). Animals are split into five habitat zones and have plenty of room to roam. Highlights include a tree-top walk over the park.

Getting there It's a ten-minute journey via bus; take #284/285 from outside the railway station. Alternatively, if you're travelling during summer, consider taking a zoo-themed 30-minute boat ride (*Colomabrug;* \ *0477 36 48 20;* ⊕ *Apr–Jun & Sep every 40min 09.30–17.30 Sat–Sun, Jul–Aug every 40min 09.30–17.30 daily*), which departs from behind the railway station every 40 minutes.

LIER

It's a hard heart that isn't charmed by Lier. This compact town, equidistant between Antwerp and Mechelen, is officially older than Brussels, having received its town charter in 1227, 15 years prior to the capital. It was also the stage for one of the most famous marriages in history. To prevent arguments breaking out between the competing cities of Gent, Brussels, Brugge and Antwerp it was decided that Philip the Fair and Johanna of Castille would marry in Lier. The story goes that they fell in love at first sight – she was 16, he was 18 – and Philip insisted the marriage took place that very same evening. Presumably so the lustful teenager could consummate the marriage as soon as possible! Among their six children was Charles V, who would rise to become Holy Roman Emperor.

The town has a strong association with lace – between 1820 and 1950 3,000 women were employed at home making it – and you can visit a workshop in the pretty *begijnhof*. You also shouldn't miss Lier's pride and joy, an 80-year-old clocktower known as the Zimmertoren. If you can, visit in spring when the surrounding orchards are in full bloom and a traditional racing-pigeon market is held on the Grote Markt – such markets are very rare these days.

GETTING THERE AND AWAY

By car From Antwerp follow signs for the R10, then join the N1 and follow it south for 3km, then turn right onto the N10 to Lier (*21km; ⏱ 30min*). From Mechelen follow the N14 north (*17km; ⏱ 22min*).

By train Antwerp (*13/31/38/46/51min past the hour Mon–Fri, 19/26/43/47min past the hour Sat–Sun; ⏱ 14min*); Mechelen (*direct 5min past the hour Mon–Fri, ⏱ 16min; on the hour/6min past the hour Sat–Sun, ⏱ 40min*); Leuven (*5min past the hour daily; ⏱ 50min*); Brussel-Noord/Bruxelles-Nord (*direct 47min past the hour Mon–Fri, ⏱ 30min; via Antwerp, 42min past the hour Sat–Sun; ⏱ 50min*).

TOURIST INFORMATION

Tourist information 57 Grote Markt; 03 800 05 55; e toerisme@lier.be; www.toerismelier.be; ⏱ Apr–Oct 09.00–17.00 Mon–Sat, 09.00–16.00 Sun, Nov–Mar 09.00–12.30 & 13.30–17.00 Mon–Fri. Small, friendly office tucked under the Stadhuis. Can book a guided tour with Huge Broes (€50/2hr), a distinguished member of the community who lives in the *begijnhof*.

Bike rental Fietspunt, 32 Leopoldplein (railway station); 03 488 18 51; ⏱ Apr–Sep 07.00–19.00 Mon–Fri, 09.00–13.00 Sat–Sun, Oct–Mar 07.00–19.00 Mon–Fri; €9.50/day with €25 deposit

WHERE TO STAY, EAT AND DRINK

Look out for *Lierse vlaaikes*, little round cakes with a hard, crunchy casing and a soft spiced filling made with cinnamon, nutmeg, coriander and cloves. The best place to try the local Caves and St Gummarus beers is **St Gummarus** (*2 Timmermansplein*).

Hotel Florent (22 rooms) 45 Florent van Cauwenberghstraat; 03 491 03 10; www.hotelflorent.be. Right in the centre of town, this new-build has smart, functional rooms & dishes up a great b/fast in the Grand Café downstairs. €€€

Sogno D'Oro (2 rooms) 17 Bril; 03 488 00 85; www.sognodoro.be. Two beautiful suites located above family-run Italian restaurant Annaloro. Both have eastern touches – Buddha statues & fretwork lamps – but Suite Alto on the top floor is possibly the better of the 2, with a mezzanine open-plan bedroom & bathroom with views of Sint-Gummaruskerk. B/fast is taken in your room. €€€

De Nieuw Schapestal 3 Koning Albertstraat; 03 489 02 20; ⏱ 12.00–14.00 & 18.00–22.00 Mon, Thu–Sun. Modern bistro with romantic pink/purple lighting & a Flemish/oriental fusion menu. €€€

Leysen 41 Mechelsestraat; 03 480 51 19; ⏱ 08.00–18.00 Mon, Tue & Thu–Sun. Scruffy bakery/café which always serves *Lierse vlaaikes*.

WHAT TO SEE AND DO

Grote Markt Lier's half moon-shaped main square is studded with historic buildings, most notably the **Stadhuis** (1740), perched in the southeastern corner, and the attached **Belfort** (1369). The interior of the town hall sports an elaborate oak spiral staircase and painted ceiling in the Council Chamber, but these can only be visited by groups. Behind these stands the **Vleeshuis** (1418) or Butchers' Hall.

Zimmertoren (*18 Zimmerplein;* 03 800 03 95; www.zimmertoren.be; ⏱ 09.00–12.00 & 13.30–17.30 Tue–Sun; admission: adult/under 16 €2.50/1.50*) It's fair to say that Lier local Louis Zimmer, the self-taught clockmaker after whom this tower is

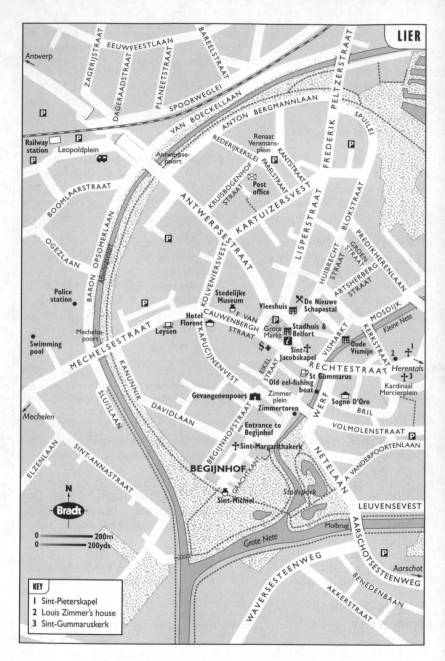

named, was a clever chap. To this day, his clocks remains some of the most intricate and advanced ever produced.

First you'll visit the 4m-high Wonder Clock which has no fewer than 92 astronomical dials. When it was dismantled and shipped to the Rockefeller Center in New York for the 1939 World Fair, it took them two years to put it back together. The clock stayed in America during World War II and was returned to Lier in 1954.

Pick out the third clock from the bottom in the middle row: it takes 25,800 years to make one full rotation which means it's the slowest-moving mechanism in the world. The room also contains a replica of Zimmer's workshop and Clock of the Landings of the Moon, the last clock he ever made (at the age of 80) and which is now set at the hour of his death.

Back outside, across the courtyard is the much-photographed Zimmertoren. The bottom half belonged to the city walls and dates from the 13th century. Zimmer donated the Centenary Clock in 1930 to mark 100 years of Belgian independence. It took him five years to build and features 13 dials which, from 12 o'clock, tell you the phases of the moon, the 19-year lunar cycle, the difference between actual time and solar time, the monthly zodiac sign, the solar cycle, the days of the week (clue: Greek god Jupiter stands for Thursday), where in the world it's light, the months of the year (clue: hay gatherer stands for July), the day of the month, the season, whether it's high tide or low tide, how many days have passed since the new moon, and the position of the moon in the sky.

Inside the tower, on the first floor, is the equally complicated Jubilee Clock with 12 dials and, on the second floor, the Astronomical Clock with 57 dials. Look for the audio buttons mounted on the wall, which provide explanations of the various parts. On the third floor are the mechanical parts of the Centenary Clock and the portraits of 12 historical Belgian figures that are paraded when the clock strikes twelve.

Stedelijk Museum (*14 Florent van Cauwenberghstraat;* ✆ *03 800 03 96;* ◷ *10.00–12.00 & 13.00–17.00 Tue–Sun; admission: adult/concession/19–25/under 18 €4/3/1/free, audio guide Dutch only*) The town's art museum has been injected with life thanks to a series of Pieter Brueghel the Younger paintings on loan from Antwerp's Museum voor Schone Kunsten until 2017. Pieter copied many of his father's artworks and two – of the chaotic *Spreekworden* (Proverbs), dating from 1607 – form the highlight of the exhibition. The one on the right belongs to Lier; the other is from Antwerp. Brueghel made slight changes to each painting, so it's an interesting game of spot the difference. Also on display are Constant Permeke's muddy and moody *De Boer (The Farmers)* and *De Pelgrims (The Pilgrims)*.

Begijnhof (*Begijnhofstraat;* ◷ *daily; admission free*) Entered via a blue-doored archway, Lier's *begijnhof* was founded in 1212 and is very pretty indeed. Almost immediately you'll come across the 17th-century Rococo-style Sint-Margaritakerk (◷ *only during services*), but keep walking south until you reach the convent and

---

SHEEP HEADS

In the 14th century, Duke of Brabant John II wanted to thank the town residents for their loyalty during fights with neighbouring Mechelen. As a reward they could choose to have a cattle market or a university. The town opted for the cattle market, at which point the duke is claimed to have sighed: 'Oh, the sheep heads!' The market brought them great wealth initially, but the university privileges were bestowed on Leuven instead and the city became famous worldwide. How different the fortunes of the town might have been had they chosen differently. A bronze herd of sheep can be found wandering along Schapenkoppenstraat in commemoration of the event.

turn left in Hellestraat. Here you'll find a **lace workshop** (*4 Hellestraat;* ⊕ *13.30–16.30 Tue & Thu, closed 15 Dec–31 Jan; admission free*) run by elderly ladies who live in the *begijnhof*. They don't speak much English, but they give you a warm welcome and are happy for you to watch and take photos.

Sint-Gummaruskerk (*Kardinal Mercierplein; www.sintgummaruskerktelier.be;* ⊕ *4 Apr–1 Nov 10.00–12.00 & 14.00–17.00 daily; admission free*)

A splendid 14th-century church which took 200 years to complete. It's rich interior houses the relics of St Gummarus, a knight who died in 774AD after performing several miracles and who is honoured as a healer of broken bones and marriage problems. His relics are paraded though town every year on the first Sunday after 10 October. Of the church's many artworks, perhaps the most beautiful are the intricate stained-glass windows gifted by Maximilian I and the young emperor-to-be Charles V when they visited in 1516.

Sint-Pieterskapel (*Heilige-Geeststraat;* ⊕ *09.00–17.00 daily; admission free*)

In the shadow of Sint-Gummaruskerk and dating from 1225, this is the oldest building in Lier. It stands on the site of the wooden chapel built by St-Gummarus when he arrived in the 8th century.

Boat trip

Until 1974 Lier fishermen patrolled the River Neter catching eels from squat black barges and selling their haul at the local fish market. When the practice was banned, the fishermen joined together to form De Koninklije Moedige Bootvissers (*Schapekoppenstraat;* ❧ *03 480 80 75;* ⊕ *Apr–Oct 14.00–17.00 Sat, 14.00–18.00 Sun; admission: adult/under 12 €2.50/1.50*) and now offer boat tours on the original barges.

Cycling

Lier's surrounding countryside is particularly beautiful in springtime when the fruit orchards come into bloom. Hop onto the saddle and follow the *Boomgaardroute* (30km; €2), a bike trail starting from Lier railway station that takes you through the fruit-growing villages of Ranst, Broechem, Emblem, Cremde and Wommelgem. You can buy cherries, pears, and apples from stalls along the route.

The longer *Pallieteren Langs de Nete* (49.6km; €2) route follows the River Nete and leads you to the quaint village of Gestel.

Alternatively, join a self-guided **cycling dinner tour** (⊕ *1 Apr–3 Oct Fri–Sun; €32pp*), which starts with breakfast in the Grote Markt, followed by a starter in the village of Nijlen, lunch in Kessel, a snack in Gestel and dessert back in Lier. You don't need to make a reservation – just pitch up at 09.00 at the tourist office – but you'll need to rent bikes from the railway station prior to starting.

HERENTALS

Hermit-like Herentals once had a thriving cloth trade and you can still see the 16th-century Lakenhalle and old city gates of Zandpoort and Bovenpoort, but today it's an unassuming place which quietly goes about its business.

GETTING THERE AND AWAY

By car From Antwerp take the N12 east out of town and merge onto the E313; after 13km take exit 20 (direction Herentals-West) and follow N13 into town (*33km;* ⊕ *30min*). From Mechelen follow the N14 north to Lier and then take the N13 to Herentals (*37km;* ⊕ *43min*).

By train Antwerp (*13/38/46min past the hour Mon–Fri & 19/26min past the hour Sat–Sun;* ⊕ *35min*); Lier (*5 trains every hour Mon–Fri & 34/42min past the hour Sat–Sun;* ⊕ *15min*); Mechelen (*5min past the hour Mon–Fri & on the hour via Antwerp Sat–Sun;* ⊕ *34min*); Brussel-Noord/Bruxelles-Nord (*47min past the hour Mon–Fri,* ⊕ *52min; 42min past the hour via Antwerp Sat–Sun;* ⊕ *1hr 4min*).

TOURIST INFORMATION

i Tourist information 35 Grote Markt; \014 21 90 88; e toerisme@herentals.be; www.uitinherentals.be; ⊕ 09.00–12.30 Mon, 09.00–12.30 & 13.30–16.00 Tue–Fri, 10.00–14.00 Sat. There are public toilets here. With 4 weeks'

notice, the English-speaking staff can arrange a guide (€50/2hr).

&& Bike rental Fietspunt, railway station, 1 Stationsplein; \014 32 14 45; ⊕ 07.00–19.00 Mon–Fri.

✗ WHERE TO EAT AND DRINK Order a bottle of the dark-blond herby Hertalse Poorter (6.5%), which is actually brewed by Brouwerij Slaghmuylder in Ninove, the other side of Brussels.

✗ Stadspoort 12 Stadspoortstraat; \ 014 23 35 56; ⊕ 11.00–23.00 Wed–Sun. Intimate family-run corner-café which overlooks Bovenpoort – the 15th-century city gate – & serves Flemish classics like *stoofvlees* cooked in Grimbergen beer, rabbit & *tomates-crevettes*. €€€

✗ Posterijen 13 Grote Markt; \ 014 23 29 99; ⊕ 10.00–00.00 Mon, Wed–Sun. This 100-year-old building served as the post office before owner Dirk van Kerkhoven converted it into a restaurant over 18 years ago. High ceilings & old oval tables. Their 2-course *dagmenu* is excellent value & served until 15.00. €€€

WHAT TO SEE AND DO The old Cloth Hall or **Lakenhalle** (*Grote Markt;* ⊕ *with guide or during exhibitions*) stands in the centre of the eyelet-shaped Grote Markt and dates from 1514, but underwent extensive renovations in the 18th century. Walk north along Hofkwartier, turn right into Begijnenstraat and enter Herental's small *begijnhof*. Established in 1212, it's still undergoing renovations and is quite quaint, although the heart symbol 2003 written in red tiles on the church's new roof isn't very tasteful.

If you fancy a mini adventure, catch a bus and visit the 22m-high **Toeristentoren De Paepekelders** (*Lichtaartsesteenweg;* ⊕ *May–Sep 10.00–18.00 daily, Oct–Apr 10.00–16.00 Sat–Sun; admission €1*), a wooden lookout tower (and café) buried in the pine woods a kilometre north of town. It was built in 1985 and has lovely views from the top: on a clear day locals say you can see Brussels' Atomium. To get there take bus #212 (direction Turnhout) from the bus stop on Hofkwartier, just north of the Grote Markt, and get off at Herentals-Kerkhof opposite the cemetery. From there it's a short walk to the tower past 12 statues, including Christ carrying the Cross.

To the east of town is Belgium's second-largest theme park, **Bobbejaanland** (*45 Olensteenweg;* \ *014 55 78 11; www.bobbejaanland.be;* ⊕ *9 Apr–15 Jul & 16 Aug–4 Sep, 10.00–17.00 daily, 16 Jul–15 Aug 10.00–19.00 daily; admission: adult/child from 1–1.40m/under 1m €28/24/free*). Bus #305 departs from Herentals railway station and drops you right outside the park.

GEEL

In the 13th century the sarcophagus of martyr St-Dymphna (see box, page 318), the patron saint of mental disorders, was unearthed in Geel. The town became a major pilgrimage site and it wasn't long before a hospital was established to care for the many patients who came to the town seeking a cure. It's rumoured that Vincent van Gogh was nearly admitted here. Originally run by Augustinian nuns, it stayed open for over 650 years and is one of three such hospitals that can still be visited in western Europe.

The city also boasts a smattering of Art Nouveau homes; ask the tourist office for a detailed brochure.

GETTING THERE AND AWAY

By car From Antwerp follow the E313 east and take exit 23 (direction Geel-West) and take N19 to Geel (*48km;* ⊕ *40min*). From Leuven take the N19 north, past Aarschot (*45km;* ⊕ *56min*). From Hasselt follow the E313 and take exit 24 (direction Geel-Oost) and join N174 to Geel (*42km;* ⊕ *33min*).

By train Antwerp (*direct 13min past the hour Mon–Fri, 19min past the hour Sat–Sun;* ⊕ *40min*); Lier (*29min past the hour Mon–Fri, 34min past the hour Sat–Sun;* ⊕ *29min*); Leuven (*via Antwerp 35min past the hour Mon–Fri,* ⊕ *1hr 24min; via Lier 5min past the hour Sat–Sun,* ⊕ *1hr 54min*); Hasselt (*via Mol 2min past the hour, Mon–Fri,* ⊕ *57min; via Lier/Mol 10min past the hour Sat–Sun,* ⊕ *1hr 49min*).

TOURIST INFORMATION

☑ Tourist information 1 Markt; ☎014 56 63 80; e toerisme@geel.be; www.geel.be; ⊕ 09.00– 12.00 & 13.00–16.00 Mon–Fri, 09.00–12.30 Sat, Apr–Sep 10.00–14.00 Sun.

🏠 WHERE TO STAY, EAT AND DRINK

Geel bakeries prepare one of my favourite regional cookies, *Geels hartjes*: two heart-shaped butter biscuits filled with apricot jam and marzipan. The local beer is Zeuntbier (7.5%), a light blond that goes well with the Zeuntpaté and bitter Zeuntkaas (paté and cheese).

🏠 **Corbie** (24 rooms) 54G Markt; ☎ 014 56 33 00; www.corbie.be. Hip 3-star boutique hotel whose all-white en-suite rooms are punctuated by the odd bright-red chair or lime-green lamp. €€€

✗ **Mille Paste** 15 Markt; ☎ 014 58 46 84; ⊕ 12.00–14.00 & 18.00–22.00 Wed–Fri, 18.00–22.00 Sat, 12.00–14.00 & 17.00–22.00 Sun. Upmarket Italian restaurant behind St-Amandskerk. If you're after something cheaper, the attached La Cucina sells pizza. €€€€

THE LEGEND OF ST DYMPHNA

Dymphna was the daughter of a 7th-century Irish king. When she was 14 years old her mother died and her father, having loved her deeply, sought to replace her with a similar-looking woman. When one couldn't be found he began to pursue his daughter, who apparently was the spitting image of her mother. He was determined to marry her, but when Dymphna heard of her father's intentions she fled the castle with her tutor Gerebernus and sailed to Europe. She landed at Antwerp and made it as far as Geel, but was betrayed by an innkeeper in Westerlo who told the king's agents where she was. Gerebernus was murdered and when Dymphna refused to travel home with the king, he cut off her head. Locals buried them both in a cave and in the 13th century her white sandstone sarcophagus was uncovered; a piece of it can be seen in the Gasthuismuseum (see opposite). If you're dubious about the verity of the legend, then bear in mind that in 1974 the relics were carbon dated and found to be the thigh bones of a young women and an elderly man who died between 700 and 800AD.

✘ **Flore** 52 Markt; ☏ 014 58 80 80; ⏱ 07.00–17.00 daily. Smartest brasserie on the main square with black interior & a lovely old till on reception. Serves the usual mix of steaks & salads. €€€

Verlooy 121 Pas; ☏ 014 58 57 28 ; ⏱ 07.00–17.30 Mon, Wed–Sat, 07.30–16.00 Sun. Best bakery for buying *Geels hartjes*.

WHAT TO SEE AND DO

Gasthuismuseum (*1 Gasthuisstraat;* ☏ *014 56 68 40; www.gasthuismuseum.net;* ⏱ *14.00–17.30 Tue–Fri & Sun; admission: adult/concession/6–12/under 6 €3/2.50/1.50/free, inc audio guide*) A ten-minute walk east from the Grote Markt, this fascinating museum is housed in the old St-Dymphna Hospital, which was founded in 1286 by Geel's feudal lord, Hendrik II Berthout, built on the spot where St Dymphna was martyred (see box opposite), and run by Augustinian nuns until 1552. You can wander through the original rooms, including the scullery, kitchen, pharmacy and former bakery.

The last room of the tour contains a series of panels depicting the legend of St Dymphna and the silver chest used to parade her relics through town every five years. The next procession takes place in May 2015.

Sint-Dimpnakerk (*St-Dimpnaplein;* ⏱ *Apr–Sep 10.00–12.00 & 14.00–17.00 Tue–Fri, 14.00–17.00 Sun, Oct–Mar 10.00–12.00 Tue; admission free*) A 14th-century church which contains the relics of St-Dymphna and Gerebernus and, above the altar, an enormous multi-panel retable carved from wood depicting her legend.

TURNHOUT

Just 11km shy of the Dutch border, Turnhout is the capital of the Kempen, an area of moorland spread between the provinces of Antwerp and Limburg that is largely undeveloped due to its poor soil. However, the town didn't suffer a lack of visitors in the past: the Dukes of Brabant built a castle here so they had somewhere to stay during hunting trips to the Kempen forests, and Maria of Hungary later used it to host lavish parties. By the end of the 16th century, Turnhout had been left impoverished by outbreaks of war, fire and plague, but got back on its feet in the 19th century by carving out a niche as the foremost producer of playing cards. It will enjoy its turn in the spotlight in 2012 when the town will be moonlighting as Flanders' Capital of Culture.

GETTING THERE AND AWAY

By car From Antwerp follow the E313, merge onto E34 and take exit 23 (direction Turnhout-West) (*45km;* ⏱ *37min*). From Geel follow the N19 north (*20km;* ⏱ *24min*). From Lier take the N14 north, merge onto the E34 and take exit 23 (*42km;* ⏱ *40min*).

By train Antwerp (*46min past the hour Mon–Fri,* ⏱ *52min; 26min past the hour Sat–Sun,* ⏱ *49min*); Lier (*6/22min past the hour Mon–Fri, 42min past the hour Sat–Sun;* ⏱ *33min*); Geel via Herentals (*1/25min past the hour Mon–Fri,* ⏱ *37min; 1min past the hour Sat–Sun,* ⏱ *1hr 14min*).

TOURIST INFORMATION

🛈 **Tourist information** 44 Grote Markt; ☏ 014 44 33 55; e toerisme@turnhout.be; www.turnhout.be; ⏱ 09.00–16.30 Mon–Fri, 13.00–16.00 Sat–Sun, Apr–Sep also 10.00–12.00 Sat–Sun. Large, modern office with a free computer terminal where you can check email. They can organise a guide (€50/2hr) with a week's notice, & they sell the *Het Land van Turnhout* cycling map (73km; €1.50), which takes in Arendonk, Beerse, Ravels & Vosselare.

🚲 **Bike rental** Fietspunt, 1 Stationstraat, platform 1 of railway station, ☎ 014 88 29 00, ⏰ 07.00–19.00 Mon–Fri; Fietshuis Hema, 36 Gasthuisstraat, m 0484 16 01 22, ⏰ 09.00–19.00 Mon–Fri, 09.00–18.00 Sat.

🏠 WHERE TO STAY, EAT AND DRINK

🏠 **Bon-Bon Nuit** (3 rooms) 10 Victoriestraat; m 0494 78 88 37; www.bonbonjournuit. be. Award-winning dbl rooms located above a rustic chocolate shop. Choose from the traveller-themed Transatlantique, the spacious Parisien Le Voyage with Jacuzzi bath & views of Heilig-Hartkerk & Jacuzzi bath, or the romantic Baroque-style Le 7ième Ciel in the attic with a claw-foot bath. Also have a wellness room offering various treatments. €€–€€€

✖ **De Weerelt** 17–19 Warandestraat; ☎ 014 72 48 65; ⏰ 12.00–22.00 Tue–Sat. Scandinavian-style restaurant with wooden floors, tables & modern fireplaces. As the name suggests, 'The

World' menu includes flavours from all over the globe. Offers b/fast & cheaper meals can be had in the brasserie. €€–€€€€

✖ **De Waterput** 75 Grote Markt; ☎ 014 65 25 55; ⏰ 10.00–late daily. For a quick, cheap bite to eat, locals recommend this funky pizzeria with lime-green walls & white chairs. Pasta, pittas, sandwiches & salads also appear on the extensive menu. €€

☕ **Café St Pieter** 60 Grote Markt; ⏰ 08.00–01.00 Mon–Fri & Sun, 07.00–02.00 Sat. Spacious bar/café run by the Smulders family since 1906. Lots of wood panelling, heavy wooden beams, yellowing walls, decent beers & light meals. €

WHAT TO SEE AND DO

Sint-Pieterskerk (*Grote Markt;* ⏰ *07.00–22.00 daily; admission free*) The red-brick St Peter's Church was established in the 13th century and has undergone several enlargements – all that remains of the medieval church is the bottom half of the 62m-high tower. Inside you'll find a remarkable 19th-century pulpit featuring fishermen hauling in their catch; a 17th-century statue of Our Lady who usually stands on a snake-wrapped globe, but is moved before and after processions; and – in the St-Anna chapel behind the altar – an anonymous 16th-century triptych showing the martyrdom of St Apollonia (centre) and St Agatha (right), and the decapitation of another unnamed saint (left).

Kasteel van de Hertogen van Brabant (*Kasteelstraat*) Northwest of the main square, this grand moat-surrounded castle was first built in 1110 and used as a lodge by the Dukes of Brabant when they went hunting in the Kempen forest. Under the rule of the Hapsburgs, Maria of Hungary spent a lot of time here and it was known as the 'Hof van Plaisanterie'. In the 18th century it fell into decay and wasn't restored until after World War I. Today it houses the town's law courts.

Begijnhof (*Begijnenstraat*) A five-minute walk north from the Grote Markt, Turnhout's large *begijnhof* is one of Flanders' best. It was founded in 1300, largely destroyed by fire in 1562 during the Reformation, and fully restored in the 17th century. One of the houses now operates as a fascinating **museum** (*56 Begijnhof;* ☎ *014 42 12 48;* ⏰ *14.00–17.00 Tue–Sat, 11.00–17.00 Sun; admission: adult/under18 €2.50/free*) with an introductory video in English about the lives of the béguines and a tour of the rooms including a cellar, and a traditional kitchen with a model of a béguine making lace.

Elsewhere in the compound is a yesteryear **café** (*76 Begijnhof;* ☎ *014 42 12 48;* ⏰ *09.30–18.30 Thu–Sun*), and house No 66, which belonged to the last béguine who died in 2002. On 24 December ever year the *begijnhof* streets are lit with candles.

Taxandriamuseum (*28 Begijnenstraat;* ✆ *014 43 63 35;* ⏰ *14.00–17.00 Tue–Sat, 11.00–17.00 Sun; admission €2.50*) Housed in the Huis metten Thoren, a 16th-century burgher mansion, this regional history museum smartly displays its collection of coins, paintings, porcelain, armour and relics. Throughout 2012 a special exhibition will be on show to celebrate Turnhout's turn as Capital of Culture, and then the permanent collection will return.

Nationaal Museum van de Speelkaart (*18 Druivenstraat;* ✆ *014 41 56 21;* ⏰ *14.00–17.00 Tue–Sat, 11.00–17.00 Sun; admission €2.50*) Turnhout is the largest manufacturer of playing cards in the world. The first were printed here in 1826 and this museum, housed in an old card factory, displays an old steam-powered printing press and the various guises of the cards, from political propaganda and advertising to fortune telling and their use in magic tricks.

Natuurpunt (*1 Graatakker;* ✆ *014 47 29 50;* ⏰ *10.00–12.00 & 13.00–17.00 Tue–Sat; admission free*) An information centre about the Kempen region with a small taxidermy museum.

8

Limburg

Flemish Primitive painter Jan van Eyck, tennis champion Kim Clijsters and cycling world champion Tim Boonen all hail from Limburg, Flanders' least populated and most overlooked province. To the south sits the regional capital Hasselt, famous for the production of *jenever*, and the historic towns of Sint-Truiden and Tongeren – Belgium's oldest settlement. East of Hasselt are the pine woods and heather-laden moors of Hoge Kempen, Belgium's only national park, and to the north lies the Kempen region, once famous for its coal mines and speckled with unassuming villages. I've not covered the industrial town of Genk, but have included Maaseik – a secluded town in Limburg's easternmost corner which is worth investigation.

HASSELT

Hasselt was founded in the 7th century and is the capital of the Limburg province. It's famous for the production of *jenever* – a highly alcoholic grain spirit (page 48) – which has been made here since the 19th century. It originally was just flavoured with juniper berries, hence the name, but today there are hundreds of flavours. You can try a large selection of them at the annual Jeneverfeesten held in mid-October, or join a *jenever*-themed city walk.

At the beginning of the 20th century, the city expanded rapidly when huge deposits of coal were discovered. The mines rose to become some of the biggest in Europe and, at their peak, employed 70% of Limburg's residents. The last mine closed in 1976 and since then the city has reinvented itself as a fashion hotspot, backed up by a fashion museum.

GETTING THERE AND AWAY
By car From Brussels follow the E40 east out of the city and take the exit for the E314 (toward Genk/Hasselt); after passing junction 26 turn off the motorway onto the E313 and take exit 27 (direction Hasselt-West) for the centre (*82km;* ⊕ *1hr*). From Antwerp follow the E313 east and take exit 27 (direction Hasselt-West) (*78km;* ⊕ *55min*).

By train Brussel-Zuid/Bruxelles-Midi (*7/36min past the hour Mon–Fri, 36min past the hour Sat–Sun;* ⊕ *1hr 15min*); Antwerp (*31min past the hour Mon–Fri, 43min past the hour Sat–Sun;* ⊕ *1hr 7min*); Leuven (*13/34/38min past the hour Mon–Fri, 5min past the hour, every hour & 36min past the hour, every 2hrs Sat–Sun;* ⊕ *50min*). The city is easy to explore on foot, but if you'd like to catch a lift from the railway station make use of the De Lijn buses, which can be used free of charge within the city centre.

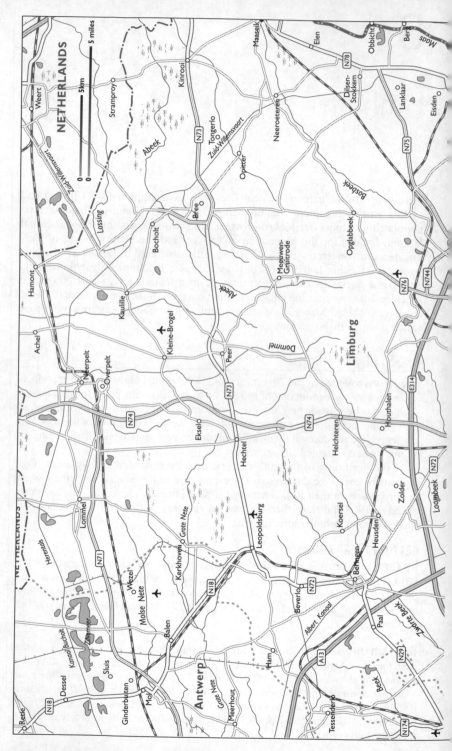

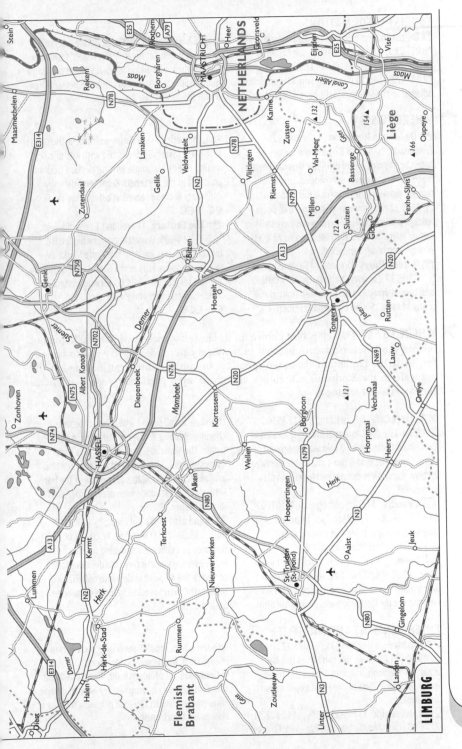

TOURIST INFORMATION

☑ Tourist information 3 Lombaardstraat; ✆ 011 23 95 40; e toerisme@hasselt.be; www. hasselt.eu; ⊕ Apr–Oct 09.00–17.00 Mon–Fri, 10.00–17.00 Sat, 10.00–14.00 Sun. Modern office adjacent to the Stadhuis. Sells *Bokrijk-Kiewit* cycle map (€2.50) for Domein Kiewit nature reserve & can book tickets for the historic Hasselt, fashion or *jenever*-themed walking tours. It's worth booking a guide (€50/2hr) so you can climb the Beiaardtoren & visit the tomb of Heilig Paterke.

WHERE TO STAY

⌂ De Groene Hendrickx (22 rooms) 25 Zuivelmarkt; ✆ 011 28 82 10; www.lodge-hotels.be. An old *jenever* distillery that has been converted & had a new wing added. Lovely contrast between the modern & old. Rooms 11, 21, 22, & 12 have impressive original oak-beam ceilings, while the all-modern rooms have striking feature walls. My favourites were rooms 25 & 31 with gin bottle displays. €€€

⌂ 't Hemelhuys (5 rooms) 15 Hemelrijk; ✆ 011 35 13 75; www.hemelhuys.be. Rustic B&B tucked away in a quiet corner, right in the centre of town. Set up by friends Liesbeth & Ann, they offer a very warm welcome & the snug rooms are tastefully decorated with lots of oak, quality linens & antique writing desks. L'Occitane products in the bathroom & homemade croissants & bread served at b/fast. Free Wi-Fi. €€–€€€

⌂ The Century (10 rooms) 1 Leopoldplein; ✆ 011 22 47 99; www.thecentury.be. Smart, functional 2-star south of the Grote Markt. B/fast taken downstairs in the Grand Café & there's a smart restaurant (€€€€) serving oysters, lobsters & an interesting 'wild' menu too. €€–€€€

✕ WHERE TO EAT

Hasselt is best known for its Hasseltse *jenever* which you'll find not only in the Jenevermuseum bar, but in the local cafés too. The city is also famous for its divine cinnamon-flavoured *speculaas* biscuits – which can be tried at the Tuincafé in the Stadsmus museum – and cooks up a particularly good *stoofvlees* (beer-soaked stew) too.

✕ Theater Café 5 Kunstlaan; ✆ 011 85 90 75; ⊕ 08.30–late daily. Informal brasserie located in the Cultuur Centrum, a 10-min walk southeast of town. Serves the best & most affordable *stoofvlees* in town. Replica VW camper van for kids to play on too. €€

⌑ t'Pandje 3 Paardsdemerstraat; ✆ 011 22 38 37; ⊕ 10.00–18.30 Mon–Sat. Interior design shop with a cosy 8-table café serving salads, paninis & spaghetti at the back. €€

⌑ Boon 13 Paardsdemerstraat; ✆ 011 42 21 99; ⊕ 10.30–18.00 Tue–Sat. Stylish café/shop which hand-makes all its own chocolates on site (you can see the kitchen), & has an extensive hot chocolate list all served with a free chocolate, chocolate mousse & glass of water to refresh the palate. The Kumabo is a whopping 80% dark chocolate drink. Hand-roasted arabic coffee also available. Solid chocolates are on sale at the front – try the 'Hasselt' made with praline, *speculaas* & juniper berries. €

✕ Juan Luis 25 Walputstraat; ✆ 011 20 12 66; ⊕ 18.00–22.00 Thu–Sat, 17.00–22.00 Sun. Operates as a delicatessen during the day, but in the evening you can tuck into delicious tapas served to the 4 quaint tables with red-checked tablecloths, & surrounded by hams suspended from the ceiling. €

ENTERTAINMENT AND NIGHTLIFE

♀ Drugstore 8 Grote Markt; ✆ 011 22 80 08; ⊕ 08.00–01.00 daily. You can't miss this bar thanks to the neon-lit brand names plastered across its façade. One of the most popular spots for a drink.

♀ Het Hemelrijk 11 Hemelrijk; ✆ 011 22 28 51; ⊕ 18.00–late Mon, 12.00–late Tue–Sun. Chunky wooden tables, candlelight & over 300 beers to choose from. Recommended by locals.

♀ Café Café 42 Meldertstraat; ⊕ 15.00–04.00 Tue–Sun. Converted syrup factory with an urbane atmosphere. Live DJs Thu–Sat playing a mixture of alternative & rock music.

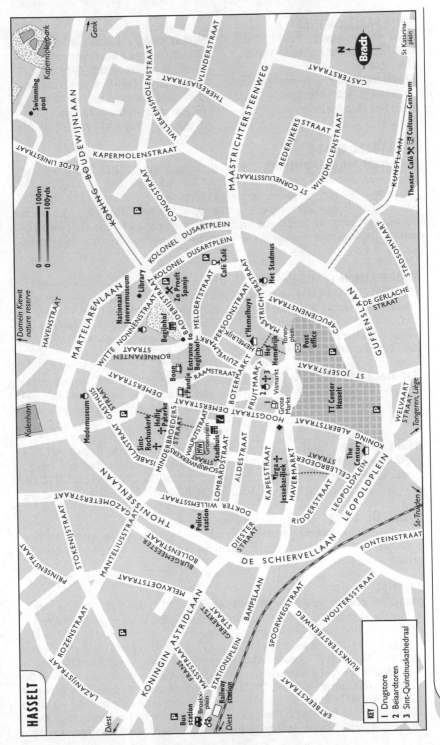

HASSELT

Genk

Kapermolenpark

Swimming pool

Elfde Liniestraat

Domein Kiewit nature reserve

KONING BOUDEWIJNLAAN

KAPERMOLENSTRAAT

WILLEKENSMOLENSTRAAT

THERESIASTRAAT

VLINDERSTRAAT

CONGOSTRAAT

MARTELARENLAAN

HAVENSTRAAT

KOLONEL DUSARTPLEIN

KOLONEL DUSARTPLEIN

Library

Nationaal Jenevermuseum

BADDERIJSTRAAT

MELDERTSTRAAT

Café Café

Zo Proeft Spanje

Het Stadmus

MAASTRICHTERSTEENWEG

REDERIJKERS STRAAT

ST CORNELIUSSTRAAT

WINDMOLENSTRAAT

Beginhof

WITTE NONNENSTRAAT

BONNEFANTEN STRAAT

Beginhoft

Boon

'Pandje Entrance to

RAAMSTRAAT

ZUIVELMARKT

BOTERMARKT

'Hemelhuys

Het Hemelrijk

MAASTRICHTERSTRAAT

ST PERSOONSTRAAT

Toren-plein

Post office

CAPUCIENENSTRAAT

DE GERLACHE STRAAT

GUFFENSLAAN

STADSOMVAART

Kolenhavn

Modemuseum

GASTHUIS

DEMERSTRAAT

Sint-Rochuskerk

Heilig Paterke

MINDERBROEDERS STRAAT

WALPUTSTRAAT

SCHRIJNWERKERSSTRAAT

DEMERSTRAAT

HOOGSTRAAT

FRUITMARKT

Vismarkt

Grote Markt

2 3

ISABELLASTRAAT

THONISSENLAAN

TIGGAZOMETERSTRAAT

DOKTER WILLEMSSTRAAT

LOMBARDSTRAAT

Stadhuis

Groenplein

ALDESTRAAT

KAPELSTRAAT

Virga Jessebasiliek

HAVERMARKT

CELLEBROEDERSTRAAT

KONING ALBERTSTRAAT

TT Center Hasselt

ST JOSEFSTRAAT

WELVAART STRAAT

Tongeren, Liège

Police station

DIESTER STRAAT

RIDDERSTRAAT

The Century

LEOPOLDPLEIN

LEOPOLDPLEIN

St-Truiden

PRINSENSTRAAT

ROZENSTRAAT

STOKENIJSTRAAT

MELKVOETSTRAAT

MANTELIUSTRAAT

BURGEMEESTER BOLLENSTRAAT

KONINGIN ASTRIDLAAN

GERAERTST STRAAT

BAMPSLAAN

DE SCHIERVELLAAN

FONTEINSTRAAT

SPOORWEGSTRAAT

WOUTERSSTRAAT

RIJKSTERSTEENWEG

ERTBEEKSTRAAT

LAZANIJSTRAAT

FRANS MASSTRAAT

STATIONSPLEIN

Broeks-plein

Railway station

Bus station

Diest

Diest

Theater Café Cultuur Centrum

St Katarina-plein

CASTERSTRAAT

KUNSTLAAN

N

Bradt

100m
100yds
0

KEY

1 Drugstore
2 Beiaardtoren
3 Sint-Quintinuskathedraal

Limburg HASSELT

327

OTHER PRACTICALITIES

$ Bank KBC, 7 Havermarkt; ⏰ 09.00–12.30 & 14.00–16.30 Mon–Wed & Fri, 10.20–12.30 & 14.00–18.00 Thu

♻ Bike rental Bikes can be rented free from the Stadhuis (⏰ 10.00–17.00 Mon–Sat); you just have to fill in a form & leave your passport as a deposit.

Markets General market, Kolonel Dusartplein, ⏰ 08.00–13.00 Tue & Fri; antiques market Kolonel Dusartplein; ⏰ Apr–Oct 08.00–13.00 Sat

➕ Pharmacy 8 Grote Markt; ☎ 011 22 33 90; ⏰ 08.30–18.00 Mon–Fri, 08.30–17.30 Sat

✉ Post office 49 Maastrichterstraat; ⏰ 09.00–18.00 Mon–Fri, 09.00–15.00 Sat

WHAT TO SEE AND DO

Nationaal Jenevermuseum (*19 Witte Nonnestraat;* ☎ *011 23 98 60; www. jenevermuseum.be ;* ⏰ *Apr–Oct 10.00–17.00 Tue–Sun, Nov–Mar 10.00–17.00 Tue–Fri, 13.00–17.00 Sat–Sun; admission: adult/concession 12–26/under 12 €4.50/3.50/1/ free*) Housed in one of the town's former steam-powered distilleries, the Jenever Museum explains the traditional production process and displays old posters and bottles. The highlight though is enjoying a few cheeky tots in the wood-panelled bar afterwards.

Modemuseum (*11 Gasthuisstraat;* ☎ *011 23 96 21; www.modemuseumhasselt.be;* ⏰ *10.00–17.00 daily; admission: adult/13–18/ under 12 €5/2/free*) Displays progress through the decades from the 18th century, showing how fashion has changed. It's particularly proud of its *robe à la française*, a tailored coat and multi-layered skirt dating from the mid-18th century. The tourist office can also book tickets for the city's fashion-themed walking route.

Het Stadsmus (*2 Guido Gezellestraat;* ☎ *011 23 98 90; www.hetstadsmus.be;* ⏰ *Apr–Oct 10.00–17.00 Tue–Sun, Nov–Mar 10.00–17.00 Tue–Fri, 13.00–17.00 Sat–Sun; admission free, audio guide €1*) Small museum explaining the city's history.

Heilig Paterke (*19 Minderbroedersstraat;* ☎ *011 24 10 63;* ⏰ *09.00–11.30 & 13.30–16.00 Mon–Fri, 09.45–11.30 & 13.30–16.00 Sat–Sun; admission free*) A chapel housing the tomb of Valentinus Paquay, a friar who lived and died in Hasselt in 1905. He was beatified by Pope John Paul II in 2003.

Wissel Distillery (*12–14 Normandiëstraat;* m *0476 59 95 25;* e *koen@ stokerijwissels.be; www.stokerijwissels.be; admission €5*) This 1920s' *jenever* distillery is the last artisanal outfit in Hasselt. Group visits only, but ask the tourist board to match you up with other visitors.

Day trips

Abdijsite Herkenrode (*4 Herkenrodeabdij;* ☎ *011 23 96 70; www. abdijsiteherkenrode.be;* ⏰ *visitor centre: 10.00–17.00 Tue–Sun, garden: Apr–Oct 10.00–17.00 Tue–Sun; admission: adult/concession/12–18/under 12 €7/5/4/free, inc entry to both*) Founded around 1180 by the Count of Loon and run by Cistercian nuns, this monastery – located 4km northwest of town – was reconstructed in the 15th century, but fell into disrepair when the nuns were expelled during the French Revolution in 1799. In 1972 the buildings were bought by a group of canonesses who built a new monastery and contemplation centre, and set about restoring the old buildings. You can now visit the original stables, coach house and English-style garden. In 2009 St Joseph, a commercial brewery based in Bree, started brewing a beer for the abbey; you can pick up a few bottles of the award-winning Herkenrode Tripel and Herkenrode Bruin at the shop.

You can cycle there, or take free bus #H1 (*direction Henegauwberg-Kermt; 3min past the hour;* ⊕ *34min*) or bus # 23 (*direction Hasselt-Heusden; 28min past the hour;* ⊕ *35min*) from Hasselt railway station, alighting at Kuringen Herkenrode Abdij with the former or Herkenrode with the latter. From there it's a 1km walk.

Natuurdomein Kiewit (*108 Putvennestraat;* ☏ *011 21 08 49;* ⊕ *daily; admission free*) One-hundred-acre nature reserve home to woodpeckers, squirrels, a herb garden and bee hives, laced with walking trails. Take bus #2 (direction Alken/Terkoest-Kiewit) from Hasselt railway station and get off at Kiewit Kinderbroederij.

Alden Biesen (*6 Kasteelstraat;* ☏ *089 51 93 93; www.alden-biesen.be;* ⊕ *Apr–Oct 09.00–17.00 daily, Nov–Mar 10.00–17.00 daily; admission: adult/12–18/under 12 €3/2.50/free*) This huge castle complex is one of Belgium's largest and features a moat-surrounded 13th-century fortress and formal rose-filled gardens. Visit in mid-August and you'll witness jousting contests and chariot races, which form part of Limburg's Folklore Festival. To get there catch the train to Bilsen and then arrange for the Belbus (☏ *011 85 03 00*) to pick you up and drop you off. By car follow the N79 east out of town, join the E313 (direction Antwerp) and take exit 31.

SINT-TRUIDEN

The pleasant town of Sint-Truiden owes its success to the crumbling St-Trudo Abbey which sits at its centre. It was built here, on the banks of the Cicindria River, in the 7th century by a Frankish noble who is claimed to have cured a woman's blindness. When he died his relics were interred in his self-named abbey and it became an important site of pilgrimage. The steady flow of visitors brought wealth and involvement in the linen-production trade. The town lost its standing in the mid 15th century when Charles the Bold took charge and destroyed the city walls. The town's monuments suffered further damage during the French Revolution and World War I. However, you can still visit the three most important buildings – the Stadhuis, Abdij and Onze-Lieve-Vrouwekerk – which are pinpointed by the three towers pointing skyward.

Finally, like Lier, Sint-Truiden is a well-known fruit town. The Haspengouw – an area of countryside on its eastern outskirts – is particularly beautiful in spring when the apple and pear orchards are filled with blossom, and between September and October when the fruit is being harvested. Rent a bike and explore.

GETTING THERE AND AWAY
By car From Hasselt follow the N80 southwest (*18km;* ⊕ *23min*). From Leuven follow the N3 east past Tienen and turn off onto the N80 for the town centre (*40km;* ⊕ *45min*).

By train From Hasselt (*35min past the hour Mon–Fri, 1min past the hour Sat–Sun;* ⊕ *15min*); Leuven (*38min past the hour Mon–Fri, 5min past the hour Sat–Sun;* ⊕ *31min*); Brussel-Zuid/Bruxelles-Midi (*7min past the hour Mon–Fri, 36min past the hour Sat–Sun;* ⊕ *1hr 2min*).

TOURIST INFORMATION
ℹ Tourist information Grote Markt; ☏ 011 70 18 18; e info.toerisme@sint-truiden.be; www. toerisme-sint-truiden.be; ⊕ Mar–Dec 10.00–12.30 & 13.00–18.00 daily, Jan–Feb 10.00–12.30

& 13.00–16.00 daily. Sells regional products. There's also an information kiosk inside the railway station, or you can download a free Sint-Truiden iPhone/iPad app.

Bike rental At the railway station; ⏱ 15 Mar–15 Oct 09.00–19.00 Mon–Fri, 09.00–17.00 Sat–Sun, 16 Oct–14 Mar 07.00–19.00 Mon–Fri; €10/day.

Market Grote Markt; ⏱ 08.00–13.00 Sat

WHERE TO STAY, EAT AND DRINK

Fruit – particularly apples – features heavily in Sint-Truiden's regional products thanks to its surrounding orchards. Look for the local Pipo apple juice, *kattenkop* (apple cake) and *stroop*, a kind of thick marmalade. Bink beer is brewed just south of the town and famous for its *bloesem* (7.1%) beer mixed with honey and local pear syrup.

Stayen (55 rooms) 168 Tiensesteenweg; 011 68 12 34; www.stayen.com. Good-value 3-star on southwestern edge of town. Rooms are a calming mix of whites & chocolate browns. Frustratingly dbls are composed of 2 twin beds pushed together, but suites come with iPod dock & swish espresso machine. €€

De Bink 39 Grote Markt; 011 76 60 20; ⏱ 11.00–22.00 Tue–Sun. Respected brasserie run by brothers Bert & Rob, who serve a mixture of light sandwiches, hearty steaks & filling pastas.€€–€€€

Pacific 4 Grote Markt; 011 67 14 90; ⏱ 09.00–00.00 daily. Warm interior of wooden floors & black tables. Serves *stoofvlees* cooked in local Bink beer & *kattenkop*. €€

t'Begijntje 62 Begijnhof; 011 69 57 53; ⏱ 11.00–20.00 Tue–Fri, 10.00–22.00 Sat–Sun. Located inside the *begijnhof*. On the down side it has a rather modern décor – bar some old wooden ceiling beams – but on the plus side they serve lots of Sint-Truiden-specific snacks like *croque haspengouw*, *kattenkop* & *begijnhof* beer. €€

Venise 12 Grote Markt; 011 65 46 81; ⏱ 08.00–22.00 Mon, Wed–Sun. Has a dated interior, but locals – particularly the elderly – flock to this tearoom for its ice creams & *kattenkop*. €

WHAT TO SEE AND DO

Stadhuis (*Grote Markt*; ⏱ *Mar–Dec 10.00–18.00 daily, Jan–Feb 10.00–16.00 daily; free*) The façade of Sint-Truiden's distinctive orangey-red Spanish-style Town Hall dates from the 18th century and was built around the medieval hall and *belfort*, which was erected in 1606 and houses a 50-bell carillon.

Onze-Lieve-Vrouwekerk (*Grote Markt*; ⏱ *07.30–18.00 daily; free*) First built in the 11th century, the Church of Our Lady has a beautiful fresco of the Last Judgement above the choir and the **schatkamer** (treasury) (⏱ *14.00–16.30 Sat, 14.00–17.00 Sun; free*) contains the relics of St-Trudo.

Abdijsite (*1 Diesterstraat*; ⏱ *Mar–Dec 10.00–18.00 daily, Jan–Feb 10.00–17.00 daily; admission: adult/concession/under 12 €3/2/free*) St-Trudo Abbey was largely destroyed during the French Revolution – all that remains are the Romanesque belltower and Baroque gateway. Thanks to a metal staircase, which winds itself in and out of the time-worn tower, you can climb the 193 steps to the top for wonderful views of the main square. The tower ticket also grants you access to the underground chapel and **crypt**, which belonged to the Romanesque church that once stood on the site and contains spooky coffin slots carved into the brick. The entrance is directly across the patch of lawn down a small ramp. The chicken coop to your right might seem odd; it belongs to Koen Vanmechelen, an honorary citizen of Sint-Truiden.

If you book a guide, you'll also be able to visit the sumptuous **Keizerszaal** (⏱ *18 Mar–29 Sep 14.00–17.00 Sat–Sun*) whose walls and ceiling are covered in 18th-century frescoes.

Sint-Agnes Begijnhof (*Entry via Speelhoflaan & Schurhoven;* ☉ *daily; admission free*) Founded in 1258, Sint-Truiden's *begijnhof* is unique thanks to the Romanesque **Begijnhofkerk** (☉ *10.00–12.30 & 13.30–17.00 Mon–Fri, 14.00–17.00 Sat–Sun, closed 1 Oct–16 Mar; free*) whose walls are decorated with 38 stunning murals and pillar paintings dating from the 13th to the 17th century. It also houses Belgium's oldest organ.

Cycling and walking The countryside to the east of Sint-Truiden is particularly beautiful between April and May when the apple and pears orchards, which spread towards Tongeren, come into bloom. The tourist office sells a couple of cycling (*Fruit Fietsroute*; 35km; €2), walking (*Fruit wandelroute;* 10km; €2) and driving (*Fruit auto route*; 70/102km; €2) maps tailored to visiting the prettiest areas.

TONGEREN

Tongeren is Flanders' oldest city. It was home to the Eburones, a Gallic tribe who protested furiously when the Romans arrived and tried to take over. One of their princes, Ambiorix, rose to fame for his bravery on the battlefield. He even impressed Roman Emperor Julius Caesar who described him in his memoirs as the 'bravest of all Gauls'. Of course, this didn't stop Caesar crushing the tribe and forcing them into slavery. Ambiorix managed to escape and, consequently, is embraced as a Flemish hero. The Romans named the town Aduatica Tungrorum and when Brussels was still no more than a few dirt lanes, Tongeren was a bustling Roman outpost connected to the imperial highway. It was also one of the first towns in the Low Countries to adopt Christianity after the appointment of Bishop St Servatius in 342AD. Under the protectorship of Liège, the city continued to do well, allowing for the construction of the medieval city walls. However, the town fell off the map when Louis XIV's army razed large sections of the city and didn't enjoy revival until Belgian independence in 1830.

Tongeren is an instantly likeable town, which has embraced its Roman history with gusto. It now boasts one of Europe's best museums and one of its largest antiques markets (☉ *06.00–13.00*), with more than 300 stalls covering Leopoldwaal, Veemarkt and Maastrichterstraat on Sundays.

GETTING THERE AND AWAY
By car From Hasselt follow the N20 south (*20km;* ☉ *24min*).

By train From Hasselt (*44/57min past the hour Mon–Fri, 4/56min past the hour Sat–Sun;* ☉ *22min*); Leuven (*direct 13min past the hour Mon–Fri,* ☉ *1hr 8min; via Aarschot/Liège-Guillemin 5/27min past the hour Sat–Sun,* ☉ *1hr 15min*); Brussel-Zuid/Bruxelles-Midi via Hasselt/Liège-Guillemins.

TOURIST INFORMATION
🛈 **Tourist information** 5 Via Julianus; 📞 012 80 00 70; e info@toerismetongeren.be; www. tongeren.be; ☉ Apr–Sep 08.30–12.00 & 13.00–17.00 Mon–Fri, 09.30–17.00 Sat–Sun, Jul–Aug 08.30–17.00 Mon–Fri, 09.30–17.00 Sat–Sun, Oct–Mar 08.30–12.00 & 13.00–17.00 Mon–Fri, 10.00–16.00 Sat–Sun. Modern office inside the Julianus Shopping Centre. Ask about a guided tour with a *béguine*.
🚲 **Bike rental** Tourist office. For a €10 deposit they rent bikes for free & you can keep them for up to 3 days if you're staying in town. Electric bikes €29/day with €150 cash deposit. They also sell the *Rijk Verleden* (€2), a compilation of 7 cycling

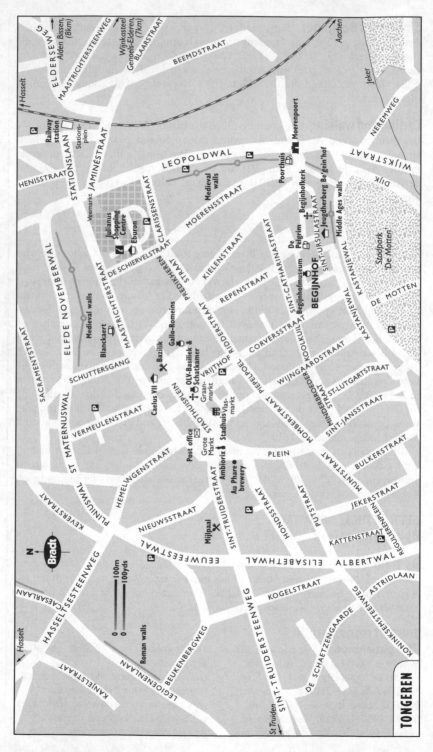

maps; No 6 *Langs Demerbronnen en Waterburchten* (23.5km) takes you past Genoels-Elderen castle and No 4 *Langs Kastelen en Romaanse Kerkjes* (50km) takes you around Tongeren.

🏠 WHERE TO STAY, EAT AND DRINK

Tongeren bakeries produce two local biscuits: the *Tongerse moppen* (flavoured with honey, aniseed and herbs) and dodecahedron-shaped *Tongerse koekje* modelled on an artefact in the Gallo-Romeins museum.

🏠 **Eburon** (52 rooms) 10 De Schiervelstraat; ☎ 012 23 01 99; www.eburonhotel.be. Close to the tourist office, this sleek contemporary 4-star starred in its own TV show & is housed in a converted convent. Choose from the Comfort or the larger Select rooms decorated in bright whites, lavenders & olive greens, with en-suite bath & rainshower, Bose iPod dock, coffee machine, free Wi-Fi & TV. Brasserie Tinto next door belongs to the hotel. €€–€€€

🏠 **Caelus VII** (7 rooms) 7 Kloosterstraat; e info@caelus.be; www.caelus.be. Family-run boutique hotel set in a renovated mansion due to open in March 2012, just off the Grote Markt. Looks set to blow the competition out the water thanks to its location & excellent price/quality. €€

🏠 **Be'gein'hof** (10 rooms, 76 beds) 1 Sint-Ursulastraat; ☎ 012 39 13 70; www.vjh.be. Youth hostel inside the *begijnhof* used mainly by school groups. A mix of 4-, 6-, 8- & 12-bed dorms with sinks in rooms & shared showers & toilets. Bar/café serving snacks. Dorm bed €15.

✘ **Mijlpaal** 25 Sint-Truiderstraat; ☎ 012 26 42 77; ⏰ 12.00–14.00 & 19.00–21.00 Mon, Thu–Fri & Sun, 19.00–21.00 Sat. Michelin-starred kitchen run by a husband-&-wife team. It's intimate, clean & classic, & the delicate portions delicious. The 3-course midweek lunch is good value at €30 a head. €€€€€

✘ **Bazilik** 1 Kloosterstraat; ☎ 012 21 33 24; ⏰ 10.00–23.00 daily. Charming Victorian-style brasserie a few steps from the Gallo-Romeins museum. Has sweeping staircase, black-&-white tiled floor & a please-all menu of salads, pastas, fish & meat. €€€

✘ **De Pelgrim** 9 Brouwersstraat; ☎ 012 23 83 22; ⏰ 11.00–23.00 Wed–Sun. Anette has run this characterful restaurant inside the *begijnhof* for 18 years. The house dates from 1632 & has a décor to match. Order the spare ribs or the steak – they're house specialities. €€

🍽 **Blanckaert** 62 Maastrichterstraat; ☎ 012 23 14 78; ⏰ 07.00–18.00 Tue–Sat, 07.00–14.00 Sun. Bakery well known for selling *Tongerse moppen* & *koekjes*. €

🍺 **Poorthuis** 112 Kielenstraat; ☎ 012 39 02 55; ⏰ 10.30–02.00 Mon, Fri & Sat, 07.00–02.00 Thu, 06.00–02.00 Sun. Local drinking den which sits in the shadow of Moerenpoort & has a good selection of beers.

WHAT TO SEE AND DO

Grote Markt At the centre of the Grote Markt stands a bronze 19th-century statue of Gallic warrior **Ambiorix** gazing sternly at **Onze-Lieve-Vrouwebasiliek** (⏰ 09.00–17.00 *daily*), which was established in 1240 and took 300 years to complete. The south transept, choir and nave still date from this era. On entering, worshippers touch the hands and feet of the Virgin Mary carrying a skeletal grown-up Jesus, which dates from 1400 and is housed in the first chapel on the left. However, the church's holiest treasure is a 15th-century statue of the Virgin and Child in the north transept. Behind them hang a set of manacles which, legend has it, were chained to Turkish slaves in the Holy Land who were miraculously transported here after praying to the Virgin for help. Finally, the **schatkamer**, or treasury (⏰ *Apr–Sep 10.00–12.00 & 13.30–17.00 daily, closed Mon morning; admission: adult/concession/6–12/under 6 €2.50/2/0.50/ free*), is one of the richest in Belgium. Look for the 6th-century jewelled buckle found at the bottom of a broom cupboard in 1869, an 11th-century wooden carving of Christ's head and a 14th-century wooden triptych.

Before leaving the square, it's worth visiting **Au Phare** (*21 Grote Markt; m 0497 99 83 38; www.phare-stadsbrouwerij.be; ⏰ 10.00–late daily, admission free*) a well-known bar that's being converted into a micro brewery so that the local Amburon beer (7%) can be brewed inside the city instead of at Halen, the other side of Hasselt.

Gallo-Romeins Museum (15 Kielenstraat; \ 012 67 03 30; www. galloromeinsmuseum.be; ⊕ 09.00–17.00 Tue–Fri, 10.00–18.00 Sat–Sun; admission: adult/under 26 €7/1) Winner of the 2011 European Museum Award, this impressive building is dedicated to all things Roman – from the collection of flints and reindeer-skin teepee on the ground floor to the Romans' arrival in Tongeren in 10BC on the third floor. You're given a comprehensive explanation book in English when you purchase your tickets.

Sint-Catharina Begijnhof (Sint-Ursulastraat; ⊕ daily; admission free) Consisting of just seven streets, Tongeren's begijnhof certainly squeezes a lot in. As well as the begijnhof church, you'll find a youth hostel and De Pelgrim restaurant (see page 333). However, the real gem here is a preserved 17th-century béguine's house which has been opened as the Beghina Museum (12 Onder de Linde, Begijnhof; \ 012 21 32 59; www.begijnhofmuseumtongeren.be; ⊕ 10.00–12.30 & 13.30–17.30 Tue–Sun; admission: adult/concession/12–18/6–12/under 6 €3.50/3/2/1/free). For 50 years it belonged to Maria Emerix, the daughter of a wealthy Bilzen lord, and her maid. Start in the attic, which was used to store grain and dry laundry, and work your way down. Aside from the nook-and-cranny charm of the place, there are some elaborate Liège stucco mosaic-tile fireplaces on the first floor, a 16th-century triptych of The Adoration, and a 14th-century statue of St Catherine of Alexandria, the patron saint of the begijnhof. When you join a guided tour, you can try a glass of the begijnhof beer – the béguines used to drink up to four litres a day instead of the disease-ridden local water – and a havermout (a traditional hard-as-rock oatmeal biscuit). Not suitable for disabled travellers.

Moerenpoort (Leopoldwal; ⊕ Apr–Sep 13.00–17.00 Wed–Sat, 09.30–12.00 & 13.00–17.00 Sun, Oct–Mar 13.00–1600 Sat, 10.00–12.00 & 13.00–16.00 Sun; admission: adult/concession €2/1) This squat watchtower is the last of the city's six gates and dates from 1379. It houses a three-floor museum detailing the city's military history and offers access to the top of the tower, which has super views of the begijnhof.

Ancient city walls Sections of Tongeren's medieval city walls can be see along Elfde Novemberwal, Leopoldwal and behind the begijnhof on Kastanjewal. Construction of towers posted at regular intervals along the wall was funded by individual guilds. The tower seen on Kastanjewal is known as Lakenmakerstoren, and was built by the cloth weavers.

Sections of surviving Roman walls can be found further out along Caesarlaan, Legioenenlaan and Cottalaan.

Genoels-Elderen (9 Kasteelstraat, 3770 Riemst; \ 012 39 13 49; www.wijnkasteel. com; ⊕ 09.00–18.00 Tue–Sat; admission: €5, but you can pay more to sample a larger selection of wines) The Romans brought their viticulture with them and successfully grew grapes on the slopes surrounding Tongeren. The practice died out in the 17th-century when Europe entered a mini Ice Age as depicted in the frosty paintings of Flemish artists at the time. It was revived in the 1950s and the castle now produces a very palatable Chardonnay and Pinot Noir. On the two-hour guided tour departing at 14.00 you visit the castle, the distillery, the vineyards and the ancient cellars, and

finish up with a tasting session. Reservations are essential, as they need to match individual visitors up with other groups. To get there by car follow the N79 east out of town; when you cross the motorway take the first left onto Sint-Maartenstraat and carry straight on until you reach the castle (*7.3km*; ⏱ *12min*).

MAASEIK

Snuggled up against the Dutch border and far away from other towns, Maaseik is rarely covered by guidebooks and what a shame. Its pretty market square is lined with medieval houses, the local church conceals an exquisite 8th-century hand-painted gospel, which is the oldest in the Low Countries, and it has great restaurants. What's more you can weave across the border and explore the waterways by bike or boat and go hiking in Hoge Kempen, Flanders' only national park.

GETTING THERE AND AWAY
By car From Hasselt take the N75 towards Genk, then follow signs for the N76 and merge onto the E314 (direction Aken/Aachen) and take exit 32 (direction Genk-Oost). Follow N75 for 15km then join N78 to Maaseik (*44km*; ⏱ *48min*).

TOURIST INFORMATION
🖸 **Tourist information** 1 Markt; ☎ 089 81 92 90; e toerisme.maaseik@maaseik.be; www.maaseik.be; ⏱ Apr–Oct 09.00–17.00 Mon–Fri, 10.00–12.30 & 13.30–17.00 Sat–Sun, Nov–Mar 09.00–12.00 & 13.00–17.00 Mon–Fri, 11.00–15.00 Sat–Sun. Very friendly office inside the Stadhuis which can arrange hotel bookings &

has a public toilet. There are numerous walking & cycling tours for the area, such as the *Aldeneik* and *Maaseik Natur* walking route which starts in Maaseik town centre & takes you along the river to Aldeneik (€2), but do ask for a full list.
♻ **Bike rental** Standard/tandem/electric €8/18/19/day from tourist office.

🏠 **WHERE TO STAY, EAT AND DRINK** Maaseik is famous for its *knapkoek*, butter biscuits sprinkled with large sugar crystals.

🏠 **Van Eyck** (33 rooms) 48 Markt; ☎ 089 86 37 00; www.hotel-vaneyck.be. Pleasant hotel on the main square. Rooms are spacious & contemporary; the suites have stunning oak-beamed ceilings & steam rooms. Only downside is it costs €18/day to use the internet. €€€
🏠 **B&B Agnetenklooster** (5 rooms) 17 Sionstraat; ☎ 089 56 43 27; www. hetagnetenklooster.be. Historic home that's been renovated by owner Patricia Indekeu. My favourite rooms are the smaller (& cheaper) Relindis, the regal Bibliotheeksuite & the Agnes up in the attic. The others have twin beds. Cash only. €€€
✗ **De Soeten Naam Jesus** 1 Vullerstraat; ☎ 089 56 23 10; ⏱ 17.00–22.30 daily. Underground tavern with vaulted brick ceiling. Opt for the ribs or steak. €€€€€
✗ **Tiffany's** 19 Markt; ☎ 089 56 40 89; ⏱ 12.00–13.30 & 18.00–21.00 Tue–Fri & Sun,

18.00–21.00 Sat. Run by Fabia & Philippe since 1984 this homely dining room has touches of Art Nouveau, fine glassware & porcelain plates. There's a set menu every day & a good wine list. €€€
✗ **Trappenhuys** 62 Bosstraat; ☎ 089 50 18 04; ⏱ 11.00–21.00 Tue–Sat, 12.00–21.00 Sun. Enter via thick velvet curtains into a cosy candlelit brasserie with wood-panelled bar & a comfort-food menu of pasta, soup, toasties & huge hamburgers. €€
♀ **Café Majestic** 10 Bospoort; ☎ 089 56 40 53; ⏱ 10.30–late Mon, Wed–Sun. Looks just like a normal house, but this bar – located on the left after passing the Dexia bank – is a real local hangout. If you time your visit correctly it'll be alive with locals singing carnival songs in the local Mezeik dialect.
Vanwijck 7 Hepperstraat; ☎ 089 56 48 68; ⏱ 08.00–12.10 & 13.30–18.00 Mon–Sat. Rustic bakery selling homemade *knapkoek*.

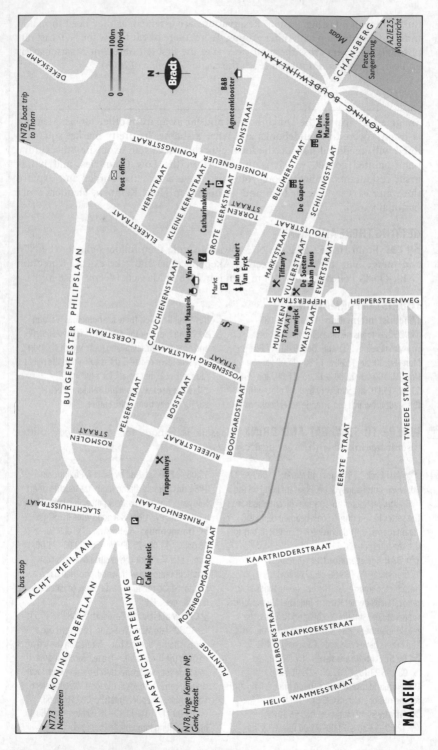

WHAT TO SEE AND DO

Musea Maaseik (*5 Lekkerstraat;* ✆ *089 56 68 90;* ⏱ *Apr–Oct 10.00–17.00 Tue–Sun, Nov–Mar 10.00–16.00 Tue–Sun; admission: combi ticket for Musea Maaseik & Catharinakerk adult/concession/8–18 €5/4/2)* The Musea Maaseik houses the Regionaal Archeologisch Museum (RAM) and the Apotheekmuseum. The pharmacy is a charming wood-panelled room with hundreds of drawers and porcelain bottles and was the oldest privately owned apothecary in Belgium. It's currently undergoing renovation, but you watch the artists at work through a glass screen; they're carefully stripping away the cabinets' old layer of dark paint to reveal the original blue and yellow paintings underneath.

RAM is a well-maintained history museum with recreated scenes, interesting artefacts and a brilliant hands-on education centre for children in the basement. Pick up the glossy explanation book in English from reception.

Catharinakerk (*Kerkplein;* ✆ *089 56 68 90;* ⏱ *Apr–Oct 13.00–17.00 Tue–Sun, Nov–Mar 13.00–16.00 Tue–Sun; admission free)* A modern-looking neo-Baroque church which houses elaborate confession boxes and an old carillon machine. However, the real treasure is found in the **kerkschatten** or treasury (*admission: adult/concession/8–18 €5/4/2, inc entry to Musea Maaseik*), down a flight of stairs to the left of the altar. On display is a very rare 8th-century gospel – the oldest of its kind in the Low Countries – known as the *Codex Eyckensis*. It was written and painted by Sts Harlindis and Relindis – the daughters of Frankish Lord Adelard, who founded the town – who became abbesses at the Aldeneik hamlet convent to the west of Maaseik. Split into two books, the pages are incredibly fragile and the colour and detail exquisite. A video presentation shows how the books were restored, and an adjoining room contains a number of religious treasures, including the arm-shaped relics of Harlindis and Relindis – odd cases with hands carved from wood and panels of glass showing the radius and ulna.

Van Eycktentoonstelling (*23 Capucienenstraat;* ✆ *089 81 92 90)* Jan van Eyck – one of Europe's best 15th-century painters – was born in Maaseik in 1395. His older brother Hubert, who is believed to have collaborated with Jan on Gent's *Adoration of the Mystic Lamb* altarpiece, was also born here. A statue of the brothers stands on the Markt. This church houses life-size photographs of all Jan's major artworks, but can only be visited as part of a guided tour (*€3pp*) which departs every Sunday at 14.00 from the tourist information office. Tours are currently only given in Dutch, but it's still worth attending just to see the pictures.

Also of note in town are two 17th-century houses **De Drie Marieen** (*77 Bleumerstraat*) and **De Gapert** (*47 Bleumerstraat*).

Day trips

Watermills The surrounding area has 16 watermills, 12 of which still remain in working order. The village of Neeroeteren, 3.7 miles west of Maaseik, has two: **Neermolen** (*Elerweg;* ⏱ *May–Sep 14.00–17.00 1st & 3rd Sun, Jul–Aug 14.00–17.00 Sat–Sun; admission €1*), which was first built in 1330 and grinds grain, and **Klaaskensmolen** (*Kleeskensmolenweg;* ⏱ *May–Jun & 1–14 Sep 12.00–20.00 Sat–Sun, Jul–Aug 12.00–20.00 daily, tours at 13.00, 15.00 & 17.00; admission €1*), which dates from 1548 and is Flanders' last working sawmill. You can drive there, but why not rent bikes and follow the route marked on the Fietsroute *Molens langs de Bosbeek* (55km; €1.50) sold at the tourist office?

Cross-border trips In summer you can enjoy a tour of the waterways aboard the *Paep van Meinecom III* (✆ *089 56 75 03; www.marec.be;* ⊕ *Jul–Aug departs Ophoven at 13.30, 15.30 & 17.30, departs Thorn 14.30, 16.30 & 18.30; return ticket: adult/ child €7.50/6)*, which departs from Harbour De Spaenjerd in Ophoven, 4km north of Maaseik, and takes one hour to sail via Stevensweert to historic **Thorn**, a pretty Dutch village of whitewashed cottages across the border.

Alternatively, create your own cross-border trip using the *Grensoverschrijdend* Fietsroutenetwerk (35km; €6) map, which includes Thorn, Wessem, Maasbracht and Stevensweert. To get across the water you can use the foot passenger ferry (⊕ *Apr–Oct)* at Veerpont and the car ferry (⊕ *all year)* at Berg.

Hoge Kempen National Park (*www.nationaalpark.be;* ⊕ *Apr–Oct 10.00– 17.00 daily, Nov–Mar 11.00–15.00 daily; admission free)* Twenty-four kilometres southwest of Maaseik spreads Flanders' only national park, which was established in 2006. The Hoge Kempen is 5,700ha of moorland covered in purple heather, pine woods and lakes home to deer, snakes, frogs, toads and goshawks. There are several trails, but ask the tourist office for either the *Station As* or the *Mechelse Heide*; they start closest to Maaseik and each costs €2. The Station As route leads you through forest; the Mechelse Heide route offers panoramic views of the moorland.

If you'd like to see the area properly, you can hire a ranger for a two-hour guided walk (⊕ *daily; €60/guide)*, or follow the 72km self-guided trail that runs around the entire circumference of the park.

Getting there The park has four gates, the closest to Maaseik being Station As gate (*124 Stationstraat, 3665 AS*) and Mechelse Heide gate (*280 Joseph Smeetslaan, 3630 Maasmechelen*). To get there you can cycle, drive or catch bus #9 (see website for full details).

Where to stay
🏠 **De Edelsteen B&B** (5 rooms) 10 Longblookstraat, 3690 Zutendaal; ✆ 089 69 90 00; www.deedelsteen.be. Charming country-chic rooms, & can arrange bike hire (€15/day) & packed lunches. €

FLANDERS UPDATES WEBSITE

For the latest travel news about Flanders, please visit the new interactive Bradt Flanders website: http://updates.bradtguides.com/flanders which will supplement the printed Bradt guidebook providing a forum whereby the latest travel news can be publicised online with immediate effect. It is a free service, but its success will depend greatly on the input of readers, whose collective experience of Flanders' tourist attractions and facilities will always be broader than those of any individual author.

Appendix 1

LANGUAGE

DUTCH (FLEMISH) With its strings of consonants and conjugated vowels, Dutch makes for bewildering pronunciation sessions and the complex series of growls, slurs and throat-clearing sounds necessary for proper pronunciation are difficult to replicate. As a general rule, place stress on the beginning of a word, devoice consonants at the ends of words and try to listen to a native speaker and follow their vocalisations whenever you can.

The pronunciation of vowels in Flemish is broadly the same as in English. However, Flemish is littered with diphthongs (double sounds) that involve complicated contortions of the mouth and tongue; it's nearly impossible to find the proper equivalent sounds in English words, but here are the fundamentals:

Vowels

a	like 'a' in 'allotment'	ie	like 'ee' in 'free'
aa	like 'ar' in 'arrow'	ieu	pronounced ee-oo
ae	like 'ar' in 'cart'	ij	like 'ei' – see above
au	like 'ow' in 'cow'	oe	like 'oo' in 'stool'
ee	like 'ai' in 'sail'	oo	like 'oa' in 'coat'
ei	like 'ay' in 'way'	ou	like 'ou' in ' about'
eie	like 'ay' in 'hay'	ui	like 'ui' in 'alleluia'
eu	like 'err' in 'herring'	uu	lIke ' oo' in 'soot'
eeu	pronounced ay-ooh		

Consonants

ch	like 'ch' in 'chip'	v	like 'f' in 'follow'
kh	like 'ch' in Scottish 'loch'	w	like 'v' in 'vacuum'
g	like 'g' in 'grow'	sch	like the 'sk' in English 'skip' - 's'
j	like 'y' in 'yes'		is soft, but 'k' is pronounced with
ng	like 'ng' in 'string'		throat-clearing as if you're about
nj	like 'nio' in 'onion'		to spit.

FRENCH You'll need to speak some French while staying in Brussels. The pronunciation of French letters and diphthongs is very similar to English. Some variants are listed below:

Vowels

a	like 'a' in 'back'	è	ever so slightly different to 'e', it
e	like 'e' in 'pet'		sounds like 'e' in 'envoy' with a
é	like 'a' in 'say'		descending tone
		eu	like 'u' in 'yurt'

i	like 'e' in 'email'	ou	is pronounced as 'oo' in 'mood'
o	like 'o' in 'pot'	u	say 'ee', but shape your mouth to
au	is pronounced as 'o' in 'over'		say 'oo'

Consonants

ch	is pronounced as 'sh'	ll	is often not pronounced
c	is pronounced as 's' in 'c'est' and	w	is pronounced as 'v'
	'k' in 'combien'	r	roll the tongue – imagine Sean
h	is silent		Connery saying 'really'
th	the 'h' is not pronounced, so it's		
	just 't'		

ENGLISH	DUTCH	FRENCH
Essentials		
Hello	Hallo	Bonjour
Goodbye	Tot ziens	Au revoir
Good morning	Goedemorgen	Bonjour
Good afternoon	Goedemiddag	Bonjour
Good evening	Goedenavond	Bonsoir
Good night	Goedenacht	Bonne nuit
My name is …	Mijn naam is…	Je m'appelle…
I am from…	Ik ben van…	J'habite à …
How are you?	Hoe gaat het?	Ça va?
Very well, thank you	Goed, dank u wel	Très bien, merci
And you?	En met u?	Et toi?/Et vous?
Nice to meet you	Aangenaam kennis te maken	Enchanté(e) m/f
See you later	Tot straks	À bientôt
Thank you	Dank u wel	Merci (beaucoup)
What's your name?	Wat is u naam?	Comment vous appelez-vous?/Comment tu t'appelles?
I don't understand	Ik begrijp het niet	Je ne comprends pas
Do you speak English/ French/ Spanish?	Spreekt u engels/ frans/spans	Parlez-vous anglais, français/espagnol?
I don't speak French/Dutch	Ik spreek geen Frans/ Nederlands	Je ne parle pas français/ néerlandais
Could you speak more slowly please?	Kunt u wat langzamer preken, a.u.b?	Pouvez-vous parler plus lentement, s'il vous plaît?
What is this called?	Hoe noemt dit?	Comment ça s'appelle?
What is that?	Wat is dat?	Qu'est que c'est ça?
Could you repeat that?	Zou u dat kunnen herhalen?	Pouvez-vous répéter ça?
Could you write it down?	Kunt u het opschrijven?	Pouvez-vous écrire ça?
Yes	Ja	Oui
No	Nee	Non
No, thank you	Nee, dank u	Non, merci
Please	Alstublieft (a.u.b)	S'il vous plait
You're welcome	Graag gedaan	Je vous en prie
Excuse me	Pardon	Excusez moi
I'm sorry	Sorry/het spijt me	Désolé(e)/pardon
I don't like…	Ik hou niet van…	Je n'aime pas…
Cheers!	Proost!	Santé!

Requests

I would like …	Ik wil…	Je voudrais…
Can I have …?	Kan ik krijgen, a.u.b…	Est-ce-que je peux avoir…
Where is …?	Waar is … ?	Où est … ?
Where are …?	Waar zijn … ?	Où sont … ?
When do you …?	Wanneer gaat u…?	Quand vous …?
I like …	Ik hou …	J'aime bien …

Time

today	vandaag	aujourd'hui
tonight	vanavond	ce soir
tomorrow	morgen	demain
yesterday	gisteren	hier
morning	de morgen	matin
afternoon	de middag	après-midi
evening	de avond	soir
night	de nacht	nuit
now	nu	maintentant
next	volgende	puis
early	vroeg	tôt
late	laat	tard
later	later	plus tard
What time is it?	Hoe laat is het?	Quelle heure est il?
When do you close?	Wanneer sluit u?	À quelle heure vous fermez?
When do you open?	Wanneer opent u?	À quelle heure vous ouvrez?
one minute	een minuut	une minute
one hour	een uur	une heure
half an hour	een half uur	une demi-heure
a day	een dag	un jour
a week	een week	une semaine
a month	een maand	un mois
a year	een jaar	une année

Numbers

0	nul	zéro
1	een	un(e)
2	twee	deux
3	drie	trois
4	vier	quatre
5	vijf	cinq
6	zes	six
7	zeven	sept
8	acht	huit
9	negen	neuf
10	tien	dix
11	elf	onze
12	twaalf	douze
13	dertien	treize
14	veertien	quatorze
15	vijftien	quinze
16	zestien	seize

17	zeventien	dix-sept
18	achttien	dix-huit
19	negentien	dix-neuf
20	twintig	vingt
21	eenentwintig	vingt et un
30	dertig	trente
40	veertig	quarante
50	vijftig	cinquante
60	zestig	soixante
70	zeventig	soixante-dix
80	tachtig	quatre-vingt
90	negentig	quatre-vingt dix
100	honderd	cent
1,000	duizend	mille
first	eerste	premier
second	tweede	deuxième
third	derde	troisième
fourth	vierde	quatrième
fifth	vijfde	cinquième
sixth	zesde	sixième
seventh	zevende	septième
eighth	achste	huitième
ninth	negende	neuvième
tenth	tiende	dixième

Days of the week

Monday	maandag	lundi
Tuesday	dinsdag	mardi
Wednesday	woensdag	mercredi
Thursday	donderdag	jeudi
Friday	vrijdag	vendredi
Saturday	zaterdag	samedi
Sunday	zondag	dimanche

Months/seasons

January	januari	janvier
February	februari	février
March	maart	mars
April	april	avril
May	mei	mai
June	juni	juin
July	julli	juillet
August	augustus	août
September	september	septembre
October	oktober	octobre
November	november	novembre
December	december	décembre
spring	de lente	printemps
summer	de zomer	été
autumn	de herfst	automne
winter	de winter	hiver

Family

mother	moeder	*mère*
father	vader	*père*
sister	zus	*soeur*
brother	broer	*frère*
grandmother	grootmoeder	*grand-mère*
grandfather	grootvader	*grand-père*
stepsister	stiefzuster	*belle-soeur*
boyfriend	vriend / lief	*ami*
girlfriend	vriendin / liefje	*amie*
I am single	Ik ben vrijgezel	*Je suis célibataire*
I am married	Ik ben getrouwed	*Je suis marié(e)*
friend	vriend	*ami(e)*

Countries/nationalities

I am ...	Ik ben ...	*Je suis ...*
I come from ...	Ik kom uit ...	*Je viens d' ...*
Britain/British	Groot Brittannië/Brits	*Grande-Bretagne/ britannique*
England/English	Engeland/Engels	*Angleterre/anglais(e)*
Scotland/ Scottish	Schotland/Schots	*Ecosse/ecossais(e)*
Wales/ Welsh	Wales/Welsh	*Pays de Galles/gallois(e)*
Ireland/Irish	Ierland/Iers	*Irlande/irlandais(e)*
America/American	Amerika/Amerikaans	*Amérique/américain(e)*
Canada/Canadian	Canada/Canadees	*Canada/canadien(ne)*
Australia/Australian	Australië/Australisch	*Australie/australien(ne)*
New Zealand	Nieuw-Zeeland/ Nieuw-Zeelander	*Nouvelle-Zélande/ néo-zélandais(e)*
South Africa	Suid Afrika/ Suid Afrikaans	*L'Afrique du Sud/ sud-africain(e)*
Belgium	België/Belgisch	*Belgique/belge*
France/French	Frankrijk/Frans	*France/français(e)*
Germany/German	Duitsland/Duits	*Allemagne/allemand(c)*
Flanders/Flemish	Flaanderen/Vlaams	*Flandre/flamand(e)*
The Netherlands	Nederland/Nederlands	*Les Pays-Bas/hollandais(e)*

Public transport

I would like a ticket to ...	Ik zo graag een ticket naar ...	*Je voudrais un billet pour ...*
single	enkel	*simple*
a return	heen en terug	*aller-retour*
How much is it?	Hoeveel kost het?	*C'est combien?*
What time does the ... leave?	Om welk uur vertrekt de ... ?	*À quelle heure le ... part?*
Will you tell me when to get off?	Wil je me zeggen wanneer ik mag afstappen?	*Pouvez-vous me dire quand je dois descendre?*
delayed	vertraging	*retardé*
cancelled	geanuleerd	*annulé*
first class	eerste klas	*première classe*
second class	tweede klas	*deuxième classe*
platform	peron	*quai*
ticket office	kaartjes balie	*bureau de vente*

343

timetable	uurrooster	horaire
from	van	de
to	naar	à/pour
How far is … ?	Hoe ver is … ?	C'est loin … ?
How do I get to … ?	Hoe geraak ik van naar … ?	Comment je peux aller à … ?
Where is the … ?	Waar is de … ?	Où est/sont le/la/les … ?
Is it near?	Is het kort bij?	C'est près?
bus station	busstation	gare routière
railway station	treinstation	gare
airport	luchthaven	aéroport
port	haven	port
bus	bus	bus
train	trein	train
plane	vliegtuig	avion
boat	boot	bateau
ferry	ferryboot	ferry
taxi	taxi	taxi
arrivals	aankomst	arrivées
departures	vertrek	départs

Private transport

I'd like to rent …	Ik zou graag een … huren	Je voudrais louer …
car hire	auto verhuur	location de voitures
driving licence	rijbewijs	permis de conduire
Where is the nearest service station?	Waar is het dichst bijzijnde benzinne station?	Où est la station service la plus proche?
diesel	diesel	gazole
leaded petrol	gellode benzine	essence super
unleaded petrol	loodvrijë benzine	essence sans plomb
car	auto	voiture
motorbike	moto	moto
bicycle	fiets	vélo
car park	parkeerplaats	parking
traffic lights	werkeerslichten	les feux
level crossing	oversteekplaats / zebrapad	passage à niveau
roundabout	rond punt	rond-point
I've broken down	Ik heb auto pech	Je suis en panne
I've run out of petrol	Ik zit zonder benzine	Je suis en panne d'essence
I have a puncture	Ik heb een punctuur	J'ai une crevaison

Directions

Is this the road to …?	Is dit de weg naar …?	Est-ce que c'est la route pour … ?
Where is it?	Waar is het?	C'est où?
straight ahead	rechtdoor	tout droit
right	rechts	à droite
left	links	à gauche
north	noord	nord
south	zuid	sud
west	west	ouest
east	oost	est

344

behind	achter	derrière
in front of	rechtover	devant
near	dichtbij	près de
opposite	tegengesteld	en face

Signs

entrance	ingang	entrée
exit	uitgang	sortie
push	duwen	poussez
pull	trek	tirez
open	open	ouvert
closed	gesloten	fermé
toilets	toiletten/wc	toilettes
information	informatie	information

Accommodation

Where is a cheap/good hotel?	Waar is een goedkoop/ goed hotel?	Où je peux trouver un hôtel pas cher/un bon hôtel?
Could you write the address?	Kan je het adres opschrijven?	Pouvez-vous écrire l'adresse?
Do you have any rooms available?	Heeft u nog kamers vrij?	Vous avez des chambres?
I'd like …	Ik zou graag …	Je voudrais …
a single room	enkele kamer	une chambre simple
a double room	dubbele kamer	une chambre double
a room with two beds	een kamer met twee bedden	une chambre avec deux lits
a room with an en-suite bathroom	slaapkamer met douche	une chambre avec salle de bain
I have a reservation	Ik heb een reservatie	J'ai une réservation
Is breakfast included?	Is het ontbijt inbegrepen?	Est-ce que le petit déjeuner est inclus?
Which floor?	Welk verdiep?	Quel étage?
What room number?	Welk kamer nummer?	Quel numéro de chambre?
Do you have a quieter room?	Heb je een rustigere kamer?	Est-ce que vous avez une chambre calme?
Do you have a room with air conditioning?	Heb je een kamer met airconditioning?	Est-ce que vous avez une chambre avec climatisation?
key	sleutel	clé
porter	portier	porteur
reception	receptie	réception
I would like to checkout	Ik zou graag uitboeken	Je voudrais régler la note

Eating out

Do you have a table for … people?	Heeft u een tafel voor … personen?	Est-ce-que vous avez une table pour … personnes?
I would like to reserve a table	Ik zou gaar één tafel reserveren, alstublieft	Je voudrais réserver une table, s'il vous plaît
breakfast	ontbijt	petit-déjeuner
lunch	middagmaal	déjeuner
dinner	diner	dîner
snack	snack	casse-croûte

Please may I see the menu?	Kan ik de kaart krijgen alstublieft?	Est-ce-que je peux voir le menu?
Do you have a childrens menu?	Heb je een kindermenu?	Vous avez un menu pour enfants?
smoking/non smoking	rokers/niet rokers	fumer/non fumer
I am a vegetarian	Ik ben vegetarisch	Je suis végétarien(ne)
waiter	kelner	monsieur
waitress	serveerster	madame/mademoiselle
dish of the day	dagschotel	plat du jour
soup	soep	potage
starter	voorgerechten	entrée
main course	hoofdgerechten	plat principal
dessert	nagerechten	dessert
Please may I have...	Kan ik ... krijgen, a.u.b	Est-ce que je peux avoir ...
glass	glas	un verre
cup	kop/tas	une tasse
knife	mes	un couteau
fork	vork	une fourchette
spoon	lepel	une cuillère
plate	bord	une assiette
the menu	menu	le menu
the wine list	de wijn kaart	la carte des vins
where are the toilets?	Waar zijn de toiletten?	Où sont les toilettes?
I'm full	Ik zit vol	J'ai assez mangé(e)
It's delicious	Het is heel lekker	C'est délicieux
Enjoy your meal	Smakelijk	Bon appétit
Please may I have the bill	De rekening, alstublieft	L'addition, s'il vous plaît
tip	drinkgeld	un pourboire

Basics

bread	brood	(du/le) pain
butter	boter	du/le beurre
olive oil	olijfolie	l'huile d'olive
pepper	peper	du/le poivre
salt	zout	du/le sel
sugar	suiker	du/le sucre
vinegar	azijn	du/le vinaigre
cheese	kaas	du/le fromage
egg	ei	l'oeuf
jam	konfituur	de la confiture

Preparation

rare (bloody and practically kicking)	saignant	saignant
medium rare	a point	à point
well done	bien cuit	bien cuit
plain (without sauces)	natuur (zonder saus)	nature (sans sauces)
minced	fijngehakt	haché
stuffed	gevuld	farci
steamed	gestoomd	à la vapeur
roasted	gebraden	rôti

boiled	gekookt	bouilli
stewed	gestoofd	mijoté
fried/ baked	gebakken	frit/au four
smoked	gerookt	fumé
grilled	gegrild	grillé

Fruit / *fruits* / *vruchten*

apple	appel	pomme
banana	banaan	banane
blackcurrant	zwarte bes	cassis
grapes	druiven	raisins
lemon	citroen	citron
orange	sinaasappel	orange
peach	perzik	pêche
pear	peer	poire
pineapple	ananas	ananas
raspberry	framboos	framboise
strawberry	aardbei	fraise

Vegetables / *groenten* / *légumes*

asparagus	asperges	asperges
beans	haricots	bonen
broccoli	brocoli	broccoli
cabbage	chou	witte kool
carrot	carotte	wortel
chicory	endive	witloof
chips	frites	frieten
garlic	ail	look
green beans	haricots verts	prinssessebonen
leek	poireau	prei
lettuce	laitue	kropje
mushroom	champignon	champignon
onion	oignon	ui
peas	petits pois	erwten
potato	pomme de terre	aardappel
rice	riz	rijst
spinach	épinards	spinazie
tomatoes	tomates	tomaat

Fish & seafood / *vis & schaaldieren* / *poisson & fruits de mer*

bass	zeebaars	loup/bar
cod	kabeljauw	morue
crab	krab	crabe
eel	paling	anguille
fish	vis	poisson
haddock	schelvis	églefin
herring	haring	hareng
lobster	kreeft	homard
mackerel	makreel	maquereau
mussels	mosselen	moules
oyster	oester	huître

plaice	schol	plie/carrelet
prawns	garnaal	crevettes
salmon	zalm	saumon
sardines	sardine	sardines
scallop	Sint - Jacobschelp	coquille St-Jacques
sole	zeetong	sole
squid	inktvis	seiche
trout	forel	truite
tuna	tonijn	thon

Meat — vlees — viande

beef	rundsvlees	boeuf
chicken	kip	poulet
duck	eend	canard
goose	gans	oie
ham	hesp	jambon
horse	paardevlees	cheval
kidney	nier	rognon
lamb	lam	agneau
liver	lever	foie
pork	varkensvlees	porc
rabbit	konijn	lapin
sausage	worst	saucisse
snails	slakken	escargots
steak	steak	steak/bifteck
turkey	kalkoen	dinde
veal	kalfsvlees	veau
venison	ree(bok)	cerf/chevreuil

Dessert — dessert — dessert

cake	taart	gâteau
ice cream	ijskreem	glace
pancake	pannekoek	crêpe
waffle	wafel	gaufre
whipped cream	slagroom	crème fouettée/Chantilly

Drinks — drankjes — boissons

white wine	witte wijn	vin blanc
red wine	rode wijn	vin rouge
medium	half droog	demi-sec
sweet	zoet	doux
dry	droog	sec
house wine	huiswijn	vin de table
a bottle of wine	een fles wijn	une bouteille de vin
still water	platwater	eau plate
sparkling water	bruisentwater	eau gazeuse
beer	bier	bière
coffee	koffie	café
tea	thee	thé
milk	melk	lait
decaffineated	caffeïne vrij	déca

348

hot chocolate	warme chocomelk	chocolat chaud
orange juice	sinaasappelsap	jus d'orange
ice	ijs	glaçons

Sightseeing

How much is admission?	Hoeveel is de inkom?	Combien est l'entrée?/
		C'est combien l'entrée?
castle	kasteel	château
church	kerk	église
art gallery	kunst gallerij	galerie d'art
museum	museum	musée
cemetery	begraafplaats / kerkhof	cimetière
palace	paleis	palais
square	plein	place
town hall	stadhuis	mairie
theatre	theater	théâtre
library	bibliotheek	bibliothèque
ticket please	ticket alstublieft	billet, s'il vous plaît
student	student	étudiant(e)
adult	volwassen	adulte
child	kinder	enfant

Shopping & practicalities

How much does this cost…?	Hoeveel kost dit?	Quelle est le prix de … ?/
		C'est combien ce … ?
Do you have…?	Heeft u … ?	Est-ce que vous avez …?
Do you have this in…?	Heeft u dit in…?	Est-ce que vous avez ça en … ?
see colour		
chemist/pharmacist	apotheek	pharmacie
market	markt	marché
newsagents	nieuwsagentschap	magasin de journaux
bookshop	boekhandel	librairie
bakery	bakkerij	boulangerie
grocers	kruidenierswinkel	épicerie
clothes store	kledij winkel	magasin de vêtements
larger	grooter	plus grand(e)
smaller	kleiner	plus petit(e)
too big	te groot	trop grand(e)
too small	te klein	trop petit(e)
I am looking for a…	Ik zoek een…	Je cherche un(e)…
bank	bank	banque
post office	postkantoor	poste
church	kerk	église
embassy	ambasade	ambassade de…
money exchange office	geldwisselkantoor	bureau de change
tourist office	touristenkantoor	office du tourisme
internet café	internet café	café internet
stamp	postzegel	timbre
phonecard	belkaart	carte de téléphone
postcard	ansichtkaart	carte postale
lace	kant	dentelle

Appendix 1 LANGUAGE

A1

Colours

black	*zwart*	*noir(e)*
blue	*blauw*	*bleu(e)*
brown	*bruin*	*marron*
green	*groen*	*vert(e)*
orange	*oranje*	*orange*
red	*rood*	*rouge*
white	*wit*	*blanc/blanche*
yellow	*geel*	*jaune*

Adjectives

cheap	*goedkoop*	*pas cher/chère*
expensive	*duur*	*cher/chère*
ugly	*lelijk*	*laid(e)*
beautiful	*mooi*	*beau/belle*
bad	*slecht*	*mauvais(e)*
good	*goed*	*bon(ne)*
difficult	*moeilijk*	*difficile*
easy	*gemakkelijk*	*facile*
old	*oud*	*vieux/vieille*
new	*nieuw*	*nouveau/nouvelle*
boring	*saai*	*ennuyeux*
interesting	*interessant*	*intéressant(e)*
big	*groot*	*grand(e)*
bigger	*groter*	*plus grand(e)*
small	*klein*	*petit(e)*
hot	*heet*	*chaud(e)*
cold	*koud*	*froid(e)*
slow	*langzaam*	*lent(e)*
quick	*snel*	*rapide*
empty	*leeg*	*vide*
full	*vol*	*plein(e)*

Health

I need a doctor	*Ik zoek een dokter*	*J'ai besoin d'un médecin*
dentist	*tandarts*	*dentiste*
It hurts here	*Het doet hier pijn*	*J'ai mal ici*
Do you have anything for…?	*Heb je iets voor…?*	*Est-ce que vous avez quelque chose pour … ?*

headache	*hoofdpijn*	*mal à la tête*
sore throat	*keelpijn*	*mal à la gorge*
blocked nose	*verstopte neus*	*nez bouché*
cough	*hoest*	*toux*
pain	*pijn*	*douleur*
skin rash	*huiduitslag*	*éruption de boutons*
constipation	*geconstipeert/verstopt*	*constipation*
upset stomach	*maagpijn*	*mal au ventre*
sunburn	*zonnebrand*	*coup de soleil*
diarrhoea	*buikloop/diaree*	*diarrhée*
nausea	*onwel*	*nausée*
prescription	*voorschrift*	*ordonnance*

Help!	Help!	Au secours!/aidez-moi!
Call a doctor!	Bel een dokter!	Appelez un docteur!
There's been an accident	Er was een ongeluk	Il y a eu un accident
I'm lost	Ik ben verloren	Je suis perdu
Go away!	Laat mij gerust/Ga weg!	Partez!
police	politie	police
fire	vuur	feu
ambulance	ambulance/ziekenwagen	ambulance
thief	dief	voleur
hospital	ziekenhuis	hôpital
I'm not feeling well	Ik voel me niet lekker	Je ne me sens pas bien
I'm hurt	Ik ben gekwetst	Je suis blessé(e)

pharmacy	apotheek	pharmacie
paracetamol	paracetamol	paracétamol
antibiotics	antibiotica	antibiotiques
antiseptic	antiseptisch	antiseptique
tampons	tampon/OB	tampons
condoms	condoom	préservatifs
contraceptive	voor behoedsmiddel	contraceptif
sunblock	zonnen craime	écran total
I am …	Ik ben…	Je suis…
asthmatic	astmatisch	asthmatique
epileptic	epeleptie	épileptique
diabetic	diabeetisch	diabétique
I'm allergic to…	Ik ben alergies aan…	Je suis allergique à …
penicillin	penicilline	pénicilline
nuts	nooten	noix
bees	bijen	abeilles

Travelling with children

Is there a…?	Is er een … ?	Est-ce qu'il y a…?
baby changing room	babyverschoonkamer	une pièce pour changer le bébé?
a childrens menu?	kindermenu	un menu enfants?
Do you have … ?	Heb je een … ?	Est-ce que vous avez … ?
nappies	pampers	couches
potty	potje	pot de bébé
babysitter	kinder oppas	babysitter
highchair	kinderstoel	chaise haute/chaise bébé
Are children allowed?	Zijn kinderen toegelaten?	Est-ce que les enfants sont acceptés?

Appendix 2

GLOSSARY

FLEMISH

abdij	abbey
begijnhof	convent occupied by béguines (members of a sisterhood living as nuns without vows; they retain the right to return to the secular world)
belfort	belfry
beurs	stock exchange
brouwerij	brewery
burgher	upper-class merchant
burgomaster	mayor
dienst voor toerisme	tourist office
eetcafé	café serving snacks
grote markt	central town square
hal	hall
huis	house
jenever	gin
kaai	quay
kasteel	castle
kerk	church
koning	king
korenmarket	corn market
kunst	art
lakenhalle	cloth hall
markt	market
ommegang	procession
o.v.(originele versie)	non-dubbed film
paleis	palace
polder	low-lying land reclaimed from the sea
poort	gate
plaats	square or open space
schone kunst	fine arts
stadhuis	town hall
steen	fortress
toren	tower
toeristische dienst	tourist office
tuin	garden

MISCELLANEOUS

Art Deco
A decorative architectural style established during the 1930s, it is characterised by geometric designs, bold colours, and the use of plastic and glass.

Art Nouveau
An architectural style whose heyday ran between 1880 and 1914. It is characterised by the depiction of leaves and flowers in flowing, sinuous lines.

Baroque
Similar to Renaissance-style architecture, it has a freer application and is characterised by bold, curving forms and elaborate ornamentation. It was popular from the early 17th to mid-18th centuries.

Benedictine
A religious order of the Roman Catholic Church, which follows the teachings of St Benedict.

Carolingian
Refers to the Frankish dynasty founded by Pepin the Short in 751AD and ended in 911AD.

Cistercian
A religious order of the Roman Catholic Church, which follows the teachings of St Stephen Harding. Originally more ascetic than Benedictines, they were renowned for eating and working in perpetual silence.

diptych
A work of art across two panels attached by a hinge. Often made of wood, they were a popular choice for early religious paintings.

fresco
The art of painting on fresh, moist plaster on the wall, with pigments dissolved in water.

Gothic
Followed on from Romanesque and is denoted by pointed arches, steep roofs, and windows large in proportion to the wall spaces. Prevalent in western Europe from the 12th to 16th centuries.

guild
Association of people of the same trade or craft that provides social security, protects mutual interests, and maintains standards of morality or conduct. A trade union of sorts.

Neoclassical
Neoclassical architecture is inspired by Greek and Roman influences and is characterised by a grandeur of scale, dramatic use of columns and a preference for blank walls.

Renaissance
Period from the 14th to 16th centuries often thought to mark the transition from medieval to modern times.

Rococo
Similar to Baroque, it refers to an elaborate style of art and architecture characterised by lots of scrolls, foliage and animals. It originated in France in the early 18th century.

Romanesque
The first style to follow Roman and Byzantine architecture, it is characterised by massive walls, round arches, and relatively simple ornamentation and was particularly popular during the 11th and early-13th centuries.

sgraffiti
A technique of layering, tinting and texturing plaster usually applied to the façade of a building.

triptych
A panel painting divided into three sections which are hinged together. The central panel features the main theme of the work and is flanked by two lesser, but related, paintings.

Appendix 3

It's a long-standing joke: how many famous Flemings can you name? Quite a few it turns out! The list below is just the tip of the iceberg. Nobel Prize winners, record breakers, movie stars: Flanders has produced them all.

JACQUES BREL (1929–78) Cheekily adopted by the French as their own, this talented singer-songwriter was born in Schaarbeek, Brussels. He achieved fame following the release of *Quand on n'a que l'amour* in 1956. He occasionally wrote songs for his Flemish homeland, most notably *Le Pays Plat*. Renowned for his deep emotional singing voice and occasional film roles, the singer died of lung cancer in 1978 and was buried within yards of Paul Gauguin's tomb on the Marquesas Islands in French Polynesia.

PIETER BRUEGHEL THE ELDER (1525–69) Unlike his contemporaries, Dutch-born Brueghel chose not to incorporate Renaissance themes into his work. Despite visiting Italy twice, he preferred to stick with northern painting traditions and became famous for immortalising the Flemish landscape and its people. His early work is intricate in design and detail and painted from a bird's eye view, while his later pieces depict just one or two figures seen at eye level and are larger in scale. His sons Pieter Brueghel the Younger and Jan Brueghel became renowned artists in their own right.

HUGO CLAUS (1929–2008) Hailing from Brugge, this experimental writer, poet, playwright, painter and film and theatre director was one of the most prolific Dutch artists of the 20th century. Originally writing under the pseudonym Dorothea van Male, he published his first novel in 1971 and 12 years later, under his real name, he released his most famous work *Het Verdriet van België* (*The Sorrow of Belgium*). He wrote more than four anthologies of poems, 20 novels, and 60 plays. Although he was frequently nominated for the Nobel Prize for Literature, the award eluded him.

JAMES ENSOR (1860–1949) One of the founding members of Les XX (see box, page 24), Ensor spent most of his life in his home town of Oostende. Forbidden by his family to marry the love of his life and frustrated by his lack of success, Ensor became increasingly morbid. In his paintings, skeletons and masks (his mother had sold them in the family shop) are coupled with warped perspectives to create incredibly unsettling compositions. His masterpiece, *Christ's entry into Brussels*, was considered so scandalous – it depicts the second coming of Christ being used for political gain and Ensor features on the face of Christ – that he was expelled from Les XX and unable to unveil it for 30 years. It ended well though: when the painting was finally shown in 1929, Ensor was knighted by Albert I.

AUDREY HEPBURN (1929–93) Edda van Heemstra Hepburn-Ruston was born in the Ixelles district of Brussels, the only child of an Englishman and a Dutch baroness. A talented ballerina, the elfin brunette turned to acting after the severe malnutrition she suffered during World War II put a dent in her dancing career. Her wit, charm and intelligence – she was fluent in French, Italian, English, Dutch and Spanish – quickly caught the attention of studio directors and in 1953 she won an Academy Award for her role as Princess Ann in *Roman Holiday*. Also famous for her roles as Holly Golightly in *Breakfast at Tiffany's* and Eliza Doolittle in *My Fair Lady*, Hepburn became one of Hollywood's leading actresses throughout the 1950s and '60s.

HERGÉ See Georges Remi.

VICTOR HORTA (1861–1947) Born in Gent, Victor Horta was one of the first designers to apply the Art Nouveau techniques of the decorative arts to architecture. He studied interior design in Paris and, upon his return to Brussels, set about incorporating the Impressionist and Pointillist styles he had picked up there into glass and metalwork. Studying at the Academy of Fine Arts, Horta was soon taken on as an assistant by his professor Alphonse Balat – architect to King Léopold II.

JACKY ICKX (1945–) Brussels-born Jacques Ickx was a Formula One driver active between 1967 and 1979. He notched up 25 podium appearances and won the 24 hours of Le Mans race six times. At the 1970 Spanish Grand Prix his car crashed; Ickx managed to escape but received serious burns. He retired in 1979, but still participates in low-profile races.

GEORGES LEMAÎTRE (1894–1966) Roman Catholic priest Georges Lemaître proposed the Big Bang theory and the expansion of the universe in 1927, two years before Edwin Hubble.

RENÉ MAGRITTE (1898–1967) Magritte – who is renowned for his quirky, question-provoking Surrealist art – began drawing at the age of 12 and went on to train at the Académie Royale des Beaux-Arts. Magritte's family life was torn apart when his mother committed suicide by drowning herself in the River Sambre when he was just 14 years old. He was present when her body was dredged from the river and the sight of her face covered by her dress was to haunt most of the figures depicted in his early paintings. His first exhibition in 1927 was critically panned and, smarting from the failure, he moved briefly to Paris where he met André Breton, one of the founders of the Surrealist movement. With renewed inspiration, Magritte returned to painting after World War II and enjoyed much greater success.

GERARDUS MERCATOR (1512–94) Born Gheert Cremer, the Flemish cartographer, better known by his Latin name, developed the Mercator projection in 1569: a flat chart showing the lines of latitude and longitude which revolutionised nautical navigation. He is also credited with producing the first globes – made from papier-mâché and tinted with watercolours – and the first modern atlas.

EDDY MERCKX (1945–) Possibly the greatest cyclist of all time, Merckx – nicknamed 'the cannibal' for his tendency to ride flat out during races – won the Tour de France five times, the Giro d'Italia five times and has been crowned world champion three times. In 1969 he was involved in a crash that killed his pacer and left Merckx with a twisted pelvis and cracked vertebrae; he returned to cycling but was plagued by constant pain. He retired from the professional circuit in 1978 and today runs a bicycle factory.

GEORGES REMI (1907–83) Better known by his *nom de plume* **Hergé** – created by the French pronunciation of his reversed initials – Remi was born in Etterbeek, Brussels. After leaving school, he joined the staff of the Catholic newspaper *Le XXe Siècle* and was put in control of the paper's children's supplement *Le Petit Vingtième*. Dissatisfied with the paper's existing comic-strips, he was commissioned to write a new series. The result was Tintin, a character inspired by Hergé's brother Paul (an officer in the Belgian Army) and who first appeared in *Tintin in the Land of the Soviets* in 1929. Hergé pioneered the use of bold colours and the *ligne claire* style that rendered Tintin ageless. He used the intrepid reporter, accompanied by his lovable fox terrier Snowy, as a vehicle to explore contemporary issues of the period and often spent months researching before committing to a plot. *The Adventures of Tintin* has been translated into over 70 languages and sold over 230 million copies. Hergé died in 1983, leaving his 24th strip, *Tintin and Alph-Art*, unfinished.

PIETER PAUL RUBENS (1577–1640) Born in Germany of Belgian parents, Rubens moved to Antwerp at the age of ten with his mother, second wife to William of Orange I. He began painting at the age of 14 and was declared a master painter at 21. Visits to Italy and Spain followed, where he encountered and studied the works of the great Renaissance artists. The death of his mother in 1608 saw his return to Antwerp and he set up a workshop to satisfy the widespread demand for his vigorous paintings characterised by their flowing movement and luminous colour. Rubens' personal contribution to the 2,000 works he is rumoured to have produced was often limited to the painting of the hands and faces of the main subjects; his apprentices would complete the body of the work using Rubens' sketches.

JEAN-CLAUDE VAN DAMME (1960–) Renowned for his martial arts and his ability to do full splits while performing stunts, the 'Muscles from Brussels' enjoyed Hollywood success during the 1990s with films like *Timecop* and *Universal Soldier*. He's equally famous for his perfect posterior which he flashed in his breakthrough film *Bloodsport*. As a child he trained in martial arts and ballet, and won the Mr Belgium body-building contest in 1978.

HENRI VAN DE VELDE (1863–1957) This neo-Impressionist painter – who was invited to become a member of Les XX (see box, page 24) – is famous for pioneering the Art Nouveau movement in Belgium, along with Victor Horta. He designed the Boekentoren university library in Gent.

ROGIER VAN DER WEYDEN (1399–1464) Born in Tournai, van der Weyden was originally known as Rogier de la Pasture, but converted to the Dutch equivalent when the reigning Dukes of Burgundy awarded him the title of Brussels' *stadsschilder* (town painter). His popularity increased when, at the age of 51, he made a pilgrimage to Rome, picking up commissions from the Medici and Este families along the way. By the time of his death in 1464, van der Weyden was one of the richest and most celebrated painters in Europe.

JAN VAN EYCK (1390–1441) Born near Maaseik, van Eyck was court painter to Philip the Good, Duke of Burgundy, and travelled widely on diplomatic missions to Prague, Portugal and Spain. Renowned for his unparalleled application and layering of oil glazes, van Eyck's work is incredibly detailed and incandescent. His most famous works are the Gent altarpiece *The Adoration of the Mystic Lamb*, and the intriguing *Arnolfini Portrait*. It's said that his brother Hubert, who little is known about, completed the lion's share of the work on the Gent altarpiece.

Appendix 4

FURTHER INFORMATION

BOOKS
History and culture

Ascherson, N *The King Incorporated* Granta Publications, 1999. A sharp, lively and insightful account of the life of Léopold II and his exploitation of the Belgian Congo.

Blom, JCH (ed) *History of the Low Countries* Berghahn Books, 2006. A dense and thorough examination of Belgium, Luxembourg and the Netherlands' collective history, ranging from the Merovingian dynasty to modern day. Peppered with paintings by leading artists of the period.

Bainbridge, T *The Penguin Companion to European Union* Penguin, 2002. An academic set of mini-essays, covering everything from treaties to key issues, policies and prominent personalities.

Hill, R *The Art of Being Belgian* Europublic, 2005. A Belgian resident for over 40 years, Hill puts pen to paper with sympathetic observations on Belgian character, values and lifestyle.

Holt, T& V *Major and Mrs Holt's Battlefield Guide to Ypres Salient* Pen & Sword Books Ltd, 1997. An easy and invaluable read that covers the salient in detail and contains three good itineraries, a pull-out map, plus some interesting anecdotes.

Pearson, H A *Tall Man in a Low Land* Abacus, 2000. One man's laugh-out-loud account of his travels around Belgium with his wife and young daughter.

Mason, A *The Xenophobe's guide to the Belgians* Oval Books, 2009. A light-hearted quick read to get you under the skin of the Belgian psyche.

Middleton, N *Travels as a Brussels Scout* George Weidenfeld & Nicholson Ltd, 1998. I interviewed Middleton when I was at university – then, as now, he writes with ineffable laidback charm. The travelogue describes his myth-busting tour of Europe – with the question 'are Belgians really boring?' on his list.

Taylor, AJP *The First World War: An Illustrated History* Penguin Books, 1974. This classic textbook guide to World War I is concise, but Taylor's style is rather dry in places and his opinions biased and largely out of date now. However, the numerous photos and diagrams still make it a worthwhile read.

Literature and art

Alpers, S *The Making of Rubens* New Haven, 1995. An unconventional critique of the master's art.

Bronte, C & E *The Belgian Essays* Yale University Press, 1997. The Bronte sisters travelled to Brussels in 1842 and the experiences they had are credited with shaping their successful writing careers. All 28 essays produced feature in their original French and are accompanied by an English translation.

Claus, H *The Sorrow of Belgium* Penguin Books Ltd, 1994. This seminal work tells the story of a Flemish child (Claus's alter ego) caught up in the German occupation of Belgium in World War II.

Conrad, J *Heart of Darkness* Oxford University Press, 2007. The classic tale of Marlow's journey up the Congo River and into the soul of man – a creative take on life in the Congo under Belgian rule.

Conscience, H *The Lion of Flanders* Fredonia Books, 2003. A historical romance hailed as one of Hendrik Conscience's masterpieces.

Dernie, D *Victor Horta* Wiley-Academy, 1995. A treat for architects, this volume covers 19 of Horta's Art Nouveau projects and includes design plans and photos.

De Vos, D *The Flemish Primitives: The Masterpieces* Princeton University Press, 2003. Lavishly illustrated, De Vos assesses and brings to life the new techniques employed by these masters of art.

Gablik, S *Magritte* Thames & Hudson Ltd, 1985. Gablik lived in Magritte's house for six months, 20 years prior to writing this book, which examines the artist's work and philosophies. There is a disappointing lack of colour photos.

Harbison, C *Jan van Eyck: The Play of Realism* Reaktion Books, 1995. Explores the histories of the characters that appear in van Eyck's masterpieces.

Lesko, D *James Ensor: The Creative Years* Princeton University Press, 1985.

Meuris, J *Magritte* Taschen, 2004. A complete history of the Surrealist's artistic development.

Thompson, H *Tintin: Hergé and his Creation* John Murray, 2011. A dual biography of cartoon character Tintin and his creator Hergé.

General

Beek, van Nicolas and Capart, Nathalie *Secret Brussels: Walking off the Beaten Track* Jonglez, 2011. Just translated from the French version, this superb slimline guide takes you behind the scenes of Brussels.

Blyth, Derek *Live & Work in Brussels* Crimson Publishing, 2007. Excellent guide for expats, with detailed information on how to find a home, setting up a business etc.

Webb, T *Good Beer Guide Belgium* Campaign for Real Ale, 2009. Honest, humorous and well written, this is the definitive guide to Belgian beer – it covers all the breweries, the best cafés and the beer festivals.

WEBSITES The majority of Flemish websites offer an English translation of the text. When you do encounter one in Dutch (or French for Brussels), use Google Translate (*www.translate.google.com*).

www.visitflanders.co.uk Official UK Flanders tourism website

www.visitbrussels.com Official Brussels tourism website

www.use-it.be Funky website for young travellers looking for places to sleep and eat in Flanders' main cities. Printable online maps too.

www.dekust.org Tourist information covering the entire Flemish coast

www.eurotunnel.com Official website for car trains from Folkestone to Calais

www.eurostar.com Official website for Eurostar trains from London to Brussels

www.stib.be Public transport network in Brussels

www.delijn.be Public transport network in Flanders

www.b-rail.be Booking website for all train travel in and out of Belgium

www.bnb-brussels.be B&Bs in Brussels, with online reservation and 360° views of hotel rooms

www.camping.be List of campsites in Flanders

Index

Entries in **bold** indicate main entries; entries in *italics* indicate maps